SHARE MARKETS
AND
PORTFOLIO THEORY

Ray Ball is Professor of Accounting at the University of Rochester

Philip Brown is Professor of Finance at the University of Western Australia

Frank J. Finn is Professor of Finance at the University of Queensland

R.R. Officer is AMP Professor of Finance at the University of Melbourne

SHARE MARKETS AND PORTFOLIO THEORY

READINGS AND AUSTRALIAN EVIDENCE

Second edition

Edited by
Ray Ball
Philip Brown
Frank J. Finn
R.R. Officer

University of Queensland Press

First published 1980 by University of Queensland Press
Box 42, St Lucia, Queensland, Australia
Second edition 1989

Typeset by Midland Typesetters, Maryborough
Printed in Australia by Globe Press, Melbourne

Cataloguing in Publication Data

National Library of Australia

Share markets and portfolio theory.

  2nd ed.
  Bibliography.

  1. Securities — Australia. 2. Capital market —
  Australia. I. Ball, Ray, 1944– .

332.63'2'0994

ISBN 0 7022 2163 5

FF13A40

Contents

Tables

Figures

Preface

Research in finance experienced a major shift in the mid-1960s toward an empirical base. Key factors in the shift were the development of the postulates of modern portfolio theory by Markowitz, the work of Sharpe and Lintner on the two-parameter model of security returns, the construction of the CRSP data file at the University of Chicago, and the ingenious experiment of Fama, Fisher, Jensen and Roll. Immediately, researchers were able to use factual data to address questions such as: "What are the implications of a change in dividend policy for a company?", "What effect do earnings announcements have on share prices?", "What happens to share prices if audit reports are qualified", "What is the effect of takeovers on the values of acquiring and acquired firms?", and "What is risk?".

Since 1970, a good deal of research of this type has been conducted in Australia. A key factor was the construction by Philip Brown of a file of returns on Melbourne industrial and commercial shares — a project which has since led to the construction of several large data bases in Australia, and which has facilitated a large amount of empirical work on Australian data.

The body of empirical work of this type investigating the Australian capital market is now large and robust. Much of it has been published in various journals in this country and overseas. The purpose of this book is to draw together the major contributions to date, making them readily accessible to practitioners, researchers and students. The book also contains several contributions which have not been published elsewhere, including historical data on returns in Australian capital markets since 1882. This edition also includes material on multifactor asset pricing models and several so-called "anomalies" to asset pricing.

The chapters in this volume cover a broad range of material ranging from introductory to advanced readings in finance. While a number of the important contributions to the first edition have been retained in the second edition, the majority of chapters in this edition have been written since publication of the first edition. The book can be used as a text for courses in capital markets and portfolio theory and courses in finance with an emphasis on empirical evidence, and it can be used as complementary material to accompany the more standard textbooks in undergraduate courses in financial management, investments, financial statement analysis and the like. Also, much of the material in the book, especially parts 4, 5 and 6, should be of use to practitioners in finance, including financial managers, security analysts and portfolio managers.

R. Ball, P. Brown, F. Finn, R. Officer

PART 1
Introduction and overview

1 The stock market: Introduction to market concepts and overview of Australian evidence

R.R. Officer and Frank J. Finn

An understanding of the broad economic and financial principles that underly the operations of a stock market is a necessary prerequisite for comprehending the studies that are reported in this book of readings. This chapter is aimed at providing an overview of the issues that have concerned empirical researchers in the area of portfolio theory and share market efficiency over the past decade or two. Readers interested in a more rigorous derivation of the concepts are referred to the sources cited at the end of the book. The chapter also attempts to dispel some of the more commonly held misconceptions about the formation of share prices on stock markets.

The role of a stock market

A market is a place where individuals can exchange economic goods and services. The motive for the exchange is the belief by persons participating in the exchange that they will end up as well as or better off than they were before the exchange took place. If this condition was not met by the exchange then there would be no inducement for the parties to participate in the exchange. Moreover, if the market is competitive and there are no externalities, i.e., no one other than the parties participating in the exchange is affected by the exchange, then we would have what is known as a *pareto optimum*.[1] An exchange that is consistent with a *pareto optimum* will imply a more efficient allocation of goods, services and resources as a result of the exchange than before the exchange took place.[2] These remarks are true for all markets whether the exchange is a simple barter arrangement or the more sophisticated dealings found in capital markets such as the stock exchange.

As an illustration of the mechanism by which markets can create the environment for the efficient allocation of resources, consider the following: in most markets the form of the exchange is one in which the consumer pays money in exchange for goods and services. In effect, consumers vote with dollars for the goods and services they want. Goods that are in high demand command a "price premium" so that producers of the goods are induced to put more resources into the production of more goods. Conversely, goods that are

in low demand incur a "price penalty" so that producers are encouraged
to reduce the flow of resources going into the production of these goods.
The result is that resources are directed to where they provide greatest utility.[3]
It is an objective of society, as illustrated in the drafting of trade practices
legislation, to have markets that are unencumbered by externalities and barriers
to entry so that society's resources are allocated in an efficient manner.

The stock market, just like any other market, has a role to perform in
the efficient allocation of resources. The stock market's role is to allocate
capital (a factor of production) among public companies and between those
companies and other assets. A company whose product is in demand can
be expected to have a "high" price placed on its shares because of the expected
future profits. The company whose share price is "high" will find it relatively
easy to raise capital to expand its operations and increase the supply of
its product. The converse is true for the shares of a company whose product
is not in demand. Ultimately, it is the consumers' spending power, together
with the product range and cost, which dictate long-term share market
movements. In the shorter term, the share market is influenced by investors
trying to predict the direction of consumer spending, i.e., demand, and
production techniques and costs, i.e., supply. It is the shorter-run movements
in share prices, based on investors' expectations of the future, which have
led to the suggestion that the stock market is just a lottery with no useful
role to perform, a suggestion which is quite fallacious.

The price of a share

When investors buy shares, they are overwhelmingly concerned with what
they can expect to get from their investment. They are profit maximisers
or equivalently they are attempting to increase their wealth. The price an
investor is prepared to pay for a share is often described as that price which
reflects the net cash flow he or she expects to get from the investment
discounted for time and risk, that is, the price is equivalent to the net present
value of the share. As an operational model this common description of
a share's value is rather empty. To give substance to such a model of valuation
we need to describe how the expected returns and the discount rate are
derived. As we might expect, this is where most people differ in their opinion
of a share's value. The expected net cash flows resulting from an investment
in a company's shares can be expected to be affected by anything that will
affect the performance of the company. This will include all those variables
that go into the day to day operations of the firm as well as those variables
that affect the economic environment in which the firm operates. These
variables will range from changes in world exchange rates to a change in
the operating capacity of a piece of equipment. The number of variables
is obviously immense. More significantly, it has not been demonstrated that
we can successfully whittle down the list of variables to just a few known
or easily forecastable factors which explain most of the expectations about
future returns or cash flows. A similar problem arises when we try to estimate
the appropriate rate of discount.

The fact that there is a large number of variables affecting the expected
return from a share market investment does not imply that we ignore these

variables. Obviously, any new information about future returns will be relevant to current prices and therefore relevant to investment decisions.[4] Further, since most news can usually be distinguished into good or bad we can usually indicate the direction of the market's response to information. However, because of the forecasting problems associated with valuation models we are not in a position to discuss with any accuracy the extent to which the market responds to information, i.e., the magnitude of the price movement in response to any particular piece of information.[5] This leaves us with the subject of how quickly the market responds to new information—the efficiency of the market.

The efficient market concept[6]

Share prices change in response to new information that alters investors' expectations about future returns from share market investments. This gives rise to the notion of the efficiency of the share market. There are two aspects of market efficiency: the type of information that the market is reacting to and the speed with which the market responds to that information. The type of efficiency exhibited by a market will depend on the source of the information and this is ultimately related to the cost to investors of that information—this will be discussed in more detail later. The degree of efficiency shown by a market is measured by the speed with which the market incorporates the new information into its price structure. For example, suppose the main factory of a company listed on the exchange is destroyed by a spectacular fire overnight. If the effect of this fire is reflected in the price of the firm's stock next morning on the exchange, then the market is said to have efficiently incorporated news of the fire into the firm's share price. On the other hand, there may be some information concerning the company that is slowly incorporated into price, typically because the information is known to few people who may be hesitant in operating on the information; they may be company staff or insiders or they may be people who have insufficient money to take full advantage of the information. Therefore, a market may exhibit different degrees of efficiency for different types of information.

The concept of efficiency does not imply a perfect market.[7] It is the opportunity to capitalise on inefficiencies in the market that encourages investors to gather information. The utilisation of this information promotes efficiency and assists in the optimal allocation of resources within the market. However, even if all the inefficiencies are removed, the condition of the market is still one of uncertainty; prices reflect expected returns and returns are not perfectly predictable in advance. Therefore, in an efficient market, although it immediately incorporates all known information into its price, the price is based only on expectations about future returns. Further, expectations are rarely a precise description of actual occurrences.

We often see company failures and prices moving in such a manner that with hindsight we are led to remark that the market was irrational and inefficient when in fact what is meant is the expectations of a previous period were not realised. Even though expectations may not be realised, at the time they were formed they were an unbiased estimate of the future performance of the company. If at any point in time expectations were biased, that is, if we could confidently predict that the expectations of the market are above or below future realisation, then this would imply an investment strategy which would enable the investor to consistently outperform the market. For example, if it were believed that the market always overestimates the impact of a change in government on the effect of listed companies, then an obvious strategy would be to take the reverse of the share market's attitude so that the investor is buying when the market anticipates an adverse political impact on the share prices or selling when the market expects a positive impact. Such a trading strategy would ensure above-normal returns if in fact the strategy is based on a substantive fact. Moreover, the abnormally high returns the investors could expect from such a strategy would encourage new investors to adopt the strategy and investors who had been using that strategy would increase the size of their investment in the strategy. The volume of trades based on such a strategy would tend to correct the bias that was initially observed. Therefore, we do not expect that any bias in expectations will persist over any substantial period of time. Thus, although markets on occasions will rapidly change direction, this does not imply that the market is being inefficient or irrational; the change in general reflects inherent uncertainty about future returns and changing expectations as new information is brought to bear on the fortunes of listed companies.

The notion that any inefficiency existing in the share market will be self-correcting once the inefficiency is recognised is clearly important to the concept of stock market efficiency. This is at the basis of the scepticism of claims made of consistently superior investment performance based on a particular trading rule or investment strategy. Knowledge of the inefficiency will spread and the pressure of trading by investors, both in number and quantity of investment, will eliminate any pattern or inefficiency on which the strategies are based.

The adjustment of share prices to new information

The adjustment of a share's price to new information does not necessarily require any trading. The adjustment can be immediate so that it is not necessary to have a "path" to the new price that could be exploited by a trader. In the example already given, the effect of the factory fire would have been implicitly incorporated into the price of the company's shares before trading commenced. Both buyers and sellers, being aware of the fire, would have adjusted their price expectations before placing orders on the market. When trading commenced, price quotations would reflect the new circumstances which were not the same as those underlying the closing price of the previous day.

The notion that share market prices change to reflect new information needs to be qualified. Information is not costless. Further, there are usually transactions costs (brokerage fees and stamp duties are the most obvious) of operating in the share market. If these costs together with the information costs outweigh the expected benefit from using that information, then there would be no incentive for traders to operate purely on such information and the market price would not reflect all relevant information. Nonetheless, there will usually be some traders who intended operating irrespective of the development, of the new piece of information, e.g., the AMP Society has millions of dollars to invest each week of which a significant proportion finds its way into the share market. For these traders the opportunity cost of utilising the information is zero. Thus, the extent to which transactions costs inhibit market prices from reflecting new information is not as great as it might appear at first sight. We will discuss the effect of information costs shortly when information sources are examined.

The spread of information needed for a price change

The adjustment of share prices to new information does not require that all traders in the market are aware of the information. Consider the earlier example of a factory fire, and imagine the situation facing a trader who comes to the market to buy shares in the company without being aware of the fire. The buyer may expect to pay around yesterday's closing price. However, potential sellers would compete against one another to make the sale by cutting their offer prices until the price actually transacted fully reflected the effect of the fire. In fact, the number of traders possessing the new information may be a very small segment of the total market and still the market price can immediately adjust. Therefore, an efficient stock market does not require that every buyer and every seller be fully informed. This is an extremely important but often overlooked condition. The treatment of business transactions is often debated at length in the belief that a misinterpretation of the accounting reports of a firm by the "average investor" will lead to an error in the market price. It is the competition among informed traders that will cause a share price to adjust so that it reflects the new information. The number of competitors necessary to make the market efficient will vary depending on the cost and rewards from utilising the information. In the limit, one informed trader may be sufficient to ensure market efficiency providing the share market is thin (few trades being made) and/or he has sufficient capital to trade until he considers the full effect of the information is reflected in the price and there is no further reward from acting on this information. In practice it may take a number of competing traders to effect the full change in price. With respect to accounting reports, there are obviously sufficient investors with the necessary skills to understand such reports.[8] These investors are unlikely to be misled by changes in accounting profits that merely reflect a change in accounting procedures but do not have any real effect on the firm's true profit. Such investors are in a position to adjust their investment strategies according to their interpretation of the reports, so that any tendency for the market to move out of line with the more "accurate" statement of profits will be corrected by them. In other words, the opportunity for profitable trading when the market misinterprets information will induce these traders to take out strategies which will tend to correct the error in the market price. Whether in fact this is carried out in practice is really an empirical issue which will be discussed in more depth shortly.

The concept of normal returns from holding shares

If the stock market efficiently incorporates new information into the price of shares, then it should be intuitively clear that investors with this information cannot expect to earn a greater return from operating in the market than those without the information (where the information is the only distinguishing characteristic between the groups), i.e., there is no direct benefit from possessing the information once it has been incorporated into price.[9] In the economist's terminology, no monopoly profit can be extracted from this information after its incorporation into price so that the expected return to investors with the information is the same as those without it. If the stock market reacts efficiently to all pieces of new information, it implies that the investor who has a well-diversified portfolio could only expect to get a return comparable to the return indicated by a market index, or, more particularly, the return indicated by the market portfolio (a portfolio consisting of all shares listed). Over the period 1882 to 1987, the average rate of return for shares or portfolios of shares representing average risk has been slightly in excess of 11 per cent; this includes the reinvestment of dividends and adjustments made for bonuses and rights issues.[10] However, we need to clarify what is meant by risk before we can attach much meaning to comparisons of rates of return.

The discussion of market efficiency has so far made no specific mention of the role of risk. Clearly, risk is a very real part of a stock market's environment and any change in price reflects not only the expected effect of new information but also the risk or degree of uncertainty surrounding that information. In fact, most of the interest in models of share market behaviour are structured with price or rate of return as some function of the risk of the share. Part 3 of this book contains examples of these models ranging from risk in the Australian industrial market (chapter 4), to risk in the mining market (chapter 5), to risk in the international market (chapter 6). Over the last two decades there has been much research into how to define and measure risk, with methods of controlling for risk ranging from a single-factor measure as illustrated by Ball, Brown and Officer in chapter 4, to multifactor measures as summarised by Sinclair in chapter 9. More recent research has also focused on several anomalies to these models of risk and return. Anomalies categorised as size effects, January effects, and day-of-the-week effects are discussed in chapters 7 and 8.

When we talk of an investor earning only normal profit or returns in an efficient share market, we mean the profits or returns are adjusted for risk. Normal returns do not necessarily mean the same level of returns because different amounts of return will be associated with different amounts of risk. The greater the risk the greater the return required, since investors are on the whole risk averse. Therefore, the normal returns of about 11 per cent for the period 1882 to 1987 referred to earlier relate specifically to a share or portfolio with the same level of risk as the market portfolio; greater returns can be expected but only for greater risk—and for some this additional risk is going to be disastrous. To illustrate we only have to look at the performance of fund managers over the last few years. During the couple of years up to October 1987, some fund managers achieved extremely high returns, but with the severe downturn in the share market in October 1987 it was these same managers who were hardest hit. The conservative managers, those who had invested in low-risk portfolios, were less severely affected by the share market downturn.[11]

Although there are a number of theories as to what constitutes risk, most would agree that variability of returns will be one of the most important components of risk. Investors who adopt high-risk strategies can expect to have highly variable returns. Moreover, in any sample of investors with high-risk investments, we would expect to find some who have profited substantially and some who have had substantial losses. The fact that some investors realised high returns or profits does not necessarily mean they were more astute investors. We expect some to be winners by pure chance. If we took a sample of gamblers playing roulette with a perfectly balanced wheel, we would expect to find winners and losers. Moreover, if the game has been going on long enough there will be some substantial losses and some substantial gains made. However, we do not usually believe that the winners have more skill in the game than the losers and with a perfectly balanced wheel we know this is highly improbable. In fact, if we took all the winners over one period and observed their performance over the next period we would expect to find an equal distribution of winners and losers. The point being made is that with the share market, as with the roulette wheel, we should not just sample winners *ex post*, i.e., we should be careful about listening to those who claim to have made abnormal returns in the market: the sample is biased— losers do not boast. In fact, if we are going to concentrate on such a sample of winners then we should examine their performance in the next and subsequent periods before deciding whether or not they possess some extraordinary skills in share market investment.

Therefore, high returns do not necessarily mean they are abnormal since they may be associated with high risk. This type of behaviour is most clearly demonstrated in the market for corporate debentures. Highly rated debentures will be offered at lower rates of interest than poorly rated issues. Clearly, the lower interest rate on a quality debenture does not necessarily mean that these debentures are a poorer investment than debentures that are paying more. Both are probably paying normal returns when the risk differences between the issues are taken into account.

In a fully efficient capital market there is no opportunity for an investor to make abnormal returns from information he receives, since the effect of the information is already impounded into share market price. This implies that for investors to make greater than normal returns they must be able to capitalise on inefficiencies that might exist in the market. With this in mind the next section looks at some of the different types of information that are considered relevant to share prices and the degree of efficiency with which that information is impounded into prices.

In investigating the efficiency of the market, many of the studies which follow compare actual returns surrounding an information event to a benchmark of the expected or normal returns. Since the benchmark requires a model of risk and return to define normal returns, the studies become by construction joint tests of market efficiency and the model of asset pricing used to define normal returns. Thus a finding of abnormal returns subsequent to an information event could be due to market inefficiency in adjusting to information, the use of an incorrect model of asset pricing, or both.

Information sources and stock market efficiency

Fama (1970a), in an important review of the empirical work supporting the efficient-market hypothesis, sets out a structure and interpretation of what efficiency means in the context of market behaviour. Fama followed a suggestion by Harry Roberts that the degree of efficiency exhibited by a market could be structured into three main classes:

Weak form efficiency: A market is said to exhibit this type of efficiency when there is no information contained in historical price patterns that is not already impounded into share price. That is, there is no opportunity to make abnormal returns by studying historical price patterns.

Semi-strong form efficiency: This is efficiency with respect to publicly available information about a firm or group of firms, e.g., the annual accounting statement. A market that exhibits semi-strong form of efficiency implies that additional information cannot be extracted from the direct application of information contained in publicly available documents relevant to the company.

Strong form efficiency: A market that is said to be efficient in the strong form is one that is efficient with respect to all information about a company whether it is publicly available or not; it includes information known only to officers of the company (insiders).

The above classification system has been widely adopted in the literature on financial markets. It is, however, a classification of convenience, rather than being based on any substantive rules emanating from the theory. Information can be thought of as a continuum of types, so that any classification system using discrete classes is essentially drawing arbitrary barriers between types of information. The distinguishing characteristic of any classification system of market efficiency that is based on information types will be the relative cost or difficulty in obtaining the information. That is, the investor, in seeking information, will imply the standard decision rule of marginal cost being less than or equal to marginal revenue, so that as long as the expected return from information is greater than its expected cost the information will be sought after. However, once the expected return becomes less than the expected cost of the information, then the information will not be incorporated into share prices. This has led Grossman and Stiglitz (1976) to state that costless information is both a necessary and sufficient condition for the information to be efficiently incorporated into price. Moreover, in their analysis the market never fully adjusts, implying that all information of relevance is costly. What Grossman and Stiglitz seem to overlook is that although all relevant information may be costly, once it is acquired it is a sunk cost to the holder of the information. Therefore, the opportunity cost of using this information for these investors (assuming no effect of transactions cost) is zero, which fulfils the necessary and sufficient condition for the information to be efficiently incorporated into price. This means that once an investor considers the expected return from information outweighs its expected cost, he will seek the information out and, once it is acquired, will fully utilise that information until there are no further rewards to utilising the information, i.e., the market is fully adjusted to that piece of information. Of course, this still allows the possibility that there may be pieces of available information whose cost outweighs any expected returns. This information will not be incorporated into price as there are insufficient or zero investors already with the information to effect a full price adjustment.

The classification system set out in Fama's paper implies some sort of cost/return stratification. Weak form information is readily available and generally at a low cost. Semi-strong form information is available and in general we would expect it to be more costly to obtain than weak form information, although this will not necessarily apply to all types of semi-strong form information. Finally, strong form information is difficult, by definition, to get hold of and likely to be very costly for outsiders. Under competitive markets for information, the cost of information is going to have a direct bearing on the returns to information, or more particularly high returns to information are likely to be associated with the high cost of obtaining that information, although the reverse is not necessarily true.

As the amount of evidence accumulates about the efficiency of markets with respect to different types of information, we might expect that a simple classification scheme based on Fama's categories will be inadequate. A scheme which more explicitly looks at the cost of extracting information and the returns from utilising such information will need to be adopted. However, it is convenient to use the classification scheme that has received wide acceptance in the literature for a brief introduction to studies of the efficiency of the Australian share market contained in this book.

Historical prices (weak from efficiency)

Some markets analysts, chartists or technical analysts believe they can forecast what the market is going to do in the future based on what the immediate past pattern of prices has been. Such a phenomenon, if it exists, implies the market is inefficient in incorporating the simplest of information sources, past prices, into the current price. The alternative hypothesis, that price changes are independent of each other and so past price changes cannot be used to predict future prices, is popularly known as the random walk hypothesis. This hypothesis is the most thoroughly tested proposition of share market price behaviour. The evidence supporting the theory as a reasonable approximation of price behaviour in the share markets is voluminous. Most of the earlier studies concentrated on the behaviour of United States stock markets, particularly the New York Stock Exchange, and a review of this evidence supporting the theory can be found in Fama (1970a). The studies have been replicated in share markets in most of the world's developed countries and the results found in these other share markets have been generally consistent with those found in the United States. In Australia there have been a considerable number of studies testing the theory, many of them unpublished. Officer (chapter 15) and Ball (chapter 16) provide some of the more thoroughly documented studies.

Praetz (1969) was the first to thoroughly document tests on the random walk hypothesis for Australian share market data. He tested weekly series of prices for sixteen separate industrial groups listed on the Sydney Stock Exchange from 1958 to 1966, twenty leading shares over the same period from the Melbourne and Sydney Stock Exchanges and monthly series of two price indices from the Sydney Stock Exchange from 1875 to 1966. Praetz concluded that the random walk theory was not strictly adhered to (there was some evidence of dependence) but "it [serial correlation] is not widespread nor large, nor do we feel it could be exploited for gain".

Officer examined 651 shares of the Melbourne Stock Exchange over the period 1958–70. The prices are the final monthly trading prices of each share adjusted for bonuses, calls, dividends, rights, etc. Officer demonstrated that the presence of a seasonal, although it is contrary to the random walk hypothesis, does not necessarily contradict the efficient-market hypothesis in its weak form. Further, Officer showed that much of the apparent serial correlation between rates of return (implying there is some information in previous returns for forecasting future returns) found in other studies is probably a result of data misspecification and other experimental errors. This helps to explain the apparent anomalies that have been found in previous studies on the random walk hypothesis.

Ball specifically examined the use of filter rules as an investment strategy. In a filter rule a buy or sell strategy is initiated on the direction and extent of immediate past movements in the prices of a share. The efficient market hypothesis implies that the use of such rules will not enable any abnormal returns to be earned. Using 126 industrial shares of the Melbourne Stock Exchange over the period 1958–70, Ball was able to conclude that filter rules do not appear to have been profitable. Ball also showed that some of the apparent anomalies found in overseas tests of filter rules, e.g., Alexander (1961), could be explained by experimental problems rather than evidence inherent in the actual data.

Most of the tests of the weak form of efficiency, including the random walk theory, are testing for linear dependence of price changes.[12] Most charting techniques assume some form of linear dependence. Ball and Officer (chapter 17) compare charts formed by plotting series of random numbers with charts formed by plotting share price changes for a number of listed companies. The comparisons will be surprising to some chartists.

However, the form of dependence of price changes can be more complex than a linear relationship. Therefore, there is no single test or set of tests that can exclude all forms of dependence. If a form of dependence more complex than linear is thought to exist then the only sure way of testing whether extra normal returns can be made is by way of a direct test of the trading rule based on this dependence. Ball, Brown and Finn (chapter 33) examined the investment recommendations of a chartist and other investment analysts whose recommendations are documented in the press. Their examination of the evidence suggests that the chartist tended to recommend buying after a price rise had already occurred and selling after a price fall. The net result is that the investor is no better off adopting the chartist's strategy than if he had used some other method of selecting shares to buy and sell, such as a random method of selection.

Public information (semi-strong form efficiency)

This category of market efficiency includes published accounting information, economic indicators and other forms of information that are obviously publicly available. It does not include information that might be contained in these reports but requires such specialised analytical skills that few, if any, are able to use the information. If the stock market is efficient with respect to public information then by or at the time the information is released to the public it will have been incorporated into share prices, so that investors utilising such information subsequent to its release cannot earn extraordinary returns. Only a limited number of investors are followers of charting techniques. However, a far greater number believe they can utilise information such as annual reports to earn themselves greater than normal profits. We must turn to the empirical evidence to see whether or not these beliefs are justified.

The studies of the semi-strong form of market efficiency have involved different methodology to that used to test weak form efficiency. The tests have typically been based on the use of the capital asset pricing model or variations of it, as described by Ball, Brown and Officer (chapter 4) and Sinclair (chapter 9). The residuals of the market model have been used to determine whether or not a piece of information has had a specific effect on share prices independently of other general economic or marketwide effects. Brown illustrates the general methodology of these types of tests in chapter 18. Refinements of the methodology and the use of different controls in estimating the specific effects of information events are discussed by Shevlin (chapter 12) and Sinclair (chapter 13).

Fama (1970a) reviews a substantial portion of the then existing United States empirical evidence of semi-strong form efficiency. This volume concentrates on Australian studies that have occurred since that date. Among the earliest and more important of the Australian studies have been those by Brown (1970, 1972) who studied the influence of annual and half-yearly profit reports on share market prices. Brown's annual report study (chapter 18) was analogous to the study conducted by Ball and Brown (1968) in the United States. The results of these studies, covering the two countries, are very similar. Brown concluded, "There appears to be no point to waiting [to invest] until the audited details of profits are published . . . because by then all price adjustments have been made and it is too late." The half-yearly report study (Brown 1972) did not contradict this statement nor did the study by Brown and Hancock (chapter 19) conducted on daily data.

Brown, Finn and Hancock (chapter 21) examined the relationship between dividend changes, earnings reports and share prices. This study was unable to separate out the information effects of dividends and earnings on prices. Moreover, the paper highlighted the difficulties in attempting to extract the effect of the informational content of dividends on share price because of the close association between earnings and dividends. Although the paper was unable to demonstrate clearly the informational impact of dividend announcements, the results were not in conflict with the efficient-market hypothesis with respect to dividend information.

Ball, Brown and Finn (chapter 23) studied the effect of bonus issues and rights issues on share price and provided evidence consistent with the efficient-market hypothesis with respect to capitalisation changes. The study concluded that there were substantial changes in share prices around the announcement of capitalisation changes. Moreover, if these changes could have been anticipated then abnormal returns could have been earned. However, although there was some anomaly in the evidence for share splits, overall "the evidence also suggests that the market's reaction to the information contained in the announcements of share capitalisation changes is fully reflected in share prices by the end of the announcement month, if not sooner." The implication behind this statement is that if daily, instead of monthly, data had been used the full adjustment would have occurred on the day of the announcement. Although clearly we would need daily data to prove the statement, the studies of Brown and Hancock (chapter 19) and Brown, Finn and Hancock (chapter 21), using daily data did show that the price adjustment to dividends and earnings' changes was complete by the end of the day of announcement.

Sharpe and Walker (chaper 25) examined the effect of a revaluation of assets by a company on its share price. The study concluded that share market prices failed to anticipate the revaluation of a company's assets, and the valuation announcement itself did have some effect on share prices. Although this is no *prima facie* evidence of inefficiency, it does suggest that investors by examining a company's assets and revaluing them at their market value could adopt investment strategies that would enable them to earn abnormal returns. However, in an examination of the methodology adopted by the Sharpe and Walker study, Brown and Finn (chapter 26) point out the difficulty of attributing price changes to the valuation announcement itself, since information about other variables, including earnings, dividends and bonus issues, is almost invariably released contemporaneously with the revaluation announcement.

Dodd and Officer (chapter 28) examined the effect of takeovers on share market prices. As well as examining the share price behaviour of successful and unsuccessful bidder and target companies separately, they also addresed the policy issues of the net economic benefit of takeovers and the effect of increased regulation of takeover activity. Dodd and Officer show that takeovers are value-creating investments, a result which questions regulatory proposals to restrict takeovers. They also conclude that shareholders of both bidding and target companies earn positive returns at the time of a takeover, with larger returns accruing to target company shareholders.

Overall, the evidence to date supports market efficiency with respect to publicly available information. This is not to say there has not been or will not be a breakdown in this form of market efficiency. However, what it does suggest is that it is not common. Moreover, if there has been some degree of inefficiency with respect to public information, then it is likely that by the stage there is sufficient data for a thorough examination it has been recognised by share traders and its effect has been eliminated. Similarly, any future development of inefficiency with respect to public information is not likely to last for very long; once its presence is recognised there are usually sufficient rewards to encourage investors to trade on the inefficiency and thus remove it from the market.

Non-public information (strong form efficiency)

The most obvious way of making extra-normal profits in the share market is to have access to a source of relevant information that is known to few or preferably no others. Such information is unlikely to have been incorporated into the current share price, typically because of the difficulty (cost) of acquiring it. The trader with this information is in a position to anticipate future share price movements before the information becomes public. The most common source of non-public information is known as "inside information", i.e., information that is only likely to be known and available to officers of the company to which the information relates.

Insofar that most insider information is available only to company officers, it typically relates only to one specific company and it is an irregular event. This makes it difficult for the insider to consistently make abnormal returns. Investment analysts, fund managers, brokers and other professional investors are likely to have access to inside information only for a limited number of companies, although even in these cases the information is often second-hand or at least not directly obtained from top management. Such groups are likely to receive a lot of information purporting to be inside information which in fact is not. The problem then is to distinguish insider information from rumour. The task is far from easy, which probably explains why the evaluation of fund managers and other professional investors fails to uncover evidence of consistent abnormal returns to the funds under their control. The literature contains many studies evaluating the performance of managed funds in Australia and overseas. Two studies included in this volume are by Robson (chapter 30) and Bird, Chin and McCrae (chapter 31). The absence of evidence of consistent abnormal returns to managed funds is not really surprising, in that one would hardly expect non-public information to be available to a fund or a fund manager on such a scale that it would enable him to significantly affect the performance of the fund. Evidence of abnormal performance is likely to be on a scale such that the information is not readily available for assessment by academic studies. Further, the amount of evidence required is unlikely to be sufficient to draw strong statistical inferences about the degree of profitability of such portfolios even if the researcher had access to data on them. This has meant that research into the strong form of market efficiency has had to be at the level of selected pieces of information on share prices rather than the overall performance of an investor's portfolio.

An example of examining price responses in relation to particular information is provided in a study by Scholes (1969). Scholes examined the effect on prices of large block sales of shares in particular companies. He concluded that the price response was not a function of the size of the block of shares being sold but was related to the identity of the seller. He found that the greatest price reduction was associated with sales by corporations and their officers and the least by banks and insurance companies (as a group). He argued that this was related to the probability of these groups having relevant information about the company resulting in a sale of its shares. Ball and Finn (chapter 29) similarly concluded that any price effects associated with block transactions on the Sydney Stock Exchange were not a function of the size of the block, but could reasonably be argued to be due to information effects.

It is illegal to trade on insider information in the United States and in Australia the Securities Industry Code, administered by the National Companies and Securities Commission, prohibits insider trading. In spite of this, the United State evidence suggests that insider trading has not been eliminated from the market. A number of studies claim to have found evidence of insider trading and the profitability to the insiders of that trading.[13] Jaffe (1974) suggested that trading on inside information is widespread and insiders violate security regulations. Moreover, Jaffe's results suggest a breakdown in the semi-strong form of market efficiency in that the *Official Summary of Security Transactions*, published by the Securities and Exchange Commission of the United States, contains information about insider trading, that if acted upon, will yield abnormal returns. A subsequent unpublished paper by Marsh (1977) criticises Jaffe's methodology and casts doubts on his conclusions. Nonetheless, it would be surprising in the light of the publicity surrounding Jaffe's results that, if these are an accurate record and not due to experimental error, abnormal returns could still be earned by making use of information contained in the *Official Summary*. Indeed, following Jaffe's study, the Value Line Investment Survey in the United States included an "index of insider decisions" for each firm covered in its weekly publication. The public nature of this information should ensure that it is quickly incorporated into share prices.

Not all information that is non-public is based on insider information. Neiderhoffer and Osborne (1966) showed that the specialist[14] on the floor of the New York Stock Exchange made extra-normal profit. These results are perhaps not surprising considering the barriers to entry into that occupation at the time the study was conducted. One of the more common possible sources of non-public information would be information regarding changes in government policy before they are publicly announced. In particular, dramatic changes in the exchange rate are likely to have a profoundly differential effect across shares which could be utilised by traders to make abnormal returns. However, there is no published evidence supporting widespread use of such information. Moreover, there are considerable empirical problems with establishing an adequate control for testing the profitability of strategies based on information of economywide events. To date there have been no studies published specifically investigating the use of non-public sources of information in Australian share markets in the framework outlined. However, if we examine the studies conducted on the efficiency of the market with respect to public information, we invariably find price rises preceding the date of the public announcement of that information. This is evidence of "leakages" in the information, i.e., the use of non-public information in investment decisions. Moreover, the fact that the price rises and is sustained on the public announcement of such information implies trading on the "leaks" has been profitable.

In view of the consistency of results found between the United States and Australia for other forms of efficiency it would be surprising if the results found in the United States for studies specifically examining non-public information were inconsistent with the behaviour in Australian share markets with respect to this type of information. In fact, because of the less restrictive laws against insider trading in Australia, it is likely that this information is used more extensively by corporate officers in Australia than in the United States—although this is supposition only.

It is perhaps worth pointing out that although insider trading is generally frowned upon it does serve a useful purpose. By utilising insider information, traders speed the adjustment of share prices to new information and therefore ultimately speed the adjustment of resources to the demands of the capital market, even though this may be at some cost to the investor who is not in a position to utilise such information. Moreover, as we have seen from the United States evidence, it is extremely difficult to stamp out and it may be that the cost of trying to do so will be greater than the benefits attributable to preventing income redistribution from those without inside information to those that have it.

In conclusion

The examination of the evidence relating to stock market efficiency raises the obvious question of what is the implication of this evidence for share market investment strategies. The evidence to date suggests that public information has been incorporated in the current share prices by or at the time it becomes public. This means the investor is unlikely to be able to adopt investment strategies arising out of the use of public information that will lead to making abnormal profits. This implies the investor should take the current share price as an unbiased estimate of the value of the share, reflecting currently available public information. He should then seek out information which he believes is not incorporated into price. In respect to individual companies this information is most likely to be obtained from company visits and detailed discussions with company officers since this is the source of much of the relevant non-public information. Finn (chapter 32) provides evidence showing potential benefits to security analysts of information obtained from company visits. At the level of information affecting all companies, i.e., macroeconomic or marketwide factors, close scrutiny of government policies both here and abroad leading to an anticipation of changes in such policies is likely to be the major source of information that might lead to making abnormal returns. This search for non-public sources of information does not imply that the investor should neglect the already existing sources of public information. A knowledge of such information is usually essential for investors to be in a position to recognise useful non-public information when they come across it and to guide them in the direction of likely sources of such information. Consequently, profit and loss statements, balance sheets and other forms of public information are of value to investors.

A second important aspect of the evidence on market efficiency relates to claims of superior performance by investment analysts. Close scrutiny of the basis on which claimants of superior performance support their claims is likely to uncover the validity of any claims of abnormal returns and superior skills. There is always an element of chance in investment: superior performance may be due to a series of fortunate but chance occurrences. It is the role of performance evaluation to judge whether superior performance has been achieved and it is a role for efficient-market theory together with statistical inference to separate out the elements of skill that could have led to the superior performance from those which could be attributable to luck. Methodology for carrying out such tests is provided in discussions of performance measurement by Robson (chapter 30) and Bird, Chin and McCrae (chapter 31) and in a study by Ball, Brown and Finn (chapter 33) on a series of investment recommendations that have appeared in the press.

Readers who are disappointed at not finding *the solution* to successful investment in shares after reading this chapter should console themselves with the conclusion that there is no strategy or formula that guarantees great success. There never will be. The efficiency of the market guarantees the ephemerality of such strategies. However, an understanding of the principles of market behaviour should protect them against incautious investments brought about by misplaced confidence. Readers who have had their appetites whetted for a serious examination of the evidence supporting these conclusions should read on.

Acknowledgments

This chapter has benefited considerably from the comments of Ray Ball and Philip Brown.

Notes

1. A *pareto optimum* is a weak condition of welfare maximisation. The optimum is achieved when it is impossible by an exchange of goods and/or resources to make someone better off without making someone else worse off.
2. Although the achievement of a *pareto optimum* is a sufficient condition for better resource allocation, it is not a necessary condition.
3. This is a rather loose use of the concept of utility. Unless everyone is better off, or at least no worse off, by an exchange, i.e., a *pareto optimum*, then there is no way we can be certain that resources put to one use can provide greater utility than alternative uses because we are unable to make interpersonal comparisons of utility. That is, we cannot aggregate individuals' utilities to form society's total utility; therefore, the only way we can be sure society's utility has increased by an exchange is when there is no one made worse off as a result of the exchange.
4. This implies the task of compiling a list of expected net cash flows from now into the future and discounting them to get a present value or price of the stock which is in some sense the right price, is not an appealing procedure. There are just too many unknown factors affecting the variables in the equation for such an estimate to be any more than one investor's estimate of price and an extremely subjective one at that. This method of evaluation is sometimes interpreted as the fundamentalist approach to share valuation, but it is only an extreme interpretation of fundamental analysis and the fact that it is not a recommended form of analysis does not refute the logic of a fundamental approach.
5. Some current research investigates the magnitude of price responses to certain types of information, e.g., Collins, Kothari and Rayburn (1987) and Freeman (1987). However, this research is still in early stages.
6. For a more rigorous and detailed discussion see Fama (1970a).
7. Stigler (1966, p. 88) lists four criteria for a perfectly competitive market—perfect knowledge, a large number of buyers and sellers, product homogeneity and product divisibility. Fama and Miller (1972, p. 277) give a more complete and a more relevant definition for stock markets; in short their definition implies firms and investors are price takers in a frictionless market.
8. Some evidence in support of this is provided by Ball and Brown in chapter 27.
9. This does not mean the information is valueless. The information may complement other information so that together they enable profitable strategies to be developed. The "other information" in this case would not be reflected in prices until it was complemented.
10. See Officer (chapter 14).
11. In the first edition of this book, the decade 1967–77 was referenced to illustrate this point. In the

early years of that decade some fund managers achieved extremely high returns, but with the severe downturn in the share market in the early 1970s it was these same managers who were hardest hit. The illustration retains its importance in the second edition, only the dates have been changed.

12. Linear dependence means a relationship that is linear in the parameters; e.g.:

$$\text{price } (t) = \beta \, [\text{price } (t-1)^2]$$

where β is the parameter relating the square of price in period $t-1$ to price at period t is not a linear relationship. But price $(t) = [\text{price } t-1]$ is a linear relationship.

13. For example, Lorie and Neiderhoffer (1968) and Jaffe (1974).

14. Specialists are responsible for matching buy and sell orders on the New York Stock Exchange— they operate on a limited number of stocks. Located on the floor of the Exchange their role is to facilitate trading by evening out temporary imbalances in buy and sell orders. Their monopoly profit comes from a knowledge of unfilled limit orders.

PART 2
The distribution of share returns

2 The distribution of stock market returns: Tests of normality

Michael D. Stokie

Introduction

The monthly returns of 578 individual securities listed on the Melbourne Stock Exchange 1958–73 were examined for normality by Praetz and Wilson (1978). They performed separate tests for kurtosis (peakedness), skewness, and overall goodness-of-fit to a normal distribution, and they found significant evidence of non-normality.

In this chapter, the Praetz and Wilson findings are re-examined. It is shown that much of the reported non-normality can be attributed to a high incidence of zero returns, especially in the less frequently traded smaller companies, and also to parameter non-stationarity over the 16-year period studied. The influence of these two factors is reduced by applying the tests to the group of 40 leading securities in three 5-year periods.

The theoretical aspects and empirical results for each of the three tests are set out in the following sections, and the results are then summarised. The main finding is that there are no conclusive grounds for rejecting normality in the monthly returns of leading securities over 5-year periods. This is of importance because normality of security returns is the simplest assumption leading to the Market Model and the Capital Asset Pricing Model as described in Fama (1976). It is also a basic assumption for some tests of the mean variance efficiency of market indices reported for example in Roll (1979), Stokie (1981) and Gibbons (1982).

Testing for kurtosis in the return distributions

Test outline and description of data

The data file of Melbourne Stock Exchange industrial securities is described in Praetz and Wilson (1978). It contains monthly rates of return adjusted for dividends, bonus issues, etc., for 578 securities with data in more than

Reprinted from the *Australian Journal of Management* (December 1982), 159–78, by permission of the author and the publisher.

60 of the 191 months in the period from 1958 to 1973. This is the group of securities used by Praetz and Wilson, and it will be referred to as Group A.

Monthly return data are available in all 191 months for 144 of the 578 securities; this group will be designated Group B. The 40 securities from Group B that have the highest capitalisation at December 1973 constitute Group C; these securities are listed in table 2.5.

The variable studied is the natural logarithm

$$x_{it} = ln\,(1 + r_{it}) \tag{1}$$

where r_{it} is the return on security i during month t. The log transformation is suggested in Praetz (1969, p. 126) to reduce skewness in the often positively skewed return distribution.

The test for departure from normality owing to significant kurtosis is based on the distribution of the standardised 4th moment

$$b_2 = m_4/m_2^2 \tag{2}$$

in random samples of n observations from a univariate normal population, where for a sample $\{x_i\}$ of mean m_1 we define $m_r = \Sigma(x_i - m_1)^r/n$. The distribution of the kurtosis statistic

$$K_n = (b_2 - 3)\,(n/24)^{1/2} \tag{3}$$

is approximately unit normal, with the approximation more and more uncertain the smaller n is and the further it is taken out into the tails of the distribution. This is discussed in D'Agostino and Pearson (1973, p. 613) and in Praetz and Wilson (1978, p. 82). Using extensive computer simulation and curve fitting, D'Agostino and Pearson have provided charts of more accurate probability levels of b_2 out to the 0.1 per cent point for sample sizes n from 20 to 200, and these are used in this study.

Influence of zero returns on kurtosis: 1958–73

There are many securities in the data file with a high incidence of exactly zero monthly returns. A zero return might be due to a genuine constancy of trading price from the end of one month to the next or it could be due to the absence of trading during the month, a market thinness effect.[1] A further possible cause could be error in or rounding off near-zero returns in the data file.

Table 2.1 compares the frequency of zero returns in each of the three groups of securities. In Group A, 38 per cent of the securities have an incidence of zero monthly returns of at least 10 per cent. The highest incidence of zeros is 30–35 per cent and this occurs in the returns of four of the securities. In Group B, the proportion of securities with at least 10 per cent of monthly returns being zero drops from 38 per cent to 14 per cent. In Group C, the decreased incidence of zero returns is even more striking with only one of these 40 leading securities having over 10 per cent of its 191 monthly returns being zero. Group A includes Group B which in turn includes Group C, so the high incidence of zero returns in Group A must occur predominantly in the less well established and smaller companies.

Now a comparison is made between the incidence of zero returns in each group of securities, and the proportion of securities in that group which fail the kurtosis test. For each security its kurtosis statistic K_n is calculated using

Table 2.1 Frequency distribution of zero monthly returns in different groups of securities

Proportion of security's monthly returns which are zero	Number (percentage) of securities in each group with the given proportion of zero returns		
	Group A 578 securities returns in more than 60 months	Group B 144 securities returns in all 191 months	Group C 40 leading securities with 191 months
0–5%	95 (16%)	33 (23%)	16 (40%)
5–10%	267 (46%)	91 (63%)	23 (58%)
10–15%	148 (26%)	14 (10%)	1 (2%)
15–20%	39 (7%)	4 (3%)	—
20–25%	18 (3%)	2 (1%)	—
25–30%	7 (1.2%)	—	—
30–35%	4 (0.7%)	—	—
over 35%	—	—	—
Total	578 (100%)	144 (100%)	40 (100%)

(3) for the longest available period of data. In Groups B and C this is for 191 months, but in Group A the period of between 61 and 191 months varies for each individual security. The proportion of securities which fail the kurtosis test for normality is given for each group in table 2.2.

Table 2.2 Numbers (percentages) of securities with significant positive kurtosis at the 1% level in the distribution of returns over various time periods

Period of monthly returns		Group A (578 securities)	Group B (144 securities)	Group C (40 leading securities)
1958–1973	191 months	364 (63%)*	85 (59%)	21 (53%)
1959–1963	60 months	—	—	6 (15%)
1964–1968	60 months	—	—	7 (18%)
1969–1973	60 months	—	—	7 (18%)

* Praetz and Wilson (1978) reported 68% for Group A, 1958–73. The difference arises from their use of the normal approximation in the distribution of b_2, whereas the D'Agostino and Pearson probability levels are used here.

The comparison of tables 2.1 and 2.2 suggests that performance on the kurtosis test might be related to the incidence of zeros in the security's set of monthly returns. A more detailed examination of this correspondence has been undertaken for Group B in which all securities have return data over 191 months, and the details are reported in Stokie (1981, pp. 101–5). It shows a tendency for very high kurtosis statistics to occur in the 20 Group B securities having the highest incidence of zero returns. Of these 20 securities, 16 (80 per cent) fail the kurtosis test at the 1 per cent level, whereas only 69 of the remaining 124 securities (56 per cent) in Group B fail the same test. The first 6 all fail the kurtosis test.

For a more objective assessment of this apparent trend, the 144 securities of Group B were ranked according to the number of zero monthly returns in the period 1958–73 and also according to their kurtosis statistics in that period. The correlation coefficient between the two rankings was $r = 0.215$. Any inference from this statistic must be made with caution because there is no evidence that the properties under consideration follow a bivariate normal distribution, and in fact the number of zero returns is not even continuously distributed. An appropriate large sample test of the independence of the two variables represented by the rankings is made by considering the statistic

$$t = \frac{r\sqrt{(n-2)}}{\sqrt{(1-r^2)}} \tag{4}$$

which is approximately Student t-distributed on $(n - 2)$ degrees of freedom if the two variables are independent. For $r = 0.215$ and $n = 144$, this statistic is $t = 2.62$, which is significant in an upper one-sided test at the 1 per cent level.

An alternative approach is to use the Kendall tau coefficient described in Winkler and Hays (1975, pp. 866–74) and based on the number of inversions in order for pairs of securities in the two rankings. This statistic has the advantage with respect to tests for independence that the sampling distribution of τ converges fairly rapidly to a normal form as the sampling size n increases. After corrections for ties in the rankings and for continuity, the Kendall tau statistic was $\tau = 0.152$ and the corresponding standardised normal value was $z = 2.70$ which is significant at the 1 per cent level. Thus the apparent relationship between the incidence of zero returns and the kurtosis statistic is sustained.

Weekly returns would seem particularly susceptible to a high number of zero returns. Dyer (1975, p. 13) found significant kurtosis in the *weekly* returns of 100 leading companies, but the incidence of zero returns averaged 18 per cent in all securities and the greatest incidence was 62 per cent for Australian Newsprint Mills Holdings Ltd. Dyer (1975, pp. 13, 23) does notice and discuss the influence of zero returns. The findings of widespread significant kurtosis by Dyer and also by Praetz (1969) based on weekly returns are perhaps attributable in a substantial part to this aggregation of returns of zero. Fama (1965) also rejects normality but uses daily returns which might be even more susceptible to this effect.

Clustering effect of discrete prices

Securities are traded at discrete prices and this can cause clustering in the monthly returns. Neiderhoffer (1965, 1966) discusses this effect.[2] As an example, consider a security with a current price of $2.00 and having sample mean monthly return 0 and a typical standard deviation 0.05. The smallest possible monthly price variation of one cent will produce a standardised log-return statistic of $z = ln(201/200)/0.05 = 0.10$ or $z = ln(199/200)/0.05 = -0.10$. So no standardised statistic can occur within 0.10 either side of the sample mean other than at the mean itself. This clustering effect is now examined.

Simulation illustrating the effect of zero returns

It is argued above that the kurtosis statistic K_n will be influenced by a high incidence of zero returns and possibly also by the central clustering effect of discrete price data. But how marked will this effect be? The following analysis with simulated data has been performed to give some quantitative assessment of these factors.

Three classes of data, *X, Y, Z*, were obtained. The *X*-data consisted of a computer-generated sample of 200 random normal deviates. These correspond to standardised monthly log-returns following a continuous normal distribution over a period of about 16 years. Each sample was transformed to have zero mean and unit variance.

The *Y*-data set made allowance for central clustering owing to discrete prices. The sample of *Y*-values was exactly the same as the *X*-values except that the *Y*-value was set to zero if the corresponding *X*-value was in the central interval $(-0.05, 0.05)$, and it was set to the endpoints 0.10 if the *X*-value was in the intervals $(0.05, 0.10)$ and $(-0.10, -0.05)$ respectively. In 10,000 different samples of 200 random deviates, the proportion of zero returns resulting from this clustering procedure averaged 3.7 per cent of each sample and in no sample did it exceed 5 per cent.

The *Z*-data allowed for the effects of market thinness and inaccurate data differentiation by artificially introducing a higher incidence of zero returns. The *Z*-data coincided with the *Y*-data but in each sample an additional number of randomly chosen returns was set to zero. A data set which had a total proportion a per cent of zero returns was denoted by Z_a. Data sets Z_a of random samples of 200 random deviates were constructed for $a = 5, 6, 7, 8, 9, 10, 15, 20$.

For each set of data *X, Y, $\{Z_a\}$* the kurtosis statistic K_n as given in (3) was calculated. The process was repeated for 10,000 different randomly generated samples of *X, Y, Z_a* data. Table 2.3 sets out the effect of increased incidence of zero returns on the kurtosis statistic K_{200} in 10,000 random samples of 200 normal deviates.

Table 2.3 The effect of increased incidence of zero returns on kurtosis statistic K_{200} in 10,000 random samples of 200 normal deviates

	Percentage of zero returns in each sample of 200 returns	Number of samples with non-normal kurtosis at 1% level of significance	Average kurtosis statistic K_{200} in 10,000 samples
X	0%	114	−0.100
Y	3.78% (average)	113	−0.103
Z_5	5%	129	0.005
Z_6	6%	157	0.098
Z_7	7%	174	0.193
Z_8	8%	200	0.297
Z_9	9%	250	0.403
Z_{10}	10%	308	0.512
Z_{15}	15%	842	1.119
Z_{20}	20%	2,032	1.841

The average kurtosis statistic and the total number of samples with significantly non-normal kurtosis at the 1 per cent level are virtually unchanged between the *X* and *Y* data sets. This leads to the conclusion that kurtosis measurement is not sensitive to any clustering effect owing to the discrete nature of prices. However, the Z_a-data shows that the kurtosis statistic is sensitive to further increases in the incidence of zero returns. The actual proportion of non-significant samples falls increasingly short of the expected proportion of 99 per cent as the incidence of zero returns grows from 5 per cent to 20 per cent, and in like manner the average value of the K_n statistic also increases with a.

The effect of parameter non-stationarity on kurtosis testing

Significant kurtosis in the monthly returns over a 16-year period has been reported in table 2.2 for between 53 per cent and 63 per cent of the securities in the three groups under consideration here. This has been partly attributed to a high incidence of zero returns, which would explain the gradation between the three groups. Nevertheless, the incidence of kurtosis in the 40 leading securities of Group C remains high at 53 per cent even though this group has a low incidence of zero returns.

It is possible that non-stationarity of the population mean return and standard deviation of returns for individual securities over the 16-year period could account for some of the observed positive kurtosis. Praetz (1969) found evidence of non-stationarity from year to year in all variances and in one-sixth of the means in his study of weekly return data for 20 Australian securities 1958–66.

The evidence regarding parameter stationarity for the Group C securities in the 16-year period 1958–73 is examined in Stokie (1981), where it is concluded that for most leading securities the mean and variance parameters of their monthly log-return distribution are stationary over 5-year periods, but the variances are non-stationary in a 16-year period.

Testing for kurtosis in 40 leaders over 5-year periods

In order to avoid the effects of a high incidence of zero returns and of parameter non-stationarity, the kurtosis test is applied to the monthly returns of the 40 leading securities over three 5-year periods. The results are set out in table 2.2.

In the period 1959–63 only 6 of the 40 securities have significant positive kurtosis at the 1 per cent level, and in the other two periods there are 7 such securities.[3] These rates of non-normality are considerably less than the rate in table 2.2 for the same securities over a 16-year period. This endorses the claim made above that apparent positive kurtosis might be observed in long-term security returns as a result of parameter non-stationarity.

In summary, table 2.2 shows that up to 34 of the 40 leading securities do not have significant positive kurtosis at the 1 per cent level, and in this sense the distribution of their monthly log-returns over 5-year periods is compatible with the normal distribution.

Testing for skewness in the return distributions

The test for departure from normality owing to significant skewness of returns is based on the distribution of the standardised 3rd moment:

$$b_1^{1/2} = m_3/m_2^{3/2} \tag{5}$$

in random samples of n observations from a univariate normal population.

The distribution of the skewness statistic

$$Sn = (b_1 n/6)^{1/2} \tag{6}$$

is approximately unit normal. D'Agostino and Pearson (1973, pp. 618–22) have given an improved approximating method for the probability integral of $b_1^{1/2}$ which is more accurate for small n. The approximation is represented by the transformation

$$X(b_1^{1/2}) = \delta \sinh^{-1} (b_1^{1/2}/2) \tag{7}$$

where X is a standardised unit normal deviate and λ, δ are tabulated functions of the sample size n.

Praetz and Wilson (1978, p. 88, table 1) used (6) and found 28 per cent of the Group A securities were significantly skewed at the 1 per cent level. The present study has used (7) and found that the proportion of securities whose returns are significantly skewed at the 1 per cent level drops to 19 per cent for Group B and even further to 13 per cent for the 40 leading securities in Group C. These results are based on monthly returns over the 16-year period 1958–73, and are summarised in table 2.4.

It was possible to confirm that a high incidence of zero returns does not contribute to skewness by considering the rankings of the 144 Group B securities according to the number of zero monthly returns in the period 1958–73 and also according to their skewness statistics in that period. The correlation coefficient between the two rankings was $r = 0.088$ which, using (4), corresponded to $t = 1.05$. This was not an extreme value for the Student t-distribution on 142 degrees of freedom and so the hypothesis of independence in the two rankings was sustained.

The alternative approach using the Kendall tau coefficient gave $\tau = 0.06$ and the corresponding standardised normal value was $z = 1.06$ which was not significant. Both approaches confirm that skewness, unlike kurtosis, is not produced by a high incidence of zero returns. This is not unexpected because, to the extent that the sample mean return is at or near zero, the clustering of several returns at zero will not contribute to skewness.

Table 2.4 Numbers (percentages) of securities with skewed returns over various time periods

Period of monthly returns		Group A (578 securities)	Group B (144 securities)	Group C (40 securities)
1958–73	191 months	161 (28%)	27 (19%)	5 (13%)
1959–63	60 months	—	12 (8%)	2 (5%)
1964–68	60 months	—	14 (10%)	4 (10%)
1969–73	60 months	—	15 (10%)	2 (5%)

Much of the apparent skewness can be attributed to parameter non-stationarity, however. Allowance for this possible effect is made by testing for skewness over 5-year periods instead of the 16-year period 1958–73, and the results are given in table 2.4.

There is a clear reduction in the proportion of skewed returns when the period of 191 months is replaced by a 60-month period and only a few securities have significantly skewed returns at the 1 per cent level over a

5-year period.[4] In summary, there is little evidence of skewness in the monthly log-returns of securities over 5-year periods.

Chi-squared test for normally distributed returns

Sensitivity of χ^2-test to choice of partition

In studying the monthly returns of securities, Praetz and Wilson (1978) used a partition of the standardised log-returns having 16 classes with endpoints at 0, ±0.2, ±0.4, ±0.6, ±0.8, ±1.0, ±1.4, ±2, ±∞. Some authors, for example Winkler and Hays (1975, p. 824), recommend the use of a partition with equiprobable classes. For 16 classes such a partition has endpoints at 0, ±0.15, ±0.32, ±0.49, ±0.68, ±0.89, ±1.15, ±1.53, ±∞. Using exactly the same return data for the 40 leaders over the 1958–73 period as Praetz and Wilson studied, a chi-squared goodness-of-fit test for normality of returns with partitions of 14, 15 and 16 equiprobable classes finds that the number of securities with significantly non-normal returns at the 1 per cent level is respectively 4, 7 and 8. The Praetz and Wilson partition (P & W) leads to 4 Group C securities being judged non-normal at the 1 per cent level.

This shows only fair agreement when different partitions are used. However, the true extent of the sensitivity of the χ^2-test to the partition chosen is better revealed by a detailed examination of the χ^2-statistics for each of the 40 leading securities. These are set out in table 2.5.

Table 2.5 Chi-squared statistics in testing returns of 40 leaders for normality, 1958–73, using different partitions of N classes

Security	Equiprobable partition			P & W
	$N = 14$	$N = 15$	$N = 16$	$N = 16$
1. Ampol Petroleum	21.6	26.1	19.5	17.8
2. Associated Pulp & Paper	16.7	28.3*	16.2	22.6
3. Associated Securities	18.9	8.6	21.4	11.3
4. Australian Consolidated Industries	10.6	14.8	28.9*	18.2
5. Australian Guarantee Corporation	20.3	15.3	28.9*	29.0*
6. Australian Paper Manufacturers	13.0	16.3	11.3	19.0
7. Bank of Adelaide	42.6*	43.3*	49.7*	39.7*
8. Bank of NSW	18.0	13.0	11.0	16.6
9. Blue Metal Industries	17.5	18.5	16.7	16.8
10. Brambles Industries	18.7	25.4	31.2*	19.2
11. AMATIL (British Tobacco)	16.5	21.7	18.3	18.5
12. BHP	24.6	15.9	21.9	22.5
13. Burns Philp	16.5	18.0	24.4	10.6
14. Carpenter (WR)	15.6	18.0	15.2	24.4
15. Coles	10.9	14.4	15.5	19.9
16. CSR	11.4	10.4	12.1	13.9
17. Commercial Bank of Australia	21.6	14.6	32.7*	12.3
18. Commercial Banking Co. of Sydney	29.0*	32.1*	31.2*	31.4*
19. Commonwealth Industrial Gases	18.9	15.5	24.5	17.0
20. Dunlop Australia	20.6	25.4	29.7*	21.7
21. EZ Industries	18.1	22.8	16.2	22.7
22. Fairfax (John)	23.5	31.6*	18.0	27.3
23. F & T Industries	17.7	10.0	20.7	19.2
24. Hardie Asbestos	24.1	17.5	26.4	26.4
25. Herald & Weekly Times	19.4	29.6*	18.8	27.2

Security	Equiprobable partition			P & W
	$N = 14$	$N = 15$	$N = 16$	$N = 16$
26. Industrial Acceptance	10.6	12.8	7.6	8.0
27. ICI	12.4	12.8	17.0	8.6
28. Jones (David)	25.5*	29.3*	27.7*	30.6*
29. Morris (Philip)	14.2	17.8	24.4	17.2
30. Myer	19.0	17.8	25.0	13.2
31. National Bank of Australia	15.3	18.9	18.7	16.3
32. Queensland Press	13.1	15.6	18.3	17.4
33. Repco	6.7	6.5	10.1	10.5
34. South Australian Brewery	13.0	23.0	21.5	19.3
35. Swan Brewery	23.5	23.6	23.7	24.4
36. Tooheys	5.2	5.6	12.0	4.6
37. Tooth & Co.	28.8*	21.4	26.5	23.6
38. Union Carbide	13.7	19.7	13.8	19.3
39. Waltons	16.9	31.2*	22.2	23.7
40. Woolworths	10.3	12.3	18.5	15.8
Upper 1% point χ^2_{N-3}	24.7	26.2	27.7	27.7

* Denotes significant at 1% level.

There was good agreement with all four partitions for the securities Bank of Adelaide, CBC Sydney and David Jones which were significant in all cases. However, there were 9 other securities which would be judged to have non-normal returns using one partition but would not be significant using the other three partitions. For 25 of the 40 securities the highest χ^2-statistic was at least 50 per cent greater than the lowest. The Commercial Bank of Australia is seen to be very sensitive to the choice of partition. Its monthly return data has been examined in an attempt to find why its χ^2-statistic was so partition-sensitive and this is discussed below.

Illustration of partition sensitivity for CBA

The sample mean and standard deviation of monthly log-returns for Commercial Bank of Australia in the 191-month period 1958–73 were $\bar{x} = 0.0083$ and $s = 0.058$. Each monthly return was standardised using $z_t = (x_t - \bar{x})/s$. The frequency table of these observed standardised returns using partitions with 15 and 16 equiprobable classes is given in table 2.6.

This table shows that market changes in the observed frequencies using the two different partitions occur at Classes 7 and 8 and also at 10 and 11. The substantial fluctuation in the χ^2-statistic is directly caused by these changes.

The observed frequency in any class of partitioned data will always be subject to slight variations if the partition points are relocated, but the variation here appears to be very high. There are two main reasons for this: a high incidence of zero returns in the CBA profile of monthly returns and the clustering effect associated with discrete prices.

The monthly returns for CBA include 14 (7 per cent) zeros. On the standardised scale $x = 0$ corresponds to $z = (0 - 0.0083)/0.058 = -0.143$. This means that there is a block of 14 returns which all plot at the same position -0.143 and this block is in Class 8 for the 16-class partition but

Table 2.6   Frequency table of standardised returns for CBA, 1958–73, using different partitions

16 equiprobable class parition		15 equiprobable class partition	
Class Interval	Observed Frequency	Class Interval	Observed Frequency
1 −∞ to −1.534	9	1 −∞ to −1.501	12
2 −1.534 to −1.151	20	2 −1.501 to −1.111	19
3 −1.151 to −0.887	5	3 −1.111 to −0.842	4
4 −0.887 to −0.675	12	4 −0.842 to −0.623	13
5 −0.675 to −0.489	12	5 −0.623 to −0.431	12
6 −0.489 to −0.319	9	6 −0.431 to −0.253	10
7 −0.319 to −0.153	5	7 −0.253 to −0.084	17
8 −0.153 to 0.000	24	8 −0.084 to 0.084	16
9 0 to 0.153	14	9 0.084 to 0.253	15
10 0.153 to 0.319	17	10 0.253 to 0.431	13
11 0.319 to 0.489	7	11 0.431 to 0.623	12
12 0.489 to 0.675	11	12 0.623 to 0.842	12
13 0.675 to 0.887	13	13 0.842 to 1.111	11
14 0.887 to 1.151	11	14 1.111 to 1.501	16
15 1.151 to 1.534	13	15 1.501 to ∞	9
16 1.534 to ∞	9	—	—
Total frequency	191	Total frequency	191
Expected frequency in each class	11.94	Expected frequency in each class	12.73
χ^2-statistic	32.7	χ^2-statistic	14.6

in Class 7 for the 15-class partition. The movement of this block across the class boundary when the $N = 15$ partition replaces the $N = 16$ partition is a major factor underlying the substantial change in the χ^2-statistic.

A typical price for CBA shares in the 1958–73 period was \$2.00, or £1 prior to 1966. A 5-cent or sixpence variation in price would give a monthly price relative of 0.975 or 1.025 and some clustering around these points would be expected due to such preferred trading units. CBA has eight monthly price relatives in the interval 1.024 to 1.026 and on the standardised scale these correspond to z-values between 0.266 and 0.299. With the 16-class partition these eight returns all lie in the class interval (0.153, 0.319) but cross the boundary of the corresponding class interval (0.084, 0.253) with the 15-class partition. This block movement of returns clustered around preferred price movement (5 cent) positions is the predominant cause of the observed frequency fluctuations around Class 10.

Corresponding to a downward preferred movement of 5 cents, CBA has nine monthly price relatives clustered in the interval 0.972 to 0.978. This corresponds to a standardised z-interval −0.633 to −0.527, and so this block of values lies in Class 5 with either partition. These values do not influence the χ^2-statistic in a markedly different fashion for equiprobable partitions of size 15 or 16 classes, but they could perhaps do so with other partitions.

This particular example with 191 monthly returns for CBS has illustrated the manner in which the χ^2-statistic for the goodness-of-fit of a normal distribution to monthly return data can be very sensitive to the choice of partition if there is a high incidence of zero returns or if there has been a clustering of returns as a result of preferred trading fluctuations. This is investigated further below using simulated data.

Simulated data illustration of partition sensitivity in χ^2-test

Consider once again the sets of data *X, Y, Z* described in detail above. The *X*-data is a sample of 200 simulated random normal deviates. Set *Y* allows for some clustering owing to discrete price movements, and Set *Z* allows for this clustering and also an increasing incidence of other zero returns.[5]

For each data set, a normal distribution was fitted to the 200 simulated returns and the χ^2-statistic for the goodness-of-fit test was calculated using partitions with 17, 18, 19 and 20 equiprobable classes. This process was repeated for different randomly generated samples. In most instances the χ^2-statistic increases as the data set is changed from *X* to *Y* to *Z*, so the statistic is satisfactorily detecting movement of the data away from normality. However, within each data set there is quite a wide fluctuation in the χ^2-statistics for the different partitions, partly due to changing degrees of freedom. For the normally distributed *X*-data these fluctuations are not large enough erroneously to reject normality. Within any one sample of *Y*-data there is also a reasonably high level of consistency in accepting normality, but with the *Z*-data having moderate levels of zero returns there is considerable conflict between the results with different partitions. When a high incidence of zero returns is present, the modified data become so badly non-normal that any partition suffices to detect the sample as being non-normal.

This indicates that a rejection of normality because of a significant χ^2-statistic with just one particular partition may be unsound if there is a moderate incidence of zero returns.

In the tests reported subsequently, normality of the return distributions will not be rejected unless the data gives χ^2-statistics which are significant at the 1 per cent level for at least two of four different partitions.

This criterion is ad hoc in nature and has the further disadvantage that it increases the significance level (α). It is particularly difficult to determine this increase in terms of α because of the strong dependence of partition results and also the distorting influence of the varying number of zero returns. In order to estimate α, the above simulation was continued for 10,000 samples of 200 random returns, and separately for 10,000 samples of 60 random returns using partitions of 9, 10, 11 and 12 equiprobable classes. The size-60 samples simulate monthly returns over 5-year periods, and for these samples the $\{Z_a\}$ data sets are constructed with $a = 5, 6^2/_3, 8^1/_3, 10, 11^2/_3, 13^1/_3,$ 15, 20 corresponding to actual numbers of zero returns from 3 to 10.

The results are set out in table 2.7 and show that α will not be greater than 5 per cent provided the percentage of zero returns in each sample does not exceed about 6 per cent in samples of 200 returns or about 10 per cent in samples of 60 returns.

χ^2-test for normality in 40 leaders over 5-year periods

The goodness-of-fit test for normality in the distribution of returns is restricted to the 40 leading securities of Group C in order to avoid as much as possible the distorting influence of a high incidence of zero returns. Monthly returns are considered over 5-year periods to avoid or reduce non-stationarity in the security parameters.

The χ^2-test is performed in each period with four different partitions of

Table 2.7 Results of χ^2-test for normality in data sets X, Y, Z for 10,000 simulated samples using partitions with different numbers of equiprobable classes

Simulation over 200 months			Simulation over 60 months		
Percentage of zero returns in each sample of 200 returns	Normal in at least 3 partitions	Non-normal in at least 2 partitions	Percentage of zero returns in each sample of 60 returns	Normal in at least 3 partitions	Non-normal in at least 2 partitions
0%	9,923	77	0%	9,924	76
3.78% (Av.)	9,957	243	3.41% (Av.)	9,915	85
5%	9,735	265	5%	9,921	79
6%	9,450	550	6.67%	9,872	128
7%	8,715	1,285	8.33%	9,763	237
8%	7,334	2,666	10%	9,538	462
9%	5,058	4,942	11.67%	9,031	969
10%	2,525	7,475	13.33%	8,179	1,821
15%	0	10,000	15%	6,773	3,227
20%	0	10,000	20%	1,024	8,976

$N = 9, 10, 11, 12$ equiprobable classes, and normality of returns is rejected if the χ^2-statistic is significant at the 1 per cent level for at least two of the four partitions. It is seen from table 2.1 that the percentage of zero returns is under 10 per cent for all but one of the 40 Group C securities, so that above simulation indicates that the significance level α associated with this criterion for non-normality should not exceed 5 per cent.

Table 2.8 Number of leading securities with non-normal returns in each 5-year period, and having significant χ^2-statistics at the 1% level for at least two of four different partitions with $N = 9, 10, 11, 12$ equiprobable classes

Period of monthly returns	Group C (40 leading securities)
1959–63	2
1964–68	4
1969–73	2

The results are given in table 2.8. Just 4 securities have non-normal returns in one period and only 2 securities in each of the other periods. Praetz and Wilson (1978) reported non-normality in 50 per cent of the 578 Group A securities over the 16-year period 1958–73. This much greater incidence is attributed to the combined effects of zero returns and parameter non-stationarity. There is little evidence of non-normality in the returns of leading securities over 5-year periods when judged by chi-squared tests.

Summary of test results and conclusions

Three tests of normality have been performed on the monthly log-returns of 40 leading securities in three different 5-year periods, 1959–63, 1964–68 and 1969–73. The tests were for kurtosis or peakedness, for skewness, and for overall goodness-of-fit. The level of significance was 1 per cent for the kurtosis and skewness tests, and for the goodness-of-fit test a special criterion was developed and its level of significance was estimated to be not more than 5 per cent. Securities which exhibited non-normality in any of the tests in any period are listed in table 2.9.

Table 2.9 Leading securities with significantly non-normal returns according to different tests in various 5-year periods

Period	Kurtosis test at 1% level	Skewness test at 1% level	Goodness-of-fit test at 5% level (estimate)
1959–63	AGC Bank of Adelaide Carpenter CBC Sydney EZ Industries Waltons	Amatil Fairfax	Bank of Adelaide CBC Sydney
1964–68	Ampol Bank of Adelaide Herald David Jones Philip Morris National Bank SA Brewery	Bank of Adelaide ICI Philip Morris National Bank	Ampol David Jones Myer Qld Press
1969–73	Assoc. Pulp & Paper ACI Brambles BHP Burns Philp Dunlop Swan Brewery	Ampol BHP	Ampol Dunlop

In any given 5-year period, between 8 and 10 securities fail at least one of the tests. It is much less common for a particular security to fail two of the tests, and this occurs for only 2 securities in 1959–63, 5 in 1964–68, and 3 in 1969–73. No security fails all the three tests in any one period. Only 2 securities exhibit prolonged non-normality over two successive periods and neither maintains this over all three periods; these securities are Ampol Petroleum and Bank of Adelaide.

In summary, this chapter has found no conclusive grounds for rejecting the normal distribution as a representation of the monthly log-returns of most leading Australian industrial securities over 5-year periods.

Other studies have consistently found that a high proportion of securities have non-normally distributed returns. Such findings have been attributed to a high incidence of zero returns, especially for weekly data or for monthly data in the less frequently traded smaller companies, and to parameter non-stationarity over long periods.

In particular, the finding of normality here contrasts with the underlying market view in Epps and Epps (1976) that variations in the rate of information releases to the share market *a priori* suggest that non-normal kurtosis will be observed. Epps and Epps use transaction volume as a manifestation of the rate of information releases, and in a study of 20 United States common stocks they show that there is a stochastic dependence between transaction volume for a security and its log-return from each transaction to the next. The log-returns are viewed as following a mixture of distributions and having pronounced positive kurtosis.

These contrasting findings seem to be related to the frequency at which returns and prices are measured. Epps and Epps examine events in a very short time span: their largest sample consists of the price changes for the stock American Telephone & Telegraph which occur in 1,078 transactions over a 5-day trading period, and their longest trading period for any stock covers only four weeks.

Non-normal distributions seem appropriate for log-returns when these are measured over short time intervals such as at each transaction, daily, weekly or even monthly for smaller sparsely traded firms. Such behaviour appears to "average out" over longer intervals so that monthly log-returns of individual leading securities do not exhibit pronounced non-normality.

Acknowledgments

Comments and suggestions by R. Ball, R. Officer and P. Praetz are gratefully acknowledged. I am indebted to P. Brown for permission to use his data file on industrial securities, 1958–73.

Notes

1. No exhaustive examination of zero returns was made. However, an examination of zero returns for some securities indicated that a genuine constancy of trading price with sales at the same level in adjacent months was relatively rare; most zero returns reflected an absence of trading during the month. There is a seasonal effect here; see Ball and Brown (1978).
2. Typical US stocks are priced between $10 and $50, and trading occurs in increments of 1/8 of $1. Australian shares have much lower unit prices, usually under $5, and trading occurs in increments of one cent. There is some tendency for changes in the higher-priced Australian securities to be in multiples of 5 cents.
3. The evidence is less decisive if the 5 per cent level of significance is used. At this level, the numbers of securities with non-normal kurtosis in the three periods are 20, 14, 11 respectively.
4. The numbers of securities with significant skewness at the 5 per cent level are somewhat greater being 10, 6, 6 in each of the three periods, compared with 2, 4, 2 at the 1 per cent level.
5. This is not quite the pattern observed for CBA. In the Z-data the clustering of discrete prices around the mean and the high incidence of zeros coincide because the sample mean is at (or near) zero. With CBA, these two blocks of data were about 0.14 standard units apart.

3 Asymmetry in Australian equity returns

William L. Beedles

Introduction

Evaluating investments on the basis of their expected mean returns and
(co)variances has come to dominate much of the modern theory of finance.
The two-moment paradigm has proven to be such a powerful aid to the
pedagogy and research of the field that it is prominently displayed in even
introductory textbooks (Peirson and Bird 1976).

Several circumstances exist in which exclusive reliance on mean and
variance can be justified. (1) If investor preferences are quadratic, then
moments higher than the second carry no weight in the allocation decision
(Chiang 1967, pp. 255–59). But quadratic preferences imply that risky assets
are inferior goods, so this characterisation is typically rejected as implausible.[1]
(2) If risks are infinitesimal (Pratt 1964), then the third and higher moments
are smaller than the second by at least an order of magnitude and hence
can be safely ignored. (3) Indeed, risks need only be "small" for the two-
moment characterisation to be adequate for many practical problems (Tsiang
1972). But focusing on small risks ignores a class of interesting problems.
Much entrepreneurial behaviour might be explained by positive asymmetry.
Paying a loading fee to avoid catastrophic losses—negative asymmetry—
is a common justification for the phenomenon of insurance (Friedman and
Savage 1948).

These difficulties with traditional normative justification for mean and
variance analysis underpin much of the extensive study of the distributional
properties of investment outcomes. If asset returns are normally distributed,
then the third and higher moments are superfluous and the pricing regime
pioneered by Sharpe (1964), Lintner (1965b) and Mossin (1966) is potentially
useful.[2] Thus, much energy has been devoted to the positive question: Are
returns asymmetric?

Although some debate continues to be waged, the consensus in the United
States is that positive asymmetry is a prevalent empirical phenomenon, at

Reprinted from the *Australian Journal of Management* 11, no. 1 (June 1986), 1–12, by permission
of the author and the publisher.

least for post-World War II data; see Beedles and Simkowitz (1980) for an overview. But affairs are somewhat less settled in Australia. Stokie (1982a, p. 165; see chapter 2 in this book) has concluded "there is little evidence of skewness in the monthly log-returns of securities over 5-year periods." But his results are subject to another interpretation. For a set of 144 continuously traded securities (i.e., with a transaction in every month of his 191 sample period), he found on average (over three contiguous subperiods) that 9.49 per cent of his sample firms were significantly symmetric at the 1 per cent level.[3] In other words, the actual frequency was nearly an order of magnitude larger than expected by chance alone. Censoring the data further by focusing on the 40 firms with the largest capitalisations, he found 6.67 per cent were significantly asymmetric, once more a much higher frequency than expected by chance at the 1 per cent level.[4] Some might thus enjoy comfort by concluding from the extant literature that asymmetry is more pronounced than Stokie recognizes.[5]

The purpose of these introductory comments is twofold. First, studying investment return distributional properties is important since the results can be used to assess the appropriateness of the popular two-moment pricing structure. Second, the matter is one of continuing debate in Australia. The empirical results reported in the next section are intended to contribute to that debate.

Empirical results

The first intent here is to answer the question: Are Australian share returns asymmetric? The conclusion reached is: Yes, they are. Then attention is turned to descriptions of cross-sectional and time-series properties of asymmetry estimates. The database used throughout is from the file of listed Australian ordinary shares, maintained by the Centre for Research in Finance at the Australian Graduate School of Management, University of New South Wales. The version employed includes monthly returns covering January 1974 to December 1984.

The existence of asymmetry

The general procedure here is to examine various subsets of the population of firms in an attempt to see if the measured asymmetry is caused by a peculiarity in the data. To begin, any firm with at least 25 monthly returns any time during the 11-year study period was considered (sample *A*). The first three moments of the return distribution were computed using all the returns available for the particular share.[6] Summary measures are reported in the first line of table 3.1.

A total of 1,335 (= *N*) firms satisfied the 25-returns criterion. The average estimated standard deviation of monthly returns was 18.18 per cent, and the average skewness was 1.7710.[7] Of the sample of 1,335, 1,179 (= 87.64 per cent) had returns distributions that were positively asymmetric. Of these, 1,002 (75.06 per cent of the total sample) had estimates that were so large that the null hypothesis that they were drawn from a Gaussian distribution

Table 3.1 Asymmetry features of various samples of Australian shares listed during January 1974 to December 1984

	N	$\overline{sd}$*	$\overline{sk}$†	Percentages		Significant at 0.05	
				$sk>0$	$sk<0$	$sk>0$	$sk<0$
A:	25 observations required; returns; discrete compounding						
	1335	0.1818	1.7710	87.64	12.36	75.06	6.29
A':	25 observations; residuals; discrete compounding						
	1335	0.1731	1.7241	89.21	10.79	77.45	6.07
A":	25 observations; residuals, continuous compounding						
	1335	0.1413	0.3213	64.20	35.80	41.27	20.90
B:	25 residuals; continous compounding; industrials only						
	738	0.1060	0.2150	61.92	38.08	37.94	23.44
B':	25 residuals; continous compounding; resources firms only						
	597	0.1848	0.4526	67.00	33.00	45.39	17.76
C:	25 residuals; continous compounding; 30 largest industrials						
	30	0.0670	0.6795	83.33	16.67	40.00	3.33

* $\overline{sd}$ = average estimated standard deviation

† $\overline{sk}$ = average estimate skewness

could be rejected at the 5 per cent level. Similarly, 84 (6.29 per cent) of the shares were so *negatively* skewed that normality could be rejected.

These data can be used to support the claim that significant asymmetry is prevalent in Australia; 5 per cent of the distributions would be expected to reject the null by chance alone, while in fact 81 per cent (= 75 + 6) do. The results can further be used to support the claim that positive asymmetry predominates; seven times more are positive as are negative, twelve times more when attention is restricted to those that display significant asymmetry.

But these results may overstate the case for two reasons. First, cross-correlations among the shares may be causing the results. In other words, a positively asymmetric common factor may produce the observed propensity for positive asymmetry in the individual series. To address this possibility, the features of the residuals of the single-factor market model[8] are reported under row A' of the table. As expected, the standard deviation of the residuals is less, viz., 17.31 per cent, as is average skewness. But significant and positive asymmetry is still clearly predominant.

A second "technical" adjustment involves the use of continuously compounded data rather than the discrete form. When this transformation is made, the results are as expected and dramatic; data are reported in the third line of table 1 (A"). As noted in Praetz (1969) and Fama (1976), the effect of using the natural log of unity plus the periodic returns is to "draw in" the extreme observations. Thus, the average estimated standard deviation is reduced by a third to 14.13 per cent, and average skewness is decreased by a factor of five. Only about two-thirds of the sample firms have positively asymmetric log residuals. But significant asymmetry is still much more common than expected by chance: 62 per cent (= 41 + 21) have estimates of adequate magnitude to reject the null of normality; about twice as many are significantly positive as are significantly negative.

Thus, in sum, significant and positive asymmetry appears to be a pervasive feature of Australian ordinary share returns. But such conclusions must be offered cautiously since reasons exist to suspect that they hold only for a subset of the economy. Specifically, Ball and Brown (1980) found noteworthy differences in the second moments of indices composed of industrial and commercial enterprises and mining firms. Perhaps the same conclusion holds in the present context; asymmetry may be more prevalent in resources companies than in industrials.

To evaluate this possibility, the entire sample of 1,335 data series have been divided into two groups, listed as B and B' in table 3.1. The results are as might be expected. The standard deviation of return of the average resources company is nearly 75 per cent larger than the average industrial (18.48 per cent versus 10.60 per cent), and average skewness is twice as large. But in terms of total frequency of significance, the difference is slight; normality could be rejected for 61 per cent of the industrial and for 63 per cent of the resources firms.

Perhaps the most noteworthy data concern the relative frequency of positive and negative asymmetry. More than twice as many resources firms are positively skewed as are negative, and the proportion is about the same when attention is focused on significantly asymmetric distributions. Although frequency of positive skewness is somewhat less for the industrial firms, it is still much more common than the negative variety.

A final aside is worthy of mention. The average estimated skewness of the industrial group, 0.2150, is the smallest of the several samples investigated here. Moreover, while a minimum of 25 observations has been required, typically a data series covers about 60 months. For $T = 60$ the critical 5 per cent significance value for skewness is 0.492 (Pearson and Hartley 1966). The point is this: For the industrials, the average firm is clearly not significantly skewed, and it is this type of subsample, industrials, that has been most clearly studied by Stokie. So this perhaps explains why the two of us reach such different generalizations; significant positive asymmetry is much less pronounced when attention is restricted to industrial firms.

But that prospect is not completely satisfactory in that Stokie (1982a) has paid special attention to large industrials, which is the object of sample C in table 3.1. For these firms, the average monthly standard deviation is only 6.70 per cent. But asymmetry estimates are positive for all firms (16.67 per cent), and 12 of the distributions are significantly positively asymmetric, versus only one significant negative.

To summarise all of this, note that the data from *any* of the samples presented in table 3.1 indicate that significant skewness occurs much more frequently than chance would suggest. And further note that *positive* asymmetry seems to dominate. In any of the samples studied here, positive skewness occurs about twice as often, and frequently more, than does negative. And among those that are significant, positive estimates typically occur twice as often as negative.

Thus, although some may find symmetry to be an adequate distributional approximation, the preponderance of evidence here points to asymmetry, and especially positive asymmetry, as the prevalent empirical phenomenon among Australian ordinary shares. Attention can now be turned to the details of this phenomenon.

The details of asymmetry

All of the tests of the previous subsection were cross-sectional in nature: given data for some period, what was the nature of the returns or residuals *across firms*. In this subsection the view is broadened in two ways: (1) What is the nature of the cross-sectional distribution *across subperiods*, i.e., attention is focused on the stationarity of the skewness phenomenon. (2) In addition to individual securities, how do asymmetry characteristics change as large holdings are studied, i.e., attention is focused on the impact of *diversification*.

The first issue is addressed by studying residuals over the entire 132-month sample period and over contiguous 33-month subperiods. All firms with at least 25 returns during the specified sample period are considered.

Table 3.2   Selected observations from cross-sectional distributions of asymmetry estimates for Australian shares for various subperiods

	Subperiod				
	1/74–12/84	1/74–9/76	10/76–6/79	7/79–3/82	4/82–12/84
Smallest	−7.219	−5.476	−5.314	−5.331	−5.421
0.1 percentile	−1.301	−1.499	−0.930	−0.952	−0.972
0.2 percentile	−0.483	−0.857	−0.417	−0.239	−0.450
0.3 percentile	−0.127	−0.439	−0.161	0.012	−0.113
0.4 percentile	0.072	−0.201	0.054	0.233	0.100
0.5 percentile	0.265	0.000	0.261	0.428	0.278
0.6 percentile	0.466	0.112	0.387	0.679	0.458
0.7 percentile	0.699	0.320	0.587	1.010	0.603
0.8 percentile	1.115	0.556	0.985	1.529	0.912
0.9 percentile	2.003	1.015	1.584	2.631	1.680
Largest	9.547	5.334	5.469	5.383	5.404
Mean	0.321	−0.152	0.246	0.601	0.267
Pos. percentile	0.358	0.500	0.373	0.291	0.350
Percentage significantly skewed at 5% level:					
positive	41	17	28	42	29
negative	21	24	14	13	15

The first step in the examination simply involves ranking the firms on the basis of the estimated skewness for each of the subperiods, and reporting selected observations from the distributions in table 3.2. Consider the first data column for illustration, where the smallest estimated value is −7.219; the estimate that divides the group into the smallest 10 per cent and largest 90 per cent is −1.301, and so forth; the largest estimate is 9.547.

Examining the distributions across subperiods is instructive since these data parallel those of Beedles and Simkowitz (1980) for US shares. Five features are particularly noteworthy. (1) For the extremes, the smallest is always negative and the largest positive; this is the same as for United States stocks. (2) The 30th percentile is always negative; in the United States, the 20th is always negative, but the 30th is sometimes positive (especially when post-World War II data are examined). Comparing this smallest always-negative 30th percentile with its symmetric parallel, the 70th, the positives are with one exception greater in magnitude than the negatives, which is also usually found for United States stocks. (3) The median (50th percentile) and the mean are always positive, as is the case in the United States. (4) Going from smallest to largest, the estimates "become positive" between the 29th (7/79–3/82) and 50th (1/74–9/76) fractiles. For United States data, this occurs at a lower point, typically between the 25th and 35th fractiles. (5) About half again as many stocks display significant positive skewness as display significant negative, considerably less than in the United States.

These data can be used to advance three conclusions. First, asymmetry, especially of the positive and significant varieties, is a *persistent* empirical phenomenon for Australian shares. Second, compared with the United States, negative asymmetry is much more prevalent in Australia. And third, the cross-sectional distribution of skewness is quite stationary, although somewhat less so than for the United States.

Although the data of tables 3.1 and 3.2 may be descriptively interesting, their major value is the base they set for looking at the economics of asymmetry. The matter comes to bear in the following way. The fact that individual assets are positively asymmetric is not particularly important if the act of diversification increases or leaves unchanged the asymmetry of the resulting portfolio. In other words, portfolio policy based on mean and variance alone prescribes extensive diversification since the effect is to decrease variance, leaving unchanged the mean simple return and increasing the geometric mean return. If diversification increases or leaves unchanged asymmetry, the same total-diversification strategy is optimal. But matters are considerably complicated if the act of diversification *reduces* asymmetry since then the investor must *choose* the number of assets to hold on the basis of *comparative* attitudes towards the three moments. Moreover, Simkowitz and Beedles (1978) showed that this diversification effect on asymmetry is ultimately an empirical question; they found that for United States data, adding stocks tended to reduce asymmetry and that hence the optimal level of diversification may be less than total, at least for some investors.

The procedure employed to examine the Australian diversification effect follows Simkowitz and Beedles (1978). All firms listed throughout a given study period are analysed. The "N" individual asset return series (i.e., one-stock portfolios) have been randomly combined to form $N/2$ two-stock portfolios, $N/5$ five-stock portfolios, and so forth, until one portfolio containing all the stocks has been constructed (i.e., one N-stock portfolio). The results are in table 3.3.

The resulting data for the first (1/74–9/76) subperiod can be described for illustration. For the 782 shares studied, their average estimated standard deviation is 14.25 per cent per month; the average (cube root of the) third moment is −0.0077.[9] When 391 two-stock portfolios are examined, the average standard deviation declines to 11.57 per cent; the mean asymmetry

Table 3.3 Averages of estimated standard deviations (*sd*) and cube root of third moments (*m3*) for portfolios of varying sizes for various subperiods

	Portfolio size							
	1	2	5	10	20	40	100	*Np*
1/74–12/84								
# of ports	410	205	82	41	20	10	4	1
sd	0.1458	0.1176	0.0935	0.6798	0.0694	0.0618	0.0551	0.0512
m3	0.0521	0.0964*	0.0878	0.0712	0.0619	0.0401	0.0.218	−0.0134
1/74–9/76								
# of ports	782	391	156	78	39	19	7	1
sd	0.1425	0.1157	0.0886	0.0735	0.0629	0.0563	0.0516	0.0478
m3	−0.0077	0.0339	0.0382*	0.0219	0.0071	−0.0159	−0.0339	−0.0374
10/76–6/79								
# of ports	922	461	184	92	46	23	9	1
sd	0.1132	0.0925	0.0721	0.0592	0.0498	0.0418	0.0353	0.6275
m3	0.0348	0.0665	0.0669*	0.0611	0.0529	0.0406	0.0308	0.0279
7/79–3/82								
# of ports	754	377	150	75	37	18	7	1
sd	0.1337	0.1106	0.0889	0.6764	0.0663	0.0590	0.0529	0.0468
m3	0.0589	0.0796*	0.0796*	0.6700	0.0509	0.0344	0.0114	−0.6263
4/82–12/84								
# of ports	697	348	139	69	34	17	6	1
sd	0.1458	0.1173	0.0896	0.0760	0.0656	0.0586	0.0517	0.0502
m3	0.0472	0.0704*	0.0679	0.0605	0.0514	0.0405	0.0384	0.0344

* denotes maximum asymmetry.

is 0.0339. The process continues, so that traversing that data of table 3.3 from left to right reveals the effect of diversification on risk and asymmetry.

Three substantive conclusions emerge. (1) Variance declines with diversification; this simply confirms the well-known analytic effect of diversification and the empirical results first reported by Evans and Archer (1968). (2) Maximum asymmetry occurs at an "interior" level of diversification; depending on the subperiod, the largest average estimated third moment occurs with a portfolio size of two or five stocks. This brings into sharp focus the complication that arises from considering three moments. For investors who are exclusively, or at least primarily, concerned with mean and variance, the standard prescription to diversify completely is seen to be appropriate. But for those who strongly favour the long-shot nature of equities, less extensive diversification may be appropriate. (3) In the United States, maximum average asymmetry occurs at the one-stock level, but that is seen not to be the case with Australian data; the measure increases, and then decreases, with diversification. This phenomenon simply reflects the propensity noted earlier for Australian shares to be dominated more often by dramatic negative returns.

In any event, the result seems unavoidable that asymmetry exists to an adequate extent that it may impinge on the behaviour of investors and hence the types of investigations that we students of financial economics conduct. The final section is a commentary on the potential usefulness of asymmetry in judging pricing studies.

Commentary

The last twenty years have witnessed an explosion of scientific research into the pricing of financial instruments. These studies have for the most part focused on the effects of information on the performance of shares (i.e., mean return) after the impact of (systematic) variance has been neutralized. The last decade has seen attention shifted to various "special factors", for examples, yield (Ball 1978a; Basu 1983), size (Banz 1981; Reinganum 1981a), transaction charges (Stoll and Whaley 1983; Shultz 1983), and seasonality (Brown et al. 1983; reproduced in this book at chapter 7).

The present effort has focused on asymmetry as a special factor. The major conclusions are:

1. Asymmetry has strong theoretical backing as a factor affecting the value of assets. Unfortunately, to date, no equilibrium model has been developed that holds much empirical content; the Kraus and Litzenberger (1976, 1983) three-moment pricing structure has not been very useful for United States shares (see Beedles 1979; Friend and Westerfield 1980) or Australian (see Ball, Brown and Officer 1976a; reproduced in this book as chapter 4). Thus, empirical studies of the phenomenon are by necessity descriptive rather than tests of forcefully justified null hypotheses.
2. Asymmetry appears to be a feature that pervades the return distributions of Australian ordinary shares. Although positive asymmetry is the dominant attribute, Australian equities exhibit a greater tendency to negative skewness than do United States shares.
3. The act of diversification reduces risk, which is welfare-enhancing. But after a point, diversification also reduces asymmetry, which dissipates welfare. Thus, some investors can be expected to hold less than completely diversified portfolios, which is in direct conflict with conventional guidance produced by a two-moment characterisation of investor preferences.

Thus, in sum, the most substantive message of this chapter is that asymmetry appears to be a variance worthy of careful scrutiny by students of asset pricing. The hope is that future empirical studies will, where possible, (1) consider the asymmetry characteristics that result from a proffered investment strategy, (2) consider asymmetry characteristics at various diversification levels, and (3) consider the stationarity of asymmetry (along with the other moments). In light of the normative and empirical support that exists, attention to asymmetry would appear to be properly a matter of routine.

Acknowledgments

This chapter was completed in part while the author was on leave from the University of Kansas as a visiting professor at Monash University and the Australian Graduate School of Management, University of New South Wales. Workshop participants at the Australian National University, Flinders University, Monash, the AGSM, and the University of Queensland provided helpful diagnostic comments on earlier versions. While not suggesting culpability, special appreciation is due to D. Anderson, R. Ball, P. Brown, R. Brown, P. Dodd, F. Finn, F. McDougall, R. Officer, N. Sinclair and M. Tippett. Particular intellectual debts are owed to P. Praetz and M. Stokie.

Notes

1. Keep in mind that any preference function displaying non-increasing absolute risk aversion implies a preference for (aversion to) positive (negative) asymmetry.
2. Kwon (1985) takes a different approach to avoid assumptions about preferences and distributional properties.
3. From Stokie (1982a, table 4, p. 172), 12, 14 and 15 firms were significantly asymmetric in the three subperiods; $[(12 + 14 + 15)/3]/144 = 0.0949$.
4. Again from Stokie's (1982a) table 4, the numbers were 2, 4 and 2 for the subperiods; $[(2 + 4 + 2)/3]/40 = 0.0667$.
5. This harsh reinterpretation of Stokie's work is softened on the basis of empirical results reported later in the chapter.
6. In other words, if the number of observations was 25 or more, $T \geq 25$, then all returns were used. Firms with $T < 25$ were not considered.
7. Skewness is the estimate third moment divided by the cube of the estimated standard deviation, and is thus a measure of asymmetry standardized by distribution scale. This metric was selected to reflect asymmetry because it is amenable to significance testing. See Simkowitz and Beedles (1980) for discussion of measurement issues and D'Agostino and Pearson (1973) for a transformation that is used when dealing with small ($T < 20$) samples.
8. See Sharpe (1963); an equally weighted index has been used.
9. The third moment is reported rather than skewness value (1) so that the magnitude of the data is similar to the standard deviation, and (2) because no significance tests are conducted.

PART 3
Risk and return

4   Asset pricing in the Australian industrial equity market

Ray Ball, Philip Brown and R.R. Officer

The aim of this chapter is to evaluate several asset-pricing models in an Australian context. The study is restricted to the industrial equity market, and in particular to shares listed on the Melbourne Stock Exchange, for two reasons: data are neither reliable nor available in other segments of the capital market; and non-equity securities present greater estimation problems because their relevant pricing parameters are more susceptible to change. The models themselves make no distinction among various legal types of assets.

The asset-pricing models describe partial price equilibrium in the market for securities, under the assumption that securities' uncertain future prices can be described in terms of moments of their probability distributions.[1] The most common version is the "mean-variance" model, in which only two moments are assumed to be relevant.

The asset-pricing models rest upon the twin assumptions of rational behaviour and perfect markets. In this context, a perfect market is one in which there are no transactions costs and all individuals are price-takers. Information is not assumed to be a free good and, as a result, investors are assumed to possess less-than-complete information: the outcomes of their investment decisions are uncertain.[2]

In most respects, the "mean-variance" model performs well in describing relative prices on the Melbourne exchange. Since the share market provides one of the rare sources of reliable data for evaluating the disciplinary matrix of economics, these results are encouraging.[3]

Models

Let there be only two points in time: now and the future (denoted by $t-1$ and t, respectively). Let households' future wealths be random variables for which the first K moments exist. Denote the aggregate future wealth of the economy by V_{et}, where the tilde ($\sim$) denotes a random variable, and the

Reprinted from the *Australian Journal of Management* 1, no. 1 (April 1976), 1–32, by permission of the authors and the publisher.

kth moment of aggregate wealth by μ_{kt}. Let $\mu'_{ikt} = \partial\mu_{kt}/\partial v_{l,t-1}$ be the marginal effect of an individual security i upon the kth moment of aggregate wealth (i.e., the effect on uncertain wealth at time t of varying, at time $t-1$, the amount invested in an individual security).

The "asset-pricing models" consist of the set of valuation equations in which the present value of any security is a linear function of the marginal effect of that security upon the K appropriate moments of aggregate future wealth:

$$V_{i,t-1} = \sum_{k=1}^{K} \omega_{kt}\, \mu'_{ikt} \text{ for all } i \tag{1}$$

where: ω_{kt}, $k = 1, \ldots, K$ are constants for all securities and households (and can be interpreted as valuation coefficients).

The two-moment model

In the two-moment, "mean-variance" model, the specific form of (1) can be shown to be.[4]

$$V_{i,t-1} = \omega_{1t} E(\tilde{V}_{it}) + \omega_{2t}{}^{cov}(\tilde{V}_{it}, \tilde{V}_{et}) \tag{2}$$

$$\omega_{1t} = [1 + E(\tilde{R}_{zt})]^{-1} \tag{2a}$$

$$\omega_{2t} = [E(\tilde{R}_{et}) - E(\tilde{R}_{zt})].\, V_{e,t-1}/\{[1 + E(\tilde{R}_{zt})]\,\text{var}(\tilde{V}_{et})\} \tag{2b}$$

where: R denotes rate of return $(1 + \tilde{R}_t = \tilde{V}_t/V_{t-1})$; $\tilde{R}_z$ is the rate of return on an arbitrary reference security with $\text{cov}(\tilde{V}_{zt}, \tilde{V}_{et}) = O$; E, var and cov denote the expectation operator, variance and covariance; and the equality holds for all securities $i = 1, \ldots, N$.

In conducting empirical work, it is common to express these models in rate-of-return form. In the mean-variance model, the equivalent to (2) is:

$$E(\tilde{R}_{it}) = \theta_{1t} + \theta_{2t}\sigma_{iet} \text{ for all } i \tag{3}$$

where: θ_{1t} and θ_{2t} are constants for all securities and households in period t; and σ_{iet} is the covariance between the rate of return on security i and the rate of return on the aggregate wealth of economy, in period t. This model can be rewritten as:

$$E(\tilde{R}_{it}) = E(\tilde{R}_{zt}) + [E(\tilde{R}_{et}) - E(\tilde{R}_{zt})]\,\beta_{it} \text{ for all } i \tag{4}$$

where:

$$\beta_{it} = \sigma_{iet}/\sigma^2_{et} \tag{4a}$$

and where: σ^2_{et} is the variance of the rate of return on aggregate wealth in period t. Equation (4) is merely a restatement of (3) which allows some intuitive interpretation of the model's parameters.

Common interpretation of the two-parameter model treats the three elements of the RHS of (4), viz. β_{it}, $E(\tilde{R}_{zt})$ and $[E(\tilde{R}_{et}) - E(\tilde{R}_{zt})]$, as determinants of the expected return on the LHS. We take the three in turn.

First, β_{it} is interpreted as the relative non-diversifiable risk of security i in period t. As first appreciated by Sharpe (1964), it is identical to the slope in the familiar regression model:

$$\tilde{R}_{it} = \alpha_{it} + \beta_{it}\tilde{R}_{et} + \tilde{\epsilon}_{it} \tag{5}$$

$$0 = E(\tilde{\epsilon}_{it}) \tag{5a}$$

$$= E(\tilde{\epsilon}_{it}\tilde{R}_{et}) \tag{5b}$$

The rationale for this apparent coincidence lies in the assumptions of rational behaviour and frictionless trading. Roughly speaking, any potential risk in the economy which can be removed by trading among investors will immediately be removed.[5] Since the only potential risk which investors cannot remove by diversification is due to economy-wide effects (by definition, one cannot diversify wider than the economy), no other potential source of risk will be rewarded in the capital market: it will have been removed. Thus, the total non-diversifiable risk in a closed economy is $\text{var}(\tilde{V}_{et})$ or, in rate-of-return form, σ^2_{et}; and $\text{cov}(\tilde{V}_{it}, \tilde{V}_{et})$ and σ_{iet} are the contributions to security i to aggregate risk in the respective wealth and rate-of-return formulations. On the assumption of universally well-diversified investment portfolios, the covariances are relevant to security pricing. A security whose value is "very sensitive" to economy-wide effects has a "high" slope on $\tilde{R}_e$ in the regression function (5), and therefore adds risk to a portfolio which is well-diversified and which as a result consists only of those economy-wide effects.

Because $\sigma^2_{et} = \Sigma_j v_j \sigma_{jet}$ (where the summation is across all securities $j = 1, \ldots, N$ and where $v_j = V_{j,t-1}/V_{e,t-1}$), it follows from (4a) that $\beta_{it} = \sigma_{iet}/\Sigma_j v_j \sigma_{jet}$. Thus: the aggregate variance risk of the economy is the weighted average of the various σ_{jet}, the weights being value-determined; σ_{iet} is the contribution of security i towards aggregate risk; and β_{it} is the contribution of security i relative to that of the average security. For this reason β_{it} is referred to as the relative non-diversifiable risk of security i.

Second, $E(\tilde{R}_{zt})$ is the expected return on an hypothetic security which is riskless in the sense that its price variation does not add risk to the economy.[6] Because σ_{zet} is therefore zero, the expected return on z is the intercept in (3), and must be the expected return that households obtain from securities as an inducement for factors other than risk-bearing.[7] All securities must offer such an inducement.

Third, $[E(\tilde{R}_{et}) - E(\tilde{R}_{zt})]$ is the expected value of the risk premium per unit of relative, non-diversifiable risk. By definition, $\beta_{zt} = 0$. Likewise, $\beta_{et} = \sigma_{eet}/\sigma^2_{et} = 1$. Because the spread in relative risk between the reference securities (or mutual funds) e and z is therefore unity, the difference in their mean returns is a standardized risk premium per unit of relative risk.[8] All risky securities must offer additional expected return as a compensation.

The three-moment model

The assumptions that uncertain future consumptions can be described in terms of distribution functions, that households behave rationally and that capital markets are perfect, together transform our view of the world from one of N securities into one of a limited number of capital goods. In the two-moment case, there are two goods: risk and expected return. Apart from differences in risk, all securities become perfect substitutes.

We will also be interested in the three-moment model, which is expressed in rate-of-return form as:

$$E(\tilde{R}_{it}) = \phi_{1t} + \phi_{2t}\sigma_{iet} + \phi_{3t}\sigma_{ieet} \text{ for all } i \tag{6}$$

where: ϕ_{1t}, ϕ_{2t}, and ϕ_{3t} are constants for all securities and households in period t; and σ_{ieet} is the coskewness of $\tilde{R}_{it}$ and $\tilde{R}_{et}$. Apart from differences in covariance and coskewness, securities are perfect substitutes.

The number of moments necessary to describe asset pricing in the securities market is an empirical issue. Third and higher moments would be irrelevant under either of two conditions: (i) they did not exist (as in the case of normal return distributions); or (ii) households' utility functions were such that they were ignored (as in the case of quadratic utility-of-wealth functions). Kraus and Litzenberger (1976) provide an inexact derivation of the three-moment-model, though exact derivations are available.

Role of individual-security moments

In the context of the asset-pricing models, moments of individual securities' return distributions, other than the mean, are not important determinants of asset pricing. Consider the role of individual-security variance in the two-moment model. Whereas variance is important at the portfolio level, in that the variance of future consumption is determined exclusively by the amount invested in a portfolio and the variance of the rate of return on that portfolio, the variance of return for individual securities is essentially irrelevant. This can be demonstrated by decomposing a security's covariance risk as follows:

$$\sigma_{iet} = \Sigma_j v_j \sigma_{ijt}$$
$$= {}_j\Sigma_{i} v_j \sigma_{ijt} + v_i \sigma^2_{it} \tag{7}$$

where the summation is across all the $(N-1)$ securities other than i itself, and $v_i\sigma^2_{it}$ is the element which has been removed from the complete summation. Risk problems are exclusively determined by the σ_{iet}, and the individual-security variance is weighted by a factor of v_i in determining that covariance. This weight is the value of security i relative to the total value of the economy, and is therefore small. In contrast, the weight given to security i's covariances with all other securities is ${}_j\Sigma_{i} v_j = (1 - v_i)$. The risk of an individual security is almost completely determined by its sensitivity to the same phenomena as other securities.

Note that any security i, *considered in isolation*, would produce risk for a consumer in accordance with its own variance of rate of return, σ^2_{it}. This interpretation of a security's risk is commonly espoused: for example, oil exploration is deemed to be risky because the outcomes from exploration are highly uncertain (exhibit high variance). The covariance interpretation of a security's risk involves two breakthroughs: first, the consideration of a security within the framework of a diversified portfolio of securities, due to Markowitz (1952, 1959); and second, the application of marginal analysis to demonstrate the marginal effect of covariances on portfolio variances, due to Sharpe (1964), Lintner (1965a) and others. Similar statements can be made, with even greater force, about the irrelevance of individual-security skewness in determining portfolio skewness.

Summary

The asset-pricing models possess four types of testable assertions: (i) that individual-security moments are irrelevant in their pricing; (ii) that "marginal moments" such as covariance and coskewness are relevant instead; (iii) that cross-sectional relationships between mean returns and these "marginal moments" are linear; and (iv) that the coefficients of these cross-sectional relationships have certain signs. We now describe the data available for testing these assertions and later we discuss possible limitations of the data. Finally, we describe the tests conducted and the major results.

Data

The data consist of monthly rates of return (adjusted for dividends, stock splits, bonus issues etc.) for all the industrial and commercial equities listed on the Melbourne Stock Exchange and which had a listed capital exceeding a million dollars at any time over the study period of January 1958 to December 1970, inclusive. The total data file comprises 651 equities.[9] A maximum of 155 monthly rates of return is available for each equity, but not all issues were continuously traded over the period and hence the number of available observations differs among the sample members.

Evidence from the United States[10] suggests that at least 60 observations of monthly returns are necessary to obtain minimum-error estimates of the β's, but the use of more observations over a longer time period encounters problems of non-stationarity. Because we were limited to a maximum of 155 observations, and because we reduced the effect of estimation errors by a grouping procedure described later, we decided to accept individual equities with as few as 48 monthly return observations. Eliminating the 100 equities with fewer than 48 monthly returns reduced the sample to 551 individual equities.[11]

The surrogate used for the return on aggregate economic wealth is an equally weighted average of the 651 individual-equity returns, constructed as:

$$\tilde{R}_{mt} = \Sigma_i \tilde{R}_{it} / N_t \tag{8}$$

where: N_t is the number of equities with data for month t (a maximum of 651); $\tilde{R}_{it} = (\tilde{p}_{it} - p_{i,t-1}) / p_{i,t-1}$; and p_{it} is the price of equity i at the end of month t, adjusted for the full amount of dividends, rights and bonus issues.

Whereas a sample of only 551 individual equities' pricing is investigated, the index used as surrogate for aggregate wealth is compiled from the records of all 651 equities. The sample average β therefore differs slightly from the population mean of unity.

Testable implications

The asset-pricing models assert relationships among statistics of the *ex ante* multivariate distribution of returns for some holding period and for all securities. The sample of observed returns for 551 equities over 155 months provides estimates of these statistics. For example, tests of the two-moment model employ sample estimates of the mean expected return and the population β's for the equities.

The sample is limited in two respects: the class of securities (equities) and the time period sampled (1958–70). Both of these are a potential source of difficulty in testing the *ex ante* relationships. Neither difficulty has been explored in the United States tests.

The time period sampled

Suppose for the moment that securities differ in relative risks, but that the asset-pricing model does not hold; i.e., that relative risks are not related to *ex ante* expected returns. Suppose also that we sample a time period in which the return on aggregate wealth exceeded its expected value; i.e., $R_e > E\,(\tilde{R}_e)$ for the period.

Consider two securities, A and B, such that $\beta_{Ae} > \beta_{Be}$. If relative risks are independent of expected returns, the difference in risks is no reason to hypothesise that $E\,(\tilde{R}_A) \neq E\,(\tilde{R}_B)$. However, simply because of the definition:

$$\beta_{ie} \equiv \sigma_{ie}/\sigma^2_e \equiv E\,\{[\tilde{R}_i - E\,(\tilde{R}_i)]\,[\tilde{R}_e = E\,(\tilde{R}_e)]\}/\sigma^2_e$$

knowledge that the sample observation of the variate $[\tilde{R}_e - E\,(\tilde{R}_e)]$ was positive allows us to predict that:

$$E\,\{[\tilde{R}_A - E\,(\tilde{R}_A)]\mid R_e > E\,(\tilde{R}_e)\} > E\,\{[\tilde{R}_B - E\,(\tilde{R}_B)]\mid R_e > E\,(\tilde{R}_e)\}$$

Even if the two-moment asset-pricing model does not explain return differentials, there can thus be a relationship between β's and average returns at a tautological level. In the above example, the relationship was positive for a period in which $\tilde{R}_e$ exceeded its expectation. It would have been negative if the opposite had been supposed.

In order to avoid observing risk-return relationships which are purely tautological, the researcher must be confident that the return on aggregate wealth did not differ significantly from its expectation over the sample time period (taken as a whole). To take the Fama and MacBeth study as an example, one would expect the entire 34-year sample to provide a better test of the asset-pricing model than the 5-year samples.

Our sample period covers only 13 years, or 155 months. Whether or not this sample size is sufficiently large to avoid the problem of tautological relationships is unknown. It also is difficult to assess whether or not the 155 monthly observations are independent. We can only assume that we have sampled a representative time period, as various studies on New York Stock Exchange data have implicitly assumed.

The securities sampled

We would prefer to have a representative sample of all securities in the economy, but reliable data are available only for industrial equities (shares). The use of equity data alone might limit the tests which can be conducted, and the aim of this section is to speculate upon these limitations.

First, the industrial equity data probably represent a broad spectrum of aggregate wealth. There are 651 firms on the file, each owning many securities;

i.e., land, buildings, cash, commodities, government securities and durables (automobiles, furniture, etc.). The data file includes firms engaged in various forms of manufacturing, some of whose features are more closely allied to mining, agriculture, finance, real estate and service industries than any other. The number and diversity of the assets represented on the equity market leads us to speculate that the file, taken as a whole, is an approximately efficient portfolio of securities.[12]

Second, the mix of securities on the file is unlikely to duplicate the proportions $\{v_i\}$ which various securities bear relative to aggregate economic wealth. In spite of the number and diversity of assets covered by equity ownership, the equity file therefore is unlikely to have an average relative risk of unity, and in this sense the sample probably misrepresents the population of securities.

Thus, for the purpose of empirical testing we assume that the file is an efficient but unrepresentative portfolio of securities. To determine the implications of this assumption for the tests which we conduct, we make use of the result of Black (1972, p. 450) that rates of return on all efficient portfolios are exact linear functions of $\tilde{R}_{zt}$ and $\tilde{R}_{et}$. Denoting the sample average return for our data by $\tilde{R}_m$, adding the *second* subscript to the β's to denote the index with which a security is covarying (either the true index e or our surrogate m), and dropping the time subscript, this means that:

$$\tilde{R}_m = (1 - \beta_{me}) \tilde{R}_z + \beta_{me} \tilde{R}_e \qquad (9)$$

where: B_{me} is the covariance between $\tilde{R}_m$ (our surrogate market index) and $\tilde{R}_e$ (the true index), standardised by σ^2_e.

Thus, the index which we use, $\tilde{R}_m$, can be viewed as a weighted average of $\tilde{R}_z$ and $\tilde{R}_e$, with the weights being unknown. With some manipulation, (9) can be shown to imply that, for all securities:

$$\beta_{im} = (1 - \beta_{me}) \beta_{iz} \sigma^2_z/\sigma^2_m + \beta_{me} \beta_{ie} \sigma^2_e/\sigma^2_m \qquad (10)$$

Using the result obtained in Appendix A that the β_{iz} are equal to $(1 - \beta_{ie})$, (10) can be shown to imply:

$$\beta_{im} = (1 - \beta_{me})\sigma^2_z/\sigma^2_m + \beta_{ie} [\beta_{me} (\sigma^2_z/\sigma^2_m + \sigma^2_e/\sigma^2_m) - \sigma^2_z/\sigma^2_m] \qquad (11)$$

for all securities which is of the form:

$$\beta_{im} = \delta_1 + \delta_2\beta_{ie} \text{ for all } i \qquad (12)$$

where δ_1 and δ_2 are constants for all i. The relationship between our index and the true index, which is assumed in (9), therefore implies a linear (but not proportional) relationship between our β's and the true β's. Because the values of the constants in (12) are unknown, tests of the asset-pricing model must be limited. In particular, one can only predict that the relationship between average returns and the estimated relative risks is linear; it is not possible to predict the sign of either the cross-sectional intercept or the slope of the empirical risk-return relationship.[13]

Testable hypotheses

With these sample limitations in mind, we now consider the major testable implications of the two-moment model.

Hypotheses 1: Effect of covariance.[14] The two-moment model hypothesises the following:

(a) A positive relation between expected return $E(\tilde{R}_i)$ and the true relative risk β_{ie} is hypothesised. The data (described above) do not in themselves allow us to assert a positive relation between $E(\tilde{R}_i)$ and β_{im}, though for reasonable values of σ^2_z, σ^2_e and β_{me} we would expect a positive relation to hold for our share price data.

(b) The relation between $E(\tilde{R}_i)$ and β_{ie} in (4) is linear. Given the linearity of (11), this implies the testable prediction that the cross-sectional relationship between $E(\tilde{R}_i)$ and β_{im} is linear.

(c) While we could hypothesise that the expected zero-covariance rate $E(\tilde{R}_z)$ is positive, we offer no test because it is difficult to obtain an unbiased estimate of $E(\tilde{R}_z)$. This can be seen from equation (12): the existence of an intercept in (12) implies that a security j with $\beta_{jm} = 0$ will not ordinarily have a "true" zero covariance ($\beta_{je} \neq 0$). Equation (11) shows that it will be possible to successfully identify a zero-covariance security only if either $\beta_{me} = 1$ (if our data file is a perfect surrogate for the economy's wealth), or if $\sigma^2_z = 0$ (if the Sharpe formulation of the model is correct). We therefore decline "intercept tests".[15]

Hypothesis 2: Effect of individual-security variance. All versions of the asset-pricing model, including the two-moment model, hypothesise that individual-security variance is essentially irrelevant. This follows from (7), in which the effect of variance on covariance, at the security level, is seen to be small. We therefore test the hypothesis that individual-security variance does not command a risk premium.

Hypothesis 3: Effect of coskewness. The three-moment version of the asset pricing model hypothesises a negative relationship between securities' expected returns and coskewnesses. In contrast, the two-moment model (4) hypothesises that coskewness is irrelevant either because return distributions are not skewed or because households ignore skewness. We test these hypotheses by estimating the cross-sectional relation between expected return and the relative coskewness statistic, $\psi_i = \sigma_{imm}/\sigma^3_m$.

Estimation

Estimation of firms' relative risks and other relevant statistics involves several problems. These problems, and the estimation procedures used to solve them, are discussed in this section.

Estimation of covariance risk effects

The β's are estimated for the 551 equities' monthly returns for the period February 1958 to December 1970 by implication using an ordinary least-squares estimator of the regression equation (5).[16] The estimates of the regression coefficients, including the β's, are subject to sampling variation; for example, the mean standard error of estimate for the 551 β's is 0.410, compared with the mean $\hat{\beta}$ of 0.996. Because the estimated β's are subsequently used as independent variables in a cross-sectional regression

(13) of average returns on β-risks, this sampling variation is troublesome: if the population-relative risks are measured with error, then the cross-sectional regression encounters the familiar errors-in-the-variables problem involving assessments of the strength of the cross-sectional risk-return relationship which are biased toward zero.[17]

To minimise the errors-in-the-variables problem, we adopted the standard technique of *grouping* the data, using 20 groups of equities. The rationale is to reduce the variance of the measurement error, on the assumption that the errors of the individual $\hat{\beta}$'s are independent within each group and that the error for the average $\hat{\beta}$ of the group therefore exhibits much less variance.[18] The grouping technique was first used in this context by Black, Jensen and Scholes (1972). Grouping minimises the *bias* involved in the cross-sectional regression of returns on relative risks. In order to maximise the *efficiency* of the cross-sectional regression, grouping was conducted on the basis of the ranked individual $\hat{\beta}$'s. The firms were sorted on the basis of their $\hat{\beta}$'s and then made up into 20 groups of 27 equities in each group.[19] We then ensure a relatively wide range for the independent variable in the cross-sectional regression (13). This means that the between-group variation is maximised relative to the within-group variation, so that the effect of β-risk on return is more apparent (i.e., the regression is more efficient).

Grouping on the basis of $\hat{\beta}$'s, however, does not allow the errors in measurement to be independent within each group: positive measurement errors tend to be sorted into high-β groups and conversely for negative measurement errors. This causes an aggregation of sampling errors of a particular type in extreme-β groups which leads to an upward bias in the slope coefficient of the cross-section regression. Bias in the cross-sectional regression can be avoided only if the variable used for grouping is independent of measurement error in the independent variable of the cross-sectional regression. For this reason, an odd/even procedure was adopted: equities were sorted and grouped by $\hat{\beta}$'s which were estimated from only the *odd* months of data (the 2nd, 4th, 6th, . . ., 154th months), and the average β of each of the ranked groups was then estimated from the *even* months of data (the 1st, 3rd, 5th, . . ., 155th months).

This technique ensures that the estimates of systematic risk for the groups, denoted by $\hat{\beta}_g$, are obtained from the same 1958–70 time period that is used to estimate the average returns to which they will be related,[20] and also that the errors are essentially independent across equities. The result is that, for the entire 155-month period, we have estimates of group relative risks which we assume are unbiased and essentially error-free.

Estimates of the average β's for the 20 groups, $\hat{\beta}_g$, are shown in columns (1) and (2) of table 4.1, for odd and even months. The reduction in standard deviation across groups from 0.490 and 0.152 (a reduction in variance from 0.240 to 0.023) gives an indication of the regression associated with ranking on the $\hat{\beta}$'s. The average $\hat{\beta}$'s for the odd months include the dispersion due to ranking partly upon sampling variation which is equivalent to measurement error, whereas the rankings in the even months are independent of the measurement error.

Note the end effect of the regrouping procedure upon the estimates of relative risk. First, the average β of 0.976 remains sufficiently close to the population mean of unity, indicating that the grouped estimates are unbiased. Second, the average standard error of estimate falls from 0.410 for individual securities to 0.072 for the 20 groups, which is a reduction in variance of 97 per cent. Bearing in mind that the bias in the slope of the cross-sectional risk-return regression (13) increases with this variance (see note 17), it can be concluded that grouping has achieved most of its objective.

Figures 4.1 and 4.2 give plots of the even-month regressions of R_g on R_m for the representative groups 5 and 15; the slopes of these regressions are $\hat{\beta}_5$ and $\hat{\beta}_{15}$ respectively. The linear regressions appear to be well specified.

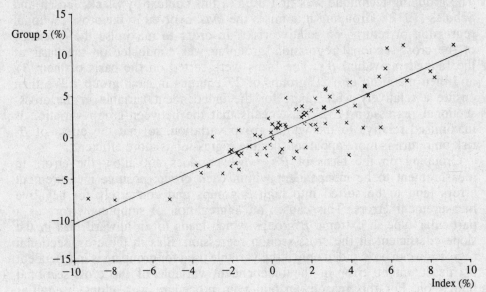

Figure 4.1   Group 5 monthly return and the Index monthly return

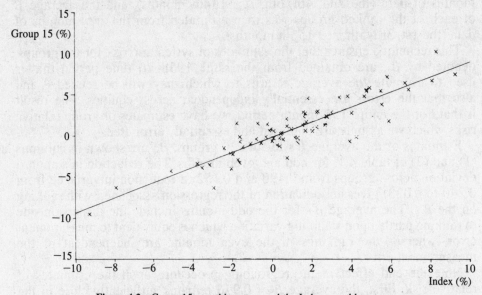

Figure 4.2   Group 15 monthly return and the Index monthly return

The final step is the cross-sectional regression:

$$\bar{R}_g = \gamma_0 + \gamma_1 \hat{\beta}_g + e_g \tag{13}$$

where: $\bar{R}_g$ is the average return on the 27 equities in group g over the 155-month period; $\hat{\beta}_g$ is the average estimated β for group g, derived from every second (even-month) observation over the 155-month period; γ_0 and γ_1 are regression constants, such that:

$$(\gamma_0 + \gamma_1) = R_m \tag{14}$$

for the period;[21] the e_g is the disturbance term for group g. Results from this regression are given as regression number 1a in table 4.3. The regression is also estimated for subperiods of the total 155-month period in tables 4.4–4.6, with the same $\hat{\beta}_g$ as in (13) and table 4.3, but with subperiod average returns (i.e., estimates of expected returns over smaller periods).

Estimating curvilinearity

The asset-pricing model implies a *linear* relation between $\bar{R}_g$ and $\hat{\beta}_g$. A standard method of testing for non-linearity is to add a β^2 term to (13). However, because all the $\hat{\beta}_g$ are in the region of unity, we would expect some collinearity between β and β^2. This is confirmed from the results shown as model 1 in table 4.2: the $\hat{\beta}_g$ and $\hat{\beta}^2_g$ are almost perfectly positively correlated.[22]

The effect of β^2 is estimated in a two-step procedure. The residuals from (13) are regressed against $\hat{\beta}^2$:

$$e_g = \gamma_0^| + \gamma_1^| \hat{\beta}_g^2 + e_g^| \tag{15}$$

with the asset-pricing model's implication being that $\gamma_1^| = 0$. Results from fitting (15) to the total period and the subperiods are shown as regression 1b in tables 4.1–4.6. Because of the relatively small residual variation of β^2_g around β_g, we do not expect to see a significant second-step result for β^2_g.

Estimating the effect of the variability of individual securities

The same procedures described above for estimating β were followed for estimating the average standard deviation of all equities in each group. Each of the 551 equities' standard deviation of monthly returns was estimated for the *odd* months over the entire period. On the basis of these standard deviations, equities were sorted into 20 separate groups and the average standard deviation of the equities in each group was estimated for the *even* months.[23] The results of these procedures are shown in columns (7) and (8) of table 4.1. A comparison of the cross-sectional standard deviation of the groups' average standard deviations for the odd and even months provides a puzzle: the large reduction in cross-sectional dispersion that was evident for β's in table 4.1 is not evident here.[24]

The sorting of shares into groups on the basis of their standard deviations gives the standard deviation maximum variation between groups. This ensures that the precision of the estimates for the cross-sectional regression of average standard deviation on $\bar{R}_g$ does not suffer from grouping. This contrasts with

Table 4.1   Grouped data for cross-sectional regressions, 1958-70

Obser-vations	Grouped by covariance						Grouped by std. devn.			Grouped by coskewness		
	Odd	Even	Even	Even	Total	Total	Odd	Even	Total	Odd	Even	Total
Statistic	$\hat{\beta}_g$	$\hat{\beta}_g$	$\hat{r}^2_g$	$\hat{\beta}^2_g$	$\bar{R}_g$	$(\sigma^3_g)^2/$ $(\sigma^2_g)^3$	Av S.D.	Av S.D.	$\bar{R}_g$	$\hat{\psi}_g$	$\hat{\psi}_g$	$\bar{R}_g$
	(1)	(2)	(3)	(4)	(5)	(6)	(7)	(8)	(9)	(10)	(11)	(12)
Group 1	2.158	1.439	0.824	2.071	0.0174	0.109	0.1378	0.1444	0.0165	3.000	−0.495	0.0196
2	1.739	1.101	0.808	1.213	0.0119	0.183	0.1136	0.1120	0.0111	2.787	0.253	0.0149
3	1.543	1.087	0.772	1.182	0.0138	0.173	0.1037	0.1061	0.0099	2.350	−0.077	0.0113
4	1.390	0.923	0.712	0.852	0.0124	0.141	0.0976	0.0960	0.0128	2.083	0.870	0.0104
5	1.311	1.157	0.745	1.339	0.0117	0.049	0.0926	0.0967	0.0102	1.964	0.328	0.0104
6	1.216	1.021	0.826	1.043	0.0111	0.035	0.0884	0.0872	0.0128	1.736	1.583	0.0108
7	1.160	1.013	0.813	1.026	0.0093	0.346	0.0849	0.0868	0.0113	1.580	0.575	0.0119
8	1.099	0.977	0.777	0.955	0.0094	0.231	0.0810	0.0788	0.0113	1.368	1.240	0.0087
9	1.039	0.855	0.759	0.731	0.0091	0.071	0.0785	0.0807	0.0099	1.216	1.076	0.0095
10	0.992	1.038	0.839	1.078	0.0102	0.356	0.0758	0.0785	0.0097	1.037	0.624	0.0092
11	0.946	0.892	0.761	0.795	0.0094	0.155	0.0738	0.0777	0.0117	0.925	0.586	0.0099
12	0.873	0.967	0.818	0.935	0.0091	0.381	0.0712	0.0773	0.0102	0.820	1.089	0.0107
13	0.826	1.061	0.745	1.126	0.0105	0.395	0.0693	0.0716	0.0100	0.661	1.170	0.0107
14	0.754	0.860	0.702	0.739	0.0099	0.213	0.0671	0.0700	0.0108	0.467	1.461	0.0099
15	0.701	0.987	0.807	0.974	0.0108	0.127	0.0651	0.0714	0.0081	0.332	0.867	0.0095
16	0.620	0.804	0.661	0.646	0.0108	0.285	0.0629	0.0718	0.0099	0.098	1.084	0.0106
17	0.525	0.844	0.717	0.712	0.0082	0.493	0.0601	0.0701	0.0094	−0.038	0.463	0.0105
18	0.433	0.865	0.710	0.748	0.0094	0.254	0.0575	0.0631	0.0094	−0.313	1.380	0.0089
19	0.341	0.791	0.747	0.625	0.0077	0.003	0.0539	0.0644	0.0092	−0.709	1.332	0.0088
20	0.149	0.840	0.625	0.705	0.0086	0.370	0.0477	0.0577	0.0091	−1.149	2.447	0.0103
Mean	0.991	0.976	0.758	0.975	0.0105	0.219	0.0791	0.0831	0.0107	1.011	0.893	0.0108
S.D.	0.490	0.152	0.058	0.329	0.0022	0.138	0.0219	0.0202	0.0018	1.145	0.649	0.0024
Market index	1.000	1.000	1.000	1.000	0.0105	0.357			0.0105	1.000	1.000	0.0105

Fama and MacBeth (1973) who tested the explanatory power of additional variables on data still grouped on the basis of β.

The β_g's of these groups, sorted on standard deviation, are then estimated from the complete 155 months of data. A stepwise regression procedure is used to test whether any variation in the returns of the groups that is not explained by the β's of the groups can be explained by the standard deviations estimated from the even months. That is, using cross-sectional regressions the average returns are regressed on the $\hat{\beta}$'s and the residuals are then regressed on the average standard deviation of the group. The results are shown in regression numbers 2a and 2b in tables 4.3–4.6.[25] The relationship

Table 4.2   Relationships among independent variables

Model	Intercept (t-statistic)	Slope (t-statistic)	Adjusted r2	Durbin-Watson
1. $\hat{\beta}^2_g = f(\hat{\beta}_g)$	−1.1253 (−20.9)	2.1516 (39.4)	0.99	2.5
2. $\text{av.}\hat{\text{sd}}. = f(\hat{\beta}_g)$	−0.0081 (−0.8)	0.0924 (9.5)	0.82	2.0
3. $\hat{\psi}_g = f(\hat{\beta}_g)$	4.4049 (5.7)	−3.5307 (4.6)	0.51	2.1

between $\hat{\beta}_g$ and the average standard deviation is shown as model 2 in table 4.2. As expected, the averages are highly correlated.

The implications of the asset-pricing model is that the slope from the second step (i.e., the coefficient for the average standard deviation) is zero. This can be seen from the regression model (5), which implies:

$$\sigma^2_i = \beta^2_i \sigma^2_e + \sigma^2 \epsilon_i$$

Because σ^2_e is common to all groups, the average standard deviations of the groups can only differ with their average β's and with the average standard deviations of their disturbance terms. The β's represent undiversifiable risk, and should earn a risk premium which is removed in the first step of the regression 2a. The disturbances represent diversifiable risk, and hence the asset-pricing model implies that there is no second-stage relation between average returns and standard deviations.[26] Given rational behaviour and frictionless markets, no diversifiable risk is borne by households and no price is attached to it.

Estimating the effect of coskewness

The same procedure is used in estimating the pricing of coskewness. Estimates of the relative coskewness of each share in the sample are made for the odd months over the entire file. Groups are formed on the basis of relative coskewness and an average coskewness parameter for each group is estimated over the even months.

The results of these procedures are shown in columns (10) and (11) of table 4.1. Note the large differences in the estimates of relative coskewness for odd and even months. The cross-sectional standard deviation of the average ψ_g's falls from 1.145 to 0.649. Furthermore, a binary classification of each group's average ψ as above or below unity (the population mean), for the odd and even estimates, reveals reversals of sign for 14 of 20 groups: relative coskewness on the odds appear, if anything, to be negatively correlated with relative coskewnesses on the even months, in spite of the fact that the odd and even months are interspersed over exactly the same time period. The suspicion is that the relative coskewnesses do not exist: that the *estimated* relative coskewnesses are measurement error, pure and simple. This is confirmed by the results presented below.

The β_g are then estimated from the full 155 months of data for each of the groups sorted on coskewness. Cross-sectional regressions are run on the $\hat{\beta}_g$ of each group and the residuals are then regressed on the $\hat{\psi}_g$ estimated from the odd months. The relationship between the $\hat{\beta}_g$ and $\hat{\psi}_g$ is shown as model 3 in table 4.2. The correlation between $\hat{\beta}_g$ and $\hat{\psi}_g$ is lower than that found by Kraus and Litzenberger (1976) for United States data, who estimated an r^2 for β_g and $\hat{\psi}_g$ of 0.94, compared with 0.51 in our results.

The implication of the two-moment asset-pricing model is that the slope for the second step (i.e., for the estimated relative coskewness) is zero, either because the return distributions are not skewed and therefore the coskewnesses are undefined (which would make the estimates pure error) or because skewness is not rewarded in households' utility functions. The three-moment model (6) implies a negative slope for the second stage, indicating households' preferences for positive skewness. Results from the two stages are given in regressions 3a and 3b of tables 4.3–4.6.

Summary of experimental design

Methods of testing various implications of the asset-pricing models have been outlined. Generally speaking, they involve cross-sectional regressions of sample average returns on sample estimates of various other parameters of the return distributions. They also involve a grouping technique which minimises the effect of sampling variation in the estimates, and a stepwise procedure in which relative risk is always forced to enter the regression before the other parameters.

The experimental stance we have adopted is one of testing *within the context* of the two-moment asset-pricing model. All experiments must be conducted within one such context;[27] we have selected the two-moment model because it is a simple and powerful tool for organising one's view of the capital market and because the evidence presented by Fama and MacBeth (1973) from United States data is consistent with the model.

This experimental stance explains the stepwise regression procedure. Because the experiment occurs within the context of the two-moment model, the experimental results must be either consistent with or anomalous for that model. Consistency would be evidenced by a positive, linear relation between mean returns and relative risks. Anomaly would be evidenced by an *additional* relation between mean returns and other parameters of the return distributions. Correlation between relative risks and other parameters is not anomalous for the two-moment theory, and hence any observed first-step relation between mean returns and the other parameters (i.e., before removing the influence of relative risk) is not anomalous and is of no experimental interest. Simple multiple regression will not give us the required experiment: for example, we could not determine whether a positive coefficient for standard deviation were consistent with or anomalous for the asset-pricing model without knowing if it were due to positive correlation between standard deviation and relative risk.

Results

Background results

Before proceeding to discuss the results for the six regressions over the various time periods, some background interpretation and evidence is offered.

First, figures 4.3 and 4.4 provide normal probability plots of the rates of return of group five[28] (which is representative of the groups taken as a whole) and the market index. The actual returns are plotted against a standard Normal variate, and hence perfect Normality of the return distributions would be indicated by perfectly linear plots. The plots suggest that Normality is a reasonable approximation and, in particular, there is little sign of skewness. There is some evidence of leptokurtosis but, using the arguments of Fama and MacBeth (1973, pp. 619–24) and Officer (1972), we accept normality as an approximation for the present purposes.

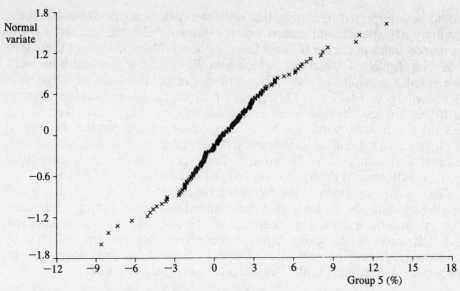

Figure 4.3 Normal probability plot of Group 5 monthly return

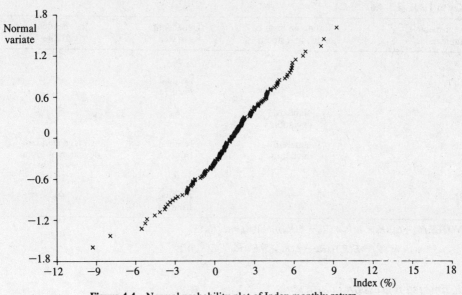

Figure 4.4 Normal probability plot of Index monthly return

To further test for skewness, the statistic $(\sigma^3_g)^2/(\sigma^2_g)^3$ was calculated for the 20 equity groups (grouped according to β's) and for the market index. The statistic is a non-negative standardised skewness estimator, taking the value of zero for a perfectly symmetric normal variation. The large-sample standard deviation for the statistic is $\sqrt{(6/155)} = 0.197$, assuming normality and where "large" means approximately twice our sample size of 155. The estimates are arrayed in column (6) of table 4.1; only 2 of the 20 groups' skewness statistics are more than 2 standard deviations from zero and 10 exceed zero by more than 1 standard deviation, using the large-sample estimate of the standard deviation (which is probably an underestimate). These results should be interpreted in conjunction with the *co*skewnesses discussed in the summary of experimental design which exhibited behaviour consistent with the market index not being skewed. Overall, there is little evidence of skewness.

Second, figures 4.1 and 4.2, which plot R_g against R_m, reveal how well-diversified a portfolio of only 27 securities can be. It should be noted that: (i) according to Black's (1972) proof of equation (9), returns on efficient portfolios are less-than-perfectly correlated with $\tilde{R}_e$ (due to the effect of $\tilde{R}_z$); and (ii) the plotted portfolios have been constructed in such a fashion as to almost guarantee their inefficiency.[29] Nevertheless, the plots reveal little residual variation for the 20 groups. This visual impression is confirmed by the coefficients of determination arrayed in column (3) of table 4.1.

Thus, before considering the following results on asset pricing, it is worth bearing in mind the evidence that the return distributions are approximately Normal, that the evidence on skewness of the distributions is at best mixed, and that most of the gains from perfect diversification are obtained by moderately diversified portfolios. These background results appear to be favourable with respect to the two-moment asset-pricing model.

Key to Tables 4.3–4.6

Regression number	Sorting on basis of individual stocks'	Dependent variable	Independent variable
1a	$\hat{\beta}$	$\bar{R}_g$	$\hat{\beta}_g$
1b	$\hat{\beta}$	residual from 1a	$\hat{\beta}^2{}_g$
2a	standard deviation	$\bar{R}_g$	$\hat{\beta}_g$
2b	standard deviation	residual from 2a	average standard deviation of group
3a	$\hat{\psi}$	$\bar{R}_g$	$\hat{\beta}_g$
3b	$\hat{\psi}$	residual from 3a	$\hat{\psi}_g$

NOTES: $\beta_g = E[\ (\tilde{R}_g - E(\tilde{R}_g))\ (\tilde{R}_m - E(\tilde{R}_m))]/E[(\tilde{R}_m - E(\tilde{R}_m))^2]$

$\hat{\psi}_g = E[\ (\tilde{R}_g - E(\tilde{R}_g))\ (\tilde{R}_m - E(\tilde{R}_m))^2]/E\ [(\tilde{R}_m - E(\tilde{R}_m))^3]$

Estimated regression coefficients

Table 4.3 summarises the six cross-sectional regressions. The general conclusion is that the two-moment asset-pricing model is a good descriptor of asset pricing on the Melbourne market for industrial equities over the 1958–70 period. Results from subperiods of the total period, in tables 4.4–4.6, confirm this conclusion.

Evidence on pricing of covariance-risk. The sign of the cross-sectional coefficient for the β_g is positive for the 155-month period (regression 1a, table 4.3), being 0.01204, or 1.2 per cent per month. This relationship between risk and average return over 1958–70 is plotted in figure 5.

While no tests are offered on the intercept, the sum of the intercept and the slope is approximately equal to the average return on the market index

Table 4.3 Specification tests, complete period Feb. 1958 to Dec. 1970 (155 months) (mean monthly market return = 0.01052)

Key	Interecept (*t*-statistic)	Slope (*t*-statistic)	Adjusted r^2	Durbin–Watson
1a	−0.00123 (−0.7)	0.01204 (6.4)	0.68	1.8
1b	−0.00014 (−0.2)	0.00014 (0.2)	0.00	1.8
2a	0.00460 (2.9)	0.00615 (3.9)	0.42	2.9
2b	−0.00121 (−0.9)	0.01453 (0.9)	0.00	2.7
3a	−0.00116 (−0.4)	0.01205 (3.7)	0.40	2.3
3b	0.00045 (0.6)	−0.00051 (−0.8)	0.00	2.1

Table 4.4 Specification tests, period Feb. 1958 to Apr. 1962 (51 months) (mean monthly market return = 0.01663)

Key	Intercept (*t*-statistic)	Slope (*t*-statistic)	Adjusted r^2	Durbin–Waton
1a	−0.00838 (−1.7)	0.02562 (5.1)	0.57	2.2
1b	−0.00027 (−0.1)	0.00027 (0.1)	0.00	2.2
2a	0.01322 (3.9)	0.00372 (1.1)	0.01	2.3
2b	−0.00158 (−0.6)	0.01905 (0.6)	0.00	2.2
3a	−0.00214 (−0.4)	0.01959 (3.3)	0.34	2.1
3b	−0.00014 (−0.1)	0.00015 (0.1)	0.00	2.1

Table 4.5 Specification tests, period May 1962 to Aug. 1966 (52 months) (mean monthly market return = 0.00483)

Key	Intercept (*t*-statistic)	Slope (*t*-statistic)	Adjusted r^2	Durbin–Watson
1a	0.01038 (4.2)	−0.00568 (−2.3)	0.18	2.5
1b	0.00004 (0.0)	−0.00004 (−0.0)	0.00	2.5
2a	0.00962 (4.6)	−0.00498 (−2.4)	0.20	2.2
2b	0.00151 (0.9)	−0.01821 (−0.9)	0.00	2.1
3a	0.00192 (0.5)	0.00285 (0.7)	0.00	1.8
3b	0.00055 (0.6)	−0.00062 (−0.7)	0.00	2.0

Table 4.6   Specification tests, period Sept. 1966 to Dec. 1970 (52 months) (mean monthly market return = 0.01023)

Key	Intercept (*t*-statistic)	Slope (*t*-statistic)	Adjusted r^2	Durbin–Watson
1a	−0.00584 (−1.5)	0.01645 (4.2)	0.46	2.1
1b	−0.00019 (−0.1)	0.00020 (0.1)	0.00	2.1
2a	−0.00880 (−2.5	0.01966 (5.6)	0.62	2.5
2b	−0.00356 (−1.3)	0.04248 (1.3)	0.04	2.4
3a	−0.00329 (−0.7)	0.01386 (2.8)	0.27	1.6
3b	0.00093 (0.9)	−0.00104 (−1.1)	0.01	1.2

(see heading, table 4.3) as predicted by equation (14). This provides a check on our estimation procedures: the equality would be exact if we had exhaustively sampled the 651 equities in the market index, and the closeness of the approximation indicates that our sample selection procedures have introduced little bias. The approximation is close throughout tables 4.3–4.6.

These results are for groups constructed from ranked β's (regression 1a). Regressions 2a and 3a differ from 1a only in the method of grouping the data, and their results are all similar (at least for the entire period, in table 4.3). All indicate general risk-aversion in the market, in that higher-β equities earned substantially higher average returns over the 1958–70 period.[30]

Over short intervals, average rates of return provide less-precise sample estimates of expected values. This is evident in the results for subperiods in tables 4.4–4.6 which are not independent of the total-period results: they merely differ in level of aggregation, and the coefficients in table 4.3 are averages of those in tables 4.4–4.6. The risk premiums in tables 4.4–4.6 (and plotted in figures 4.6–4.8 are 0.02562, −0.00568 and 0.01645 respectively, averaging almost exactly the 0.01204 for the total period. The behaviour of these coefficients is as predicted by the two-moment model. For example, in the second subperiod (May 1962 to Aug. 1966), the mean monthly marketwide return is only 0.483 per cent, which is less than the average for the entire period and probably is less than its expected value. During this subperiod, the *ex post* premium per unit of relative risk is negative. This is what one would expect: when the economy does worse than expected, the high-β securities are by definition very sensitive to this result and the low-β securities are not, with the result that the risk premium per unit of β is negative. In the first subperiod (Feb. 1958 to Apr. 1962), the market return is 1.663 per cent per month, and the *ex post* risk problem is large and positive.

However, these subperiod results could be purely tautological, as explained above in "Testable Implications". As a result, they contribute no reliable evidence in relation to the asset-pricing theory.

Evidence on linearity. As predicted by the asset-pricing model, the cross-sectional relationship between β-risk and average return over the 155-month period is linear. This is confirmed by a visual inspection of figure 4.5, which plots regression 1a, and by the low second-step slope of 0.00014 or 0.014 per cent per month for β^2 in regression 1b of table 4.3.[31]

With only 20 groups, the range of β_g might not be sufficient to pick up any non-linearity. A sample of the results for the whole period but using 40 groups is given in table 4.7. There remains no relationship between return and $\hat{\beta}^2_g$ that cannot be explained by $\hat{\beta}_g$, in that the second-step slope is only -0.008 per cent per month.

Table 4.7 Selected results for cross-sectional regressions on 40 groups of shares

Key	Intercept	Slope	Adjusted r^2	Durbin–Watson
1a	0.00532	0.00520	0.16	1.5
	(1.8)	(5.6)		
1b	0.00008	−0.00008	0.00	1.5
	(0.1)	(−0.1)		
Relationship between $\hat{\beta}^2$ and $\hat{\beta}$ for the 40 groups $\hat{\beta}^2 = f(\hat{\beta}_g)$]				
	−1.0089	2.0412	0.98	1.9
	(−25.1)	(49.8)		

The same linearity is evident for individual subperiods, including those reported in tables 4.4–4.6, and also for subperiods when equities are placed into 40 groups (the latter results are not reported). These results are in contrast to those of Fama and MacBeth (1973), Blume and Friend (1973), and Friend and Blume (1970) who found some evidence of non-linearity for some periods in the United States. The difference in the results may reflect the restricted period studied in our tests, the differences in countries and equity markets studied, or differences in estimation methods.[32] The United States studies also found that the low-β groups had positive residuals in the equivalent regression to 1a (plotted as figures 4.5–4.8) and that high-β groups had negative residuals. We find no evidence of this type in the Melbourne equity data. Again, the difference could be due to data, or it could be due to estimation techniques.

Evidence on pricing of individual variance. Regression 2b in table 4.3 shows no relationship between average returns, after controlling for the effect of relative risk, and equities' standard deviations. The common supposition that securities' own standard deviations determine their risks is not supported by the evidence: very little of the residual variation from regression 2a is explained by the average standard deviations in regression 2b. The coefficient of 0.01453, given the average standard deviation for all equities of 0.0831, implies that an equity with a *double*-average standard deviation received a premium of 0.00121 or 0.012 per cent per month over the 1958–70 period. Further, the subperiods reveal little evidence of any relationship between standard deviation and average return: the coefficient for regression 2b in

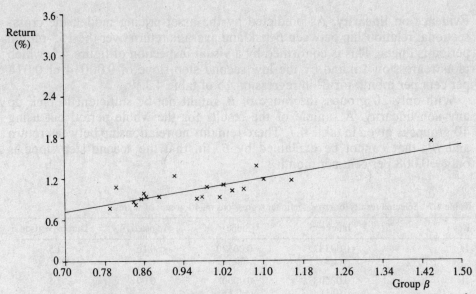

Figure 4.5   Covariance risk and average monthly return, Feb. 1958 to Dec. 1970—groups ranked on $\hat{\beta}$

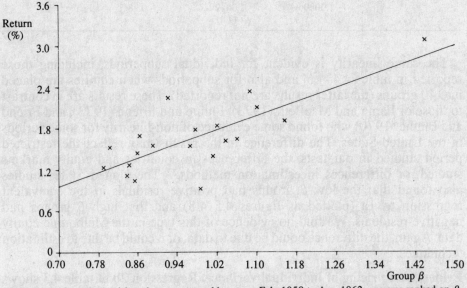

Figure 4.6   Covariance risk and average monthly return, Feb. 1958 to Apr. 1962—groups ranked on β

tables 4.4–4.6 changes sign from subperiod to subperiod. Overall, the marginal analysis of the asset-pricing model is well-supported.

Evidence on pricing of coskewness. Regression 3b of table 4.3 shows that equities' coskewnesses are not important determinants of their pricing, once the effect of covariance has been controlled. While the sign of the slope coefficient is as predicted by the three-parameter model (negative), the coefficient of −0.00051 is small. A security with *double*-average coskewness on average earned 0.046 per cent per month less than the average security, over the 1958–70 period. Similar results are obtained for subperiods.

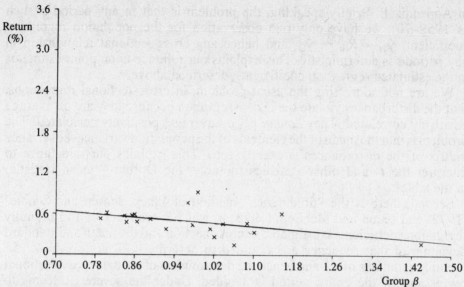

Figure 4.7   Covariance risk and average monthly return, May 1962 to Aug. 1966—groups ranked on β

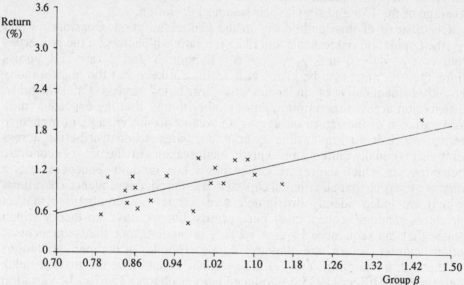

Figure 4.8   Covariance risk and average monthly return, Sept. 1966 to Dec. 1970—groups ranked on β

Significance of regression coefficients

We are aware of no reliable method of describing the regression coefficients in more detail. In particular, we cannot obtain reliable estimates of their standard deviations. We discuss three possible estimators.

First, there is the standard OLS estimator for the various cross-sectional coefficients' variances. This provides the estimates of the t-statistics which are presented in parentheses in tables 4.3–4.6. It seems that little reliance can be placed upon these statistics for regressions 1a, 2a, 3a and 3b, owing to a peculiar problem in this experiment which is described in more detail in Appendix B. Briefly speaking, the problem is that in any period t (such as 1958-70), we have only one observation for the population regression coefficient, $\tilde{\gamma}_{1t} = \tilde{R}_{mt} - \tilde{\gamma}_{0t}$, and hence any cross-sectional relationship in any period t is deterministic. This explains our reliance upon point estimates in the estimated regression coefficients, described above.

We are not addressing the usual problem, in cross-sectional regressions, that the disturbances violate the i.i.d. assumption because they are on average positively correlated. They *cannot* be, on average, positively correlated. The problem is that the mean of the elements of the population variance–covariance matrix of the disturbances is exactly zero. This explains our reluctance to interpret the t- and other statistics (notably, the Durbin–Watson statistic) in the tables.

Second, there is the "time series" method of Black, Jensen and Scholes (1972) and Fama and MacBeth (1973) in which a sequence of 155 monthly regression coefficients is estimated in cross-section and the mean and standard deviation of that sequence are assumed to describe it. There are now 155 monthly estimates of $\tilde{\gamma}_1$, and hence the determinism of a single cross-sectional regression for the entire period is avoided. Under the severe (it seems to us) assumption that the monthly coefficients are i.i.d., the t- statistic for the mean of the 155 monthly coefficients is $\tilde{\gamma} / [s(\gamma) \sqrt{155}]$, where $\tilde{\gamma}$ is the average of the 155 and $s(\gamma)$ is their standard deviation.

Our distrust of this method lies in the i.i.d. assumption. Consider $\tilde{\gamma}_0$ and $\tilde{\gamma}_1$, the population riskless rate and risk premium, which possess the properties that $\text{cov}(\tilde{\gamma}_0, \tilde{\gamma}_1) = 0$ and $\tilde{\gamma}_0 + \tilde{\gamma}_1 = \tilde{R}_m$. If both $\tilde{\gamma}_0$ and $\tilde{\gamma}_1$ are i.i.d. across time, then $\tilde{R}_m$ must also be i.i.d. Yet it seems unlikely that the market index is either identically *or* independently distributed across time. *Identical* distribution across time implies, among other things, that the expected value and variance of the return on aggregate wealth do not change, in monetary terms, which is an implausible assumption. *Independent* distribution across time seems equally unlikely and equally inconsistent with theories of economic behaviour, in which aggregate yields follow non-random sequences. It is a mistake to argue that an efficient capital market produces sequences of returns which are independently distributed across time.[33] A competitive market produces random sequences of pure profits, but we have no theory which states that the sequence $\{\tilde{\gamma}_{1t}, t = 1, 2, \ldots\}$ is random, nor that sequences of other "market factors" are random.[34] Some examples of the many violations of the i.i.d. assumptions are: (a) the seasonal variation in the market index described by Officer (1975; reproduced here as chapter 15); (b) the variation in yields over the "business cycle" which both monetarists and non-monetarists seek to explain; and (c) the secular decline in the risk premium which is reported by Fama and MacBeth (1973, pp. 627-28).

Results from this "time series" method are reported in table 4.8. Note that the mean of the 155 monthly coefficients is, in each of the six cases, exactly equal to the coefficient for the single whole-period regression reported in table 4.3. The standard deviation derived under the independence assumption is also reported, as are the first 12 serial correlation coefficients for the sequence of monthly regression coefficients (though we do not accept that the serial correlations are a reliable guide to the variance–covariance matrix for the coefficients).

Table 4.8 Time-series tests on regression slope coefficients

Key	Average of 155 coeff.	Std. devn. of 155 coeff.	Serial correlation—various lags												Student prob.	Wilcoxon prob.
			1	2	3	4	5	6	7	8	9	10	11	12		
1a	0.01204	0.00484	0.25	0.06	0.13	0.11	0.08	0.02	0.15	0.27	0.16	0.18	0.11	−0.02	0.01	0.03
1b	0.00014	0.00012	−0.16	−0.12	−0.01	−0.13	0.19	0.10	−0.01	0.04	−0.01	0.02	0.01	−0.03	0.26	0.34
2a	0.00615	0.00329	0.28	0.06	0.10	−0.02	0.07	0.19	0.10	0.12	0.13	0.02	0.15	0.12	0.06	0.19
2b	0.01453	0.00834	−0.07	0.00	0.17	0.09	0.09	0.06	0.14	0.01	0.17	−0.02	0.07	−0.02	0.08	0.33
3a	0.01205	0.00538	0.12	0.11	0.01	−0.07	−0.04	−0.01	0.00	−0.14	−0.10	−0.01	0.01	0.02	0.02	0.00
3b	−0.00051	0.00046	0.01	0.05	0.12	0.02	−0.05	0.00	−0.01	−0.10	−0.07	0.01	0.07	0.03	0.26	0.73

The third method is a non-parametric version of the "time series" method, in which the Wilcoxon matched-pairs test is substituted for the t-test. The statistic reported is the probability, under the null hypothesis that the regression slope in each month is zero, of observing the actual sequence of coefficients. The test is described in Siegel (1956). It does not have the defect of the parametric t-test of assuming that the sequence of coefficients is identically distributed. Results are reported in table 4.8.

We leave readers to draw their own conclusions from the three sets of tests. In particular we know of no reliable method of estimating the 155 x 155 variance–covariance matrix of the sequence of 155 coefficients for the parametric time-series method, and therefore cannot attempt a generalised least-squares estimate.

Conclusions

By adopting a marginal approach to an individual security in a diversified portfolio of securities, and assuming that expected value and variance are sufficient to describe return distributions, the two-moment asset-pricing model asserts that expected value and covariance uniquely determine the pricing of individual securities. More specifically, the model asserts a positive, linear relation between the expected values of rates of return on securities and their covariances with the rate of return on aggregate economic wealth. We find evidence of such a relationship in the Australian industrial equity market over the period 1958–70.

The asset-pricing models assert that individual securities' variances of rate of return play no independent role in their pricing. Again, the evidence is reasonably consistent with this assertion.

The models assume that all households behave rationally in the context of frictionless capital markets. Irrational behaviour might include failure to take advantage of diversification, so that individual-security variances would increase in importance (in the limit, a one-security portfolio's risk is exclusively determined by that security's variance). Transactions costs might inhibit diversification efforts, again increasing the importance of individual-security variance. Thus, the empirical finding that individual-security variance does not influence asset pricing, in contrast to popular belief, provides support for the disciplinary matrix of economics.

The assumptions of the economic discipline, and the assumption of the two-moment model that mean and variance are sufficient, obviously are violated in reality. For example, human capital is a significant proportion of aggregate wealth, yet it cannot be traded in continuous amounts without transaction costs, as is assumed. To take another example, brokerage fees for buying and selling Australian shares are usually in the order of 2 per cent of the amount transacted and, as a result, consumer/investors just as obviously do not form perfectly diversified portfolios. We are aware of these types of considerations. But it would be incorrect to conclude that the asset-pricing model is unlikely to describe observable *price* behaviour. It is just as obvious that most consumer/investors are nevertheless quite widely diversified: human capital, for example, is portable across many industries and therefore is not dependent upon only one sector's outcome; and many consumer/investors own a house, the land on which it is built, furniture, clothes, and automobile, some cash and maybe some piano lessons as well as marketable securities. Just how widely diversified consumer/investors' portfolios have to be, in order for assets to be priced as if they are *perfectly* diversified, is not obvious (though we offer some evidence on the matter in figures 4.1 and 4.2). Furthermore, many of these assets are such that consumer/investors might in any case hold them for production reasons (e.g., cash, houses, furniture) and hence the marginal transaction costs from diversification for consumption/investment reasons could be close to zero. In any event, the question is best settled by the evidence, and the Australian evidence seems consistent with the two-moment model.

Appendix A

The version of the two-moment model (4) due to Black (1972) implies (adding a second subscript to β's as per the "Testable Implications" section)

$$\tilde{R}_i = (1 - \beta_{ie})\tilde{R}_z + \beta_{ie}\tilde{R}_e + \tilde{\epsilon}_i \tag{A.1}$$

where $\tilde{\epsilon}_i$ is a well-behaved disturbance for security i. Thus $\tilde{R}_i$ can be viewed as a weighted sum of three independent random variates. It follows that σ_{iz} can be viewed as a weighted sum of three covariances

$$\sigma_{iz} = (1 - \beta_{ie})\sigma_{zz} + \beta_{ie}\sigma_{ez} + \sigma_{ez}$$

where σ_{iz} is the covariance between $\tilde{R}_i$ and $\tilde{R}_z$, σ_{zz} is σ^2_z (the variance of $\tilde{R}_z$), σ_{ez} is zero (z has zero relative risk), and $\sigma_{\epsilon z}$ is also zero (ϵ is a well-behaved disturbance). Substituting

$$\sigma_{iz} = (1 - \beta_{ie})\,\sigma^2_z,$$

dividing both sides by σ^2_z, and nothing that $\beta_{iz} = \sigma_{iz}/\sigma^2_z$, we obtain

$$\beta_{iz} = 1 - \beta_{ie} \tag{A.2}$$

which is the desired result. Note that (A.1) and (A.2) imply

$$\tilde{R}_i = \beta_{iz}\tilde{R}_z + \beta_{ie}\tilde{R}_e + \tilde{\epsilon}_i \tag{A.3}$$

and for efficient portfolios

$$\tilde{R}_p = \beta_{pz}\tilde{R}_z + \beta_{pe}\tilde{R}_e \tag{A.4}$$

Appendix B

Consider the population cross-sectional regression for period t

$$R_{it} = \gamma_{0t} + \gamma_{1t}\beta_{it} + \epsilon_{it} \quad i = 1, \ldots, N \tag{B.1}$$

where

$$R_{et} = \gamma_{0t} + \gamma_{1t} \tag{B.2}$$

Assume equal weighting for simplicity, so that

$$R_{et} = \Sigma_i R_{it}/N \tag{B.3}$$

and therefore

$$1 = \Sigma_i \beta_{it} / N \qquad (\text{B.4})$$

Summing (B.1) across all securities gives

$$\Sigma_i R_{it} = N\gamma_{0t} + \gamma_{1t}\Sigma_i\beta_{it} + \Sigma_i\epsilon_{it}$$

which, together with (B.1), (B.2) and (B.3) implies

$$0 = \Sigma_i\epsilon_{it} \qquad (\text{B.5})$$

The following then obtains

$$0 = \text{var}(\Sigma_i\epsilon_{it}) \qquad (\text{B.6})$$

$$= \Sigma_i\Sigma_j\text{cov}\,(\epsilon_{it}, \epsilon_{jt}) \text{ and} \qquad (\text{B.7})$$

$$\Sigma_i \text{ var}\,(\epsilon_{it}) = -\Sigma_i \Sigma_{j\neq i} \text{ cov}\,(\epsilon_{it}, \epsilon_{jt}) \qquad (\text{B.8})$$

Note that we are dealing with *population* statistics for time t, not with some time sequence. Equation (B.8) is (B.7) with the diagonal elements of the variance–covariance matrix of the disturbances separated out, and (B.7) is an expansion of (B.6).

The cross-sectional regression is usually set up with β as the independent variable and γ_{1t} as the slope. The OLS estimator for $\text{var}(\gamma_{1t})$ assumes, among other things, that

$$cov\,(\epsilon_{it}, \epsilon_{jt}) = \begin{cases} 0 \text{ for } i \neq j \\ \\ \text{var}\,(\epsilon_t) \text{ for } i = j \end{cases}$$

which clearly is violated by the result in (B.7) that the sum of the elements of the variance–covariance matrix is zero. As seen in (B.8), the off-diagonal elements must, on average, be slightly negative, not zero as OLS assumes.

Thus, if the population regression coefficients are to be interpreted as in (B.2), as the asset-pricing theory dictates, then the OLS estimator is inappropriate. Because the mean element of the population variance–covariance matrix is zero, the variance of the OLS coefficient does not exist.

Acknowledgments

The financial support of the Australian Research Grants Committee and the Reserve Bank of Australia is gratefully acknowledged. We are indebted to E. Fama, F. Finn, G. Foster, and R. Watts for helpful comments and to G. Smith for computer programming.

Notes

1. The terms "asset" and "security" are used synonymously throughout this chapter.
2. The assumption of costless information (perfect certainty) would not allow phenomena such as persistent differences in yields of securities, which might be caused by (say) differences in their risks. The models distinguish perfect knowledge of *present* market prices from imperfect (uncertain) knowledge of *future* prices.
3. There are various reasons for the scarcity of other data sources. First, the *capital* market provides richer data than other markets for at least two reasons: (1) the asset-pricing models assert that

securities are perfect substitutes, apart from risk differences and possibly other quantifiable differences, thus allowing an investor to replicate any one security by linear combinations of any other securities (in contrast, price theory does not, in its standard form, allow perfect substitutability of consumption goods, and therefore denies cross-sectional testing); and (2) security rates of return and risk differentials are readily measurable, due to the frequency with which transactions prices are available from (say) the stock exchanges, whereas frequent and accurate transactions price data are not available for most commodities. Second, the *share* market provides the best data from among the various arms of the capital market, for the two reasons given in the text.

4. Fama and Miller (1972) provide a proof. See Jensen (1972) for a review of the relevant literature.

5. A more accurate general interpretation is provided by the portfolio separation theorem of Cass and Stiglitz (1970). The statements in this paragraph are accurate in the Sharpe (1964) formulation described in note 6.

6. In the formulation attributed to Sharpe (1964) and others, a further restriction is placed upon the riskless security: that its future price be known in advance and that its rate of return therefore be a constant.

7. With quadratic utility-of-wealth functions for all households, the riskless-rate in the two-period case can be shown to equal $\Sigma_p[(\theta_{p0} - \theta_{p1}) / \theta_{p2}] / \Sigma_p (\theta_{p1} / \theta_{p2})$, where: θ_{p0}, θ_{p1} and θ_{p2} denote, respectively, partial derivatives of expected utility of consumption with respect to immediate consumption, mean of future consumption and variance of future consumption; and the summation is across all households $p = 1, \ldots, P$.

8. With quadratic utility functions, the risk premium can be shown to equal $-2V_{e,t-1}\sigma^2_{et}/\Sigma_p(\theta_{p1}/\theta_{p2})$. Because $V_{e,t-1}$, σ^2_{et} and all the θ_{p1} are positive, and all the θ_{p2} are negative (assuming universal risk aversion), the risk premium is positive. Together with the implication of (4) and $E(\tilde{R}_{it})$ is linear in β_{it}, this provides the major testable assertion of the model.

   Due to the appearance of $V_{e,t-1}$ in this expression, the risk premium rises with wealth, which means that risky securities are treated as inferior goods. Some find this an unattractive feature.

9. The file was prepared by Philip Brown and is described in Brown (1974). Monthly last sale prices were used to calculated rates of return. The theoretical value of a rights, bonus or convertible note issue was used when appropriate to adjust for changes in the basis of quotation. Dividend payout changes were checked, as were all bonus, rights and priority issues. Extensive filter tests have been applied: for every share, the largest ten rates of return (ignoring their signs) have been checked, as have all continuously compounded rates of return exceeding 20 per cent in absolute value; and each rate of return series has been checked for "excessive" negative serial dependence.

   The file is currently being expanded and upgraded in quality. The expanded file will contain data for 300 more securities for 1958–70, 950 securities for 1971–73, and *all* securities listed on an Australian mainland stock exchange since January 1974. The upgrading will incorporate, where possible, a flag to denote whether the last sale took place on the last trading day of the month, and the traded value of bonus, rights and other issues (the traded value is usually less than the theoretical value, because of: differences in dividend entitlements in the timing of payments, and in transactions costs; and the fact that the purchaser of a "right" acquires a share option with an option value). Needless to say, some errors will remain undiscovered, particularly in the dividend part of the file, as records of "ex dividend" dates are not entirely reliable.

10. Gonedes (1973) and Fama and MacBeth (1973).

11. The results cited in the text are based upon the sample selection already mentioned, with the following modification: a security which is delisted from the Exchange in a particular month is assumed to disappear six months earlier, essentially because of an extreme errors-in-the-variables problem. Many of these securities were the subjects of successful takeovers. It is to be expected that the β's of such securities would be non-stationary as a result of the takeover offer. The β of the offeree security would approach the β of the offeror company as the probability of takeover approaches unity. In essence the firm will usually change its risk class. We would expect this to reduce the efficiency of the estimates of β. This could lead to a downward bias in the slope and an upward bias in the intercept of the cross-sectional model resulting from errors in estimating the independent variable (the β's).

   Tests, where the exclusion procedure was not followed, confirm the bias discussed above. The average r^2 for the one-factor model regressions (5) for individual equities fell slightly, from 0.126 to 0.123. The cross-sectional r^2 for regression number 1a in table 4.3 fell from 0.68 to 0.48, with the slope falling from 0.01204 to 0.01051 and the intercept rising from −0.00123 to 0.00055.

   The results above are not precisely comparable because the dependent variables are not exactly equivalent—owing to the exclusion method.

12. In the context of the two-moment model, an efficient portfolio is not dominated by any other portfolio in mean-variance space. See Markowitz (1952, 1959).

13. The studies using US data seem to have overlooked these limitations. In effect, they have assumed that the index of NYSE returns is the true index.

14. The various hypotheses are numbered in correspondence with the numbering of the regressions described below.

15. Most of the United States studies have included tests on the zero-covariance rate. They have all found higher-than-expected average returns for a zero-covariance investment, though the conclusions drawn from this finding have differed (compare, for example, Fama and MacBeth (1973, pp. 630–33) and Blume and Friend (1973, pp. 30–31)). We believe that these results reveal more about the sign of the intercept in (12) than they reveal about the asset-pricing model: i.e., that the data used in these studies estimate a security with zero covariance with $\tilde{R}_m$ which probably has a positive covariance with $\tilde{R}_e$.

    Most of the studies have not only tested the hypothesis that the average zero-covariance return has positive sign, but also that it is equal to the average return on short-term Treasury bills over the same period. Thus, average returns on zero-covariance shares are compared with average returns on bills which have approximately zero variance and which are offered as approximations to Sharpe's riskless rate. The anomalous feature of these tests is that they cannot be construed as tests of the Sharpe version of the asset pricing model over and above that of Black, as Fama and MacBeth, for example, do (see pp. 613–14 and 630–33). Clearly, if a zero-variance security exists, then *both* versions of the model imply that all other securities with zero covariance have the same expected return. Evidence of shares earning higher average returns than bills with identical covariance either supports the claim of Blume and Friend (1973, p. 32) that the share and bill markets are segmented, or supports our claim that the estimated zero-covariance share portfolio actually has a positive covariance.

16. For reasons explained below, the regressions for each equity were run only on the odd months of data (i.e., 77 of the 155 available months, though not all equities had complete data). The odd/even procedure was suggested by E.F. Fama.

17. See most standard econometric texts, including Johnston (1972, pp. 281–91).

18. See, for example, Johnston (1972, pp. 284–85), and Black, Jensen and Scholes (1972, Appendix).

19. Of the 551 equities, the 11 with the extreme $\hat{\beta}$'s were eliminated, leaving 540 equities: 20 portfolios of 27. Forming 20 groups for the cross-sectional regressions represents a trade-off between fewer groups and greater accuracy of $\hat{\beta}_g$, or more groups and greater range of the independent variable in the regression. Some test runs were made with 10 and 40 groups. A report on the results for 40 groups will be made when the effect of β^2 is discussed below. In general there was nothing in the results that suggested 20 groups were inappropriate.

20. In contrast with Fama and MacBeth (1973), who estimate the β_g and average returns from different time periods, possibly encountering problems and non-stationarity in the β's. This would be a particular problem if risks were not linearly related across time. Preliminary evidence indicates a non-linear relation between subperiod risks in our data, which implies that the method of Fama and MacBeth would not be appropriate.

21. See Fama and MacBeth (1973, pp. 625–27).

22. The same holds for the Fama and MacBeth (1973) study, in which the correlation between β and β^2 is almost perfect in each of their periods.

23. Note that the statistic estimated for each group is the average of the individual equities' standard deviations, *not* the standard deviation of the group average return. Given equation (9), and assuming that the groups are efficient portfolios, the latter would be perfectly ranked with the group β's, and no test of the ability of consumer/investors to diversify would be provided.

24. Two solutions offer promise. The first is that sample estimates of population parameters are more precise for standard deviations than for covariances. The second is that errors in recording price data affect adjacent months' rates of return and, while their effect on β's is random in sign (and would therefore create the sort of mean-reversion seen in the data), their effect on standard deviations is positive in adjacent months (and would not create any reversion, which is consistent with the data). However, we believe that there are few price recording errors on the file.

25. Regressions 1a, 2a and 3a differ in that the equities are grouped on different bases, and hence the β_g and $\bar{R}_g$ are different. There are minor differences in the samples, because the eleven eliminations described in note 19 depend upon the method of ranking and grouping.

26. In the context of the Black (1972) assumptions concerning borrowing and lending, the disturbances of different securities impound common variation but the differences among firms are all due to relative risks and are removed in the first step.

27. Kuhn (1969) demonstrates that there is no neutral language, there are neutral concepts, and there is no experimental observation which has a neutral existence which is independent of the experimenter's conceptual apparatus.

28. Grouping in this case is on the basis of β's, and hence the groups correspond to those in columns (1)–(6) of table 4.1.

29. The reason being the considerable overlap between industry classifications and β-classes (see King 1966), and hence portfolios formed on the basis of ranked β's do not effectively diversify out of return variation due to industry effects.

30. Note that the various statistics are not strictly comparable across regressions 1, 2 and 3: the dependent variables (the average group returns) are not identical, due to the different bases of grouping. This is clearly demonstrated by the varying slopes for regressions 1a, 2a and 3a of tables 4.4–4.6. All

have β as the independent variable, but are grouped on different variables, and occasionally give quite different and seemingly contradicting results. For example, compare 1a and 2a in table 4.4. (The slopes *within* the stages of the stepwise regressions, i.e., 1a and 1b, 2a and 2b, 3a and 3b, are comparable.)

31. The almost identical values for the intercept and slope of regression 1b, in all the tables 4.3–4.6, reflects the facts that: the regression passes through the means; the mean of the dependent variable (the residual from regression 1a) is zero; and the mean β^2 is very close to unity (see table 4.1).

32. See note 20.

33. See Fama (1970a) for a definition of "efficiency" in this context. Fama and MacBeth (1973, p. 625) seem to argue that efficiency implies independence.

34. The random-walk model therefore applies only to sequences of pure profits, such as the sequence of disturbances from a time-series version of (5) known as the "market model". Its empirical success for the return sequences for individual securities, as documented in Fama (1970a), is presumably due to the high variances of the disturbance terms relative to the variances of the individual-security returns, especially with daily data.

5 Risk and return from equity investments in the Australian mining industry: January 1958 to February 1979

Ray Ball and Philip Brown

In this chapter we report the compilation of a database of rates of return on all equity investments listed on the Sydney mining market. The period covered is from the end of January 1958 to the end of February 1979. We also report the results of the first research using the database, which addresses the question of the historical risks and average returns from Australian mining equity investments.

Outline of study design

The initial phase of the project consisted of collecting actual monthly rates of return on every share listed on the mining boards of the Sydney Stock Exchange at any time over the period from the end of January 1958 to the end of February 1979. Having collected these data, the next phase consisted of investigating issues such as the historical returns and risks from mining. Further work is yet to be done on several more-detailed issues. Before turning to the results that have been obtained to date, it will be helpful to outline some features of the study design, so that its strengths and weaknesses can be appreciated at the outset.

Equity investments

Limiting the study to equity investments (i.e., ordinary and preference shares) is a practical necessity. Data on returns from non-equity participation, such as debenture or overdraft financing, simply are not available.

Furthermore, data on non-equity participation are not relevant. Initially, it might seem that ignoring debt might lead to a misleading impression of mining returns; and that the differences in debt/equity ratios of mining and other companies might make a comparison of their respective equity returns somewhat misleading. This would be true if we were to evaluate the absolute level of mining returns, or if we were to simply compare average returns

Reprinted from the *Australian Journal of Management* 5, nos. 1 and 2 (October 1980), 45–66, by permission of the authors and the publisher.

across sectors. But if we compare mining and other returns in relation to risks, then the analysis no longer is misleading: both risks and returns will be increased by the existence of debt. Provided the holders of debt securities are not overrewarded or underrewarded, on average, for the risks they bear, then the risk-return relationship for equities should reflect the risk-return relationship for investments in total. In highly geared situations (that is, with high proportions of debt financing), any excess returns from mining will show up in a concentrated fashion in the returns to equity capital; and any risk attached to return-seeking in mining will show up in a concentrated fashion in the risk of equity capital.

Sydney exchange

The Sydney exchange was chosen because of its proximity to the researchers. Frequent use was made of the exchange's facilities throughout the data collection phase. In assessing the representativeness of our sample, one must bear in mind the substantial amount of multiple listing on the exchanges, the similarity of the quoted prices for multiple-listed securities, and the likelihood that the sample of 1,028 securities will be representative of all listed mining securities. Note that from January 1972 onward, the Sydney exchange listed all mining shares listed on the Australian Associated Stock Exchanges.

Listed and unlisted investments

In using rates of return from stock exchange data, we omit data on returns from investments in mining by unlisted companies or other unlisted entities. Consequently, we tend to omit two numerically large segments:
1. Unlisted companies (normally, where the investment does not perform well enough to warrant subsequent listing); and
2. The pre-listing experience of listed companies.

We do not expect the magnitude of the bias involved to be relatively large, for three reasons. First, unlisted operations are relatively unimportant. Although the number of unlisted operations has at various stages been large, their aggregate value, relative to the aggregate value of the listed investments, is small. Our conclusions below are based on "value-weighted" averages, which would give little weight to unlisted operations, even if data on them were available. Consequently, inclusion of the relatively large number of unlisted operations would have a relatively small impact on the results. Second, we place some importance on comparisons between industrial and mining equities, both of which exclude the pre-listing experience of securities. That is, industrials as well as miners have pre-listing experiences. Third, we note that pre-listing experience cuts both ways: while our data do not include the pre-listing profits of companies that floated after earning substantial returns, they also omit the losses of ventures that did not get off the ground.

Time period: January 1958 to February 1979

The time period was chosen on the following grounds: (1) at the time of commencing the project, December 1977 was the latest practicable completion

date, and it was desirable to collect the most current data available; (2)
a 20-year period was the maximum possible, given the budgetary constraints
on the project, and hence the starting point was selected as January 1958;
(3) a subsequent revision of the database became feasible in March 1979,
so that data then were collected up to the end of February 1979; and (4)
the resulting period should be long enough to be representative of the range
of experience one can expect of the mining sector.

Although the period was not chosen to include specific episodes (for
example, discovery) or to exclude others (for example, wars), we note that
January 1958 to February 1979 did cover a large range of experience in
the mining industry. The period 1958–65 might be considered static and
relatively stable; 1966–73 included both "boom" and "bust", and could be
considered neither static nor stable; 1974–77 might be considered static and
relatively unstable; and 1978–79 has seen a substantial rise in prices.
Nevertheless, the sampling of time was not a function of these outcomes.

One problem with using equity prices in this context is that their initial
values in our file (either at January 1958 or at the time of initial listing,
for subsequent issues) incorporate expectations of future profitability. Thus,
subsequent share market returns do not precisely reflect the performance
of companies' capital investments over that period. Rather, they reflect
equilibrium expected returns on equity over the period and the effects of
changes in shareholders' assessments of the values of companies' capital
investments.

Because our beginning date of January 1958 predates the substantial growth
of the Australian mining industry over recent times, we can therefore interpret
the mean equity returns as applying to a period of *ex post* growth. The
capitalised values of equities at the beginning of the sample period are unlikely
to have incorporated accurate expectations of the events of the next two
decades, even though we would expect them to have been unbiased.[1]

Calculation of rates of return

Rates of return were calculated as capital gains and losses, adjusted for
dividends and for all other changes in the basis of quotation. The latter included
returns of capital, calls, bonus elements of rights issues, bonus issues, priority
issues, consolidations, and share splits.

No adjustment was made for the differential tax effects of capital gains/
losses versus dividends, for tax deductibility of calls, or for other special
tax treatments. There are several important reasons for not making such
adjustments:

1. It is not obvious that there is a differential treatment of dividends versus
   capital gains/losses. If capital gains occur because investors assess a higher
   present value to future dividends than previously, then tax *is* paid on capital
   gains: when the increase in future dividends occurs. This is an area of
   some debate, and it is not clear whether or not an adjustment should
   be made.[2]
2. Even if such an adjustment were made, the problem would remain that
   some investors are taxed differently from others. Some institutions are
   taxed on capital gains and not on dividends; some investors are taxed
   on both; others effectively avoid taxation on both sources; and the marginal

income tax rates varied considerably across investors during the period investigated. The effect of these tax differences upon equity returns also is an area of some debate, and it is not clear exactly what adjustment should be made.

3. Little systematic, reliable work has been done on the effects of tax deductibility of calls and other special taxation provisions in mining.

In summary, the treatment of taxation differentials is far from satisfactory—but, given the lack of any strong grounds for specific methods of treatment, we have little alternative. On a brighter note, we hope that the collection of this file will be an impetus to systematic, reliable work on the effects of taxation differentials.

Methods of adjustment for changes in the basis of quotation, such as returns of capital and share consolidations, provide much less controversy. Consequently, all such feasible adjustments were made. This aspect of the project was most time-consuming.

Use of monthly data

The choice of a monthly frequency of observation of returns was the result of a trade-off among several factors. The basic factors were the decrease in reliability as observations become more frequent (that is, as the interval between observations decreases) and, owing to the increased relative frequency of "no trades" and other problems,[3] the increase in detail of information as the interval decreases. In assessing the extent to which these factors are important, we took into account the fact that a continuously compounded monthly return is the average of a series of continuously compounded returns over shorter intervals, such as days. Consequently, the loss of information in monthly data relative to daily data is considerably less than the numerical reduction in data points.

A monthly frequency normally is chosen for this type of data file. The principal commercial and industrial files in the United States[4] and in Australia[5] provide monthly data. Daily data are used for estimation of short-run phenomena, but such a high frequency of observation cannot be justified in this project—which seeks to measure long-run average returns and risks.

Coverage of equity types

All types of equity issues are included, with two important provisos. First, data have been collected on "foreign" corporations and oil corporations, but they are not included in the calculations for the results outlined below. Here, a "foreign" corporation is a corporation whose assets consist entirely of operations outside of Australia. Second, mining equities listed on the industrial boards are not included at this stage.[6] Note that preference shares are included in the file and in the calculations.

Description of data files

The initial stage of data collection resulted in the creation of five primary files: a "Names" file; a "Dividends and Returns of Capital" file; a "Calls" file; a "Rights and Reconstructions" file; and a "Prices" file. Data collection was conducted carefully and with considerable checking. Prices are either last sales or, where there is no last sale, averages of bid and ask prices, provided the spread did not exceed 10 per cent of the bid price. The next stage was the construction of a '"Price Relative" file, which is accessed for data on historical returns. The total number of separately listed securities on the Price Relative File is 1,029, few of which were listed for the entire period.

The primary data sources used were: the *Sydney Stock Exchange Gazette* and the *Australian Stock Exchange Journal* for calls, new issues, capital reconstructions, dividends and prices; and the Weekly Dividends Declared List, the Weekly Capital Reconstructions List and the Capital Changes Appendage to the Weekly Dividends Declared List, all published by the Sydney Stock Exchange.

The Price Relative File has been filtered in order to isolate and check any changes in successive price that exceed 40 per cent. A smaller filter would have been preferable and would have been consistent with the practice employed in constructing the industrial price relative files. However, the mining market throws up a considerably greater relative frequency of correct large monthly price changes, with the effect that the cost of checking the prices thrown up by even a 40 per cent filter is relatively high. If additional resources become available, it will be possible to apply a finer filter. In the meantime, the expected relative frequency of errors on the file is greater than on the industrial file, though we believe it to be low.

Historical risks and average returns

The first application of the file has been to array the historical experience for mining equities. Some of the more general results are discussed in this section.

Number of mining equities listed on monthly basis

Table 5.1 arrays the number of mining equities listed separately on the Sydney board, on a month-by-month basis over the period. The number ranges from a minimum of 68 (in mid-1966) to a maximum of 473 (in February 1972). The decline to 227 at the end of February 1979 (a decline of 52 per cent from the peak) is evidence of the erratic fortunes of the industry. It is important to note that the table records the number of separately listed securities, not the lesser number of mining corporations with listed securities.

Number of recorded returns on monthly basis

In order to calculate a monthly return, opening and closing prices must be available, and accurate data on changes in the basis of quotation must be available as well. Table 5.2 arrays the number of mining equities for which such a calculation could be made, on a month-by-month basis over the period.

The numbers reported in table 5.1 constitute upper bounds to the numbers in table 5.2. Because of low turnover and other problems in obtaining monthly returns, the numbers in table 5.2 average about 70 per cent of those in table

Table 5.1   Number of mining equities listed, on monthly basis

Year	Jan.	Feb.	Mar.	Apr.	May	Jun.	Jul.	Aug.	Sept.	Oct.	Nov.	Dec.
1958	81	81	99	99	99	99	99	99	99	97	97	99
1959	99	99	98	98	95	94	94	93	92	92	92	93
1960	93	91	90	90	88	88	88	85	85	85	84	83
1961	82	83	82	79	79	79	79	79	79	81	81	79
1962	77	75	74	74	75	76	73	73	73	73	73	74
1963	74	74	74	75	74	73	72	72	72	72	72	70
1964	71	71	70	71	69	70	70	69	70	70	70	71
1965	69	69	69	71	72	70	71	69	69	69	74	73
1966	72	74	73	72	68	68	68	68	69	70	71	77
1967	76	77	78	77	80	80	79	80	80	79	82	81
1968	80	81	81	81	87	86	89	94	94	98	105	106
1969	107	117	121	122	134	143	147	151	160	172	187	209
1970	223	250	263	269	278	292	297	302	319	348	366	391
1971	404	407	412	421	425	423	426	429	428	428	428	427
1972	471	473	471	463	463	461	452	453	454	450	449	449
1973	445	438	432	430	422	412	402	397	398	389	385	384
1974	383	380	368	355	354	354	346	344	341	338	338	337
1975	326	318	315	309	305	301	300	297	293	280	277	273
1976	271	265	259	259	257	259	250	248	248	246	246	241
1977	237	236	235	235	232	232	233	232	230	225	226	223
1978	223	224	227	227	223	221	222	222	221	222	223	226
1979	229	227										

Table 5.2   Number of recorded returns, on monthly basis

Year	Jan.	Feb.	Mar.	Apr.	May	Jun.	Jul.	Aug.	Sept.	Oct.	Nov.	Dec.
1958			67	72	73	72	69	70	70	70	69	69
1959	72	73	74	73	71	70	71	71	72	72	71	65
1960	64	65	68	72	69	70	68	68	68	67	66	66
1961	65	67	66	69	70	66	65	65	65	66	67	66
1962	69	64	62	64	63	65	66	65	62	60	60	62
1963	63	60	61	63	61	61	63	63	62	62	61	52
1964	48	52	55	59	60	59	60	59	60	60	62	61
1965	62	63	60	61	63	67	66	65	64	62	64	70
1966	67	64	60	54	51	51	52	59	56	58	59	61
1967	66	65	65	66	65	71	71	71	72	74	73	72
1968	73	70	79	72	75	78	79	83	88	88	88	100
1969	101	100	106	114	118	127	135	142	145	150	160	181
1970	200	209	230	254	262	262	273	281	289	300	315	331
1971	347	350	354	358	381	382	380	382	387	379	369	360
1972	352	381	388	383	382	392	392	395	366	363	359	365
1973	353	350	345	339	330	335	324	308	279	271	244	225
1974	205	209	224	227	225	225	216	196	158	148	144	159
1975	156	159	171	176	176	187	190	174	154	159	151	156
1976	159	166	167	172	172	177	181	177	168	170	160	148
1977	141	143	143	147	148	158	161	162	147	142	142	147
1978	144	145	147	151	154	156	177	186	184	191	188	186
1979	185	187										

5.1, ranging from a minimum of 48 observations (January 1964) to a maximum of 395 (August 1972).

Monthly returns from mining equities, January 1958 to February 1979

Tables 5.3 and 5.4 display indexes of the profitability over time for the average listed mining security. Figures 5.1 and 5.2 reproduce the indexes graphically.

Table 5.3 Weighted monthly mining index, 1958–79

Year	Jan.	Feb.	Mar.	Apr.	May	Jun.	Jul.	Aug.	Sept.	Oct.	Nov.	Dec.
1958	100.00	94.54	97.05	91.56	91.56	100.81	100.35	102.33	97.26	108.83	111.52	113.91
1959	119.71	121.38	125.01	127.96	142.97	141.43	145.20	155.52	156.33	177.11	171.64	165.87
1960	176.80	169.26	174.06	184.02	191.53	187.62	189.16	192.96	191.04	176.48	165.85	162.87
1961	168.60	169.40	167.24	180.01	190.68	190.12	196.35	201.87	194.61	191.30	187.12	192.15
1962	196.68	205.34	199.85	197.62	195.08	184.79	190.01	187.07	177.84	184.64	184.41	193.63
1963	197.32	199.16	202.78	204.54	214.89	220.89	252.97	263.86	265.53	273.45	282.10	296.12
1964	317.58	337.97	357.14	350.61	329.92	348.30	379.43	374.32	358.90	362.61	377.62	409.60
1965	369.61	365.84	358.52	355.08	376.39	345.85	365.66	380.50	369.42	398.56	409.91	420.49
1966	460.16	439.23	428.46	452.01	442.31	494.32	488.75	475.39	491.90	491.56	479.91	501.66
1967	501.81	478.72	468.43	505.75	589.11	644.33	731.25	724.60	780.59	887.14	932.65	966.38
1968	1071.81	977.71	1076.36	1322.41	1519.56	1683.00	1664.98	1722.23	1332.29	1327.30	1434.77	1577.56
1969	1715.64	1692.10	1747.40	1782.51	1597.71	1559.39	1534.04	1505.51	1598.48	1757.44	1882.33	2306.18
1970	2188.54	2123.18	2016.35	1709.97	1482.02	1793.37	1768.94	1790.94	1892.54	1664.22	1572.61	1487.68
1971	1330.30	1228.92	1330.73	1261.80	1123.55	1106.20	1024.64	920.29	741.11	743.22	711.39	836.75
1972	795.93	913.66	922.63	868.16	906.73	962.93	841.80	839.83	826.68	864.25	887.70	835.25
1973	915.31	819.99	810.30	792.02	813.31	795.50	799.39	665.88	648.00	635.89	581.91	555.63
1974	660.50	733.69	690.53	674.69	565.50	538.47	469.82	494.37	393.10	517.42	547.43	534.68
1975	585.20	592.72	576.46	572.81	649.03	608.69	602.28	611.48	650.75	640.23	706.57	718.86
1976	706.94	695.99	743.23	803.43	827.98	817.09	939.10	908.23	860.03	785.36	795.12	855.08
1977	880.15	869.61	943.73	936.68	956.11	922.66	849.18	807.66	789.49	796.49	766.17	798.88
1978	747.39	706.35	753.74	814.56	936.40	912.72	997.32	1110.28	1135.22	1029.42	1014.19	1073.30
1979	1156.78	1222.56										

Table 5.4 Unweighted monthly mining index, 1958–79

Year	Jan.	Feb.	Mar.	Apr.	May	Jun.	Jul.	Aug.	Sept.	Oct.	Nov.	Dec.
1958	100.00	98.66	93.78	91.38	88.97	92.21	93.27	97.28	99.56	102.84	106.23	107.08
1959	109.55	107.06	106.81	108.17	113.87	110.03	111.91	112.34	117.65	120.01	122.21	121.87
1960	123.68	120.54	118.02	117.37	116.46	115.99	116.31	116.29	115.10	113.67	109.24	109.75
1961	113.69	110.65	109.20	112.23	111.86	113.38	115.82	119.89	123.33	130.41	133.99	140.66
1962	143.87	156.52	155.28	149.99	150.23	147.31	154.09	155.52	145.79	152.19	149.66	151.10
1963	148.87	155.84	154.45	158.05	164.30	165.05	172.93	177.57	184.77	188.60	199.26	223.18
1964	226.11	239.99	244.77	240.85	236.93	226.54	253.98	252.10	254.26	259.29	265.17	283.77
1965	278.03	275.06	263.08	264.41	280.83	269.84	283.04	293.34	283.96	294.04	295.16	308.98
1966	339.41	333.90	323.57	334.82	340.27	377.72	407.12	415.64	409.11	402.92	397.36	427.06
1967	441.95	416.55	399.19	430.98	460.26	503.34	557.18	579.74	594.81	800.25	873.12	827.54
1968	1047.25	1001.80	1008.01	1170.68	1535.16	1619.36	1573.19	1607.13	1249.88	1040.98	1239.28	1242.82
1969	1668.19	1677.54	1843.69	1917.93	1657.80	1409.96	1466.97	1321.42	1454.14	2439.46	2501.93	3248.32
1970	3692.40	3322.75	2519.46	1918.09	1413.09	2285.89	2303.69	2361.85	2708.66	2182.19	1843.89	1572.16
1971	1195.26	940.16	1223.76	1163.02	923.37	849.44	904.07	811.72	650.06	574.01	528.70	593.54
1972	606.84	583.41	631.34	618.16	650.83	688.51	713.37	711.71	737.62	855.74	830.28	771.62
1973	793.65	731.61	697.15	649.39	599.68	561.11	656.94	596.63	561.44	557.16	549.18	510.32
1974	628.40	705.69	696.71	677.66	579.64	462.08	456.36	465.52	447.06	521.04	632.79	610.72
1975	697.32	802.76	769.61	746.99	777.91	698.48	808.42	902.69	990.17	1121.16	1061.74	1176.28
1976	1207.72	1206.60	1149.91	1193.61	1276.86	1250.76	1567.70	1659.43	1637.32	1486.56	1391.83	1402.23
1977	1420.39	1460.91	1532.53	1487.37	1667.11	1639.23	1680.56	1706.88	1723.37	1773.88	1775.68	1892.81
1978	1943.74	1943.61	1985.43	2361.86	3531.68	3217.06	3976.38	5039.24	5408.85	4511.15	4133.28	4355.96
1979	4752.28	5161.15										

Table 5.3 reports an index that is weighted by proportionate market capitalisations. Table 5.4 reports an unweighted index. For reasons given below, the value-weighted index is the correct index to employ.

All indexes reported for mining equities are estimated as truncated means of individual equities' performances. The cross-sectional distributions are truncated by omitting the top and bottom 5 per cent (the extreme) rates of return, to reduce the effects of data errors which, in spite of elaborate care and checking, must arise with a small frequency in the source records, in transcription and in calculation. Truncation tends to exclude a security in its last month of listing, or when a stag profit/loss occurs, which is a price we are prepared to pay in order to reduce the higher data-error problem of mining equities; however, because monthly return distributions are approximately symmetric, no biases are introduced by the truncation.[7]

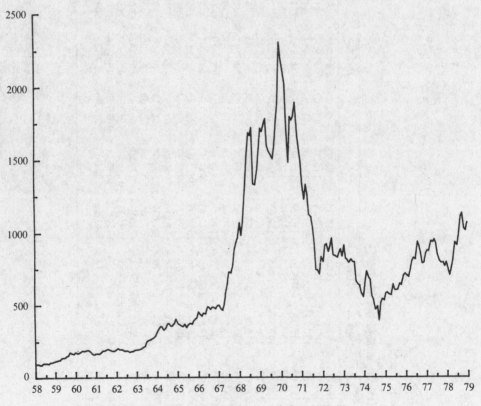

Figure 5.1 Weighted mining index, 1958–79

The value-weighted mining index is calculated as follows:
(i)   Let R_{jt} and N_t be the (discrete) rate of return on equity j and the number of equities in month t.
(ii) Let $K_{j,t-1}$ be the dollar value of market capitalisations of equity j at the end of the previous month, $t-1$.

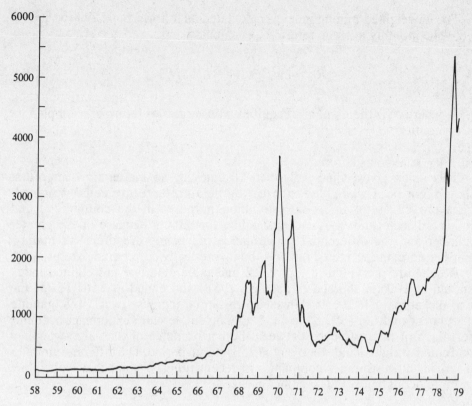

Figure 5.2   Unweighted mining index, 1958–79

(iii) The monthly average return R_{mt} is calculated as:

$$R_{mt} = \log_e \left[\sum_{j=1}^{N_t} (1 + R_{jt}) K_{j,t-1} / \sum_{j=1}^{N_t} K_{j,t-1} \right]$$

$$= \log_e \left[\sum_{j=1}^{N_t} Q_{j,t-1} (1 + R_{jt}) \right]$$

where $Q_{j,t-1}$ is security j's proportion of the total market value at the beginning of the month.

(iv) The index begins at 100 ($I_1 = 100$).

(v) Successive observations of the index are given by:

$$I_t = I_{t-1} e^{R_{mt}}$$

The value-weighted index started at 100 (at the end of January 1958) and ended at 1222.56 (at the end of February 1979). As figure 5.1 and table 5.3 reveal, the periods 1957–66 and 1972–77 were relatively calm for the mining market, whereas 1967–71 was a period of fluctuating fortunes. In 1978 a 34.3 per cent increase was experienced in the value-weighted index, from 798.88 to 1222.56.

The unweighted mining index is calculated as follows:
(i) The monthly average return R_{mt} is calculated as:

$$R_{mt} = \log_e \left[\sum_{j=1}^{N_t} (1 + R_{jt}) \,/N_t \right]$$

where N_t is the number of equities whose rates of return are sampled in month t.
(ii) $I_1 = 100$ as before.
(iii) $I_t = I_{t-1} e^{R_{mt}}$ as before.

This index gives equal weight to all equities, no matter how important they might be. Unweighted indexes (by default, these are equal-weighted) have proven useful for some estimation purposes in the commercial and industrial sector, but they are misleading for mining because of the greater number and the differential performance of "penny dreadfuls" in mining. Furthermore, the weighted index is the theoretically correct index to use.[8]

Results are presented in figure 5.2 and table 5.4. The unweighted index started at 100 (at the end of January 1958) and ended at 5161.15 (at the end of February 1979). It showed a substantial increase over 1978, gaining 130.1 per cent from 1892.81 to 4355.96. This single year's experience accounts for much of the difference between the performance of the value-weighted and equal-weighted indexes over the 253-month period. The difference implies a larger gain to smaller companies in recent times, a point that we explore in more detail below ("The Effect of Size").

Year-by-year record

Table 5.5 reports "index relatives" for holding periods of various lengths over 1958–78. These results are based upon the value-weighted index. From this table, one can determine the average annual rate of return from any one December in the period to any other. These annual averages are reported in table 5.6, using continuously compounded returns. For example, the average annual rate of return over the 7 years, 1969–76, was −14.2 per cent, calculated as $(1/7) \log (0.37)$.

Average return from mining equities, January 1958 to February 1979

Little is known about the profitability of mining as a whole. We know that, historically, a few mining companies have done very well. But we also know that a large percentage of mining investment is irretrievably lost. We do not know what the average or total result has looked like.

In this section, we concentrate on the value-weighted index, because it is the correct index for our purpose; that is, we are interested in the performance of investments in mining in total.

Between the end of January 1958 and the end of February 1979, the value-weighted index rose from 100 to 1222.56. Thus, the total return over a 253-month period, including dividends and capital gains and losses, could be estimated at 1122.56 per cent. This figure is difficult to interpret, since we are used to thinking in terms of annual and perhaps also monthly rates of return. Although there is no obvious method of turning a 253-month sequence of returns into an average return that can be said to be typical for the average

Table 5.5 Indexes over various holding periods, 1958–78

Year	1958	1959	1960	1961	1962	1963	1964	1965	1966	1967	1968	1969	1970	1971	1972	1973	1974	1975	1976	1977	1978
1958	100																				
1959	145	100																			
1960	142	98	100																		
1961	168	115	117	100																	
1962	169	116	118	100	100																
1963	259	178	181	154	152	100															
1964	359	246	251	213	211	138	100														
1965	369	253	258	218	217	142	102	100													
1966	440	302	308	261	259	169	122	119	100												
1967	848	582	593	502	499	326	235	229	192	100											
1968	1384	951	968	820	814	532	385	375	314	163	100										
1969	2024	1390	1415	1200	1191	778	563	548	459	238	146	100									
1970	1306	896	913	774	768	502	363	353	296	153	94	64	100								
1971	734	504	513	435	432	282	204	198	166	86	53	36	56	100							
1972	733	503	512	434	431	282	203	198	166	86	52	36	56	99	100						
1973	487	334	341	289	286	187	135	132	110	57	35	24	37	66	66	100					
1974	469	322	328	278	276	180	130	127	106	55	33	23	35	63	64	96	100				
1975	631	433	441	374	371	242	175	170	143	74	45	31	48	85	86	129	134	100			
1976	750	515	525	445	441	288	208	203	170	88	54	37	57	102	102	153	159	118	100		
1977	701	481	490	415	412	269	195	189	159	82	50	34	53	95	95	143	149	111	93	100	
1978	942	647	659	558	554	362	262	255	213	111	68	46	72	128	128	193	200	149	125	134	100

Note: Holding periods start and end at the end of December on the years indicated by the row and column headings. Figures given in the body of the table are the ending values of $100 invested at the beginning of the holding period. The figure of 412 in the 1962 column and 1977 row, for example, indicates that $100 invested in the weighted-average mining index at the end of December 1962 would have returned $412 at the end of December 1977—with complete adjustment for changes in the basis of quotation, and with dividends reinvested. This implies a continuously compounded annual average return of 9.4 per cent between 1962 and 1977. Annualised mean returns (continuously compounded) for all holding periods are given in table 5.6.

Table 5.6 Average annual continuously compounded rates of return over various holding periods, 1958–78

Year	1958	1959	1960	1961	1962	1963	1964	1965	1966	1967	1968	1969	1970	1971	1972	1973	1974	1975	1976	1977
1959	37.6																			
1960	17.9	−1.8																		
1961	17.4	7.4	16.5																	
1962	13.3	5.2	8.7	0.8																
1963	19.1	14.5	19.9	21.6	42.5															
1964	21.3	18.1	23.1	25.2	37.5	32.4														
1965	18.7	15.5	19.0	19.6	25.8	17.5	2.6													
1966	18.5	15.8	18.7	19.2	23.8	17.6	10.1	17.7												
1967	23.8	22.0	25.4	26.9	32.2	29.6	28.6	41.6	65.6											
1968	26.3	25.0	28.4	30.1	35.0	33.5	33.7	44.1	57.3	49.0										
1969	27.3	26.3	29.4	31.1	35.4	34.2	34.6	42.5	50.8	43.5	38.0									
1970	21.4	19.9	22.1	22.7	25.5	23.1	21.5	25.3	27.2	14.4	−2.9	−43.8								
1971	15.3	13.5	14.9	14.7	16.3	13.0	10.2	11.5	10.2	−3.6	−21.1	−50.7	−57.5							
1972	14.2	12.4	13.6	13.4	14.6	11.5	8.9	9.8	8.5	−2.9	−15.9	−33.9	−28.9	−0.2						
1973	10.6	8.6	9.4	8.8	9.6	6.3	3.4	3.5	1.5	−9.2	−20.9	−35.6	−32.8	−20.5	−40.8					
1974	9.7	7.8	8.5	7.9	8.5	5.4	2.7	2.7	0.8	−8.5	−18.0	−29.2	−25.6	−14.9	−22.3	−3.8				
1975	10.8	9.2	9.9	9.4	10.1	7.4	5.1	5.4	4.0	−3.7	−11.2	−19.4	−14.5	−3.8	−5.0	12.9	29.6			
1976	11.2	9.6	10.4	10.0	10.6	8.2	6.1	6.5	5.3	−1.4	−7.7	−14.2	−9.2	0.4	0.6	14.4	23.5	17.4		
1977	10.3	8.7	9.4	8.9	9.4	7.1	5.1	5.3	4.2	−1.9	−7.6	−13.3	−8.9	−0.8	−0.9	9.1	13.4	5.3	−6.8	
1978	11.2	9.8	10.5	10.1	10.7	8.6	6.9	7.2	6.3	1.0	−3.9	−8.5	−4.1	3.6	4.2	13.2	17.4	13.4	11.4	29.5

Note: This table gives average continuously compounded annual returns over the holding periods defined for table 5.5.

month in the sequence, the superior method for share market returns is to calculate an average continuously compounded return for the period.[9] The implicit assumption is that we are using 253 sample observations to estimate the mean of a lognormal variate.

We report estimates of average continuously compounded monthly and annual rates of return over various periods. Results are summarised in table 5.7. For the value-weighted index over the full period, the average return was 0.0099 (or 0.99 per cent) per month, which is equivalent to 0.1188 (or 11.88 per cent) per year on average.

Table 5.7 Summary of continuously compounded monthly returns, various indexes

Index	Period*	Number of months	Mean	Standard deviation
Industrials—weighted	1/64–12/73	119	0.0045	0.0419
Industrials—unweighted	1/58–12/73	191	0.0107	0.0309
Mining—weighted	1/64–12/73	119	0.0047	0.0826
Mining—weighted	1/58–2/79	253	0.0099	0.0737
Mining—unweighted	1/58–2/79	253	0.0156	0.1072
Statex-Actuaries Accumulation	3/72–2/79	83	0.0057	0.0687

* From month-end to month-end.

Note that these figures apply to the value-weighted index. They therefore include small equities as well as those of the large, established corporations— and give the correct weights to both.

Risk from mining equities, January 1958 to February 1979

Little is known about the risk of mining investments. We know that risk is relatively high (relative to industrial and commercial ventures). But how high?

On the assumption that monthly rates of return from mining equities are lognormally distributed, the standard deviation of the continuously compounded returns correctly measures risk.[10] Using the value-weighted index of monthly returns, we estimate the monthly standard deviation over the period as 0.0737 (that is, 7.37 per cent per month). If one assumed independence of returns across time, this would imply an annual standard deviation of approximately 25 per cent.

On a monthly basis, the standard deviation of 7.37 per cent can be compared with the arithmetic average return of 0.99 per cent. To get a better understanding of this risk-return ratio, it seems reasonable to make a comparison with its contemporaneous equivalent in non-mining investments, to which we turn in the next section.

Comparison of mining with industrial and commercial, 1964–73

How good has been the average return of the mining industry, taken as a whole, in relation to the risks that have been involved? We know of no absolute answer to this question, and address it in terms of a comparison of the risk-return relationship of mining with that of industrial and commercial equities.

The industrial and commercial data are taken from an updated version of the file compiled by Philip Brown. The file contains rate-of-return data on 909 Melbourne-listed industrial and commercial equities. From this file, a value-weighted index was constructed, in an equivalent manner to the mining index described above. The industrial and commercial value-weighted index is available only over the period February 1964 to December 1973, so the risk-return comparison is made over that 10-year period. A longer comparison will be available when further development of the industrial file has been completed.

Over 1964–73, the following parameters are estimated (monthly figures):

	Mining	Industrial
Average return	0.0047	0.0045
Standard deviation	0.0826	0.0419

The average rates of return over the decade were surprisingly similar. The difference of 0.0002 per month is approximately one quarter of 1 per cent per year and is not significantly different from zero, with a t-statistic of 0.06. In contrast, mining equities were riskier (considered by themselves) than their industrial and commercial counterparts. On a monthly basis, their standard deviation of return was approximately twice as large; the ratio of variances was 3.89 and the hypothesis that they are equal was rejected at trivial significance levels, using an F-test.

The period of overlap in this comparison is only 10 years. Work is under way to update the industrial and commercial file to February 1979, which will allow a 15-year comparison, with the advantage of it being both longer and more recent. In the meantime, a longer overlap can be approximated by "splicing" our industrial and commercial index onto the Statex-Actuaries Accumulation Index. Using the spliced index, an estimate of the average return on industrial and commercial equities over the period January 1958 to February 1979 is 12.7 per cent per year, as compared with the 11.9 per cent figure earlier reported for mining.[11] Thus, over a period of more than two decades, it does not appear that mining equities have earned higher returns on average than their lower-risk (considered by themselves) industrial and commercial counterparts.[12] This result surprised us.

Several factors are relevant to the interpretation of these figures. First, there is the effect of measurement error. Because not all securities record their month-end closing prices at the same point in time (that is, they are not continuously traded), individual months' returns are measured with error. This measurement error will average out in the average of 119 months returns reported above, so that the average returns reported in this study are not thereby biased. However, the error has an unknown effect on the reported standard deviation for mining relative to industrial and commercial equities, owing to the different rates of turnover in the respective markets.

Second, we note that the standard deviation of the index return measures the risk *of the index*—that is, of the mining market taken as a whole. Because it is possible to diversify away much individual-equity risk by owning more than one equity investment, the average risk of the individual equities is not as relevant as the risk of the equities in total.

Third, we have not indicated the degree to which the risks from mining (as a whole) can be reduced by diversifying into other sectors. That is, we have not measured the "systematic" risks of the respective indexes. The degree of effective diversification is an important determinant of the amount of risk that mining investments add to the economy.

Is mining risk diversifiable?

Little is known about the degree to which the risk of mining investments can be reduced by diversification. In addition to being relevant to determining the effect of mining on the risk of the economy, this issue is relevant to policy issues such as the foreign investment guidelines. To what degree can Australian investors reduce mining risk by diversification, if they are asked to bear that risk (for example, via minimum Australian-ownership provisions)?

In this section, we offer results on the extent to which the historical risks from mining investment were absorbable, via diversification, in the Australian economy. The data used are the value-weighted indexes, during the "overlap" period of 1964–73 inclusive.

The basic result is that the correlation between the value-weighted indexes (mining, and industrial and commercial) was +0.72. Thus, 52 per cent of the monthly variation in one index could be explained by contemporaneous behaviour of the other. The implication is that the two sectors are sensitive to the same phenomena—though to varying degrees. As a result, there seems less opportunity to diversify out of mining risk than we had expected.

It is often said that the mining and industrial markets are separate markets. These results indicate that they have different degrees of risk, but are nevertheless highly related. One is almost a levered version of the other.

The source of the high correlation between mining returns and industrial and commercial returns is not known to us. An hypothesis that is consistent with the data is that the demand for mining products is a derived demand, arising from industrial activity.

Projection of past experience into the future can, of course, be hazardous. In this instance, the degree of hazard involved depends upon whether the mining and industrial sectors and the relationship between them has changed over time. It also depends upon whether the 10-year period 1964–73 was typical; for example, mining returns over January 1958 to February 1979 showed a higher average than for 1964–73, a result that also held for industrial and commercial equities. Nevertheless, there do appear to be messages in the historical record. First, we were surprised by the small difference in average returns from mining versus industrial and commercial investments. Second, the variability of mining returns was relatively high, as expected. Third, there was a surprisingly high degree of undiversifiable risk in mining investment, owing to its surprisingly high degree of dependence upon the same phenomena as industrial and commercial investment.

The effect of size

As a test of the hypothesis that size and rate of return are related, we calculated the means and standard deviations of six portfolios formed from the ranks of corporations based upon capitalised market value of equity. Ranking was conducted monthly, beginning at the end of January 1958. Portfolios of ranked corporations 1–8, 9–16, ... were formed and denoted as portfolios 1, 2, ... The rate of return on each portfolio was calculated for March 1958, skipping one month to avoid the bias involved in using the January closing price in both the ranking and in the subsequent February return (the bias arises from errors in observing prices). The above procedure then was rolled forward, with the portfolios for April 1958 being based upon a reranking by size at the end of February 1958. The effect is to give a time series of up to 252 monthly rates of return for portfolios that are continuously ranked by size. We avoided ranking once at the beginning or once at the end, for efficiency and bias reasons respectively.

Only the top six portfolios had continuous data over the 1958–79 period. Results for these portfolios are presented in tables 5.8 and 5.9.

Table 5.8 Relation between size, average return and standard deviation

Rank of portfolio	Months of data	Monthly average	Monthly standard deviation
1	252	0.01266	0.07651
2	252	0.01320	0.10055
3	252	0.01371	0.08928
4	252	0.01423	0.09455
5	252	0.00864	0.11224
6	252	0.01238	0.13957

Table 5.9 Ratios of pairwise differences between size-ranked portfolio average returns to the standard deviations of the differences*

Portfolio	1	2	3	4	5
2	−0.11				
3	−0.22	−0.09			
4	−0.32	−0.18	−0.10		
5	0.69	0.79	0.88	0.94	
6	0.04	0.10	0.17	0.25	−0.51

* Difference is defined as average return of column portfolio less average return of row portfolio.

Table 5.8 arrays the means and standard deviations of the portfolios, ranked by size. The Spearman rank-order correlations are:

size rank/average return	0.37
size rank/standard deviation	−0.83
average return/standard deviation	0.54

For a one-tailed test and sample size of 6, the 0.05 limit for this statistic is 0.90. The conclusions are: there was a weak negative relationship between size and average return (the smaller corporations earned higher average returns); there was a strong positive relation between size and standard deviation (the smaller corporations had more volatile returns); and there was a positive relation between average return and standard deviation. However, note the small sample sizes.

Table 5.9 reports ratios of differences in average returns to standard deviations of the differences, estimated from the time series. For each pair of portfolios there are 252 return differences and hence a *t*-test with 250 d.f. is appropriate. None of the 15 pairwise differences is significant.

Summary and conclusions

The principal objectives of the research reported in this chapter were fourfold. The first aim was to create a detailed, reliable and objective data file which will stimulate research into the mining sector. The second aim was to obtain a reliable, objective assessment of the risk and the rate of return from equity ownership in Australian mining investment over a relatively long period. The third aim was to attempt a crude comparison of risk and return: of whether or not the historical rewards to risk-taking in mining have been consistent with those elsewhere in the economy. The final aim was to shed some light in passing upon the relation between size and market performance.

The data support several major conclusions. First, we were able to calculate a comprehensive average return, continuously compounded. After allowing for dividends, capital gains and losses, capital contributions and all other changes in basis of quotation, the average return on mining equity investments over 1958–79 was 11.9 per cent per annum. For reasons given in the body of this report, averaging across equities was conducted so as to give appropriate weights to individual equities. Second, the standard deviation of mining returns was relatively high. The comparison of average return against standard deviation for mining investments relative to industrial and commercial investments appeared to be unfavourable, though we did not measure "systematic" risks. Third, the high degree of correlation between the mining and industrial and commercial returns implies that much of the risk from mining investments could not be absorbed into a diversified industrial and commercial portfolio. Fourth, larger mining corporations (measured in terms of market capitalisation of equity) tended to have lower standard deviations of return, but no clear relationship between size and average return was apparent.

We do not know what to make of the second conclusion. The mining market (considered by itself) appears to have been substantially riskier than its industrial and commercial counterpart, without earning a commensurate risk premium. There is evidence that this result holds for more than the 10-year period for which a precise measurement was possible: it appears to extend over the 21-year period 1958–79 and possibly back two decades before that. Current research is directed at testing this conclusion further. In the meantime, we suggest four possible explanations. First, favourable tax treatment of mining investment, such as the tax deductibility of calls, might imply that pre-personal tax returns should not be compared across sectors. Second, the failure could lie in the mean-variance model, and in particular the unfavourable risk/return comparison could be due to hedging behaviour of investors in mining. Third, the high variance of mining returns implies that the result could be specific to the time sample chosen. Fourth, the differences in "systematic" risk between mining and industrial indexes might not be well measured by differences in their standard deviations. The anomaly requires further investigation.

Acknowledgments

We wish to acknowledge the generous financial support of CRA Services Ltd, the assistance of the Sydney Stock Exchange, the comments of the referees and the work of our research assistants on this project, David Firth and (especially) Jill Henry.

Notes

1. See note 11 for evidence on this point. In particular it seems unlikely that we would have reached different conclusions concerning mean returns in mining relative to industrial and commercial equities, if we had initiated the experiment 20 years earlier.
2. The argument that some adjustment should be made is developed further in Ball (1979).
3. See Gibbons and Hess (1979) and French (1980).
4. The file prepared by the Center for Research in Security Prices, University of Chicago. See Fisher and Lorie (1968).
5. The file prepared by Philip Brown.
6. We do not believe this exclusion has an important effect on our results. The "industrials" concerned (notably, Bellambi Coal, BHP, Coal and Allied Industries, Comalco, CSR, E-Z Industries, Thiess and Peko-Wallsend, the latter for the period December 1963 to January 1969) are represented on the industrial price relative file, so we were able to construct an unweighted index of their returns over the period January 1956 to December 1973 (the period covered by the industrial file). The continuously compounded average return on this index was 0.01075 per month. The equivalent for the weighted mining index over that period was 0.00898. Thus, for 16 of the 21 years, it appears that there would have been only a small effect of including the "miners" listed as industrials. We also note that several of these companies were predominantly "industrials" over that period.
7. To provide a check, we performed the basic calculations both with and without truncation. We found little difference in the monthly average and standard deviation of return for the value-weighted index, which were:

	truncated	*not*
mean	0.0099	0.0111
standard deviation	0.0737	0.0743

   Note that the truncation was applied on a monthly basis; in particular, it did not exclude the same companies each month and therefore did not act to exclude the extreme performers over the whole period.
8. The reasoning is obvious: any other weights do not exactly duplicate the entire market portfolio. Note that it is not correct to exclude the "penny dreadfuls" from the index because of their relative lack of importance. The correct solution is to give them a relatively unimportant proportional effect: to use the value-weights. Note also that there are possible second-order effects which influence the choice of an index. An example is the additional accuracy of a value-weighted index, owing to the higher turnover of the largest issues.
9. For an appreciation of the problems involved see Praetz (1973a). The justification for using continuously compounded returns is the observed lognormality of security return distributions (see note 10). In a misleading sense, it can be argued that a time-series mean of N continuously compounded returns reflects only two data points: the beginning and ending values of the series. However, it is more informative to view the ending value as the sum of the beginning value and N independently drawn growth rates.
10. Monthly returns from Australian industrial and commercial equities are close to being lognormally distributed, with changing standard deviation over time. See Praetz and Wilson (1978). Research is under way to determine whether similar results apply to mining equities.

11. An indication of the pre-sample experience of mining companies relative to others can be obtained from Lamberton's (1958) data. The following are continuously compounded growth rates of his indexes over the 21-year period December 1936 to December 1957:

Index	Description	Monthly average return
13	Non-ferrous metals	0.0039
14	Fuel	0.0024
15	All ordinaries	0.0033

Note that the "all ordinaries" includes the other indexes. An average for indexes 13 and 14, using Lamberton's weights, is 0.0030 per month. This is quite close to the 0.0033 average for the "all ordinaries". Together with the results for January 1958 to February 1979, these numbers do not point to large differences in average returns.

12. The calculation is as follows. The equal-weighted index of 909 equities on Version II of Philip Brown's industrial and commercial file averaged 1.070 per cent per month (12.84 per cent per year, continuously compounded) over the 191 months, February 1958 to December 1973. From January 1974 to February 1979, the Statex-Actuaries Accumulation Index averaged 1.015 per cent per month (12.18 per cent per year, compounded) over a total of 62 months. Chaining the two indexes together, we obtain a "rough" estimate of 1.056 per cent per month (12.68 per cent per year, compounded) over the total of 253 months.

6 International diversification: An *ex post* and *ex ante* analysis of possible benefits

John Watson and John P. Dickinson

Introduction

An investor investing solely in the stock market of a single country cannot reduce the risk of his investment portfolio (for a given expected return) below the minimum level as determined by the capital market line for that country. However, an investor may be able to improve the balance between risk and return on his single-country portfolio by investing in the stocks of other countries.

This aspect of portfolio diversification has been the subject of many papers including those by Agmon (1972, 1978), Grubel (1968), Lessard (1973), Levy and Sarnat (1970), Makridakis and Wheelwright (1974) and Solnik (1974). These papers have presented some contrasting evidence and opinion as to the relative merits of international portfolio diversification. In addition, the emphasis in the literature to date has been on an *ex post* rather than *ex ante* analysis of the possible benefits of international diversification.

The purpose of this study is to examine both on an *ex post* and on an *ex ante* basis the possible benefits (in terms of reduced risk or increased return) of diversifying investments internationally. As was pointed out by Cohn and Pringle (1973, p. 63):

> Little empirical work has been done in the way of constructing internationally diversified portfolios and analysing their returns . . ., and there is far too little empirical evidence yet available to permit any definitive conclusions.

The data

Monthly data were collected for the period December 1969 to December 1977 on a representative industrial stock market index for each of the following eight countries: Australia, Denmark, Germany, Japan, New Zealand, South Africa, the United States and the United Kingdom.[1] Typically these indices include a large number of securities and therefore are representative of a

Reprinted from the *Australian Journal of Management* 6, no. 1 (June 1981), 125–34, by permission of the authors and the publisher.

well-diversified domestic portfolio. The monthly exchange rates between Australia and each of the other seven countries were also obtained for the period of the study.[2]

Because the risks on foreign investment stemming from war, confiscation of resources, and political instability could not be quantified, they were disregarded. Consequently, the risk measure (standard deviation of returns) used in the subsequent calculations might understate foreign investment risk.[3]

Methodology

Monthly rates of return (r_t) were calculated for the stock markets of each country as follows:

$$r_t = \log_e (IN_t/IN_{t-1}) \cdot (EX_{t-1}/EX_t) \tag{1}$$

where IN_t is the stock market index for period t, and EX_t is the exchange rate in period t (expressed as the number of units of a foreign currency required to buy \$A1).

The monthly rates of return for each country were then used to calculate the geometric mean rate of return and the variance in the rates of return for each country, and the correlation between the monthly rates of return for the eight countries.

For purposes of analysis, the data collected were split into two 4-year periods (January 1970 to December 1973, and January 1974 to December 1977) and four 2-year periods (January 1970 to December 1971, January 1972 to December 1973, January 1974 to December 1975, and January 1976 to December 1977).

The use of subperiods permitted an *ex ante* analysis of international diversification. This was done by making use of historical data for a prior subperiod to select an internationally diversified portfolio which could then be examined in the light of its actual performance in the following subperiod. Implicit in this procedure is the assumption that *ex post* data are all that investors need (and use) in order to estimate the expected values and standard deviations of returns. Although this may be a dubious assumption, evidence presented later in the study lends support to the premise that portfolio risk and return estimates based on historic data are reasonable predictors of future outcomes.

Results

Ex post *analysis*

From the calculations of each country's mean return and standard deviation of monthly returns and inter-country correlation coefficients, *ex post* efficient portfolios (with no short sales, as they are not permitted in many countries, including Australia) were calculated using a "Markowitz-type" analysis for the period January 1970 to December 1977.[4] These portfolios form the *ex post* efficient frontier shown in figure 6.1 which also depicts the mean returns and standard deviations of returns both on the 8 stock market indices and

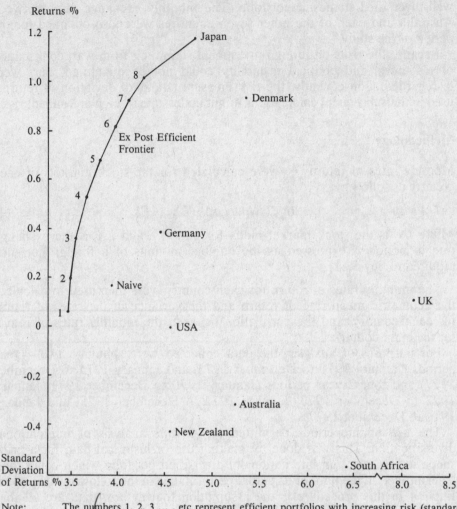

Figure 6.1 Portfolio returns and standard deviation of returns for the period January 1970 to December 1977

Note: The numbers 1, 2, 3 . . . etc represent efficient portfolios with increasing risk (standard deviation of returns) — 1 represents the minimum variance portfolio.

also on a naive international portfolio (equal investment in each country). The naively diversified international portfolio was included as a yardstick against which to measure the effectiveness of the "Markowitz" diversified international portfolios.

Figure 6.1 shows that an Australian investor could have gained substantially through international diversification over the period of this study. All portfolios on the *ex post* efficient frontier dominate the Australian stock market index (as well as the stock market indices for all the other countries in the study except Japan). For example, the minimum-variance international portfolio had a mean return of 0.06 per cent monthly compared with a mean monthly return of −0.31 per cent on the Australian index. Similarly the average monthly standard deviation of returns on the minimum-variance international portfolio was 3.45 per cent compared with an average monthly standard deviation of returns of 5.24 per cent on the Australian index. This represents a 34 per cent reduction in risk or an absolute difference of 1.79 per cent.

The naive international portfolio also dominated the Australian index. The return on the naive portfolio was 0.17 per cent compared with −0.31 per cent on the Australian index. Similarly, the standard deviation of returns on the naive portfolio was 3.83 per cent compared with 5.24 per cent on the Australian index. This represents a 25 per cent reduction in risk or an absolute difference of 1.31 per cent.

Comparing the naive portfolio with the *ex post* efficient frontier showed that for a similar level of return there was a portfolio on the efficient frontier which had a standard deviation of return that was approximately 12 per cent (or in absolute terms 0.46 per cent) lower than that of the naive portfolio. Alternatively, for a similar level of risk there was a portfolio on the efficient frontier which had a return that was approximately 382 per cent (or in absolute terms 0.65 per cent) higher than that of the naive portfolio. Therefore the *ex post* efficient frontier dominated the naive international portfolio. Nevertheless, an investor may consider the increase in risk (or decrease in return) on the naive portfolio to be compensated for by the fact that it is a relatively simple and computationally inexpensive method of selecting an internationally diversified portfolio.

Figure 6.1 also revealed that the Japanese stock market index performed exceptionally well over the period of the study, having the highest return of all portfolios. An Australian investor investing solely in the Japanese index could have reduced his risk (standard deviation of returns) from 5.24 per cent to 4.78 per cent at the same time increasing his average monthly return from −0.31 per cent to 1.18 per cent.

However, this observation is made with hindsight. To place the analysis on an *ex ante* basis and to test further the effectiveness of international diversification, the following procedure was adopted.

Ex ante *analysis*

Firstly, taking the 4-year subperiods of the study, the *ex post* efficient frontier was calculated for the period January 1970 to December 1973. The weights for the various portfolios in this *ex post* efficient frontier were then applied to the data for the second 4-year subperiod (i.e., January 1974 to December 1977). The resulting returns and standard deviations of returns could then be considered as *ex ante* results on a selection of internationally diversified portfolios.

The returns and standard deviations of returns on the *ex post* efficient portfolios for the period January 1970 to December 1973 and the results for the same portfolios for the period January 1974 to December 1977 are shown in figure 6.2 together with the returns and standard deviations of returns on the eight country indices and on the naive portfolio for the same periods.

Note, in figure 6.2, that in analysing the *ex ante* performance of the international portfolios and country stock market indices, the standard deviations of returns for the first subperiod (January 1970 to December 1973)

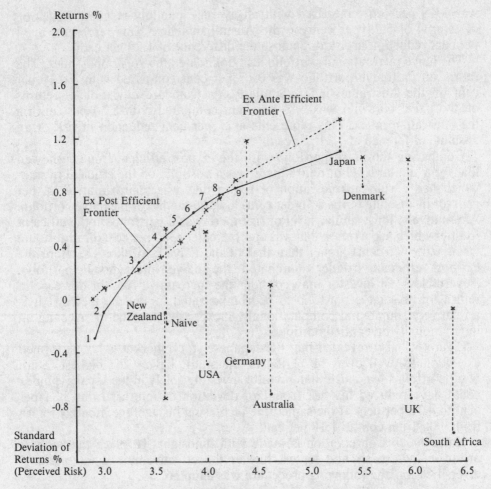

Figure 6.2   Portfolio returns and standard deviation of returns (perceived risk) for the period January 1970 to December 1973 and January 1974 to December 1977

were considered to be the perceived risks for the second subperiod (January 1974 to December 1977). This assumption simplified the graphical representation in figure 6.2 which is focusing on the variation between predicted and actual portfolio returns for a given or perceived level of risk. It could be argued that the actual standard deviations of returns in the second period are really of no major consequence to an investor when he examines his performance in that period. What is of importance to him, is whether the return he achieved is reasonable given his expectations and his perceived risk prior to the start of the period. An alternative interpretation, where standard deviations of returns vary significantly from one period to the next, may be that an investor, in evaluating his portfolio performance, is interested not only in the risk he thought he was undertaking but also in the risk he did actually undertake.

As the standard deviation of returns, as well as the mean returns, did not vary significantly from one subperiod to the next either for the country stock market indices or for the international portfolios, the above assumption is not critical to the analysis. Indeed, over the two 4-year subperiods of the study there was only one portfolio with a mean monthly return that varied significantly, on the basis of a *t*-test, at either the 5 per cent or 10 per cent level. The portfolio concerned was the German stock market index and its mean monthly return, as depicted in figure 6.2, increased from −0.39 per cent to 1.18 per cent from the first to the second 4-year subperiod of the study. This increase was significant at the 10 per cent level but not at the 5 per cent level. With regard to actual standard deviations in portfolio returns, using an *F*-test the only exceptions were the United Kingdom stock market index, which varied significantly at the 5 per cent level, and the New Zealand stock market index which varied significantly at the 10 per cent level. Although covering only a limited number of countries over a relatively short time period, this result lends support to the premise that portfolio risk-and-return estimates based on historic data are reasonable predictors of future outcomes.

Examining figure 6.2 reveals that an Australian investor could have benefited from international diversification on an *ex ante* basis using either a "Markowitz-type" strategy or a naive strategy. Both the naively diversified and the *ex ante* Markowitz diversified international portfolios dominated the returns and standard deviation of returns on the Australian index (as well as most other country indices). For instance, in the second 4-year subperiod, the naively diversified international portfolio had a return which was 430 per cent (or on an absolute basis 0.43 per cent) higher than the return on the Australian stock market index. At the same time the perceived risk on the naive international portfolio was approximately 21 per cent (or on an absolute basis 0.97 per cent) lower than the perceived risk on the Australian stock market index.

Comparing the *ex ante* performances of the Markowitz diversified portfolios with that of the naive international portfolio it can be seen that the naive portfolio dominated the efficient frontier on an *ex ante* basis. The reason for this lies in the fact that the United Kingdom stock market index, which had the largest increase in return from the first to the second 4-year period, did not figure at all in the *ex post* efficient portfolios. Similarly Germany, which also showed substantial improvement over the two subperiods, figures only in the first three *ex post* efficient international portfolios (numbers 1, 2 and 3 in figure 6.2). Both countries had equal weighting (along with the other six countries in the study) in the naive international portfolio and therefore lifted considerably the *ex ante* performance of that portfolio.

Nevertheless, the variation in the return on the naive portfolio (from the first to the second 4-year period) was not statistically significant at either the 5 per cent or the 10 per cent level, and therefore there is no evidence to suggest that a naive diversification strategy will dominate a "Markowitz-type" diversification strategy. The results would suggest that the opposite is the more likely outcome, i.e., that an *ex ante* Markowitz diversified international portfolio, on average, will dominate a naively diversified international portfolio.

To further test, on an *ex ante* basis, the effectiveness of international diversification, the same procedure was carried out on the 2-year subperiods of the study. That is, the *ex post* efficient portfolios were calculated for each of the following 2-year subperiods: January 1970 to December 1971, January 1972 to December 1973, and January 1974 to December 1975. The weights of the efficient portfolios in each of these subperiods were then applied to the data for the following 2-year subperiod (i.e., January 1972 to December 1973, January 1974 to December 1975, and January 1976 to December 1977 respectively) to obtain *ex ante* results of a "Markowitz-type" international diversification strategy. These results were then compared with those obtained for the country indices and for the naively diversified international portfolio over the same subperiods.

With the 2-year subperiods (as with the 4-year subperiods) it was found that the mean returns and standard deviations of returns on the internationally diversified portfolios and the country stock market indices did not vary significantly from one subperiod to the next at either the 5 per cent or 10 per cent significance level. The major exceptions occurred in the first two subperiods where, based on the *t*-test, the returns on the indices of the United Kingdom and Denmark varied significantly at the 10 per cent level. However, neither of these variations was significant at the 5 per cent level. With regard to standard deviations in returns, the portfolio comprising Denmark's stock market index was the only one that varied significantly (at the 5 per cent level) and this also occurred from the first to the second 2-year subperiod.[5]

It would appear, therefore, that there is some evidence to suggest that the returns and standard deviations of returns on individual country stock market indices may vary significantly from one period to the next, particularly where the periods concerned are relatively short. For this reason an investor may not be able to rely on a strategy of simply investing in a single-country stock market index which has an *ex post* risk/return trade-off that satisfies him. In contrast, the realised returns on the internationally diversified portfolios (both the *ex ante* Markowitz-efficient and the naive) did not vary significantly from their expected returns over the various subperiods of this study. In general, the same was also true for standard deviations in returns.

Conclusion

The results of this study (bearing in mind its limitations, particularly with respect to the non-inclusion of dividends) over the period and various subperiods from January 1970 to December 1977 suggest that international diversification could have produced risk-return benefits for an Australian investor not only on an *ex post* basis but also, and more importantly, on an *ex ante* basis.

Although it is difficult to generalise from the results of a specific study such as this, it is worth noting that the evidence presented is in line with the earlier findings of Grubel (1968), Lessard (1973), Levy and Sarnat (1970) and Solnik (1974). This study therefore lends further support to a wider proposition, namely, that investors in general (i.e., from all over the world) could benefit from internationally diversifying their investment portfolios.

Unfortunately, investors in many countries are prohibited from taking advantage of the benefits available from internationally diversifying investment portfolios. This was true for Australian investors until September 1972 at which time the federal government decided that exchange control approval would be given for some modest overseas portfolio investments. The amount of such overseas portfolio investment was limited in any 12-month period to $1 million for institutional investors, public companies and the like, and to $10,000 for individual investors. Those limits were increased in April 1980 to $40,000 for individuals and $2,500,000 for listed and substantial unlisted public companies and institutions. Substantial private companies which meet certain financial standards are eligible for an annual maximum overseas portfolio investment of $250,000.

It appears, therefore, that Australian investors are now better off than they were prior to 1972. Their investment opportunity set has been increased and they are now partially able to take advantage of reducing the risk on their investment portfolios through international diversification. Needless to say, further reductions in exchange controls would benefit Australian investors, as a first approximation.

Acknowledgments

This chapter has benefited from the helpful comments of Dick Cotter and Philip Brown.

Notes

1. The monthly average stock market indices for all countries, apart from Australia, were taken from *International Financial Statistics*, International Monetary Fund. End-of-month figures were unobtainable from this source. The Australian Index was taken from the *Sydney Stock Exchange Journal* for the period December 1969 to November 1971 and from the *Australian Stock Exchange Journal* for December 1971 to December 1977. Although all the indices are not calculated in an identical manner, they are, however, basically similar in that they tend to be fairly representative of the stock markets in their respective countries and they all adjust for major capital changes, but do not adjust for dividends. The estimation error caused by the non-adjustments for dividends is likely to result in an understatement of the covariance between share markets and therefore the gains from international diversification may be overstated.
2. Exchange rates were obtained from *Banking Statistics*, Commonwealth Bureau of Census and Statistics (Canberra). A monthly average buying rate was used based on daily quotations by the Commonwealth Trading Bank of Australia. Although funds cannot be transferred at average rates, average quotations were used to be consistent with the market indices which were also monthly averages. Similarly, one would use the selling rate at the time of overseas investment and the buying rate for disinvestment, but because the difference between the two rates is a type of transaction cost, and as transaction costs have been omitted from the calculation of investment gains and losses, to be consistent they were also omitted from the calculation of exchange gains and losses.
3. Such political risk may arise only in the case of overseas investors, particularly where confiscation of resources is a likely outcome. In such circumstances the standard deviation of share market returns, taken alone, may understate investment risk for an international investor. Solnik (1973, p. 48) has argued, "The limitation of such an analysis appears clearly if one considers more unstable countries (e.g. Venezuela) where the political risk is an important determinant of the investment decision. . . . However, this problem is not crucial for Western European and American capital markets."
4. The algorithm described by Francis and Archer (1971, pp. 85–92) was used to calculate the *ex post* efficient portfolios. To obtain efficient portfolios with short selling not permitted, the following procedure was used: all countries showing negative weights in the original solution were omitted from the calculations and the efficient frontier was recomputed. This procedure was continued until an efficient frontier was derived which contained no negative weights (short sales).
5. The major cause of the significant changes in the mean returns and standard deviations of returns of some country stock market indices can be attributed to the breakdown of the Bretton Woods fixed exchange-rate system during the early period of this study. This breakdown caused significant changes as far as the exchange-rate component of country stock market returns was concerned—see equation (1).

7 Stock return seasonalities and the tax-loss selling hypothesis: Analysis of the arguments and Australian evidence

Philip Brown, Donald B. Keim, Allan W. Kleidon and Terry A. Marsh

Introduction

Recent empirical studies by Banz (1981) and Reinganum (1981a) report a significant negative relation between abnormal returns and market value of common equity for samples of NYSE and NYSE–AMEX firms respectively. Brown, Kleidon and Marsh (1983) find that the apparent relation is actually reversed over certain intervals of time, and Keim (1983) shows that the small-firm premium is always positive in January from 1963 to 1979. Keim reports that nearly 50 per cent of the average annual size effect can be attributed to the month of January, and more than half of the January effect occurs during the first week of trading. A complete explanation of the apparent size effect requires, therefore, separate explanations for both the sizeable small-firm premium every January and the smaller and non-stationary premiums in the other months.

Subsequent studies of the January effect have examined a tax-loss selling hypothesis (discussed in Wachtel 1942, Branch 1977 and Keim 1983) that the small-firm premium in the first few days of the year is a reaction to tax selling pressure at the end of the tax year for the shares of these firms. These studies have taken two different empirical approaches. First, Reinganum (1983) and Roll (1983) examine United States stock return data and report that January returns are greater for those firms with larger price declines over the previous 6- and 12-month period respectively, which they interpret as support for the tax-loss hypothesis. However, neither study controls for other variables that may affect January returns or investigates whether the phenomenon is unique to January.

A second method of obtaining evidence on the tax-loss hypothesis is to examine stock return patterns on stock markets in countries with different tax year-ends, on the assumption that international arbitrage is inhibited. Gultekin and Gultekin (1982) and Korajczyk (1982) both examine the monthly

Reprinted from the *Journal of Financial Economics* 12 (1983), 105–27, by permission of the authors and the publisher.

returns of value-weighted stock market indices in countries with widely differing tax laws and tax year-ends. Both studies find evidence of a persistent but generally less significant (than the United States) January effect in most of the countries, with Gultekin and Gultekin interpreting the evidence as support for the tax-loss hypothesis and Korajczyk interpreting it as not supportive. One drawback to these studies is that a single market index does not allow discrimination between small and large firms. Further, analysis of a value-weighted index, which is more heavily influenced by large firms, does not permit detection of the more important seasonal patterns in *small-firm* stock returns that are allegedly the result of country-specific tax laws.

In this study, we extend the discussion of the tax-loss selling hypothesis and also examine the month-to-month small-firm return premium for a sample of Australian stocks for the period 1958 to 1981. Although the basic idea behind the tax-loss selling hypothesis seems straightforward, a number of factors mitigate any impact that tax-related selling may have on stock prices. We argue that, at best, the tax-loss hypothesis leads to ambiguous predictions.

In Australia, the tax year-end is 30 June, and the tax treatment of capital gains/losses is such that the tax-loss selling hypothesis predicts a July seasonal in returns for small stocks. We find that the raw returns for most Australian stocks exhibit pronounced December–January and July–August seasonals, with the largest (and roughly equal) effects in January and July. The persistence of these seasonals across almost all size categories results in an Australian "size effect"—the smallest 10 per cent of the firms earn an average monthly premium relative to the other nine deciles of at least 4 per cent— with a month-by-month behaviour that is very different from that observed in the United States. Unlike the United States effect, the Australian size *premium* for small firms, whether measured with raw returns or with abnormal returns relative to the Sharpe–Lintner CAPM, appears fairly constant across all months.

It might be possible to construe some of our empirical results as more indicative of the degree of integration of world capital markets than as inconsistent with the tax-loss selling hypothesis. However, although this may "explain" the Australian January seasonal, it leaves unexplained the August and December seasonals. The theoretical ambiguity of tax effects and the Australian evidence presented here tend to support the conclusion that the relation between the tax year and the United States January seasonal may be more correlation than causation.

The next two sections, "Tax-loss Selling" and "Australian Taxes", discuss the tax-loss hypothesis with respect to the United States and Australia, and the following sections report the data and results. The last section briefly discusses our results in an integrated capital markets context, and contains concluding remarks.

Tax-loss selling

The tax-loss selling hypothesis has been advanced most often to explain the January effect. The hypothesis maintains that tax laws influence investors' portfolio decisions by encouraging the sale of securities that have experienced recent price declines so that the (short-term) capital loss can be offset against taxable income.[1] Small-firm stocks are likely candidates for tax-loss selling, since these stocks typically have higher variances of price changes and, therefore, larger probabilities of large price declines. Importantly, the tax-loss argument relies on the assumption that investors wait until the tax year-end to sell their common stock "losers". For example, in the United States, a combination of liquidity requirements and eagerness to realise capital losses before the new tax year may dictate sale of such securities at year-end. The heavy selling pressure during this period supposedly depresses the prices of small-firm stocks. After the tax year-end, the price pressure disappears and prices rebound to equilibrium levels. Hence, small-firm stocks display large returns in the beginning of the new tax year.[2]

There are, as Roll (1983) and others recognise, obvious problems with the above argument. The major problem is that even if it were established that there is heavy tax-related selling of a particular security at year-end, this does not necessarily imply any price decline. Realisations of capital gains and losses need not be associated with a shift in the demand functions for stocks. Although the price-pressure hypothesis suggests that a firm's common stock—being unique—has a downward-sloping demand curve, it is generally recognised that securities with similar risk characteristics will serve as close substitutes for inclusion in an investor's portfolio (see Scholes 1972). In this case, the demand curve is essentially horizontal, and tax-related selling should have no effect on security prices.

Further, the mechanics of this price-pressure argument are unclear. If sales are made purely for tax purposes (as opposed to a desire to liquidate a portfolio), then the proceeds must be reinvested somewhere. Portfolio requirements would suggest that, all else equal, it would be desirable to replace the security by one with similar characteristics. Although "wash sales" are precluded by tax laws, investment brokers publish lists of similar stocks to aid tax exchanges (Sharpe 1981, p. 205) that would weaken any price pressure effect. Sharpe concludes (1981, p. 205):

> End-of-year sales and purchases motivated by tax considerations are fairly common. Volume in securities that experienced substantial price changes during the year tends to be high as holders sell to realise gains or losses. *However, no major fall in prices appears to result from this pressure.* Buyers apparently recognise that the sellers are motivated by knowledge of the tax laws, and not some previously unrecognised news of disastrous developments affecting the companies in question. (Emphasis added.)

If the price-pressure argument were true, we should observe a general decline in prices of small-firm stocks in December even if no unusually detrimental information about them was filtering into the market. Keim (1982) finds evidence of general price increases for these shares in December.

Finally, there appear to be relatively simple ways to avoid or exploit any "low" price, if it did in fact exist. Those who sold a little before the rush would avoid the large price-pressure loss.[3] Anyone not forced to sell an underpriced security for tax purposes would stand to gain large excess returns by purchase of those securities.

Even the case for abnormal tax-loss selling of small-firm stocks at year-end is not clear-cut. It is easy to see why it would be preferable to time tax-loss sales at year-end as opposed to (say) a few days *later* (in the following year) to avoid waiting another twelve months for the benefit of the tax loss.

However, why not recognise capital losses as they occur *throughout* the year? Given the existing tax structure and wash sale rules, Constantinides (1982, p. 35) argues that "investors have an incentive to realise capital losses immediately". This would result in only a fraction of total tax-loss selling being affected by realisations in December rather than in January. Reinganum (1983, p. 9) argues that if investors do not follow a year-end policy, they "might accumulate short-term losses in excess of the (legal) amount which can be deducted from income", but this argument does not explain why the investor would not move his or her tax-loss sales back slightly to avoid the rush. Although Reinganum (1983) finds a negative relation between January returns and their per cent change in the immediately preceding months, Keim (1982) finds this relation in *all* calendar months, not just January.

There may also be tax-related selling of large as well as small-firm stocks. If *marginal* transactions costs are low or zero, it is not obvious why losses on the stocks of larger firms would not also be realised. In fact, costs associated with realising a given dollar loss may be higher for small-firm securities. This is particularly important since the limit of $3,000 on deductions for capital losses may be binding, especially for larger portfolios. Although losses can be carried forward, an investor may not want to sell only big losers (small stocks) since that would ignore possible diversification losses, and reduce the present value of the losses. In addition, it is not clear that small firms will necessarily provide the big losses, since even though they tend to have high return variance, they also typically have high *expected* returns.

Finally, Constantinides (1982) shows that, under certain conditions, some taxable investors will also find it optimal to realise capital gains on small-firm stocks as well as, or instead of, capital losses, indicating that the emphasis on tax-*loss* selling is misplaced. In short, the United States tax position is somewhat ambiguous, and certainly does not necessarily imply the year-end price pressure on small-firm stock prices relied on in the tax-loss hypothesis. Further, such pressure on prices in December does not show up in the United States data.

Australian taxes

The Australian tax year is from 1 July to 30 June for all but a few Australian taxpayers. Capital gains/losses either are treated as ordinary income/deductions and taxed at the ordinary rate (in general, if the taxpayer is classified as a "share trader"), or are not subject to taxes at all (in general, if the taxpayer is an "investor").

All tax-paying financial institutions [e.g., insurance companies, banks, and non-exempt superannuation (pension) funds] are automatically classed as share traders. Share traders pay taxes at normal rates on all realised gains and deduct all realised losses, regardless of the length of holding period. Other taxpayers may choose to nominate all or part of a portfolio as being held for trading purposes, although this does not bind the Taxation Commissioner.

The Commissioner is more likely to be persuaded that shares are held for investment purposes if they pay dividends and are not turned over frequently. Investors are not taxed on gains, nor can they deduct losses, on shares held for a year or more. Gains on shares held for less than a year are taxed, and a recent court decision[4] denies a deduction for losses on shares held less than a year. Isolated "speculative" transactions by investors, for example, purchases of shares in non-dividend-paying oil exploration companies, attract tax on any gains. Losses normally will be deductible if the investor promptly notifies the taxation authorities of the purchase.

Since the rationale for a tax effect comes from the ability of capital losses to directly offset ordinary income, "traders" in Australia appear to have similar incentives for June tax-loss selling as exist in the United States in December. In fact, the incentive may be stronger since they are not limited to the $3,000 deduction.

Certainly there appears to be no reason to predict a January seasonal based on Australian tax law. An alternative possibility is that if shares are accessible to both Australian and United States investors, then a January seasonal in the United States may show up in Australia to prevent arbitrage. However, this would create another arbitrage possibility for those not subject to United States taxes, which extends the class of those able to profit from any tax-selling induced price changes. Further, the securities of main interest, those of small firms, are unlikely to be of primary interest to foreign investors. The same arguments would apply to Australian listed stocks held by United States investors.

Data

General

The database used is a merged version of three monthly data files. In all cases, only the most senior, ordinary share is included in the merged database of 1,924 shares. The first file, Brown's "$N = 909$" file, covers the period January 1958 to December 1973, and comprises all "industrial" shares listed on an Australian stock exchange, with par value not less than $A1 million. The second "AGSM/CRA" file covers January 1958 to February 1979, and comprises all listed mining and oil shares where the company's main operations are in Australia. The third file, an early version of the AGSM Share Data File, begins January 1974, is current, and comprises all listed Australian shares. The merged file is used to construct a value-weighted market index, with the weights based on market values of equity in the previous month. A file of riskless rates of return is constructed from Australian Treasury Bills.[5]

Ten size-ranked portfolios have been constructed, with updating each month t based on market value of equity deciles in month $t-2$. Consequently, the first rate of return available for these portfolios is in March 1958. The rates of return used in this chapter are based on discrete compounding,[6] and returns are equally weighted within each of the ten size-ranked portfolios.

Not all shares were listed for the full period and fewer were traded in every month. The number of shares for which returns are available ranges from a minimum of 281 (February 1958) to a maximum of 937 (April 1974). Two events that increased the number of available securities are capitalisation changes that accompanied decimalisation of currency in February 1966, and the introduction of Australian Associated Stock Exchange uniform listing in February 1972.

Until January 1974, the smallest shares on the merged file are dominated by mining and oil shares, because of the $A1 million minimum par value imposed on the first industrial file. However, since then the inclusion of all industrial shares adds another set of small stocks. Time-series plots of rates of return for the decile of smallest firms reveal that although there are outliers around 1974, the small-firm portfolio does not show a readily apparent general increase in variance after 1974, which may indicate that small industrials are not significantly smaller than small mining and oil stocks.

In any event, there is an increase in the number of relatively small stocks in 1974. Further, the data error rate is likely to be higher in the early version of the AGSM Share Data File because it had not been validated to the same extent as the other two files.[7] To assess the sensitivity of our results to the structural change in our database, analysis was conducted on subperiods before and after January 1974, and results are reported where pertinent. Also, robust regression techniques have been used to gauge the sensitivity of our results to extreme returns.[8]

Average returns and autocorrelation

The average rate of return, OLS beta and autocorrelation functions for the value-weighted market index and all ten portfolios are given in table 7.1 for the overall period March 1958 to June 1981. This table is meant to summarise the Australian data, and allows comparison with the United States size effect studies (e.g., Banz 1981; Reinganum 1981a) and also with the earlier work of Officer (1975) who examined seasonalities in Australian industrial stocks from 1958 to 1970 (see chapter 15).

The cross-sectional pattern[9] of higher average returns for small firms in table 7.1 mirrors that reported by Banz (1981) and Reinganum (1981a) for the United States. The size effect, whatever its origin, shows up in the Australian data.[10] A significant feature relative to the statistics for the United States monthly returns is the high first-order serial correlation ranging from 0.16 for the largest firms to 0.33 for portfolio 8. These estimates are consistent with Officer (1975, p. 38) who attributes this to more severe non-trading in the Australian market than in the United States. In contrast to the United States data, the autocorrelation is less pronounced at both ends of the size spectrum than for the medium-size firms.[11] The value-weighted market index, which puts primary emphasis on the largest firms, shows similar autocorrelations to portfolio 10.

Officer (1975) finds persistence over different subperiods of significant positive autocorrelation at lags 6 and 9, and significant negative autocorrelation at lags 13 and 14. The latter were regarded as particularly surprising, but he reports that they did not appear to have any predictive ability. Over the subperiod from January 1974 to June 1981, which is outside Officer's sample period, we find only weak evidence of negative autocorrelation at these lags. Similarly, autocorrelation estimates at lags 6 and 9 vary widely in sign and magnitude across subperiods in our sample.

In short, there appears reliable evidence (and explanation) for positive first-

Table 7.1 Average monthly rates of return, ordinary least-squares beta estimates,[a] and correlograms of monthly rates of return for ten portfolios constructed by equally weighting monthly rates of return on all Australian industrial, mining and oil stocks[b] in each decile of size (measured by market value of equity),[c] and for the value-weighted market index of all Australian industrial, mining and oil stocks, over the period March 1958 to June 1981.

Size decile	Average[d] rate of return (%)	OLS beta	Autocorrelation estimates for the monthly rate of return[e]							
			$\hat{\rho}_1$	$\hat{\rho}_2$	$\hat{\rho}_3$	$\hat{\rho}_6$	$\hat{\rho}_9$	$\hat{\rho}_{12}$	$\hat{\rho}_{13}$	$\hat{\rho}_{14}$
Smallest	6.754 (0.637)	1.040	0.18	0.07	0.08	−0.03	0.14	−0.04	−0.12	−0.10
2	2.231 (0.393)	0.868	0.19	0.01	0.03	0.07	0.19	0.06	−0.02	−0.14
3	1.743 (0.305)	0.657	0.18	−0.01	0.14	0.06	0.17	0.02	−0.15	−0.14
4	1.319 (0.271)	0.661	0.28	0.06	0.04	0.07	0.23	0.04	−0.10	−0.20
5	1.476 (0.240)	0.609	0.30	0.11	0.07	0.07	0.23	0.01	−0.14	−0.23
6	1.267 (0.237)	0.613	0.28	0.05	0.07	0.05	0.21	0.07	−0.12	−0.16
7	1.150 (0.239)	0.659	0.31	0.08	0.04	0.10	0.20	0.02	−0.10	−0.18
8	1.221 (0.239)	0.678	0.33	0.07	0.06	0.04	0.21	0.01	−0.13	−0.20
9	1.181 (0.247)	0.759	0.24	0.07	0.13	0.03	0.21	0.03	−0.14	−0.17
Largest	1.023 (0.286)	0.950	0.16	0.01	0.08	−0.03	0.19	0.03	−0.09	−0.22
Index	1.073 (0.291)		0.16	0.03	0.05	0.02	0.22	0.02	−0.08	−0.20

[a] The OLS beta is computed by regressing monthly portfolio rates of return on the monthly rates of return of a value-weighted (market) portfolio over the period March 1958 to June 1981.

[b] The industrial stocks comprise all those listed on an Australian stock exchange, but prior to December 1973 include only those with a par value of at least $A1 million. The mining and oil stocks comprise all those which are listed and have their main operations in Australia.

[c] Market values of equity used for weighting rates of return in month t are computed two months prior to t, i.e., at the end of month $t − 2$, $t =$ March 1958 to June 1981.

[d] The average returns in per cent are based on 280 observations for each equally weighted portfolio of stocks in each size decile over the period March 1958 to June 1981. The standard errors given in parentheses will be biased downward because of the autocorrelation in the rates of return.

[e] The standard error of these autocorrelation estimates is approximately 0.06.

order serial correlation and this shows up in subsequent tests. Although some odd apparent correlation shows up at other lags, it is much less reliable and may be due to sampling variation. Table 7.1 also contains the sample market model beta estimates for ten portfolios. The beta estimates are downward-biased owing to the non-trading just described, and we report results using Dimson (1979) betas later.

Results

Raw data

Praetz (1973b), using spectral analysis, reports apparent seasonalities in the

Sydney All Ordinaries Index with peaks in January–February and July–August and troughs in March–April and November–December. Using time series analysis, Officer (1975, p. 46) concludes that "the results do not give a clear indication of any particular type of seasonality", although there is some evidence of correlation between the returns of March and September. However, his results (1975, table 5, p. 44) may show some effects of a January seasonal, since for his sample index the largest lag 12 serial correlation occurs for the month of January.

To test for seasonality in Australian mean monthly stock returns, we estimate the following dummy variable OLS regression:

$$R_{pt} = a_{p1} + \sum_{i=2}^{12} a_{pi}D_{it} + \epsilon_{pt}, \quad p = 1, \ldots, 10, \tag{1}$$

where R_{pt} = return on portfolio p in month t, D_{it} = seasonal dummy for calendar month i, i = February, ..., December. The intercept a_{p1} indicates average returns for January, and the dummy coeficients a_{pi} indicate the average differences in return between January and each respective month. In table 7.2, we present estimates of equation (1) for the overall period March 1958 to June 1981. The results of table 7.2 have been graphed in figure 7.1 for visual assessment. Figure 7.3 contains an analogous plot of the returns for the five market-value portfolios of NYSE stocks used in Keim (1982) for comparison with United States results.

Table 7.2 and figure 7.1 contain several important results. First, the smallest-firm portfolio 1 shows higher average returns across all months than do the other portfolios. The results in table 7.1 indicate an average monthly return of 6.75 per cent for portfolio 1 and 2.23 per cent for portfolio 2.

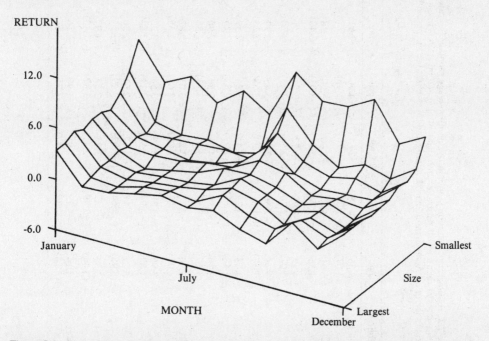

Figure 7.1 Plot of the average monthly rates of return (in per cent) for ten market-value portfolios constructed from Australian industrial and mining stocks for each month over the period March 1958 to June 1981

Table 7.2 Estimates of variation in month-by-month average monthly (%) rates of return (t-statistics in parentheses) on ten portfolios constructed by equally weighting monthly rates of return on all Australian industrial, mining and oil stocks[a] in each decile of size (measured by market value of equity),[b] and for the value-weighted market index of all Australian industrial, mining and oil stocks, over the period March 1958 to June 1981

$$R_{pt} = a_{p1} + \sum_{i=2}^{12} a_{pi}D_{it} + \epsilon_{pt}, \quad p = 1, \ldots, 10, \quad t = 1, \ldots, T.[c] \tag{1}$$

Portfolio	Jan.	Feb.	March	April	May	June	July	Aug.	Sept.	Oct.	Nov.	Dec.
Smallest	8.86 (3.67)	-4.18 (-1.22)	-2.64 (-0.78)	-4.90 (-1.45)	-2.61 (-0.77)	-4.61 (-1.36)	1.34 (0.39)	-1.25 (-0.37)	-1.03 (-0.30)	0.68 (0.20)	-3.77 (-1.10)	-2.06 (-0.60)
2	6.01 (4.55)	-5.17 (-2.77)	-5.88 (-3.18)	-5.60 (-3.03)	-6.28 (-3.40)	-5.52 (-2.98)	0.77 (0.41)	-2.77 (-1.48)	-4.63 (-2.48)	-3.40 (-1.82)	-4.27 (-2.28)	-2.21 (-1.18)
3	4.27 (4.08)	-3.99 (-2.70)	-3.72 (-2.54)	-3.58 (-2.45)	-3.31 (-2.26)	-3.57 (-2.44)	0.25 (0.24)	-2.16 (-1.46)	-3.17 (-2.15)	-2.46 (-1.66)	-3.33 (-2.25)	-1.16 (-0.79)
4	3.11 (3.37)	-2.36 (-1.81)	-2.96 (-2.29)	-3.45 (-2.68)	-2.94 (-2.28)	-1.87 (-1.45)	0.93 (0.72)	-1.60 (-1.23)	-2.66 (-2.04)	-2.43 (-1.86)	-2.19 (-1.68)	0.28 (0.21)
5	3.68 (4.48)	-3.29 (-2.83)	-3.41 (-2.97)	-3.24 (-2.82)	-2.59 (-2.25)	-2.27 (-1.98)	-0.62 (-0.53)	-1.20 (-1.03)	-3.10 (-2.66)	-2.63 (-2.27)	-2.93 (-2.52)	-1.05 (-0.91)
6	3.70 (4.57)	-2.89 (-2.53)	-4.21 (-3.71)	-3.54 (-3.13)	-2.90 (-2.56)	-1.59 (-1.41)	-1.46 (-1.28)	-2.15 (-1.88)	-3.34 (-2.92)	-2.33 (-2.03)	-3.50 (-3.06)	-1.16 (-1.01)
7	3.30 (4.01)	-2.76 (-2.37)	-3.22 (-2.88)	-3.01 (-2.62)	-2.82 (-2.45)	-2.31 (-2.01)	-0.68 (-0.58)	-1.80 (-1.55)	-2.92 (-2.51)	-2.06 (-1.77)	-3.14 (-2.70)	-0.86 (-0.74)
8	3.96 (4.87)	-3.38 (-2.94)	-3.99 (-3.51)	-3.54 (-3.11)	-3.23 (-2.84)	-2.69 (-2.36)	-1.67 (-1.45)	-2.45 (-2.13)	-4.28 (-3.72)	-2.63 (-2.29)	-3.65 (-3.17)	-1.24 (-1.08)
9	3.39 (3.98)	-3.18 (-2.64)	-3.47 (-2.92)	-2.61 (-2.19)	-2.30 (-1.94)	-2.70 (-2.27)	-1.12 (-0.93)	-2.69 (-2.24)	-3.38 (-2.81)	-1.47 (-1.22)	-2.81 (-2.33)	-0.63 (-0.53)
Largest	3.39 (3.44)	-3.47 (-2.49)	-3.31 (-2.41)	-2.58 (-1.87)	-1.97 (-1.43)	-2.56 (-1.86)	-2.03 (-1.46)	-3.42 (-2.45)	-4.29 (-3.08)	-0.91 (-0.65)	-3.24 (-2.33)	-0.61 (-0.44)
Market	3.14 (3.14)	-3.22 (-2.27)	-2.97 (-2.12)	-1.90 (-1.35)	-2.16 (-1.54)	-2.19 (-1.56)	-1.90 (-1.34)	-2.80 (-1.97)	-4.21 (-2.97)	-0.91 (-0.64)	-2.86 (-2.02)	0.31 (0.22)

	$\hat{\rho}_1$	$\hat{\rho}_6$	$\hat{\rho}_9$	$\hat{\rho}_{12}$	$\hat{\rho}_{13}$	$\hat{\rho}_{14}$	DW	F-stat.[e]	Prob > F[f]
	Autocorrelations of $\hat{e}_{pt}$[d]								
Smallest	0.22	−0.03	0.16	−0.08	−0.13	−0.12	1.57	0.75	0.686
2	0.20	0.01	0.26	−0.05	−0.04	−0.12	1.60	3.09	0.001
3	0.20	0.02	0.21	−0.06	−0.17	−0.13	1.61	2.02	0.027
4	0.29	0.02	0.33	−0.06	−0.14	−0.19	1.42	2.39	0.008
5	0.33	0.03	0.31	−0.07	−0.18	−0.23	1.34	2.05	0.025
6	0.30	−0.01	0.30	−0.02	−0.16	−0.14	1.40	2.26	0.012
7	0.33	0.06	0.26	−0.06	−0.13	−0.16	1.34	1.78	0.053
8	0.36	−0.01	0.28	−0.09	−0.17	−0.19	1.28	2.36	0.009
9	0.27	−0.01	0.24	−0.05	−0.16	−0.16	1.46	1.77	0.059
Largest	0.18	−0.06	0.21	−0.04	−0.10	−0.23	1.65	1.77	0.059
Market	0.18	−0.00	0.25	−0.06	−0.09	−0.21	1.64	1.75	0.064

[a] The industrial stocks comprise all those listed on an Australian stock exchange, but prior to December 1973 include only those with a par value of at least \$A1 million. The mining and oil stocks comprise all those which are listed and have their main operations in Australia.

[b] Size rankings are up-dated monthly and are based on market values of equity two months earlier, i.e., in month t, portfolios are formed using equity values at the end of month $t − 2$, $t = 1, \ldots, T$.

[c] For each portfolio p, the intercept coefficient $\hat{a}_{p1}$ is an estimate of that portfolio's average rate of return in January. The t-statistic for $\hat{a}_{p1}$, in parentheses under that coefficient estimate, is for the test of whether January's average rate of return is significantly different from zero. The coefficients $\hat{a}_{p2}$, $\hat{a}_{p3}, \ldots, \hat{a}_{p12}$ are estimates of the differences in average rates of return in February ($= D_{2t}$), March ($= D_{3t}$), $\ldots$, December ($= D_{12t}$), from that in January. The t-statistics under $\hat{a}_{p2}, \hat{a}_{p3}, \ldots, \hat{a}_{p12}$ test whether there is significant variation in the February, March, $\ldots$, December average rates of return relative to that of January.

[d] The standard error of these autocorrelation coefficients is approximately 0.06.

[e] The F-statistic tests the hypothesis that a_{p2} through a_{p12} are jointly equal to zero for each $p = 1, \ldots,$ 10: $F_{11,268}$ (95%) = 1.79; $F_{11,268}$ (99%) = 2.25.

[f] The Prob > F-statistic is the p-value for the F-test, i.e., it is the area to the right of the F-statistic on the $F(11,268)$ distribution. A sampling theorist would reject the null hypothesis that a_{p2} through a_{p12} jointly equal zero at the α% level if (Prob > F) < α.

Table 7.2 and figure 7.1 show that this average monthly premium of about 4 per cent seems fairly constant across all months. Although the statistical significance of these results is somewhat difficult to judge, given the high first-order autocorrelation in the residuals shown in table 7.2 and the cross-sectional dependence in the returns, it seems that the size-related premium for the smallest firms exists in all months. Note also the extra information obtained by the analysis of the size-ranked portfolios vis-à-vis the market index, which looks most like the large-firm portfolio 10.

Second, for all portfolios, the dummy coefficients in table 7.2 are negative for almost all non-January months, indicating that January does earn apparently higher returns than most other months. The main exceptions are the July coefficients for the four smallest portfolios.

Third, there appears to be more than just a January premium. For portfolio 1, the smallest firms, there is considerable sampling variation across months, so that although (say) January and July appear to earn higher returns than (say) June, the F-statistic reported in table 7.2 indicates that the null hypothesis of no difference across months cannot be rejected for portfolio 1 at conventional significance levels. However, the null hypothesis is rejected at the 5 per cent level for portfolios 2 to 6 and portfolio 8, and barely accepted at this level for portfolios 7, 9 and 10. For most portfolios, two strong seasonals emerge. December–January and July–August appear to earn consistently higher returns than do other months, with the largest returns in January and

Table 7.3 Estimates of variation in month-by-month excess monthly (%) rates of return (t-statistics in parentheses), relative to the Sharpe–Lintner capital asset pricing model, on ten portfolios constructed by equally weighting monthly rates of return on all Australian industrial, mining and oil stocks[a] in each decile of size (measured by market value of equity),[b] over the period March 1958 to June 1981

$$(R_{pt} - R_{Ft}) = a'_{p1} + \beta_p (R_{Mt} - R_{Ft}) + \sum_{i=2}^{12} a'_{pi} D_{it} + \epsilon'_{pt}, \quad p = 1, \ldots, 10, \ t = 1, \ldots, T.^{c}$$

Portfolio	Jan.	$\hat{\beta}_p^d$	Feb.	March	April	May	June	July	Aug.	Sept.	Oct.	Nov.	Dec.
Smallest	5.54 (2.53)	1.07 (0.53)	−0.74 (−0.24)	0.54 (0.18)	−2.87 (−0.95)	−0.31 (−0.10)	−2.27 (−0.75)	3.37 (1.10)	1.74 (0.57)	3.47 (1.12)	1.65 (0.54)	−0.70 (−0.23)	−2.40 (−0.78)
2	3.24 (3.20)	0.86 (−2.42)	−2.40 (−1.68)	−3.34 (−2.37)	−3.97 (−2.83)	−4.43 (−3.16)	−3.64 (−2.59)	2.40 (1.70)	−0.37 (−0.26)	−1.02 (−0.71)	−2.63 (−1.86)	−1.81 (−1.27)	−2.48 (−1.75)
3	2.05 (2.49)	0.65 (−7.03)	−1.89 (−1.62)	−1.79 (−1.55)	−2.34 (−2.05)	−1.91 (−1.67)	−2.15 (−1.88)	1.59 (1.37)	−0.33 (−0.29)	−0.43 (−0.37)	−1.87 (−1.62)	−1.47 (−1.26)	−1.37 (−1.19)
4	0.86 (1.33)	0.66 (−8.87)	−0.22 (−0.24)	−0.99 (−1.11)	−2.19 (−2.46)	−1.52 (−1.70)	−0.42 (−0.47)	2.19 (2.43)	0.25 (0.28)	0.13 (0.15)	−1.83 (−2.03)	−0.29 (−0.32)	0.07 (0.07)
5	1.57 (2.85)	0.61 (−11.69)	−1.31 (−1.69)	−1.61 (−2.09)	−2.08 (−2.71)	−1.28 (−1.67)	−0.94 (−1.23)	0.54 (0.70)	0.51 (0.66)	−0.52 (−0.67)	−2.08 (−2.69)	−1.18 (−1.52)	−1.24 (−1.61)
6	1.60 (2.99)	0.61 (−12.00)	−0.93 (−1.23)	−2.40 (−3.22)	−2.39 (−3.22)	−1.60 (−2.15)	−0.27 (−0.36)	−0.30 (−0.41)	−0.45 (−0.60)	−0.78 (−1.02)	−1.78 (−2.37)	−1.75 (−2.33)	−1.35 (−1.80)
7	1.06 (2.16)	0.66 (−11.50)	−0.62 (−0.89)	−1.35 (−1.98)	−1.75 (−2.58)	−1.40 (−2.06)	−0.87 (−1.27)	0.58 (0.84)	0.05 (0.08)	−0.14 (−0.19)	−1.46 (−2.13)	−1.24 (−1.80)	−1.07 (−1.56)
8	1.70 (3.66)	0.67 (−11.75)	−1.22 (−1.87)	−2.01 (−3.11)	−2.27 (−3.52)	−1.80 (−2.79)	−1.23 (−1.90)	−0.40 (−0.61)	−0.58 (−0.89)	−1.46 (−2.22)	−2.03 (−3.12)	−1.73 (−2.65)	−1.45 (−2.24)
9	0.89 (2.31)	0.76 (−10.23)	−0.74 (−1.36)	−1.23 (−2.28)	−1.18 (−2.19)	−0.68 (−1.27)	−1.04 (−1.94)	0.31 (0.58)	−0.58 (−1.06)	−0.19 (0.35)	−0.78 (−1.45)	−0.64 (−1.18)	−0.87 (−1.61)
Largest	0.39 (1.50)	0.95 (−3.26)	−0.41 (−1.14)	−0.50 (−1.38)	−0.78 (−2.18)	0.07 (0.20)	−0.48 (−1.35)	−0.23 (−0.64)	−0.76 (−2.11)	−0.30 (−0.82)	−0.05 (−0.14)	−0.52 (−1.44)	−0.91 (−2.52)

Portfolio	Autocorrelations of $\hat{\epsilon}_{pt}$[e]						DW	F-stat.[f]	Prob $> F$[g]
	$\hat{\rho}_1$	$\hat{\rho}_6$	$\hat{\rho}_9$	$\hat{\rho}_{12}$	$\hat{\rho}_{13}$	$\hat{\rho}_{14}$			
Smallest	0.10	0.02	0.08	−0.04	0.02	−0.08	1.80	0.97	0.477
2	0.01	0.05	0.06	−0.06	0.11	−0.05	1.98	3.89	0.000
3	−0.02	−0.05	−0.00	−0.05	−0.02	−0.11	2.04	2.02	0.027
4	−0.02	−0.00	0.13	−0.07	0.03	−0.10	2.05	3.35	0.000
5	0.03	0.02	0.17	−0.09	−0.03	−0.16	1.93	2.71	0.002
6	0.07	0.03	0.15	−0.04	0.01	−0.12	1.85	2.52	0.005
7	0.01	0.12	0.12	−0.15	0.08	−0.15	1.97	2.36	0.009
8	0.16	−0.01	0.11	−0.12	−0.03	−0.16	1.68	2.38	0.008
9	0.12	0.11	0.05	−0.06	−0.06	−0.11	1.75	1.52	0.123
Largest	−0.00	0.00	0.05	−0.05	−0.06	−0.02	2.00	1.58	0.104

[a] The industrial stocks comprise all those listed on an Australian stock exchange, but prior to December 1973 include only those with a par value of at least \$A1 million. The mining and oil stocks comprise all those which are listed and have their main operations in Australia.

[b] Size rankings are up-dated monthly, and are based on market values of equity two months earlier, i.e., in month t, portfolios are formed using equity values at the end of month $t - 2$, $t = 1, \ldots, T$.

[c] For each portfolio p, the intercept coefficient $\hat{a}'_{p1}$ is an estimate of that portfolio's average excess rate of return in January. The t-statistic for $\hat{a}'_{p1}$, in parentheses under that coefficient's estimate, is for the test of whether January's average excess rate of return is significantly different from zero. The coefficients $\hat{a}'_{p2}, \hat{a}'_{p3}, \ldots, \hat{a}'_{p12}$ are estimates of the differences in average excess rates of return in February ($= D_{2t}$), March ($= D_{3t}$), $\ldots$, December ($= D_{12t}$), from that in January. The t-statistics under $\hat{a}'_{p2}, \hat{a}'_{p3}, \ldots, \hat{a}'_{p12}$ test whether there is significant variation in the February, March, $\ldots$, December average excess rates of return relative to that of January.

[d] The t-statistics for beta are for the null hypothesis $\hat{\beta}_p = 1$.

[e] The standard error of these autocorrelation coefficients is approximately 0.06.

[f] The F-statistic tests the hypothesis that a'_{p2} through a'_{p12} are jointly equal to zero for each $p = 1, \ldots, 10$: $F_{11,268}$ (95%) = 1.79; $F_{11,268}$ (99%) = 2.25.

[f] The Prob $> F$-statistic is the p-value for the F-test, i.e., it is the area to the right of the F-statistic on the $F(11,268)$ distribution. A sampling theorist would reject the null hypothesis that a'_{p2} through a'_{p12} jointly equal zero at the $\alpha\%$ level if (Prob $> F$) $< \alpha$.

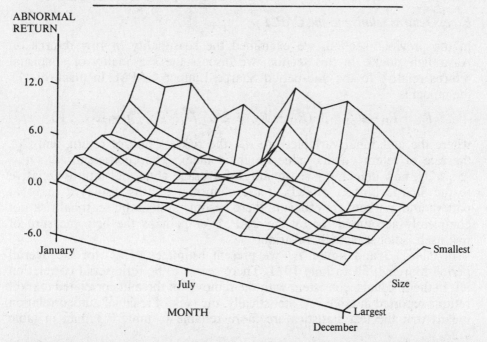

Figure 7.2 Plot of the average monthly abnormal rates of return (in per cent) for ten market-value portfolios constructed from Australian industrial and mining stocks for each month over the period March 1958 to June 1981

July. For example, for portfolio 2, the average December–January and July–August returns are 4.91 per cent and 5.01 per cent respectively, whereas the average for other months is 0.87 per cent. (Interestingly, figure 7.3 shows that the largest average returns in the United States data also occur in January and July.) The January and the July–August seasonals reported by Praetz (1973b) for a market index are confirmed across size-ranked portfolios, but we find little evidence of his reported December trough and February peak.

Examination of the returns before and after December 1973 yields subperiod results whose interpretation is qualitatively equivalent to that for the overall period.[12] The primary difference is that the sample from January 1974 to June 1981 contains more small firms, and average returns for the smaller-firm portfolios during this period are much larger than returns from March 1958 to December 1973. For example, portfolio 1 returns are, on average, 9.84 per cent per month in contrast to an average of 5.29 per cent during the earlier subperiod. For the largest-firm portfolio 10, the average first and second subperiod returns differ by only 0.94 per cent.

In summary, analysis of the raw returns indicates a strong "size effect", and the average small-firm premium appears to be roughly equal across all months. Second, there are pronounced December–January and July–August seasonals in average portfolio returns. The tax-loss selling hypothesis predicts a July seasonal based on Australian tax law, and hence we conclude that the Australian evidence is inconsistent with at least the usual form of the tax-loss hypothesis. Even if one invoked an integrated capital markets hypothesis to explain the January seasonal as a reflection of United States tax-loss selling, neither story explains the December and August results.

Excess returns relative to the CAPM

In the previous section, we examined the seasonality of raw returns on Australian stocks. In this section, we discuss the seasonality of abnormal returns relative to the one-period Sharpe–Lintner CAPM. In place of (1), the model is

$$R_{pt} - R_{Ft} = a'_{p1} + \beta_p (R_{Mt} - R_{Ft}) + \sum_{i=2}^{12} a'_{pi} D_{it} + \epsilon'_{pt}, \quad p = 1, \ldots, 10, \quad (2)$$

where the additional variables are R_{Ft}, the riskless rate of return, and R_{Mt}, the rate of return on the value-weighted index. The coefficients a'_{p1}, a'_{p2}, ..., a'_{p12}, now detect any seasonality of average abnormal returns (relative to the Sharpe–Lintner model). If the abnormal returns display a seasonal pattern and markets are efficient, there is some systematic seasonal risk not completely accounted for by the CAPM, or perhaps the beta measure of risk itself is not seasonally invariant.

In table 7.3 and figure 7.2 we present estimates of (2) for the overall period March 1958 to June 1981. There seems to be little serial correlation left in the residuals, consistent with the removal of the autocorrelated market returns reported in table 7.1. Statistically, the lack of residual autocorrelation means that the test statistics are more reliable in table 7.3 than in table 7.2.

Table 7.3 and figure 7.2 show that a "size effect" similar to that in the raw returns is also found in excess returns relative to the Sharpe–Lintner model. For portfolios 1 and 2, average monthly excess returns (across all months) are 5.66 per cent and 1.27 per cent respectively. Again, the premium of about 4 per cent per month for the smallest firms seems fairly even across months (see figure 7.2).

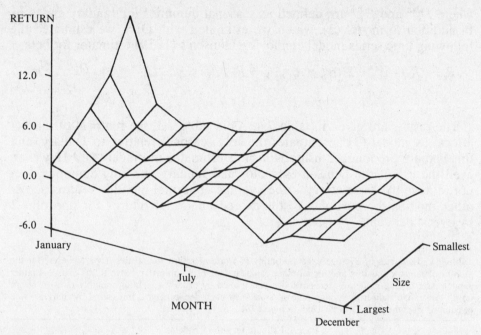

Figure 7.3 Plot of the average monthly rates of return (in per cent) for five market-value portfolios constructed by Keim (1982) from firms on the NYSE for each month over the period January 1931 to December 1978

Although average excess returns in January and July are larger than most other months in table 7.3, the effect is not as pronounced as for the raw returns in table 7.2. For example, the *F*-statistics in table 7.3 indicate that we cannot reject at conventional significance levels the hypothesis of equal excess returns across months for portfolios 9 and 10. As for the raw returns, despite relatively large absolute differences in the point estimates of average excess returns across months for portfolio 1, the sampling variation is sufficiently high that the null hypothesis of equal excess returns for all months is accepted for the smallest firms. For portfolios 2–8, the *F*-statistics indicate rejection of the null hypothesis, with the largest average excess returns in January and July.[13] The major implication of table 7.3 and figure 7.2 is that although the levels of average excess returns are generally highest around the months of January and July, the size-related premium for small firms is fairly constant across months (this is readily apparent in figure 7.2). This finding is in contrast to the strong January seasonal in the size-related premium in the United States data in figure 7.3.

The subperiods show basically similar results to the overall period, although again the size effect is more pronounced in the second period January 1974 to June 1981 in which there are more small firms.

We have also fitted a variation of (2) which examines the January and July abnormal returns separately.

$$R_{pt} - R_{Ft} = \alpha_p + \beta_p(R_{Mt} - R_{Ft}) + \gamma_{p,1} D_t^{Jan} + \gamma_{p,2} D_t^{Jul} + e_{pt}, \qquad (3)$$

$$p = 1, \ldots, 10, \quad t = 1, \ldots, T,$$

where D_t^{Jan} and D_t^{Jul} are defined as seasonal dummies for January and July. In addition to model (3), which we estimated with OLS, we estimated the following time series model employing Dimson's (1979) estimator for beta:

$$R_{pt} - R_{Ft} = \alpha'_p + \sum_{k=-1}^{+1} \beta'_{p,k} (R_{m,t+k} - R_{F,t+k}) + \gamma'_{p,1} D_t^{Jan} + \gamma'_{p,2} D_t^{Jul} + U_{pt},$$

$$p = 1, \ldots, 10, \, t = 1, \ldots, T. \tag{4}$$

The results are given in table 7.4. As in table 7.3, the removal of market effects by model (3) accentuates the July seasonal relative to January, and this is more pronounced using Dimson's estimator in model (4).[14] However, even the use of the Dimson estimator and January and July dummies does not remove the "size effect"—the average abnormal monthly returns across other months for portfolio 1 still exceed abnormal returns for portfolio 2 by over 4 per cent.

Table 7.4 Estimates of average excess monthly (%) rate of return (*t*-statistics in parentheses) for the months of January and July and for all other calendar months combined, relative to the Sharpe–Lintner capital asset pricing model, on ten portfolios constructed by equally weighting monthly rates of return on all Australian industrial, mining and oil stocks[a] in each decile of size (measured by market value of equity),[b] over the period March 1958 to June 1981

	Part A: Estimation with OLS betas			

$$R_{pt} - R_{Ft} = \alpha_p + \beta_p(R_{Mt} - R_{Ft}) + \gamma_{p,1} D_t^{Jan} + \gamma_{p,2} D_t^{Jul} + e_{pt},$$

$$p = 1, \ldots, 10, \quad t = 1, \ldots, T,$$

Portfolio	$\hat{\alpha}_p$	$\hat{\gamma}_{p,1}$	$\hat{\gamma}_{p,2}$	$\hat{\beta}_p^c$
Smallest	5.37	0.29	3.57	1.02
	(7.85)	(0.13)	(1.57)	(7.95)
2	0.62	2.67	5.04	0.84
	(1.94)	(2.49)	(4.74)	(13.93)
3	0.49	1.59	3.16	0.64
	(1.90)	(1.85)	(3.70)	(13.21)
4	0.14	0.74	2.92	0.65
	(0.69)	(1.08)	(4.30)	(16.94)
5	0.41	1.20	1.71	0.60
	(2.34)	(2.04)	(2.95)	(18.03)
6	0.21	1.40	1.09	0.60
	(1.24)	(2.46)	(1.93)	(18.75)
7	0.06	1.03	1.59	0.65
	(0.39)	(1.98)	(3.09)	(22.29)
8	0.11	1.60	1.20	0.66
	(0.75)	(3.28)	(2.47)	(24.18)
9	0.10	0.81	1.11	0.75
	(0.82)	(2.01)	(2.79)	(33.10)
Largest	−0.07	0.47	0.23	0.95
	(−0.88)	(1.71)	(0.85)	(61.76)

Part B: Estimation with Dimson betas

$$R_{pt} - R_{Ft} = \alpha'_p + \sum_{k=-1}^{+1} \beta'_{p,k}(R_{m,t+k} - R_{F,t+k}) + \gamma'_{p,1}D_t^{Jan} + \gamma'_{p,2}D_t^{Jul} + U_{pt},$$

$$p = 1, \ldots, 10, t = 1, \ldots, T.$$

Portfolio	$\hat{\alpha}'_p$	$\gamma'_{p,1}$	$\gamma'_{p,2}$	$\hat{\beta}'_{p,-1}$	$\hat{\beta}'_{p,0}$	$\hat{\beta}'_{p,1}$
Smallest	5.21	−0.72	3.51	0.47	0.95	0.02
	(7.69)	(−0.32)	(1.57)	(3.64)	(7.34)	(0.18)
2	0.56	2.03	4.96	0.26	0.81	−0.03
	(1.79)	(1.90)	(4.81)	(4.39)	(13.44)	(−0.49)
3	0.42	1.13	3.13	0.21	0.61	0.01
	(1.66)	(1.34)	(3.77)	(4.42)	(12.60)	(0.19)
4	(0.04)	(0.27)	(2.92)	(0.24)	(0.61)	(0.04)
	(0.20)	(0.42)	(4.60)	(6.52)	(16.57)	(1.09)
5	0.34	0.70	1.68	0.22	0.56	0.00
	(2.08)	(1.28)	(3.13)	(7.23)	(18.04)	(0.07)
6	0.15	1.04	1.07	0.17	0.58	0.01
	(0.93)	(1.89)	(1.97)	(5.33)	(18.31)	(0.25)
7	−0.01	0.58	1.55	0.20	0.62	0.00
	(−0.04)	(1.22)	(3.30)	(7.39)	(22.61)	(0.16)
8	0.05	1.26	1.18	0.16	0.64	0.02
	(0.34)	(2.72)	(2.60)	(6.19)	(24.08)	(0.62)
9	0.07	0.57	1.09	0.10	0.74	−0.01
	(0.62)	(1.44)	(2.81)	(4.50)	(32.71)	(−0.35)
Largest	−0.07	0.39	0.21	0.02	0.94	−0.02
	(−0.81)	(1.41)	(0.78)	(1.45)	(60.26)	(−1.04)

[a] The industrial stocks comprise all those listed on an Australian stock exchange, but prior to December 1973, include only those with a par value of at least \$A1 million. The mining and oil stocks comprise all those which are listed and have their main operations in Australia.

[b] Size rankings are up-dated monthly, and are based on market values of equity two months earlier, i.e., in month t, portfolios are formed using equity values at the end of month $t-2$, $t = 1, \ldots, T$.

[c] To maintain comparability with the Dimson beta estimates, the t-statistics for the OLS beta in this table are for the null hypothesis $\beta_p = 0$.

Summary and conclusion

Evidence from United States stock returns suggests that a large proportion of the "size effect" consists of a premium for small firms in January. Australian returns show an average premium of at least 4 per cent per month for the smallest-firm decile (portfolio 1) relative to any other decile, and this premium appears to be fairly constant across months in contrast to United States data.

Although recent research has attributed the United States January premium in large part to tax-loss selling, we have argued that there are persuasive *a priori* reasons for questioning the importance of tax-loss selling as an explanation. In Australia where the tax year-end is 30 June, we should expect a perhaps even stronger "July effect" under that hypothesis because, for market participants classified as "traders", there is no \$3,000 limit for the loss deduction. What we find is more complex than the simple tax-loss selling hypothesis predicts. Pronounced seasonals (in raw returns) occur in December–January and July–August, with the largest (and roughly equal) effects in January and July.

It is conceivable that a tax-induced January effect in the United States could show up in Australian data owing to arbitrage across capital markets. But this response is, at best, incomplete. The tax-loss selling hypothesis itself relies on an *absence* of arbitrage from those not forced to sell a particular security for tax purposes. It seems difficult to reconcile an integrated capital market, that functions so well that a United States tax-induced January seasonal shows up in even penny stocks in Australia, with simultaneous mispricing of securities to create the original United States January seasonal.

Moreover, if the January and July premiums are induced by United States and Australian tax law, what is the cause of the December and August premiums? For August, one might argue that non-trading causes the July effect to show up in August returns, or that the tax-effect is somewhat continuous and *should* appear in months subsequent to July. But if so, why is there no apparent February seasonal in both Australia and the United States, and what explains the December results?

On balance, we regard the Australian evidence as difficult to reconcile with the tax-loss selling hypothesis. Although the original hypothesis is at least consistent with the United States January premium, the story seems to be much more complicated if it is to be reconciled with the Australian data. It seems more promising to investigate possible equilibrium causes of the United States January seasonal, perhaps by comparing the relative timing of events other than tax years in Australia and the United States.

This conclusion is further supported by Keim's (1982) finding that the January effect is a significant phenomenon in every year (except two) from 1931 to 1979, even during periods (e.g., prior to World War II) when personal tax rates were relatively low and when the benefit of the capital tax loss offset was lower. The magnitude of the January effect does not seem sensitive to variations in the tax rate. In one sentence, tax-loss selling still leaves us at a loss for an explanation of the January effect.

Acknowledgments

Helpful comments have been received from Ray Ball, Robert C. Merton, Richard Fayle, and the referee, G. William Schwert. We are grateful to the Australian Graduate School of Management for access to their data files. Partial financial support was provided by the Program in Finance, Stanford University, and the General Electric Foundation Grant to the Sloan School, Massachusetts Institute of Technology.

Notes

1. Thus, the rationale for a year-end tax effect arises from the ability of capital losses to directly offset ordinary income. In the United States, realised capital gains and losses are short term if the asset has been held for one year or less, and long term otherwise. Short-term gains or losses are taxed as ordinary unearned income, and long-term gains and losses are taxed at 40 per cent of the investor's marginal tax rate on ordinary income since 60 per cent of long-term gains or losses are excluded from taxable income. Net short-term losses and net long-term gains incurred in the same year, however, offset each other. Also, net short-term losses and 50 per cent of net long-term losses are limited to a deduction level of $3,000 in any year. Unused capital losses may be carried forward indefinitely.
2. The same line of reasoning implies the potential for a late April effect as investors experience liquidity drains during the income tax filing period, although no such seasonal has been found. Constantinides

(1982, p. 38) discusses a variant of this hypothesis, under which selling pressure throughout the year is "suddenly relieved at the beginning of January". Our primary arguments apply to this variant also.

3. This is especially the case since they are free to redefine their personal tax year to differ from the usual 31 December year-end.

4. F.C.T. v. Werchon and Anor. (1982) 82 A.T.C. 4332.

5. Details of file construction and composition for all files are available from The Australian Graduate School of Management, University of New South Wales, P.O. Box 1, Kensington, NSW 2033.

6. We repeated all tests based on continuously compounded returns. For raw returns, the results are essentially unchanged from those reported, although the size premium appears larger in discrete returns. For abnormal returns we used an equally weighted market index, which removed more of the seasonal effect from small-firm portfolios than did the value-weighted index used in reported results.

7. Extreme outliers (price relatives less than 0.2 or greater than 5.0) were verified. There were 87, of which 42 proved to be correct. The rest were deleted.

8. The robust methods used follow Huber (1964) and Krasker–Welsch (1979). Outliers are defined relative to both regression and explanatory variable space. All computations have been made using the BIF and BIFMOD programs in the TROLL package (see Peters, Samarov and Welsch 1982). The results were not significantly changed.

9. Note that "the pattern" does not consist of ten independent observations (since the returns are cross-sectionally dependent), and it must be interpreted with this in mind.

10. Preliminary tests (Brown, Kleidon and Marsh 1982) indicate that the stochastic nature of the United States size effect (after allowing for a deterministic January seasonal) reported by Brown, Kleidon and Marsh (1983) does not seem to describe the Australian size-ranked portfolios. Any change in the size premium seems more akin to a steady, deterministic drift, although the stochastic component may be obscured by high volatility of Australian returns.

11. Aside from sampling variation, a possible explanation for this pattern lies in the popularity and, therefore, heavier trading volume of small-firm "penny stocks" relative to (say) the stocks of small NYSE–AMEX firms.

12. However, the second subperiod has only eight observations per month, and shows greater sample variation than does the earlier period.

13. Although the seasonals for January, July and August show up in excess returns as in raw returns, the excess returns are influenced by the seasonal pattern for the market index, and one effect is that in general the December seasonal disappears. The raw returns in table 7.2 shows that the market index has higher average returns in December than in any other month (December has the only positive dummy coefficient, 0.31 per cent). Even for the (equally weighted) largest-firm portfolio 10, the December dummy coefficient is negative. Portfolio returns are equally weighted, so large December returns for the largest firms in portfolio 10 can result in a negative dummy coefficient for portfolio 10 and a positive coefficient for the value-weighted market index. [For an equally weighted index (of continuously compounded returns), the December dummy coefficient is negative.] The removal of the large December returns for the market index leaves no residual December seasonal in excess returns. Similar effects can be seen in, say, January and July. The index shows a negative July dummy coefficient in table 7.2, and so a positive coefficient for July relative to January in the small-firm portfolios is accentuated in the excess returns in table 7.3.

14. For all portfolios other than portfolio 10, the coefficient on the lagged market index appears significant. Preliminary work showed that lags greater than 1 and leads were not significantly different from zero.

8 Daily seasonals in equity and fixed-interest returns: Australian evidence and tests of plausible hypotheses

Ray Ball and John Bowers

The objectives of this chapter are to present new evidence on the day-of-the-week seasonal in Australian equity returns, to extend the evidence to daily interest rates and to evaluate several plausible hypotheses concerning the seasonal. It is offered as a preliminary study aimed at stimulating discussion.

The first section of the chapter discusses the nature of the anomaly arising from a daily return seasonal and proposes that it can be understood only by analysing seasonals in supply parameters and in investor preferences. The second section describes alternative hypotheses. The third and fourth describe the Australian data and our results. The final section draws conclusions from this preliminary work.

Anomaly and hypotheses

The day-of-the-week seasonal was first documented by Osborne (1962, tables IV and V). Subsequent work by Cross (1973), French (1980), Gibbons and Hess (1981), Lakonishok and Levi (1982), Smirlock and Starks (1983), Keim and Stambaugh (1984), Rogalski (1984), Jaffe and Westerfield (1985) and others has confirmed the existence of a seasonal, in that equity return distributions are not independent of the day of the week or of the time of the day. One result that researchers have found to be particularly anomalous is that sample mean returns over weekends are negative.

The existence of seasonals in equity returns is not *in itself* surprising, since there is no theoretical reason to preclude seasonals in either supply or demand parameters. For example, in a simple Fisherian world, the rate of interest reflects both the marginal efficiency of investment and the marginal rate of intertemporal consumption preference (see Hirshleifer 1970, ch. 6). There is no reason to believe that the ratio of marginal utilities of present and future consumption is identical on weekends and weekdays, during daytime and during nighttime. Nor is there reason to believe that the marginal efficiency

Reprinted from Elroy Dimson, ed., *Stock Market Anomalies* (Cambridge; Cambridge University Press, 1988), 74–90, by permission of the authors and the publisher.

of investment is a constant, independent of time of day and day of week. Indeed, casual observation suggests the existence of seasonals in consumption patterns and returns on investment.

Seasonal variation in the expected value of returns from real investments is likely, particularly on weekends. If weekends are universal times of leisure, then it is likely that the marginal efficiency of investment (MEI) is lower on weekends than during the week. A proportion of the capital stock lies idle and incurs positive real holding costs on weekends (deterioration, insurance, security costs, etc.). Note that we are dealing with the *marginal* expected return on real investment—the expected return on the market-clearing marginal investment. The argument does not address the expected return on the *average* real investment. On weekends (when much of the real capital stock is idle across the world), it is plausible that at least the *marginal* expected return on real assets is lower than on weekdays, and perhaps it is negative. Note also that a similar point can be made about overnight returns. A complete treatment of these issues requires modelling the real investment market; we offer an incomplete analysis.

It is not sufficient to argue that systematical seasonals in returns are inconsistent with rational expectations. When both supply and demand for real assets are considered jointly (as they must be, to explain a seasonal in the price of capital), the equilibrium expected return on real assets is endogenous. Prices can be present values and still yield equilibrium-expected returns that display seasonals.

Nor is it sufficient to argue entirely in terms of pure-exchange models. Although modern finance concentrates on pure exchange, a source of explanations of seasonals in prices is likely to be seasonals in supply parameters. Nevertheless, pure-exchange models can provide insight. In particular, the anomalous feature of the negative mean returns over weekends on the NYSE is that the *ex post* risk premium is negative over a prolonged period. We therefore investigate daily interest rates, in the hope of finding clues about the "weekend effect".

The above argument presumes that equity returns are riskier than the interest rate over weekends. This presumption is worth checking. The second parameter of interest, therefore, is risk. Here we repeat the distinction between short and long-term effects in real asset markets and again make a simple observation, without providing an articulated supporting model. The observation is that, in a security market where the marginal investor has a long-term horizon, the risk arising from holding investments over a short interval depends upon the contribution of that interval to risk over the complete horizon, not simply the short term. Consider a world where the security markets trade at discrete intervals and the marginal investor evaluates risk over a T-period horizon. The return over this horizon is $R_{0,T} = \sum_{t=0}^{T} r_t$, where $R_{0,T}$ is return over the interval $(0,T)$, r_t is return over the discrete interval t lying in $(0,T)$ and returns are continuously compounded. Risk over this horizon is:

$$\text{var}(R_{0,T}) = \Sigma_t \Sigma_\tau \text{ covar}(r_t, r_\tau)$$

where var and covar denote variance and covariance respectively. The contribution of any single period to risk over the complete horizon depends upon that period's own return variance and its covariance with returns in other periods. A seasonal in risk is feasible. Furthermore, there is the intriguing possibility that short-term periods could have negative risk (this could occur if a period's own variance was more than offset by negative covariance with returns in other periods). We therefore investigate seasonals in the day-of-the-week covariances, as well as in the day-of-the-week means, of security returns.

Other hypotheses

In the previous section, we hypothesised that seasonals in security returns could reflect underlying seasonals in returns from real assets. This section outlines several alternative hypotheses.

Dividend seasonal

Institutional practices could cause seasonals in dividend payment and ex-dividend days. Any effect of tax on pre-tax yields (including both dividends and price changes) and error in recording dividends in the index, then, would induce seasonals in observed security returns. We therefore test for a day-of-the-week seasonal in dividends and its effect on equity return seasonals.

Money seasonal

Institutional practices in money management (e.g., payment of wages near the weekend) could cause seasonals in security returns. Although we are sceptical of this argument, because most of these practices suggest seasonals in zero-sum flows rather than stocks of real assets, we test for a day-of-the-week seasonal in interest rates and its effect on equity return seasonals.

International capital market

Sydney time on average (i.e., ignoring daylight saving in both countries) is 15 hours ahead of New York time and 18 hours ahead of Pacific Coast time. It is 10 hours ahead of GMT. The Sydney Stock Exchange claims to be the first exchange in the world to open for the week. If capital markets strike international equilibria, then it is possible that "weekend effects" on the international market would carry over into "Tuesday effects" in Sydney.

Discontinuous trading

It is not possible to observe security returns over precise daily intervals, because securities are not traded continuously in time. If there is a seasonal in trading volume, then a spurious seasonal could be observed in daily returns. We therefore investigate whether the day-of-the-week seasonal can be attributed in part to serial correlation arising from discontinuous trading.

Weekend float

Lakonishok and Levi (1982) observe that the time interval, between contracting to purchase and delivering cash for stocks, is two days longer in the case of contracts written on Fridays. Because the buyer obtains extra two-day "float" on Friday trades, Friday closing prices would incorporate the present value of the float, whereas Monday opening prices would not. This implies lower apparent returns on equities over weekends. The practice on the Sydney exchange is to effect invoicing and settlement in terms of elapsed business days after trading, so that an additional two-day float is provided on weekends. We test this hypothesis in two ways: (1) by comparing the difference in weekend and Friday returns with the interest rate over the weekend; and (2) by comparing weekend and holiday returns (holidays provide additional float).

Data

Equities

The equity data consist of 2,759 observations of the daily closing values of two Sydney Stock Exchange indexes, the Statex-Actuaries Price and Accumulation Indexes. The Sydney data are interesting because of the opportunity to replicate United States results and because the difference in timing of the weekends in Sydney and New York might provide insights into the "weekend effect". Data are available for the 11 years from 2 January 1974 until 28 December 1984. The price index does not include dividends, whereas the accumulation index does. It is possible, therefore, to derive a daily dividend yield variable for the index stocks.

The indexes are based upon an annually rebalanced portfolio of 50 stocks. The stocks are chosen annually on the basis of capitalisation, volatility and turnover: from the set of stocks that have "consistently been in the top 250 by market capitalisation for the prior two years", the fifty highest-turnover stocks in the immediately preceding year are selected. The indexes thus are comprised of relatively actively traded stocks. They are equal-weighted at the beginning of each year. There is no "small-firm effect" in the indexes.

We found considerable error in reported values of the indexes. Some error arose from typographical mistakes in publication. Other errors arose from problems that the Sydney Stock Exchange experiences in computing an index in real time. These had been corrected in subsequent output from the Sydney Stock Exchange Research Service, which we obtained. Each observation was cross-checked against newspaper reports, the *Sydney Stock Exchange Daily Official List*, the *Australian Stock Exchange Journal* and (finally) the exchange's handwritten copy supplied to the printer of the *Journal*. We now believe that we have a clean data series.

A further source of error was found in the construction of the index. Daily dividends are not reinvested in the index portfolios until the annual rebalance date. Instead, the accumulation index is valued at the simple sum of the daily closing prices of the index stocks, plus the accumulated dividends on the index for the year to date. This introduces error in measuring rates of return on the index, because the index observation and the preceding observation are displaced by a constant, the accumulated dividend to date. We discovered the error when we observed that the price index had a higher rate of return than the accumulation index on slightly more than 40 per cent of all trading days. (The difference exceeded rounding error.) We were able to develop an algorithm to correct for the error, because the daily dividend yield on the index portfolio can be inferred from the two indexes. Corrected copies of the indexes are provided in Ball and Bowers (1986a), which is available on request.

Interest rates

Clues concerning the source of seasonals in daily equity returns possibly lie in daily interest rates. Unfortunately, the rates available to us are averages—the dollar-weighted average rate on all transactions for the day. Although this is not necessarily a market-clearing rate, we are led to believe that there is little cross-sectional variation in rates within each day. Further, the average rates should capture any daily seasonal in the fixed-interest market—the averaging occurs within (but not across) days.

The data cover the period 15 April 1975 to 28 December 1985. They were made available in clean form by the Reserve Bank of Australia.

Results

All rates of return are expressed as logarithms of price relatives. Returns are measured from close of trading to close of trading on the next day that the exchange is open. Thus, returns labelled "Monday" cover the three-day period from Friday closing to Monday closing, in the absence of holidays, and have *not* been expressed as daily average equivalents. Returns on the first trading day after a holiday (or holidays) cover more than one calendar day.

Descriptive statistics: equity returns

Table 8.1 reports sample statistics by day of the week for the accumulation and price indices. The sample of 2,656 observations covers the entire period for which we have data, excluding holidays (for which there are no data) and the 102 days immediately following holidays. Following days are included in other analyses below, but they distort the day-of-the-week seasonal because there is a daily seasonal in holidays. The following conclusions are drawn from the table:

1. The five separate day-of-the-week samples are "well behaved" relative to the pooled sample of returns across all days. There is no evidence of skewness—the individual day-of-the-week skewness statistics range from -0.55 to $+1.15$ for the accumulation index, in contrast with $+6.90$ for all days pooled together. There is some leptokurtosis, though it is not stationary (compare table 8.2, for a subsample of these days) and the leptokurtosis in the individual day-of-the-week series does not approach the degree of leptokurtosis for the pooled daily returns sequence (96.4 for the accumulation and 98.7 for the price index). This suggests that a major source of leptokurtosis in pooled daily equity returns is the seasonal across days of the week.
2. The significant Box–Pierce statistics imply autocorrelation in each of the

Table 8.1 Excluding days immediately following holidays, 2 January 1974 to 28 December 1984

	$\bar{x}$	σ	Skew	Kurt	ρ_1	B–P	N
1. Accumulation index							
Mon.	−0.00007	0.01150	1.15	11.79	0.07	18.9	499
Tues.	−0.00152	0.00942	0.01	2.80	0.05	28.9	498
Wed.	0.00053	0.01009	1.19	9.83	−0.07	28.6	554
Thur.	0.00191	0.00950	−0.15	1.75	0.02	20.1	560
Fri.	0.00161	0.00918	−0.55	4.97	−0.07	26.7	545
			$F = 8.6$	$p < 0.01$			
2. Price index							
Mon.	−0.00048	0.01157	1.11	11.45	0.07	17.3	499
Tues.	−0.00160	0.00942	0.01	2.79	0.05	29.9	498
Wed.	0.00043	0.01009	1.13	9.28	−0.07	29.1	554
Thur.	0.00172	0.00951	−0.17	1.78	0.02	19.3	560
Fri.	0.00136	0.00925	−0.60	5.09	−0.08	28.1	545
			$F = 8.4,$	$p < 0.01$			

Note: Columns describe sample mean, standard deviation, standardised skewness and kurtosis statistics, first-order serial correlation in the sequence of returns for the denominated day-of-the-week, the Box–Pierce statistic for the first 15 serial correlation statistics, and sample size. Returns on holidays and days immediately following holidays are replaced by sample day-of-the-week means for purposes of calculating ρ and B–P. The F-statistic and associated probability are offered as a test of the null hypothesis that the day-of-the-week means are equal.

day-of-the-week sequences. However, the coefficients for lags up to 15 seldom exceed one standard deviation, as shown in figure 8.1.

3. There is a significant day-of-the-week seasonal in both indices. The F-statistics of 8.6 and 8.4 for the accumulation index and the price index suggest that the null hypothesis (time-invariant mean returns) can be rejected at conventional significance levels. The sample mean returns are positive on Thursday and Friday: univariate t-statistics for the accumulation index are +4.76 and +4.09 for these days). In contrast, the mean return over the other five days of the week, taken as a whole, is negative.

The sample mean return for the weekend (designated "Monday") has the same sign as in the NYSE studies, but it is not significantly different from zero. It changes sign for a subsample of this period, reported in table 8.2.

The surprises in the data, given the NYSE results, are the sample means for Tuesday and Wednesday. On a univariate basis, the Tuesday mean is negative and significant ($t = -3.60$ for the accumulation index); and the Wednesday mean is postiive but small and insignificant ($t = 1.24$). An interpretation of this result is provided below.

4. Although the seasonal is significant, it explains little of the variation in daily returns. This can be seen from the low explanatory power of the regression reported in table 8.3.

5. The day-of-the-week standard deviations also exhibit a seasonal. Although the weekdays differ significantly in volatility, the weekend variance is not in the order of three times the average weekday variance, implying either lower variances on weekend days or negative covariance among weekend returns.

6. There is a day-of-the-week seasonal in dividends, as shown by the difference

Table 8.2 Excluding days immediately following holidays, 15 April 1975 to 28 December 1984

	$\bar{x}$	σ	Skew	Kurt	ρ_1	B–P	N
1. Accumulation index							
Mon.	0.00044	0.01012	1.24	9.69	0.11	22.4	442
Tues.	−0.00116	0.00883	0.28	2.34	0.06	27.3	446
Wed.	0.00045	0.00838	−0.01	1.60	−0.02	17.9	496
Thur.	0.00198	0.00863	−0.19	1.19	0.03	16.1	499
Fri.	0.00157	0.00800	−0.48	2.32	−0.02	25.6	490

$$F = 8.7, \qquad p < 0.01$$

	$\bar{x}$	σ	Skew	Kurt	ρ_1	B–P	N
2. Price index							
Mon.	0.00006	0.01015	1.18	9.13	0.11	22.6	442
Tues.	−0.00123	0.00883	0.28	2.36	0.07	28.4	446
Wed.	0.00037	0.00839	−0.01	1.62	−0.02	17.8	496
Thur.	0.00180	0.00863	−0.19	1.14	0.02	15.7	499
Fri.	0.00134	0.00800	−0.49	2.31	−0.02	26.6	490

$$F = 8.5, \qquad p < 0.01$$

	$\bar{x}$	σ	Skew	Kurt	ρ_1	B–P	N
3. Interest rates							
Mon.	0.00081	0.00024	0.27	−0.28	0.64	2551	442
Tues.	0.00026	0.00008	0.45	−0.27	0.57	2118	446
Wed.	0.00024	0.00008	0.68	−0.17	0.46	1565	496
Thur.	0.00027	0.00008	0.54	−0.17	0.57	2186	499
Fri.	0.00029	0.00008	0.33	0.07	0.66	2651	490

$$F = 752.1, \qquad p < 0.01*$$

Note: Columns describe sample mean, standard deviation, standardised skewness and kurtosis statistics, first-order serial correlation in the sequence of returns for the denominated day-of-the-week, the Box–Pierce statistic for the first 15 serial correlation statistics, and sample size. Returns on holidays and days immediately following holidays are replaced by sample day-of-the-week means for purposes of calculating ρ and B–P. The F-statistic and associated probability are offered as a test of the null hypothesis that the day-of-the-week means are equal.

* $F = 29.0$ ($p < 0.01$) when "Monday" rates (i.e., from 3 p.m. Friday to 3 p.m. Monday) are expressed as daily averages, rather than 3-day rates.

ORDER	AUTO-CORR.	S.E. RANDOM MODEL	-1	-.75	-.50	-.25	0	.25	.50	.75	+1	ADJ.B-P
1	0.020	0.042					+ * +					0.2234
2	0.089	0.042					+ * *					4.845
3	0.037	0.042					+ :*+					5.578
4	−0.019	0.042					+ * +					5.782
5	−0.075	0.042					* : +					9.061
6	−0.024	0.041					+ * +					9.388
7	−0.025	0.041					+ * +					9.752
8	0.062	0.041					+ :*+					11.98
9	0.006	0.041					+ * +					12.00
10	0.037	0.041					+ :*+					12.81
11	0.066	0.041					+ :*+					15.37
12	0.001	0.041					+ * +					15.37
13	0.075	0.041					+ : *					18.70
14	−0.028	0.041					+*: +					19.17
15	0.017	0.041					+ * +					19.33

	-1	-.75	-.50	-.25	0	.25	.50	.75	+1

* AUTOCORRELATIONS
+ 2 STANDARD ERROR LIMITS (APPROX.)

Figure 8.1 Autocorrelation in sequence of 560 Thursday accumulation index returns, 2 January 1974 to 28 December 1984

in means of the accumulation and price indices. Approximately 40 per cent of dividends are recorded in the accumulation index on Mondays, 25 per cent on Fridays and 20 per cent on Thursdays.

The preliminary evidence thus confirms a day-of-the-week seasonal on the Sydney Stock Exchange, though it appears to take a different form than the NYSE seasonal.

Descriptive statistics: Interest rates

Table 8.2 reports equivalent sample statistics over the period for which interest rate data are available. Again, days immediately following holidays are excluded. The data suggest the following:

1. There is little skewness or kurtosis in daily interest rates.
2. There is considerable serial correlation in each of the five day-of-the-week sequences. Figure 8.2 graphs the autocorrelation function for Thursdays, which is representative of the days. This result implies significant non-stationarity in the interest rate series. Note that observations are spaced seven calendar days apart and that the result is not due to the seasonal in the means.

ORDER	AUTO-CORR.	S.E. RANDOM MODEL	-1	-.75	-.50	-.25	0	.25	.50	.75	+1	ADJ.B-P
1	0.565	0.044					+ : +		*			162.7
2	0.510	0.044					+ : +		*			352.8
3	0.541	0.044					+ : +		*			502.4
4	0.610	0.044					+ : +		*			693.3
5	0.550	0.044					+ : +		*			848.4
6	0.514	0.044					+ : +		*			1042.0
7	0.544	0.044					+ : +		*			1194.0
8	0.493	0.044					+ : +		*			1320.0
9	0.562	0.044					+ : +		*			1483.0
10	0.493	0.044					+ : +		*			1699.0
11	0.488	0.044					+ : +		*			1729.0
12	0.459	0.044					+ : +	*				1835.0
13	0.513	0.044					+ : +		*			1972.0
14	0.438	0.044					+ : +	*				2073.0
15	0.466	0.044					+ : +	*				2186.0

* AUTOCORRELATIONS
+ 2 STANDARD ERROR LIMITS (APPROX.)

Figure 8.2 Autocorrelation in sequence of 499 Thursday interest rates, 15 April 1975 to 28 December 1984.

3. Compared with equity returns, interest rates exhibit little seasonal variation in means. The *F*-statistic and the Monday (i.e., weekend) mean are misleading, because the latter is a 3-day rate. When the weekend rate is transformed in to a daily average, the weekend mean is 0.27 per cent per day and the *F*-statistic falls to 29.0. Because of the large sample sizes, the small differences in means either are significant or border on significance: for example, a univariate *t*-statistic for the difference in Tuesday and Wednesday mean interest rates (0.002 of 1 per cent) is 1.25,

Table 8.3 Dependent variable: return on index; independent variables: DOW dummies and holiday dummy; 2 January 1974 to 28 December 1984, $N = 2758$

Variable	Coefficient	t	$p <$
1. Accumulation index			
Constant	−0.00009	−0.20	0.84
Holiday	0.00253	2.15	0.03
Tues.	−0.00140	−2.25	0.03
Wed.	0.00068	1.11	0.27
Thur.	0.00192	3.14	0.01
Fri.	0.00162	2.63	0.01

$$F = 7.8, \qquad p < 0.01$$
$$\bar{R}^2 = 0.01$$

Variable	Coefficient	t	$p <$
2. Price index			
Constant	−0.00050	−1.12	0.27
Holiday	0.00237	2.02	0.05
Tues.	−0.00108	−1.73	0.09
Wed.	0.00099	1.62	0.11
Thur.	0.00214	3.49	0.01
Fri.	0.00178	2.88	0.01

$$F = 7.6, \qquad p < 0.01$$
$$\bar{R}^2 = 0.01$$

taking into account the sample covariance between Tuesday and Wednesday rates (refer table 8.7). The absence of a daily seasonal in interest rates is consistent with the regulatory policy of the Reserve Bank of Australia. Regulation of banks' balance sheets is conducted on the second Wednesday of each month, based upon the average position of the bank over the entire month. Consequently, there is no reason for the banks to vary their trading systematically with the day of the week.

4. The behaviour of the day-of-the-week interest rate standard deviations is intriguing. Whereas weekday sample standard deviations are almost identical, the weekend standard deviation is within rounding error of three times the weekday equivalent. Note that "weekends" here cover exactly three days (since holidays are excluded) and that independence of daily weekend interest rates would imply a scaling by $\sqrt{3}$. The evidence suggests a mechanism such as perfect positive correlation of interest rates across three days. This is consistent with the high serial correlation observed in the data, particularly for adjacent days (table 8.7).

Descriptive statistics: Risk premia

The anomalous nature of these results can be highlighted by calculating day-of-the-week risk premia for equities relative to the fixed-interest contract. The sample mean risk premium is negative.

The interest rate data allow a test of the "weekend float" hypothesis, which predicts that the weekend return is a three-day equity return, net of the value of a two-day float. The float value can be approximated by twice the daily average weekend interest rate and the daily equity return can be approximated by the Friday average. Thus, the hypothesis predicts a "Monday" return (using part 1 of table 8.2) of $0.00417 = 3 \times 0.00157 - 2 \times 0.00027$. This hypothesis is rejected by the data.

The preliminary evidence thus reveals little day-of-the-week seasonal in interest rates, significant serial correlation and an intriguing behaviour in the dispersion of weekend rates.

Regression analysis

There are several reasons for not taking the descriptive statistics at face value. These reasons, and our attempts to correct for them, are outlined in this section.

First, we are not satisfied with treating holidays by excluding the immediately following day. Table 8.3 reports a regression which includes these data and with five $(0,1)$ independent variables representing normal days of the week and holiday-affected returns. The "holiday" dummy variable is set to unity for days following holidays and to zero otherwise. The other four dummy variables denote Tuesday to Friday. The constant term therefore captures the mean return on those Mondays that do not follow Fridays on which the exchange was closed. The "holiday" coefficient captures the marginal mean effect of a holiday. For example, the regression prediction of the accumulation index return on a Wednesday following a Tuesday holiday is $0.00312 (= -0.00009 + 0.00253 + 0.00068)$.

The "holiday" coefficient is positive and significant, suggesting that the "weekend effect" does not carry over into holidays, as observed on the NYSE. This result is surprising when one considers that: (1) most of the holidays include weekends; and (2) the size of the coefficient is in the order of an average *weekly* return. Addition of the holiday "dummy" variable does not increase the significance of the regression. However, it slightly alters the pattern of the daily seasonal, by bringing the Tuesday and Wednesday means closer to those of the other days. All coefficients show higher t-statistics than for an (unreported) regression without the holiday variable.

Second, there is considerable positive serial correlation in index returns on successive trading days, as shown in table 8.7. First-order coefficients are in the order of $+0.30$. This result holds for the entire time series and for each day of the week, except for Friday/Monday—a result we are pursuing. Although the Statex-Actuaries Indices comprise only high-turnover stocks, there is not continuous trading in these stocks and it is essentially an equally weighted index. Thus, it is possible that measured returns are being attributed incorrectly to the days of the week. The regression reported in table 8.4 attempts to deal with this problem by introducing lagged values of the index return as independent variables.

The adjusted R^2 and F-statistic increase, largely owing to the first-order lag variable. The first three lags have significant coefficients. The "holiday" coefficient falls but remains significant at $p = 0.07$. The important result is that the Tuesday mean now looks more like the Monday (i.e., weekend) mean and the Wednesday mean now looks like Thursday and Friday. Presumably, the positive first-order serial correlation in the stock returns confounds the descriptive statistics reported in tables 8.1 and 8.2. One cannot

Table 8.4 Dependent variable: return on index; independent variable: part 1 of table 8.3 plus lagged dependent variable; 2 January 1974 to 28 December 1984, $N = 2758$

Variable	Coefficient	t	$p <$
1. Accumulation index			
Constant	−0.00055	−1.33	0.18
Holiday	0.00193	1.77	0.08
Lag 1	0.39351	20.66	0.01
Lag 2	−0.09552	−4.67	0.01
Lag 3	0.05667	2.77	0.06
Lag 4	−0.02067	−1.09	0.28
Tues.	−0.00088	−1.52	0.13
Wed.	0.00156	2.73	0.01
Thur.	0.00205	3.57	0.01
Fri.	0.00150	2.62	0.09

$$F = 54.2, \quad p < 0.01$$
$$\bar{R}^2 = 0.15$$

Variable	Coefficient	t	$p <$
2. Price index			
Constant	−0.00088	−2.11	0.04
Holiday	0.00178	1.62	0.11
Lag 1	0.39421	20.69	0.01
Lag 2	−0.09845	−4.81	0.01
Lag 3	0.06089	2.98	0.01
Lag 4	−0.02497	−1.31	0.19
Tues.	−0.00049	−0.85	0.40
Wed.	0.00181	3.15	0.01
Thur.	0.00223	3.89	0.01
Fri.	0.00165	2.87	0.01

$$F = 54.1, \quad p < 0.01$$
$$\bar{R}^2 = 0.15$$

be sure that this first-order serial correlation is due to discontinuous trading, as distinct from dependence in the unobserved true returns, but the increased sharpness of the day-of-the-week seasonal suggests that it is.

Third, the daily seasonal in dividends could present an explanation of the return seasonal if either: (1) there is a "tax effect"; or (2) the index does not record dividends at the correct time. Table 8.5 therefore repeats the regression reported in table 8.4, with the addition of the contemporaneous dividend yield on the index as one variable and its four lagged values as others. (The lagged variables correspond to the four lags of the dependent variable.) The explanatory power of the regression is not altered by introducing the dividend variables. The coefficients on the day-of-the-week "dummies" all fall slightly in absolute value, but the seasonal pattern of table 8.4 is not disturbed. The coefficients of the dividend variables flip-flop, suggesting multicollinearity.

Fourth, research, by Ariel (1984) on returns before and after the midpoints of months and various papers on "month-of-the-year effects" suggests the addition of twelve further "dummy" variables to the regression: one for position within the month and eleven to distinguish among months. In this

Table 8.5 Dependent variable: return on index; independent variables: part 2 of table 8.3 plus dividend yield; 2 January 1974 to 28 December 1984, $N = 2758$

Variable	Coefficient	t	$p <$
1. Accumulation index			
Constant	−0.00052	−1.15	0.26
Holiday	0.00202	1.85	0.07
Lag 1	0.39467	20.71	0.01
Lag 2	−0.09625	−4.70	0.01
Lag 3	0.05749	2.81	0.01
Lag 4	−0.02132	−1.12	0.27
Div(t)	−0.34835	−1.01	0.32
Div(t-1)	−0.47541	−1.37	0.17
Div(t-2)	0.90510	2.62	0.01
Div(t-3)	−0.12416	−0.36	0.73
Div(t-4)	0.49117	1.42	0.16
Tues.	−0.00093	−1.57	0.12
Wed.	0.00118	2.00	0.05
Thur.	0.00194	3.28	0.01
Fri.	0.00135	2.31	0.03

$$F = 35.7, \quad p < 0.01$$
$$\bar{R}^2 = 0.15$$

Variable	Coefficient	t	$p <$
2. Price index			
Constant	−0.00051	−1.13	0.26
Holiday	0.00203	1.86	0.07
Lag 1	0.39462	20.70	0.01
Lag 2	−0.09559	−4.67	0.01
Lag 3	0.05779	2.82	0.01
Lag 4	−0.02238	−1.18	0.24
Div(t)	−1.40557	−4.07	0.01
Div(t-1)	0.14180	0.41	0.69
Div(t-2)	0.70903	2.05	0.05
Div(t-3)	−0.03354	−0.10	0.93
Div(t-4)	0.44298	1.28	0.21
Tues.	−0.00097	−1.63	0.11
Wed.	0.00120	2.02	0.05
Thur.	0.00195	3.29	0.01
Fri.	0.00134	2.29	0.03

$$F = 36.5, \quad p < 0.01$$
$$\bar{R}^2 = 0.15$$

(unreported) regression, the adjusted R^2, the seasonal pattern and the marginal effect of the lagged returns and dividend variables do not change noticeably. The coefficient on the "holiday" variable falls to 0.00166, the coefficient on the "first-half-of-the-month" variable is 0.000498 ($t = 1.39$), and the eleven month-of-the-year coefficients are all negative (implying a positive "January effect"). Only the March coefficient is significant at $p = 0.05$.

Finally, we attempt to determine whether the equity seasonal is related to interest rates, by adding five interest rates to the above regression: the contemporaneous rate, two leads and two lags. We found no relation between daily equity returns and interest rates over the period April 1975 to December 1985.

Correlation matrices

Table 8.6 reports the correlation matrix for the five day-of-the-week sequences. Except for Friday, equity returns are significantly positively correlated with returns on the immediately following day. There is no evidence of weekend returns being negatively correlated with returns on other days of the week, thus ruling out the negative-risk hypothesis as an explanation of negative weekend returns. However, we noted above that the weekend variance is "low" relative to weekday variances. Note also that the seasonal in covariances among adjacent-day returns (i.e., the low Friday/weekend covariance) implies that the regressions reported in tables 8.4 and 8.5 are misspecified.

Table 8.6   Correlation matrices, 453 weeks without holidays, 2 January 1974 to 28 December 1984

	Mon.	Tues.	Wed.	Thur.
1. Accumulation index				
Tues.	0.340			
Wed.	−0.186	0.264		
Thur.	−0.024	0.055	0.312	
Fri.	0.007	0.008	−0.025	0.409
2. Price index				
Tues.	0.344			
Wed.	−0.189	0.265		
Thur.	−0.023	0.055	0.315	
Fri.	0.003	0.017	−0.025	0.409

In contrast, table 8.7 reveals that the positive autocorrelation in day-of-the-week interest rates (reported above) also is observed across days: adjacent days exhibit correlation coefficients in excess of +0.8. As in the case of equity returns, the Friday/Monday correlation is lower, suggesting that not all of the positive serial correlation in equity returns is due to discontinuous trading.

Table 8.7   Correlation matrices, 405 weeks without holidays, 15 April 1975 to 28 December 1984

	Mon.	Tues.	Wed.	Thur.
1. Accumulation index				
Tues.	0.303			
Wed.	-0.082	0.326		
Thur.	0.052	0.058	0.358	
Fri.	0.027	0.009	0.053	0.306
2. Price index				
Tues.	0.307			
Wed.	-0.082	0.326		
Thur.	0.055	0.057	0.358	
Fri.	0.025	0.012	0.053	0.307
3. Interest rates				
Mon.				
Tues.	0.883			
Wed.	0.688	0.858		
Thur.	0.671	0.758	0.866	
Fri.	0.713	0.702	0.652	0.812

Conclusions

Equity returns on the Sydney Stock Exchange exhibit a significant day-of-the-week seasonal. Some of the seasonal is due to a "weekend effect" in which mean returns from close of trading Friday to close of trading on Monday are negative but not significantly different from zero. This suggests an explanation in terms of a negative *marginal* efficiency of investment on weekends, owing to idle capacity. This explanation is difficult to reconcile with the other conclusion from the data, that the seasonal does not extend to daily interest rates: the weekend average interest rate is almost exactly the weekday rate on a daily average basis. Several other hypotheses are not consistent with the data.

Much of the daily seasonal is due to a significant, negative mean return on Tuesdays. This covers the period 3 p.m. Monday to 3 p.m. Tuesday, Sydney time. This is midnight Sunday/Monday to midnight Monday/Tuesday, New York time. The possibility of an international effect cannot be ruled out, since the Sydney seasonal looks like the NYSE seasonal, lagged in calendar time. The lag in trading hours, however, is not precisely one day, so we are not convinced by this explanation.

Other puzzling regularities are observed, particularly in the weekend standard deviations. For equities, weekend volatility seems "low" and for interest rates it seems "high", relative to weekdays. The latter appears to be related to the high serial correlation in daily interest rates, which suggests a similar explanation for the "low" weekend equity variance; that is, negative correlation among the three implicit weekend-day returns. Although the covariance matrix across days of the week provides no additional clues, it is possible that the patterns in standard deviation are related to the seasonals in the mean returns.

Acknowledgments

We are indebted to Maurice Levi for comments on an earlier draft. The Centre for Research in Finance, AGSM, provided financial support and the Reserve Bank of Australia provided valuable daily interest rate data.

9   Multifactor asset-pricing models

N. A. Sinclair

Introduction

Since the early 1960s, the mean-variance Capital Asset Pricing Model (CAPM) has been a dominant paradigm in modern finance. Under its auspices, researchers have studied capital market efficiency, examined risk-adjusted investment performance and estimated opportunity costs of capital for corporate capital budgeting. However, recently two major developments have pushed this paradigm to a point of crisis. First, Roll (1977) analytically proved the tautological nature of most of the testable hypotheses of the CAPM. His critique cast a shadow over all of the empirical evidence which seemed to support the CAPM and raised doubts about its potential applications. Second, CAPM pricing anomalies which transcended international boundaries and have persisted over several decades have been reported in the literature. Both developments are too important to ignore and have to some extent resulted in a search for a more general alternative paradigm.

The purpose of this chapter is to survey briefly the major multifactor asset-pricing models which have been developed in the finance literature since the mid-1960s.[1] The first section briefly outlines the mean-variance Capital Asset Pricing Model (CAPM), since it has been the dominant single factor theory and provides a benchmark for alternative multifactor theories. The second section outlines the methodology of the empirical studies in asset pricing since it is common to almost all of the tests of the alternative models. The third section describes the major multifactor asset-pricing models which have been developed to date, together with some of the empirical evidence on those models. A brief conclusion is drawn in the final section.

One-factor asset pricing

Most asset-pricing models specify *ex ante* returns as linear functions of risk in the form:

Reproduced from *Accounting and Finance* 27, no. 1 (1987), 17–36, by permission of the author and the publisher.

$$E(\tilde{R}_{jt}) = \gamma_0 + \sum_{i=1}^{k} \beta_{ij} \, \tilde{\gamma}_{it}, \; j = 1, \ldots, p \tag{1}$$

where:

$E(\tilde{R}_{jt})$ is the expected return for asset j in period t;

γ_0 is the risk-free rate or the expected return on a "zero-beta" asset;

β_{ij} is the measure of association between the return on asset j and the returns on any common risky factor i; often termed systematic factor risk;

$\tilde{\gamma}_{it}$ is the risk premium determined by the market as applying to the common risk factor i; $[E(\tilde{R}_{it}) - \gamma_0]$;

p number of securities;

k number of common sources of risk.

The best known of the models characterised by (1) is the mean-variance Capital Asset Pricing Model (CAPM) developed by Sharpe (1964) and Lintner (1965a) and based upon the portfolio theory of Markowitz (1959). The following set of assumptions (A1 to A5) are sufficient to derive the CAPM version of (1).

A1. All investors make plans, investment/consumption decisions and portfolio revisions at the beginning of a single time period which is identical for all investors.

A2. All investors are risk averse and seek to maximise the expected utility of end-of-period wealth.

A3. Mean and variance of the distribution of terminal wealth are assumed to be sufficient statistics for investors' decision rules.

A4. Capital markets are perfect in the sense that there are no impediments to trade such as transaction costs or taxes and all assets are marketed and perfectly liquid. Information on beginning-of-period prices is available to all investors without cost, and unlimited borrowing/lending opportunities are available at the risk-free rate of interest.

A5. The supply of risky assets is exogenously determined.

This set of assumptions is sufficient to derive a partial equilibrium model of risky asset pricing from the first-order conditions for a maximisation of investors' utility functions as specified by assumptions A2 and A3.[2] In equilibrium, the familiar one-period *ex ante* pricing equation is:

$$E(\tilde{R}_j) = R_f + [E(\tilde{R}_m) - R_f] \, \beta_j \tag{2}$$

where:

R_f is the exogenously determined risk-free rate;

$E(\tilde{R}_m)$ is the expected return on the market portfolio;

β_j is equal to $\text{cov}(\tilde{R}_j, \tilde{R}_m) / \sigma^2(\tilde{R}_m)$;

$\sigma^2(\tilde{R}_m)$ is the variance of return on the market portfolio; and

$\text{cov}(\tilde{R}_j, \tilde{R}_m)$ is the covariance between the returns on asset j and returns on the market portfolio.

Three important aspects of the one-period equilibrium described in (2) are worth noting. First, assumption A3 either places a quadratic restriction upon investors' utility functions or alternatively requires normality for one-period return distributions. The typical objection to these assumptions was expressed by Ross (1977, p. 190) who argued:

Neither of these assumptions is particularly appealing on intuitive economic grounds; normality has only an inappropriate (and careless) application of the central limit theorem to recommend it and quadratic utility functions are implausible for any agents, let alone for all of them.[3]

Second, a value-weighted combination of all risky assets, the market portfolio, plays a central role in (2). Assumptions A1, A2 and A3 imply that in equilibrium all investors hold Markowitz (1959) mean-variance efficient portfolios. The addition of assumption A4 and the equilibrium condition that markets clear leads to a two-fund separation in which the opportunity set of risky assets is dominated by the market portfolio as one of the funds and the risk-free asset as the other. That is, all investors are assumed to hold some fraction of their wealth in the market portfolio. Third, it follows that the only component of risk which commands a risk premium in equilibrium is the covariance between the returns on any risky asset and the market portfolio of all risky assets. All diversifiable risk has been eliminated since all investors hold mean-variance efficient portfolios.

Methodology of asset pricing

It is clear that equation (2) is a special case of (1) when $t = 1$ and $k = 1$. Empirical testing of the model requires estimation of the cross-sectional constants, γ_0 and γ_1, with the prediction that $\hat{\gamma}_0 = R_f$ and $\hat{\gamma}_1 = [E(\tilde{R}_m) - R_f]$. Fama and MacBeth (1973) suggested a general framework for testing model (2), using a cross-sectional regression of the form:

$$\tilde{\tilde{R}}_{jt} = \gamma_0 + \gamma_1 \hat{\beta}_{jt-1} + \gamma_2 \hat{\beta}^2_{jt-1} + \gamma_3 \hat{\sigma}_{jt-1} + \tilde{\epsilon}_{jt} \tag{3}$$

where:

$\tilde{\tilde{R}}_{jt}$ is the average realised return on security j in period t;

$\hat{\beta}_{jt-1}$ is an estimate of systematic risk from a time series regression of $\tilde{R}_{jt}$ on $\tilde{R}_{mt}$ using data up to $t - 1$;[4] and

$\hat{\sigma}_{jt-1}$ is an estimate of "own variance" (diversifiable risk) such as the standard deviation of total returns on security j or unexpected returns, $\tilde{v}_{jt}$ (see note 4).

Some testable implications of (2) and their empirical tests have been:

1. *Linearity of risk and return.* Support is implied by the goodness-of-fit of (3) with the last two independent variables suppressed and/or by the insignificance of $\hat{\gamma}_2$.
2. *Only systematic risk commands a risk premium.* Support is implied by the significance of $\hat{\gamma}_1$ with the last two independent variables suppressed and/ or by the insignificance of $\hat{\gamma}_3$.
3. *Intercept.* Sharpe–Lintner CAPM is supported if $\hat{\gamma}_0 = R_f$ or $\hat{\gamma}_1 = \tilde{R}_m - R_f$ with the last two independent variables suppressed.
4. *Risk and return are positively related.* Support is based upon $\hat{\gamma}_1 > 0$.

To date, the results of the empirical tests have provided mixed support for the mean-variance CAPM derived from assumptions A1 to A5.[5] Nevertheless, at least two major benefits have also accrued from this period of intensive empirical investigation. First, there has been a recognition of some fundamental econometric problems and the development of methodologies to deal with them. Second, there has been a substantial effort to enrich the theory of asset pricing by relaxing many of the original assumptions. The remainder of this chapter will examine these latter contributions.

There are many non-trivial econometric problems to be addressed when testing asset-pricing models. In the early tests of the CAPM individual security returns were used and the overall results were weak. Not only was the systematic risk factor seldom priced, but diversifiable risk measures also seemed to be significantly priced. One explanation is that these results are consistent with the inefficiency of the tests since the individual estimates of systematic risk and average (expected) returns are affected by errors. In an important paper, Miller and Scholes (1972) demonstrated that these results could also be attributed to methodological weaknesses associated with skewness in *ex post* individual security return distributions. The usual procedure in the later tests of the CAPM has been to:

1. form groups of securities to reduce the inefficiency associated with the individual risk estimates, $\hat{\beta}_j$;
2. form these groups such that maximal dispersion in the independent variable (usually $\hat{\beta}_j$) is obtained; and
3. separate the initial grouping data set from the experimental data set on the assumption that the error structure affects the ranks of the beta estimates but is independently distributed through time.

Steps 1 and 2 are designed to maximise the power/efficiency of the estimation of (3) and step 3 attempts to deal with the errors-in-variables problem.[6] When asset-pricing tests were performed in this way, consistent support was evident for all of the testable implications except the *intercept* hypothesis of the Sharpe–Lintner version of the CAPM.

Despite these seemingly successful tests of the CAPM there were two important developments which raised doubts concerning the empirical validity of the one factor CAPM. First, Roll (1977) showed that if the market index, used as a proxy for the market portfolio, was *ex post* mean-variance efficient then the equilibrium equation (2) held tautologically at even the individual security level. A simple numerical example will help demonstrate the significance of Roll's critique. Table 9.1 is based upon a sample of 91 securities with complete monthly return data on the AGSM–CRIF price relatives database between January 1974 and December 1984 inclusive.

Table 9.1 Cross-sectional regression of betas on average returns as a function of index efficiency*

Market index proxy	$\bar{R}_m$	$\sigma(\bar{R}_m)$	$\bar{\beta}_j$	$\sigma(\beta_j)$	$\hat{\gamma}_0$	$\hat{\gamma}_1$	$\bar{R}^2$
Equally weighted	1.624	4.621	0.997	0.316	1.350 (0.156)	0.002 (0.149)	0.000
Mean variance efficient	1.624	1.641	0.942	0.095	−3.053 (0.001)	4.676 (0.002)	1.000

* Standard errors in parentheses.

In table 9.1, it is clear that if the selected market index is *ex post* mean-variance efficient then individual security betas and average returns are exactly linear as Roll (1977) proved. It follows that the mean-variance efficiency of the market index is the only major testable implication of (2).[7]

Second, a number of pricing anomalies were reported which were consistent with the claim that other factors, in addition to the market factor, affected security returns.[8] The volume of evidence is too large and too important to ignore. One response to such a crisis is to examine the competing models and to assess their ability to deal with a possible multifactor equilibrium as well as the extent to which they depend upon a "market portfolio". The next section of the chapter describes some of the major alternatives to the one factor CAPM.

Multifactor asset pricing

There are several theories of asset pricing under uncertainty which lead to a multifactor equilibrium in which individuals no longer perceive the market factor as the principal source of uncertainty. This section of the chapter deals with the following contributions.[9]

1. Intertemporal factor models (relax assumptions A1 and part of A2)
2. Skewness preference model (relax assumption A3)
3. Non-standard CAPM (relax assumption A4)
    (a) Non-marketable assets
    (b) Taxation
4. Arbitrage pricing models

Intertemporal factor models

Assumptions A1 and A2 imply that each investor's utility is solely a function of consumption at the beginning of the period and wealth at the end of the period. Importantly, utility does not depend upon the state of the economy at the end of the period. That is, utility is state independent.[10] The relaxation of assumption A1 leads to a potentially richer theory. The problem is conceptually simple in that the individual is now concerned with consumption and investment in each period throughout his or her lifetime. The basic premise is that an individual maximises the expected utility of *lifetime* consumption. Two broad approaches are evident in the development of intertemporal asset pricing. First, there have been attempts to identify the theoretical restrictions that are required such that the one factor CAPM in (2) holds on a period by period basis.[11] Second, there has been a considerable effort to explicitly model the sources of uncertainty.[12] It is this approach which leads directly to multifactor asset-pricing models which imply portfolio behaviour that is fundamentally different from the CAPM.

Using "dynamic programming", Fama (1970b) modelled the investor's consumption/investment decision in a discrete multiperiod framework. Working back from the optimal decision in the terminating period, Fama derived the utility function for a representative investor in each period of his life. Fama noted that, in the model, the consumer/investor behaved as if he were a risk-averse, one-period expected-utility-of-wealth maximiser for each period of the multiperiod horizon. That is, model (2) could describe equilibrium asset-pricing intertemporally. However, it is necessary that the derived utility functions be state independent if the one-factor asset-pricing model is to hold. Fama identified three possible sources of state dependent utility as:

(a) state-dependent tastes for consumption goods;
(b) state-dependent prices of the available consumption goods;
(c) investment opportunities (return distributions) may depend on prior period events and are therefore state dependent.

Clearly, if these sources of uncertainty cannot be ignored because they create a differential demand for particular securities, then the one-period model may not hold.

Fama and MacBeth (1974) investigated the empirical validity of (c), the intuition of which they describe as:

> If the level of expected returns on investment portfolios to be available at time t is to some extent uncertain at time $t - 1$, and if the returns from $t - 1$ to t on some investment assets are more strongly related to the level of expected returns at t than returns on other assets, then the former assets are better vehicles for hedging against the level of expected returns at t.

They tested for shifts in expected real returns on the two "funds" of the one-period model (R_z and R_m) over the period 1953–72.[13] No evidence of measurable relationships between real returns on investment assets from $t-1$ to t and the level of expected returns at t was found. Therefore, restriction (c) was rejected, and a necessary (but not sufficient) condition for the multiperiod validity of the one-period model was established.

Merton (1971, 1973a, 1973b) laid the groundwork for the second approach to modelling intertemporal uncertainty. There, the following sources of uncertainty were identified:

U1. Relative prices of consumption goods;
U2. Future labour income;
U3. Future values of non-human assets, i.e., end-of-period wealth;
U4. Future investment opportunities or rates of return on invested capital;
U5. Future tastes;
U6. Range of consumption goods available in future periods;
U7. Age of death.

It was noted that financial instruments were unlikely to be created for uncertainties U5, U6 or U7. However, the other sources of uncertainty could give rise to a differential demand for securities and were therefore admissible in an intertemporal framework.[14]

In Merton (1973a), it was assumed that asset returns and changes in the investment opportunity set could be described by continuous time stochastic processes.[15] Merton demonstrated that a two-fund separation theorem characterises equilibrium only if the investment opportunity set is constant through time. When uncertainties U3 and U4 prevail, it was shown that a three-fund separation was necessary. Funds one and three provide the "service" to investors of an (instantaneously) efficient risk-return frontier and fund two allows investors to hedge against unfavourable intertemporal shifts in the investment frontier.

In Merton (1973b) the "hedging" model was generalised to accommodate all four sources of uncertainty, U1 to U4. This approach leads to a multifactor model, wherein the funds are:

F1. The "market" portfolio;

F2. A riskless asset;

F3. Hedging portfolios for unanticipated shifts in rates of return;

F4. Hedging portfolios for shifts in the wage/rental ratio; and

F5. Hedging portfolios for changes in the prices of basic groups of consumption goods.

Securities play a dual role in this model since they aid diversification and also allow investors to "hedge" against common sources of uncertainty. There will be as many funds created as there are common sources of uncertainty, and "the equilibrium-expected return on a security will be a function of the expected return on each of these funds and the statistical dependence between the security's return and the return on each of these funds" (Merton 1973b, p. 149).[16] Clearly, a major obstacle to empirical tests of Merton's multifactor model is the identification of the hedging portfolios (state variables) and the estimation of the security covariances with those portfolios. Nevertheless, the intuition that investors seek securities which offer a hedge against perceived sources of uncertainty and will pay a premium for those securities is useful when considering later developments in asset pricing.

Breeden (1979) achieved a major simplication in intertemporal asset pricing by demonstrating that within a multigood, continuous-time model with uncertain prices of consumption goods and uncertain investment opportunities, it is possible to collapse Merton's multifactor pricing model into a single-factor model. However, although the form of the model is identical to (2), the underlying common factor is no longer aggregate wealth but is now aggregate real consumption.[17] By analogy with the CAPM, the "consumption" beta determines expected returns such that assets which are positively correlated with consumption ($\beta_c > 0$) are less valuable than those which can insure against adverse movements in consumption ($\beta_c < 0$).[18] The major advantages of Breeden's model are its parsimonious factor structure and the ability to observe the central variables, both of which were also a central feature of the original CAPM.

The limited evidence on intertemporal asset pricing tends to reject the restrictions required for the multiperiod validity of the one-period, one-factor CAPM and sustains the basic intuition of the intertemporal asset-pricing models as presented by Merton and others. That evidence also suggests that the empirical methodology outlined above must be modified to deal simultaneously with temporal and cross-sectional restrictions while allowing for possible non-stationarities in the estimation of the parameters of the model.[19] A major advantage of the intertemporal models is that the theory and data are consistent with each other since prices are presumably the outcome of successsive equilibria. This point is often overlooked in empirical tests of one-period models. However, there is an obvious need for caution when applying sophisticated statistical techniques to ill-behaved data.

Skewness preference model

The relaxation of assumption A3 may be justified if investors derive utility from higher moments of securities' return distributions and/or those return distributions are skewed. Kraus and Litzenberger (1976) extended the CAPM to incorporate the effect of a second asset-pricing factor related to co-skewness in return distributions. It was suggested that investors would be willing to pay a premium for securities whose returns are positively co-skewed with the market if the market portfolio is positively skewed. However, if returns on the market portfolio are negatively skewed then securities whose returns display positive co-skewness with the market portfolio will sell at a discount. More formally, the model in Kraus and Litzenberger is of the form:

$$\tilde{R}_j = \gamma_0 + \gamma_1 \beta_j + \gamma_2 \delta_j + \tilde{\epsilon}_j, \quad j = 1, \ldots, p \tag{4}$$

where: δ_j is a second factor measuring co-skewness with the market portfolio and is estimated as:

$$\sum_{t=1}^{T} (R_{mt} - \bar{R}_m)^2 (R_{jt} - \bar{R}_j) \Big/ \sum_{t=1}^{T} (R_{mt} - \bar{R}_m)^3$$

Empirical support for the model is based upon the significance of $\hat{\gamma}_2$ and the predicted sign which should be the opposite to the sign of the skewness of the market portfolio. To date the evidence is mixed.[20] Friend and Westerfield (1980, p. 898) found that "there is some but not conclusive evidence that investors may pay a premium for positive skewness in their portfolios". This may be contrasted with the claim in Ball, Brown and Officer (chapter 4), "The suspicion is that the relative co-skewnesses do not exist; that the estimated relative co-skewnesses are measurement error, pure and simple. This is confirmed by the results."[21]

Recently, Kraus and Litzenberger (1983) reformulated their three-moment CAPM wherein the market portfolio represents aggregate consumption. Although there have been no tests of this model, it is worth noting the low explanatory power of "aggregate consumption" variables in the Marsh (1980) tests of the consumption-based CAPM.

Non-standard CAPM

There have been several extensions to the CAPM which are based upon alternatives to assumption A4.[22] An important contribution was made by Mayers (1972) who explores the equilibrium implications of individuals holding economically significant claims to assets which are not marketable, such as "human capital".[23] One major result is that systematic risk estimates are comprised of two parts; one part attributable to the variation of the firm's dollar returns with all other firms (a market factor), and the other due to the extramarket variability of total dollar returns with non-marketable assets. Mayers (1972, p. 241) concluded:

> The modified model implies that investors evaluate all risk premiums, taking into consideration the covariance of the risky asset's return with the return from their non-marketable assets. In effect, the investor modifies the risk premiums, affecting relatively more importance to those with which his non-marketable returns have the least covariation.

In short, not all individuals will necessarily choose to hold the market portfolio.[24] One of the major contributions of this class of "missing assets" models has been to identify one source of bias in systematic risk estimates which has some theoretical basis but has been largely ignored in the empirical work. Owing to the unobservability and non-traded nature of human capital, this research direction has not been as productive as others, such as the after-tax versions of the CAPM.

If individuals maximise expected after-tax returns and dividends and capital gains income are taxed differentially for at least some investors, there is an equilibrium relationship between before-tax expected returns and dividend yields. Extensions to the CAPM by Brennan (1970) and Litzenberger and Ramaswamy (1979) resulted in a model of the form:

$$\tilde{R}_j - R_F = \gamma_0 + \gamma_1 \beta_j + \gamma_2 (d_j - R_F) + \tilde{\epsilon}_j, \quad j = 1, \ldots, p \quad (5)$$

where d_j is an estimate of the dividend yield on security j. The coefficient γ_2 is predicted to be positive and if within a realistic range is typically interpreted as a "tax differential".[25]

Overall, the empirical evidence provides mixed support for the after-tax version of the CAPM. Ball et al. (1979) attribute this lack of consistency to pervasive experimental design problems. They conclude:

> The relationship found was not consistent with any of the extant hypotheses on the effect of dividends on share returns. It was consistent with either the dividend yield variable proxying for omitted variables and for other misspecifications in the two-parameter model, or to a combination of this proxy-effect and a tax differential in favour of capital gains versus dividends.

Arbitrage pricing models

Ross' (1976, 1977) arbitrage pricing theory (APT) retains the intuitive simplicity of linearity between returns and systematic risk yet does not explicitly assume quadratic utility or mean-variance sufficiency for return distributions. There are two central assumptions in the APT. First, it is assumed that the return generating process may be expressed as a linear k factor model of the form:

$$\tilde{R}_j = E(\tilde{R}_j) + \beta_{j1} \tilde{\delta}_1 + \ldots + \beta_{jk} \tilde{\delta}_k + \tilde{\epsilon}_j, \quad j = 1, \ldots, p \quad (6)$$

where:

$\tilde{R}_j$ is the realised return on the jth asset;

$\tilde{\delta}_i$ is the unanticipated realised return on factor i and $E(\tilde{\delta}_i) = 0$ since any anticipated movements in factor returns have been incorporated in $E(\tilde{R}_j)$ and are therefore already in current market prices;

β_{ji} measures the sensitivity of asset j to movements in the common factor i.

Second, it is assumed that the asset-specific return, $\tilde{\epsilon}_j$, is sufficiently independent such that $E(\tilde{\epsilon}_j) = 0$ in large well-diversified portfolios. Ross (1976, 1977) proved that if these assumptions held, then for there to be zero arbitrage opportunities, it must be that:

$$E(\tilde{R}_j) \approx \gamma_0 + \beta_{j1} \tilde{\gamma}_2 + \ldots + \beta_{jk} \tilde{\gamma}_k, \quad j = 1, \ldots, p \quad (7)$$

for constants γ_0 and $\tilde{\gamma}_i = [E(\tilde{R}_i) - \gamma_0]$ for $i = 1, \ldots, k$. In simple terms, (7) suggests that the expected return on any risky asset exceeds a constant γ_0 (perhaps the riskless rate of interest) by an amount equal to the sum of the products of the risk premium on each factor and the sensitivity of that asset to the respective factors.

However, a major consequence of the parsimonious set of assumptions upon which the APT is based is that the economic content of the model is also limited in a number of important respects. First, unlike the CAPM, the APT does not specify the number of common factors which generate systematic risk in the economy. If only one factor is considered important as in the CAPM, and the "true" market portfolio remain unobservable, then the pricing models of the two theories are empirically indistinguishable. It is also important to note that, solely on the basis of a pricing equation such as (7), the APT cannot be rejected against any specified alternative since the APT is a general k factor theory, in which k is an unspecified constant. Second, the signs and magnitudes of the $\hat{\gamma}_i$'s in (7) are unspecified by the APT, unlike the equivalent propositions of the other models. Third, the identity of the factors against which the β_j are to be measured, unlike other multifactor asset-pricing models, are not identified. Finally, although the absence of arbitrage opportunities is necessary for an equilibrium, the APT is not an equilibrium-based theory.[26]

However, in principle the APT is testable.[27] For example, Roll and Ross (1980) alphabetically selected 42 groups of 30 securities listed on the New York or American Stock Exchanges on both 3 July 1962 and 31 December 1972. Using daily arithmetic returns adjusted for all capital changes and dividend payments, the following test was conducted for each of the 42 groups:
1. the time series sample covariance matrix was computed for each group of 30 securities for the period 3 July 1962 to 31 December 1972 inclusive;
2. estimates of the number of factors and factor loadings were obtained using maximum likelihood factor analysis (MLFA); and
3. the factor loading matrix was then regressed cross-sectionally on average returns for the complete period to provide estimates of the factor risk premia which were then evaluated for significance.

To test the diversifiable risk hypothesis, the cross-sectional regressions were repeated and the standard deviation of returns included with factor loading estimates. Under the null, it was predicted that this variable would be insignificantly related to average returns. After extensive empirical investigation, including time series pricing tests and the use of interlocking data sets to overcome skewness-induced dependence of own variance on average returns, Roll and Ross (1980, p. 1100) concluded:

> The empirical data support the APT against both an unspecified alternative—a very weak test—and the specific alternative that own variance has an independent explanatory effect on excess returns.

Overall, their results were consistent with at least three but possibly four factors being priced in cross-section. Chen (1983) found support for a five-factor APT model against the "own variance" factor, the CAPM systematic risk factor and the "firm size" factor. Brown and Weinstein (1983) replicated Roll and Ross (1980) using a more powerful statistical methodology. They confirmed the finding of at least a three-factor APT and rejected both five- and seven-factor models.

Sinclair (1982) found *prima facie* support for a three-factor model using monthly returns for large samples of Australian equities. However, a number of important methodological problems were highlighted which seriously affect the interpretation of empirical tests of the APT. First, simulation results indicated that the application of maximum likelihood factor analysis (MLFA) to security return data which are affected by either infrequent trading or variance non-stationarity leads to the extraction of more than the "true" number of factors. Second, it was found that as more factors were retained in the cross-sectional regressions, more factors appeared to be significantly "priced". For example, when four factors were retained, three were "priced", but when eight factors were retained six or seven were "priced".[28] Third, it was found that the first-factor loadings proxied for the CAPM β's such that support for the APT against the CAPM seemed to rest with the statistical significance of the minor factors, none of which were intertemporally stationary.

Further methodological problems were highlighted by Dhrymes, Friend and Gultekin (1984) who re-examined the Roll and Ross data with surprising results. As in Kryzonowski and To (1983), it was shown that the number of factors depended on the number of securities in the sample. It was also found that estimates of the first-factor loadings remained relatively constant with increasing sample size, whereas estimates of the factor loadings for the remaining factors changed dramatically. Finally, the Roll and Ross (1980) conclusion that a five-factor model was adequate was not supported.[29]

It is clear that empirical tests of the APT are confounded by serious methodological problems arising from the restrictions that the factor analysis statistical model places upon the data.[30] However, Chamberlain and Rothschild (1983) demonstrated that an "approximate" factor structure may be obtained using the simpler principal components analysis on "nested" samples of securities. As the sample size increases, the eigenvalues of the "true" factors increase without bound whereas all other eigenvalues are bounded. The eigenvectors associated with the eigenvalues provide estimates of the factor loadings required to test (7). Using this simpler methodology, Luedecke (1984) and Faff (1986) could not reject a one-factor structure.

Recently, Chen, Roll and Ross (1984) attempted to extend the APT by empirically identifying the systematic factors in the economy which could be consistent with the factor structure. They set out to answer two questions:

1. Which macroeconomic variables are related to the latent factors extracted from equity returns?
2. Are the "betas" on these "state variables" significant explanatory variables in asset-pricing tests?

The "state variables" selected by Chen, Roll and Ross are easy to relate to the intertemporal "hedge" factors identified by Merton (see above). These were unanticipated shifts in inflation, the term structure, the growth rate of industrial production and the risk premia; together with changes in stock market indices, real consumption and oil prices.

These variables were used as explanatory variables for the returns on portfolios of securities which were statistically constructed to "mimic" five latent factors extracted from security return data by factor analysis (MLFA). Unanticipated shifts in the first four variables were found to be significant in the estimation period, January 1953 to December 1972, and in the holdout period, January 1973 to December 1977. Asset-pricing tests, using the methodology described above, also found these variables to be significant in explaining average returns across portfolios of securities. Neither stock market indices, aggregate consumption nor oil prices increased the explanatory power of those basic state variables.

Conclusion

The purpose of this chapter has been to identify the multifactor models that have been developed in the literature and may provide competing models to the CAPM. One broad distinction between the models examined in the section "Multifactor Asset Pricing" depends upon whether they are "equilibrium" based or "zero arbitrage" based. The former set typically arise from the explicit relaxation of one or more assumptions of the simple CAPM and often contain the CAPM as a special case. To that extent, they are also susceptible to the Roll (1977) criticisms. Further, the empirical evidence is not strongly supportive.

The "zero-arbitrage" model of Ross (1976, 1977) has been embraced by some as the natural successor to the CAPM for good reasons. The APT seems to be more general than the CAPM since it requires fewer assumptions and permits a multifactor process. It does not pivot on the market portfolio and therefore avoids the criticisms of Roll (1977). Finally, the early CAPM empirical tests can be embraced as evidence of one factor APT. In short, the APT introduces an alternative theoretical structure to asset pricing and a new empirical methodology.

However, overall acceptance of the APT has been tentative for good reasons. There are serious unresolved methodological issues involved in testing the APT which may account for the mixed evidence to date. Unless the number of factors and/or their identity is universally established, then the practical application of the APT to central issues in finance will prove more difficult than the CAPM. The testability of the APT and the extent to which it differs from the CAPM are central to an ongoing paradigm debate.

In conclusion, as Morgenstern (1963) noted, the critical problems arise where the theory confronts the data. The more complex the theory, the greater the demands it places on the available data and the statistical methodology. Relatively easy access to large computerised databases increases the possibility of a definitive test of some model, but at the same time it may increase the frequency of methodologically included artifacts. To cope with such eventualities, the existence of an accepted paradigm in modern finance is indispensable and its importance is indisputable.

Acknowledgments

The author gratefully acknowledges the comments of Philip Brown, Frank Finn and Bob Officer and absolves them from any remaining errors of fact or omission.

Notes

1. See Jensen (1972), Roll (1977) and Ross (1978b) for comprehensive coverage of the theoretical and empirical aspects of the early asset-pricing theories.
2. For example, see Fama and Miller (1972, ch. 6).
3. However, from a positive economic perspective the merits of any theory are to be judged by the empirical validity of the predictions of the theory, and not from the *a priori* reasonableness of its assumptions.
4. There exists an underlying return-generating model which is consistent with each specification of

(1). For example, if it is assumed that $\bar{R}_{jt} = E(\bar{R}_{jt}) + v_{jt}$ and that v_{jt} is distributed $N(0,\sigma)$, then the market model may be derived as an *ex post* analogue of the CAPM in equation (2). The market model has been an integral part of the literature on capital market efficiency.

5. See Douglas (1969), Friend and Blume (1970), Black, Jensen and Scholes (1972), Fama and MacBeth (1973), Blume and Friend (1973), Ball, Brown and Officer (1976a), Foster (1978a) and Gibbons (1982a). The intercept hypothesis was the most regularly rejected. However, see Roll (1977) for a critical discussion of this empirical work with particular emphasis on the sensitivity of the results to any misspecification of the market portfolio.

6. Two variations on this approach may be found in Fama and MacBeth (1973) who used "moving subperiods" and Ball, Brown and Officer (1976a) who used an "odds/evens" technique. Gibbons (1982) performed a multivariate test of the CAPM which eliminated the errors-in-variables problem and increased the precision of the estimated risk premia by as much as 76 per cent.

7. See Stokie (1982b) for evidence that none of the commonly used Australian market indices is mean-variance efficient. However, although the linearity of betas and average returns is a mathematical tautology if the index is mean-variance efficient, it may be economically deficient in two respects. First, the optimal weights assigned to many securities in the index are often negative. Second, in table 9.1 the negative estimate of $\tilde{\gamma}_0$ implies a negative nominal risk-free rate over the 1974–84 time period.

8. See the *Journal of Financial Economics*, vol. 7, 1978, and vol. 12, 1983. Basu (1977) showed that price-earnings ratio seemed to command additional risk premia, and Banz (1981) documented a "priced" size factor. It is worth noting that if a mean-variance efficient index had been used to estimate security betas, then tautologically there can be no anomalies or additional factors whatsoever! See Roll (1978) for a discussion of a "benchmark error" interpretation of this evidence.

9. With the exception of the arbitrage pricing theory (APT) these models are extensions of the CAPM derived from the relaxation of one or more of the assumptions A1 to A5. The APT may imply that the "market factor" *per se* is not a source of risk but is a composite of several risk factors.

10. In the "state-preference" approach to the theory of asset pricing, all uncertainty resides in the "state-of-the-world" which has yet to evolve. The term "states" is often used synonymously with "source of uncertainty" or "risk factor". The importance of state independence is that it implies a separation principle in which the demand for risky securities is independent of the investor's preferences. See Cass and Stiglitz (1970) for a discussion of the class of utility functions which permit separation and Ross (1978a) for a discussion of return-generating processes.

11. See Fama (1970b), Fama and MacBeth (1974) and Stapleton and Subrahmanyam (1978). Constantinides (1980) spans both approaches and particularly emphasises the need to consider non-stationarities in the parameters of the CAPM.

12. See Merton (1971, 1973a, 1973b), Roll (1973), Long (1974), Breedon (1979), Marsh (1980) and Cornell (1981). It should be noted that Roll's (1973) model is not a multiperiod model but does allow for uncertainty in the prices of consumption goods. In that model, inflation-rate uncertainty affects nominal equilibrium prices.

13. "Real" returns were used to control for uncertainty in the prices of consumption goods.

14. Uncertainties on the supply side (assumption A5) are treated as exogenous. However, see Constantinides (1980) for a set of assumptions on production technologies and consumption-investment behaviour such that the Sharpe–Lintner single-factor model holds in an intertemporal general equilibrium.

15. Other sources of uncertainty such as U1 and U2 were controlled by assuming only one consumption good and that all income was derived from capital gains (i.e., via U3).

16. Long (1974) allows there to be uncertainty with respect to the prices of many future consumption goods and investment opportunities and obtains a multifactor separation such that in equilibrium each investor holds (a) bills of maturity, (b) the stock market portfolio, and (c) "quasi-futures contracts" on each of the K consumption goods.

17. Breeden (1979, p. 292) noted that an observed aggregate consumption variable was potentially closer to true consumption than any proxy for aggregate wealth was to true wealth. Therefore, this approach circumvents the issues raised in Roll (1977) concerning the observability of the "true" market portfolio. However, Cornell (1981) argues that Breeden (1979) may not have overcome the problems of unobservable state variables and that these have merely been impounded into the consumption betas. Tests of these intertemporal models in Marsh (1980) do not provide support for any version of the model.

18. Leroy (1982, pp 192–93) also discussed the consumption-based CAPM as an important framework for considering expectations theories of asset prices. In particular, it is noted that the relationship between risk premia and the covariance between rate of return and the *marginal* utility of consumption is valid for unrestricted preferences and distributions. The validity of that relationship for *levels* of consumption holds only by virtue of the approximately linear relationship between marginal utility of consumption and the level of consumption in the framework of diffusion processes.

19. The simultaneous equation systems presented by Gibbons (1982) and Brown and Weinstein (1983) are representative of the likely directions of future empirical research in asset pricing.

20. See Kraus and Litzenberger (1976), Ball, Brown and Officer (1976a) and Friend and Westerfield (1980).
21. It is worth noting that although the explanatory power of systematic co-skewness in asset pricing is limited, total skewness appears to be highly correlated with excess returns defined with respect to the CAPM. See Beedles (1984) and the references therein. Unfortunately, total skewness lacks a convincing theoretical framework.
22. In a recent article, Elton and Gruber (1984) coined the term "non-standard" CAPM and reformulated many of these models to show that these are special cases of Roll's (1977) point concerning the efficiency of the market index. It is demonstrated that "each model arises directly from the efficiency of a particular version of the market portfolio".
23. Mayers (1972, p. 230) noted the equivalence of the form of his model to the general "missing assets" model wherein bonds, real estate and other securities are omitted from the market index. However, it should be noted that the rights to such assets are implicit in the equity prices which are typically used in the empirical work. Also, Stambaugh (1982) found the asset-pricing tests to be robust with respect to the inclusion of a previously omitted set of assets.
24. A similar discussion may be found in Merton (1973b, p. 146) who noted than an investor with a highly specialised form of labour would want to hold less of his firm's equity than is in the market portfolio and would short sell to hedge against unfavourable shifts in his labour income.
25. The theoretical and empirical issues involved with testing models such as (5) are summarised in Brealey and Myers (1984). Recent empirical evidence on the ex-dividend behaviour of Australian equities is reported in Brown and Walter (1986).
26. Since Ross's (1976, 1977) there have been other theoretical expositions of the APT by Huberman (1982), Chen and Ingersoll (1983), and Ingersoll (1984) among others. Recently, Connor (1985) has developed an intertemporal, competitive equilibrium version of the APT.
27. Empirical tests of the APT are to be found in Roll and Ross (1980), Chen (1983), Reinganum (1981b), Brown and Weinstein (1983), Luedecke (1984) and Faff (1986). With the exception of the last three papers, the empirical methodology has been analogous to that described above in the section "Methodology of Asset Pricing". However, not everyone agrees on the testability of the APT. See Shanken (1982) for a contrary viewpoint.
28. Recently, this phenomenon has also been documented by Dhrymes, Friend and Gultekin (1984). They also claim that APT pricing tests on individual risk premia or subsets of risk premia are not unambiguous and question the validity of testing the APT on small samples of securities.
29. Chen (1983) and Brown and Weinstein (1983) shared data in common with Roll and Ross (1980) and relied upon the conclusion of Roll and Ross that five factors were sufficient. However, it is also worth noting that Cho, Elton and Gruber (1984) found five or six priced factors using the Roll and Ross methodology over a different time period.
30. See Sinclair (1982) for a discussion of some of the inherent problems associated with the factor analysis of security return data.

PART 4

Estimation of relative risk

10 Market model statistics for selected companies and industry groupings

Philip Brown

This chapter contains a listing of Scholes–Williams and OLS regression statistics for 217 companies. The companies listed are all those on the Australian Graduate School of Management's CRIF Merged Price Relative File that have complete histories from 1981 until the end of 1985. The index used is the Statex–Actuaries Accumulation Index. The index was restated to assume end-of-month investment of dividends rather than end-of-year, which is the basis for the published index. All regression estimates are based on the natural logarithms of the price relatives. The results by industry group the 217 companies according to the Australian Associated Stock Exchange industry classifications. The industry statistics are the unweighted averages of the companies in each industry classification.

			Scholes–Williams		Ord. Least Squares		
Ind		Company name	Alpha	Beta	Alpha	Beta	rsq
23	aag	australian agricult	− .002	.871	.002	.637	.18
8	aal	amatil ltd	.020	.368	.017	.928	.33
5	abc	adelaide brighton	.013	.448	.009	.692	.24
1	abf	aberfoyle ltd	− .007	.861	− .008	.917	.35
22	afi	australian foundat.	.005	.685	.006	.628	.41
11	aft	afl holdings ltd	− .003	.424	− .004	.481	.21
15	agc	australian guarantee	.010	.367	.005	.622	.34
22	agl	australian gas light	− .003	1.029	− .001	.880	.40
22	ahd	amalgamated holdings	.011	.481	.016	.185	.03
15	alh	alliance holdings	.019	.351	.019	.384	.10
3	alr	alpha resources ltd	− .054	2.594	− .040	1.774	.10
8	aml	allied mills ltd	.016	.400	.015	.484	.10
22	amp	ampol ltd	− .007	.891	− .004	.741	.42
3	amx	ampol exploration	− .028	1.690	− .028	1.680	.55
13	ani	australian national	− .011	1.044	− .012	1.104	.59
15	anz	australian & nz bank	− .003	.788	− .003	.760	.43
3	aog	australian oil & gas	− .026	1.132	− .030	1.370	.38
16	apa	a.p.a. holdings ltd	.017	.304	.021	.054	0.00
14	apm	apm limited	.002	.650	.002	.655	.45
22	arg	argo investments ltd	.004	.677	.006	.591	.33
1	ark	arcadia minerals ltd	− .029	.393	− .038	.884	.06
8	arn	arnotts ltd	.022	.304	.020	.419	.09

Ind		Company name	Scholes–Williams		Ord. Least Squares		
			Alpha	Beta	Alpha	Beta	rsq
1	ash	ashton mining ltd	− .026	1.049	− .026	1.020	.32
21	asp	a.s.c. prop. trust	− .008	.563	− .006	.472	.20
23	ast	adelaide steamship	.017	.709	.019	.542	.27
1	ats	australis mining n1	− .068	2.043	− .063	1.765	.26
22	aui	australian united in	.010	.276	.013	.137	.01
20	avt	advertiser newspaper	.019	.245	.017	.329	.07
6	awa	amalgamated wireless	.001	.800	.003	.661	.29
23	bas	base resources ltd.	− .004	.713	− .003	.705	.06
23	bbs	bundaberg sugar co.	− .014	.569	− .018	.796	.30
9	bcp	bonds coats patons	.009	.460	.010	.442	.16
5	bcs	blue circle southern	.006	.762	.012	.412	.11
24	bhp	broken hill pty. ltd	− .011	1.284	− .008	1.086	.69
19	bil	brambles industries	− .003	.849	− .002	.756	.47
5	bkw	brickworks ltd	.005	.463	.008	.284	.14
23	bll	bell group ltd	.021	.981	.023	.913	.31
5	bnp	brick & pipe	.017	.298	.017	.276	.07
1	boc	bougainville copper	− .005	.618	− .010	.911	.32
23	bon	bond corporation	− .022	1.712	− .016	1.359	.32
5	bor	boral ltd	− .003	.751	− .006	.876	.63
18	bph	burns, philp & co.	− .001	.875	.003	.693	.32
3	bpt	beach petroleum n1	− .043	1.801	− .042	1.774	.38
15	bqd	bank of queensland	.004	.284	.006	.160	.03
3	brg	bridge oil ltd	− .028	1.672	− .023	1.391	.53
23	btr	btr hopkins ltd	.010	.656	.015	.357	.10
7	cat	castlemaine tooheys	.018	.482	.015	.665	.29
5	cbk	clifton brick hldgs.	.006	.596	.007	.544	.24
8	cby	cadbury schweppes	.022	.550	.019	.678	.32
11	cig	commonwealth indust.	− .007	.779	− .006	.703	.39
22	cin	carlton investments	.009	.154	.010	.130	.02
13	cly	clyde industries ltd	− .015	1.085	− .016	1.114	.66
1	cmc	comalco ltd	− .009	.591	− .014	.880	.29
22	cmi	commonwealth mining	− .009	.755	− .008	.734	.23
2	cna	coal & allied	− .047	1.931	− .038	1.458	.48
1	cng	central norseman	− .013	1.179	− .015	1.271	.36
3	cnw	canada northwest	− .031	.906	− .040	1.434	.11
17	col	coles (g.j.) & co.	.003	.782	.005	.631	.43
2	cpm	central pacific	− .073	1.516	− .070	1.384	.14
1	cra	cra ltd	− .010	.766	− .012	.923	.51
12	crg	crane (g.e.) hldgs	− .010	.730	− .006	.536	.15
5	csl	calsil ltd	.002	.554	.004	.420	.09
24	csr	csr ltd	− .021	1.077	− .019	.981	.55
2	cta	costain australia	− .032	1.718	− .022	1.154	.36
1	ctr	centaur mining	− .013	1.072	− .017	1.258	.13
1	cud	cudgen r.z. ltd	− .006	1.081	− .002	.865	.14
15	dac	direct acceptance	.013	.243	.016	.084	.01
17	dav	davis (charles) ltd	− .002	1.085	.001	.880	.29
22	djp	d.j.'s properties	.021	.387	.028	.032	0.00
23	dun	dunlop olympic ltd	.009	.781	.008	.860	.49
13	edi	evans deakin	− .014	.440	− .014	.445	.12
14	edl	edwards dunlop & co.	.003	.515	0.000	.687	.45
13	ego	eglo engineering	− .016	.125	− .018	.220	.02
6	eml	email ltd	− .007	.898	− .004	.756	.37
1	emp	emperor mines ltd	− .021	1.427	− .017	1.224	.15
1	emt	eastmet ltd	− .021	1.349	− .016	1.280	.13
23	enc	enacon ltd	.001	.534	− .008	1.068	.19
2	era	energy resources	− .012	.725	− .011	.710	.35
20	ffx	fairfax (john) ltd	.022	.527	.025	.366	.10
8	fhf	faulding (f.h.) & co	.024	.209	.024	.203	.06
3	fln	flinders petrol. n1	− .071	2.049	− .061	1.468	.23
19	flw	fleetways (holdings)	.006	.291	.008	.168	.01
14	gad	gadsden (j.) aust.	.002	.562	.003	.500	.20

Ind		Company name	Scholes–Williams		Ord. Least Squares		
			Alpha	Beta	Alpha	Beta	rsq
5	gch	goliath cement	.001	.730	.004	.555	.16
11	gci	gibson chemical inds	.006	.414	.008	.324	.15
1	gcx	gold copper expl.	− .071	1.588	− .074	1.779	.32
1	ggm	golden grove mining	− .039	1.663	− .048	2.177	.36
1	gme	Gold & mineral exp.	− .063	1.262	− .054	.750	.02
1	gmk	gold mines of kalg.	− .010	1.316	− .008	1.206	.23
17	gng	gordon and gotch ltd	.015	.175	.013	.314	.10
21	gpt	general prop. trust	.012	.329	.010	.478	.43
10	gud	g.u.d. holdings ltd	.007	.296	.006	.311	.08
1	gvm	golden valley mines	− .060	2.042	− .058	1.903	.28
5	hah	hardie (james) inds.	− .005	.858	− .004	.802	.51
8	hak	harris (keith)	.001	.522	.009	.052	0.00
22	hew	heller (walter e.)	.020	.347	.024	.110	.01
1	hgd	hill 50 gold mine n1	− .039	1.295	− .041	1.428	.31
6	hil	hills industries ltd	.007	.320	.006	.362	.13
4	hkr	hooker corporation	.007	.644	.005	.713	.25
6	hmx	hanimex corporation	− .011	.431	− .019	.908	.23
12	hnd	henderson's indust.	.007	.775	.011	.526	.11
4	hol	holland (john)	.001	.666	.004	.520	.18
15	hsd	hastings deering	.009	.110	.010	.059	0.00
3	hsi	hawkstone investment	− .041	1.351	− .028	.568	.03
3	hte	hartogen energy ltd	− .050	2.125	− .044	1.747	.55
5	hum	humes ltd	.004	.616	.003	.666	.29
20	hwt	herald & weekly	.016	.396	.014	.523	.24
14	hyl	hygienic-lily ltd	.002	.126	.005	− .022	0.00
13	ica	international comb.	− .005	.562	− .005	.566	.23
11	ici	ici australia ltd	− .006	.829	− .005	.764	.40
2	imc	international mining	− .051	.917	− .055	1.116	.14
4	jen	jennings industries	.006	.739	.008	.630	.26
17	jod	jones (david) ltd	.024	.803	.029	.532	.17
13	jpl	johns perry ltd	.001	1.056	.003	.966	.40
4	jry	jonray holdings ltd	.027	.662	.038	.041	0.00
22	jsc	jasco holdings ltd	.019	.107	.016	.285	.07
22	key	keywest investments	.008	.793	.011	.582	.05
4	krn	kern corporation ltd	.002	1.205	.009	.767	.24
1	ktr	kitchener mining n1	− .046	1.238	− .048	1.367	.18
4	kup	kurts (peter) prop	.018	.620	.014	.829	.18
4	lei	leighton holdings	− .006	.866	− .004	.781	.29
3	len	lennard oil n1	− .040	1.083	− .038	.995	.05
4	llc	lend lease corp.	− .001	.990	.003	.797	.54
16	lme	lumley (edward) ltd	.023	.305	.025	.217	.04
22	lti	latec investments	− .006	.483	− .002	.246	.02
3	mag	magellan petroleum	− .061	2.207	− .054	1.793	.50
22	mat	matine ltd	.016	.291	.017	.244	.05
19	may	mayne nickless ltd	− .006	1.033	− .005	1.023	.54
13	mbr	martin bright steels	− .015	.778	− .010	.493	.10
23	mcp	mcpherson's ltd	− .003	.831	− .004	.838	.48
15	mer	mercantile credits	.009	.488	.007	.591	.21
1	mex	metals exploration	− .050	1.812	− .050	1.867	.33
3	mgt	magnet group limited	− .052	1.560	− .050	1.400	.11
1	mim	m.i.m. holdings ltd	− .021	.861	− .024	1.042	.45
2	mkl	mary kathleen	− .021	.867	− .011	.319	.01
16	mlc	m.l.c. ltd	.019	.312	.021	.206	.02
7	mld	mildara wines ltd	.009	.301	.013	.111	.01
1	mln	mallina holdings ltd	− .028	.605	− .028	.605	.04
16	mmt	mercantile mutual	.014	.379	.018	.184	.02
5	mnr	monier ltd	− .004	.841	− .002	.721	.41
7	mph	morris (philip)	.008	.888	.013	.624	.15
3	mro	meridian oil n1	− .026	1.684	− .025	1.633	.26
22	msa	moore business sys.	.005	.529	.007	.391	.11
1	mta	mount arthur molyb.	− .034	.109	− .035	.188	0.00

		Scholes–Williams		Ord. Least Squares		
Ind	Company name	Alpha	Beta	Alpha	Beta	rsq
1	mtn metana minerals	− .028	2.732	− .020	2.287	.26
1	mtr metramar minerals	− .008	1.116	− .021	1.873	.23
19	mwm mcilwraith mceacharn	− .006	.867	0.000	.510	.12
17	myr myer emporium ltd	.008	.741	.011	.601	.20
24	nbh north broken hill	− .016	.972	− .017	1.038	.59
12	ncl national consol.	− .006	1.126	− .002	.896	.38
20	ncp news corp. ltd.	− .003	1.244	.001	1.000	.19
1	ngm norseman gold mines	− .032	1.415	− .029	1.276	.24
12	nio nilsen (oliver j.)	.006	.402	.009	.230	.02
1	nkm north kalgurli mines	− .018	1.707	− .012	1.368	.26
1	nmx newmcx exploration	− .021	.622	− .019	.498	.02
1	nrn nicron resources ltd	− .035	1.441	− .036	1.499	.13
20	nsr northern star hldgs	.012	.307	.013	.273	.02
12	nuc nucleus ltd	− .040	1.888	− .033	1.454	.23
3	oip oakwood internat	− .017	.907	− .010	.548	.02
22	olm olims consolidated	.009	.304	.013	.060	0.00
22	ops opsm industries ltd	− .001	.794	.002	.620	.31
3	osh oil search ltd	− .013	1.091	− .013	1.099	.14
2	pcm pancontinental min.	− .042	1.370	− .040	1.267	.34
1	pcr placer development	− .007	.649	− .001	.341	.06
3	pen petro energy ltd	− .035	1.767	− .032	1.594	.17
13	phh parbury henty holdgs	.016	.189	.010	.522	.11
6	pih philips industries	0.000	.253	− .004	.487	.13
24	pko peko-wallsend ltd	− .023	.947	− .023	.981	.40
8	pma plumrose (australia)	.038	.093	.041	− .089	0.00
21	pml p.m.l. prop. trust	.008	.355	.012	.123	.02
5	pnc pioneer concrete	− .008	.984	− .008	1.021	.69
4	pnd paynter dixon hldg	.008	.510	.009	.469	.16
22	pno p&o australia	− .004	.478	− .004	.464	.17
23	pns pioneer sugar mills	− .013	.649	− .013	.633	.21
1	pos poseidon ltd	− .023	1.459	− .022	1.380	.31
3	ppl pancontinental pet.	− .057	2.311	− .048	1.811	.38
1	prn pelsart resources n1	− .032	1.490	− .031	1.423	.19
5	qcl queensland cement	.007	.645	.012	.363	.11
22	qnt qintex ltd	.021	.562	.027	.225	.02
20	qpr queensland press ltd	.013	.563	.012	.636	.21
8	quf q.u.f. industries	.021	.427	.022	.385	.07
6	rhm rheem australia ltd	.008	.551	.008	.572	.16
8	rnc reckitt & colman	.002	.645	.002	.625	.39
7	rth rothmans holdings	.034	.419	.031	.582	.19
1	sam samantha exploration	− .018	1.307	− .020	1.445	.13
7	sbq s.a. brewing hldgs	.015	.567	.016	.485	.15
21	sdp schroder darling pr.	.007	.226	.009	.096	.03
13	shr shearer (john) hldgs	.005	.287	.005	.289	.05
12	sid siddons industries	.003	.470	.002	.536	.26
2	smi smith (howard) ltd	− .025	1.279	− .021	1.032	.44
22	sol soul pattinson (w.h.)	.003	.414	.005	.312	.09
1	spg spargos exploration	− .029	1.382	− .025	1.171	.18
6	sph simpson holdings ltd	.005	.430	0.000	.727	.24
2	spp southern pacific	− .081	2.101	− .068	1.345	.15
18	sst steamships trading	− .004	.743	.001	.435	.17
3	sto santos ltd	− .023	1.460	− .020	1.282	.55
5	swh softwood holdings	.001	1.049	.003	.967	.38
5	tab taubmans industries	.002	.781	.005	.608	.30
13	tma tubemakers of aust.	− .011	1.070	− .009	.951	.55
19	tnt thomas nat. trans.	− .004	.981	− .004	.947	.46
19	tpt transpec holdings	.005	.289	.004	.328	.05
4	trg trio group ltd	.004	.315	.001	.454	.14
23	tth tooth and co. ltd	.013	.307	.016	.145	.03
3	upr united petroleum	− .004	.525	− .011	.899	.07
1	vam vam ltd	− .041	1.374	− .035	1.052	.14

Ind		Company name	Scholes–Williams		Ord. Least Squares		
			Alpha	Beta	Alpha	Beta	rsq
1	vlt	valiant consolidated	− .046	1.471	− .043	1.299	.15
8	weg	weston (george)	.011	.521	.011	.535	.38
8	wjm	white (joe) maltings	.005	.132	.004	.193	.04
17	wlw	woolworths ltd	.005	.736	.006	.685	.38
1	wmc	western mining corp.	− .018	.856	− .024	1.232	.60
12	woi	wormald internat.	− .005	.805	− .005	.826	.47
3	wpl	woodside petroleum	− .042	1.637	− .038	1.412	.45
3	wpm	weeks petroleum ltd	− .028	1.656	− .028	1.631	.50
5	wrw	wright (walter) ind.	− .001	.147	− .003	.269	.06
4	wsf	westfield holdings	.012	1.059	.013	1.046	.36
5	wyl	wattyl limited	.007	.736	.014	.338	.11
1	yor	york resources n1	− .056	.783	− .056	.800	.04

Results by industry

Ind	N	S–W		OLS		
		Alpha	Beta	Alpha	Beta	rsq
1	38	− .029	1.216	− .029	1.222	.223
2	9	− .043	1.380	− .037	1.087	.268
3	21	− .037	1.581	− .033	1.395	.289
4	11	.007	.752	.009	.641	.236
5	17	.003	.662	.004	.577	.267
6	7	0.000	.526	− .001	.639	.221
7	5	.017	.531	.018	.493	.158
8	11	.017	.379	.017	.365	.162
11	4	− .002	.612	− .002	.568	.287
12	7	− .006	.885	− .003	.715	.231
13	10	− .006	.664	− .007	.667	.283
14	4	.002	.463	.002	.455	.275
15	7	.009	.376	.009	.380	.160
16	4	.018	.325	.021	.165	.020
17	6	.009	.720	.011	.607	.262
18	2	− .003	.809	.002	.564	.245
19	6	− .001	.718	0.000	.622	.275
20	6	.013	.547	.014	.521	.138
21	4	.005	.368	.006	.292	.170
22	20	.007	.522	.009	.380	.137
23	12	.001	.776	.002	.738	.245
24	4	− .018	1.070	− .017	1.021	.558
All	217	− .007	.842	− .006	.767	.228

Note: Industry number reference is from AGSM. It refers to the AASE classification number.

11 The relationship between accounting variables and systematic risk and the prediction of systematic risk

A. D. Castagna and Z. P. Matolcsy

Introduction

Capital market theory predicts that systematic risk is the only relevant measure of risk for the pricing of securities.[1] The models of price equilibrium which emerge from this theory provide the framework for the empirical studies which support the notion that capital markets are efficient (Fama 1970a). These developments question the traditional role of historical accounting information in security valuation, thus providing a stimulus to seek alternate roles for historical accounting information.[2] The aim of this chapter is twofold: first, to conduct a number of tests of association between accounting information and systematic risk; and second, to develop and evaluate the performance of a number of models for the prediction of systematic risk.

The need for an inquiry along these lines is suggested by Beaver, Kettler and Scholes (1970) who state: "Previous research would suggest that financial statement ratios can be used as measures of default risk, but little is known of their associations with the concept of risk as defined in portfolio theory." The theoretical foundation and empirical support for the determinants of systematic risk is examined by a number of researchers. Hamada (1969, 1972) provides the theoretical analysis and empirical support for the relationship between capital structure and systematic risk. Lev (1974) provides empirical support for the association between operating leverage and systematic risk; and Rubinstein (1973) demonstrates the existence of a positive relationship between operating risk and systematic risk. Beaver, Kettler and Scholes (1970) develop accounting measures of risk based upon growth, earnings variability and dividend payout, among other measures, and compare the predictive ability of those variables against the predictive ability of the market measure of risk. The results of the Beaver, Kettler and Scholes (BKS) study indicate that, for United States data, a model based upon accounting measures of risk outperforms a predictive model based upon the market

Reprinted from the *Australian Journal of Management* 3, no. 2 (October 1978), 113–26, by permission of the authors and the publisher.

measure of systematic risk. Other researchers subsequently investigate the relationship between the market measure of risk and accounting measures of systematic risk, and between the market measure of risk and other financial characteristics.[3] These studies confirm the association between the market measure of risk and historical accounting information. The results of three major United States studies are summarised in table 11.1.

Table 11.1   Results of three US studies for the tests of correlation between market-determined measures of risk and accounting variables

1(a) Beaver, Kettler and Scholes (1970, table 5)

Variables	1947–1956 period		1957–1965 period	
	Individual level	Portfolio level	Individual level	Portfolio level
Earnings variability	0.66	0.90	0.45	0.82
Dividend payout	−0.49	−0.79	−0.29	−0.50
Leverage	0.23	0.41	0.22	0.48
Asset growth	0.27	0.56	0.01	0.02
Asset size	−0.06	−0.09	−0.16	−0.30
Liquidity	−0.13	−0.35	0.05	0.40

1(b) Bildersee (1975, table 3)

Variables	Coefficient
Debt to equity	0.364
Preferred stocks/Common stocks	0.221
Sales/Common equity	0.319
Current assets/Current liabilities	−0.261
Standard deviation of earnings-to-price ratio	0.319

1(c) Thompson (1976, table 4)

Variables	Individual security level	Portfolio level
Averages of 1960–1968 ratios		
Dividend payout	−0.37	−0.76
Asset growth	0.21	0.56
Total debt/Total assets	0.24	0.53
Pretax interest coverage	−0.23	−0.41

The results presented in this chapter indicate some similarities with the results of the United States studies. They also indicate some important dissimilarities which may reflect the underlying structural differences between the Australian and United States corporate sectors.

The experimental design is now outlined and the observed relationships between historical accounting information and systematic risk are later examined. The chapter concludes with the development and evaluation of the performance of a number of predictive models of systematic risk.

Experimental design: Sample

The study is based on a random sample of 140 companies which meet the following selection criteria:

1. Each company must have been listed on the "industrial" section by the Australian Associated Stock Exchanges. Companies primarily involved in banking, finance and mining were omitted.
2. Each company must have been in continual existence for the 10-year period 1967–76. This criterion permitted an examination of structural changes which might have occurred during the period. In addition, it facilitated the implementation of validation tests for the predictive models developed in this study.
3. Each company must have had a 30 June balance date to facilitate contemporaneous comparisons.

The selection criteria outlined above are biased towards the more successful, older companies. The extent and direction of this bias on the results is difficult to ascertain.

Data

The thirteen variables examined were twelve accounting-based variables and a measure of trading volume. They are selected from the ACD Maxi File, described in Castagna (1976). These variables are listed in table 11.2, together with their mean values for two 5-year subperiods of 1967–71 and 1972–76, and for the 10-year period 1967–76. With the exception of the leverage measures, there is no established theoretical foundation to justify the variables selected. Accordingly, the criteria for selecting the remaining variables and the guidance for the *a priori* expectations between these variables and systematic risk are formulated upon the empirical studies of previous researchers.[4]

Table 11.2 List of variables and their mean values over the indicated periods

Variables	1967–71 Mean	1972–76 Mean	1967–76 Mean
Debt/Equity (at book value)	47.80	48.68	48.50
Debt/Total assets	18.56	20.33	19.44
Debt/Market value of common equity	45.45	55.99	53.24
Liquid ratio	0.99	0.96	0.97
Current ratio	1.59	1.54	1.57
EBIT/Total assets	13.68	13.75	13.71
Return to s/hold. fund	9.30	9.44	9.33
Payout ratio	55.28	53.36	54.74
Interest cover	41.76	18.85	38.44
EPS growth	7.02	8.65	9.05
EPS volatility	13.66	30.91	31.97
Log. asset size	9.63	10.31	10.04
Trading volume	824.62	565.45	692.01
Beta	0.98	1.03	1.00

The first three variables are measures of financial structure. The measure of debt in each instance incorporates total short- and long-term financial debt, including bank overdraft. A positive relationship is expected between financial structure and systematic risk because of the results of Hamada (1969, 1972). The liquid and current ratios reflect measures of liquidity. The current ratio is measured by total current assets divided by total current liabilities. The liquid ratio excludes stocks and bank overdrafts from the measures of total current assets and total current liabilities, respectively. An inverse relationship between the measures of liquidity and systematic risk is expected, based on the studies of Beaver, Kettler and Scholes (1970) and Bildersee (1975).

The measures of profitability are the ratio of earnings before interest and tax (EBIT) to total assets, and the return to shareholders' funds, the latter being defined as net profit available to ordinary shareholders divided by total shareholders' funds. In a competitive economy, a positive relationship is expected between the measures of profitability and systematic risk. A negative relationship is expected between the dividend payout ratio and systematic risk, as dividend payout presumably reflects management's perceptions association with future earnings. Interest coverage is measured as the ratio of EBIT to interest. This variable reflects the ability to meet fixed-interest commitments and is expected to be negatively related to systematic risk. The posited relationship between the measures of profitability, dividend payout ratio, interest coverage and systematic risk is supported by the studies of Beaver, Kettler and Scholes (1970) and Thompson (1976).

The growth in earnings per share (EPS) is measured by the slope of a trend line derived from an EPS series. The standard error of the trend estimate is the measure of volatility in the growth of EPS. There is an expected positive relationship between the growth and volatility of EPS and systematic risk. The reasons posited for these expectations are that high earnings growth can be achieved only at a higher risk in a competitive economy.[5] In addition, the higher the volatility of growth in earnings, the greater the risk of not being able to service fixed commitments.

Company size is approximated by the logarithmic transformation of total assets. There is an expected inverse or zero relationship between size and systematic risk. Theory suggests that large companies would be less risky than small companies only if the average systematic risk of the assets in which they invest is lower than that of small companies. Empirical evidence (Castagna and Matolcsy 1977) suggests that the frequency of failure is higher with small companies, although there is no theoretical link between company failure and systematic risk.

Trading volume reflects the activity and marketability of a company's security. It is difficult to establish the expected relationship between trading volume and systematic risk because of some interpretational conflicts. For example, given the relative thinness of the Australian market, one can suggest that the more marketable a security, the less its holding risk. Alternatively, one can suggest that the greater the incidence and frequency of trading, the greater a security's price volatility and, consequently, the greater its relative riskiness.

Systematic risk is estimated through the "market model" using an ordinary least-squares technique, from a regression of a security's rate of return (R_i) with the market rate of return (R_m) over time (t). The market model is:

$$R_{it} = \alpha_i + \beta_i R_{mt} + \epsilon_{it}$$

where α_i and β_i are constants, and ϵ_i is a disturbance term. Month-end prices adjusted for capitalisation changes are used to estimate R_{it}, and R_{mt} is approximated by the unweighted return[6] of all companies which constitute the ACD Maxi File.

There is evidence that the estimates of the β coefficient (systematic risk) are biased and tend to revert toward the mean of unity.[7] A number of interdependent sources of measurement error contribute to the bias in the estimated β coefficient, particularly in a "thin" market. These include errors in the estimates of security returns and in the construction of a market index. In addition, the procedure of expressing the independent variable (R_{mt}) as the sum of the dependent variables (R_{it}) in the estimation of systematic risk violates the independence of errors assumption in ordinary least-squares regression.[8]

The association between the accounting variables and systematic risk

The product moment and rank correlation between the estimates of systematic risk and each variable are computed at the individual-security level and at the portfolio level for the periods 1967–71, 1972–76 and 1967–76. The portfolios comprise 5 and 10 securities each, and are derived by ranking (from highest to lowest) the estimated systematic risk of the individual securities. This results in 28 portfolios with 5 securities and 14 portfolios with 10 securities. The results of the association tests for each period are contained in tables 11.3 to 11.5.

Table 11.3 Association between market determined measure of risk and the accounting and non-accounting-based variables

| | Period 1967–71 | | | | | |
| | Individual level | | Portfolio of 5 securities | | Portfolio of 10 securities | |
Variables	Product mom. correlation	Rank correlation	Product mom. correlation	Rank correlation	Product mom. correlation	Rank correlation
Debt/Equity	0.17	0.06	0.37	0.15	0.53	0.24
Debt/Total assets	0.16	0.03	0.28	0.15	0.39	0.12
Debt/Market value	−0.05	−0.05	−0.09	−0.18	−0.01	−0.16
Liquid ratio	−0.09	−0.08	−0.18	−0.06	−0.23	−0.09
Current ratio	−0.07	−0.02	−0.14	0.00	−0.18	0.06
EBIT/Total assets	0.05	0.08	0.11	0.03	0.15	0.13
Return to s/hold. funds	0.13	0.19	0.25	0.35	0.34	0.38
Payout ratio	−0.18	−0.18	−0.31	−0.19	−0.46	−0.62
Interest cover	−0.05	−0.04	−0.10	−0.02	−0.16	−0.11
EPS growth	0.19	0.13	0.33	0.30	0.38	0.46
EPS volatility	0.01	0.02	0.03	0.03	0.05	0.00
Log. asset size	0.20	0.22	0.39	0.42	0.57	0.56
Trading volume	0.31	0.36	0.65	0.62	0.81	0.79

In each period, the results confirm the expected positive relationship between systematic risk and the variables: debt to equity, debt to total assets, EBIT to total assets, return on shareholders' funds, and growth in EPS. The expected positive relationship between systematic risk and earnings growth volatility are not consistent at either the individual or the portfolio level in the three time periods. This finding is difficult to interpret. We suggest that the

Table 11.4 Association between market determined measure of risk and the accounting and non-accounting-based variables

| | Period 1972–76 | | | | | |
| | Individual level | | Portfolio of 5 securities | | Portfolio of 10 securities | |
Variables	Product mom. correlation	Rank correlation	Product mom. correlation	Rank correlation	Product mom. correlation	Rank correlation
Debt/Equity	0.33	0.25	0.67	0.49	0.73	0.55
Debt/Total assets	0.32	0.23	0.68	0.51	0.71	0.62
Debt/Market value	0.03	0.06	0.06	0.14	0.04	0.20
Liquid ratio	−0.19	−0.12	−0.33	−0.23	−0.36	−0.28
Current ratio	−0.16	−0.07	−0.27	−0.07	−0.36	−0.10
EBIT/Total assets	0.05	0.11	0.16	0.25	0.30	0.39
Return to s/hold. funds	0.17	0.20	0.44	0.43	0.68	0.50
Payout ratio	−0.16	−0.11	−0.30	−0.29	−0.41	−0.34
Interest cover	−0.18	−0.12	−0.38	−0.45	−0.47	−0.51
EPS growth	0.09	0.09	0.20	0.33	0.26	0.40
EPS volatility	−0.15	−0.10	−0.36	−0.29	−0.40	−0.36
Log. asset size	0.49	0.48	0.76	0.68	0.90	0.85
Trading volume	0.36	0.32	0.54	0.55	0.64	0.57

Table 11.5 Association between market determined measure of risk and the accounting and non-accounting-based variables

| | Period 1967–76 | | | | | |
| | Individual level | | Portfolio of 5 securities | | Portfolio of 10 securities | |
Variables	Product mom. correlation	Rank correlation	Product mom. correlation	Rank correlation	Product mom. correlation	Rank correlation
Debt/Equity	0.19	0.19	0.39	0.19	0.49	0.20
Debt/Total assets	0.31	0.17	0.60	0.30	0.64	0.38
Debt/Market value	0.04	0.02	0.09	0.10	0.15	0.16
Liquid ratio	−0.15	−0.09	−0.29	−0.18	−0.39	−0.10
Current ratio	−0.14	−0.03	−0.30	−0.15	−0.36	0.02
EBIT/Total assets	0.05	0.09	0.14	0.23	0.28	0.38
Return to s/hold. funds	0.24	0.23	0.50	0.43	0.65	0.55
Payout ratio	−0.20	−0.10	−0.37	−0.26	−0.56	−0.33
Interest cover	−0.10	−0.10	−0.27	−0.25	−0.35	−0.38
EPS growth	0.27	0.27	0.50	0.47	0.57	0.57
EPS volatility	−0.07	0.06	−0.18	−0.16	−0.25	−0.27
Log. asset size	0.46	0.45	0.80	0.82	0.91	0.90
Trading volume	0.41	0.36	0.77	0.63	0.83	0.73

unexpected relationship between systematic risk and earnings volatility might be a function of the measurement errors associated with the least-squares estimate of earnings volatility. The expected positive relationship between debt-to-market value and systematic risk is confirmed in the periods 1972–76 and 1967–76. However, there is a consistent but statistically insignificant (at the 5 per cent level) negative relationship at both the individual and portfolio level in the period 1967–71. In addition, table 11.2 shows that the average debt-to-market value ratio is lower during this period than the average for the periods 1972–76 and 1967–76. This result might reflect the peculiarity of the stockmarket condition during the "boom" period of the late sixties. Trading volume is positively related to systematic risk, which suggests that the more frequently traded securities have, on average, a higher price volatility than the market.

The results confirm the expected negative relationship between systematic risk and the variables: liquid ratio, current ratio, payout ratio and interest coverage.[9] The expected relationship between asset size and systematic risk is not confirmed. The evidence indicates a significant positive relationship in all periods, which is contrary to the United States findings (Beaver, Kettler and Scholes 1970). There could be a number of economic factors that explain the unexpected relationship between size and systematic risk. For example, the relatively small size of the domestic market has led to concentration in key industries in order to achieve economies of scale. Paradoxically, this development has promoted not only the size of companies in many of the key industries, but also the sensitivity of large companies to anticipated and actual changes in the economic climate. Another possible explanation is that large companies in Australia undertake projects which are more risky than the projects undertaken by small companies. The pursuit of this line of inquiry is beyond the scope of this chapter, but forms the basis of a further study.[10]

The prediction of systematic risk

This section develops and evaluates the performance of a number of market-based models of systematic risk. Models based on accounting variables are not considered as the timing of the interaction between accounting variables and systematic risk has not yet been specified.[11] The motiviation is to establish benchmarks for the evaluation of future studies concerned with the performance of accounting-based versus market-based models of systematic risk.

Four market-based models that make differing assumptions about the behaviour of systematic risk are developed and evaluated. The total sample period is divided into three subperiods, and the models are developed over two periods of 40 months, January 1967 to April 1970 and May 1970 to August 1973. The predictive ability of the models is evaluated in a third non-contemporaneous period, September 1973 to December 1976, by comparing the actual versus the predicted beta estimates for this period.

The performance evaluation criteria are the calculated mean value of errors, the mean square value of errors, and the mean absolute value of errors, where the error is the difference between the predicted and actual systematic risk of the sample companies. In addition, the Wilcoxon rank sign test for significance is calculated for each of the error metrics.

The first model to explain systematic risk assumes the existence of stability (or no change) from the prior period's measure of systematic risk. Essentially, this model implies that the best predictor of future systematic risk is the current measure of systematic risk (i.e., $\beta_3 = \beta_2$). The second model implies that the best predictor of systematic risk is unity (i.e., $\beta_3 = 1$), as this is the prior for all betas. The third and fourth models assume the need to specifically adjust for the mean reversion tendencies of systematic risk. The third model utilises the cross-sectional information of the first and second subperiods in its formulation (i.e., $\beta_2 = a + b\beta_1 + \epsilon$). The fourth model utilises a Bayesian revision procedure to adjust the estimates of systematic risk. The extent of adjustment depends upon the variance of the sample regression coefficients:

$$\beta_3 = [\bar{\beta}_2 / S^2 (\bar{\beta}_2) + \beta_{i2} / S^2 (\beta_{i2})] / [S^{-2} (\bar{\beta}_2) + S^{-2} (\beta_{i2})]$$

where: $\bar{\beta}_2$ is the sample mean of the β estimates in period 2; $S^2 (\bar{\beta}_2)$ is the variance of the sample mean; β_{i2} is the β estimate of company i in period 2; and $S^2 (\beta_{i2})$ is the variance of the β estimate for company i in period 2.[12]

Table 11.6 Summary of forecast errors

	$\beta_3 = \beta_2$	$\beta_3 = 1$	$\beta_3 = 0.541 + 0.464\beta_2$	$\beta_3 = f(\beta_2, \bar{\beta}_2, S^2_{\beta_2}, S^2_{\bar{\beta}_2})$
Mean value of error	0.053	0.027*	0.035*	0.054
Mean square value of error	0.175	0.217	0.140	0.170
Mean absolute value of error	0.342	0.341	0.280	0.336

*The sum of the regression coefficients is not unity and the mean value of error is not zero as the market index comprised the unweighted return of all companies on the ACD maxi file.

The performance of these models is listed in table 11.6. The third model outperforms all others on the basis of mean square and mean absolute errors. The Wilcoxon rank sign tests indicate that these error metrics are significantly lower, at the 1 per cent level, for the third model relative to the other models. However, the mean error for the third model compared with that of the second model is higher but not statistically significant. These results confirm the predictive superiority of models which adjust for the convergence characteristics of systematic risk by utilising cross-sectional information. In this respect, the findings are similar to those of Blume (1975).

Conclusion

The tests of association conducted in this study confirm a relationship between accounting variables and systematic risk. The results indicate both the similarities and dissimilarities to the results of United States-based studies. The study also suggests the need for further research in a number of areas: first, to explain the positive relationship between size and systematic risk; second, to explore the lead/lag relationship between accounting variables and systematic risk; and, finally, to compare the performance of correctly specified accounting-based models relative to that of market-based models of systematic risk.

Acknowledgments

The helpful comments of George Foster and Joe Winsen and the programming assistance of Clarke Gerber are acknowledged. The financial support of the

Special Projects Grant of the Commerce Faculty, University of New South Wales is also gratefully acknowledged.

Notes

1. Systematic risk is defined as the covariance of security returns with the market returns, divided by the variance of returns for the market. See Sharpe (1964), Lintner (1965a) and Mossin (1966).
2. For example, studies of the usefulness of accounting information for the prediction of company failures, such as Altman (1968), and company acquisitions, such as Castagna and Matolcsy (1976).
3. For example, Gonedes (1973), Bildersee (1975), Beaver and Manegold (1975). See Foster (1978b, ch. 9) for an overview of this research.
4. Beaver, Kettler and Scholes (1970), Bildersee (1975) and Thompson (1976).
5. If the growth in EPS measures expansion rather than actual growth, then this expected relationship might not hold.
6. Alternatively, the market rate of return is approximated by a weighted index using the Sydney All Ordinaries Index. The resulting estimates of systematic risk are systematically lower, notwithstanding the high observed rank correlation coefficients between the weighted and unweighted market returns (0.85). The rank correlation coefficients between the systematic risk estimates based on the weighted and unweighted market returns are 0.823, 0.960 and 0.903 for the periods 1967–71, 1972–76 and 1967–76, respectively. A possible explanation for this difference could be the somewhat arbitrary and constant weighting which is assigned to the industry groups that are included in the All Ordinaries Index. The results based on the All Ordinaries Index are not reported.
7. Blume (1975) provides economic reasons to explain the mean reversion tendencies of the β coefficient: namely, that a company's new investment projects have a β closer to unity than the existing portfolio of projects, or that the existing portfolio of projects move closer to unity over time.
8. These and related issues have been raised by Ball (1977) and Roll (1977).
9. Table 11.3 shows that there is a positive but insignificant relationship between current ratio and systematic risk for the period 1967–71.
10. A positive relationship between size and systematic risk also is supported in a pilot study which uses the beta estimates of Brown and Walter (1974).
11. Beaver, Kettler and Scholes (1970) and Holthausen (1976) do not explicitly consider the lead/lag relationship between accounting variables and systematic risk in developing accounting-based models. This introduces a bias in the validation tests of the predictive ability of accounting-based versus market-based models of systematic risk. The lack of explicit recognition of the lead/lag relationship could explain the reported superiority of accounting-based models. The specification of the lead/lag relationship between accounting variables and systematic risk is the subject of an independent inquiry. A preliminary examination of accounting-based models is reported in Castagna and Matolcsy (1978b).
12. For a more detailed discussion on the Bayesian revision procedure refer to Vasicek (1973).

12 Measuring abnormal performance on the Australian securities market

T.J. Shevlin

Introduction

Brown and Warner (BW) (1980) used Monte Carlo techniques to examine the performance of the methodologies employed in empirical testing of the semi-strong form of the efficient-market hypothesis. The BW study was based on monthly return data from the New York Stock Exchange. This chapter reports the results of similar tests carried out on Australian security return data. The results generally but not fully support those reported by BW.

There have been numerous studies carried out testing the share market response to the public release of information. Most studies have found that the particular share market studied was efficient with respect to the information release.[1] These studies are tests of a joint hypothesis: firstly, that the market is efficient with respect to the information being released, and secondly, that the methodology used in the test is "correct". This chapter is concerned with testing the second part of this joint hypothesis.

Most tests of the semi-strong EMH compare the actual security returns observed around the event date (the date when the information first became publicly available) with the expected or normal returns if there had been no event. The residual or difference between the observed and expected returns is the excess or abnormal rate of return.[2] It is the calculation of these expected returns that is of concern in this study. Various methods are tested; all, however, are consistent with (but need not depend on) the assumption that the capital asset-pricing model determines equilibrium-expected returns.

It is possible that different models of expected returns could lead to different inferences about the market reaction to public releases of information. Ball (1972a), Brown, Finn and Hancock (1977) and Brenner (1979) in their event studies examined different modelling procedures. Generally, the results were consistent between the procedures within each study.

Reprinted from the *Australian Journal of Management* 6, no. 1 (June, 1981), 67-107, by permission of the author and the publisher.

However, a more thorough and robust analysis of the abnormal performance methodologies can be carried out by the controlled simulation of "events". The procedure involves constructing 250 portfolios of N securities each (by random selection of securities and "event" dates), then introducing abnormal returns into the security returns and assessing the performance of the different methodologies in deteching this abnormal performance. When there is no abnormal performance introduced, the null hypothesis of no abnormal performance should be accepted; and when abnormal performance is simulated, the null hypothesis should be rejected. With 250 replications or portfolios, it is possible to assess the performance of the methodologies by their Type I errors—rejecting the null when it is true—and Type II errors—accepting the null when it is false. To detect these errors it is necessary to apply significance tests to the abnormal returns calculated under the different methodologies. Various significance tests are studies.

The test procedure enables an estimate to be made of the power of the different methodologies. The power of a test is defined here as the probability, for a given level of Type I error and a given level of abnormal performance, that the null hypothesis of no abnormal performance will be rejected. This probability is estimated by the frequency of rejections of the null hypothesis across the 250 portfolios.

This chapter is organised into sections. First, there is a discussion of the measurement of abnormal performance and the methodologies tested are defined. The next section outlines and defines the significance test statistics employed to test the significance of portfolio abnormal returns. The experimental design and data employed in this research are outlined in the next section. The results are presented in the following sections. Various tests have been carried out: each is discussed and detailed tables are included illustrating the performance of the models and significance tests under the different simulated conditions. The conclusions are presented in the last section.

The measurement of abnormal performance

A security's abnormal return performance can be calculated only by reference to some benchmark or normal return. It is therefore necessary to specify some model or process that generates these normal returns. BW specify three different processes; under each process the difference between a security j's observed rate of return in period t $(\tilde{R}_{jt})$ and its normal (or *ex ante* expected) rate of return $E(\tilde{R}_{jt})$ is referred to as the security's abnormal return or residual $\tilde{u}_{jt}$. That is,

$$\tilde{u}_{jt} = \tilde{R}_{jt} - E(\tilde{R}_{jt}), \tag{1}$$

where the tilde denotes a random variable.

In an efficient market realised returns should not systematically differ from *ex ante* expected returns, which means that $E(\tilde{u}_{jt}) = 0$. Further $\tilde{u}_{jt}$ is assumed to be independent of all other variables in the model generating the equilibrium-expected returns, and in this sense we refer to the abnormal performance measured $\tilde{u}_{jt}$ as being unbiased for each model.

In an attempt to isolate the effect of some event on security returns, it is necessary to form those securities which have experienced the event into portfolios. This is because some securities in the portfolio may have experienced positive abnormal returns and others negative abnormal returns owing to the occurrence of other events. However, a cross-sectional average

$$A\tilde{R}_t = \frac{1}{N} \sum_{j=1}^{N} \tilde{u}_{jt} \qquad (2)$$

of these abnormal returns will have an expected value of zero. Whether it is zero or not (or significantly different from zero) is a function of the variance of the residuals which in turn is a function of the types of events (or information releases) causing the security prices to change. The smaller the variance (of the residuals), the more powerful the test in detecting abnormal performance. Models that reduce this variance may therefore be more powerful.

In event studies, the event date is designated $t = 0$ and time is then measured relative to this date. In this study, as in most event studies, abnormal returns are examined for a period surrounding the event month; the event period studied here is the 12 months either side of $t = 0$. By calculating the cumulative abnormal returns,[3] defined as

$$C\tilde{A}R_t = \sum_{t=-12}^{+12} A\tilde{R}_t \qquad (3)$$

we can assess firstly whether the market reacted at all to the public release of the information (the information content of the variable under study), and secondly the timing of any observed market response (the efficiency of the market).

The definitions of the models excamined in this chapter are:

General Model	*Specific empirical model*	*Notation*	
Mean-adjusted returns	mean-adjusted model	$\tilde{u}_{jt} = \tilde{R}_{jt} - \tilde{R}_j$	(4)
Market-adjusted returns	zero-one model	$\tilde{u}_{jt} = \tilde{R}_{jt} - \tilde{R}_{mt}$	(5)
Market- and risk-adjusted returns	market model	$\tilde{u}_{jt} = \tilde{R}_{jt} - (\hat{a}_j + \hat{\beta}_j \tilde{R}_{Mt})$	(6)
	cross-sectional model	$\tilde{u}_{jt} = \tilde{R}_{jt} - (\tilde{\gamma}_{0t} + \tilde{\gamma}_{1t}\tilde{\beta}_j)$	(7)

The mean-adjusted returns model assumes that the expected return for security j is equal to the mean returns ($\bar{R}_j$) of that security over some previous period. A simple method and the method employed here is to calculate $\bar{R}_j$ over the 30-month period preceding the start of the event period.[4]

The market-adjusted returns model assumes that expected returns are constant across all securities, but not necessarily constant over time. In effect this model assumes that the individual security returns are explained only in terms of market variability. Tests were conducted using an equally weighted index of market returns which was calculated as an average of all the security returns on the Brown price file (described below).

The market- and risk-adjusted returns models are usually based on the presumption that some version of the capital asset pricing model (CAPM) generates returns. The market model is usually related to the Sharpe–Lintner version of the CAPM and the cross-sectional model is normally developed from the more general version of the two-parameter CAPM as presented by Black (1972). However, as pointed out by Officer (1980), the market model need not be interpreted in the CAPM framework. Similar arguments are advanced for the cross-sectional model by Ball, Brown and Finn (1977).

In the market model, α_j and β_j are estimated using ordinary least-squares (OLS) regression [5] with α_j being the intercept term and β_j the slope coefficient referred to as the security's systematic or relative risk.

In the cross-sectional model $\tilde{\gamma}_{0t}$ is the return on any portfolio that has zero covariance with the market: $E(\tilde{\gamma}_{0t}) = E(\tilde{R}_{zt})$ in the Black CAPM, the expected return on a zero β portfolio. $\tilde{\gamma}_{1t}$, is an estimate of the *ex post* difference between the returns on the market and zero β portfolio. It is expected risk premium per unit of β. Note that $\tilde{\gamma}_{0t}$, $\tilde{\gamma}_{1t}$, referred to here as the marketwide factors, are estimated from cross-sectional OLS regression methods,[6] and that they differ from calendar month to calendar month, but for a given calendar month they are the same for all securities.

If we compare the equations for the market and cross-sectional models we can observe that the residuals from the one-factor market model contain variation in the market factors $\tilde{\gamma}_{01}$, $\tilde{\gamma}_{1t}$. Thus it is argued (e.g. see Ball 1972a) that if one is interested in the effect on a security's return of an event specific to a given firm, this effect can probably best be studied more precisely using the residuals of the two-factor cross-sectional model.

It is expected that the models based on the risk/return relationship would be more powerful in detecting abnormal performance, because they bring into account additional information about the process determining expected (and realised) returns. However, these models may not dominate the simpler mean-adjusted returns models and, to a lesser extent, the market-adjusted returns model for the following reasons.

Firstly the market portfolio R_{Mt} in the CAPM cannot be observed directly; rather, some surrogate measure needs to be employed in empirical tests. The surrogate employed here, and that which is commonly used, is an equally weighted index of the returns of securities listed on some stock exchange.

Secondly, there are measurement problems associated with estimating a security's systematic risk. These estimates are subject to sampling error, and although these measurement errors need not introduce any systematic bias into empirical tests, with small samples the error may be so large as to reduce the power of the more precisely specified return models.[7]

Thirdly, at the empirical level there are several variants as to how to allow for the risk/return relationships of the CAPM in computing the residuals. The variants to be tested here are the market model and the cross-sectional model.[8] Which one is better, if either, is an empirical question which it is hoped will be resolved in this paper.

Finally, as pointed out by BW (1980, p. 210) the residuals of a model need to satisfy the additional assumptions which must be made in order to test the hypothesis of no abnormal performance. If the assumptions of the significance tests are not met, then the model may not be appropriate.

It is possible to reconcile the simpler methodologies with the more fully specified CAP models. The expected returns under the mean-adjusted returns model will be consistent with the CAPM when security j has constant (over time) systematic risk and the efficient frontier is stationary. The market-adjusted returns model is consistent with the CAPM if security j has unit systematic risk (hence the reason it is referred to as the zero-one model).

Assessing the significance of portfolio abnormal returns

To be able to talk in terms of accepting or rejecting the null hypothesis, it is necessary to be able to test whether the observed result is statistically significantly different from the value postulated in the null hypothesis.[9]

When data may appropriately be analysed by a parametric test (e.g., the t-test) that test will be more powerful than any other in rejecting the null hypothesis (H_0) when it is false. Sufficient conditions to make the t-test the most powerful one are that the residuals must be independently and identically distributed. However, it is argued (e.g., Dodd 1976; Ball, Brown and Finn 1977) that it is unlikely that the residuals (of each of the models) are identically (and normally) distributed across time and securities. Alternative statistical tests which do not make this strong assumption are the non-parametric tests. These distribution-free statistical tests do require, however, that the sample observations be independent. Both parametric and non-parametric test statistics were employed to assess the significance of portfolio abnormal returns.

Thus far, the null hypothesis has been defined in general terms only, as no portfolio abnormal performance. More specifically, two different hypotheses were examined, referred to as event-month tests and event-period tests. In the event-month tests the null hypothesis is that the portfolio does not exhibit normal performance in the event month $t = 0$; that is H_0: $\tilde{A}R_{t=0} = 0.0$.

In the event-period tests the null hypothesis is H_0: $\overline{AR} = 0.0$ where $\overline{AR} = C\tilde{A}R_t / t$. In effect, the null to be tested now is whether the mean monthly portfolio performance $\overline{AR}$ over the event interval (covering a number of months) is significantly different from zero.

Significance test definitions

In the hypothesis tests, the t-test was calculated as:

Event-month tests	Event-period tests
$(A\tilde{R}_t - \mu) / S_{A\tilde{R}_t}$	$(\overline{AR} - \mu) / S_{A\tilde{R}}$

where $S_{A\tilde{R}_t}$, $S_{\overline{AR}}$ are the sample estimates of the population standard deviations, and μ is the population mean and is assumed equal to zero.

Three different methods of estimating the standard error were examined; table 12.1 shows these.

The standard error estimate of the distribution of residuals around the portfolio mean in the event month ($t = 0$) only is used in t-test -1. An alternative method of estimating the standard error, t-test -2, employs the distribution of the company residuals around the securities' own abnormal performance calculated over the event period. It is argued that this brings into account more information about the variance of the residuals. The third t-test procedure attempts to take into account cross-sectional dependence between the residuals. As the method is reasonably crude in its attempt at adjusting for

Table 12.1 Methods of estimating standard error

Test	$S_{A\tilde{R}_t}$ calculated as	$S_{\overline{AR}}$ calculated as*	
−1.	$\dfrac{1}{N^{1/2}}\ (\dfrac{\sum\limits_{j=1}^{N} (\tilde{u}_{jt} - A\tilde{R}_t)^2}{N-1})^{1/2}$	$\dfrac{1}{N^{1/2}}\ (\dfrac{\sum\limits_{j=1}^{N} (\tilde{u}_j - \overline{AR})^2}{N-1})^{1/2}$	(8)
−2.	$\dfrac{1}{N}\ (\sum\limits_{j=1}^{N} [\dfrac{1}{24} \sum\limits_{t=-12}^{+12} (\tilde{u}_{jt} - \tilde{u}_j)^2])^{1/2}$ =	$\dfrac{1}{N^{1/2}}\ (\dfrac{\sum\limits_{j=1}^{N} (\tilde{u}_j - \overline{AR})^2}{N-1})^{1/2} / \sqrt{25}$	(9)
crude-dependence-adjusted t	$(\dfrac{1}{24} [\sum\limits_{t=-12}^{+12} (A\tilde{R}_t - \overline{AR})^2])^{1/2}$ =	$\dfrac{1}{N^{1/2}}\ (\dfrac{\sum\limits_{j=1}^{N} (\tilde{u}_j - \overline{AR})^2}{N-1})^{1/2} / \sqrt{25}$	(10)

$* \ \bar{u}_j = \dfrac{1}{25} \sum\limits_{t=-12}^{+12} \tilde{u}_{jt}; \quad \overline{AR} = \dfrac{1}{25} \sum\limits_{t=-12}^{+12} A\tilde{R}_t = \dfrac{1}{N} \sum\limits_{j=1}^{N} \bar{u}_j$

cross-sectional dependence, and following BW, the best procedure is termed the crude-dependence-adjusted t-test.[10]

t-test −1 is distributed Student-t with $N−1$ degrees of freedom, where N is the number of securities in a portfolio, whereas t-test −2 and the crude-dependence-adjusted t-test are distributed Student-t with 24 degrees of freedom (at least in relation to the definitions of the standard errors above, where they were estimated over the 12 months either side of the event month).

It is possible in the latter two t-tests to estimate the standard error from pre-event-period residuals, event-period residuals or some combination thereof.[11] Tests were conducted using event-period residuals, as defined above, and also with the standard errors estimated from the residuals over the t_{-42} to t_{-13} (pre-event) period. The resulting test statistics, designated (pre), are distributed Student t with 29 degrees of freedom.

Two non-parametric tests were also examined: namely, the sign test and Wilcoxon matched-pairs signed-ranks test.[12] In applying the sign test, attention is focused only on the sign of the residuals. Under H_0 we expect the number of securities with positive residuals to equal the number of securities with negative residuals. If too few scores of one sign occur, H_0 is rejected. Probabilities can be determined by reference to the binomial distribution. When $N > 25$ the normal approximation to the binomial distribution can be used. That is,

$$Z = \frac{(X \pm 0.5) - \mu_x}{\sigma_x} \tag{11}$$

where μ_x = mean = $N/2$,
  σ_x = standard deviation = $(N^{1/2})/2$,
  X = the number of positive residuals in the event month
and $(X \pm 0.5)$ is a correction for continuity.[13]

The sign test simply employs the direction of the securities' abnormal returns.

If the relative magnitude, as well as the distribution of the abnormal returns (score) is utilised, a more powerful test can be constructed. The Wilcoxon test does this by ranking the scores based on their absolute values; after this ranking, each score has its sign attached to it. The sum of the ranks of the positive residuals and the sum of the ranks of the negative residuals are then calculated. Under H_0 we expect these two sums to be about equal. When $N > 25$ we can assess the significance of the difference in sums by calculating

$$Z = \frac{T - \mu_T}{\sigma_T}$$ (12)

where T = the sum of the positive signed ranks,
   μ_T = mean = $N(N + 1)/4$
   and σ_T = standard deviation = $(\frac{N(N + 1)(2N + 1)}{24})^{1/2}$

Under both non-parametric tests, Z is approximately normally distributed with zero mean and unit variance.

Finally, most of the tests carried out in this study are concerned with positive abnormal performance. Since the predicted direction of the abnormal returns is positive, the region of rejection is one-tailed.

Data description and experimental design

The data on which this research is based is the Brown file of monthly price relatives.[14] Initially, the natural logarithm of price relatives was employed, $\tilde{R}_{jt} = ln(P_{jt}/P_{j, t-1})$. This gives rates of return under continuous compounding which are simple to work with and, secondly, and more importantly, given the arguments for the need for normality in the parametric t-tests, as returns are often positively skewed owing to their being in the range -1 to $+ \infty$, a log transformation helps to reduce this skewness.[15] For consistency the values of the market index and marketwide factors ($\tilde{\gamma}_{ot}$ $\tilde{\gamma}_{1t}$) were also calculated and expressed in natural log form.

Not all of the 909 equities on the Brown file were continuously traded over the 16-year period (owing to takeovers, new listings, etc.). To avoid problems of missing data and to allow sufficient observations from which to estimate the parameters of the various models, securities were included on the population list from which portfolios were constructed only if they had a minimum 96 monthly price relatives over the period. This criterion left 456 securities available for constructing portfolios.

Basically, portfolios were constructed using similar procedures as BW (1980, pp. 211–12). An unrestricted random-sampling approach was employed to construct each portfolio.[16] It was unrestricted because the sampling was conducted with replacement; this means a security can appear more than once in a particular portfolio which accords with actual event studies when a particular security experiences the event more than once but at different points in calendar time.

For each security, an hypothetical 'event' month was generated, again using an unrestricted random-sampling approach. To allow for at least a minimum period over which model parameters could be estimated, the first 42 months of data for each security were omitted from the available months from which the event month was selected. Events were assumed to occur with equal probability in each of the remaining months of data available for that security. Within each portfolio (and also across portfolios) events occur in different calendar months for the different securities.

The null hypothesis of no abnormal performance is true and therefore should be accepted when actual rates of return are used. This is because, on average, with a large number of portfolios each constructed by random selection of securities and event-dates, no abnormal performance (given some benchmark of normal) should be exhibited. This allows us to detect Type I errors—rejection of the null when it is true—for each of the methodologies.

To allow us to assess the performance of the methodologies when the null hypothesis is not true, we need to introduce abnormal performance into the security returns. Two different procedures were used; the first procedure simply added a constant to the actual rate of return of the security in the event month. To introduce, for example, a 10 per cent level of abnormal performance for each security in the portfolio, 0.10 is added to the actual rate of return experienced by each security in the month in which that security's hypothetical event is assumed to occur.[17]

The second procedure tested attempts more closely to match the simulation with our expectations of share market reactions to releases of information. Share prices of a group of securities that experience some firm-specific event (e.g., an earnings announcement) will not, it is hypothesised, all react by the same percentage amount (nor possibly in the same direction). The degree of reaction at the date of announcement will be a function of many factors, not the least being the prior information or beliefs held by investors about the firm's announcement and the uncertainty about the implications arising from the announcement for the future price of that security. If, for example, the market participants had overanticipated a firm's earnings, then in the actual announcement period it is possible the announcement might induce a negative price shift.[18] To simulate abnormal performance under these conditions, instead of adding a constant percentage to all securities, amounts were generated on the basis of a normal distribution with a mean equal to the required portfolio abnormal performance. The variance of the distribution was increased as the mean increased so as to hold constant the relative dispersion of the distribution (as measured by the coefficient of variation).

For a given level of abnormal performance introduced into each portfolio the null hypothesis of no abnormal performance is tested for each methodology. If the null is not rejected, this is classified as a Type II error—failure to reject the null when it is false.

It is necessary, when trying to assess whether the different methodologies sytematically result in Type I or Type II errors, not only to take one portfolio but also to make numerous replications with different portfolios. Hence we construct 250 portfolios and concentrate on the proportion of Type I and Type II errors in the 250 replications to assess the ability and power of the methodologies to detect abnormal performance.

Event-month test results

The frequency of rejections of the null hypothesis of no abnormal performance

Table 12.2 Comparison of alternative abnormal performance methodologies—percentage of rejections of the null hypothesis H_0: $AR_{t=0} - 0.0$; based on 250 portfolios of 30 securities each; abnormal performance simulated by adding a constant to all securities in t_0.

Methodology and test statistic	Actual level of abnormal performance in month 0, the event month							
	Significance test level $\alpha = 0.05$				Significance test level $\alpha = 0.01$			
	0%	3%	5%	10%	0%	3%	5%	10%
Zero-one model								
t-test -1	4.0%	65.6	94.0	100.0	1.6%	38.4	82.0	100.0
t-test -2	7.2	58.0	93.2	100.0	1.2	30.4	74.0	100.0
t-test -2 (pre)	8.8	61.2	95.6	100.0	2.8	38.4	77.6	100.0
Crude-dep-adj t	7.6	57.2	90.4	100.0	1.2	23.6	64.8	100.0
Crude-dep-adj t (pre)	9.6	62.0	94.4	100.0	3.2	38.4	78.8	99.6
Sign test	3.2	64.8	94.0	100.0	0.0	40.4	82.0	100.0
Wilcoxon test	4.4	78.0	98.0	100.0	2.0	48.8	89.6	100.0
Market Model								
t-test -1	3.6	65.6	93.2	100.0	1.2	35.2	80.4	100.0
t-test -2	7.2	58.0	92.0	100.0	2.4	30.4	73.6	100.0
t-test -2 (pre)	9.6	64.0	94.4	100.0	4.4	38.8	77.6	100.0
Crude-dep-adj t	7.2	55.6	89.2	100.0	1.2	21.2	66.4	100.0
Crude-dep-adj t (pre)	10.8	64.0	93.6	100.0	4.0	37.6	78.8	100.0
Sign test	3.2	64.4	90.8	100.0	0.4	36.4	81.6	100.0
Wilcoxon test	4.4	75.2	97.6	100.0	1.2	45.2	87.6	100.0

in the event month are rejected in table 12.2 at both the 5 per cent and 1 per cent significance levels using a one-tailed test. Abnormal performance in this test was based on adding a constant amount to all securities.

When there is no abnormal performance simulated, the four methodologies record slightly different rates of rejections. For a methodology to perform satisfactorily it should record a rejection rate of the null hypothesis at approximately the significance test level.

Generally, the sign test, the less powerful of the two non-parametric test statistics examined, performs quite poorly in that it does not reject often enough across the methodologies. At $\alpha = 0.05$, i.e., 5 per cent probability of rejecting the null hypothesis when it is true, the sign test ranges from 2.8 per cent for the mean-adjusted model to 4 per cent for the cross-sectional model. The other non-parametric test, the Wilcoxon signed-ranks statistic, performs well across the different methodologies with an average rejection rate of approximately 5 per cent.

The results for the parametric t-tests are also included in the table for completeness. In this set of tests, where securities and event dates have been selected at random, it is expected that there will be little cross-sectional dependence between residuals. The similarity in rejection rates for the t-tests indicates that this expectation is valid. The tests also indicate that the pre-event t statistics reject the null too often, when it is true, across all four methodologies at both the 5 per cent and 1 per cent significance test levels.

It is important to note that the proportion of rejections when the null is true will not be exactly equal to the significance test level. The rejection rate itself is a random variable with a sampling distribution. Brown and Warner (1980, p. 216) state that if (i) the test statistics are correctly specified and (ii) the proportion of rejections are normally distributed, the rejection rates with 0 per cent abnormal performance should be between 2 per cent (0 per cent) and 8 per cent (2.2 per cent) approximately 95 per cent of the time when testing at the 0.05 (0.01) level.

Some idea of this variation in rejection rates can be obtained if we look at the behaviour of the rejection frequencies in each of the 25 months in the event period. Each of the months in the event period could be treated as event months given that the portfolios were constructed on a random basis. Note, however, these 6,250 portfolios and events (250 x 25) are not strictly independent; for each portfolio there are 25 consecutive event months. If we allow the random-walk hypothesis, it could be argued that each of the event months is independent. Nevertheless, the results in table 12.3 are presented only as a guide to the average rejection rates across the 250 portfolios in each of the successive 25 months of the event period. The figures in table 12.3 show the variability of the rejection rates for a given methodology and significance test. For example, under the market model, with $\alpha = 0.05$, the Wilcoxon test has a highest rejection frequency in any one event month of 8.5 per cent, a lowest rejection frequency of 2.8 per cent and averages 4.592 per cent across all 25 event months for the 250 portfolios.

The results in table 12.3 generally support those drawn above with reference to table 12.2. The sign test simply does not reject the null often enough. The pre-event period t statistics reject the null hypothesis too often.[19] In the absence of abnormal performance no methodology appears superior or inferior to the other methodologies in rejecting the null hypothesis.

As the level of abnormal performance is increased from 0 per cent to 3 per cent to 5 per cent all four models record similar rejection fequencies. With 5 per cent abnormal performance, at $\alpha = 0.05$, the null is rejected on average 92 per cent of the time across all methodologies using t-test -1. The Wilcoxon test performs somewhat better averaging around 96 per cent. At higher levels of abnormal performance the crude-dependence-adjusted t-test performs poorly for each methodology at both $\alpha = 0.05$ and $\alpha = 0.01$ test levels. While the power of the methodologies appeared to increase with the use of the pre-event t statistics (as evidence by the higher rejection rates recorded by these statistics with 3 per cent and 5 per cent abnormal performance simulated) the level of Type I error when there was no abnormal performance varied between the test statistics, making power comparisons difficult and misleading. With 10 per cent abnormal performance simulated, the null is rejected 100 per cent of the time at $\alpha = 0.05$.[20]

The distributional properties of the significance test statistics

The t-tests are based on the Student-t statistic whose distribution varies with sample size. As N increases the t distribution becomes less "flat" and when $N > 120$ the t distribution is virtually identical to the normal distribution. The t distribution is symmetrical regardless of sample size. With large samples ($N > 25$) both the non-parametric tests assume the distribution for the test statistics in hypothesis testing is normally distributed about a mean of zero with unit variance. If the distribution of the test statistic is misspecified then the null hypothesis when true could be rejected with some frequency other than that given by the significance level of the test.

Table 12.3 Details of the percentage of rejections of the null hypothesis of no abnormal performance in each of the 25 months of the event period.*

Methodology and test statistic	Significance test level					
	$\alpha = 0.05$			$\alpha = 0.01$		
	HRR†	LRR†	Mean	HRR	LRR	Mean
Zero-one model						
t-test -1	8.4%	4.0	5.472	2.4%	0.0	0.896
t-test -2	8.4	3.2	4.864	2.0	0.0	0.928
t-test -2 (pre)	9.6	4.0	6.208	3.6	0.4	1.824
Crude-dep-adj t	9.2	2.8	5.296	2.4	0.0	0.896
Crude-dep-adj t (pre)	10.8	4.4	6.928	4.0	0.8	2.208
Sign test	5.6	1.6	2.944	1.2	0.0	0.480
Wilcoxon test	8.4	2.4	5.104	2.4	0.0	0.992
Market model						
t-test -1	8.8	2.8	4.880	2.4	0.0	0.736
t-test -2	8.8	3.2	4.944	2.0	0.4	1.008
t-test -2 (pre)	10.0	3.6	6.432	4.4	0.4	2.064
Crude-dep-adj t	9.2	3.2	5.072	2.4	0.0	0.864
Crude-dep-adj t (pre)	12.0	4.0	7.280	4.4	0.4	2.448
Sign test	5.2	1.2	2.416	1.2	0.0	0.416
Wilcoxon test	8.4	2.8	4.592	3.2	0.0	0.944
Cross-sectional model						
t-test -1	7.6	2.4	5.152	2.8	0.0	0.880
t-test -2	8.0	2.4	4.832	2.0	0.0	0.864
t-test -2 (pre)	12.0	3.6	7.920	4.4	0.4	2.272
Crude-dep-adj t	8.4	2.4	5.408	2.4	0.0	0.928
Crude-dep-adj t (pre)	12.8	4.0	8.224	6.0	0.8	2.768
Sign test	4.8	1.6	3.008	1.2	0.0	0.576
Wilcoxon test	7.6	2.8	5.056	2.4	0.0	0.992
Mean-adjusted model						
t-test -1	8.8	3.2	6.272	2.8	0.0	1.024
t-test -2	9.6	3.2	5.872	3.2	0.0	1.264
t-test -2 (pre)	10.4	5.2	7.696	4.0	0.8	2.256
Crude-dep-adj t	10.0	3.6	6.320	3.6	0.0	1.408
Crude-dep-adj t (pre)	12.4	6.0	8.576	5.2	0.8	2.704
Sign test	5.6	1.2	3.200	1.6	0.0	0.640
Wilcoxon test	8.0	3.6	5.728	3.2	0.4	1.104

* The results are derived from the same tests as underlying table 12.2. The mean is simply calculated as the sum of the number of rejections per 250 portfolios for $t = -12, +12$ divided by 25.

† The highest (lowest) rejection rate HRR (LRR) is simply the observed highest (lowest) rejections of the null hypothesis per 250 portfolios in any of the individual event months $t = -12, +12$.

With the simulation of 250 portfolios it is possible to compute descriptive statistics of the empirical sampling distribution of the test statistics. Following BW (1980), the mean, standard deviation, skewness and kurtosis coefficients[21] as well as two goodness-of-fit statistics, the chi-squared test and the Kolmogorov–Smirnov D statistic,[22] were used to test the empirical sampling distributions for departures from normality.[23] Several different partition sizes were tested, and following Winkler and Hays (1975, p. 824), equiprobable classes were used within each partition size.

The results of the tests are presented in table 12.4. When there is no abnormal performance present the mean of all the test statistic distributions under each model is not significantly different from zero at the 5 per cent significance test level. The distributions of the pre-event versions of the t statistics are more dispersed than their event-period counterparts. Although only one of the distributions displays signs of significant kurtosis at $\alpha = 0.05$, the pre-event t statistic distributions are more peaked than the event-period distributions. Most of the t statistic distributions are not symmetrical, with the pre-event distributions being more highly skewed.[25] Further, the t statistic distributions appear to be less skewed under the simple mean-adjusted model than in the more sophisticated risk/return models. The goodness-of-fit tests reject the null of normality for the sign test distributions at $\alpha = 0.05$ across all four models.[26]

Table 12.4 Descriptive statistics and summary measures of the empirical sampling distributions of the significance test statistics—based on 250 portfolios of 30 securities each; continuously compounded rates of return; 0% abnormal performance.

A. Model and test statistics	Mean	Standard deviation	t stat for mean	Skewness	Kurtosis
Zero-one model					
t-test −1	0.018	0.091	0.267	−0.038	3.015
t-test −2	0.069	1.066	1.026	0.182*	3.043
t-test −2 (pre)	0.088	1.148	1.218	0.312*	3.267
Crude-dep-adjust t	0.064	1.051	0.968	0.137†	2.772
Crude-dep-adjust t (pre)	0.098	1.184	1.311	0.287*	3.233
Sign test	−0.005	0.844	−0.085	−0.016	3.104
Wilcoxon test	0.021	1.034	0.316	−0.062	2.880
Market model					
t-test −1	−0.010	1.118	−0.147	−0.138†	3.249
t-test −2	0.051	1.084	0.745	0.157†	3.046
t-test −2 (pre)	0.071	1.196	0.944	0.266*	3.277
Crude-dep-adjust t	0.045	1.064	0.662	0.110†	2.830
Crude-dep-adjust t (pre)	0.079	1.236	1.008	0.225*	3.372
Sign test	−0.033	0.867	−0.593	0.123†	3.210
Wilcoxon test	−0.033	1.072	−0.485	−0.113*	2.906
Cross-sectional model					
t-test	−0.031	1.102	−0.452	−0.014	3.191
t-test 2	0.040	1.075	0.592	0.301*	3.326
t-test −2 (pre)	0.054	1.214	0.698	0.351*	3.423
Crude-dep-adjust t	0.030	1.044	0.456	0.211*	2.782
Crude-dep-adjust t (pre)	0.060	1.263	0.754	0.314*	3.695†
Sign test	−0.025	0.873	−0.445	0.209*	3.412
Wilcoxon test	−0.020	1.072	−0.297	0.068	2.733
Mean-adjusted model					
t-test −1	0.028	1.069	0.407	−0.161*	2.967
t-test −2	0.084	1.072	1.235	0.076	3.025
t-test −2 (pre)	0.100	1.159	1.362	0.203*	3.263
Crude-dep-adjust t	0.091	1.066	1.352	0.072	2.929
Crude-dep-adjust t (pre)	0.112	1.199	1.473	0.184*	3.434
Sign test	−0.008	0.847	−0.156	0.041	3.048
Wilcoxon test	0.011	1.021	0.176	−0.072	2.801

B. Model and test statistics	Chi-squared			Kolmogorov–Smirnov D-statistic		
	$k = 10$	$k = 14$	$k = 18$	$k = 10$	$k = 14$	$k = 18$
Zero-one model						
t-test −1	10.40	16.45	19.71	0.036	0.037	0.032
t-test −1	4.48	9.39	20.29	0.016	0.027	0.032
t-test −2 (pre)	5.68	14.54	30.37†	0.036	0.041	0.036
Crude-dep-adjust t	4.64	11.18	14.82	0.024	0.031	0.032

Table 12.4 (continued)

B. Model and test statistics	Chi-squared			Kolmogorov–Smirnov D-statistic		
	$k = 10$	$k = 14$	$k = 18$	$k = 10$	$k = 14$	$k = 18$
Crude-dep-adjust t (pre)	13.20	13.54	23.02	0.056	0.041	0.044
Sign test	91.44	76.03*	103.81*	0.164*	0.077	0.092†
Wilcoxon test	8.72	16.34	18.99	0.032	0.035	0.028
Market-model						
t-test -1	13.20	14.54	25.33	0.036	0.037	0.032
t-test -2	6.40	10.51	16.11	0.028	0.033	0.032
t-test -2 (pre)	10.72	16.78	25.33	0.040	0.045	0.052
Crude-dep-adjust t	7.20	7.82	15.54	0.032	0.021	0.028
Crude-dep-adjust t (pre)	10.96	22.50	25.18	0.044	0.061	0.056
Sign test	103.68*	91.49*	125.12*	0.184*	0.117*	0.132*
Wilcoxon test	6.96	10.29	16.11	0.032	0.025	0.032
Cross-sectional model						
t-test -1	5.68	10.29	13.09	0.032	0.029	0.028
t-test -2	9.44	16.00	26.19	0.032	0.045	0.044
t-test -2 (pre)	12.88	20.70	33.10†	0.048	0.061	0.064
Crude-dep-adjust t	10.96	13.98	22.88	0.036	0.037	0.044
Crude-dep-adjust t (pre)	15.44	23.84	41.89	0.052	0.061	0.068
Sign test	95.44*	71.78*	100.06	0.164*	0.071	0.080
Wilcoxon test	10.08	23.62	23.46	0.040	0.045	0.036
Mean-adjusted model						
t-test -1	3.68	5.02	12.80	0.024	0.021	0.024
t-test -1	4.80	15.55	14.53	0.032	0.043	0.032
t-test -2 (pre)	6.48	15.10	20.29	0.044	0.037	0.040
Crude-dep-adjust t	6.64	11.18	18.27	0.032	0.037	0.040
Crude-dep-adjust t (pre)	9.04	20.59	18.70	0.048	0.061	0.048
Sign test	118.24*	77.49*	112.88*	0.188*	0.109*	0.124*
Wilcoxon test	5.36	9.50	7.62	0.032	0.023	0.020

* Statistic is significant at the 5% level.
† Statistic is significant at the 1% level.

Overall, the initial tests using continuous rates of return indicated that the simple mean-adjusted model performed as well as the more fully specified risk/return models. Further, the sign test and crude-dependence-adjusted t-test are much less powerful in detecting abnormal performance than the Wilcoxon[27] and t-tests -1 and -2. Most of the t statistic distributions appeared to violate the underlying theoretical distributions assumed in the hypothesis testing. As a result of the above findings, later tests will include results only for t-test -1, t-test -2 (pre) and the Wilcoxon test (unless there is some specific reason for doing otherwise).

Event-period tests

In nearly all studies of semi-strong market efficiency the researchers have studied the share market reaction not only in announcement period but also for several period either side of the event period in an attempt to determine the information content of the variable under study and for any signs of market inefficiency. A popular method used to examine returns around the event date is the cumulative abnormal return (CAR) method.

Simulation results—CAR

To fully understand the properties and behaviour of CAR when the null
hypothesis is known to be true, CARs were constructed using the average
residuals calculated in the simulation tests reported in table 12.2. The CAR

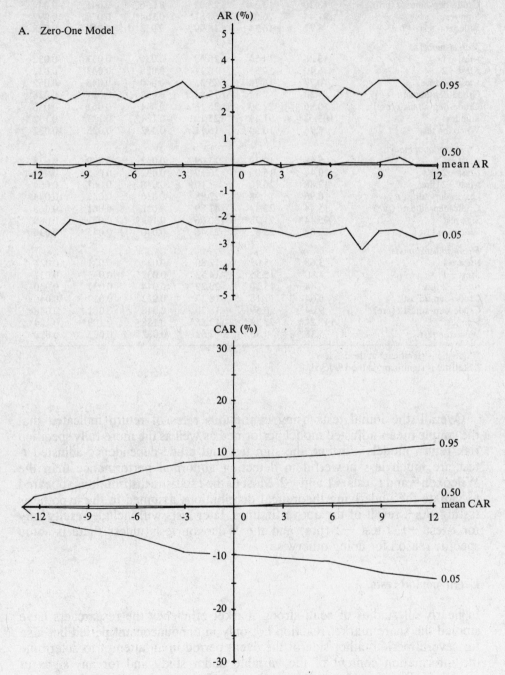

Figure 12.1 Selected fractiles of average and cumulative average residuals − 0% abnormal
performance

was cumulated from $t - 12$ to $t + 12$. Given that there were 250 portfolios we derive 250 CAR's. By sorting the monthly CAR's into ascending order we can graph selected fractiles of the distributions of the CAR. In figure 12.1 the 0.05, 0.50 and 0.95 fractiles of the AR and CAR are graphed for the 4 different models in the 4 panels.

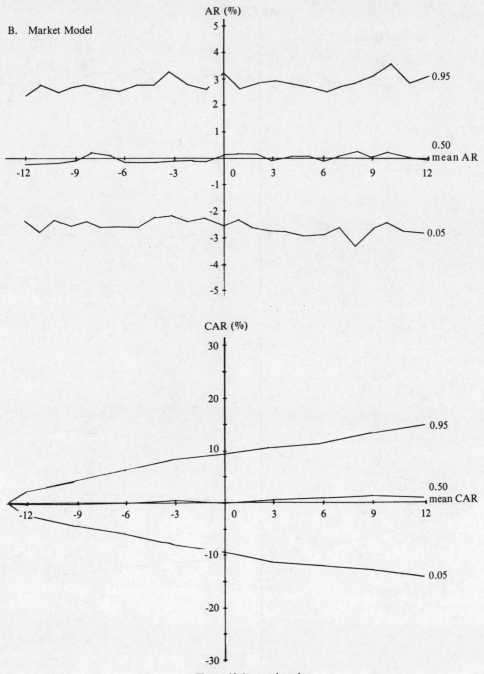

Figure 12.1   continued

The first point to note is that for all models at the 0.05 and 0.95 fractiles, CAR departs more and more from zero as we approach the end of the event period. However, the CAR appears to be reasonably symmetric around the mean CAR for each mode. Recall that, with a large number of portfolios or replications each constructed by random selection of securities and event dates, no abnormal performance should, on average, be exhibited. In terms

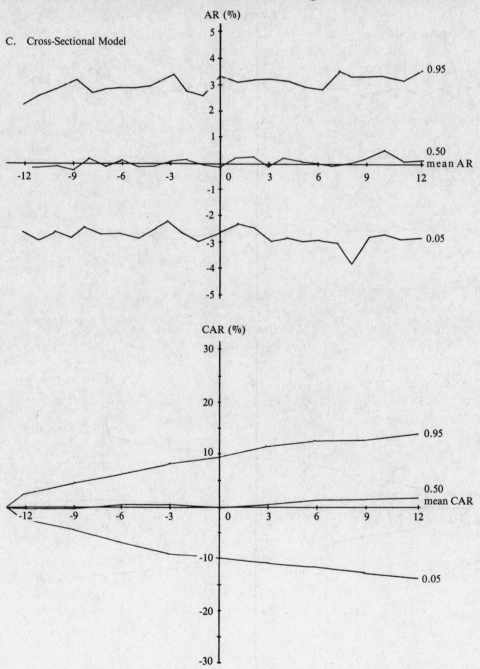

Figure 12.1   continued

of the CAR this means that the 0.50 fractile (the mean CAR) should be approximately equal to 0 per cent at the end of the cumulation period. Reference to figure 12.1 indicates that this is the case for all models except the mean-adjusted model where there is a slight upward drift in the mean CAR of around 5 per cent. This indicates that there may be some bias present in this model.[28]

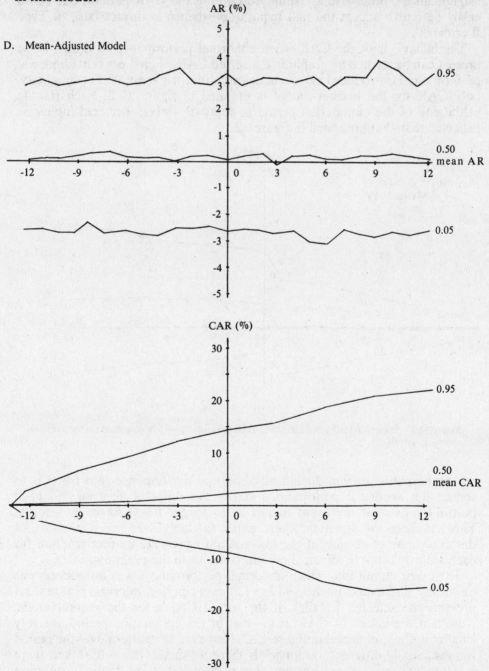

Figure 12.1   continued

The behaviour of the CAR in figure 12.1 highlights the point that CAR (for a given portfolio) is by construction like a random walk and thus can easily give the appearance of "significant" positive or negative abnormal performance when there is none present. This indicates that it is necessary to apply significance tests to the average residuals to determine their "significance", otherwise, by simply observing the CAR pattern, one could easily be led to accept the null hypothesis when it is in fact false (a Type II error).[29]

The behaviour of the CAR when abnormal performance is known to be present can be studied by graphing the sorted CAR when 5 per cent abnormal performance is introduced into each security's return in month 0. For simplicity, only CAR for the market model is graphed in figure 12.2. Each fractile at the end of the cumulation period is approximately 5 per cent higher as expected than that presented in figure 12.1.

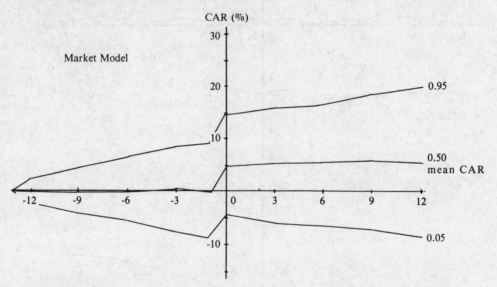

Figure 12.2 Selected fractiles of cumulative average residuals — 5% abnormal performance in the event month

An alternative to introducing all abnormal performance into $t = 0$ is to spread the abnormal performance across the different securities in each portfolio such that the event month is no longer $t = 0$ for each security. This simulates the situation where either (a) the researcher is not sure of the exact date of release of the information or (b) the market reaction for each security is not in identical months (relative to the event month).[30]

The event month into which abnormal performances was introduced was uniformly distributed in the $(-12, +12)$ event-period interval. Figure 12.3 presents the selected fractiles of the sorted CAR's for the market mode. Note that the values of CAR at the end of the cumulation period are very smaller to those obtained in figure 12.2. However, the pattern over the period is substantially different: no longer is there a "spike" in $t = 0$; rather, there is a gradual cumulation. Further, this pattern is not substantially different from that obtained under the null hypothesis presented in figure 12.1. Again this illustrates it is essential that signficance tests be applied to the portfolio abnormal returns.

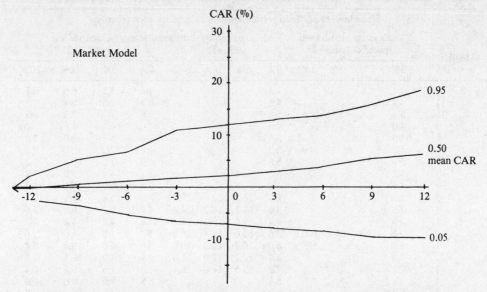

Figure 12.3 Selected fractiles of cumulative average residuals — 5% abnormal performance uniformly distributed across event period (-12, +12)

Assessing event-period abnormal performance

There are at least two ways to test the significance of portfolio abnormal returns over the event period:

(a) Test the significance of each monthly portfolio abnormal return. This procedure is a simple extension of testing $A\tilde{R}_{t=0}$ as presented in the event month tests; now $A\tilde{R}_t$ is tested for $t = -12, +12$.

(b) Test the significance of the mean monthly portfolio abnormal return over the event period.[31] This involves testing whether $\overline{AR}$ is significantly different from zero. The procedure is referred to here as event-period tests.

To gain an insight into the performance of the first method the frequency of rejections of the null hypothesis (of no abnormal performance in month t) in each of the 25 months of the event period is reported in table 12.5. The rejections are based only on the market model because to include all models would obscure the performance of the procedure itself.[32]

When all abnormal performance is introduced only into the event month $t = 0$, the procedure is quite powerful in detecting abnormal performance. For example, with 10 per cent abnormal performance simulated the null is rejected in month 0 100 per cent of the time, whereas in the other months of the event period the null is rejected at approximately the significance test level of 5 per cent. However, as the period over which abnormal performance is simulated increases from 0 to (−3, +3) to (−12, +12) the rejection rate of the null falls. When the abnormal performance is distributed uniformly across the (−12, +12) interval even with 20 per cent abnormal performance the null is rejected in each month only 7–10 per cent of the

Table 12.5 Market model abnormal returns over the event period—percentage of rejections of the null hypothesis AR_t = 0.0 in each month of the event period $(-12, +12)$; rejections based on t-test -1, one-tailed significance tests at α = 0.05; abnormal performance based on the noraml distribution.

| | Mean level of portfolio performance introduced for each security: | | | | | | | | | | | |
| | in the event month $t = 0$ (spiked distribution) | | | | uniformly distributed across the interval $(-3, +3)$ | | | | $(-12, +12)$ | | | |
Month relative to $t = 0$	0%	1%	5%	10%	0%	5%	10%	20%	0%	5%	10%	20%
−12	4.4				4.4				4.4	5.2	6.0	6.8
−11	4.4				4.4				4.4	4.8	8.4	7.2
−10	5.6				5.6				5.6	7.2	7.2	9.2
−9	4.0				4.0				4.0	4.4	6.8	8.0
−8	3.6				3.6				3.6	5.2	6.0	7.6
−7	5.2				5.2				4.8	7.2	10.0	8.0
−6	5.6				5.6				6.0	7.2	8.4	7.2
−5	3.2				3.2				3.2	4.4	7.2	7.2
−4	3.6				3.6				3.6	6.0	6.0	9.2
−3	8.8				8.4	16.4	22.4	27.6	8.8	8.8	11.6	12.4
−2	3.6				3.6	11.2	14.0	24.4	4.0	5.2	6.8	7.6
−1	4.0				4.4	9.6	17.2	25.2	3.6	4.8	6.4	7.2
0	3.6	18.4	86.8	100.0	3.6	12.0	16.4	26.4	3.2	4.8	6.0	7.6
1	5.6				6.0	10.4	17.2	26.0	5.6	6.0	8.8	8.4
2	4.4				4.4	12.2	17.6	26.4	4.4	4.0	6.8	8.0
3	7.2				7.2	13.6	18.0	26.4	7.2	7.6	9.2	10.4
4	6.8				6.8				6.8	7.6	9.6	10.0
5	5.2				5.2				5.2	6.8	6.0	8.0
6	4.0				4.0				4.0	5.6	7.2	6.4
7	5.2				5.2				5.2	6.8	8.0	8.8
8	2.8				2.8				2.8	4.8	4.8	8.4
9	7.2				7.2				7.2	8.4	9.6	10.8
10	4.4				4.4				4.4	5.2	8.0	8.4
11	5.2				5.2				4.8	6.0	8.0	8.0
12	4.4				4.4				4.0	6.8	6.8	8.4

time. Thus we can conclude that if the market reaction is not concentrated within one or two months the ability to detect abnormal performance under this procedure is substantially lowered.

The results for the second procedure are reported in table 12.6[33] where the percentage of rejections of the null $(\overline{AR} = 0.0)$ is reported for each of the 4 models. When no abnormal performance was simulated the rejection frequencies of the null of no abnormal performance in the $(-3, +3)$ interval varied slightly across the models and test statistics. With the introduction of 5 per cent abnormal performance, rejection rates increase but are substantially less than those recorded in the event-month tests. At this level of abnormal performance the zero-one model appears to be the most powerful. However, when the level of abnormal performance is increased to 10 per cent and 20 per cent the market and cross-sectional models record rejection rates similar to the zero-one model. The mean-adjusted model tends to reject the null less often than the other methodologies at higher levels of abnormal performance.

With no abnormal performance simulated in the $(-12, +12)$ interval, the Wilcoxon test records too-high rejection frequencies across all methodologies.[34] Further, the mean-adjusted model rejected the null too often when true. These rejecction frequencies are consistent with the plots of CAR presented in figure 12.1, where the mean CAR for the mean-adjusted model drifted upwards. With the introduction of abnormal performance the zero-one and cross-sectional models appear to be slightly more powerful than the other models.

From the rejection frequencies reported in tables 12.5 and 12.6 it appears that when abnormal performance is spread across more than one or two months, event-period tests (of $\overline{AR}$ = 0.0) are more powerful than individual month tests (of $\overline{AR}_t$ = 0.0 for t = 12, +12). For example, under the market model when there was 20 per cent abnormal performance uniformly distributed across the 25-month event period, the null (of $\overline{AR}$ = 0.0) was rejected approximately 65 per cent of the time which far exceeded the individual-month test results of 7–10 per cent.

Table 12.6 Tests on mean monthly portfolio abnormal returns over the event period—percentage of rejections of the null hypothesis*, H_0: $\overline{AR}$ = 0.0; abnormal performance based on the normal distribution, and uniformly distributed across the event interval; one-tailed significance tests at α = 0.05.

Methodology and test statistic	Event interval							
	(−3, +3)				(−12, +12)			
	0%	5%	10%	20%	0%	5%	10%	20%
Zero-one model								
t-test −1	5.2%	43.2	76.2	98.0	6.8%	23.2	40.0	72.8
t-test −2 (pre)	2.8	34.8	79.6	99.2	5.2	20.4	38.4	74.8
Wilcoxon test	8.4	48.4	84.8	99.6	16.4	38.4	57.6	84.8
Market model								
t-test −1	5.6	36.8	77.2	97.2	4.4	16.8	34.0	58.4
t-test −2 (pre)	3.6	41.2	79.2	99.2	9.2	24.0	42.4	71.2
Wilcoxon test	5.2	42.4	80.0	98.4	10.0	28.4	46.0	73.2
Cross-sectional model								
t-test −1	6.0	38.8	73.6	96.8	9.2	24.0	39.6	71.6
t-test −2 (pre)	5.2	37.2	78.0	99.2	8.4	24.0	40.0	75.2
Wilcoxon test	7.2	43.2	79.2	98.4	15.6	36.8	56.4	81.2
Mean-adjusted model								
t-test −1	5.6	34.0	67.6	95.2	8.4	17.6	27.2	55.2
t-test −2 (pre)	10.2	45.2	74.4	98.4	23.6	37.2	52.8	76.8
Wilcoxon test	5.6	30.4	65.6	96.8	13.2	26.8	38.0	62.0

* The null hypothesis relates to the same interval as that over which abnormal performance is introduced.

Descriptive statistics of the sampling distributions of test statistics from the (−12, +12) event-period tests are presented in table 12.7. Generally they are consistent with the rejection frequencies reported in table 12.6. The Type I errors reported by each of the models is reflected in the means of the test statistic distributions being significantly greater than zero (at α = 0.05). Most of the distributions are skewed, and the goodness-of-fit tests also reject the null of normality for most of the distributions.

From these event-period tests it is evident that the power of the methodologies is reduced compared with the event-month tests reported earlier. The Wilcoxon test leads to Type I errors and appears unsuitable in tests for abnormal performance over a 25-month event period. The mean-adjusted model and, to a less extent, the cross-sectional model reject the null when true, far too often in the event-period tests. In these event-period

Table 12.7 Descriptive statistics of the sampling distributions of the event-period significance test statistics—based on 250 portfolios of 30 securities each; continuously compounded rates of return; 0% abnormal performance, uniformly distributed across the event period (−12, +12).

Model and test statistics	Mean	Standard deviation	t-stat for mean	Skewness	Kurtosis
Zero-one model					
t-test −1	0.143	1.077	2.101†	−0.045	2.583
t-test −2 (pre)	0.097	1.101	1.387	−0.188*	3.040
Wilcoxon test	0.505	1.129	7.077	−0.213*	2.523
Market model					
t-test −1	0.085	1.053	1.270	−0.174*	2.848
t-test −2 (pre)	0.084	1.281	1.040	−0.229*	3.141
Wilcoxon test	0.293	1.113	4.168*	−0.113†	2.650
Cross-sectional model					
t-test −1	0.247	1.114	3.503*	−0.129†	2.973
t-test −2 (pre)	0.220	1.155	3.010*	−0.122†	2.946
Wilcoxon test	0.502	1.123	7.069*	−0.210*	2.813
Mean-adjusted model					
t-test −1	0.347	1.071	5.120*	−0.143†	3.156
t-test −2 (pre)	0.531	1.631	5.147*	−0.288*	3.245
Wilcoxon test	0.475	1.115	6.739*	0.011	2.813

	Chi-squared			Kolmogorov–Smirnov D statistic		
	k = 10	k = 14	k = 18	k = 10	k = 14	k = 18
Zero-one model						
t-test −1	16.40	14.32	21.73	0.056	0.033	0.032
t-test −2 (pre)	12.80	16.56	28.06	0.044	0.049	0.036
Wilcoxon test	107.84*	100.90*	127.28*	0.184*	0.133*	0.124*
Market model						
t-test −1	11.92	17.34	21.01	0.048	0.045	0.036
t-test −2 (pre)	28.72*	38.40*	45.78*	0.052	0.057	0.052
Wilcoxon test	38.64*	43.33*	46.93*	0.100†	0.065	0.064
Cross-sectional model						
t-test −1	29.04*	26.53†	31.95†	0.088†	0.057	0.048
t-test −2 (pre)	34.16*	35.04*	38.58*	0.084	0.069	0.048
Wilcoxon test	80.48*	84.54*	97.90*	0.140*	0.113*	0.112*
Mean-adjusted model						
t-test −1	38.24*	46.02*	42.03*	0.072	0.065	0.048
t-test −2 (pre)	157.36*	210.54*	244.06*	0.216*	0.217*	0.208*
Wilcoxon test	79.44*	74.69*	77.31*	0.152*	0.113*	0.084

* Statistic is significant at the 5% level.
† Statistic is significant at the 1% level.

tests the zero-one model appears to be slightly more powerful, and the test statistics better behaved for this model than the other models.

Event-month clustering

When events occur for a group of securities in the same calendar month it is referred to here as "event month clustering". Examples of how clustering may occur include company specific announcements coinciding or if there is some change in government policy that affects some firms but not others. The implications of clustering in tests for abnormal performance are outlined by BW (1980, pp. 232–33) with the main point being that there is no longer cross-sectional independence between security rates of return within a portfolio.

To examine the effect of clustering, 250 portfolios of 30 securities each were constructed as previously but now each security in a portfolio shared the same calendar month as the event month, which was randomly selected between July 1961 and December 1972. For each portfolio a new event month was selected but with only 138 event months available some portfolios shared a particular calendar month.

While all abnormal performance was introduced into $t = 0$ both event-month ($A\tilde{R}_{t=0} = 0.0$) and event-period ($\overline{AR} = 0.0$) tests were conducted. The results are presented in table 12.8. In the event-month clustering substantially increases the rejection frequencies (or Type I error) for the mean-adjusted model. t-test -1, t-test -2 (pre) and the Wilcoxon test, which all assume cross-sectional independence in returns, reject the null 25.2 per cent, 23.2 per cent and 24.8 per cent of the time respectively at $\alpha = 0.05$. With a crude adjustment for the dependence the rejection rate of the t-test is 6.8 per cent. However, with the introduction of abnormal performance the crude-dependence-adjusted t-test rejects the null far less often (i.e., is less powerful) than the other significance tests.

Table 12.8 The effect of event-month clustering on the percentage of rejections of the null hypothesis—abnormal performance normally distributed in the event month; one-tailed significance tests at $\alpha = 0.05$.

Methodology and test statistic	Event-month tests			Event-period tests		
	0%	3%	5%	0%	5%	10%
Zero-one model						
t-test -1	5.2%	66.0	91.6	11.6%	25.2	44.8
t-test -2 (pre)	5.2	68.8	94.0	8.8	24.8	45.6
Crude-dep-adj t (pre)	6.4	68.0	92.8	8.8	24.8	46.4
Wilcoxon test	8.0	71.2	92.8	20.4	43.2	65.6
Market model						
t-test -1	4.8	64.8	89.6	10.4	16.8	31.2
t-test -2 (pre)	6.8	68.0	93.2	11.6	24.4	41.6
Crude-dep-adj t (pre)	8.0	68.0	92.8	11.2	23.6	41.6
Wilcoxon test	7.2	68.0	92.0	14.0	30.0	47.2
Cross-sectional model						
t-test -1	5.2	65.6	88.4	9.6	26.0	46.0
t-test -2 (pre)	8.0	68.0	91.6	8.4	26.0	46.0
Crude-dep-adj t (pre)	8.8	68.0	92.0	9.2	26.0	48.4
Wilcoxon test	5.6	68.0	90.0	16.8	36.8	60.0
Mean-adjusted model						
t-test -1	25.2	64.4	82.8	38.8	43.6	48.4
t-test -2 (pre)	23.2	64.4	83.6	42.4	46.4	51.2
Crude-dep-adj t (pre)	6.8	28.8	52.0	31.6	35.2	36.8
Wilcoxon test	24.8	70.4	84.4	42.4	47.2	50.4

With the exception of the mean-adjusted model the performance methodologies take into account marketwide factors. It appears that in the event-month tests the effects of event-month clustering and hence cross-sectional dependence on the market-adjusted performance methodologies and the associated significance tests are minimal.[35]

In the event-period tests (of $\overline{AR}$ = 0.0), the mean-adjusted model again rejects the null, when true, too often (around 40 per cent). With an adjustment for cross-sectional dependence the model still rejects the null in 31.6 per cent of the portfolios. However, as previous event-period test results indicate, the mean-adjusted model is totally unsuited in event-period tests for abnormal performance. Similar arguments apply to the Wilcoxon test statistic. However, the market-adjusted methodologies also now reject the null, when true, too often. The methodologies all appear unsuited (as they all record Type I errors) to tests for abnormal performance over a 25-month period when the securities in the portfolio have common event dates.

Systematic risk clustering

BW (1980, pp. 236–39) examine the effect of clustering of securities within portfolios by systematic risk (β). They argue that, because Fama (1976) has provided empirical evidence of a positive relationship between the variance of returns and β, tests for abnormal performance will be more powerful for low-β securities than high-β securities.[36]

To examine the effect of clustering of securities by systematic risk, tests were carried out on portfolios that were constructed by reference to β values. Two different sets of 250 portfolios of 30 securities each were generated as previously but now with the additional restriction that only securities with the required β values (estimated by OLS regression) be included in the portfolios as follows:[37]

$$\text{low-risk portfolios} \qquad \beta < 1.00$$
$$\text{high-risk portfolios} \qquad \beta > 1.00$$

Both event-month and event-period tests were conducted (with all abnormal performance introduced into $t = 0$). The percentage of rejections of the null with $\alpha = 0.05$ are presented in table 12.9. In the event-month tests, the methodologies, with the possible exception of the cross-sectional model, appear to be more powerful for the low-risk portfolios. For example, with 3 per cent abnormal performance the market model rejects the null under the Wilcoxon test 75.2 per cent of the time for the low-risk portfolios and only 60.0 per cent of the time for the high-risk portfolios. It is also evident in these tests that t-test -1 is less powerful than t-test -2 (pre) and the Wilcoxon test.

Overall, these event-month results are consistent with those reported by BW (1980, table 7). Note that the simple mean-adjusted model performs as well as, if not better than, the more sophisticated models in the presence of systematic risk clustering. This is surprising given that both the market and cross-sectional models explicitly adjust for risk. That these models do not outperform the mean-adjusted model may be the result of several factors including (a) measurement error in the β's and/or (b) stationarity in the β's resulting in the simple mean-adjusted model capturing the effect of risk differentials in the expected return $\overline{R}_j$.

In the event-period tests, the mean-adjusted model continues to record Type I errors. The Wilcoxon test statistic also continues to perform poorly. Overall it appears that the cross-sectional model is sensitive to the risk of

Table 12.9 The effect of clustering by risk on the percentage of rejections of the null hypothesis—abnormal performance normally distributed in the event month; one-tailed significance tests at $\alpha = 0.05$.

Methodology and test statistic	Event-month tests					
	Low-risk $\beta < 1.00$			High-risk $\beta > 1.00$		
	0%	3%	5%	0%	3%	5%
Zero-one model						
t-test -1	4.0%	68.4	90.8	2.8	52.8	86.4
t-test -2 (pre)	6.0	73.6	93.6	4.8	56.0	91.2
Wilcoxon test	4.4	77.6	96.0	2.0	62.0	90.4
Market model						
t-test -1	2.4	64.8	89.6	3.2	54.0	85.2
t-test -2 (pre)	4.8	71.6	94.0	6.4	55.2	90.8
Wilcoxon test	2.4	75.2	95.2	1.6	60.0	89.2
Cross-sectional model						
t-test -1	2.8	57.2	86.4	3.2	57.6	83.2
t-test -2 (pre)	4.8	62.8	90.4	7.2	60.8	89.6
Wilcoxon test	2.8	64.4	91.2	2.4	63.6	90.4
Mean-adjusted model						
t-test -1	3.6	64.8	89.2	3.6	48.4	83.6
t-test -2 (pre)	7.2	69.2	94.0	7.2	56.0	87.6
Wilcoxon test	3.6	68.0	94.8	2.4	56.4	88.0
	Alpha		Beta	Alpha		Beta
Mean ($N = 7500$)	0.0015		0.760	-0.0015		1.234
Standard deviation	0.0015		0.070	0.0022		0.086

Methodology and test statistic	Event-period test					
	Low-risk $\beta < 1.00$			High-risk $\beta > 1.00$		
	0%	3%	5%	0%	3%	5%
Zero-one model						
t-test -1	7.2%	22.0	39.2	4.8%	16.8	34.8
t-test -2 (pre)	6.4	18.4	40.0	4.8	15.2	33.6
Wilcoxon test	17.6	35.6	63.2	11.2	31.6	49.2
Market model						
t-test -1	5.6	17.6	36.8	5.6	13.6	26.4
t-test -2 (pre)	8.8	24.8	46.4	8.4	21.6	38.0
Wilcoxon test	12.8	28.8	52.8	7.6	20.8	37.6
Cross-sectional model						
t-test -1	1.6	9.6	24.0	16.0	36.4	50.0
t-test -2 (pre)	1.6	9.2	24.0	18.4	38.0	52.0
Wilcoxon test	5.6	24.4	41.2	26.8	44.4	65.6
Mean-adjusted model						
t-test -1	12.0	22.0	34.4	8.4	15.2	26.8
t-test -2 (pre)	21.6	38.0	57.2	24.0	37.2	50.4
Wilcoxon test	17.2	32.4	49.2	13.6	24.8	35.2

the securities in the portfolio. When β is low, abnormal returns are low, and when β is high, abnormal returns are high. The zero-one and market models are less sensitive and appear to be more powerful for the low-risk portfolios.

Additional simulations

In addition to the above tests, further tests were conducted to examine the robustness and validity of the results under different simulated conditions. Tables of results are not presented (although they are available from the author); only the main points of the analysis are noted.

The results discussed previously relate to portfolios containing 30 securities each. Tests were carried out with portfolio sizes of 15 and 50 securities respectively so as to examine the sensitivity of the methodologies and significance tests to portfolio size. When the null is true there is little difference in rejection rates across the different portfolio sizes. With the introduction of abnormal performance, as portfolio size increases so do the rejection frequencies recorded by each model.[38] For example, with 1 per cent abnormal performance the market model rejects the null hypothesis, using t-test -1, 12.0 per cent, 19.6 per cent and 22.8 per cent of the time as N goes from 15 to 30 to 50. Thus it can be concluded that the methodologies are more powerful in detecting abnormal performance in larger portfolios than smaller portfolios, which is consistent with the BW (1980, table 9) results.

The performance of the market- and risk-adjusted models depends heavily on the estimate of each security's systematic risk. This variable could be quite important in an actual event study; however, in this study there is no reason to expect a change in a security's systematic risk consequent upon a simulated event. Only minor testing of the importance of this variable was therefore conducted; it was found that the use of the 60 months before or the 60 months after the event period to estimate α and β had little effect on the performance of the models.

When a researcher cannot *a priori* predict the direction of the market reaction to an event, it is necessary to conduct two-tailed significance tests. As expected, when two-tailed testing was examined the power of the methodologies was lowered, which is consistent with the findings of BW (1980, table 5).

In tests similar to BW (1980, table 10) an examination of the consistency between methodologies in rejecting the null for a given portfolio indicated that the methodologies are reasonably consistent in detecting abnormal performance. Similarly, the different significance tests are reasonably consistent in rejecting the null for a given portfolio.

Simulations introducing negative abnormal performance were carried out to test the power of the methodologies to detect the market's response to bad news. The rejection frequencies were similar to those reported previously in table 12.2 in tests for positive abnormal performance. This indicates the methodologies are equally powerful in tests for positive or negative abnormal performance.

All tests of the mean-adjusted returns model used the simple non-standardised version defined in equation (4). BW (1980, p. 250) found that without the standardisation there was too much mass in the left-hand tail of the t statistic distributions. The tests conducted and reported here indicate that with respect to Australian security returns the simple mean-adjusted model test statistic distributions are no more skewed (and in fact may be less skewed generally, see table 12.4) than the distributions for the other models. Nevertheless, the performance of the standardised version was examined to determine if the power of the methodology was increased by such a procedure. Overall, the results in both event-month and event-period tests of abnormal performance indicate that there is little difference in the performance of the two models in either their ability to detect abnormal performance or in the behaviour of the test statistic sampling distributions. In either version it is unsuitable for event-period tests.

All tests and results reported previously were conducted using continuous rates of return. Simulations were conducted without the natural log transformation (that is, using arithmetic rates of return) to examine the sensitivity of the methodologies and test statistics to such transformations. In the event-month tests the Wilcoxon test recorded very low rejection rates when the null was true and the mean of the distribution under each of the models was significantly negative (at least at the $\alpha = 0.05$ level). This negative bias in the Wilcoxon test statistic was also reported by BW (1980, table 2). The distributions of the t statistics are also much more skewed and the t-test -2 (pre) distribution for each model leptokurtic. With the introduction of abnormal performance there was little difference in the rejection rates reported using continuous rates of return. In the event-period tests with 0 per cent and positive abnormal performance the rejection frequencies and CAR of each of the models were similar under both continuous and arithmetic rates of return.

Conclusions

This chapter reported the results of various tests on methodologies which have been used in empirical tests of the semi-strong efficient market hypothesis. The methodologies tested were the zero-one model, the market model, the cross-sectional model and the mean-adjusted mode. Further, the applicability and performance of parametric and non-parametric significance tests was examined. Two different non-parametric tests, the Wilcoxon signed-ranks statistic and the sign test, and various different versions of the parametric t-tests were employed to test the null hypothesis of no abnormal performance.

All tests conducted involved constructing 250 portfolios by random selection of securities and event dates and then simulating abnormal returns for the securities. The performance of the different methodologies in detecting this abnormal performance was assessed by studying the proportion of Type I errors and Type II errors recorded by the different methodologies.

As a variety of different tests and conditions were simulated it is difficult to generalise about the results. The main points that might be noted are as follows. In the event-month tests the methodologies performed as well as one another with the exception of the mean-adjusted model in the event-month clustering tests. This result is consistent with BW (1980). In the event-period tests the zero-one model tended to perform as well as, if not better than, the market and cross-sectional models, with the mean-adjusted model being totally unsuited to this test period. As BW did not provide much detail about the performance of the methodologies in event-period tests, it is not possible to compare the two studies in this area.

In relation to the significance test statistics the results are not so clear.

In event-month tests, the t-tests based on the event-period estimates of the standard error appeared to perform better than their pre-event-period counterparts. In event-period tests for abnormal performance the pre-event t-tests continued to record Type I errors. Generally, t-test -1 did as well as the more complicated t-test -2, both of which were generally superior to the crude-dependence-adjusted t-test. The Wilcoxon test statistic performed satisfactorily when using continuous rates of return. Without the log transformation the Wilcoxon test appeared to be inferior to the t-tests. However, nearly all test statistic distributions were, in one way or another, found to violate the underlying theoretical distribution assumed in hypothesis testing.

When the data requirements and the costs of computation of the residuals of each of the models are considered the results indicate that, in most situations, the zero-one and market models provide the researcher with "the best" tools for studying the share market response to information releases. Similarly, with respect to the choice of significance tests, t-test -2 (pre) is recommended. Although t-test -1 and t-test -2 both performed as well as t-test -2 (pre), the last is more theoretically defensible.

Overall, it is possible to conclude that tests for abnormal performance are most powerful when (i) the market reaction is concentrated within one or two months of the announcement date, which announcement date is accurately determined, and (ii) the researcher conducts the tests in each of these months rather than test for the mean abnormal returns over an extended event period.

Acknowledgments

This paper has benefited from the comments and criticisms of R. Brown, P. Praetz and S. Brown. As supervisor for my M.Ec. thesis, I am indebted to R. Officer. P. Brown also allowed access to the "$N = 909$" version of his price-relative data file. Any errors or omissions remain, of course, the responsibility of the author.

Notes

1. See Officer (1979) for a summary of Australian studies of the semi-strong EMH. Note, however, that some studies have reported results inconsistent with efficient-market behaviour; see Ball (1978a) for a review of some of this anomalous evidence.
2. An alternative approach to residual analysis is that formulated by Gonedes (1974) and Gonedes, Dopuch and Penman (1976).
3. See Fama et al. (1979) for a description of the CAR procedure. A similar technique employed by Ball and Brown (1968) is the abnormal performance index (API).
4. That is, over t_{-42} to t_{-13}. BW used a standardised version of this model $u_{jt} = (R_{jt} - R_j)/S_{Rj}$ where S_{Rj} = standard deviation of the returns of security j around R_j. This version also was tested here; as the results are not particularly sensitive to the standardisation procedure, only the results for the simple model are reported. Further, the simple model was used by Masulis (1980). He referred to it as the comparison period returns approach and gives a theoretical justification for the approach (see pp. 153-57).
5. United States evidence (see Gonedes 1973, and Fama and MacBeth 1973) suggests 60 monthly observations of returns are necessary to obtain minimum-error estimates of the relative risk of a security. Initially these parameters were estimated for each security as follows:
   (a) for u_{jt} $t = -12, 0$, α_j and β_j were estimated using observations from the period t_{-72} to t_{-13}.
   (b) for u_{jt} $t = +1, +12$, α_j and β_j were estimated over the 60-month period t_{+13} to t_{+72}.
6. Estimates of the monthly marketwide factors were derived by similar procedures as outline in Ball, Brown and Officer (1976a).

7. The effect of portfolio size on the power of the methodologies is investigated and reported below. A further point to note is the problem of dealing with risk changes consequent upon the event. See Ball (1972a) and Dodd (1976) for further discussion.

8. These two variants are the simplest methods. More complex methods are available (see Brown and Warner 1980). Further, there are several different methods of implementing the market model (see Brenner 1979, and Collins and McKeown 1979).

9. Alternatively, as Dodd (1976, p. 19) argues: "Because the residuals (and therefore the average and cumulative average residuals) are *ex post* observations of random variables, averages are not sufficient statistics to describe the stock market reaction."

10. t-test -1 was adopted from an elementary statistical test, Karmel and Polasem (1970). t-test -2 and the crude-dependence-adjusted t-tests were adopted from Brown and Warner (1980, see their Appendix A).

11. It could also be argued (although it is not pursued here) that a fourth alternative exists, namely, the use of post-event-period residuals. Note that BW argue for and use pre-event residuals.

12 These two tests are outlined in Siegel (1956). See also Ball, Brown and Finn (1977) for a discussion of the usual approach to the implementation of the Wilcoxon test in event studies. Both these statistics usually work with the difference between the residuals of matched pairs. It is, however, possible to work directly with the security's own score; this implies that the matched security has a zero abnormal return over the same period. This latter approach is adopted in this simulation study.

13. The correction for continuity is necessary because the normal distribution is for a continuous variable whereas the binomial distribution involves a discrete variable. $X + 0.5$ is used when $X < N/2$. See Siegel (1956).

14. This file was compiled by Philip Brown and is further described in Ball, Brown and Officer (1976a, fn. 9). The main reason for using monthly data as opposed to daily data is that a comprehensive file of daily price relatives is simply not available in Australia. Other reasons for using monthly data are given by Brown and Warner (1980, p. 211).

15. See Praetz and Wilson (1978) and Fama et al. (1969, p. 4, fn. 8) for further discussion.

16. The intrinsic random number generator on a VAX-11/780 computer was used to facilitate this unrestricted random-sampling approach.

17. This simple procedure is similar to BW's. However, they make a further slight adjustment (see their fn. 9) so as to leave the mean returns across their study period unaltered. They carry out simulations with and without this adjustment and the results do not appear sensitive to the adjustment.

18. This discussion touches upon a more fundamental problem faced by researchers, namely, the determination in a particular situation of what is "good" news and what is "bad" news. For example, are increased earnings by company A good or bad news? (See Ball and Brown 1968.)

19. In this regard, when there is no abnormal performance present both the pre-event and event-period t statistics should reject at approximately the same rate as their pair. That is, the standard error should be very similar in the absence of an event. That the rejection rates are not similar suggests that the pre-event-period estimates of the standard errors are lower. This is consistent with evidence (e.g., see Praetz and Wilson 1978) that the variance of the distribution of security returns increased over the period 1958–73.

20. This test was replicated adding abnormal performance based on the normal distribution. The rejection frequencies across all models tended to fall, especially for 3 per cent and 5 per cent abnormal performance levels; for example, at $\alpha = 0.05$ ($\alpha = 0.01$) with 5 per cent abnormal performance simulated, the Wilcoxon test rejection rates are on average 5 per cent (12–14 per cent) lower. Among the test statistics, t-test -2 and the crude-dependence-adjusted t are least affected by the method of simulating abnormal performance. Otherwise, the results are consistent between the two procedures.

21. See Praetz and Wilson (1978) for the definition and setting of critical points for both the skewness and kurtosis coefficients.

22. See Siegel (1956) for the definitions and critical points for the goodness-of-fit test statistics.

23. Strictly, the tests of the t statistic distributions should be for departures from the t distribution (with the degrees of freedom depending on the t-test). However, for our purposes, the above tests provide some indication of the test statistic distributions.

24. Note that, instead of equiprobable classes a better test might have been constructed by concentrating on the tails of the distributions.

25. The differences in direction of the skew are due to the methods of calculating the standard errors.

26. The distributions of the test statistics when 1 per cent abnormal performance is simulated are as expected. The means of the test statistics across all four models are significantly greater than zero at $\alpha = 0.01$. Further, the goodness-of-fit tests reject at $\alpha = 0.01$ the null of normality (0, 1) for all test statistic distributions (see Brown and Warner 1980, table 2 and fn. 19).

27. The relatively good performance of the Wilcoxon test reported here contrasts with that reported by Brown and Warner (1980, pp. 217–22). However, the BW tests were based on arithmetic rates of return, whereas continuous rates of return were used here. Tests using arithmetic rates of return (reported briefly below) confirm the BW results.

28. This bias is consistent with a rising market. If the market returns are rising over time, then the expected return for securities based on past returns will be too low, resulting in positive abnormal returns (see also Brown and Warner 1980, fn. 35).

29. Given the portfolio construction procedures employed in this study, the fractiles of the CAR (AR) actually trace out probabilities for tests of the null hypothesis in sample sizes of 30. If a researcher found, in a particular study, CAR (AR) lying above the 0.95 fractile in figure 12.1, he could reasonably conclude that the abnormal returns were significant at the one-tailed 5 per cent level.

30. That is, for some securities the market may have anticipated the release of the information, for others it may have been surprised and for others it simply may have been inefficient in impounding the information effects of the announcement. This also raises the point that the behaviour of the CAR is not representative of the cumulative residuals for individual securities. The months in which the market reacts (relative to the event month) differ from security to security, and this explains any persistent upward (or downward) drift in CAR in the months preceding the announcement and why this drift could not be used to earn abnormal returns.

31. Approach (a) was employed by Ball, Walker and Whittred (1979), and approach (b) was adopted by Brown and Warner (1980). See also Dodd (1976).

32. The performance of the testing procedure was the same for all models.

33. In table 12.6 the abnormal performance was uniformly distributed across the event interval. Following Brown and Warner (1980, p. 225), other distributions were examined. It makes little difference to the rejection frequencies when the null is true. When abnormal performance is introduced, the rejection rates continue to be very similar, except for the crude-dependence-adjusted t statistic calculated over the event period. This similarity is easily explained in terms of the calculation of AR (a simple equally weighted average of the monthly portfolio abnormal returns) and the standard errors of the t-tests being unaffected by the time-shape of the distribution of abnormal performance across the event period. See the section "Significance Test Definitions".

34. The Wilcoxon test statistic was calculated as earlier defined in equation (12) but now with T calculated as the sum of the ranks of the sorted absolute values of the individual security mean monthly abnormal returns $\bar{u}_j$.

35. These findings are consistent with those reported by Brown and Warner (1980). Note, however, as BW point out (p. 235), the above results are based on the random selection of securities for inclusion of portfolios. In actual event studies securities are not selected at random; there may be securities with known common event months which are drawn from a common industry group having positively correlated returns. Thus it may not be sufficient just to abstract from market effects while ignoring the other cross-sectional dependencies.

36. The intuitive reasoning being "that a given level of abnormal performance should be easier to detect when 'normal' fluctuations in sample security returns (and the standard errors of parameter estimates such as β are small rather than large)" (Brown and Warner 1980, p. 236).

37. The exact procedure adopted was that for portfolio selection purpose each security's β was estimated from all observations available for that security. Next an event date was randomly generated and β was re-estimated, over t_{-72} to t_{-13}, for the purposes of the abnormal performance tests. By forming portfolios on the basis of β over the entire 1958–73 period, the expected value of the measurement error in β over the $(-72$ to $-13)$ period should be minimised for the different risk portfolios. For further discussion see Black, Jensen and Scholes (1972).

38. It was pointed out earlier that there may be measurement error in β, which with small sample sizes might lead to errors, reducing the power of the more precisely specified return models. An inspection of the rejection rates indicated that if there are any errors they are minimal, as the power of *all models increased as sample size increased.*

13 An empirical examination of the required number of leading and lagged variables for ACM beta estimation

N. A. Sinclair

Introduction

The aim of this chapter is to examine empirically Dimson's (1979) suggestion for obtaining unbiased systematic risk measures, the aggregated coefficients method (ACM). Dimson (1979, p. 198) claimed that this method of estimation obtained "an unbiased estimate of the systematic risk of a share, when the share and some or all of the securities in the market are subject to infrequent trading".

Econometrically, estimating the market model when there is infrequent trading in the market index is tantamount to an error-in-variables problem. It is well known that ordinary least-squares (OLS) estimators are then biased and inconsistent.[1] The source of the problem is measurement error in the market index owing jointly to infrequent trading of its constituent securities and the method of index construction. Many alternative estimation techniques specifically set out to reduce the effects of this error. The inclusion of lagged market terms in the market model, or the construction of a market proxy with only end-of-period traded firms, provide simple examples. Also, the calculation of market returns over variable trade-to-trade time intervals or the Scholes and Williams (1977) estimation method provide more elaborate examples.[2]

In comparison to these methods of adjusting for non-trading bias, Dimson's (1979) ACM appears to require less prior information such as actual times of trading, and in certain cases involves less data loss. Simply stated, the method requires a multiple regression of security returns on contemporaneous, lagged and leading market returns and the summation of the slope coefficients. That is, estimate the β_j from

$$\tilde{R}_{it} = \alpha_i + \sum_{j=-m}^{n} \beta_{ij} \tilde{R}_{I_{t+j}} + \tilde{\epsilon}_{it} \tag{1}$$

where m and *n* are pre-specified numbers of lagged and leading terms

Reprinted from the *Australian Journal of Management* 6, no. 2 (December, 1981), 119–26, by permission of the author and the publisher.

respectively. The $\tilde{R}_{it}$ is the return on security i in month t, and $\tilde{R}_I$ is the return on a market index. Dimson's (1979) adjusted estimate of beta may then be obtained as

$$\beta^* = \sum_{j=-m}^{n} \hat{\beta}_j \tag{2}$$

No prior information need be available on the trading frequencies of the constituent securities of the index or on the particular times of trading of any security.[3] The major prior information required concerns the appropriate number of lagged and leading terms to include in (1). Overspecification of the number of terms leads to a relatively inefficient estimator, and underspecification allows some non-trading bias to persist.

As in Blume (1975, p. 790), a bias ratio such as

$$\widehat{\text{VAR}} \, (\beta_j) / \text{VAR}(\hat{\beta}_j) \tag{3}$$

provides a convenient cross-sectional measure of the extent of bias in the estimates of systematic risk. If any $\hat{\beta}_j$ has zero measurement error, then (3) reaches a maximum of unity, which corresponds to there being zero bias.[4] All of the cross-sectional variance in $\hat{\beta}_j$ would then be attributable to true differences in securities' relative risks. An estimate of the numerator, the variance of the true β_j, may be obtained from a partitioning of the observed cross-sectional variance in beta estimates,

$$\widehat{\text{VAR}} \, (\beta_j) = \text{VAR} \, (\hat{\beta}_j) - \text{MEAN}(\text{var} \, [\hat{\beta}_j]), \tag{5}$$

assuming independence of the true coefficients β_j and the estimation errors var$(\hat{\beta}_j)$, calculated as the squared standard error of the β_j in (1).

Dimson (1979, table 9, p. 218) estimated (3) and (5) using monthly security return data for 300 securities with no more than one missing observation in the period January 1955 to December 1974. With five leads and five lags, 230 months of data were available. From an empirical examination of (3), Dimson (1979, p. 219) concluded, "This study indicates that with monthly UK data a leading and several lagged market terms are needed . . . if risk measures are to take account of the effects of infrequent trading." Specifically, assuming that a reasonable cutoff point for (3) was approximately 20 per cent, then it was concluded that four lagged terms and one leading term would be required in (1), for Dimson's sample of UK securities.

Unfortunately, the use of (3) and (5) to establish priors concerning the appropriate number of leading and lagged terms in (1) has complications. Dimson (1979) did not discuss the potentially confounding effects which also impact on (3). Firstly, to enable the second term in (5) to proxy for $\sigma^2 \, (\epsilon)$ in (4), it must be assumed that the standard errors of the estimated $\hat{\beta}_j$ are constant across securities. This assumption may not be tenable simply because cross-sectional differences in size are often associated with heteroscedastic error variance. Secondly, this error variance, ceteris paribus, is likely to be a decreasing function of the number of observations, and conclusions reached on the basis of (3) are therefore likely to differ depending on the number of time series observations available to estimate (1) for each security. Further difficulties are introduced by increasing the number of time series observations, since it is likely to involve non-stationarity of the error variance. If OLS estimators are then obtained, the variance of these estimators will be biased.[5] In short, the second term in (5) is an accurate approximation only under some tenuous assumptions, and is unlikely to be unbiased. For that reason the unequivocal interpretation of (3) seems dubious.[6]

The empirical approach to establishing priors is also confounded by a number of important experimental issues. Any sample of securities will be affected to some extent by the phenomenon under investigation. Conclusions based on that sample will follow directly from the degree of infrequent trading in the sample and the selected index. The inferential problems associated with this empirical approach are clearly demonstrated in the results below.

It is therefore difficult to generalise with respect to setting priors on the required number of leading and lagged terms. An alternative benchmark involving the evaluation of the t statistics associated with (1) may avoid the constant cross-sectional variance assumption inherent to (4) but may not be unaffected by infrequent trading related to variance non-stationarity. The results of this investigation are also presented below. Briefly, the results demonstrate that the setting of priors for ACM beta estimation is not a straightforward exercise and that the extent of generalisation to a wider database is limited.

Data

All securities on Philip Brown's $N = 909$ price relatives file with complete monthly return observations in the time interval February 1958 to December 1973 inclusive were analysed. Eighty-one securities satisfied this criterion.[7] Both an equally weighted $N = 909$ index and a sample-based index ($N = 80$) were used in (1).

Results

Results are presented in tables 13.1 and 13.2. Table 13.1 shows the value of (3) for each of five leads and lags in (1). To demonstrate the effect of index choice, results are also presented in table 13.1 using a sample-based index in (1), calculated excluding the security of interest.

Table 13.1 Percentage of cross-sectional variance of estimated coefficients attributable to true differences between coefficients

| Lag/lead | $\widehat{\text{VAR}}\,(\beta_j)/\text{VAR}(\hat{\beta}_j)$ | | |
	Dimson (table 9)	$N = 909$ index	$N = 80$ index
−5	9	24	17
−4	21	6	6
−3	33	20	15
−2	23	31	34
−1	61	51	51
0	85	64	69
1	21	14	7
2	10	3	15
3	11	*	19
4	5	52	46
5	28	30	31

* $\widehat{\text{VAR}}\,(\beta_j)$ estimated negative in (5).

Table 13.2   Number of significant *t* statistics for *N* = 909 index and *N* = 80 index in (1)*

Lag/lead	N = 909 index α = 0.01	N = 80 index α = 0.01
−5	3	4
−4	2	3
−3	5	1
−2	3	4
−1	19	6
0	11	15
1	3	4
2	1	3
3	3	3
4	2	4
5	2	4

* Sample size of 81 securities.

As an alternative benchmark, table 13.2 contains a summary of the number of significant *t* statistics on the coefficients from (1). Non-synchronous beta coefficients were tested agains zero, and the expectation for the synchronous beta was assumed to be unity. Given the nature of the investigation on a relatively small sample of securities, the type I error rate was set at α = 0.01.

To further illustrate the effect of sample selection, table 13.3 re-examines the issue for two subsamples selected on the basis of the relative frequency of non-end-of-month trades.

Table 13.3   Two subsamples at different levels of infrequent trading using the *N* = 909 index

Lag/ lead	40 relatively frequently traded securities $\widehat{VAR}$ $(\beta_j)/$ VAR$(\hat{\beta}_j)$	α = 0.01	Lag/ lead	41 relatively infrequently traded securities $\widehat{VAR}$ $(\beta_j)/$ VAR$(\hat{\beta}_j)$	α = 0.01
−5	10	1	−5	30	2
−4	*	0	−4	23	2
−3	7	1	−3	28	4
−2	13	1	−2	41	2
−1	10	14	−1	50	5
0	70	8	0	53	3
1	18	2	1	10	1
2	4	0	2	3	1
3	*	1	3	0	2
4	*	0	4	64	2
5	19	1	5	35	1

* $\widehat{VAR}$ (β_j) estimated negative in (5).

Discussion

Table 13.1 discloses that between 64 and 69 per cent of the variance in the contemporaneous beta coefficient may be attributed to true differences between securities' systematic risk. Interpreted as a measure of bias, the magnitude of expression (3) implies that an unbiased estimate of the contemporaneous beta would need to be between 36 per cent and 31 per cent closer to unity than the original estimate.[8] For example, if an original beta estimate of 1.3 is obtained, then an unbiased estimate would be approximately 1.19. Interpreted as in Dimson (1979), it would appear from table 13.1 that three lagged terms and no leading terms are required to adequately adjust for infrequent trading bias.[9] The unexpectedly high explanatory power of the four- and five-period leading coefficients is most likely artifactual.

However, results presented in table 13.1, using a sample-based index, indicate that only two lagged and no leading terms appear necessary. This difference is to be expected since the selected sample trades more frequently than the larger and less well traded $N = 909$ index. The relatively small explanatory power of the lead one coefficient from the sample-based index implies that the present sample trades less frequently than Dimson's.

Evaluation of the t statistics, presented in table 13.2, does not lend unequivocal support to the conclusion reached in table 13.1. If the $N = 909$ index is used then the frequency of significanct t statistics across lagged coefficients appears to indicate that only one lagged term is required. Use of the $N = 80$ index reduces the importance of the lagged coefficient, and is consistent with less infrequent trading bias in the $N = 80$ index relative to the $N = 909$ index. In turn this may imply that these results understate the incidence of infrequent trading bias for a more "typical" sample of the $N = 909$ index. If this were the case, then, as a general rule, it is better to err on the side of overinclusion in (1) since merely a loss of efficiency occurs in the ACM beta estimates. However, an alternative involving the construction of a relatively frequently traded index should not be overlooked, and in the absence of reliable priors may be a preferred alternative.

Evidence that (3) is not independent of the incidence of infrequent trading in the selected sample is presented in table 13.3. Relatively frequently traded securities have 70 per cent of the variance in the contemporaneous beta coefficient attributable to real differences in securities systematic risk coefficients, compared with 53 per cent for relatively infrequently traded securities. Using (3) it would appear that for a sample of frequently traded securities no lagged terms are required, whereas for infrequently traded securities possibly five lagged terms appear necessary. As expected, the use of (3) leads to differing conclusions concerning the required number of leads and lags, depending on sample selection and the frequency of trading in the sample relative to the index.

Evaluation of significant t statistics ($\alpha = 0.01$) appears more consistent across subsamples using the $N = 909$ index. With this criterion, one lagged term appears adequate, and the use of a more frequently traded index diminishes the problem substantially as illustrated in table 13.2.

Conclusion

In an attempt to provide priors for the use of Dimson's (1979) aggregated coefficients method of estimating systematic risk measures, two criteria were examined. Following Dimson (1979), a bias ratio was calculated. In addition a simple aggregation of significant t statistics on lagged and leading market terms was also carried out. Both criteria indicated clearly that at least one lagged term would be required to adjust for non-trading bias. However, the extent of generalisation across other non-synchronous terms appears hazardous since the first criterion was shown to be affected by sample selection. In terms of rigorously establishing the priors for examination of the larger database both the present study and Dimson's (1979), to a lesser extent, have low external validity.[10] The simpler yardstick provided by the number of significant coefficients was consistent across subsamples and lends support to the conclusion that at least one lagged term but possibly two lagged terms are required if systematic risk estimates are to be adjusted for non-trading bias.

Acknowledgments

The author acknowledges helpful suggestions from R. Ball and F. Finn.

Notes

1. Alternative estimators to OLS are discussed by Johnston (1972). Alternative methods applied to security return data to adjust for bias in systematic risk measures are reviewed in Dimson (1979).
2. Dimson (1979, pp. 206-10) compared the estimation efficiency of these alternatives across trading frequencies and concluded that the ACM was among the most efficient unbiased estimators.
3. Dimson (1979, p. 206) noted that if more informed priors were available, a Bayesian adjustment of the $\hat{\beta}_j$ could be performed.
4. If a cross-sectional regression were specified as

$$\hat{\beta} = b_0 + b_1 [\beta + \epsilon] + \epsilon \tag{4}$$

where β is the true beta measured with error ϵ, then an OLS estimate of b_1 is biased. Plim $\hat{b}_1$ is $\frac{\sigma^2 \beta}{\sigma^2(\beta + \epsilon)} \beta_1$. The ratio term is analogous to (3) and when numerator and denominator are equal, there is no measurement error, and $\hat{b}_1 = b_1$, assuming that cov $(\epsilon, \beta) = 0$.
5. It is also likely that variance non-stationarity is not independent of infrequent trading which further complicates the use of (3) to give any "indication of the maximum number of lags and leads which are required to avoid bias in the estimator" (Dimson 1979, p. 205). See also Dimson (1979, fn. 9, p. 199) for speculation on the incidence of heteroscedasticity in market-model residuals and the incidence of infrequent trading.
6. Blume (1975, p. 794) also alluded to the shortcomings associated with the use of (3) for a similar purpose.
7. It is possible that this sample has a low variance across trading frequencies owing to survivorship bias. Evidence presented below seems consistent with this claim.
8. See Blume (1975, p. 791) for details of this adjustment.
9. Dimson (1979, p. 223) used approximately 20 per cent as a cutoff point for (3).
10. Dimson's (1979, p. 212) sample was approximately 16 per cent of the securities in the larger database.

PART 5

Price response in share markets—efficiency and valuation issues

A. Time series properties of rates of return

14 Rates of return to shares, bond yields and inflation rates: An historical perspective

R.R. Officer

The accompanying tables and graphs give an historical perspective of the behaviour of the returns to a portfolio of equities (shares), the yields on 10-year government bonds, and inflation rates over the period 1882–1987 inclusive (106 years).

Table 14.1 shows 10-yearly average annual rates for these variables and includes the average annual rate for the entire period 1882–1987 inclusive. A brief description of how the figures in the tables and graphs were constructed follows.

The arithmetic average nominal equity rate of return is the simple annual average rate of return for an investor who invested in the portfolio at the start of the year and liquidated at the end of each year. The average real rate of return was derived by deflating the nominal annual rate of return by the rate of change in prices over the year using the Fisher equation. The geometric nominal rate of return for the equity portfolio reflects the rate of return investors would have experienced if they had invested in the

Table 14.1 10-year average annual rates, equity returns, bond yields and inflation, 1882–1987

| Time period | Equity rate of return | | | | Average 10-year bond yields | Equity premium over bond yields | Price changes geometric average |
| | Arithmetic average | | Geometric average | | | | |
	Nominal	Real	Nominal	Real			
1882–1987	13.06	9.56	11.76	8.26	5.21	7.94	3.23
	(17.01)	(16.31)			(2.86)	(16.86)	
1882–1887	14.45	15.17	10.82	12.16	3.76	10.68	−1.20
1888–1897	9.52	10.65	6.19	7.90	3.46	6.06	−1.58
1898–1907	12.34	11.23	11.33	10.23	3.46	8.87	1.00
1908–1917	10.35	5.48	7.97	3.47	4.05	6.30	4.35
1918–1927	17.16	15.74	15.81	15.32	5.53	11.64	0.42
1928–1937	12.78	13.77	9.81	11.36	4.33	8.45	−1.39
1938–1947	8.96	5.33	8.83	5.41	2.94	6.02	3.24
1948–1957	11.99	4.09	9.20	2.38	4.15	7.83	6.66
1958–1967	14.52	12.04	11.49	9.20	4.92	9.60	2.10
1968–1977	7.68	−0.85	0.85	−7.04	7.32	0.36	8.48
1978–1987	24.45	14.79	18.52	10.24	12.58	11.87	7.52

Note: All of the above figures are in percentage terms. Figures in parentheses are standard deviations.

portfolio at the start of the 10-year period and liquidated at the end of the 10-year period. The geometric average real rate of return to equities was found by taking the nominal rate and deflating it by the geometric average rate of price changes over the period using the Fisher equation.

The average 10-year bond yields represents the average annual redemption yield on long-dated government securities.

The equity premium over bond yields represents the difference between the arithmetic nominal return to shares and the average annual yield on long-dated government securities. This premium is often used in the capital asset pricing model as a reflection of the price of risk, i.e., the rate of return premium earned by the market portfolio over the risk-free rate of return.

Price changes reflect the geometric annual average rate of change in prices over each of the 10-year periods.

A similar set of figures to table 14.1 is given in table 14.2, except that 5-year averages are used.

Table 14.2   5-year average annual rates, equity returns, bond yields and inflation, 1882–1987

Time period	Equity rate of return				Average 10-year bond yields	Equity premium over bond yields	Price changes geometric average
	Arithmetic average		Geometric average				
	Nominal	Real	Nominal	Real			
1882–1987	13.06	9.56	11.76	8.26	5.21	7.94	3.23
	(17.01)	(16.31)			(2.86)	(16.86)	
1882–1887	14.45	15.17	10.82	12.16	3.76	10.68	−1.20
1888–1892	10.18	12.33	3.96	7.03	3.56	6.62	−2.87
1893–1897	8.86	8.98	9.71	8.71	3.37	5.49	0.93
1898–1902	9.49	7.26	7.74	5.73	3.35	6.15	1.91
1903–1907	15.18	15.19	10.85	9.88	3.58	11.60	0.89
1908–1912	13.17	9.35	9.01	5.86	3.72	9.45	2.98
1913–1917	7.53	1.61	4.91	−0.43	4.46	3.07	5.37
1918–1922	16.32	13.83	13.80	13.19	5.66	10.66	0.53
1923–1927	18.01	17.65	12.01	11.80	5.42	12.59	0.18
1928–1932	3.26	7.12	−1.24	3.23	5.13	−1.87	−4.32
1933–1937	22.31	20.42	14.95	12.92	3.70	18.61	1.79
1938–1942	0.90	−3.61	1.42	−2.56	3.11	−2.21	4.09
1943–1947	17.02	14.27	10.88	8.63	2.77	14.24	2.07
1948–1952	8.85	−3.86	3.96	−6.04	3.51	5.33	10.64
1953–1957	15.13	12.04	12.96	10.39	4.79	10.33	2.33
1958–1962	15.34	13.35	10.58	9.00	4.98	10.36	1.46
1963–1967	13.70	10.73	7.75	5.11	4.86	8.84	2.51
1968–1972	10.82	5.93	0.73	−3.28	5.76	5.06	4.15
1973–1977	4.55	−7.62	6.73	−3.69	8.89	−4.34	10.82
1978–1982	18.96	8.51	11.10	2.92	11.54	7.42	7.95
1983–1987	29.93	21.06	14.76	8.71	13.62	16.31	5.56

Note: All of the above figures are in percentage terms. Figures in parentheses are standard deviations.

The graphs represent annual figures for those that are described in the tables plus 10-year moving averages where the 10-year period changes by one year at a time.

10 YEAR TREASURY BOND YIELDS
(1882–1987)

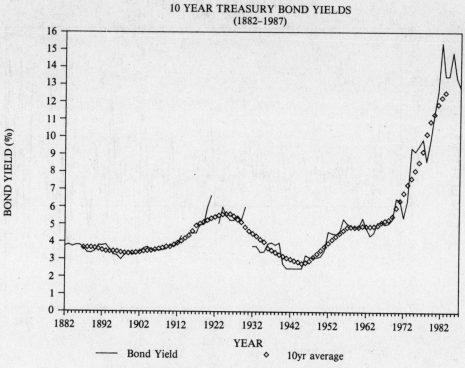

Figure 14.1   10-year Treasury bond yields (1882–1987)

INFLATION RATES
(1882–1987)

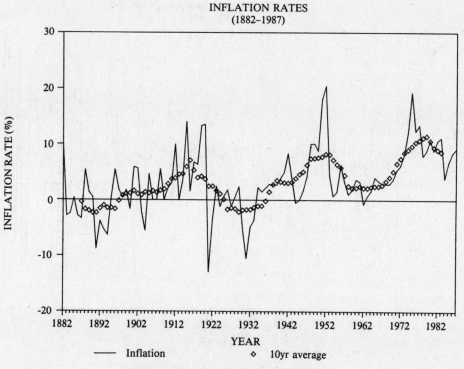

Figure 14.2   Inflation rates (1882–1987)

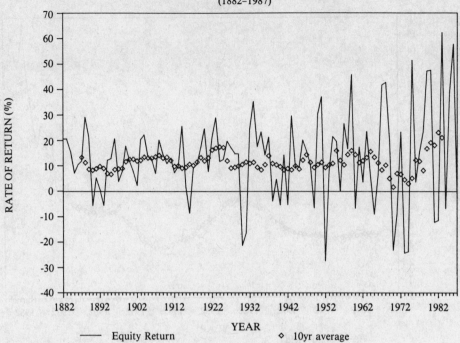

Figure 14.3   Annual equity rates of return (1882–1987)

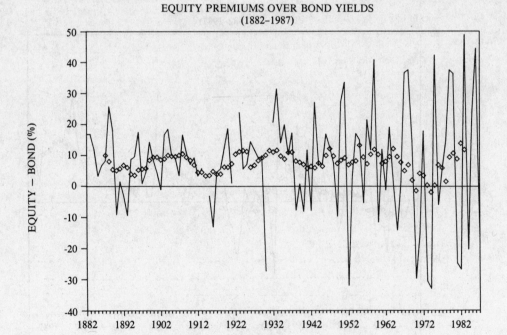

Figure 14.4   Equity premiums over bond yields (1882–1987)

Data

Annual share returns

Annual share returns were constructed from a share market accumulation index; such an index reflects both dividend returns plus capital gains. The index was constructed for the period 1882–1987 (106 years) inclusive from a variety of sources. The early period made use of data developed by Lamberton (1958) and this was linked to an accumulation index of fifty leading shares from the AGSM price file (1958–1974) and the AGSM Value Weighted Accumulation Index (1975–1987). The use of different indexes can present problems. There is always doubt as to compatibility when such a mix of indexes is used. A large number of checks were made for consistency and compatibility of indexes. All of the checks suggested movements in the above indexes were relatively closely and contemporaneously related.

There are also doubts as to the accuracy of the data in earlier parts of the period particularly for shares. The base data were monthly share price data from which annual indexes were constructed adding in dividends. Using annual data and the various relationships found, Officer (1985) dispels much of the concern about incorrectly drawing inferences because of poor-quality data, at least on an annual basis.

Inflation rates

Three series were used to construct an annual price index. The period 1882–1901 was constructed from an implicit gross product deflator (see Butlin 1962, table 13). From 1902 to 1948 a retail price index was used (see Commonwealth Year Book 1981) and from 1949 to 1987 the Consumer Price Index was used. The series were linked as rates of change (yields). A number of tests were conducted on various indexes before deciding on this group and where the indexes overlapped tests were made on their relationships. As might be expected the correlations were high.

Bond yields

The intention was to use long-term Commonwealth Bond yields to approximate the behaviour of interest rates. Under generally accepted theories of the term structure of interest rates, changes in these yields will reflect changes in yields generally across the term structure. Moreover, we would expect the yields on company debentures to be similarly affected. For the period 1882–1914, yields were taken from New South Wales government securities traded on the London capital market (Hall 1963). For the period 1915–1949 the yields were on Commonwealth Government Securities maturing in five years or more (see Reserve Bank bulletins). Finally, for the period 1950–1982, yields were taken from 10-year rebateable Commonwealth Government Bonds (see Reserve Bank 1982) and from 1982–1987 non-rebateables were used. The reason for switching between rebateables and non-rebateables was the lack of trading and/or availability of data on one or other of these security types—the typical difference between the yields of the two types is low, of the order of 5 per cent of the security's total yield, which implies the effective tax rate of traders in these securities is also low, approximately 5 per cent.

15 Seasonality in Australian capital markets: Market efficiency and empirical issues

R. R. Officer

Introduction

The implication of seasonality in share prices is part of the conventional wisdom that usually surrounds stock markets. Along with beliefs in "four-year cycles", "recessions straddling two fiscal years", "resistance levels in market indices" and other folklore, beliefs in "April and June downturns", and "post-Christmas bulls" are fairly widespread. Nevertheless, there has been little worthwhile empirical study on such issues for Australian share markets. An exception is a paper by Praetz (1973b) who reported finding a seasonal pattern in the Sydney All Ordinaries Index and a number of other industrial share groups of two peaks and two troughs. The pattern he found using spectral methods was not large but indicated peaks in January–February and July–August and troughs in March–April and November–December.

This chapter examines possible economic implications of a seasonal in Australian capital markets and the problems of obtaining adequate data and the traps of using indices. The chapter also reports extensive testing for seasonality in the time domain, as distinct from the frequency domain used by Praetz in his spectral analysis, of shares and bonds.

Seasonality and the efficiency of the stock market

An efficient market is one in which prices fully reflect available information. Different types of efficiency may be described depending on what set of information is said to be fully reflected in prices. In this chapter we will be dealing with the "weak form" of efficiency, i.e., the information set is historical prices and any pattern apparent in the series.[1] An implication of an efficient market is no abnormal returns can be made from this information because current prices already reflect the information. Models describing efficiency are said to be "fair game" models. The theory of "fair game" models

Reprinted from the *Journal of Financial Economics* 2 (1975), 29–51, by permission of the author and the publisher.

has been developed by Samuelson (1965, 1973) and Mandelbrot (1966). The clearest discussion of the theory of efficient markets and the evidence for their existence is given by Fama (1970a). Fama's paper gives much of the background for this section of the chapter.

As Praetz suggests, his study is unique in that there has been no well-supported evidence of a seasonality in any other of the world's share markets. The lack of a seasonal in share prices is generally considered to be evidence consistent with the "weak form" of efficiency in these markets. In a market that exhibits the "weak form" of efficiency no abnormal returns can be made from any information contained in the historical price series. The presence of a seasonal component is usually considered evidence of inefficiency or, as Praetz (1973b, p. 77) suggests, a market imperfection. The argument usually runs that if speculators knew of a seasonal they would make use of it to make abnormal returns and in doing so would effectively remove the seasonal. This would cause returns to fluctuate randomly. An example of such a process is the random-walk model,

$$\tilde{r}_{jt} = \mu_j + \tilde{e}_{jt}, \tag{1}$$

where $\tilde{r}_{jt} = (\tilde{p}_{jt} - p_{j,t-1}) / p_{j,t-1}$ is the rate of return (yield) on share j over the period $t-1$ to t, and p_{jt} is the price adjusted for bonus issues, dividends, etc. The tilde indicates a random variable.

μ_j is the normal rate of return for share j, assumed to be constant, so that

$$E(\tilde{r}_{jt}) = \mu_j.$$

$\tilde{e}_{jt}$ is the residual and it is assumed to have the properties

$$E(\tilde{e}_{jt}) = 0,$$

$$\text{cov}\,(\tilde{e}_{jt}, \tilde{e}_{j,t-k}) = 0, t = 1, 2, \ldots \text{ and } k < t.$$

It then follows that

$$\text{cov}\,(\tilde{r}_{jt}, \tilde{r}_{j,t-k}) = 0.$$

A further property of the model is

$$E\,(\tilde{r}_{jt}) = E\,(\tilde{r}_{jt} | r_{j,t-1}, r_{j,t-2}, \ldots),$$

i.e., the marginal return is equal to the conditional return. This property implies that the past series $\{r_j\}$ provides no information about the expected return that is not already incorporated in the return.

Suppose a seasonal develops in the process generating the yields; this implies for model (1),

$$E\,(\tilde{r}_{jt}) \neq E\,(\tilde{r}_{jt} | r_{j,t-1}, r_{j,t-2}, \ldots),$$

$$E(\tilde{e}_{jt}) \neq 0,$$

$$\text{cov}\,(\tilde{e}_{jt}, \tilde{e}_{j,t-k}) \neq 0, k = \text{the period of the seasonal}.$$

A speculator who becomes aware of such a seasonal can buy $E(\tilde{e}_{jt}) > 0$ type shares or sell $E(\tilde{e}_{jt}) < 0$ type shares, so that his expected return, $E(\tilde{r}^*_{jt}) = E(\tilde{r}_{jt} | r_{j,t-1}, r_{j,t-2}, \ldots)$, is greater than the normal return, i.e., $E(\tilde{r}^*_{jt}) > E(\tilde{r}_{jt})$.

The speculator will continue to operate so long as abnormal returns are being earned. However, his actions will raise $E(\tilde{e}_{jt}) > 0$ type share prices or lower $E(\tilde{e}_{jt}) < 0$ type share prices until in period $t-1$ prices will have fully adjusted so that normal returns are again being earned and the process is once more a random walk.

The presence of a seasonal in share prices is not in itself sufficient to reject the hypothesis of an efficient market. For example, a seasonal may be well known and still exist in an efficient capital market simply because the opportunity cost of capital may be different at different times of the year.[2] An example of a generating process of stock returns in which there is an intrinsic seasonal is

$$\tilde{r}_{jt} = v_{jt} + \tilde{e}_{jt}, \tag{2}$$

where $v_{jt} = \mu_j + \sigma_t$ is the normal rate of return for time t, μ_j is a deseasonalised normal rate of return and σ_t is the seasonal component assumed constant at a particular time $t \in T$, and $\Sigma \, \sigma_t = 0$, where T indicates which seasonal component is appropriate, e.g., for a quarterly seasonal $T = 1, 2, 3, 4$. The properties of the model are:

$$E\,(\tilde{r}_{jt} | r_{j,t-1}, r_{j,t-2}, \ldots) = v_{jt},$$

$$E\,(\tilde{r}_{jt} | r_{j,t-1}, r_{j,t-2}, \ldots) \neq E\,(r_{jt}),$$

$$E(\tilde{e}_{jt}) = 0,$$

$$\mathrm{cov}\,(\tilde{e}_{jt}, \tilde{e}_{j,t-k}) = 0,$$

$$\mathrm{cov}\,(\tilde{r}_{jt}, \tilde{r}_{j,t-k}) \neq 0.$$

Model (2) still describes a "fair game" process, $E(\tilde{e}_{jt}) = 0$, but the time series $\{r_j\}$ is no longer a random walk. Because the intrinsic seasonal component is built into expectations of returns, there is no way a speculator can make abnormal returns from operating on the seasonal component.

Clearly, if the process under investigation is assumed to form expectations as in model (1), but in fact model (2) is the generating process, then the wrong conclusions about the efficiency of the market will be drawn from an analysis of the series $\{r_j\}$. In the absence of knowledge about the true generating process, the simplest way of testing the series for efficiency is to see whether abnormal returns can be made from trading rules based on the historical series.[3]

Artifacts induced by index construction[4]

The outcome of studies of the time series behaviour of share prices is critically dependent on the "cleanliness" of the data, i.e., actual market figures (traded prices) taken at some fixed time interval, for example the end-of-week closing price. These prices should then be adjusted for any cash outlay, bonus issue or the like. The failure to use "clean" data can often lead to spurious relationships which wrongly suggest profitable trading rules.

Positive first-order serial correlations

One of the best known examples of such spurious relationships was pointed out by Working (1960). If the average price over a time interval is taken to form a price series, i.e., the average weekly traded price of a share, then even though the underlying series may be a pure random walk, first differences or rates of return of price series will have a first-order serial correlation.

The same type of phenomenon described by Working can exist with an index even though the index may have been constructed from aggregating "clean" share-price series. Share prices change in response to changes in information. A share price or yield index is a surrogate for the market factor, and the market factor represents common movements in all shares, i.e., it responds to information that affects all shares. Not all shares are traded at the same time, in fact, in relatively "thin" markets like those in Australia, shares in fairly major companies can go for some days without a trade. The result is an index which, instead of measuring the market factor at a single point in time, is really taking an average of the true market factor over the time interval represented by the earliest and the latest of the sales made in the component shares.

As an illustration of this phenomenon, suppose an index has a particular value on 30 June 1974, but one of the shares in the index was last traded on 25 June, then the index is some average of the market factor over the period 25–30 June. *Ceteris paribus*, we would expect such an index to exhibit positive first-order serial correlation with the value of the index which included any of the period 25–30 June in its value, even though it may be centred well outside the period. This explains why monthly rates of return can exhibit serial correlation even though there may be only a few days of commonality. For example, the end-of-month June figures for the index include the entire period 25–30 June, but the end-of-month July rate of return will also include this period in any share that was not traded between 25 June and the end of the month. It does not require a whole month of non-trading in some of the component shares for a rate of return index to exhibit first-order serial correlation, a day or so near the end of the month is sufficient.

As a result of the phenomenon described above, the presence of first-order serial correlation in a share index may lead to the incorrect rejection of the random-walk hypothesis. Evidence of this type of artifact of index construction and a method of overcoming it will be described in the empirical section of the chapter.

Bias induced in serial correlation

Slight negative first-order serial correlations are often observed in "clean" data series. This is due in part to the bias in the expected serial correlation coefficient of a random series. The bias is of the order[5]

$$E(\hat{\rho}_{j1}) = -1 \ / \ (n-1),$$

the magnitude of bias is a function of the number of observations (n). However, of more importance is the negative first-order serial correlation induced by data errors. If a price is wrongly recorded higher (lower) than the actual price, then in a random series the next price recorded has an expected value less (greater) than the wrongly recorded price. The result is that price increases tend to be followed by price decreases and vice versa, leading to the observation of negative first-order serial correlation coefficients.

Obviously one of the major sources of data errors is the failure to correct for adjustments made to a share's value due to dividends, bonus issues, rights, returns of capital, calls, new issues, etc. The Sydney Stock Exchange All Ordinaries Index fails to adjust for dividends. We would expect that the price of a share going ex-dividend will drop by an amount determined by the product of the dividend and marginal tax rate of the marginal trader. Since many institutional investors (i.e., insurance companies) are not taxed on dividends, and they make up a substantial proportion of the market, it has been suggested that the price will fall by the amount of the dividend. Moreover, companies tend to pay out dividends over similar months, i.e., March–April, September–October, which could induce a "seasonal" in the index as share prices go ex-dividend.

Tests of seasonality in share returns

Data

The data source is an as yet unpublished price file of 651 companies' shares of the Melbourne Stock Exchange over the period 1958 to 1970 inclusive. The file was prepared by Professor Philip Brown of the University of Western Australia. The prices are the final monthly trading price of each share adjusted for bonuses, calls, dividends, rights, etc., so that data can be considered "clean" under the description of the previous section.

The monthly return for each share is calculated as

$$r_{jt} = (p_{jt} - p_{j,t-1}) \, / \, p_{j,t-1},$$

where p_{jt} is the price of stock j for month t, and $t-1$ represents the previous month. One hundred and fifty-five monthly returns were derived for each share covering the period February 1958 to December 1970.

Serial correlations

A standard method of detecting seasonality in time series observations is by serial correlations (autocorrelation). Serial correlation coefficients were estimated as $\hat{\rho}_{jk} = \text{cov} \, (r_{jt}, \, r_{j,t-k}) \, / \, \text{s.d.} \, (r_{jt}) \, \text{s.d.} \, (r_{j,t-k})$,[6] where $\hat{\rho}_{jk}$ is the estimate of the serial correlation coefficient for the jth firm ($j = 1, \ldots,$ 126) and the k lag in months ($k = 1, \ldots, 36$). The 126 firms selected were those that had complete data for the entire period of the file, i.e., 155 monthly observations from 1958 to 1970.

The market model

It is useful for understanding the analysis of serial correlations if we represent the generating process of stock market returns by the market model,[7] i.e.,

$$\tilde{r}_{jt} = \alpha_j + \beta_j \tilde{r}_{mt} + \tilde{e}_{jt},$$

as previously the r_{jt} is the rate of return for stock j at time t, α_j and β_j

are parameters specific to stock j, r_{mt} is the return to the market factor—the market factor is the common denominator of movements in the return for all shares. e_{jt} is the disturbance term—it is that component of a share's return that is specific to that share. The model is assumed to have the following properties:

$$E(\tilde{e}_{jt}) = 0,$$

in effect this property implies that no share consistently earns abnormal returns or losses;

$$cov\,(\tilde{e}_{jt}, \tilde{e}_{j,t-k}) = 0,$$

this property implies that no stock has a seasonality that is specific to that stock, i.e., the market is not segmented;

$$cov\,(\tilde{e}_{jt}, \tilde{r}_{mt}) = 0,$$

this property is defined by the model;

$$cov\,(\tilde{e}_{jt}, \tilde{r}_{m,t-k}) = 0,$$

this implies that no stock consistently leads or lags the market; if the property did not exist it would imply an inefficient market.

Adopting the market model and employing the above assumptions we can show that the serial correlation of a particular stock for lag k, i.e., ρ_{jk}, must be less than or equal to the serial correlation of the market factor for the same lag, i.e. $|\rho_{mk}| \geqslant |\rho_{jk}|$.

Serial correlation has been defined as

$$\rho_{jk} = cov\,(\tilde{r}_{jt}, \tilde{r}_{j,t-k})\,/\,\text{s.d.}\,(\tilde{r}_{jt})\,\text{s.d.}\,(\tilde{r}_{j,t-k}).$$

Substituting the market model for r_{jt} and $r_{j,t-k}$ and making use of our assumptions, including stationarity of $\tilde{r}_j$ and $\tilde{r}_m$, we can show that:

$$\rho_{jk} = \frac{\beta^2{}_j\,cov\,(\tilde{r}_{mt}, \tilde{r}_{m,t-k})}{\beta^2{}_j\,var\,(\tilde{r}_m) + var\,(\tilde{e}_j)}$$

$$= \frac{[cov^2\,(\tilde{r}_j, \tilde{r}_m)\,/\,var^2\,(\tilde{r}_m)]\,cov\,(\tilde{r}_{mt}, \tilde{r}_{m,t-k})}{[cov^2\,(\tilde{r}_j, \tilde{r}_m)\,/\,var^2\,(\tilde{r}_m)]\,var\,(\tilde{r}_m) + var\,(\tilde{e}_j)}$$

and since $\rho_{mk} = cov\,(\tilde{r}_{mt}, \tilde{r}_{m,t-k})\,/\,var\,(\tilde{r}_m),$

$$\rho_{jk} = \rho_{mk} \left\{ \frac{[cov\,(\tilde{r}_j, \tilde{r}_m)\,]^2}{[cov\,(\tilde{r}_j, \tilde{r}_m)\,]^2 + var\,(\tilde{e}_j)\,var\,(\tilde{r}_m)} \right\}$$

Since the values of $[cov\,(\tilde{r}_j, \tilde{r}_m)\,]^2$, $var\,(\tilde{e}_j)$ and $var\,(\tilde{r}_m)$ are all positive, ρ_{jk} must be the same sign as ρ_{mk}, and moreover, $|\rho_{mk}| \geqslant |\rho_{jk}|$. When $var\,(\tilde{e}_j) = 0$, i.e., there is no disturbance term, then j is the market factor or a surrogate for it and $\rho_{mk} = \rho_{jk}$.

The analysis above indicates that while it may be difficult to detect seasonality by examining individual shares, the "portfolio effect" will make the presence of any seasonality more apparent when we examine an index or portfolio of shares. It is with this in mind that we first examine the distribution of serial correlation coefficients for 126 individual shares and then examine the serial correlations of a return index of the 126 companies.

Serial correlations for individual share returns

Table 15.1 gives the deciles of the monthly serial correlation coefficients for the returns to 126 companies.[8] The coefficients were sorted by months of lag and not by companies to give the distribution. The mean and standard deviation are also shown. An approximation of the standard deviation of the serial correlation coefficient is given[9] by $1/n^{1/2}$, and for the data in table 1 this is approximately 0.0803. This is remarkably close to the estimate provided by the sample data, lending support to the notion of a single generating process for the serial correlation of share returns.

Table 15.2 gives the results for the two half-periods, each of 77 months. There does not appear to be any substantial difference between the periods, with the possible exception of the 12-month lag—where a 0.076 coefficient becomes—0.001 in the second period.

Table 15.1 The distributions of monthly serial correlation coefficients of shares in 126 firms over the period 1958–70 inclusive (155 monthly returns)

I. Deciles *

Fractiles	1	2	3	4	5	6	7	8	9	10	11	12
							Lag (k)					
0.9	0.063	0.105	0.156	0.120	0.122	0.189	0.141	0.109	0.164	0.102	0.121	0.149
0.8	0.005	0.069	0.118	0.069	0.089	0.149	0.101	0.089	0.114	0.072	0.091	0.122
0.7	−0.020	0.038	0.096	0.036	0.065	0.112	0.061	0.068	0.090	0.039	0.069	0.090
0.6	−0.039	0.004	0.051	0.007	0.047	0.089	0.048	0.054	0.061	0.028	0.042	0.063
0.5	−0.053	−0.025	0.027	−0.006	0.024	0.077	0.036	0.019	0.041	0.001	0.018	0.035
0.4	−0.080	−0.041	0.003	−0.022	0.049	0.043	0.016	0.007	0.019	−0.019	−0.010	−0.012
0.3	−0.112	−0.066	−0.009	−0.047	−0.032	0.024	−0.016	−0.013	−0.008	−0.044	−0.031	−0.099
0.2	−0.130	−0.104	−0.038	−0.092	−0.048	−0.015	−0.039	−0.040	−0.033	−0.085	−0.058	−0.045
0.1	−0.171	−0.151	−0.075	−0.133	−0.090	−0.082	−0.067	−0.072	−0.062	−0.104	−0.087	−0.074

II. Mean and standard deviation of monthly serial correlation coefficients

−0.063	−0.020	0.034	−0.008	0.021	0.062	0.032	0.025	0.044	−0.001	0.018	0.039
(0.091)	(0.094)	(0.097)	(0.088)	(0.086)	(0.102)	(0.085)	(0.078)	(0.089)	(0.089)	(0.087)	(0.093)

* The serial correlation coefficients were sorted separately for each month's lag, for example, the 0.5 fractile (the median) does not represent a single firm but it is the median value for each month's lag.

Overall, the results are reasonably similar to those obtained by Kendall (1953) for United Kingdom data and Moore (1962), Alexander (1961) and Fama (1965) in the United States. On the basis of this evidence alone we would be hard pressed to reject the random-walk hypothesis for individual shares. However, two points are worth making:

1. There appears to be some evidence of small data errors as the first-order serial correlation does show the largest negative coefficient. This effect was discussed above in "Artifacts Induced by Index Construction".

Table 15.2 The mean, median and standard deviation of monthly serial correlation coefficients for two half-periods *

I.						Lag (*k*)						
	1	2	3	4	5	6	7	8	9	10	11	12
Mean	−0.028	−0.015	0.039	0.011	0.015	0.043	0.025	0.004	0.030	−0.006	−0.005	0.076
Median	−0.030	−0.033	0.033	0.010	0.011	0.042	0.017	0.013	0.037	−0.008	−0.023	0.064
S.D.	0.128	0.113	0.139	0.129	0.109	0.149	0.098	0.127	0.110	0.122	0.121	0.124

II.												
Mean	−0.108	−0.039	0.009	−0.041	0.009	0.056	0.021	0.031	0.041	−0.010	0.020	−0.001
Median	−0.113	−0.044	0.005	−0.057	0.003	0.056	0.036	0.049	0.036	−0.019	0.018	0.015
S.D.	0.110	0.121	0.113	0.112	0.128	0.114	0.117	0.114	0.123	0.114	0.118	0.118

* Half-periods I (February 1958–June 1964) and II (July 1964–November 1970).

2. The largest positive serial correlation occurred at 6-months lag. This provides some indication, albeit slight, of the phenomenon described by Praetz (1973b); although, if we took this coefficient at its face value, then it would explain less than half of one per cent of the total variation in the monthly return to the average share.

Serial correlations for index returns

A simple arithmetic index of the 126 companies' share returns was created. The index in effect is a portfolio of 126 shares, each with the same weight in the portfolio, and it serves as a surrogate for the market factor. The results

Table 15.3 Serial correlations for an index of 126 shares (DEX126) and the Sydney All Ordinaries Index (SYD)

Months lag	2/1958–12/1970		2/1958–6/1964		7/1964–11/1970	
	DEX126	SYD	DEX126	SYD	DEX126	SYD
1	0.256	0.181	0.301	0.217	0.197	0.162
2	−0.001	−0.038	0.029	−0.040	−0.056	−0.041
3	0.068	0.034	0.135	0.011	−0.017	0.046
4	−0.090	−0.177	0.019	−0.030	−0.215	−0.256
5	0.023	−0.095	0.006	−0.043	0.004	−0.122
6	0.204	0.135	0.183	0.006	0.197	0.217
7	0.051	0.071	0.018	−0.051	0.051	0.139
8	0.100	0.097	0.010	−0.030	0.157	0.170
9	0.221	0.155	0.148	0.011	0.265	0.227
10	0.022	0.042	−0.071	−0.069	0.074	0.094
11	0.055	0.031	−0.039	−0.115	0.112	0.101
12	0.122	0.047	0.240	0.062	0.020	0.048
13	−0.157	−0.147	−0.075	−0.080	−0.236	−0.178
14	−0.256	−0.278	−0.396	−0.328	−0.166	−0.258
15	−0.171	−0.213	−0.220	−0.285	0.150	−0.182
16	−0.064	0.003	−0.182	−0.051	0.009	0.030
17	0.026	0.059	−0.156	−0.025	0.150	0.099
18	0.100	0.132	0.128	0.033	0.077	0.179
19	0.107	0.126	0.098	0.014	0.110	0.179
20	−0.056	0.016	−0.115	0.017	−0.020	0.015
21	−0.166	−0.153	0.122	0.053	−0.366	−0.250
22	−0.230	−0.194	−0.021	−0.013	−0.374	−0.282
23	−0.092	−0.064	−0.083	0.010	−0.105	−0.099
24	0.055	0.020	0.068	0.229	0.043	−0.068

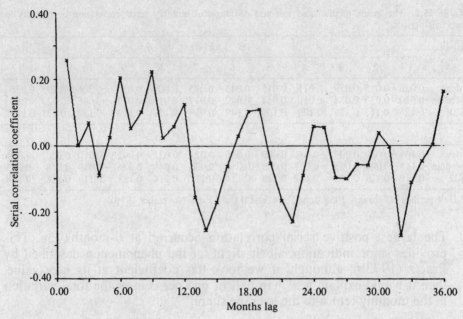

Figure 15.1 Correlograms of serial correlations for DEX126; period Feb. 1958 to Dec. 1970; data from table 15.3.

of serial correlation for lags up to 24 months for this index, labelled DEX126, are shown in table 15.3 and figure 15.1 gives correlograms over 36 months for DEX126. For comparison, the serial correlations for the Sydney All Ordinaries Index, labelled SYD, are also shown. The period tested was from February 1958 to December 1970, which was divided into two subperiods for further testing.

The comments on the results are restricted to DEX126. The Sydney All Ordinaries Index, although it shows somewhat similar behaviour to DEX126, is too unreliable because of composition changes and the failure to reinvest dividends to accurately draw inferences when the effects we are looking for are so small. Two principal observations can be made from the results:

1. The first-order serial correlation coefficient is quite large (0.256) and positive. This is in contrast to the individual shares, whose average first-order serial correlation was small and negative. The reversal in the sign contradicts the proof given in the market model, above. However, the large positive first-order serial correlation of the index is interpreted as clear evidence of the non-trading phenomena discussed in positive first-order serial correlations. It should not be interpreted as evidence of a deviation from the random-walk hypothesis.[10]

2. An approximation of the standard deviation of the serial correlation coefficient was discussed above, for the full period $1/n^{1/2} = 0.080$ and for the half-periods $= 0.114$. On the basis of this approximation, the 6- and 9-month serial correlations appear to be signficantly greater than zero. This is substantiated by the two half-periods. Results for further splits in the period are not shown but they also indicated a persistence in these two coefficients, particularly the 6-month coefficient. The results

for the 12-month coefficient are not so conclusive. The strong negatives for 13 and 14 were perhaps surprising in their persistence, but under the tests described in the next section they did not appear to have any predictive ability.

Since there appear to be some serial correlation coefficients that are significant, the next step is to examine whether these are just chance occurrences for the periods examined. If not, they should have some persistence that enables us to forecast returns more accurately, although, on the evidence so far, we cannot expect too much from the forecasts. The maximum returns any one of the coefficients, by itself, is likely to forecast is only about 5 per cent of the total variations—a model constructed over a number of parameters may fare better. To test these propositions we turn to the Box and Jenkins methods of univariate forecasting.[11]

Forecasts of the index

The positive first-order serial correlation has been attributed to the presence of some non-trading in stocks making up the index. This is an artifact of index construction and one we want to get rid of. The procedure used was to fit a simple first-order autoregressive model, i.e.,

$$z_t = \beta_0 + \beta_1 z_{t-1} + a_t,$$

where the z's are the index rates of return. If the true process was a random walk but the artifact caused a first-order relationship, then this model would ensure that the residuals (a_t) behave as a random-walk series. The forecasts of this model were then used as the control for testing more complicated models.

On the basis of the serial correlation coefficients a number of autoregressive, moving-average and mixed models of the Box–Jenkins type were tried. The method used was to estimate the models over the first half of the data (77 observations) and then use the models to make one-month-ahead forecasts over the second half of the data.[12] The results for selected models are shown in table 15.4.

The models were selected on the basis of the coefficient of determination (r^2) for both fitted and forecast data, mean absolute errors and their standard deviations, and mean errors and standard deviations.

There is no absolute criterion for making the decision regarding whether one model is "significantly" superior to another model. A t-test on the basis of errors is not valid because errors are not independent between models. For forecast results, which is what we are concerned with, no adjustment is necessary for degrees of freedom, therefore, r^2, F-values and the mean absolute errors and standard deviations indicate if one model is better than another. What these measures do not clearly indicate is "how much" better is one model than another, i.e., we cannot put a significance level on the degree of superiority.

Model 3, the mixed autoregressive moving-average model, gives the best results, forecasting about 7 per cent more of the total variation in returns than the control (model 1).[13] Similar results to those in table 4 were obtained when 143 months were used to select appropriate models and estimate the

Table 15.4 Selected models and their performance in forecasting the index of 126 share price relatives

Model

$$\hat{Z}_t = \hat{\beta}_0 + \hat{\beta}_1 Z_{t-1}$$
$$\hat{Z}_t = \hat{\beta}_0 + \hat{\beta}_1 Z_{t-1} + \hat{\theta}_1 a_{t-6}$$
$$\hat{Z}_t = \hat{\beta}_0 + \hat{\beta}_1 Z_{t-1} + \hat{\theta}_1 a_{t-6} + \hat{\theta}_2 a_{t-9} + \hat{\theta}_3 a_{t-12}$$

Parameter estimates (period February 1958 to May 1963)

Model	$\hat{\beta}_0$	$\hat{\beta}_1$	Q	MAE	r^2	$\hat{\theta}_1$	$\hat{\theta}_2$	$\hat{\theta}_3$
	0.70876	0.30093	49.5	0.0215	0.101			
	(0.11219)	(0.11057)		(0.0199)				
	0.67872	0.33058	38.3	0.0206	0.132	0.146911		
	(0.11617)	(0.11448)		(0.0200)		(0.12151)		
	0.60891	0.40037	27.7	0.0199	0.209	0.18724	0.16538	0.187056
	(0.12275)	(0.12082)		(0.0189)		(0.13062)	(0.13389)	(0.14112)

Forecast results (period June 1963 to December 1970)

Model	MAE	r^2	F-value
1	0.0244	0.028	2.20
	(0.0287)		
2	0.0235	0.055	4.39
	(0.0210)		
3	0.0224	0.097	8.06
	(0.0200)		

Notes:

R_j Price relatives have a one-to-one correspondence with rates of return, i.e., $R_j = 1 + r_j$

Q For a discussion of this statistic see Box and Jenkins (1970, p. 290); it is approximated by χ^2 with $(k-m)$ degrees of freedom, whereas $k = 36$ and m = the number of parameters. For 30 degrees of freedom and 5 per cent level of significance, $\chi^2 = 43.8$, where the null hypothesis is there is zero serial correlation in the residuals of the model.

MAE The mean absolute deviation, i.e., $1/n \sum_{t=1}^{n} |z_{jt} - \hat{z}_{jt}|$, with the standard deviation in parenthesis; $n = 77$.

r^2 The coefficient of determination; it is a very rough guide of fit for the period over which the parameters were estimated. However, for the forecast period it estimates the proportion of total variation explained by the model.

F Value indicates the signficance of r^2, e.g., $F(1.70)$ at 5 per cent level is 3.98.

parameters, leaving 12 months to test their forecastability—these results are not shown.

On the basis of the tests conducted there is some evidence of a 6-month seasonal and to a lesser extent a 9-month and 12-month. There is no evidence of a quarterly seasonal. However, the procedures used here, where the tests were conducted on the whole series, may mask a greater seasonal effect which occurs only between certain months. For example, suppose that only the months of March and September show any relationship, the returns of all other months being completely independent of one another. An analysis of the whole series is likely to seriously dilute the relationship between March and September returns, to the extent that the 6-month serial correlation coefficient is so small that it is not accepted as being different from zero. To investigate the possibility of this occurring, the relationships between months were examined on a month-by-month basis. For example, if March was related only to September, then the 13-year period gave 25 observations in the series of March–September returns. The tests were conducted for 3-, 6-, 9- and 12-monthly relationships.

A breakdown of serial correlations by month

Tables 15.5 and 15.6 give the results of the month-by-month relationship for lags of 3, 6, 9 and 12 months for the index and the average of the 126 companies on the index. Once again the "portfolio effect" of the index on the serial correlation coefficients is obvious. The approximate standard deviation shown in table 15.5 is really only for large numbers. With only 12 observations its validity must be treated with some scepticism. There is also the negative bias $[-/(n-1)]$ to be considered, which becomes important with so few observations. The size of this bias is shown in table 15.6.

Table 15.5   Serial correlation by months for lags 3, 6, 9, and 12 months of the index of 126 shares

	Jan.	Feb.	March	April	May	June	July	Aug.	Sept.	Oct.	Nov.	Dec.
Lag 3 months (av. no of obs. 49, *approx. S.D.* = 0.143*)*												
	−0.063	0.159	−0.091	−0.056	0.153	−0.072	−0.065	0.162	−0.067	−0.064	0.174	−0.083
Lag 6 months (av. no. of obs. 24, *approx. S.D.* = 0.204*)*												
	−0.039	−0.142	0.267	0.000	0.191	−0.156	−0.037	−0.083	0.268	0.000	0.180	−0.146
Lag 9 months (av. no. of obs. 16, *approx. S.D.* = 0.250*)*												
	0.452	0.218	−0.106	0.052	0.315	0.157	−0.145	0.245	0.061	0.483	0.330	0.061
Lag 12 months (av. no of obs. 12, *approx. S.D.* = 0.289*)*												
	0.554	−0.236	0.454	0.225	−0.198	−0.347	−0.406	0.096	−0.143	−0.377	0.011	−0.166

Note: The results within any one lag, except for the 12-month lag, are not independent of each other. For example, the month indicates the starting month, so that for the 6-month lag, the March figure starts relating March 1959 to September 1958, then September 1959 to March 1959 and so on until September 1970 is related to March 1970. The September figure starts relating September 1958 with March 1958 and continues until September 1970 is related to March 1970. Thus the serial correlation figures shown in the table for a 6-month lag for March and September differ in only one observation.

Table 15.6   Mean and standard deviation of serial correlations by month for lags 3, 6, 9, and 12 months for 126 companies' shares*

	Jan.	Feb.	March	April	May	June	July	Aug.	Sept.	Oct.	Nov.	Dec.
Lag 3 (n = 49, *bias* = −0.021)												
	−0.010	0.036	−0.021	−0.009	0.035	−0.015	−0.007	0.037	−0.014	−0.009	0.039	−0.017
	(0.173)	(0.161)	(0.148)	(0.174)	(0.159)	(0.150)	(0.168)	(0.160)	(0.148)	(0.170)	(0.160)	(0.148)
Lag 6 (n = 24, *bias* =−0.043)												
	−0.038	−0.030	0.008	0.019	0.022	−0.021	−0.040	−0.022	0.009	0.013	0.021	−0.014
	(0.216)	(0.208)	(0.203)	(0.191)	(0.180)	(0.188)	(0.212)	(0.207)	(0.202)	(0.191)	(0.180)	(0.184)
Lag 9 (n = 16, *bias* =−0.067)												
	0.011	−0.096	−0.120	−0.099	−0.167	−0.092	−0.119	−0.047	−0.099	0.013	−0.036	−0.028
	(0.247)	(0.227)	(0.259)	(0.249)	(0.262)	(0.256)	(0.248)	(0.234)	(0.262)	(0.320)	(0.253)	(0.276)
Lag 12 (n = 12, *bias* =0.091)												
	0.013	−0.036	−0.028	0.011	−0.096	−0.120	−0.099	−0.067	−0.092	−0.119	−0.047	−0.099
	(0.320)	(0.253)	(0.276)	(0.247)	(0.227)	(0.259)	(0.249)	(0.262)	(0.256)	(0.248)	(0.234)	(0.262)

* See note to table 15.5.

The results do not give a clear indication of any particular type of seasonality. No month or lag is so consistently high that we could point to it as the cause of the relationships found in the previous section. However, a type of pattern appears to be emerging in relation to the 6-month lag in both tables. The months March, April and May show a closer relationship to the months September, October and November than any of the other relationships. This is particularly true for the March–September relationship when the period was split and examined in two halves—these results are not shown. The months showing the relationship are the months when dividend payments are normally made. For example, in 1970 out of the sample of 126 firms 11 paid dividends in January, 13 in February, 43 in March, 34 in April and 8 in May; in the sceond half of the year payments made were 12 in August, 43 in September, 35 in October and 12 in November. Over the whole period for all firms, the average dividend payments were made in March and September—these are also the months for which the 6-month serial correlation coefficient is greatest for the index.

A possible explanation for the results is some type of dividend effect, i.e., a tax effect on dividends—it will be remembered that the data fully adjust the returns for dividends.[14] The mixed nature of the results could possibly be due to all the firms not paying out dividends in the same month. We would not expect to get a single peak in the serial correlation for any particular month, or even lag, under these circumstances. We will examine the possibility of a dividend effect more thoroughly in the next section.

An explanation for some of the high serial correlations for 9- and 12-month lags is not so apparent, except these results are not consistently high between periods (the results of half-periods are not shown) or between tables 15.5 and 15.6. They may just be chance relationships, but the lack of a clear lead on them encourages us to pursue the possibility of a dividend effect.

Examining for a dividend effect

The removal of shares' yields from the index in the month that dividends were paid should give a clear indication of the presence of a "dividend effect" by the behaviour of the serial correlations of the reconstructed index. The weighting of the index will be changed by such a procedure. The minimum number of companies in the reconstructed index in any one month was 73, but typically it was well over 100 of the 126 companies in the original index. An index of this number of companies will still fully reflect the market factor and it is unlikely that changing the composition will produce any substanital bias in the results.[15]

Table 15.7 Serial correlations of the index in which the return to a share in a month of a dividend payment has been removed (period Feb. 1958 to Dec. 1970)

Lag											
1	2	3	4	5	6	7	8	9	10	11	12
0.259	−0.003	0.040	−0.090	0.036	0.216	0.067	0.093	0.193	−0.011	0.062	0.153

Results by month for 6-month lag ($n = 24$)											
Jan.	Feb.	March	April	May	June	July	Aug.	Sept.	Oct.	Nov.	Dec.
−0.067	−0.204	0.293	−0.027	0.191	−0.153	−0.064	−0.143	0.292	−0.028	0.181	−0.142

The results, in terms of serial correlations, of this "surgery" on the index are given in table 15.7. If these results are compared with those in tables 15.3 and 15.5, it becomes clear that the removal of the dividend month return from the index has had very little effect on the pattern of serial correlation coefficients. There does not appear to be any "dividend effect". A further possibility associated with the dividend was the presence of a non-trading effect.[16] For example, if the dividend was added back into a share's return in the month it was paid, but the share was not traded between then and the end of the month, then the return would be biased upward since the end-of-the-month price would not be an ex-dividend price. The following month, when the share does go ex-dividend, would be biased downward. The end result would be correlation between months in which the dividend was paid and the following month. To check on the possibility of this phenomenon the returns from both the dividend month and the month following were removed from the index. The results are now shown but it had no effect on the pattern of serial correlations observed.

Further possibilities

The average monthly return for March and September, the two months showing greatest correlation, over the thirteen years of the sample was −0.007, whereas for the other ten months the average monthly return was 0.014. This is a fairly surprising result and it suggests it may be worthwhile examining cross-temporal correlations and also standard deviations. For example, if March–September returns are negatively correlated with other months' returns, then portfolio theory would be consistent with a negative return of those months. However, this is not the case; although nine of the thirteen years show negative returns for March–September, compared with only two for the other months, the returns are positively correlated.

Another possibility for explaining the seasonal is a lower market factor risk in those months' returns that are correlated, i.e., the stock market has lower risk relative to all other assets in those months. If this was the case, we might expect lower standard deviations for these months than for the market factor in general, but again this hypothesis is not verified by the data.

The results to date are consistent with a "seasonal effect" of a type that is not intrinsic to the share market. As a check on whether it is a general capital market effect an examination was made on bonds.

Test of seasonality on some bond data

A complete description of the data used in this section of the study can be found in Dunsdon (1973). The bonds were government's with approximately nine years to maturity. Monthly holding periods yields were calculated from the final trading day of the months' prices on the bond quote sheet of the Melbourne Stock Exchange; adjustments were made for coupon payments. Where traded prices were not available, buyer and seller quotes, price of last trade and the price of the next trade were all recorded.[17] This enabled the construction of four series of monthly yields on the bond data: (1) actual traded figures, (2) where traded price was missing a buyer quote was inserted, (3) a linear interpolation between trades for missing observations, and (4) the nearest traded price. The period over which data was collected was July 1964 to December 1972.

The same type of serial correlation analyses conducted on shares was conducted on each of the four bond series. No substantial differences were found between the four. An example of the results obtained for the traded series where missing data was filled by the nearest trade (typically within two days) is shown in table 15.8. The results do not show any clear pattern of behaviour; certainly the pattern is not comparable to that found for shares. Where a high serial correlation exists for the whole period, it typically disappears in one of the half-periods, i.e., it is not consistently present. The generally poor quality of the bond data could be a significant factor in the failure to find a pattern of results similar to shares.

Table 15.8   Serial correlations of monthly holding period yield of the bonds

	Lag											
	1	2	3	4	5	6	7	8	9	10	11	12
Period 8/64–12/72 (n = 83)												
	0.334	0.128	0.110	0.107	0.072	0.041	0.137	0.210	0.102	0.224	0.064	−0.020
Period 8/64–10/68 (n = 40)												
	−0.006	0.141	−0.039	−0.167	0.073	−0.095	0.159	−0.029	−0.079	−0.017	0.013	−0.046
Period 11/68–12/72 (n = 42)												
	0.387	0.122	0.133	0.131	0.063	0.058	0.130	0.231	0.116	0.251	0.069	−0.020

Conclusions

On the basis of the evidence, particularly the performance of the forecasting model,[19] there appears to be a seasonal in the Australian share market. The apparent seasonal pattern is not precisely as Praetz (1973b) described it, but the different form of analysis and data could account for this.

It was shown that the presence of a seasonal in share prices is not sufficient for rejecting the efficient-market hypothesis. Moreover, the lack of evidence from the world share markets of any seasonal must lead one to reserve final judgment until tests can be carried out on the forecasting model with individual shares whose precise dates of trading are known. Also, it is possible that the seasonal was just a function of the period under study, although it did appear that the forecasting model was doing just as well in the twelve months of 1970 as in the 1960s.

If further testing still leads to the conclusion of a seasonal, then the next step would be to determine the underlying cause. The evidence that it is not present in the bond market is very weak. It is possible that share and bond markets are sufficiently segmented to allow a seasonal in one but not the other; but it is easier to think of arguments why they should not be segmented. It was suggested that if a seasonal is present then it is probably related to the varying opportunity cost of money through the year. This in turn should be reflected in some of the economic indicators, although if the effect is small, and it appears to be, these indicators may not be of a sufficient quality to show it. Only further tests will resolve the issue.[20]

Acknowledgments

Many of the concepts developed in this chapter have benefited from discussions with Ray Ball, Philip Brown and Frank Finn. I am also indebted to M. N. Bhattacharya for helpful suggestions and assistance with the forecasting models and Geoff Smith for some programming. It has benefited from comments by Peter Praetz and from seminar discussions in the Departments of Economics and Commerce, University of Queensland.

The share price data were provided by Philip Brown of the University of Western Australian and W. K. Dunsdon, now with GMH in Melbourne, provided the bond data.

Money for the research came from a Reserve Bank Grant and the Australian Research Grants Committee.

Notes

1. For the most part we will be dealing with yields (rates of return) which are in effect proportional price changes.
2. Seasonality in the opportunity cost of capital is most likely to be caused by some regular aspect of government monetary or fiscal policy (or the failure of it) which will affect the yields on all securities.
3. This is usually done by comparing the trading-rule return against a buy-and-hold return. But even these tests are usually not conclusive since it is difficult to control for risk differences between the trading rule and the control, a point usually neglected in studies that have been done on trading rules (i.e., filter tests). These problems along with some evidence have been examined by Ball (1974).
4. This section does not purport to give an exhaustive set of artifacts that can arise in using share indices but restricts itself to those that may be relevant to this study.
5. Kendall and Stuart (1968, p. 434).
6. The precise formulation used was:

$$\hat{\rho}_{ik} = \frac{\sum\limits_{t=1+k}^{n} \left[\left(r_{jt} - \sum\limits_{t=1+k}^{n} r_{jt} / (n-k) \right) \left(r_{j,\,t-k} - \sum\limits_{t=1+k}^{n} r_{j,\,t-k} / (n-k) \right) \right]}{\left[\sum\limits_{t=1+k}^{n} \left(r_{jt} - \sum\limits_{t=1+k}^{n} r_{jt} / (n-k) \right)^2 \cdot \sum\limits_{t=1+k}^{n} \left(r_{j,\,t-k} - \sum\limits_{t=1+k}^{n} r_{j,\,t-k} / (n-k) \right)^2 \right]^{1/2}}$$

7. Fama (1968) discusses the model.
8. Results are shown only for lags up to 12 months; in fact, lags up to 36 months were calculated but they did not reveal any pattern that was inconsistent with lags up to 12 months.
9. Box and Pierce (1970, p. 1510).
10. Unpublished results obtained by Ball and Officer indicate this serial correlation is a function of the frequency of trading in the shares in the index. Smaller-sized portfolios made up of only popular stocks have a smaller first-order serial correlation coefficient.
11. See Box and Jenkins (1970) and Nelson (1973).
12. There is insufficient space to go into details of these procedures; a simple description of them can be found in Nelson (1973).
13. To give some idea of the magnitude of its forecast superiority, the model's investment performance was tested against the control on the basis of a simple trading rule. The rule was when the models forecast a monthly rate of return less than a short-term money market rate (taken as 6 per cent), the rule specified investing at this rate; when they forecast above 6 per cent, the rule specified investing in the market. The results over the period June 1963 to December 1970 showed the model outperformed the control by about 3.5 per cent in yield, i.e., 12 per cent versus 8.5 per cent per year on a monthly basis.

14. It was pointed out earlier that the marginal tax bracket of the marginal trader will determine the extent of a tax effect. It was also pointed out that much of the institutional business is not taxed on dividends.

15. In fact, the results do not suggest any bias.

16. I am indebted to Ray Ball for suggesting this possibility.

17. Bond markets in Australia are extremely thin with respect to the number of traders. It is very difficult to get a complete series of fixed interest securities of any maturity.

18. Due to the thinness of the market.

19. We could further improve on this model by taking specific account of those months of the year that show a closer relationship to each other than the others.

20. A possible explanation for the seasonality that has only come to light after the paper was accepted for publication is a data problem associated with a rights issue. The value of a right was estimated at the theoretical value; however, it has been observed that where a trade is recorded in rights, a consistent disparity of about 2½ per cent between the recorded price and the theoretical price exists. Further, rights tend to be issued around the months a seasonal was observed. The issue was brought to the author's attention by Philip Brown.

16 Filter rules: Interpretation of market efficiency, experimental problems and Australian evidence

Ray Ball

This chapter estimates the efficiency of the Melbourne share market with respect to filter rules. Several problems of interpretation and experimental design are encountered and hence the chapter also describes those problems and the solutions chosen for them.

The major conclusions of the chapter are: (i) early studies of filter rules on the New York Stock Exchange contain latent anomalous evidence of filter rules earning excess returns, in spite of the contrary interpretation in the literature; (ii) the apparent anomaly is due to incorrect experimental method, an example of which is the buy-and-hold control; and (iii) the apparent anomaly disappears when the experimental method outlined in this chapter is applied to the Melbourne prices.

Definitions

Fama and Blume (1966, p. 227) define a filter of x per cent in the following manner: "If the daily closing price of a particular security moves up at least x per cent, buy and hold the security until its price moves down at least x per cent from a subsequent high, at which time simultaneously sell and go short. The short position is maintained until the daily price rises at least x per cent above a subsequent low at which time one covers and buys. Moves less than x per cent in either direction are ignored." Advocates of filter rules believe that these strategies earn positive rents.[1]

The efficient-market theory denies the existence of such rents. As interpreted here, the theory states that security markets are in equilibrium with respect to information which is acquired without private cost. If equilibrium is described in terms of an "expected return" model in which securities' prices are set so that they earn equilibrium expected rates of return, then the expected excess return (rent) from utilising privately costless (public) information is zero.[2] The efficient-market theory thus is treated as a joint implication of

Reprinted from *Accounting Education* 18, no. 2 (November 1978), 1–17, by permission of the author and publisher.

the theory of pure exchange and the assumption that information about filter strategies has no private cost.

Strictly speaking, filter rules cannot be modelled in this fashion, because filter rule information is not strictly a public good. The private costs of applying filter rules to share price data include: (i) the time required to read stock exchange quotation sheets or newspapers; (ii) subscription costs to quotation services or newspapers; (iii) the costs of applying the filter rules to the price data; and (iv) brokerage and other costs incurred in acting upon the buy/ sell recommendations of the filters.

The efficient-market theory's prediction that filter strategies do not increase investor returns would thus seem unreasonable if the private costs of implementing filter rules (or their competitors) were more than trivial. Fortunately for this version of the efficient-markets theory, the private costs of filter rules do appear to be negligible. With the exception of brokerage charges, the private costs are small in relation to the amounts invested in the strategies. And the brokerage charges are not relevant if one argues that the volume of trading in the share market is sufficient to ensure the existence of traders with motives other than trading on information, so that the marginal brokerage cost of employing the filter rule is essentially zero.

We will thus assume that filter rule strategies are public goods, accessible at zero cost to traders, and turn to the modelling of this version of the efficient-market theory.

Consider the class of "expected return" models, in which equilibrium solutions for securities' expected returns, over the interval $(t-1, t)$ in discrete time, are given by

$$E(\tilde{r}_{it}) = f(\alpha_t, \psi_{it}), \tag{1}$$

for $i = 1, \ldots, N$. Here, N is the number of securities, α_t is the set of determinants of securities' expected returns whose values are common to all securities, and ψ_{it} is the set of determinants whose values vary across securities. Let ϕ_{t-1} be made known without cost to market participants, prior to the formation of prices at time $t-1$. Assume that ϕ does not alter either (i) the functional form f or (ii) the values of the determinants of securities' expected returns. Symbolically,

$$E(\tilde{r}_{it}|\phi_{t-1}) = f(\alpha_t|\phi_{t-1}, \psi_{it}|\phi_{t-1}) \tag{2}$$

$$\alpha_t|\phi_{t-1} = \alpha_t \tag{2a}$$

and $\qquad\qquad \psi_{it}|\phi_{t-1} = \psi_{it} \quad$ for all i. $\qquad\qquad$ (2b)

It follows from (1) and (2) that:

$$E(\tilde{r}_{it}|\phi_{t-1}) = E(\tilde{r}_{it}) \quad \text{for all } i. \tag{3}$$

If ϕ_{t-1} is the sequence of historical prices for a security, then (3) becomes

$$E(\tilde{r}_{it}|r_{i,t-1}, r_{i,t-2}, \ldots) = E(\tilde{r}_{it}) \quad \text{for all } i. \tag{4}$$

This model of the efficient-market theory is evaluated in the present chapter. It would be contradicted if filter rules sytematically earned rents (i.e., if (4) were an inequality).

This is a comparative-statisics model, with equilibrium expected returns marginal with respect to past outcomes for returns being compared with equilibrium expected returns conditional upon such outcomes. Sufficient condition for the equality of the conditional and marginal expected returns is that the sequence of past return outcomes (upon which the filter strategy is conditional) only influences security prices via its effect on rents, not via any relation with the determinants of rate-of-return equilibrium.

The two-parameter model is a familiar member of the class of "expected return" models, and thus fits within the above framework. The model states:

$$E(\tilde{r}_{it}) = r_{ft} + [E(\tilde{r}_{mt}) - r_{ft}] \beta_{it} \quad \text{for all } i, \tag{5a}$$

where $\beta_{it} = \text{cov}(\tilde{r}_{it}, \tilde{r}_{mt}) / \text{var}(\tilde{r}_{mt})$, m denotes the market portfolio and f denotes riskless securities. If we assume ϕ_{t-1} does not alter the *form* of the equilibrium described by the two-parameter model, then

$$E(\tilde{r}_{it}|\phi_{t-1}) = r_{ft}|\phi_{t-1} + [E(\tilde{r}_{mt}|\phi_{mt}) - r_{ft}|\phi_{t-1}]\beta_{it}|\phi_{t-1}. \tag{5a}$$

If we further assume that

$$E(\tilde{r}_{mt}|\phi_{t-1}) = E(\tilde{r}_{mt}) \tag{6}$$

$$r_{ft}|\phi_{t-1} = r_{ft} \tag{6a}$$

$$\beta_{it}|\phi_{t-1} = \beta_{it} \quad \text{for all } i, \tag{6b}$$

then we obtain, by simple substitution,

$$E(\tilde{r}_{it}|\phi_{t-1}) = E(\tilde{r}_{it}) \quad \text{for all } i, \tag{7}$$

which is (3). In the context of the two-parameter model, sufficient conditions therefore are: (i) that ϕ_{t-1} does not alter the form of price equilibrium; and (ii) that ϕ_{t-1} is independent of the riskless rate, the expected return on the market portfolio and the relative risks of securities. These conditions are important in this study (and many other studies) of efficiency.[3]

What happens if the assumptions in (6) are not met, i.e., if ϕ_{t-1} is not independent of β_i, r_f or $E(\tilde{r}_{mt})$? Let ϕ_{t-1} be the announcement of impending war, which is assumed to increase the variance of $\tilde{r}_{mt}$, making risky securities riskier relative to the riskless security. Other things remaining equal, this might increase the risk premium, so that $[E(\tilde{r}_{mt}|\phi_{t-1}) - r_{ft}|\phi_{t-1}] > [E(\tilde{r}_{mt}) - r_{ft}]$. Then, the efficient-market theory could not be modelled as in (7), since $E(\tilde{r}_{it}|\phi_{t-1}) > E(\tilde{r}_{it})$ for $\beta_{it} > 0$. Researchers now need a more elaborate model to test market efficiency, since the two-parameter model is silent on the determination of equilibrium values for the risk premium.

To summarise, this chapter adopts the usual comparative-statics model of market efficiency and the two-parameter model to describe securities' equilibrium expected returns. To the extent that the *ex post* return sequence $\{r_{i,t-1}, r_{i,t-2}, \ldots\}$ is not independent of the equilibrium expected values of β_{it}, $E(\tilde{r}_{mt})$ and r_{ft} (and therefore of $E(\tilde{r}_{it})$), the experiment is not a complete evaluation of efficiency.[4] Earlier experiments on filter rules are excessively ambitious in this regard.

Experimental problems

Four issues are now discussed involved in testing market efficiency in the context of the two-parameter model.

Buy and hold as an experimental control[5]

Alexander's initial study (1961) compared the profitability of filter strategies to a buy and hold (BH) on the same securities. Subsequent studies have employed essentially the same experimental control. But the filter and BH strategies only have equal expected returns in an efficient market when securities' expected returns are equal to zero. With positive expected returns, the BH return exceeds the expected filter return.

When the filter is long, it earns the same rate of return as BH, which is a long position. When the filter is short, it earns the negative of the BH return.[6] Returns on the filter and the BH therefore can be equal only if the security earns zero return during short positions, and the expected returns from filter and BH strategies, in an efficient market, are equal only if unconditional expected returns are equal to zero.

To assess the order of the resulting bias in the BH control, observe that

$$E(T\tilde{R}_{jt}|F) = [1 - p(S)] \, E(T\tilde{R}_{jt}|L) - p(S) \, E(T\tilde{R}_{jt}|S) \tag{8}$$

where: $T\tilde{R}_{jt}$ is the total return from j over interval t; L, S denote long and short positions; F, BH denote filter and buy-and-hold strategies; and $p(S)$ is the probability of being in a short position. Market efficiency, as modelled in (4), implies

$$E(T\tilde{R}_{jt}|L) = E(T\tilde{R}_{jt}|S) = E(T\tilde{R}_{jt}|BH) = E(T\tilde{R}_{jt}), \tag{9}$$

for equal dollar amounts long or short. Substituting in (8) gives

$$E(T\tilde{R}_{jt}|F) = [1 - 2p(S)] \, E(T\tilde{R}_{jt}|BH). \tag{10}$$

For a very small filter, with $p(S)$ approximately equal to 0.5, the expected cash flow is approximately zero. For a very large filter, with $p(S)$ approximately zero, it should be essentially impossible to generate a difference between filter and BH returns.[7] This raises the question of whether the anomaly apparent in the Fama and Blume study is due to the incorrect BH control. Their filter rules earned less than BH, as predicted by equation (10).

An unbiased experimental control is described as follows.[8] First, all securities are sorted on β, estimated over all available data. Second, a set of filter strategies is calculated for each security and each filter size. Third, these strategies are applied to: A. the "subject" security, from which the filter strategies were formed; B. the "control" security with the next-highest β; and C. the "control" security with the next-lowest β. These are referred to as securities A, B and C, respectively. It is assumed that $\beta_A = \frac{1}{2} \, (\beta_B + \beta_C)$. Finally, the average returns from applying A's strategy to the three securities are determined and A's average return is compared with the simple average of B's and C's average returns (Fama and Blume 1966).

One qualification is necessary. Because A and its experimental control have essentially the same risk, their expected returns share in common

$\beta_A E(\tilde{r}_{mt}|r_{A,t-1}, r_{A,t-2}, \ldots)$. Thus, we cannot estimate the profitability of filtering any return variation that is due to the market index.[9] This limiation is unavoidable in the context of the two-parameter model and the usual partial-equilibrium model of efficiency. In order to study filtering of the market index, a model of its *equilibrium* time series behaviour would be necessary.

Describing excess returns

We now discuss two related issues: the definition of the rate of return on a short position, and the validity of using geometric mean returns when both long and short positions are involved. The first issue is one of defining rate of return *within* the duration of a position, and the second is one of reducing a sequence of such returns across positions to an average rate per unit of time.

Fama and Blume (1966, p. 232) define the short rate as the negative of the long rate. Dryden (1969, p. 322) disagrees, claiming that

$$(1 + \bar{r})^n = \begin{cases} p_t / p_{t-n} & \text{for a long position,} \\ (2p_{t-n} - p_t) / p_{t-n} & \text{for a short position,} \end{cases} \tag{11}$$

where $\bar{r}$ is a geometric average return per unit of time. This difference is easily resolved in favour of Fama and Blume. Dryden incorrectly treats a short sale as an investment, with an outlay of p_{t-n}. But a short sale involves borrowing, with a *receipt* of p_{t-n}. Consider his example, a short sale for 100 of a security which moves to 121 at the end of two periods. His erroneous calculation of an 11.1 per cent loss, using equation (11), is: $(1 - 0.11)^2 = (200 - 121)/100$. This assumes that the investor invests 100, loses 21 when the price rises by that amount, and thus ends with 79, giving: $79 = 100(1 - 0.111)^2$, when in fact he neither begins with 100 nor ends with 79. He receives 100 and repays 121 at the end of two periods, borrowing at a geometric mean cost of 10 per cent per period.[10]

A more difficult problem arises in pooling rates of return from mixed borrowing and lending positions over time. Fama and Blume (1966, p. 232) pool across positions, using

$$(1 + \bar{\bar{R}})^N = \prod_{k=1}^{K} (1 + r_k)^{n_k}$$

where: $k = 1, \ldots, K$ are the K individual (short or long) positions of duration $n_1, n_2, \ldots, n_k$ time periods; $N = \Sigma_k n_k$ is the total duration of all positions; $(1 + r_k)^{nk}$ is unity plus the total return on position k of duration n_k periods (r_k is thus the geometric mean return over the duration of the position); and R is the geometric mean return over all positions for the security (i.e., over N periods in which K positions occur). But the statistic $\bar{R}$ has no meaning, unless positions in the sequence are either long or short. We see this in two ways.

First, in terms of strategies, (12) assumes that $1 is invested at the beginning of position $k = 1$ and is reinvested at subsequent rates $(r_1, r_2, \ldots, r_K)$. But short positions involve borrowing, not investing: -1, not $1, is invested or reinvested for short positions. Equation (12) incorrectly asumes the maintenance of only positive (long) positions.

Second, in terms of prices, (12) is meaningful in stringing together price relatives for either borrowing or lending, but no such relationship can be defined for a mixture of both. For a sequence of long positions, $_t p_\tau = {}_t p_{t+1} \cdot {}_{t+1} p_{t+2} \cdot \cdots \cdot {}_{\tau-1} p_\tau$, where $_w p_s$ is the price at w for forward delivery of \$1 at s, $\tau > t$ and $s > w$, (i.e., the investments are all long).[11] In terms of rates of return, $(1 + {}_t r_\tau) = (1 + {}_t r_{t+1}) \cdot (1 + {}_{t+1} r_{t+2}) \cdots (1 + {}_{\tau-1} r_\tau)$, which is the form of (12). Similar statements can be made about short positions. Short selling (borrowing) involves present delivery, and the relevant price is of the form $_s p_w$ where $s > w$. This price is the future amount to be repaid at s for delivery of \$1 at the prior time w. Then, $_\tau p_t = {}_\tau p_{\tau-1} \cdot {}_{\tau-1} p_{\tau-2} \cdot \cdots \cdot {}_{t+1} p_t$ and $(1 + {}_\tau r_t)^{-1} = (1 + \tau r_{\tau-1})^{-1} \cdot (1 + {}_{\tau-1} r_{\tau-2})^{-1} \cdots (1 + {}_{t+1} r_t)^{-1}$. Again, (12) has some basis for a sequence of short positions. But there is no sensible interpretation of a product of prices drawn from the two sequences $\{_w p_s\}$ and $\{_s p_w\}$, such as $_1 p_2 \cdot {}_2 p_3 \cdot {}_4 p_3 \cdot {}_5 p_4 \cdot {}_6 p_5 \cdot {}_6 p_7$, which is precisely what (12) does when these are both long and short positions.

A clean solution is to avoid geometric means. The method chosen here is simply to pool all rates of return in long positions with the negatives of all rates for short positions. When the simple average of the pooled returns is compared with its equivalent for the control securities, the result is an arithmetic average excess return.

The method used to describe dispersion is the non-parametric Wilcoxon matched-pairs signed-ranks test. The advantage of the test relative to the parametric "t" is that the "independently distributed" component of the i.i.d. assumption is avoided. The disadvantage is a loss in power efficiency, which is not great for our sample size.[12]

The estimated probability of observing the particular sample of N average differences between filter and control securities, under the assumption that the expected returns on the filter and control securities are identical, is therefore reported. The null hypothesis is that the expected excess return on the filter rule is zero. A two-tailed test is used because market efficiency implies no particular sign for any anomalous return behaviour, a point to which we now turn.[13]

Sign of excess returns

In models of efficiency such as (3) and (4), the conditional mean return is equal to the marginal. When it comes to applying the models, much of the empirical work has interpreted them, somewhat loosely, as implying that the conditional is *less than* or equal to the marginal.

For example, Fama and Blume applied filter and BH strategies to the 30 common stocks comprising the Dow Jones Industrial Averages. Filter sizes ranged from 1/2 of 1 per cent to 50 per cent. Before transaction costs, 23 of the 24 filter sizes earned lower returns (averaged across securities) than BH (table 3). The single exception was the smallest filter: 1/2 of 1 per cent. For 28 of the 30 securities, the filters earned lower returns (averaged across filters) than BH (table 2). After deducting transaction costs, the differences were even more decisive. Fama and Blume (1966, p. 240) conclude: "The market is working rather efficiently from an economic viewpoint."[14]

The implicit modelling of market efficiency is thus along the lines

$$E(\tilde{r}_{it}|\phi_{t-1}) \leqslant E(\tilde{r}_{it}). \tag{13}$$

Historically, there has been an inconsistency between the explicit modelling and the actual interpretation of the efficient-market theory.

In terms of strategies, the existence of negative excess returns from a strategy is evidence of positive excess returns which could be earned by reversing that strategy.[15] In terms of theory, a model of the efficient-market theory (i.e., (3) or (4)) states that, in equilibrium, a specific type of *equality* obtains and the model is violated by inequalities of both signs.

Transactions costs

The role of transactions costs in the efficient-market theory is not obvious, as indicated in the first part of the chapter. Historically, transactions costs have not been handled consistently. Efficiency has been modelled along the lines of (3), which equates expected *gross* returns (i.e., ignoring brokerage and other costs). But the experiments and their interpretations frequently have relied upon brokerage costs to "explain" experimental anomalies. In the absence of an explicit theory of the effects of these costs on market equilibrium, this approach is understandable, but it is not very rigorous.

Fortunately, the experimental design described earlier avoids the transactions costs issue. Identical positions are taken in both the filter and the control securities. Costs of transacting therefore are identical for the filter and the control, and the difference between their returns is independent of their common cost of transacting. The issue of transactions costs arises in the BH control only because the filter and BH take different positions and transact with different frequencies. In the context of the present experiment, the efficient-market theory makes the unambiguous prediction that the difference between the filter and control securities' returns is zero.

Data

The sample is monthly data for 126 industrial equities listed on the Melbourne Stock Exchange over the interval January 1958 through December 1970.[16] Prices are adjusted for dividends and changes in the basis of quotation. The data are taken from Philip Brown's Melbourne file.

The relatively low turnover on the Melbourne market creates an upward bias in the control-security returns relative to the filter-security returns. To establish the bias, consider the filter security A and the control security B. Let the price of A increase in response to "good" news, and let a "buy" position be triggered by the filter rule. Conditional upon A's price increase, the expectation is that the price of B increases, due to "market" and "industry" effects and due to pairing on β's. Now, because of the low turnover, *recorded* price response for B might lead, lag, or be coincident with A's, even if the implicit market prices change in unison. If B's recorded price leads or is coincident with A's, then in subsequent periods the expected returns on A and B are equal, due to the pairing on β. But if B's recorded price lags A's, then, subsequent to the triggering of the "buy" for A, the *recorded* rate

Table 16.1 Buy-and-hold control for filter strategies execution one interval after triggering strategy

Filter size	No. of months		Average monthly return					Wilcoxon probability	Average monthly returns		Wilcoxon probability
	Long	Short	Long	Short	Filter	BH	Difference		Paired securities	Difference	
	(1)	(2)	(3)	(4)	(5)	(6)	(7)	(8)	(9)	(10)	(11)
0.005	10,649	8,615	0.00928	0.01080	0.00030	0.00996	−0.00966	0.00	0.00125	−0.00095	0.29
0.01	10,725	8,532	0.00955	0.01044	0.00069	0.00995	−0.00926	0.00	0.00137	−0.00068	0.64
0.02	10,935	8,289	0.00979	0.01016	0.00119	0.00995	−0.00876	0.00	0.00169	−0.00050	0.73
0.04	11,194	7,913	0.01038	0.00937	0.00220	0.00996	−0.00776	0.00	0.00234	−0.00014	0.83
0.08	11,947	6,845	0.01078	0.00824	0.00385	0.00986	−0.00601	0.08	0.00356	+0.00029	0.63
0.16	12,448	5,722	0.01062	0.00685	0.00512	0.00943	−0.00431	0.79	0.00414	+0.00098	0.11
0.32	14,064	3,159	0.00918	0.00696	0.00622	0.00877	−0.00255	0.26	0.00516	+0.00106	0.13
0.64	14,815	277	0.00758	0.02262	0.00702	0.00785	−0.00083	0.00	0.00746	−0.00044	0.65

Key to columns: (1), (2) Number of months for all securities in which filter was long and short
(3), (4) Average *market* return while filter was in stated position: i.e., short positions earned minus the rate shown
(5) Average return from filter = [(1) x (3) − (2)x(4)] / [(1)+(2)]
(6) Average buy-and-hold return = [(1)x(3) + (2)x(4)] / [(1)+(2)]
(7) = (5)−(6)
(8), (11) Two-tailed probability of the observed returns for filter and control if their expected returns are equal
(9) As per (5), averaged over 2 control securities
(10) = (5)−(9)

Table 16.2 Risk-adjusted return from filter strategies execution at trigger price

Filter size	Average monthly return		
	Filter security	Paired securities	Difference
0.005	−0.00063	0.00447	−0.00510
0.01	−0.00029	0.00454	−0.00483
0.02	−0.00022	0.00455	−0.00477
0.04	−0.00004	0.00446	−0.00450
0.08	0.00128	0.00525	−0.00397
0.16	0.00377	0.00445	−0.00068
0.32	0.00544	0.00513	+0.00031
0.64	0.00718	0.00713	+0.00005

or price change for *B* is expected to exceed that for *A*. The direction of the bias is unequivocal: it is against the filter rule. We therefore report two sets of results: one set which delays the calculation of excess returns by one period (assuming that all control securities have traded in the interval), and the other which executes the calculations immediately. Immediate execution is unrealistic, in that it assumes that buying and selling occurs at the price which triggered the decision, whereas a trader would have to wait for the next transaction. Delaying until the next transaction with available data also is unrealistic, because of the monthly frequency of the data.

Results

In general, the evidence is consistent with market efficiency, with estimated excess returns from filter rules being insignificantly different from zero. There are six major results.

First, columns (1) through (8) of table 16.1 give results for the conventional BH control. They demonstrate the inappropriate control which BH provides, being essentially as predicted by equation (10). The smallest filter is short almost as frequently as it is long, indicating that securities' monthly return distributions on average are roughly symmetric around 0.005. This filter produces approximately zero net cash flow: it is borrowing almost as frequently as it is lending, and rates of price change are essentially independent of the position it takes. In contrast, the largest filter has a low probability of being short, is long most of the time, and its average return is almost the same as the average return from BH. Over the entire range of filter sizes, the difference between the average filter and BH returns is monotone decreasing with the filter size. For all filter sizes, the difference is of the correct sign: negative. These results are to be expected in an efficient market, since the probability of being in a short position decreases with filter size, and the bias in the BH control is always negative and increases with the probability of being short.

Second, columns (9) through (11) of table 16.1 give results for the risk-adjusted control, which is offered in preference to BH. The differences between the filter security and the average paired-security returns are, on average, quite small. The largest (in absolute terms) average difference (0.00106) is approximately one-tenth of one per cent per month. The smallest average difference in absolute terms (0.00014) is approximately one-seventieth of one per cent per month. Three of the eight differences are positive.[17]

The Wilcoxon test gives some indication of the strength of any relationship between filter strategies and excess returns: under the null hypothesis that the pairwise differences in securities' expected returns are zero, the probability of sampling differences equal to or greater than the observed differences (based on a two-tailed test) is a minimum of 0.11 (for the 16 per cent filter) and a maximum of 0.83 (for the 4 per cent filter). These results are consistent with market efficiency with respect to filter rules. If there is any excess return from operating filters, then it would appear to be small.

Third, it is instructive to compare the average excess returns under the BH control with those under the paired-security risk control. As evidence on experimental design, the results speak for themselves.

Fourth, similar (unreported) results are derived from dividing the 156-month period into three 52-month subperiods. Strategies are closed at the end of each of the subperiods, and filter positions must be triggered anew in each subperiod. The subperiods are thus treated in the same fashion as the total period. Again, the results appear to be consistent with market efficiency. The average return differences tend to reflect the total-period results: they are on average quite small, and they are predominantly negative for small filters and positive for large filters.

Fifth, some indication of the effect of discrete price quotation can be seen from table 16.2. Here it is assumed that transactions in both filter and control securities occur at the price which triggered the filter position. As hypothesised, the smallest filters in table 16.2 earn substantially less, on average, than the control securities. For the smallest filter, the difference is 0.005, or approximately 6 per cent per year. For the largest filter, the difference is approximately zero.

Finally, some evidence on the short-run profitability of filter rules can be obtained from comparing the average returns for the filtered securities in tables 16.1 and 16.2. For example, the difference for the 0.005 filter is -0.093 per cent per month ($-0.00093 = -0.00063 - 0.00030$). Except for the largest filter, which essentially is a BH strategy, the differences are all negative. Since the differences are due exclusively to the one month delay in execution for table 16.1, the implication is that, on average, there is a slight price reversal in the month following the triggering of a filter position. This is consistent with the slight negative first-order serial correlation observed in securities' returns, a phenomenon which could be due to data errors occurring with low frequency.[18] It certainly is inconsistent with filter rules being profitable in the short run.

Summary and conclusions

If market efficiency is interpreted as a simple statement about price equilibrium in the securities market, providing testable implications of the theory of pure exchange, then the early filter rules studies indicate persistent anomaly. The anomaly takes the form of filter rules earning systematically less than their experimental control (buy and hold) or, in the case of one small filter, systematically more.

Happily, interpreting market efficiency in this manner also leads to a rejection of the early experimental methods. Taking advantage of work on the two-parameter model which was not available in their time, changing the method of averaging returns across trading sequences and ignoring transactions costs, we find that the anomalies observed in the earlier experiments tend to disappear. Filter rules do not appear to have been profitable on the Melbourne exchange over 1958–70.

Some caveats are required. First, not all researchers will accept this interpretation of market efficiency. Some, for example, would prefer to incorporate private costs of information usage. Second, the data used in this study are of monthly frequency, and cannot satisfy the claims of those who claim that filtering works on intramonthly variation. Third, this study abandoned all pretence at evaluating filter rules on the market index, which accounts for approximately 20 per cent of the average security's return variance. Finally, lest we lose historical perspective, the filter-rule studies of the early 1960s might be criticised in hindsight on several grounds, but they were key studies in their time and they were undertaken before subsequent experimental techniques became available.

Acknowledgments

Financial assistance of the Australian Research Grants Committee and the Reserve Bank of Australia was received and appreciated. The study was completed for the Seminar on Portfolio Management at Macquarie University, 18–23 February 1973. Valuable criticism was received from P. Brown, E. Fama, F. Finn, M. Jensen, G. Foster, R. Officer, M. Rozeff and R. Watts.

Notes

1. The form of short selling assumed in Fama and Blume and in this chapter is a "pure" form, involving pure borrowing and without several institutional restrictions. In Australia, short selling is illegal.
2. Publicly-available information, having no private cost, is exploited until, at the margin, the private gain from its use is zero. Such an assertion cannot be made about "inside" information, which is defined as information which has a positive private cost of reproduction (and therefore is not a public good).
3. The model of (3) and (7) will be recognised as that of Fama (1970a).
4. Joint tests of market efficiency and the two-parameter model involve accepting the strictures of assumptions equation (6). Acceptance of the strictures is an inevitable consequence of believing that the equilibrium time sequences

$$\{E(\tilde{r}_{mt}), E(\tilde{r}_{m,\,t+1})\ldots.\}\,,\{r_{ft}, r_{f,\,t+1},\ldots\}\text{ and }\{\beta_{it}, \beta_{i,\,t+1},\ldots\}$$

   are unknown. Because the assumptions necessary for the two-parameter model are sufficient for market efficiency as we have defined it, with the exception of the assumption that past price data are costless to investors, the test essentially is not joint: it amounts to a test of the two-parameter model.
5. The conventional BH control is a long position in the same security upon which the filter strategy is being executed. The long position is opened coincidentally with the initial filter strategy, and is continued until the filter is closed. In the meantime, the filter may shift between short and long positions, but the BH remains in a long position. Both are opened and closed on the same dates. Since this experiment was conducted, Praetz (1976b) has published an expression that is equivalent to (10).
6. Consider a security whose price moves from \$100 to \$108 and which pays a \$2 dividend. There is a \$10 profit for a long position and a \$10 loss for a short position. The cash outlays required of long and short positions are of equal magnitude and of opposite sign, involving lending and borrowing of \$100. This assumes that the short seller reimburses the buyer for any dividend he would have received if he had held a long position, and that proceeds from short sales are made available to the borrowers (see note 1).
7. The expected value of the amount to be outlaid, conditional upon the filter strategy, is $[1 - 2p(S)\,]\,I$, where I is the amount to be either invested or shorted (usually taken as \$1 for experimental purposes). For a small filter, borrowing and lending with approximately equal frequency, the expected outlay is approximately zero.
8. The experimental control used here is similar to that of Black and Scholes (1973a) who compare the return on the subject security with the return on a relatively large portfolio with similar relative risk. Their procedure can be expected to provide a more efficient estimator for the marginal expected return on the RHS of (4), and is preferable on these grounds. Both provide an unbiased estimator, in the context of the two-parameter model, provided the assumptions (6) are satisfied by the data. At the time of conducting the present experiment (late 1972), I was, unfortunately, unaware of this procedure. To some extent, the limitation on efficiency is avoided by the sample size (see "Results" in this chapter).
9. The early versions of the Dow Theory applied only to filtering the index, though it was gradually and substantially modified over time to deal with individual securities. Because only approximately

20 per cent of the variation in individual securities' monthly returns, on average, is due to the market factor, the deficiency created by pairing on β's is relatively unimportant.

10. In Dryden's formulation, an additional problem is that r is imaginary if $p_t > 2p_{t-n}$.

11. See Fama and Miller (1972, pp. 29–31).

12. See Siegel (1956, pp. 61–62 and 75–83).

13. An additional problem arises from using more than one filter size or filter strategy. Return differences are not independent across filter sizes and strategies, and hence the *joint* distribution of differences across filters is relevant. For example, the probability of triggering a 2 per cent filter in a given month, conditional upon having triggered a 5 per cent filter in that month, is unity (greater than the unconditional probability). These filters cannot be viewed as providing independent evidence of market efficiency. Without computing the joint distribution of the return differences, one approach is for the reader to choose a single filter size in advance, and to draw inferences concerning market efficiency from its results.

14. For similar interpretations, see Fama (1970a, pp. 395–96) and Jensen and Benington (1970). Jensen and Benington reason: "Since the point at issue is whether or not the trading rules perform significantly better than the B & H policy the fact that they don't on the average even perform as well means we need not bother with any formal tests of significance." (p. 480).

15. This statement appears false when BH is used as a control. But this simply reflects the bias of BH; denoting a reversed filter rule by *RF*, equation (10) becomes $E(T\check{R} \mid RF) = [1 - 2p(L)] E(T\check{R} \mid \text{BH})$. Correct experimental procedure would reverse the sign of the control when the filter strategy is reversed, so that both the filter and the control returns change sign. The difference between filter and control therefore changes sign.

16. The sample is described in chapter 15. There is survivorship bias, but it is common to both the filter and control securities and causes no problem in this experiment.

17. Do not be misled by the agreement in sign of excess returns among the first four filters: returns are not independent across filters, and hence, agreement in signs among adjacent filter sizes is to be expected. See note 13.

18. See chapter 15 and Ball and Brown (1978).

17   Try this on your chartist

Ray Ball and R. R. Officer

You might have heard about the Random Walk Hypothesis. It says that share prices look a lot like cumulated random numbers—the type of thing you would get if you had a kitty of $10.00 and added or subtracted $1.00 depending upon the toss of a coin. Don't be thrown by the word "random", and in particular don't think it means "chaotic", because a random walk is what share prices in a well-behaved share market should look like. Why?

Suppose that the charts for Share A tell us that past price behaviour of Share A suggests a future increase. If this were true, then the increase should occur today (or yesterday) as investors become aware of the change to gain. And the increase today should be such that, today, there is no more chance to profit; i.e., there should not be any "free lunches" sitting around in the form of predictability of future share prices. Thus, future share price changes should be independent of past price changes, which is what a random walk is—a series in which each movement is independent of every other movement.

Because some people apparently believe in "free lunches", or something for nothing, we have constructed a painless little test of ability to discriminate between free caviar and free chiko rolls. The eleven graphs on the following pages were created by plotting, over time: (1) the prices of five industrials listed on the Stock Exchange of Melbourne; and (2) six cumulated random numbers.

Each of the eleven series was scaled to start at $1.00 to avoid easy identification. This was done by dividing the whole series by the starting price. The time period was disguised also.

The real share prices were adjusted for dividends, splits, bonuses, etc. The particular issues were chosen randomly from the list.

The cumulated random numbers were generated by computer. They simulate six price series, where each change in price is independent of each preceding change in price. That is, no amount of analysis of past price changes is useful in predicting future price changes in each of these series—the future

Reprinted from *Superfunds* (June 1978), by permission of the authors and publisher.

is *constructed* to be independent of the past. As was the case with the actual share prices, the simulated prices were all scaled to start at $1.00.

Figure 17.1   Charts of price series

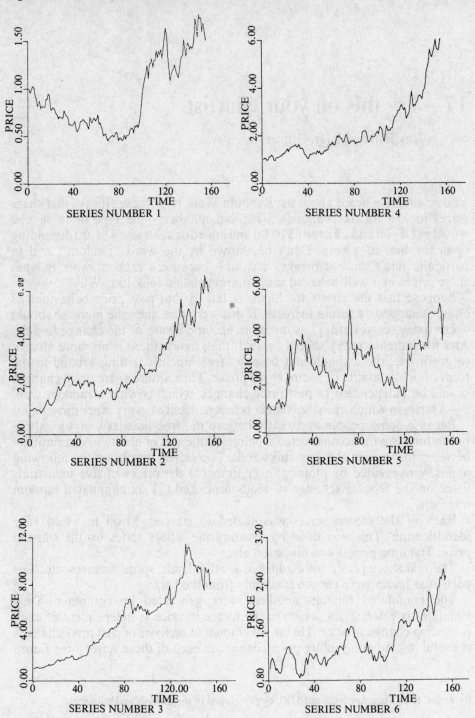

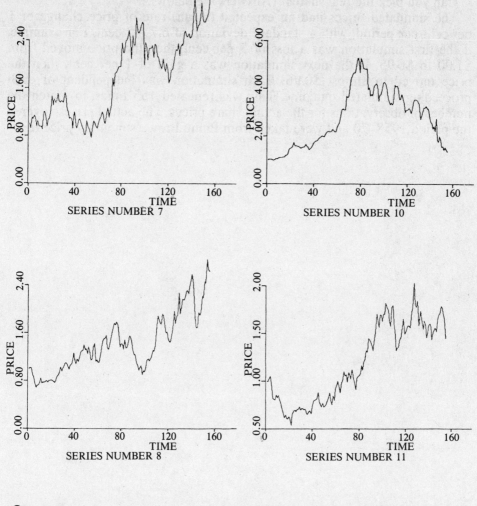
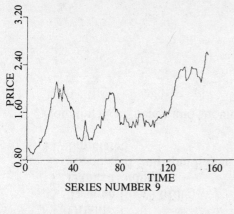

Figure 17.1 Charts of price series

Can you pick the real shares? (Answers are below).

The simulated prices had an expected (mean) rate of price change of 1 per cent per period, with a standard deviation of 6.7 per cent. For example, if the first simulation was a loss of 5 per cent, then the price moved from $1.00 to $0.95. If the next simulation was a gain of 1 per cent, then the price moved to almost $0.96. Each simulation was independent of each proceeding simulated outcome. This was repeated 155 times, to match the number of observations for the actual share prices. The actual prices covered the period 1958-70 and were taken from Philip Brown's monthly price file.

Note the nice "heads and shoulders" in the simulated series?

Answers

1. Simulated	2. Simulated
3. OPSM	4. Simulated
5. Tasman Board Mills	6. Simulated
7. Danks Holding	8. Simulated
9. Associated Pulp and Paper	10. Australian Fertilizers
11. Simulated	

PART 5

B. Information and share prices

18 The impact of the annual net profit report on the stock market

Philip Brown

Introduction

Theories about the fundamental determinants of share prices have existed for many years. One of the more impressive is that put forward by Miller and Modigliani (1966), which relates the total market value of the firm to, among other things, its future earnings. But, like most others, the Miller–Modigliani (MM) theory is silent on *how* and *when* the investor learns about future earnings. This is not intended as a criticism of MM, because when testing their theory they were able to bypass these questions.

Nevertheless the questions remain and are interesting, for if the phenomena which trigger price movements on the stock market were identified, then security analysts could focus their efforts to gather and process information and hence perform their tasks more efficiently. Some early work, based on data for firms listed on the New York Stock Exchange (NYSE), has been done. For example, Fama et al. (1969) investigated ". . . the process by which common stock [ordinary share] prices adjust to the information . . . that is implicit in a stock [share] split"; Scholes (1969) examined the stock market's reaction to large block sales; Ball and Brown (1968) assessed the relevance to investors of the annual report of net profit; and Brown and Kennelly (1972) extended the Ball and Brown results to interim reports.

This chapter will be concerned mostly with efforts to further the research of Ball and Brown, and Brown and Kennelly. It reports tentative findings on the impact of the annual net profit report on the prices of shares listed on stock exchanges in Australia.

Experimental design

The experimental design is similar to that described in detail in Ball and Brown (1968, pp. 160–65).

Reprinted from *The Australian Accountant* (July 1970), 277–83, by permission of the author and publisher.

It is (1) assumed that future Earnings (Net Profit) Per Share is relevant to investors, who (2) forecast future Earnings Per Share (EPS) from known data, but (3) react to errors in their forecast, as errors are revealed, by adjusting the price at which their shares are traded.

The ability of investors to make advance predictions determines the amount of information contained in an EPS report at the time of its release. Thus, if investors could predict exactly the contents of an annual report say, six months before its release, then, apart from confirming their prediction, the release of the report is of no consequence. Conversely, the greater the discrepancy between actual EPS and the EPS as forecast by investors, the greater the amount of information contained in the EPS report; and presumably the greater the impact of the report's announcement on share prices. Basically, the impact of the annual net profit report is assessed by relating this discrepancy, or EPS forecast error, to the adjustment in share prices associated with its announcement.

There are two parts to the experimental design. First, in the absence of explicit knowledge of investors' EPS forecasts they must be simulated by mechanical rules. Second, investors' reactions (via share price adjustments) must be measured and related to the errors in "their" forecasts as those errors are revealed.

Forecasting future EPS

It is difficult to develop efficient mechanical rules for forecasting EPS without some knowledge of the behaviour of earnings through time. Ball and Watts (1968) concluded, after a detailed study of several hundred firms listed on the NYSE, that EPS appears to behave as if it is generated by a process which is either a random walk or at least "very close" to it. Unfortunately, to my knowledge, no similar study has been conducted in Australia, although I am hopeful some results will be known soon. In the meantime I have fallen back on the Classical Naive Model, which assumes simply that the world does not change.[1] In other words, it predicts that tomorrow will be the same as today which, in the present context, reduces to the forecast that this year's EPS will be the same as last year's.

For example, suppose investors forecast, on the basis of News Ltd's EPS of 20 cents for the year ended 30 June 1967, that EPS for 1967–68 will also be 20 cents. If actual EPS proves later to be 25 cents, then there will be a forecast error of +5 cents. Moreover, when the actual EPS is announced and investors realise they have underestimated EPS (that is, they have made a positive forecast error), they will react by adjusting the price of News Ltd upwards. On the other hand, if actual EPS proves to be only 15 cents, then there will be a forecast errors of −5 cents, suggesting that the price of News Ltd will decline—other things being equal.

Investors' reactions

The difficulty when measuring investors' reactions is that those "other things" are not always equal. It is a well-known fact, for example, that share prices, and therefore rates of return from investing in shares, tend to go up and down together, behaving as if they are all subject to common expectational influences. Some factors which contribute to this related movement in Australia are changes in monetary and fiscal policy (the Federal Budget), in foreign investment ("London Support"), in interest rates (at home and abroad) and in the rate of overall economic activity. Therefore, when measuring investors' reactions to a particular firm's profit report, an adjustment should be made for that part of the movement in the price of the firm's share which is due to fluctuations and drifts in the stock market in general.

The adjustment procedure is the same as that used elsewhere. For each particular share it consists of three steps. First, estimate, using past price data, the normal relationship[2] between the rate of return[3] on this share and the rate of return on a market index. Second, for any particular month which is of interest, predict, from this normal relationship, how much the rate of return on this share should have been, given whatever change happened to take place in the market index. Third, compare the actual rate of return on this share with the rate of return predicted under step two. The result, the extent to which the actual rate of return is greater or less than the predicted rate of return, reflects the impact of new information about this particular share. Continuing the example of News Ltd will help clarify the procedure.

Suppose, when there is no change in the market index, that the price of a share in News Ltd, on average, increases by one-half of 1 per cent per month; whereas if the market index increases by say 1 per cent, the price of that same share increases by a further 1½ per cent. Now take any particular month, for example August 1963 when the market index increased by about 5 per cent. Then other things being equal the price of News Ltd shares should have increased ½ + (1½ x 5) = 8 per cent. If, in fact, the shares rose by only 4 per cent, then they did not rise as much as they normally should have risen, implying that some adverse information concerning that particular firm, News Ltd, must have been received by investors during August.

The argument applies equally to months when the market index decreases, as, for example, it did in November 1960. If the market declined by 10 per cent, then we would have expected News Ltd shares normally to change by ½ + (1½ x −10) = −14½ per cent. If News Ltd shares declined by only 10 per cent, then shareholders in effect have ended up some 4½ per cent better off than they normally would have expected. This 4½ per cent, obtained by subtracting the predicted (or "normal") return from the actual return, is defined as the "abnormal rate of return". And it is clear that the sign of the abnormal rate of return determines whether the sum of information received about News Ltd in any one month has been deemed, on balance, to be "good" or "bad" news: if positive, then it was "good", if negative, then it was "bad".

Summary

The two parts can now be assembled in the following way. Because of the nature of the forecasting rule, investors will have forecast this year's EPS as soon as last year's EPS was known; which for convenience is assumed to be exactly twelve months prior to this year's announcement.[4] In the intervening time (that is, between last year's and this year's announcements) the shareholder would have received many pieces of information of various types—for example, an interim dividend, the half-yearly profit report, routine newspaper items—some of which, in particular the half-yearly profit report, would have improved his ability to forecast this year's EPS.

An improved ability to forecast the final outcome would result in an early realisation of any forecast error, such that investors would adjust share prices some time before the annual report's announcement. For this reason abnormal rates of return are tracked from a starting point twelve months prior to the announcement date. Further, by studying the behaviour of the abnormal rates of return over the full twelve months, we can measure the relevance for investors of both the content of the annual report and the timing of its release.

At this stage we are more interested in what happens on average rather than what happens as a result of any one particular annual report or in any one particular year. Thus data for more than 100 firms over a 10-year period are the base for this report.

Data

Three types of data are required: annual EPS; EPS announcement dates; and share prices.

Annual EPS data were extracted from the 1968 and 1969 editions of Ian Potter & Co.'s *Australian Company Reviews*. The 1968 edition lists EPS since 1958 for 138 separate companies. Eight mining companies were excluded[5] because they will be the subject of a special study in the near future.

EPS announcement dates were obtained for the ten years 1959–68 from two sources: the *Official Record* of the Melbourne Stock Exchange and records maintained by the Research and Statistical Bureau at the Sydney Stock Exchange. These dates correspond to the month in which each preliminary profit statement was released to the press, subject to the proviso that, if the press release was made within the last five calendar days of the month, the profit statement was assumed to have become available to the general public in the following month.[6]

Share price data corresponding to the last recorded sale for each month since January 1958, were extracted from publications of the Adelaide, Melbourne and Sydney stock exchanges. Data were also collected for all dividends and rights to issues (whether bonus or cash issues of deferred, ordinary or preference shares, issues of debentures and convertible unsecured notes, etc.). The price, dividend and rights[7] data were then expressed in the form of monthly price relatives, with each relative defined as the ratio of the end-of-month price cum dividends and rights to the beginning-of-month price (that is, the end-of-month price from the previous month).

A share-price relative so defined is just the (adjusted) proportion by which the price changed in the particular month, plus unity. For example, in October 1960, News Ltd issued approximately three million 5-shilling ordinary shares to existing shareholders on the basis of 1-for-1 at a 3-shilling premium. The last recorded share sales were 30s.6d. (September, cum rights) and 18s.3d. (October, ex rights). Based on the October ex rights price of 18s.3d., the theoretical value of the rights attached to one of the old shares was 10s.3d. The shares had already been quoted ex the final dividend for 1959–60 in

September, hence the price relative for October was 28s.6d. (= 18s.3d. + 10s.3d.) divided by 30s.6d., or 0.934. The rate of return was −0.066, or a loss of 6.6 per cent for the month.

For statistical reasons it is essential that each share be actively traded for a number of years.[8] I arbitrarily selected five years, or 60 monthly price relatives, as a minimum,[9] which excluded a further 12 firms, leaving a total of 118.

Some properties of the 118 are interesting. Table 18.1 gives the month-by-month results from investing $100 at the end of January 1958 (spread equally over all firms for which prices were quoted).[10] It shows that the Potter survey must include a number of firms which, historically, have been extremely successful. Table 18.2 gives the deciles of the distributions of: (1) the square of the coefficient of simple correlation between the monthly rate of return on each security and the monthly rate of return on the market index;[11] and (2) the coefficient of first-order autocorrelation in the estimated abnormal rates of return, that is, the residuals from the OLS regression implied in (1). The median r^2 value (0.5 decile, in table 18.2) indicates that about 20 per cent of the variance in the monthly rate of return on the "typical" share can be associated with widespread movements in share prices.[12] The distribution of the coefficients of first-order autocorrelation suggests that there is very little relationship, if any, between abnormal rates of return in consecutive months.[13]

Results

The easiest way to reduce the obvious complexity of the results is to treat the 12 months leading up to the announcement of the annual report as the basic unit of time. The results can then be summarised, by month relative to the annual report announcement, in the form of (a) Abnormal Performance Indexes[14] and (b) chi-square statistics calculated from a two-by-two classification by the sign of the EPS forecast error and the sign of the abnormal rate of return. Abnormal Performance Indexes (APIs) are computed separately for three portfolios, the first consisting of all EPS reports which contain "good" news (that is, when EPS increased over the previous year), the second consisting of all EPS reports which contain "bad" news, and the third consisting of all EPS reports regardless of what they contain. This last portfolio provides a control.

Suppose, for example, that News Ltd's EPS for the year to 30 June 1964 was 10 cents, and for 1964–65 15 cents. Thus, according to our forecast rule the 1964–65 net profit report, announced in September 1965, contained "good" news. Now assume that the relevant monthly abnormal rates of return for News Ltd, were:

1964	October	0.001	1965	April	−0.012
	November	0.002		May	0.000
	December	−0.003		June	−0.030
1965	January	0.008		July	0.000
	February	−0.004		August	0.009
	March	0.100		September	0.056

Table 18.1 Investment performance index—118 firms surveyed by Ian Potter & Co. January 1958 = 100

	Jan.	Feb.	March	April	May	June	July	Aug.	Sept.	Oct.	Nov.	Dec.
1958	100.00	102.85	102.34	103.65	102.78	106.73	110.45	114.33	117.20	117.78	122.13	125.51
1959	131.02	133.92	135.21	142.68	147.49	153.65	165.24	173.82	185.19	192.84	193.65	196.76
1960	210.53	205.47	206.73	212.91	215.58	216.50	222.05	223.43	219.61	207.72	187.57	184.08
1961	193.59	197.94	195.26	205.51	210.99	213.31	215.27	214.31	215.12	219.66	220.71	224.81
1962	238.02	247.45	245.79	247.27	246.36	239.11	241.06	243.27	238.99	247.54	249.04	256.11
1963	263.14	263.38	262.38	268.92	270.96	275.18	295.74	308.16	306.04	307.97	320.68	331.89
1964	338.61	345.27	337.92	335.41	338.41	343.40	347.73	352.75	348.45	344.11	345.82	352.58
1965	348.42	338.29	318.73	308.86	319.44	302.99	317.23	322.57	308.21	321.77	316.54	328.95
1966	330.27	330.24	322.71	331.82	320.16	324.62	332.09	322.29	319.89	321.63	321.40	337.53
1967	341.92	336.40	339.03	347.20	341.10	347.94	365.95	379.25	387.68	392.49	393.05	391.50
1968	399.75	397.24	399.16	430.96	468.34	479.49	504.01	511.06	483.72	481.41	504.06	534.21
1969	545.83	547.92	556.63	563.42	553.91	532.33						

Table 18.2 Deciles of the distributions of the squared coefficient of correlation for the rate of return regression, and of the coefficient of first-order autocorrelation in the estimated abnormal rates of return

Coefficient name	Decile								
	0.1	0.2	0.3	0.4	0.5	0.6	0.7	0.8	0.9
Rate of return regression r^2	0.08	0.11	0.15	0.17	0.21	0.22	0.25	0.27	0.23
Autocorrelation in abnormal rates of return	−0.22	−0.18	−0.14	−0.13	−0.11	−0.08	−0.05	−0.03	0.03

Then the sequence of the API for News Ltd's 1964–65 annual report would be calculated as follows:

Month relative to annual report announcement	Abnormal performance index
−11	1.001
−10	1.001 x 1.002
−9	1.001 x 1.002 x 0.997
−8	1.001 x 1.002 x 0.997 x 1.008

Finally, entries to the two-by-two contingency tables would be:

Entries to contingency tables

Month relative to annual report announcement	EPS increased over previous year		EPS decreased over previous year	
	Return > 0	Return < 0	Return > 0	Return < 0
−11	+1			
−10	+1			
−9			+1	
−8	+1			

Table 18.3 presents the three APIs (the first two are adjusted)[15] and chi-square statistics calculated for the 118 firms and those years for which data were available.[16] Figure 18.1 plots the three APIs. Several results emerge.

Table 18.3 Summary statistics by month relative to annual report announcement date

Month relative to annual report announcement	API: EPS increased over previous year	API: EPS decreased over previous year	Chi-square statistic	API: All EPS reports
−11	1.005	0.990	5.76	1.000
−10	1.010	0.992	7.42	0.997
−9	1.012	0.989	1.10	0.991
−8	1.012	0.994	0.02	0.986
−7	1.018	0.983	8.38	0.989
−6	1.025	0.965	18.86	0.991
−5	1.028	0.959	4.62	0.987
−4	1.031	0.952	0.10	0.982
−3	1.035	0.943	5.06	0.981
−2	1.036	0.940	0.45	0.978
−1	1.042	0.925	19.36	0.979
0	1.054	0.905	42.62	0.986
1	1.055	0.905	0.02	0.987
2	1.057	0.900	2.21	0.985
3	1.057	0.904	0.00	0.981
4	1.058	0.906	0.29	0.976
5	1.062	0.907	4.20	0.979
6	1.063	0.908	0.40	0.981
Number of EPS announcements	620	287	—	907

Note: Probability (chi-square $\geqslant 3.84 \mid x^2 = 0$) = 0.05, for 1 degree of freedom.
   Probability (chi-square $\geqslant 6.64 \mid x^2 = 0$) = 0.01, for 1 degree of freedom.

1. Net profit reports contain information relevant to investors. To illustrate, suppose an investor were told annual EPS twelve months in advance of the release of each EPS report and that his investment decisions had negligible effect on stock prices. Then by buying those shares which later report an increase in EPS he could have made an average 5.4 per cent p.a. more than he normally would have expected;[17] and, at the same time, he could have avoided making investments which would have returned him on average 9.5 per cent less than he normally would have expected.[18]

2. The larger values of chi-square statistics and the larger proportionate changes in the first two APIs appear to cluster in two distinct time intervals, namely months −7 and −6, and months −1 and 0. These correspond to the announcements of the half-yearly and yearly profit reports respectively. Although the greatest monthly adjustment in share prices takes place in the annual report's announcement month, the results in table 18.3 indicate that it is only about 20–25 per cent of the total adjustment for the year. Presumably investors anticipate some three-quarters of the content of the annual profit report before the month of its release. Unfortunately, owing to data deficiencies,[19] these estimates might prove inaccurate.[20] Future work will identify more precisely the date the annual report became generally available, which will improve our assessment of the roles the reports play in informing investors about EPS.

3. If the half-yearly and yearly profit reports are *themselves* the media by which the stock market becomes informed about EPS, then it appears that the market reacts speedily to adjust share prices to that information. Both the APIs and the chi-square statistics (table 18.3) suggest once the

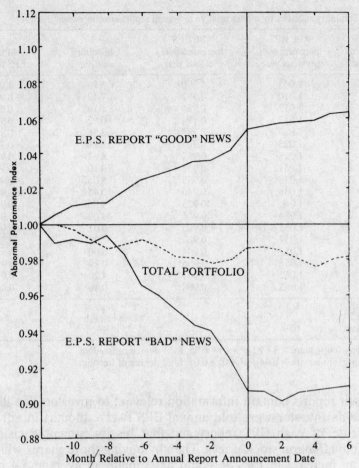

Figure 18.1   Abnormal performance indices for various portfolios

annual report has become generally available there are no further opportunities for abnormal profits. At that point the individual investor can earn further abnormal profits only by forecasting the *next* annual report more accurately or in advance of all other investors.[21]

4. It is quite possible that investors look further than twelve months into the future when predicting EPS. Moreover, EPS is certainly not the only datum on which investors base their decisions. It is of some interest, therefore, to measure the extent to which share price adjustments can be associated with (a) EPS reports, and (b) information from all other sources.

The estimation procedure is intricate so I will provide only a heuristic interpretation.[22] Suppose investor X were told every single piece of information about a firm which would be announced to the public at any time during the next twelve months, after which time the firm would announce EPS for its most recent fiscal year. Suppose further that: (a) X must either buy, or adopt a short position on, a share in the firm and hold it until the annual report is released; and (b) X's decision has no effect on share prices. Then X would have earned on average 14.6 per cent more than he normally could have expected.[23]

On the other hand, suppose investor Y is also clairvoyant, but only with respect to annual EPS. That is, he can foresee an EPS report twelve months in advance of its announcement, but he can foresee no other news. If Y is identical to X in all other respects (that is, he is permitted to decide on an investment strategy only once and his decisions do not influence share prices), then Y who acts only on EPS information would have earned on average 6.9 per cent more than he too normally would have expected.[24]

I conclude that approximately half the annual adjustments in share prices can be related to EPS reports and, by implication, that approximately half are related to information from other sources.

5. The above results for the Australian stock market are remarkably consistent with results obtained for the New York Stock Exchange. From their study of the NYSE, Ball and Brown (1968, p. 176) concluded: "Of all the information about an individual firm which becomes available during a year, one-half or more is captured in that year's income number." Our preliminary estimate is the same. Ball and Brown continue: "However, the annual income report does not rate highly as a timely medium, since most of its content (about 85 to 90 per cent) is captured by more prompt media which perhaps include interim reports." Again, the estimates are entirely consistent. The annual report probably has greater impact in the month of its announcement in Australia because profit reports are made typically only once every *six* months here, compared with once every *three* months in the United States.

Finally, the tendency of the proportionately larger movements in the APIs and the relatively larger values of the chi-square statistics to cluster in the neighbourhood of the release of the half-yearly report indicates that results, such as those recently obtained by Brown and Kennelly, will likewise be obtained in Australia.

Concluding remarks

The objective of this chapter was to report on some preliminary attempts to measure the impact of the annual net profit report on the Australian stock market. We conclude: although net profit reports contain information relevant to investors, in the sense that at least half the adjustments in share prices over a 12-month period can be related to EPS reports, only about 20–25 per cent of those adjustments take place in the month in which the annual report is announced.[25] Moreover, by the time the annual report is generally available, the market has fully adjusted share prices such that no further opportunity for abnormal profit remains.

While these findings are important in their own right, there are many other questions to be investigated. A few of them are listed below.

1. What effect did the adoption of the Uniform Companies Acts have on the relevance of the annual profit report?
2. Does the amount of information contained in annual reports differ between industries—for example, mining versus manufacturing?

3. Some have argued net profit should be adjusted for "unusual items". What is the evidence?
4. How relevant is the half-yearly profit report?
5. How do EPS series behave through time?[26]
6. Of what importance are other items contained in the annual report?

This last question is particularly intriguing. It could be answered by employing discriminant analysis techniques to differentiate those firms and years in which the API was greater than unity from those in which it was less. Unfortunately this exercise requires far more data than are at my disposal.

The implications of our findings for the investing public are as follows. For the fundamentalist, there is little doubt that profit reports are important. Generally, however, the market is able to make advance forecasts of the contents of an annual report, these forecasts having greatest impact on share prices during the two months immediately prior to a report's release. Thus the investor who can develop a superior ability to forecast EPS, even if it is only from a point two months prior to the release of the report, will be in a position to make substantial gains over and above what he normally could expect—*provided he acts quickly*. There appears to be no point to waiting until the audited details of profits are published, for example, because by then all price adjustments have been made and it is too late. This does not mean that those glossy annual reports are worthless, for they contain information in addition to profits, although the value of that other information is at present unknown.

Finally, an unfortunate implication for the chartist. Little is to be gained from studying month-by-month share price adjustments for clues to future months, since, to all intents and purposes, monthly adjustments are serially independent. This means that the stock market reacts both speedily and fully to new information, such that the rewards belong to those who look to the future, and are brave enough to act quickly on what they see.

Acknowledgments

The author wishes to acknowledge the helpful cooperation of: Mr D. Patterson, formerly of the Sydney Stock Exchange; Mr D. Smalley, formerly of Messrs Ian Potter & Co.; Mr I. Steele, Stock Exchange of Perth; Mr R. Watters, Sydney Stock Exchange; and Mr F. Wray, Stock Exchange of Adelaide.

Notes

1. It should be pointed out that the Classical Naive Model is naive only in the statistical sense. Several economic time series appear to be described well by this model. It has been used extensively in applications similar to the present one.
2. Estimated by ordinary least-squares regression.
3. That is, the proportionate change in price, adjusted for dividends and rights to new issues.
4. This assumption is not an accurate description of what in fact takes place. However, for a rather subtle reason which I will not argue here, it happens to make little difference as long as the two announcements are at least about nine months apart.
5. They were: BH South, Consol Goldfields, CRA, Hammersley, Mt Isa, New BH, North BH and WMC. However, the remaining 130 firms include several firms which are classified as industrial but for which mining activities play an important part in overall operations: for example, BHP, CSR and EZ Industries.

6. The reason for this adjustment is that the price quotations are taken as the last sale for the month, which must be post-announcement for the procedure to be accurate. The effect of the assumption can be investigated in several ways, but I have not yet had the necessary time to do so.

7. The theoretical value of the rights was used in the case of issues of ordinary shares, and the actual value (that is, quoted price) of the rights in all others.

8. The reason that the distribution of the disturbance terms in the OLS regression between the investor's rate of return on an individual share and the rate of return on the market as a whole is characterised by fat tails.

9. The minimum number of monthly price relatives for firms which met the cut-off criterion turned out to be 75.

10. Expressed in the form of an Investment Performance Index, which ". . . assumes the same dollar amount is invested in each share at the beginning of the month, when the whole portfolio (including rights) is sold out. The proceeds are then re-invested and the process repeated." See Philip Brown 1969. The Stock Market in Retrospect. *Economic Activity* 12: 7.

11. For each firm, the market index is estimated by the arithmetic mean of the share price relatives for the remaining 117 firms.

12. Because the Potter survey contains firms which historically have been more successful than the average Australian firm, the estimate of 20 per cent is possibly biased downwards.

13. Some negative serial correlation is to be expected because of small data violations of the assumptions of the model we are using. However, the estimates do not vary much from those reported by Ball and Brown (1968).

14. Ball and Brown (1968, p. 168) define and illustrate the Abnormal Performance Index as follows:

$$ API_M = \frac{1}{N} \sum_{n}^{N} \prod_{m=-11}^{M} (1 + v_{nm}) $$

(where v_{nm} is the abnormal rate of return on security n in month m). Then API_M traces out the value of one dollar invested (in equal amounts) in all securities n ($n = 1, 2, \ldots, N$) at the end of the month -12 (that is, 12 months prior to the month of the annual report) and held to the end of some arbitrary holding period ($M = -11, -10, \ldots, T$) after abstracting from market effects. An equivalent interpretation is as follows: Suppose two individuals, A and B, agree on the following proposition. B is to construct a portfolio consisting of one dollar invested in equal amounts in N securities. The securities are to be purchased at the end of month -12 and held until the end of month T. For some price, B contracts with A to take (or make up), at the end of each month M, only the normal gains (or losses) and to return to A, at the end of month T, one dollar plus or minus any abnormal gains or losses. Then API_M is the value of A's equity in the mutual portfolio at the end of each month M.

15. The adjustment (for each month) was made by subtracting the third API from unity, and adding this difference to the other two.

16. Nine hundred and seven EPS reports are included.

17. Table 18.3, row for month 0, column for EPS increases:

$$ 5.4 \text{ per cent} = \frac{1.054 - 1.000}{1.000} $$

18. Similarly, -9.5 per cent $= \dfrac{0.905 - 1.000}{1.000}$

19. Recall the arbitrary rule by which the announcement month was determined.

20. For example, I suspect 20-25 per cent is too low.

21. In this connection it should be noted that the persistence in the drifts in the APIs from month -11 to month 0 (see figure 18.1) is the result of averaging over many firms and years. No such persistence is to be found in the API for the "typical" firm and the "typical" EPS report. If it were to be found, then there would be opportunities to profit by applying a mechanical trading rule (which is most unlikely on *a priori* grounds). Further, those opportunities would be evidenced by positive autocorrelation in the abnormal rates of return. However, table 18.2 shows that autocorrelation, if anything, is slightly negative.

22. See Ball and Brown (1968, p. 176) for a detailed description of the procedure.

23. That is, based on the firms and years surveyed in this report.

24. Ibid, result 1.

25. Both calculations are biased against findings in favour of EPS reports; see Ball and Brown (1968, p. 176).

26. Ibid.

19 Profit reports and the share market

Philip Brown and Phillip Hancock

Financial statements, it is claimed, contain, or should contain, information for various purposes. Yet how useful are financial statements, in fact? To help answer this question, this chapter summarises some recent Australian findings on what happens to share prices when companies release their half-yearly and yearly profit reports.[1]

Why study the share market investor?

Since share market investors are only one of many classes of potential users of financial statements, why study them? The answer is threefold: first, because the share market plays an important allocative role in the Australian economy; second, because of the ready availability of reliable data on the share market; and third, because investors are surely an important class of potential users of financial statements.

An investor forgoes present consumption in anticipation of future consumption. If he is to make his investment decision rationally, he must assess both his present position and his likely future position under alternative courses of action. For the investor who makes judgments about the present and likely future worth of different shares (which may affect his temporal positions under alternative courses of action), firms themselves supply much of the data he is likely to find useful when making his judgments. And accounting reports, and accounting data-related reports, make up a large slice of the total output of data made public by the firm.

While profit is usually only one of many figures contained in a set of accounting reports, it is nevertheless a key one as far as investors are concerned. Stated concisely, the intuitive connection between profit reports and share prices is as follows. A share's present price, it is suggested, depends on forecast future profits such that, other things being equal, the higher the forecast profit, the higher today's price.[2] Since past profits appear to play a direct

Reprinted from I. Tilley and P. Jubb, *Capital Income & Decision Making: Introductory Readings in Accounting* (Sydney: Holt, Rinehart and Winston, 1977), by permission of the authors and the publisher.

role in the formation of investors' forecasts of future profits,[3] if a profit figure, when made public, is discovered to be higher (lower) than expected, then investors would revise upward (downward) their forecasts of future profits and consequently increase (decrease) the price at which they are willing to trade the shares, again other things being equal.

Earlier evidence

Unfortunately those other things are not always equal, for a variety of reasons. Share prices are notoriously volatile, both individually and "across the board". For example, the market as a whole can reel from the declaration of war, from a shock election result, or from a surprise reversal of the terms of trade. Or the market might move less dramatically, say as a result of changes in income tax laws. Whatever the cause, share prices are forever changing, with marketwide movements accounting for varying proportions of the variance of each share's rate of return.[4] For some Australian shares, market effects account for more than half the variance in monthly rate of return, for others very little at all. In the 1960s, on average they accounted for about 20 per cent.[5]

If a share's rate of return is adjusted for changes in the market as a whole, it has been found that on average at least half the movements in Australian industrial share prices over the twelve-month period ending with the *month* of a profit report announcement can be associated with the profit report.[6] However, this earlier evidence has left open the question of whether profit reports themselves trigger share price movements, or whether share prices move either in anticipation of a profit report (i.e., some days prior to its release) or, if not in anticipation, then perhaps in response to some correlated announcement (such as a change in dividend payout or a forthcoming bonus issue[7]) made at the same time as the profit report. As we shall see, even if dividend payments etc. remain unchanged, immediate and significant share price reactions are triggered by profit reports. It is worth noting that these reactions occur despite the many real and imaginary weaknesses in present-day methods of accounting.

A note on rationality

There is a common belief that "the share market is irrational", a belief usually supported by reference to earlier market events or predictions which, with the benefit of hindsight, are later shown to have been wrong. According to the belief, even if accounting weaknesses resulted in profit figures that were completely irrelevant to investment decisions, investors who lacked the relevant information from any source would unthinkingly seize upon profit figures as if they were "the real thing", and act accordingly. In that sense share market investors are believed to act irrationally, so that share price reactions to profit reports would not necessarily imply profit reports are "useful" to them. Such a view of the share market is erroneous. Investors are confronted with alternative information sources of which profit reports are only one.

One well-documented feature of share markets is that worthwhile information sources are acted upon and worthless sources are ignored.[8] This feature is hardly surprising since the market consists of many competing investors and analysts who can profit from acting on interpretations of information relevant to the future that are better than those of their rivals. Competition between market participants quickly removes any opportunities which are recognised to be abnormally profitable, so that share prices adjust quickly and fully to relevant news as it becomes public.[9] So if, as the evidence indicates, only useful sources are acted upon and if the actions of investors are reflected quickly and fully in share prices, then (other things being equal) changes in share prices at the time of the public release of profit reports do provide evidence that profit figures are useful.

Research method

Our method of studying share price reactions to profit figures being made public consists of four steps: (1) select a set of firms and a time period for study; (2) within the time period, identify the exact date on which each profit figure was made public by each firm in the set; (3) for each profit report, measure the share price movements associated with its release; and (4) classify each profit report into one of two categories, according to whether the profit figure is higher or lower than it probably was expected to have been, and try to reach some inferential conclusion about the association between share price movements and the release of profit reports generally.

Data

Firms and time period

The set of firms chosen was the same 118 industrial firms studied earlier by one of the authors.[10] The period selected was January 1964 to December 1970 because of the ready availability of data for that period.

Announcement dates

Since September 1964 the Australian Associated Stock Exchanges have required listed companies to furnish half-yearly as well as yearly profit reports. The announcement dates used, obtained from stock exchange records, were the dates on which the half-yearly and yearly profit reports were first released to the respective companies' home exchanges. In the case of a yearly profit report this was often some weeks prior to when the printed annual report was circulated to shareholders.

There were two complications which made it difficult to identify announcement dates exactly. First, we have estimated that 10 to 15 per cent of the profit reports appeared in the press on the same day as they were released to the stock exchange, about 80 per cent appeared the next day, and the rest mainly within a day or two thereafter. Since the techniques we employed yield results which can be sensitive to errors in the announcement dates, we excluded reports for which we were unable to confirm publication in the *Australian Financial Review* (a morning paper) either on the same day as the official report was made or on the trading day immediately following it. The second complication arose because a profit report can be made to a company's home exchange after the close of the day's trading. As a result of these two complications the announcement date was accurate only to within one trading day of the date of the official report.

Share price movements

The next step was to measure the share price movements associated with each profit report. Earlier work suggested that while the Australian share market is often caught by surprise when a profit report is released,[11] it nevertheless reacts quickly in the sense that share prices are rapidly adjusted to the changed circumstances.[12] Because of these earlier results and because data collection is a painstaking exercise, we decided to confine our measurements to share price movements which occurred over the four trading days leading up to the day of each profit announcement, the announcement day itself and the six trading days which immediately followed it.

Daily closing prices were collected from the price-quotation sheets issued by the Melbourne and Sydney stock exchanges. Appropriate adjustments were made to the prices of shares which were quoted ex dividend, rights or entitlements at any time during this eleven-day period. The adjusted price series of each report was then restated in the form of daily continuously compounded rates of return.

Is profit higher or lower than expected?

The classification of Australian profit reports into one or two categories, according to whether reported profit is higher or lower than investors expected it to have been, does present some problems. In the absence of explicit knowledge of investors' profit expectations they must be simulated by a mechanical rule. Because the minimum listing requirements of the Australian Associated Stock Exchanges (AASE) have serious computational shortcomings, our mechanical rule may appear to border on the simplistic. We assumed, in essence, that investors consider the world will not change, which implies that this year's profit figure is expected to be the same as for the corresponding period last year.[13] The explanation for our assumption is as follows.

The AASE's minimum listing requirements provide, in essence, for 6-monthly reports. Prior to March 1970 the first 6-monthly report (i.e., the "half-yearly" report) was required to state only whether profit was up or down on the corresponding period in the previous year, while the second 6-monthly report (i.e., the annual report) had to contain profit for the full year in dollar terms. In March 1970 the minimum listing requirements, as they related to half-yearly reports, were amended to require firms to be more precise about the change in profit, by expressing it in percentage terms. Because the amendment occurred towards the end of the time period studied, as far as the half-yearly report is concerned we had little choice other than to assume investors expected profit for the first six months of this year to be the same as for the first half of last year, so that a report of an increase in profit was to be classified as "good" news (in the sense that profit was higher than expected) and correspondingly that a decrease in profit was "bad" news.

While classification of half-yearly reports was difficult, it proved even more difficult for reports relating to the second half of the year. For a little reflection will show that, even if companies reported on the first six months' results according to the March 1970 amendments (so that for the first half-year only the percentage change in profit was known), when the Australian investor was later told profit in dollar terms for the full year, he could not be always sure whether profit increased or decreased in the second half of the year.[14] Only on rare occasions was the Australian investor told earnings (net profit) per share, in contrast with his American counterpart.

Another difference between reporting practices in Australia and the United States is that in Australia the forthcoming dividend payment is almost always announced simultaneously with the profit report.[15] Because the effects of changes in profits and dividends were observed jointly, we controlled for dividends by considering only those profit reports made when dividends were unchanged. Clearly, the effective dividend payment could have been changed by any one of a number of ways. For example, a bonus issue may have been made to existing shareholders say in the ratio of 1 bonus share for every 4 shares already held, without changing the dividend amount per share. We excluded a profit report if the effective dividend payment was changed either directly or indirectly by this or any other means, and provided that the announcement about the change was made during the time period we were studying.

It is worth noting that dividend increases occurred far more frequently than dividend decreases, so that the expected change in dividends was greater than zero. Thus a report of "no change in dividend" would have been perceived, on average, as a disappointment. Although we have presumed dividend policy to be neutral, it is so only in the sense that all profit reports selected were made in the context of dividends that were unchanged.

Results

We identified 638 separate profit reports for which we were able to collect sufficient share price data to calculate at least one share price movement in the days surrounding the report's announcement date. Among the 638 there were 463 reports of increased profits and 175 reports of decreases. The results are summarised in table 19.1, by trading day relative to the official report date, in the form of: (1) average and cumulative average rates of return[16] for each of the two classes of profit reports (decreases/increases); and (2) frequency data and the corresponding chi-square statistics and associated probabilities obtained from a two-by-three classification of observations by the direction of the change in profit (decrease/increase) and the direction of the change in price (decrease/zero change/increase).[17]

Table 19.1 may be interpreted as follows. Suppose for illustration we focus on the column headed day -2, which is the second trading day prior to each report date. From the top part of the table, which relates to rate-of-return calculations for the 175 occasions on which profit was reported to have decreased, it can be seen that on 59 occasions the price of the share fell on day −2, on 53 occasions it was unchanged, and on 47 occasions it rose. (The last three numbers do not add to 175 since on 16 occasions a price change could not be calculated because the share was not traded on day −3 or −2.) The average rate of return, taking into account the 59 falls, 53 no changes, and 47 rises, was −0.07 per cent which, when added to the averages for the previous two days, gave a cumulative figure of −0.28 per cent for the three-day period. Similarly, the middle part of the table shows that of 463 occasions on which profit was reported to have increased, on 123 occasions the price of the share fell on day −2, on 153 occasions it was unchanged, on 117 occasions it rose, while on 70 occasions a price change could not be calculated.

Table 19.1 Daily analysis of share price reactions to 638 Australian profit reports when the dividend payment was unchanged

	Day relative to official announcement date										
	−4	−3	−2	−1	0	+1	+2	+3	+4	+5	+6
Profit decreased (n = 175)											
Rate of return (%):											
$n < 0$	62	54	59	53	72	81	57	61	52	55	43
$n = 0$	42	64	53	62	47	36	52	51	55	56	62
$n > 0$	53	44	47	47	47	38	44	43	43	39	43
Average	−0.07	−0.14	−0.07	−0.07	−0.61	−1.27	−0.34	−0.23	−0.18	−0.19	0.03
Cumulative average	−0.07	−0.22	−0.28	−0.21	−0.82	−2.09	−2.43	−2.65	−2.83	−3.02	−2.99
Profit increased (n = 463)											
Rate of return (%):											
$n < 0$	123	135	123	121	124	123	134	139	124	110	130
$n = 0$	144	144	153	149	114	107	128	148	140	144	131
$n > 0$	134	118	117	134	174	176	150	132	140	140	126
Average	−0.01	−0.12	−0.03	0.09	0.40	0.49	0.08	−0.05	0.03	0.09	−0.06
Cumulative average	−0.01	−0.13	−0.16	−0.08	0.33	0.82	0.90	0.85	0.88	0.97	0.91
All profit reports (n = 638)											
Chi-square statistic	5.49	0.60	2.11	0.97	12.16	25.74	2.94	1.96	1.86	5.76	3.02
Chi-square probability	0.06	0.74	0.35	0.62	0.00	0.00	0.21	0.38	0.40	0.06	0.22

The statistical significance of these results is summarised in the bottom section of table 19.1, where the chi-square statistic and its associated probability indicate a 35 per cent chance that changes at least as pronounced as those which took place in share prices in day −2 could have been observed even if share price changes that day were totally unrelated to profit reports. The findings in table 19.1, then, could hardly be used to justify claims for share prices moving in anticipation of the release of a profit report two days later, because of the "distinct possibility" that the results for day −2 could have been due to chance. The results for other days surrounding the announcement date, however, gave an entirely different picture.

Without labouring the point, when dividend policy was neutral, there appears to have been a strong association between the direction of the change in reported profit and the direction of share price movements concurrent with the release of the report.[18] The average drop in share prices of firms which reported profit declines was about 2 per cent from day −4 to day +1,[19] and there would have been a less than one-in-two-hundred chance (chi-square probability is 0.00, correct to two decimal places) of observing the changes in share price movements which occurred in day 0 or in day +1 if share price movements were unrelated to profit reports.

Moreover, the impact of a profit report was greatest in days 0 and +1 (within the order of accuracy of the announcement date itself) which suggests that news leakages, if they did exist, were not usually significant over the

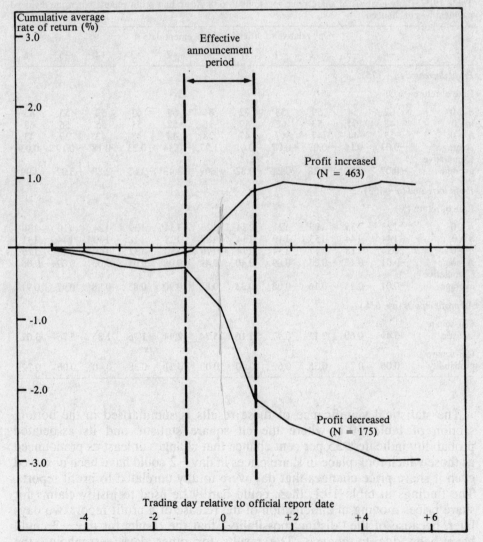

Figure 19.1 Cumulative average share price reactions to 638 Australian profit reports when the dividend payment was unchanged

four days prior to a report's release and, as a corollary, that the profit reports themselves triggered the share price movements. Once movements were triggered, share prices adjusted fully within a few days of the report (immediately in the case of "good" news?) so that the usual observations confirming the efficient market hypothesis can be made.[20]

Summary

Despite their shortcomings, accounting profit figures have been and presumably still are important to shareholders of listed companies, in the sense that the public release of a profit figure triggers a change in share prices and hence in the financial positions of shareholders.

Ackowledgments

This chapter has benefited from comments by the participants in the Workshop in Accounting Research at the University of Western Australia and by Professor Ray Ball of the University of Queensland.

Notes

1. Similar studies have been conducted elsewhere; see, as one example, Ball and Brown (1968). Three somewhat related studies which readers might find interesting are: Beaver (1968), Beaver, Kettler and Scholes (1970), and Gonedes (1973).
2. From the shareholder investor's point of view, a share certificate evidences his entitlement to future consumption (and bequest) possibilities. Moreover, the present worth of this entitlement to future consumption possibilities depends on the quantity of resources expected to be available for future consumption. This in turn depends upon the net worth of the shareholders' equity today, what the shareholders' equity is likely to be worth in the future, and what resource exchanges are expected to take place between the firm and its shareholders in the interim. Accountants generally refer to increases in the *book value* of shareholders' equity (after allowing for dividends, new capital injections, capital reductions and ignoring some types of asset revaluations made in the books of account) as "net profit".
3. Evidence on the relationship between past and future profit figures is provided by Ball and Watts (1972).
4. The rate of return is the profit or loss per dollar invested, where profit includes both dividends and capital gains.
5. See also chapter 18.
6. See chapter 18, and Brown (1972).
7. A bonus issue refers to the situation where shareholders are issued additional shares without having to pay for them. Share prices on average move up when a forthcoming bonus issue is announced, because a bonus issue usually heralds higher returns to shareholders in the years ahead. A bonus issue is differentiated from a share split inasmuch as the par (stated) value of the shares is unaltered in the case of a bonus issue. Note that new issues made to existing shareholders at a price less than the ruling market price (immediately prior to the "old" share being quoted "ex rights") contain bonus elements. This practice, of including bonus elements in new issues to shareholders, is a common one in Australia. It has the effect of prompting shareholders into action: either to sell the rights to others, or else to subscribe to the new issue.
8. Ball and Brown (1968, p. 161).
9. Similar observations about the nature of investors and the structure of the market place provide the foundation for the efficient market hypothesis; see Fama (1970). The hypothesis has serious implications for some individual analysts and it is not without its critics. However, the balance of evidence favours the hypothesis at least in its "weak" and "semi-strong" forms, which is sufficient for our purposes.
10. The 118 firms are surveyed in the 1968 edition of Ian Potter & Co.'s *Australian Company Reviews*. For a more detailed description of the firms, as well as some of the techniques used to study the firms, see chapter 18.

11. "The largest and most significant adjustment in share prices *over the six months ending with the announcement month* tends to take place in the announcement month, which leads to the inference that the most important source of information about profit is probably the preliminary report itself." Brown (1972, p. 18). Emphasis added.

12. Ibid., especially p. 24.

13. It should be pointed out that the Classical Naive Model (the world will not change) is naive only in the statistical sense. Several economic time series appear to be described well by this model, which has been used extensively in applications similar to the present one.

14. To illustrate, suppose two hypothetical companies achieved profit figures as follows:

	Company A		Company B	
	Year 1	Year 2	Year 1	Year 2
First half	$75	$90	$25	$30
Second half	25	20	75	80
Full year	100	110	100	110

Under the March 1970 minimum listing requirements, both companies would give identical profit reports in year 2: profit up by 20 per cent in the first half; profit of $110 for the full year (up from $100 in year 1). Yet Company A's profit declined in the second half, while Company B's continued to increase, albeit at a lower rate than over the first half-year. These points and proposals for change are discussed in detail in Brown (1972). The implication of our difficulties in classifying reports is obvious: our test of the usefulness of profit figures to share market investors is a joint test of accounting numbers *and* the stock exchange reporting requirements.

15. The standard report form issued by the Australian Associated Stock Exchanges encourages this practice. By way of contrast, it appears from some data we have available that only half the *quarterly* dividend and profit announcements occur in the same calendar month in the United States.

16. Market effects were not eliminated for three reasons: the probable relative unimportance of market effects in explaining the variance of daily (as opposed to, say, monthly) rates of return on individual Australian industrial shares; the shortness of the implied holding period (11 trading days); and the apparent unavailability of a reliable daily index of Australian share rates of return. We tried, twice, to adjust for market effects by subtracting two alternative Sydney Stock Exchange indices, namely the *All Ordinaries Index* (Index 15) and the *All Ordinaries Index Excluding Non-Ferrous Metals* (Index 19). On both occasions sharp movements in share prices were still observed in days 0 and +1. However, the cumulative average rates of return were decreased in the case of the first series, while they were increased in the case of the second series. Since there is no reason to prefer one price index to the other, and both sets of results are unequivocal with respect to share price movements on the announcement date, we have opted to report results without adjusting for market effects.

17. If the rate of return was negative, then the price fell; if zero, then the price was unchanged; if positive, then the price rose. Note that, if market and industry factors are present in the profit reports, then the chi-square probabilities in the last row of table 19.1 may be understated.

18. These findings cast further doubts on a study of American firms by R. Richardson Pettit, who claimed that there is "virtually no earnings effect" when the dividend effect is controlled. Pettit's method of identifying the "surprise" content of profit announcements was possibly responsible for his "surprising result". See Pettit (1972).

19. This compares with an average 0.8 per cent rise in the share prices of firms which reported profit increases. Since profit increases were more common in the 1960s than profit decreases, announcements of increased profits had lower informational content and hence less impact on share prices.

20. An important result because we rely on the hypothesis. Admittedly there was a puzzling persistence in the downward drift in the cumulative average rate of return for profit decreases and a "low" probability that the chi-square statistic for day +5 was due to chance. However, the drift was not evident in day +6.

20 On the use of naive expectations of earnings per share as experimental benchmarks

Frank J. Finn and G. P. Whittred

Random-walk earnings forecasts

This chapter describes an investigation into the relative accuracy of martingale and submartingale forecasts of annual earnings. Random-walk processes have been adopted as benchmarks against which the accuracy of earnings forecasts made by management, analysts and a variety of mechanical models have been evaluated, or as surrogates for the market's expectation of individual firm earnings in a large number of studies.[1] At present there is little underlying theory to explain the time-series properties of corporate annual earnings.[2] On *a priori* grounds we might suspect that a random-walk with positive drift, or a submartingale,[3] would better describe the behaviour of earnings over time than would a strict random-walk, or martingale, process. Inflation and the reinvestment of earnings by firms could both be expected to induce positive drift in corporate earnings over time.

The results of a good number of studies provide evidence that annual earnings or annual earnings per share (EPS) on average follow a "submartingale or some very similar process".[4] Also, Watts and Leftwich (1977) and Albrecht, Lookabill and McKeown (1977) found that full Box–Jenkins models fitted to the time series of earnings for individual firms did not provide more accurate forecasts than did the random-walk models. Since the random-walk models have stood up well, on average and for individual firms, it seems reasonable to use a single or "premier" model of earnings expectations to generate control or benchmark forecasts in experiments involving annual earnings.

A caveat may be warranted. Some evidence from the United States suggests that forecasts using interim (quarterly) earnings may outperform forecasts based on annual earnings only. Watts and Leftwich (1977) give a brief summary. This issue was not investigated here since Australian companies were not required to report interim earnings numbers prior to 1978.[5]

Reprinted from the *Economic Record* (June 1982), 169–73, by permission of the authors and the publisher.

Data and forecast models

The sample used here comprises 70 firms for which complete earnings time series were available over the interval 1960–78.[6]

Earnings per share (available to ordinary shareholders) for these firms were calculated both after taxes, and after taxes and extraordinary items, and are referred to as "operating" and "net" EPS respectively. Adjustments were made for all changes in the basis of capitalisation. Although no attempt was made to ensure a uniform classification of extraordinary items across firms, adjustments were made to the reported figures to ensure a consistent definition of extraordinary items was applied through time for any one firm.

Our sample selection procedures may have introduced some bias into the data. First, the requirement that sample members have at least 19 consecutive years of earnings data requires them to have survived for at least that long and this reduces the probability of firms with poor earnings performance getting into the sample.[7] Second, the Potter Survey from which the sample was drawn contains firms which tend to be larger and historically more successful than the average Australian firm. As a result, it may be an unrepresentative sample of firms with a lower than average expected frequency of earnings decline. If so, this would tend to bias the results against the martingale process.

The procedure used was to compare actual and predicted changes in EPS, using martingale (equation (1) below) and submartingale forecasts (equation (2)):

$$E_{t-1}(Y_{k,t}) = Y_{k,t-1} \tag{1}$$

$$E_{t-1}(Y_{k,t}) = Y_{k,t-1} + \delta_k \tag{2}$$

where:

E_{t-1} = an expectation made at time $t-1$;

$Y_{k,t}$ = EPS for firm k in period t;

δ_k = a drift factor, independent of t.

Forecasts were made for each of the eight years 1971–78, leaving up to 11 years of prior data over which to estimate the drift factor for the submartingale model.

In estimating δ_k, estimates were obtained from ten different averaging periods. To illustrate, the following ten forecasts were made for firm k for 1971:

$$\hat{Y}_{k,1971} = Y_{k,1970} + \frac{1}{N}(Y_{k,1970} - Y_{k,1970-N}), \quad N = 1, \ldots, 10.$$

In this way ten submartingale predictions were made for each firm for each of the eight years 1971–78, each prediction incorporating a drift factor ($\delta_{k\tau}$), with τ varying from one to ten prior EPS changes.

Evaluation of forecasting models

Forecasts were evaluated using the familiar mean square error (MSE) and mean absolute error (MAE) metrics. The mean error (ME) was also calculated to provide evidence on the extent of any bias in the forecasts. To date, most researchers have attempted to test the significance of error differences between competing forecasts using cross-sectional earnings data, either for each of several years individually or pooled across a number of years.

One problem with the cross-sectional tests is that they rely on the assumption that the forecast errors are cross-sectionally independent—an assumption which is unlikely to be satisfied because of market and industry influences on corporate earnings. To test for common market influences we ran the following regression for each firm in the present sample:

$$\Delta E_{k,t} = \alpha_k + \beta_k \Delta M_t + e_{kt}, \quad t = 1961, \ldots, 1978$$

where:

$\Delta E_{k,t}$ = the change in EPS for firm k from $t-1$ to t.

ΔM_t = an index computed as the equally weighted average of changes in EPS for all firms in the sample, excluding firm k, and

e_{kt} = the OLS disturbance term for firm k for period t.

The average cross-sectional dependence in our sample of Australian firms (as measured by the mean adjusted R^2), was 15.4 and 15.7 per cent for operating and net EPS respectively.

Because of this cross-sectional dependence, we turn to longitudinal or time-series tests. An appropriate design for hypothesis testing which obviates the necessity of scaling forecast errors (for example, by actual EPS or by the standard deviation of forecast errors) is a matched-pairs test, with self-pairing by firms in each forecast year using the competing forecast models.[8] For each of the ten submartingale predictions we compare the mean error metric for each forecast year, 1971 to 1978, with that produced by the no-change or martingale forecast. After taking the difference in the estimated mean errors, $\hat{d}_t$ for t = 1971 ... 78, we are left with eight yearly estimates of the mean difference in the forecast error distributions of the two models in each comparison. If we can assume that these differences represent drawings from an i.i.d. population, the statistic

$$t(\overline{\hat{d}}) = \overline{\hat{d}} / [s(\hat{d}) / \sqrt{8}]$$

where $s(\hat{d})$ = the estimated standard deviation of the eight yearly mean differences,

will be distributed as Students t with seven degrees of freedom.

Results

Table 20.1 shows the mean value of each error metric, averaged across all firms and all years for net EPS. Also shown is the Student probability, estimated by the longitudinal t-test described above, that the mean difference in errors between each submartingale model and the martingale model is zero. Table 20.2 shows the same results for operating EPS.

Two points become apparent. First, for both earnings definitions the martingale model and all submartingale models consistently underestimated realised earnings changes for the period 1971–78. Second, both the MAE and MSE metrics showed a consistent decrease in the magnitude of the forecast

Table 20.1 Martingale versus submartingale forecasts of net EPS error metrics and significance tests pooled data (N = 560)

	Martin-gale	Submartingale model									
		$\tau = 1$	$\tau = 2$	$\tau = 3$	$\tau = 4$	$\tau = 5$	$\tau = 6$	$\tau = 7$	$\tau = 8$	$\tau = 9$	$\tau = 10$
ME	−0.0151	−0.0039	−0.0054	−0.0059	−0.0053	−0.0051	−0.0056	−0.0059	−0.0062	−0.0066	−0.0071
Student probability	—	0.0950	0.0192*	0.0000*	0.0000*	0.0000*	0.0000*	0.0000*	0.0000*	0.0000*	0.0000*
MAE	0.0496	0.0712	0.0603	0.0546	0.0527	0.0515	0.0507	0.0501	0.0498	0.0494	0.0492
Student probability	—	0.0000*	0.0004*	0.0015*	0.0193*	0.0784	0.3173	0.6106	0.8415	0.8259	0.6171
MSE	0.0079	0.0161	0.0124	0.0102	0.0096	0.0091	0.0088	0.0086	0.0084	0.0083	0.0083
Student probability	—	0.0001*	0.0061*	0.0076*	0.0108*	0.0139*	0.0257*	0.0615	0.0969	0.1416	0.1770

* Significant at $\alpha = 0.05$

Table 20.2 Martingale versus submartingale forecasts of operating EPS error metrics and significance tests pooled data (N = 560)

	Martin-gale	Submartingale model									
		$\tau = 1$	$\tau = 2$	$\tau = 3$	$\tau = 4$	$\tau = 5$	$\tau = 6$	$\tau = 7$	$\tau = 8$	$\tau = 9$	$\tau = 10$
ME	−0.0138	−0.0024	−0.0037	−0.0043	−0.0042	−0.0044	−0.0049	−0.0053	−0.0056	−0.0059	−0.0064
Student probability	—	0.0067*	0.0001*	0.0000*	0.0000*	0.0000*	0.0000*	0.0000*	0.0000*	0.0000*	0.0000*
MAE	0.0386	0.0518	0.0446	0.0411	0.0394	0.0386	0.0380	0.0375	0.0372	0.0370	0.0370
Student probability	—	0.0001*	0.0076*	0.0614	0.3898	0.9920	0.3898	0.0801	0.0340*	0.0108*	0.0102*
MSE	0.0052	0.0092	0.0081	0.0068	0.0063	0.0060	0.0058	0.0056	0.0055	0.0054	0.0054
Student probability	—	0.0061*	0.0524	0.0444*	0.0614	0.0614	0.0767	0.1336	0.1936	0.2937	0.3371

* Significant at $\alpha = 0.05$

error as the number of observations used in estimating $\delta_{k\tau}$ increased (at least up to $\tau = 10$).[9] This result is consistent with that of Ball, Lev and Watts (1976) who found a monotonic decrease (to $\tau = 9$) in mean absolute error deflated by total assets. However, the relative superiority of the models depends on the error metric chosen.

For the MAE metric, the magnitude of the mean forecast errors favoured the martingale for low τ and the submartingale for high τ for both EPS variables. For the net EPS variable, the martingale performed significantly better (at $p \leqslant 0.05$) for $\tau \leqslant 4$. For $\tau > 4$ the differences in the error measures were not significant, although the magnitude of the error measures favoured the submartingale for $\tau \geqslant 9$. For operating EPS the martingale performed significantly better for $\tau \leqslant 2$, while the submartingale was significantly better for $\tau \geqslant 8$. Thus the submartingale with trend, with $\delta_{k\tau}$ estimated over a large number of preceding years, appeared to be better than the martingale as a naive standard for earnings expectations.

For the MSE metric, the magnitude of the error measures consistently favoured the martingale for both EPS variables. The differences in the error measures were significant for low τ's (i.e., for $\tau \leqslant 6$ for net EPS and for $\tau \leqslant 3$ for operating EPS), but appeared to be insignificant for higher τ's. These results point to the relative superiority of the martingale model, at least for $\tau = 1, \ldots, 10$.

In summary, the results suggest that, for the firms and period studied here, submartingale models incorporating drift factors estimated over a large number of past observations outperformed those using fewer observations. The underestimation shown by both models may be a function of the inflation rate in Australia during the forecast period 1971–78, and may not recur, especially for the submartingale models, in periods of different rates of inflation. The martingale significantly outperformed the submartingale model with the drift factor estimated over only one prior earnings change, i.e., a naive model which assumes that earnings will change by the same amount this year as last year.[10] Indeed, the martingale always outperformed the submartingale with drift factors estimated over between one to five earnings changes. However, conclusions regarding the relative superiority of the models depend on whether the researcher specifies a quadratic or linear loss function.[11]

Acknowledgments

B. B. Davis, O. M. Joy, L. L. Lookabill and R. R. Officer provided valuable comments on earlier versions of this chapter.

Notes

1. Abdel-Khalik and Thompson (1978) provide a summary.
2. One tentative explanation is provided by Beaver, Lambert and Morse (1980), who model annual earnings as a temporal aggregation of intra-period earnings.
3. Strictly speaking, the processes are different although the terms are often used interchangeably. A random walk with drift is $z_t = z_{t-1} + \delta + U_t$, where U_t is i.i.d. with $E(U_t | U_{t-1}, \ldots) = 0$, and δ is the drift factor. In the submartingale process, U_t is not restricted to being i.i.d. The submartingale includes the martingale process, with $\delta = 0$.
4. Ball and Watts (1972, p. 680).

5. From March 1970 to July 1978, the Australian Associated Stock Exchanges required firms to disclose in their half-yearly reports the relationship of profit to that of the corresponding period of the previous year in *percentage* form only. From September 1964 to March 1970, firms were required to state only whether profit was *up* or *down* on the corresponding period of the previous year.

6. The starting point for the data collection was the "earnings per share" file described in Whittred (1978). Briefly, commercial and industrial companies were selected from the 1970 edition of Ian Potter and Company's *Australian Company Reviews*.

7. Ball and Watts (1979) investigated the effects of survivorship bias similar to that described above and concluded that the effects were minimal in describing the average time-series behaviour of EPS.

8. Given the well-documented evidence on the serial independence of EPS changes, it is unlikely that the means of the forecast error distributions are serially correlated.

9. The results by individual forecast years were consistent with those reported above. For most years and error metrics the magnitude of the forecast error declined throughout the range of δ_{kr}. For the remainder, the forecast errors declined for a number of years and thereafter remained relatively steady. Full details are available on request.

10. We also compared the martingale model with the "same per cent change as last year" model. The martingale was better for each error metric (MSE, MAE, ME) and each year except one (MSE, 1971). This suggests that studies using the same amount or same per cent change as last year, such as Elton and Gruber (1972) or Sharpe and Walker (1975), may have misspecified the naive EPS expectations.

11. The results in tables 20.1 and 20.2 were replicated, almost identically, after scaling both MAE and MSE by the standard deviation of past earnings changes, where σ_k was estimated over the past ten changes in annual EPS for firm k.

21 Dividend changes, earnings reports and share prices: Some Australian findings

Philip Brown, Frank J. Finn and Phillip Hancock

Introduction

The effect of changes in a firm's dividend policy on its share price has been debated in the finance literature for many years. Most of the debate has centred on whether the firm's market value depends upon the proportion of earnings paid out in dividends; that is, the firm's dividend payout rate. This aspect of the debate is referred to as the "dividend payout *per se*" issue.

This chapter is concerned with a related issue, frequently coined the "information content of dividends" hypothesis, which states that dividend payments inform the share market about management's views of the future prospects of the firm. Changes in dividend payments contain information which enables market participants to revise their predictions of future worths, and consequently to adjust share prices when the changes are announced.

As noted below, about 98 per cent of Australian companies announce dividends and profits simultaneously. Hence we observe the information effects of dividends and earnings as joint phenomena.

Dividends, earnings, and share prices

Why should dividend changes be important to shareholders?

Lintner (1956) suggested that dividends are important to shareholders because of their close relationship to "current and reasonably foreseeable profits",[1] although he was not explicit about how present dividends were related to those future profits.[2]

Miller and Modigliani (1961) invoked the "informational content of dividends" to explain the fact that a change in a share's dividend rate was often followed by a change in its market price. In a reference to Lintner's (1956) earlier findings of corporate dividend stabilisation policies and target payout ratios, they argued that a change in a firm's dividend rate was likely

Reprinted from the *Australian Journal of Management* 2 (October 1977), 127–47, by permission of the authors and the publisher.

to be interpreted by investors as a "change in management's views of future profit prospects for the firm". (Miller and Modigliani 1961, p. 430). They concluded that the dividend change was not the cause of any price change, although it did provide the occasion for the price change, which was a response to information concerning future profits.

Ball and Brown (1968) also suggested that dividend announcements may contain information of importance to market participants. Although they were primarily concerned with the association between share price changes and the announcement of accounting income numbers, they recognised there could be some overlap between the information content of the annual income number and that of dividend announcements. In cases of overlap, they attributed the information to income, and further stated that they "consider the dividend announcement to be the medium by which the market learns about income" (1968, note 34).

Previous direct tests of the information content hypothesis

Pettit (1972) and Watts (1973) investigated the marginal contribution of information contained in dividend announcements while attempting to control for information already known through the announcement of earnings per share (EPS). Their conclusions were almost diametrically opposed. Pettit concluded that "substantial information" was conveyed by the announcement of dividend changes, while earnings announcements, when controlled for dividend changes, had virtually no effect. Watts concluded that once the earnings effect was controlled, the information content of a dividend was "trivial".[3]

Pettit (1972) classified firms into positive and negative earnings performance categories, and further classified firms within each earnings category into seven mutually exclusive dividend categories, based on the size and direction of the dividend change. Share price movements appeared to depend on the dividend categorisation, and to be independent of the earnings categorisation.[4] Pettit (1972, p. 1002) described his finding, of virtually no earnings announcement effect, as a "rather surprising result".

Brown and Hancock (1977) examined daily share price changes associated with 638 Australian profit reports announced between 1964 and 1970. They controlled for dividends by considering only profit reports made when dividends were unchanged. Their results suggested that profit announcements have had a significant association with share prices when dividend policy was neutral,[5] which is inconsistent with Pettit's results.

Close examination of Pettit's method of identifying the informational content of an earnings announcement provides a clue to why he obtained his "surprising result". Pettit's method involved a "market model" similar to those used by Ball and Brown (1968) and Brown and Kennelly (1972). However, unlike Ball and Brown and Brown and Kennelly, who estimated the relationship between the *change* in a firm's annual EPS and an index of the *change* in annual EPS experienced by all firms whose shares were traded on the share market, Pettit estimated the relationship in (de-trended) *levels* of EPS. A "market model" specification in levels of EPS was rejected by Ball and Brown and, since then, by Gonedes (1973), on several grounds, the most relevant one to us being that the residuals were autocorrelated. Since Pettit's aim was to discover the newsworthy component of each earnings report, and since Pettit's Ordinary Least Squares regression residuals typically exhibited serial dependence, it is likely his method was seriously biased.[6]

We attempted to replicate Pettit's results by using his method to classify Brown and Kennelly's earnings data. A comparison of the replication results with those derived from using an alternative method similar to that used by Brown and Kennelly suggested that Pettit's method of classifying earnings reports has led him to understate substantially the earnings effect. This bias possibly accounts for his "surprising result".[7]

Watts' (1973) evidence on the information content of dividends also had weaknesses. He assessed the marginal effect of dividend announcements on share prices by a two-step procedure. First, he related the annual dividend payment to annual earnings; then he examined the association between the unexplained (residual) component of the annual dividend payment and share price changes. Annual earnings were defined as EPS for fiscal year t, while annual dividends were defined first as the sum of all dividends per share (DPS) declared in fiscal year t (fiscal definition of dividends), and second as the sum of all DPS's declared in the last three quarters of fiscal year t and the first quarter of fiscal year $t + 1$ (overlap definition). Annual dividends were related to annual earnings by partial adjustment models, as suggested by Lintner (1956) and evaluated by Fama and Babiak (1968). Watts acknowledged that the dividend model he relied upon in his first step might have confounded the unexpected change in dividend with statistical noise, and consequently his second step might have underestimated the relationship between dividend announcements and share prices. His study was criticised by Pettit (1976) on these grounds.

A further problem resulted from the fact that Watts did not use actual announcement dates of earnings and dividends. Annual EPS, upon which Watts supposed the annual dividend depended, in many cases was unknown at the time the dividend was announced. In these cases, the association between the dividend announcement in one month and, say, the next month's announcement of earnings, suggests the dividend announcement would have pre-empted the earnings announcement, and not vice versa. Even with Watts' overlap definition of DPS, it is likely that in a significant number of cases[8] the dividend announcement would have pre-empted the earnings announcement.[9]

Hypotheses

We expect both dividend and profit announcements are important to the share market, in so far as they provide information about the future profitability of the firm. If both dividend and profit change in the same direction, we expect a stronger effect on share prices than if they were to change in opposite directions, since on the one hand they are mutually confirmatory, while on the other they would be *prima facie* in conflict. However, we do note Ball and Brown's caution (1968, note 34), and recognise that it is difficult to identify the marginal contributions of earnings and dividend announcements, since earnings and dividends may be highly correlated with themselves and with other "more fundamental" informational determinants of share prices.

We report the results of our experiments on two samples. Sample 1 included a large number of earnings and dividend announcements, with earnings and dividend changes defined somewhat simplistically on an annual basis. The results refer to monthly share price movements over 25 months centred on the announcement month, and are used to establish an overview of the association between share prices and earnings and dividend announcements. The second set of data discussed (Sample 2, which is not independent of Sample 1) comprised a smaller number of announcements in which both interim and final dividend and profit reports were considered, and both monthly and daily share prices were studied. We confine detailed discussion of results to those from Sample 2. The next section describes the data and the definitions we used.

Data and methodology

Data

All firms selected in the study had to satisfy a basic criterion of being in the $N = 651$ version of the price-relative data file compiled by Brown.[10]

Sample 1 comprised 647 dividend and profit announcements made during the period January 1963 to December 1969. Firms were selected randomly, except for cases where dividends and earnings changed in opposite directions. An extensive search was made to find firms in this category.[11] Sample 2 comprised 363 dividend and profit announcements made during the period January 1964 to December 1972. The $N = 651$ data file was found to contain 270 cases of interim or final dividend decreases (including omissions) during this period; all were included. All cases of dividend increase–profit decrease were also included. This dividend increase category was then augmented by a random selection of dividend increase–profit increase cases, such that 270 cases of dividend increases were included. Subsequently, 177 of these 540 cases were discarded, 5 because of errors later discovered in the data file, and the remainder because of classification problems discussed later, or because precise announcement dates could not be confirmed.

Report announcement dates were obtained from *The Sydney Stock Exchange Gazette* and *The Stock Exchange of Melbourne Official Record*. In all cases included in Sample 1, the dividend and profit announcements were made in the same month. Since the analysis of daily data can be sensitive to errors in announcement dates, Sample 2 excluded cases in which we could not confirm that the report was published in the *Australian Financial Review*, a morning newspaper, either on the same day as the official report was made to the stock exchange, or on the next trading day. Another complication arose because a report could have been made to the stock exchange after the last sale for the day. Consequently, our announcement dates were accurate to within one trading day. In other words, the effective announcement period for the daily analyses was the official announcement day and the next trading day.[12]

All monthly rate of return data were obtained from the $N = 651$ version of Brown's price-relative file. Daily share prices were collected separately, and require some comment.

Brown (1972) and Brown and Hancock (1977) suggested that although the Australian share market often was "caught by surprise" when a profit report was released, it nevertheless reacted quickly, in the sense that share prices adjusted rapidly. Because of these earlier results, and because of the tedious nature of data collection, we decided to confine our study of daily share price changes to those that occurred over the 4 trading days leading up to the day of each dividend announcement, the announcement day, and the 6 trading days which immediately followed it.

Daily last sale[13] prices were collected from the price-quotation sheets published by the Melbourne and Sydney Stock Exchanges. Appropriate adjustments were made (for bonus and rights issues, share splits, dividends, etc.) when the basis of quotation was changed. The adjusted price series was then restated in the form of daily continuously compounded rates of return.

Dividend and earnings variables

We needed to know what was newsworthy about the dividend and earnings announcements.

Because we did not know what investors' expected earnings would be, we simulated them by a mechanical rule. We adopted the classifical naive model,[14] and assumed investors were surprised by every change. In essence, we assumed that this period's earnings was expected to be the same as that for the corresponding period last year. An increase in earnings was thus deemed "good" news, and a decrease in earnings "bad" news.

For Sample 1, dividend and earnings changes were defined on an annual basis. EPS changes were determined by whether the annual EPS (adjusted for capital changes) was greater or less than in the previous year. Dividends were categorised as increase, decrease, or no change, by comparing the annual dividend per share (adjusted for capital changes) with that of the previous year.[15] Cases involving a "special" or "bonus" dividend payment were excluded from consideration.

Sample 1 was categorised as follows:

	DPS			
EPS	Increase	Constant	Decrease	Total
Increase	209	199	19	427
Decrease	70	100	50	220
Total	279	299	69	647

Interim and final dividend and profit announcements were studied in Sample 2. Profit reports were classified into increases and decreases relative to the corresponding period in the preceding year.[16] Six reports were excluded from further consideration because there was no basis for comparison.

Dividend payments were classified by assuming shareholders' dividend expectations were based on reports in the *Australian Financial Review*, supplemented by policy statements made by the board of directors and known to us from other sources. For instance, if a firm increased its final dividend in one year and the board stated the new rate would be maintained in the future, then the increased interim dividend in the following year was not included as a further dividend increase. When both the interim and final dividends were changed by the same amount, only the interim dividend change was categorised as a change in payout, on the assumption that the change in the final dividend would have been anticipated when the interim dividend was announced.

Capitalisation changes also present problems. Clearly, the effective dividend payment could have been changed by a bonus or rights issue, or a share split. For example, suppose a firm which had been paying a steady dividend of 10 cents per share made a bonus issue to existing shareholders in the ratio of one-for-two, and the next dividend payment was 8 cents per share. Although the firm's total dividend payout increased, shareholders could have regarded DPS as decreased.[17] Consequently, all dividend changes were excluded if a capitalisation change was made in the 12-month period prior to the dividend announcement. Also, as noted above, dividends with a "special" or "bonus" portion were excluded.

Sample 2 was categorised as follows:

	DPS			
Profit	Increase	Decrease*	Omitted	Total
Increase	148	10	—	158
Decrease	38	87	74	199
Unable to classify	2	3	1	6
Total	188	100	75	363

* but not omitted

Estimation methodology

Numerous other "information cue" studies of share price reactions to specific events have tried to eliminate distortions due to "market effects" on individual share prices. Attempts to adjust for market effects have usually been by: (a) subtracting a market rate of return index from the individual firm's rate of return (tantamount to assuming alpha = 0, beta = 1 in the "market model" popularised by Fama, Fisher, Jensen and Roll (1969); (b) applying the Fama, Fisher, Jensen and Roll market model (or some variant of it); or (c) exploiting the *ex post* (systematic) risk-return relationship, estimated as a cross-sectional relationship in unit time.

When market effects are to be removed, it is hard to know what to assume about each firm's beta, that is, its *ex post* systematic risk. Is it reasonable to assume a stationary beta in the face of a severe shock, such as the omission of a dividend? Is it any more reasonable to constrain each firm's beta to be equal to unity, an unbiased estimate in the absence of information? Perhaps not surprisingly, our results were not particularly sensitive to whichever assumption we chose to make, nor to the choice of method (market model or cross-sectional model) we used to remove market effects. Similarly, when we examined the stationarity of the Sample 1 betas around the announcement months, the largest change in the average beta for a given category was an 8 per cent increase for profit increases–dividend decreases. Results were calculated using (a) average whole-period betas for each firm to estimate the price changes around the announcement month, and (b) separate betas for the periods before and after the announcement month. The results were much the same.

Because it made little difference which way we eliminated market effects, we report only the results from the application of the cross-sectional model, assuming stationary betas over the period studied. The *ex post* risk-return parameters were taken from Ball, Brown and Officer (1976a; reproduced as chapter 4 in this book) for Sample 1. They were re-estimated for Sample 2, to take account of the time-period differences.

We report the cumulative average rate of return, after removing market effects, for each profit–dividend category. The rate of return in each month is averaged over all firms in a given category, and then cumulated for the 24-month period centred on month 0, the month of each profit and dividend announcement.

When daily price movements were examined, market effects were not eliminated from the daily rates of return for three reasons: (a) the probable relative unimportance of market effects in explaining the variance of daily rates of return on individual Australian industrial shares; (b) the shortness of the implied holding period (11 trading days); and (c) the apparent unavailability of a reliable daily index of rates of return of Australian shares for the years we studied.[18] We report the cumulative average unadjusted rates of return for the period around day 0, the day of the announcement of the official report. As noted previously, the effective announcement period was day 0 and day +1.

Results

Monthly share price changes

Figures 21.1, 21.2 and 21.3 present the monthly CAR's (cumulative average rates of return, after removing market effects) for Sample 1. Figure 21.1 shows the CAR's for firms categorised on the basis of changes in earnings only. The pattern is consistent with that found in other earnings announcement studies. Firms which announced increases in earnings on average experienced positive CAR's in the months up to the earnings announcement month, and vice versa for firms which announced decreases in earnings. The CAR for the total sample serves as a control.[19]

Figure 21.2 shows the CAR's for firms categorised on the basis of changes in dividends only. The patterns for the dividend increase and decrease categories are similar to those for the earnings increases and decreases, in that firms which announced increased and decreased dividend payments on average experienced positive and negative CAR's respectively.

The announcement of a constant dividend payment was associated, on average, with a negative CAR. This was to be expected, since dividend increases occurred far more frequently than dividend decreases, suggesting the expected change in a dividend was greater than zero. However, the

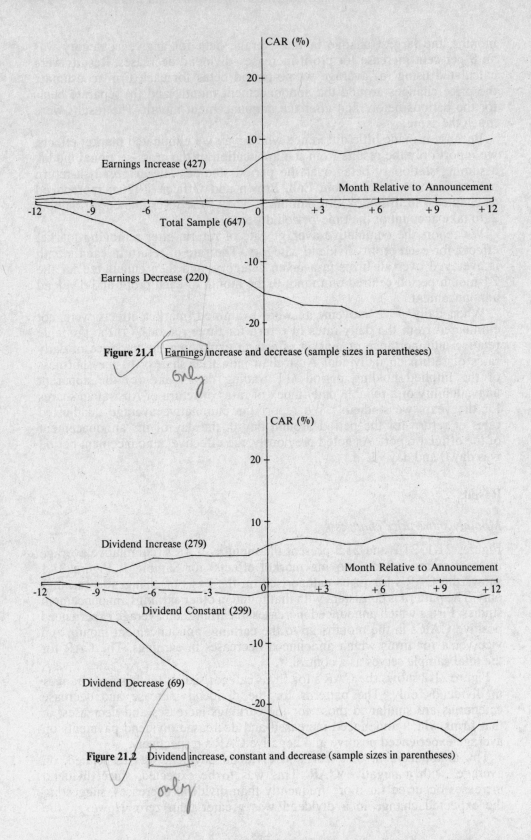

Figure 21.1 Earnings increase and decrease (sample sizes in parentheses)

Figure 21.2 Dividend increase, constant and decrease (sample sizes in parentheses)

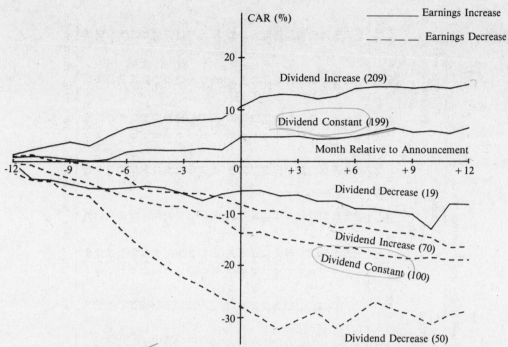

Figure 21.3 Earnings and dividends (sample sizes in parentheses)

downward drift in the CAR was "small" and occurred before the announcement month. Overall, it appears Brown and Hancock's (1977) supposition that no change in dividend signified a neutral dividend policy was not unreasonable.

Figure 21.3 shows the share price changes for firms categorised according to their joint dividend and earnings changes. Two points are worth noting. First, when dividend policy was neutral, earnings announcement appeared to have had a significant effect on share prices: firms in the earnings increase–dividend constant category experienced a positive CAR, while the CAR was negative for firms in the earnings decrease–dividend constant category. Second, when dividend and earnings changes were in the same direction, the absolute values of the CAR's were greater than those of firms which announced a constant dividend coupled with an earnings change, or firms which announced dividend and earnings changes that were in opposite directions.[20] This is in line with our previously stated expectation.

Monthly CAR's for Sample 2 are contained in Table 21.1. The patterns generally are consistent with those for Sample 1: differences in the CAR's can be attributed to the different sample sizes in the various categories, and to the fact that interim reports were excluded from Sample 1. When profit and dividend changed in the same direction, there was a similar change in the CAR, with the largest CAR change occurring in the announcement month. When profit and dividend both increased, the CAR changed in month 0 by 5 per cent. Ninety-two of the 130 shares were traded in that month at a higher price. Conversely, when profit and dividend both declined, the CAR fell in month 0 by 7.8 per cent, and 56 out of 74 shares were traded at a lower price. When dividend was omitted, the CAR fell in the announcement

Table 21.1 Monthly share price movements relative to announcement month: cross-sectional model used to remove market effects

Month relative to announcement month	Profit increase Dividend increase (N = 148)			Profit increase Dividend decrease (N = 10)			Profit decrease Dividend increase (N = 38)			Profit decrease Dividend decrease (N = 87)			Profit decrease Dividend omission (N = 74)		
	Cum ROR	No. <0	ROR >0	Cum ROR	No. <0	ROR >0	Cum ROR	No. <0	ROR >0	Cum ROR	No. <0	ROR >0	Cum ROR	No. <0	ROR >0
−11	0.013	53	75	0.018	3	6	−0.011	16	12	−0.016	43	31	−0.005	36	32
−10	0.022	59	68	0.019	4	4	−0.018	19	9	−0.025	40	34	−0.036	42	25
−9	0.023	69	57	0.008	4	4	0.005	13	15	−0.036	47	26	−0.068	48	19
−8	0.034	60	64	0.006	5	4	−0.005	16	11	−0.029	35	38	−0.059	41	27
−7	0.042	56	68	−0.006	5	5	−0.008	16	11	−0.053	49	25	−0.075	39	29
−6	0.082	45	84	0.001	5	4	−0.014	16	12	−0.075	40	33	−0.112	40	29
−5	0.102	59	70	0.031	2	7	−0.035	15	12	−0.080	41	30	−0.143	49	19
−4	0.097	65	64	0.081	2	5	−0.024	13	14	−0.099	42	30	−0.170	38	29
−3	0.102	63	65	0.012	4	1	−0.030	15	12	−0.097	44	29	−0.187	40	28
−2	0.104	62	66	−0.005	8	1	−0.024	12	15	−0.113	40	32	−0.213	41	26
−1	0.121	57	73	0.041	8	7	0.007	12	15	−0.146	48	24	−0.247	38	26
0	0.171	38	92	−0.006	6	3	0.002	14	13	−0.224	56	18	−0.372	56	11
1	0.189	59	71	−0.001	4	5	−0.016	13	14	−0.216	39	35	−0.376	38	30
2	0.198	56	74	0.031	4	5	−0.046	19	8	−0.215	40	34	−0.395	41	26
3	0.202	64	64	0.015	6	3	−0.029	13	15	−0.214	40	30	−0.405	36	29
4	0.199	69	60	0.029	3	6	−0.015	12	15	−0.206	37	33	−0.440	43	22
5	0.199	63	67	0.031	5	4	−0.052	17	10	−0.224	35	35	−0.448	39	25
6	0.221	49	81	−0.000	4	3	−0.073	16	12	−0.259	39	31	−0.485	45	21
7	0.229	51	78	0.021	4	5	−0.061	13	15	−0.267	40	30	−0.468	27	41
8	0.238	54	74	−0.002	5	4	−0.061	14	14	−0.279	36	34	−0.467	34	34
9	0.221	76	52	0.003	5	4	−0.060	15	13	−0.283	33	37	−0.458	30	38
10	0.229	53	74	0.007	2	7	−0.045	14	13	−0.254	29	40	−0.445	31	35
11	0.233	67	61	0.033	7	2	−0.055	14	13	−0.239	35	34	−0.423	34	32
12	0.236	56	71	0.028	3	6	−0.070	13	14	−0.239	28	42	−0.440	33	34

Note: The number of ROR's in most months do not sum to the sample size for each category. This is because only those firms in which a trade was recorded during the month are recorded.

month by 13.5 per cent. When profit and dividend gave conflicting signals, there appeared to be little significant change in the CAR in month 0: the CAR for the profit decrease–dividend increase category fell by half a per cent; about half the price changes were positive, and half negative.[21]

Table 21.2 Daily share price movements relative to announcement date

					Day relative to official announcement date						
	−4	−3	−2	−1	0	+1	+2	+3	+4	+5	+6
					Profit increase dividend increase $N = 148$						
Rate of return (%):											
$n < 0$	14	19	16	15	5	12	27	22	30	26	21
$n = 0$	15	30	23	29	36	26	24	36	26	41	28
$n > 0$	27	24	30	27	32	37	19	16	21	19	24
Average	0.2	0.2	0.9	0.6	1.6	2.1	−0.2	−0.2	−0.3	−0.0	0.0
Cumulative average	0.2	0.4	1.3	1.9	3.5	5.6	5.4	5.2	4.9	4.9	4.9
					Profit increase dividend decrease $N = 10$						
Rate of return (%):											
$n < 0$	2	3	3	1	2	2	3	2	2	0	3
$n = 0$	1	3	3	4	1	0	0	0	1	2	3
$n > 0$	2	1	0	0	0	1	0	2	1	4	1
Average	0.3	−0.0	−1.0	−0.3	−0.8	−6.2	−1.6	−0.4	−1.1	1.4	−0.4
Cumulative average	0.3	0.3	−0.7	−1.0	−1.8	−8.0	−9.6	−10.0	−11.1	−9.7	−10.1
					Profit decrease dividend increase $N = 38$						
Rate of return (%):											
$n < 0$	3	6	5	9	9	5	5	9	7	11	4
$n = 0$	10	8	4	3	7	3	10	8	8	7	8
$n > 0$	4	5	8	5	4	10	8	5	3	3	7
Average	0.6	−1.1	0.6	−1.2	−0.2	0.7	0.6	−0.7	−0.6	−0.6	−0.2
Cumulative average	0.6	−0.5	0.1	−1.1	−1.3	−0.6	0	−0.7	−1.3	−1.9	−2.1
					Profit decrease dividend decrease $N = 87$						
Rate of return (%):											
$n < 0$	9	12	13	9	15	18	14	11	12	10	12
$n = 0$	18	22	12	11	8	7	15	12	11	17	14
$n > 0$	10	3	6	8	6	2	10	17	5	14	15
Average	0.6	−1.0	−1.4	−0.1	−1.5	−6.1	−1.2	−0.6	0.1	0.7	0.5
Cumulative average	0.6	−0.4	−1.8	−1.9	−3.4	−9.5	−10.7	−11.3	−11.2	−10.5	−10.0
					Profit decrease dividend omission $N = 74$						
Rate of return (%):											
$n < 0$	15	11	15	11	16	24	13	10	11	8	7
$n = 0$	15	16	13	14	14	6	8	15	22	17	13
$n > 0$	7	9	6	9	7	6	13	16	14	13	14
Average	−1.0	−0.1	−1.5	0.1	−2.3	−10.4	−0.1	0.8	0.3	0.3	0.5
Cumulative average	−1.0	−1.1	−2.6	−2.5	−4.8	−15.2	−15.3	−14.5	−14.2	−13.9	−13.4
					All dividend announcements						
Chi-square statistic	6.55	4.55	13.79	1.49	16.54	37.28	0.96	5.18	2.77	6.11	1.45
Chi-square probability	0.04	0.10	0.00	0.47	0.00	0.00	0.62	0.08	0.25	0.05	0.49

Note: The number of ROR's in most days do not sum to the sample size for each category. This is because only those firms in which a trade was recorded in that day are included.

Daily share price changes

Table 21.2 and figure 21.4 present the daily share price changes for each category in Sample 2. Table 21.2 also contains the chi-square statistic for a three-by-two classification of the data, by the sign of the rate of return for each trading day and the sign of the dividend change.[22]

The Australian share market appears to have been taken largely by surprise when profit and dividend announcements were made. When profit and dividend changed in the same direction, there was a substantial price adjustment during the effective announcement period of day 0 and day 1.

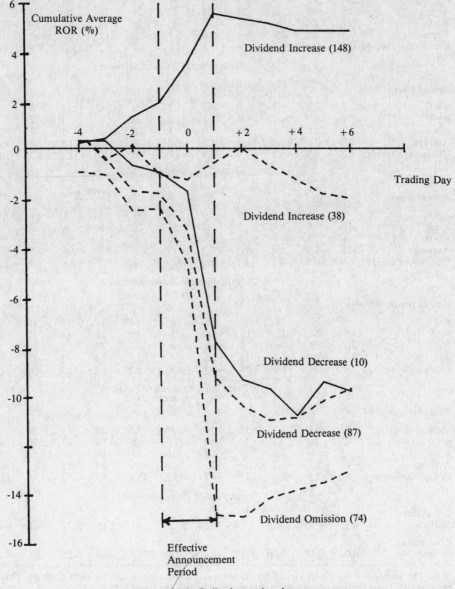

Figure 21.4 Daily share price changes

Also, the size of the price change appeared to depend on both the dividend and profit changes. For example, when profit declined and dividend was omitted, share prices on average decreased by 12.7 per cent in the announcement period, whereas when profit declined and dividend declined but was not omitted, the average price change was −7.6 per cent. The chi-square statistics in table 21.2 indicate that the probability of the price changes in the announcement period being unrelated to dividend but occurring due to chance was essentially zero.[23]

It must be remembered that dividend and profit simultaneously changed in the same direction in almost 90 per cent of all cases.[24] Thus, the results indicate a significant share price movement in the announcement period which very likely was due to investors becoming aware of a change in profit, dividend, or both.

Note the speed of the share price adjustment in all categories shown in table 21.2 and figure 21.4. Only minor price changes occurred in the days after the effective announcement period.[25]

Explaining the magnitude of the price changes

The magnitude of a share price adjustment depends on the quantity of information which triggers that adjustment. If a profit or dividend change conveys information which triggers a share price adjustment, the magnitude of that adjustment depends on the quantity of information conveyed, which, we suppose, is associated with the extent of the profit or dividend change.

Table 21.3 Profit change ratio and dividend change classification

Profit Decile	Ratio* N	Dividend change classification		
		Increase	Decrease	Omitted
1	14	10	3	1
2	28	9	5	—
3	42	6	5	3
4	56	2	12	—
5	70	2	10	2
6	84	2	10	2
7	98	—	7	7
8	112	—	6	8
9	126	1	5	8
10	140	—	2	12

* For firms with profit decreases only. Refer note 24.

To test this hypothesis, the rate of return from day −1 to +1, that is, from the day immediately preceding the announcement date to the end of the effective announcement period, was regressed on that ratio of the change in dividend to the share price at day −1. The results were as follows:

	Intercept	Dividend variable
Coefficient	−0.005	1.478
Standard error	0.007	0.185
t-statistic	−0.76	7.99
r^2		0.30
N		151

The above statistics must be interpreted cautiously, because of the influence of EPS which could not be held constant.[26] The r^2 statistic indicates that about a third of the sample variance in rate of return from day −1 to day +1 was accounted for by the sample variance in the ratio of the dividend change to share price at day −1; which is significant at the 0.001 level.

The above ratio is not obviously a good proxy for the information content of a dividend change, and might have resulted in a seriously misspecified model. The percentage dividend change is an alternative estimate of the information content of the dividend change. The rate of return from day −1 to day +1 was thus regressed on the logarithm of the ratio of the new dividend to the old dividend, excluding all cases where either the new or the old dividend payment was equal to zero. The following results were obtained:

	Intercept	Dividend variable
Coefficient	−0.008	0.148
Standard error	0.007	0.019
t-statistic	−1.13	7.56
r^2		0.35
N		107

The results of both regressions support the contention that the larger the change in dividend, the greater the associated share price adjustment.[27]

Again, we caution against reading too much into these results, since no control was made for the accompanying profit report. We did attempt to control for profit, by adding the logarithm of the ratio of the new to the old profit, to the regression—a variable which is far from an ideal measure of the information content of a profit report, since, for example, reports of losses, which are among the most newsworthy, are outside the variable's domain. The multiple regression results were as follows:

	Intercept	Dividend variable	Earnings variable
Coefficient	−0.006	0.140	0.018
Standard error	0.0078	0.029	0.018
t-statistic	−0.7469	4.81	1.00
R^2		0.38	
N		80	
r (dividend, earnings)		0.60	

Despite the measurement problems with the dividend and earnings variables, the results do indicate a positive relationship has existed between the magnitude of share price adjustments and the amount of information conveyed by dividend and profit reports.

Conclusions

Earlier studies did not resolve whether dividend announcements conveyed information to the share market additional to that conveyed by earnings reports. This chapter has highlighted the difficulties involved in attempting to attribute marginal information content to one or the other type of announcement.[28]

In Australia, dividend and profit reports are normally announced simultaneously, and have an immediate impact on share prices. There have been interactive informational effects, whereby dividend and profit changes have tended to reinforce one another. When dividend and profit signals have been *prima facie* in conflict, their joint impact on share prices has been considerably lessened.

Although it appears that the larger the change in dividend or profit, the greater has been the associated change in share price, there has been a tendency for dividend and profit changes to be positively related. It may also be true that profit and dividend have been proxies for more fundamental informational determinants of share prices, in which case attempts to isolate the information effects of either dividend or profit may well prove pointless.

Acknowledgments

An early version of this paper was presented first at the Research Workshop, Department of Commerce, University of Western Australia, in April 1974. The paper has benefited from comments by Ray Ball and an anonymous referee.

Notes

1. Lintner (1956, p. 103). In our empirical work, we differentiate between "earnings" (earnings per share) and "profit" (net income of the firm).
2. Fama and Babiak (1968) extensively tested Lintner's dividend partial adjustment model, and confirmed his observation that current dividends were strongly correlated with current (and past) profits and dividends. However, they too made little reference to the association between dividends and future profits.
3. A recent exchange (Pettit 1976 and Watts 1976) did not reconcile their opposite conclusions.
4. For example, Pettit's Abnormal Performance Index figures for month 0 for the dividend no change categories were: 0.998 for the positive earnings performance category, and 0.995 for the negative earnings performance category (Pettit 1972, pp. 1000 and 1001). This result appears to have been reinforced in the more recent study by Pettit (1976).
5. The cumulative average rate of return over the 6 days up to the end of the announcement date was -2.09 per cent for dividend decreases and 0.82 per cent for dividend increases. The chi-square probability, that the differences in the rates of return in the announcement period were due to chance, was less than 0.005 (see chapter 19, table 19.1). Brown and Hancock noted that dividend policy was neutral only in the sense that dividends were unchanged.
6. Pettit (1972, note 11) referred to autocorrelation, but dismissed the misspecification as of "only minor importance".
7. The cumulative average rate of return for EPS "bad news" (i.e., EPS lower than its expectation) at day 0 was -0.0049 (Pettit's model) compared with -0.0119 (Brown and Kennelly's model) and for EPS "good news" 0.0029 (Pettit's model) compared with 0.0052 (Brown and Kennelly's model). Moreover, Brown and Kennelly's model is probably not the most efficient now known: see, for example, their own reservations (1972, pp. 406–8).
8. See Hancock (1975, Appendix I and II). Data from the *Wall Street Journal Index* on 4,850 United States quarterly reports showed that the percentage of cases in which the fourth quarter's earnings announcement lagged the dividend announcement by 4 months or more were: 1964 35.6 per cent, 1965 30.5 per cent, 1966 29.4 per cent, 1967 31 per cent, 1968 26.5 per cent. These would all have been cases where, for the overlap definition, the dividend announcement preceded and hence possibly pre-empted the earnings announcement.
9. Watts' finding (1973, p. 195) that the overlap definition of DPS was generally more favourable

to the information hypothesis is consistent with this claim, since his overlap definition would have included fewer cases of the dividend announcement pre-empting the earnings announcement than would have been the case with the fiscal definition.

10. The file is described in chapter 4, note 9. The file initially extended over the period January 1958 to December 1970. It has recently been updated to December 1973.

11. Even then, we found only nineteen cases of earnings increase–dividend decrease.

12. It is worth noting that profit and dividends were reported on the same day in all but six of the 363 cases in Sample 2.

13. Because some shares were not traded every day, daily results were also obtained using buyer quotes only, seller quotes only, and the average of buyer and seller quotes, whenever a share was not traded on a particular day. The results obtained were consistent with those reported here, which relate to actual (transaction) prices.

14. The classical naive model is naive only in the statistical sense. The behaviour of several economic time series, including corporate income, appears to be described well by this model. It has been used in applications similar to the present one, for example, by Ball and Brown (1968), Brown and Kennelly (1972), and chapter 19 of this book.

15. This classification into dividend categories is simplistic, because it ignores the fact that an annual dividend change could have occurred when the interim dividend was paid. Both interim and final dividend announcements are considered in Sample 2.

16. Brown and Hancock in chapter 19 of this volume discuss problems in identifying whether interim or final profit numbers increased or decreased.

17. The point at issue is the amount of dividend that shareholders were expecting. If, when the bonus issue was made, directors had indicated they intended to maintain the dividend rate on the bonus-increased capital, then a dividend of 8 cents per share could be viewed as a cut in the dividend rate.

18. See chapter 19, note 16 for an elaboration of these issues.

19. For a large random sample, the average of "good" and "bad" news is expected to be neutral. Thus, the CAR should be close to zero.

20. We were surprised to see relatively large price changes in the 12 months after month 0 for some categories in figure 21.3. This was not evident in figures 21.1 and 21.2. Ball (1976) gives one possible explanation of this price behaviour, namely that the dividend is a proxy for omitted variables or other specification errors in the risk–return relationship.

21. There were too few cases in the profit increase–dividend decrease category to warrant detailed comment.

22. See chapter 19 for a similar statistic for the rate of return–profit report association.

23. It should be noted that if market and industry factors were present in the profit reports, the chi-square statistic may be overstated and the chi-square probability understated, because of possible violations of the independence assumption.

24. There was a correlation of about +0.6 between the ratios of the present-to-previous dividend and the present-to-previous profit. See also table 21.3, which shows the number of firms in each dividend change category and each profit change decile, when firms in the profit decrease category were ranked from the highest ratio to the lowest on the basis of the ratio of the new profit figure to the old profit figure.

    The number of entries in table 21.3 is less than the number in the profit decrease categories in table 21.2 because a profit change ratio could not be calculated in all cases, especially when interim profit reports were considered.

25. An efficient market is characterised by a readjustment to equilibrium prices immediately new information comes to the market (see Fama 1970a for more detail). Admittedly, the chi-square probabilities that the price changes in days 3 and 5 were due to chance were "low". However, the magnitude of the price changes was "small", and the probabilities that the price changes in days 2, 4, and 6 were due to chance were "high". This anomaly possibly warrants future investigation. It might be due to downward bias, in the chi-square probability, as discussed in note 23 above. Cf. the results alluded to in note 20 above.

26. Half-yearly EPS figures were unavailable in Australia for most of the companies we studied.

27. There is close consistency in the results, because a share's price is a proxy for future dividend receipts, which are not independent of present dividends. The slope coefficient in both regressions is biased towards zero, because of the classical errors-in-variables problem.

28. In an experiment somewhat similar to ours, Griffin (1976) classified a sample of United States reports on the basis of the signs of earnings changes, analysts' forecasts of earnings changes, and dividend changes. He attributed unique information to dividends and analysts' forecasts, based on differences in the CAR's at month 0 for various combinations of the three variables. However as pointed out by Sunder (1976), the differences in the CAR's could have been due to Griffin's lack of control for the magnitude of the earnings changes.

22 Ex-dividend day behaviour of Australian share prices

Philip Brown and Terry Walter

Introduction

Recent changes to the Australian income tax law have again focused attention sharply on the share market trade-off between dividends and capital gains. Australia is to get a dividend imputation system, whereby companies will be taxed at the company tax rate on all dividends they pay. Assuming the proposed 49 per cent company tax rate is introduced, for each $51 of eligible dividends they receive, taxpaying sharholders will be assessed $100 in income and credited with $49 tax paid.

Some have claimed the changes herald a new era for equity investment[1] and that the "strong" share market performance which followed the Treasurer's September 1985 statement can be explained, at least partly, by his proposals.

We do not address this question directly. But we do address the question of the dividend–capital gain trade-off, to the extent that it is manifest in the ex-dividend day behaviour of Australian share prices.

The most common finding in North America is that share prices fall by *less* than the amount of the dividend on the day they are first quoted ex-dividend (XD). Explanations include higher tax rates on dividends than on capital gains, investors or floor operators being "caught asleep" and errors in identifying the XD day.

If the tax rate is higher for dividends than for capital gains and if marginal investors are indifferent to the form of their *after-tax* income (that is, whether it be in the form of dividends or capital gains), then a *before-tax* preference for capital gains should be apparent when share prices fall by less than the amount of the dividend. Kalay (1982) models the relationship clearly.

The difficulty with this argument is that it glosses over questions of transaction costs, time lags that would be embedded in arbitrage operations [cum-dividend (CD) and XD trades are sequential in time] and the fact that

Reprinted from the *Australian Journal of Management* 11, no. 2 (December 1986), 139-52, by permission of the authors and the publisher.

the tax positions of investors are more complex than a simple tax-driven preference for capital gains would suggest. These issues are explored further in our literature review and our sketch of the Australian institutional background below.

The other two explanations can be dismissed readily. Although there are, no doubt, cases when the floor operator or the investor could overlook the fact that a share is quoted XD,[2] they are hardly likely to be common or pervasive events, partly because of the system safeguards[3] but more importantly because of the automatic safeguard of natural selection in a competitive environment. We protect our experiment against the third explanation, errors in XD dates, in ways which rule out the possibility of data errors driving our results.

There is a rational reason for discounting dividends on the XD day: typically dividends are not paid until a few weeks later. At most the discount would be of the order of 1 per cent, which is much less than the 20 to 25 per cent discount we observe.

Data issues are explored in the section "Institutional Background". We accessed the Centre for Research in Finance at the Australian Graduate School of Management (AGSM/CRIF) database, which includes information on 7,376 dividends paid between January 1974 and December 1984.[4]

Results from the tests we conduct on drop-off ratios (the drop-off ratio is the ratio of the CD price less the XD price, to the dividend amount) and on rates of return (calculated by adding back the full dividend to the XD price) are summarised in the section "Data". Their implications for market anomalies are explored in "Results". We conclude with "Implications for Market Anomalies".

Prior evidence

Early research by Campbell and Beranek (1955) and Durand and May (1960) documents the size of the average price decline on the XD day, relative to the dividend amount. They report drop-off ratios that do not differ greatly from 1. By contrast, Elton and Gruber (1970) estimate the drop-off ratio averages 0.78 for 4,148 observations between April 1966 and March 1967, which implies a marginal income tax rate for investors of about 35 per cent. Dividend yield (and payout ratio) is positively related to the drop-off ratio. Elton and Gruber (1970, p. 73) conclude:

> The close relationship between both measures of a firm's dividend policy and the implied stockholder bracket suggest that M&M were right in hypothesising a "clientele effect".

Kalay (1982) argues that the marginal tax rate of investors cannot be inferred from the dividend drop-off ratio and that any departure of the dividend drop-off ratio from 1 is bounded by the transaction costs of traders able to arbitrage. From 2,540 United States dividends paid in the same period studied by Elton and Gruber, Kalay estimates the drop-off ratio is not significantly different from 1. The drop-off ratio is, however, related to dividend yield.

Eades, Hess and Han Kim (1984) repeat the XD day experiment with a variety of samples. Over the period 1962 to 1981, they find strong support for the hypothesis of an XD day premium (equivalent to a market-adjusted drop-off ratio of less than 1) for the total period and the three subperiods prior to the introduction of negotiated commissions in April 1975. Results for April 1975 and later generally favour the null of no XD day premium, which is consistent with a significant drop in effective transaction costs. Taxable preferred stock dividends are priced as if dividends were taxed at a *lower* rate than capital gains, non-taxable cash distributions are found to be priced as if they impose *negative* tax on the recipients, and non-taxable stock dividends are priced on XD days as if they were taxable. Their results thus cast doubt on the tax interpretation of XD day pricing behaviour.

Eades, Hess and Han Kim extend their analysis to examine the pricing behaviour for five days on each side of the XD day. They report (p. 4):

> Abnormal returns are neither confined to the ex-dividend day nor are they confined to taxable distributions by common stocks. Indeed all samples reveal anomalous return behaviour during the ex-dividend period . . . [and] suggest that the tax interpretation . . . is inconsistent with the results of the ex-dividend day experiment.

Noti (1977) is the only published Australian study in this vein.[5] He collected share price data on 36 XD days for four companies. Noise in the data makes it difficult to draw any reliable conclusions from such a small sample.

Institutional background

The income tax positions of Australian shareholders who received dividends and realised capital gains and losses between 1974 and 1984 included all four combinations of dividends or capital gains being taxed or not.[6] Some of Australia's largest investors, such as exempt superannuation funds, paid no income tax at all. Share traders, including sharebrokers, were taxed on dividends and realised capital gains, but could deduct realised capital losses. Personal investors paid tax on dividends, but escaped tax on realised capital gains if the shares were held for at least a year. Taxpaying financial institutions, automatically classed as share traders for tax purposes, were taxed on realised capital gains, but as companies they were eligible for the dividend rebate.[7]

From 1974 until their deregulation in April 1984, brokerage rates were fixed by agreement among the sharebrokers.[8] Brokerage plus stamp duty averaged about 3 per cent for an order worth $5,000; 2.5 per cent for $15,000; 2 per cent for $50,000; 1.4 per cent for $250,000; 1.25 per cent for $500,000; and 1 per cent for $1 million. These "one-way" rates could have been halved for "round-trips" completed within a month, as might be the case with arbitrage operations. Even so, a round trip buying CD and selling XD could have consumed a large proportion of the dividend, as the ratio of the dividend amount to the CD price averaged 3.5 per cent over the period 1974 to 1984.

It is a moot point, however, whether transaction costs of this order are relevant at the margin. Brokers who arbitrage recoup their own fees, and for them the appropriate brokerage component of the marginal transaction cost is surely less than the scheduled fee.[9] Other investors may be rearranging their portfolios for reasons unrelated to XD price behaviour. For them, the relevant marginal transaction cost could be negligible.

In sum, anything seems possible. At the margin, dividends could have been preferred to capital gains for tax reasons, but the reverse could easily be true. And transaction costs might or might not have mattered.

Data

Our company names, dividend amounts and XD dates come from the AGSM/ CRIF database. Our data set includes 7,376 dividends, although many of them, typically 50 to 60 per cent, can not be used because the required share price data are unavailable. The 7,376 dividends exclude all known cases where the basis of quotation was changed [e.g., where the shares were quoted XB (ex-bonus) or XR (ex-rights)] within the experimental period, which we define as the two weeks centred on the XD day.

There is no reliable, machine-readable database which contains daily prices of Australian shares for this period. Our prices were taken from quotation sheets issued by the stock exchanges. All price changes were filtered and absolute changes greater than 10 per cent of the CD price were verified. We verified the XD dates against the flags on the quotation sheets and at the same time checked for any other changes in the basis of quotation that could have been missed by our data sources. This was done because our study is sensitive to data errors: XD date errors induce a bias towards a drop-off ratio less than 1 (an error rate of 10 per cent in the XD dates could lead us to conclude, erroneously, that dividends are discounted by 10 per cent); and including XB or XR prices could bias our results the other way if the dilution effect of the new issue is missed.

We use the Statex-Actuaries Accumulation Index (SAAI) to measure the market return.[10] We recomputed the index to allow for daily reinvestment of the full cash proceeds from any dividend or the sale of any rights, etc. It may seem odd that we calculate the market index by assuming dividends are not discounted, when our results show they almost certainly are. However, we should point out (a) although XD dates do cluster, they are nevertheless spread out, over time, for the 50 companies in the index, (b) any bias will tend to be marginal, to overstate the market return and to understate a share's market-adjusted return (equivalently, to overstate the drop-off ratio), (c) the SAAI has a bias towards larger companies and therefore a slight bias towards understating the market return (Brown et al. 1983) and (d) in any event, our conclusions are relatively insensitive to whether or not we adjust for market movements.

Results

Our results are summarised in table 22.1, which is compact and requires elaboration.

Table 22.1 covers all fiscal years, that is, 1973/74 to 1984/85. Results are presented for continuously compounded rates of return—the natural logarithm of the price relative $(PXD + Div)/PCD$, where PXD and PCD are the XD and CD prices—and for the drop-off ratio $(PCD - PXD)/Div$, both with and without market adjustments.[11] To check on the sensitivity of our

Table 22.1 Summary of results: Rates of return* and dividend drop-off ratios, 1974 to 1984

	Rate of return		Drop-off ratio	
	No adj.	Mkt adj.	No adj.	Mkt adj.
	(a) Daily price data			
Mean	0.73	0.66	0.72	0.68
Median	0.39	0.46	0.86	0.84
1st quartile	−0.47	−0.55	0.33	0.37
3rd quartile	1.93	1.81	1.14	1.18
t statistic	15.79	14.81	−10.74	−9.14
t probability	1.000	1.000	0.000	0.000
$N < 0$ 966		1,108 $N < 1$	1,674	1,904
$N = 0$ 392		zero $N = 1$	392	zero
$N > 0$ 1,674		1,896 $N > 1$	966	1,100
N 3,032		3,004	3,032	3,004
Regression:†				
• beta	—	—	0.845	0.772
• std err beta	—	—	0.028	0.28
• *r*-squared	—	—	0.23	0.21
	(b) Weekly price data			
Mean	1.39	1.06	0.46	0.59
Median	1.04	0.90	0.67	0.72
1st quartile	−0.99	−1.41	1.33	1.47
t statistic	16.04	12.77	−6.94	−6.35
t probability	1.000	1.000	0.000	0.000
$N < 0$ 998		1,148 $N < 1$	1,749	1,763
$N = 0$ 196		zero $N = 1$	196	zero
$N > 0$ 1,749		1,765 $N > 1$	998	1,150
N 2,943		2,913	2,943	2,913
Regression:†				
• beta	—	—	0.645	0.639
• std err beta	—	—	0.04	0.05
• *r*-squared	—	—	0.04	0.05

* Holding period is from the last CD sale one trading day/week before the XD day until the last sale on the XD day.

† The regression is an Ordinary Least Squares regression of the CD less the XD price (deflated by the CD price) on the dividend amount (also deflated by the CD price).

results to data errors, results are presented for *PCD* being the last sale on (a) the day before and (b) the week before the XD day.[12] For each variable, we report distributional statistics (mean, median, first and third quartiles), frequency counts, the *t* statistic and the probability of observing it under the appropriate null hypothesis (population mean return is zero; population mean drop-off ratio is one) and selected estimates from the Ordinary Least Squares cross-sectional regression of the deflated price change $(PCD - PXD)/PCD$ on the deflated dividend amount Div/PCD. The regression coefficient of the dividend variable, the coefficient's standard error of estimate and the proportion of explained variance are the three we report. There are many connections between the results in table 22.1: they are far from being independent and some combinations are no more than slightly different ways of looking at the same basic phenomenon.[13]

Whichever way we look at it, table 22.1 contains clear evidence that Australian share prices drop by *less* than the amount of the dividend when they are quoted XD, and the difference is statistically significant. The regression estimate, using market-adjusted daily data, is that the drop-off averages 77 per cent of the dividend. The t statistics are "large" by any standard; a non-parametric test (based on, say, the rate of return frequencies $N < 0$ and $N > 0$) leads to the same conclusion: that there is only the remotest possibility of observing the results by chance if the appropriate null hypothesis were true.

Table 22.1 contains evidence of skewness in the distributions (the mean drop-off ratio is less than the median in all cases) although we did not test specifically for skewness; and the data are noisy (note the inter-quartile range relative to the median). We collected weekly data to try to avoid a downward bias in the drop-off ratio due to XD date errors. Interestingly the bias, if there is one, goes the other way. However, the weekly data, as we would expect, are more noisy than the daily data (compare the lower t statistics and proportions of variance explained by the regression, or the inter-quartile ranges). For this reason we prefer to concentrate our discussion on the results from the daily data.

It makes little difference to the tenor of the results whether or not we adjust for market movements. The reason is simple enough: dividends, as we have already noted, are most often paid half-yearly and, given the history of dividend yields[14] and the (daily) return on the market since January 1974, the dividend is the dominant component of the XD day return. It does, as we expect, make more difference with a longer holding period. For example, the mean and median drop-off ratio is more sensitive to market adjustments for weekly than for daily data.

Table 22.2 gives selected statistics, for the drop-off ratio, by fiscal year (July 1 to the next June 30) after adjustment for market effects. The measures of central tendency fluctuate about 0.8. We note, in particular, that deregulation of brokerage rates in April 1984 had no obvious impact on the drop-off ratio in 1984/85.[15] In every year the drop-off ratio for an individual share was less than 1 more often than it was greater than 1, which suggests that

Table 22.2 Drop-off ratio statistics by fiscal year (July 1 to June 30), 1974–85; holding period is one trading day; adjusted for market movements

Fiscal year	Mean	Median	Beta	Regression* SE (B)	$N < 1$	$N > 1$	N
1974	0.85	0.83	0.81	0.12	92	54	146
1975	0.72	0.71	0.90	0.10	154	68	222
1976	0.85	0.87	0.84	0.08	173	106	279
1977	0.81	0.86	0.79	0.06	198	102	300
1978	0.83	0.90	0.97	0.08	184	126	310
1979	0.79	0.88	0.85	0.10	201	133	334
1980	0.77	0.83	0.51	0.11	205	131	336
1981	0.55	0.78	0.89	0.11	190	122	312
1982	0.74	0.82	0.92	0.14	134	71	205
1983	0.76	0.82	0.80	0.10	127	77	204
1984	0.52	0.74	1.08	0.10	170	77	247
1985	0.97	0.85	0.83	0.27	68	41	109
All	0.68	0.84	0.77	0.03	1,904	1,100	3,004

* Regression "beta" and "SE(B)" refer to the coefficient of the dividend variable and its standard error in the OLS regression of the deflated price change $(PCD - PXD)$ on the deflated dividend amount. The CD price, PCD, is the deflator.

dividends have been discounted relative to capital gains throughout the experimental period.

Eades, Hess and Han Kim (1984) examine the rate of return for five days on each side of the XD day. Since we had collected prices on the fifth day before and after the XD day, we also could examine returns over the same 5-day periods. Table 22.3 reports selected statistics for the market-adjusted, continuously compounded rate of return over four adjacent holding periods: day $t-5$ to day $t-1$; day $t-1$ to day t (the XD day); day t to day $t+1$; and day $t+1$ to day $t+5$. There is clear evidence in table 22.3 that positive returns, in excess of the market, occur before and after the XD day, though it appears that, in Australia, they peak on the XD day itself. Our finding differs from that of Eades, Hess and Han Kim who report that "for all but the stock dividends and splits sample, the absolute value of the ex-day excess returns are smaller than the day +1 or the day −1 returns or both" (1984, p. 21).

Table 22.3 Selected statistics for the market-adjusted, continuously compounded rates of return (%) for four adjacent holding periods, all years

Statistic	Holding period (day t is the XD day)			
	$(t-5, t-1)$	$(t-1, t)$	$(t, t+1)$	$(t+1, t+5)$
Mean	0.41	0.66	0.21	0.21
Median	0.26	0.46	0.11	0.10
1st quartile	−1.68	−0.55	−0.88	−2.00
3rd quartile	2.34	1.81	1.28	2.24
t-statistic	6.03	14.81	4.92	3.03
t-probability	1.000	1.000	1.000	0.999
$N < 0$	1,527	1,108	1,357	1,543
$N = 0$	—	—	5	4
$N > 0$	1,806	1,896	1,582	1,642
N	3,333	3,004	2,944	3,189

Table 22.4 Frequency with which the drop-off ratio of a lower yielding security was less than, equal to or greater than the drop-off ratio of its higher yielding pair; comparison is for shares quoted XD on same day

Year	Daily data				Weekly data			
	<	=	>	All	<	=	>	All
1974	86	3	85	174	67	6	97	170
1975	96	10	95	201	90	10	78	178
1976	234	21	233	488	198	14	149	361
1977	210	18	192	420	181	9	223	413
1978	211	21	181	413	204	11	197	412
1979	224	18	309	551	243	9	269	521
1980	234	26	256	516	250	4	256	510
1981	227	20	175	422	224	5	176	405
1982	99	5	99	203	88	5	136	229
1983	88	8	104	200	93	2	88	183
1984	151	12	105	268	111	3	110	224
1985	64	15	61	140	50	2	54	106
All	1,924	177	1,895	3,996	1,799	80	1,833	3,712

Elton and Gruber (1970) found the dividend drop-off ratio declined with the dividend yield, consistent with the clientele view. Lakonishok and Vermaelen (1983) and Booth and Johnson (1984) did not find the relationship in Canada. Hess (1982) found no relationship in the United States but Kalay (1982) did. Moreover, Gibbons (1982b) argues Hess' results do support, weakly, a clientele effect.

We replicate the Elton and Gruber experiment but on a daily basis, to minimise the impact of shifts in dividend yields over time. The price we pay is a coarser test, because of data sparsity. Our test is a pair-wise comparison between shares quoted XD on the same day. The clientele effect predicts that the drop-off ratio is lower for the share with the lower yield, a prediction which, under the most favourable interpretation of table 22.4, is only weakly confirmed by our daily data and is rejected by the weekly data. For example, table 22.4 reports a total of 1,924 cases that support the clientele effect and 1,895 that do not (if we ignore the 177 cases where the drop-off ratios were equal).[16]

In sum, then, we find evidence that dividends were discounted about 20 to 25 per cent, relative to capital gains, in Australia over the period 1974 to 1984, but any evidence linking the discount to the dividend yield is at best very weak.

Implications for market anomalies

Figure 22.1 displays the average rate of return on the Statex-Actuaries Accumulation Index (SAAI) by day of the week. Because XD days are concentrated on Mondays and to a lesser extent on Fridays,[17] and given the drop-off ratio is on average less than 1, we would expect a higher average return on Mondays and Fridays, other things being equal. We do not find that to be so and the puzzle, in figure 22.1, is why.[18]

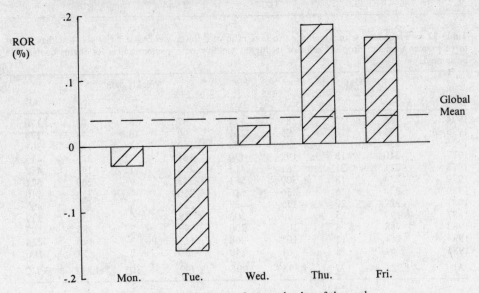

Figure 22.1   SAAI rate of return, by day-of-the-week

There is evidence in figure 22.1 of an anomalous day-of-the-week effect, as French (1980) and Keim and Stambaugh (1984) document for the United

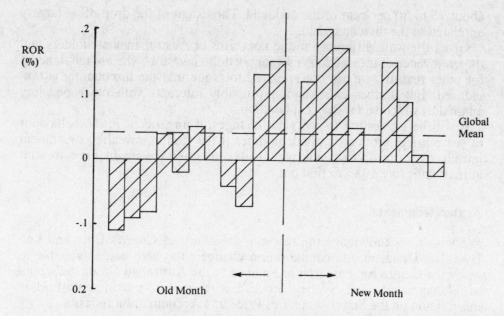

Figure 22.2   SAAI rate of return, by day-of-the-month

States and Jaffe and Westerfield (1985) show is present also in Japan, Canada, the United Kingdom and Australia.[19] But the strength of this effect is masked by the concentration of XR dates (see note 17) and the suspicion that rights adjustments can bias indexes in subtle ways (O'Brien and Young 1985).

Now consider the index seasonality question which Officer (1975) studies. Officer rejects a dividend explanation of market index seasonalities. Yet XD dates are concentrated in March–April and October, periods in which the average return on the SAAI is among the highest.[20] We wonder if the XD date concentration also has complicated measurement of the so-called January effect (see, for example, Brown et al. 1983).

Figure 22.2 explores the day-of-the-month phenomenon. Ariel (1983) reports anomalously high returns for United States stocks beginning with the last trading day of the month and continuing for the next nine days; and anomalously low returns in the previous nine days. We find a similar result (possibly beginning a day earlier), although our data are more limited in scope than his. But what causes the anomaly?

There is no simple relationship between the concentration of XD, XB and XR dates, and anomalous returns. The peaks in the XD and XB/XR date concentrations are respectively days −9, −4, 5 and 6 for dividends, and days −4 and 1 for capitalisation changes. Index returns on average are negative on days −9 and −4, less than the global mean on day 1, not much different from the mean on day 5, and about zero on day 6.

Summary

We find clear evidence that the dividend drop-off ratio in Australia is significantly less than 1. Our best guess is that prices drop, on average, by about 75 to 80 per cent of the dividend. The extent of the drop-off is largely unrelated to the dividend yield.

Given the wide difference in the tax status of Australian shareholders and the irrelevance of transaction costs for portfolio investors who are rebalancing for other reasons, we are not prepared to argue that the discounting is tax-induced. But it does exist, and it probably interacts with other puzzling anomalies which so far defy explanation.

It will be interesting to see what changes, if any, occur in the behaviour of share prices around ex-dividend dates if the Commonwealth government introduces the proposed new income tax regime. We might have to wait at least until July 1987 to find out.

Acknowledgments

We wish to acknowledge the research assistance of Charles Chin and Loh Hwa Tin. Dividend and capitalisation change data were made available to us by the Centre for Research in Finance at the Australian Graduate School of Management. The Sydney Stock Exchange Ltd provided up-to-date information on the Statex-Actuaries Price and Accumulation Indexes.

Notes

1. *Australian Financial Review*, 23 September 1985, p. 1.
2. See for example, *Australian Financial Review*, 3 May 1985, p. 74.
3. Computer-based quote screens in sharebrokers' offices and elsewhere provide XD flags against shares traded XD. Flags are also visible on the trading floors of the stock exchange.
4. Unfortunately, applicable price data required for this study are unavailable for many of them (refer to the section "Data").
5. Ball et al. (1979) take a different approach.
6. A handy reference is table 17.1 in Bruce, McKern and Pollard (1983).
7. A resident public company for tax purposes is entitled to a rebate on all dividends included in its taxable income. The way the rebate is calculated generally means the dividend is tax free. In fiscal 1982/83 only, Australian resident individual shareholders received a rebate on up to $1,000 of dividends included in their taxable incomes.
8. The fee schedule was published in the exchanges' listing manual.
9. From the enquiries we made in June 1985, processing a transaction between clients of two different sharebrokers requires preparing at least 20 pieces of paper.
10. The SAAI was not calculated on some public holidays in New South Wales when trading did take place interstate. Corrected index values were supplied by the Sydney Stock Exchange.
11. All prices are for the last sale on the day (see Kalay 1982) as opening prices and index values are unavailable. Returns are adjusted by subtracting the continuously compounded rate of return on the SAAI. The drop-off ratio is adjusted by multiplying the CD price by the ratio of the SAAI on the XD date to its value the day (or week) before.
12. We also studied the *two* weeks centred on the XD date. The results are closely similar to those reported in table 22.1.
13. The slight differences between the market-adjusted frequency counts, for the rate of return and the drop-off ratio, are due to the slightly different natures of the two market adjustments (see note 11).
14. The ratio of the dividend amount to the CD price averaged 3.5 per cent over all years. The average peaked in fiscal 1974/75 (at 4.4 per cent). Its lowest value was 2.8 per cent, in 1984/85.
15. In 1984/85 the mean drop-off ratio did increase (to 0.97) but all other indicators (median, regression coefficient, frequency counts) are consistent with a drop-off ratio less than 1; see Eades, Hess and Han Kim (1984).
16. The results in table 22.4 are calculated without adjusting for market effects. The corresponding market-adjusted numbers are: for daily data, 2,052 v. 1,919; for weekly data, 1,811 v. 1,869.
17. The percentage of XD dates, by day of the week (Monday to Friday) are 45, 11, 10, 15 and 19. The corresponding percentages for capitalisation changes are 38, 15, 14, 16 and 17.

18. Although irregular holding periods (owing to long weekends or mid-week holidays) are excluded from figure 22.1, their inclusion does not alter the picture. At a superficial level, figure 22.1 suggests investors should sell late on a Friday and buy late on a Tuesday. Ball and Bowers (1986b) have also investigated the day-of-the-week phenomenon.

19. Jaffe and Westerfield (1985) calculate their returns as the percentage change in the SAAI from one day to the next. Our results are corrected for known errors in the published index. They exclude irregular holding periods, are based on daily reinvestment of dividends and the proceeds from rights issues and other entitlements, and are expressed in continuously compounded form. Nevertheless our results exhibit the same broad pattern as those of Jaffe and Westerfield.

20. A third of the XD dates are in March–April and a fifth are in October.

23 Share capitalisation changes, information and the Australian equity market

Ray Ball, Philip Brown and Frank J. Finn

Bonus share issues, share splits and rights issues containing bonus elements are methods of changing Australian firms' share capitalisations. This chapter studies the effects of such changes on share prices, and thus replicates and extends the now classic Fama, Fisher, Jensen and Roll (1969) study of share splits on the New York Stock Exchange.

Definitions

Bonus shares are issued to existing shareholders, at zero subscription price and in proportion to their holdings. In the accounts, shareholders' reserves are reduced and paid-up capital is increased (to reflect the share issue), leaving total shareholders' equity unchanged. However, bonus issues frequently are preceded by asset revaluations, which increase shareholders' reserves.[1]

Share splits change the nominal or par values of the split shares, such that existing shareholders receive correspondingly larger numbers of shares, each share having a proportionately lower nominal value. The accounting treatment involves no alteration to either shareholders' reserves or paid-up capital.

Rights issues offer additional shares to existing shareholders, usually on a pro-rata basis, at positive subscription prices. When the subscription price is below the market price of the firm's existing shares at the time of the rights issue, it is said to contain a bonus element. Rights issues differ from bonus issues and share splits in that they increase the firm's total investment. The accounting treatment involves transfers from shareholders' reserves, to the extent of the bonus elements of the issues.

Hypotheses

Because neither bonus issues nor share splits have any direct implication for firms' investments, or future cash flows from investments, neither have

Reprinted from the *Australian Journal of Management* 2, no. 2 (October 1977), 105–25, by permission of the authors and the publisher.

a direct implication for firms' values.[2] Rights issues with bonus elements are equivalent to bonus issues plus cash issues at the ex-bonus prices of the existing shares. They thus incorporate bonus issues, with no direct implication for firms' values, and cash issues, with direct implication for future cash flows.

In contrast to this reasoning, the financial community often regards bonus issues as rewards, as evidenced by their name and by statements such as the following:

Sydney-based retailer Waltons Ltd is rewarding shareholders for a bumper year with a one-for-20 bonus share issue after achieving a sharp improvement in profit margins in the second half [of the year].[3]

Mr Brady [Chairman of Crestknit Industries Ltd] said that the company had decided to make another bonus issue for the good of shareholders and the good of the country as a whole.[4]

Not enough companies adequately reward their shareholders, either by increased dividends or by bonus issues.[5]

Share splits sometimes are regarded as means of altering market prices of shares to bring them into a more "popular" price level and so to "broaden" the market for the share, which presumably implies a higher price.[6]

In their study of share splits, Fama et al. (1969) provide a reconciliation of these contrasting views. They hypothesise that splits convey information from managements to shareholders about future cash flows, and thus have an indirect effect on firms' values. Following Fama et al., we hypothesise that, around the time of capitalisation changes, any systematic share price revision is due to information concerning future cash flows, rather than to the bonus issues, rights issues or share splits in themselves.

Our second hypothesis concerns the speed with which market prices adjust to any information contained in share capitalisation changes. A market in which prices are continuously in equilibrium with respect to available information is called "efficient".[7] Thus, in an efficient market, securities are priced to yield equilibrium expected returns, reflecting all available information concerning the expected values of future cash flows accruing to them. An efficient market is characterised by a readjustment to equilibrium prices and expected returns at or before the news of capitalisation changes: above-or-below equilibrium ("abnormal") expected returns do not occur thereafter.

Data and methodology

Characterisation of price equilibrium

The two-parameter model of Black (1972) is employed to characterise the equilibrium expected return on any asset i for any discrete period t:

$$E(\tilde{R}_{it}) = E(\tilde{R}_{zt}) + \beta_{it} [E(\tilde{R}_{mt}) - E(\tilde{R}_{zt})] \qquad (1)$$

where:

$\tilde{R}_{it}$ = rate of return on security i over period t, the tilde denoting a random variable

$\tilde{R}_{mt}$ = rate of return on aggregate wealth (usually referred to as the market portfolio)

$\tilde{R}_{zt}$ = rate of return on a security with $\text{cov}(\tilde{R}_{zt}, \tilde{R}_{mt}) = 0$

$\beta_{it} = \text{cov}(\tilde{R}_{it}, \tilde{R}_{mt}) / \text{var}(\tilde{R}_{mt})$

and where E, cov and var denote expectation, covariance and variance respectively. The risk parameter, β_{it}, is the risk of asset i relative to all assets (that is, relative to the market portfolio m) in period t. Being a partial-equilibrium model, (1) asserts that expected return is a linear function of risk β_{it}, given the constants $E(\tilde{R}_{zt})$ and $E(\tilde{R}_{mt})$.

Equation (1) can be rewritten as the so-called "two factor" model:[8]

$$\tilde{R}_{it} = \tilde{\gamma}_{1t} + \beta_{it} \tilde{\gamma}_{2t} + \tilde{e}_{it} \tag{2}$$

where:

$\tilde{\gamma}_{1t} = \tilde{R}_{zt}$

$\tilde{\gamma}_{2t} = \tilde{R}_{mt} - \tilde{R}_{zt}$

$\tilde{e}_{it}$ = disturbance term for security i in period t

$E(\tilde{e}_{it}) = 0$

$\text{cov}(\tilde{e}_{it}, \tilde{\gamma}_{1t}) = 0$

$\text{cov}(\tilde{e}_{it}, \tilde{\gamma}_{2t}) = 0$

The disturbance in equation (2), $\tilde{e}_{it}$, is the abnormal return on security i in period t, after controlling for marketwide influences on all securities and given the relative risk of security i. If a particular event under investigation is independent of the two market factors and of the security's risk, then $\tilde{e}_{it}$ incorporates the price adjustment to that event.

The standard experimental design in this area is summarised as follows. A sample of securities experiencing an event (such as the announcement of a bonus issue) is chosen. Time is defined *relative to the date at which that event takes place*. The estimated disturbance from equation (2), i.e., the residual from the two-factor model, is calculated for the variable period τ relative to the event. Thus period τ is not the same *chronological* date for all securities, and τ is allowed to vary over a "reasonable" range (say, 12 months before and after the month in which the event takes place). The average abnormal return across all N securities in the sample, for period τ relative to the event date, is given by the sample average residual, $\widetilde{AR}$:

$$\widetilde{AR}_{\tau} = \frac{1}{N} \sum_{i=1}^{N} \tilde{e}_{i\tau}$$

The abnormal behaviour cumulated from q periods prior to the event date to the end of any period τ is given by the cumulative average residual, $\widetilde{CAR}$:

$$\widetilde{CAR}_{\tau} = \sum_{t=-q}^{\tau} \widetilde{AR}_t$$

where q is the number of prior periods the experimenter wishes to investigate. For example, with $q = 12$ and monthly data, $\widetilde{CAR}_0$ is the sample average abnormal return over the 13 months up to, and including, the month of the event under investigation, which is month $\tau = 0$.

Data

Announcement dates of bonus issues, share splits and rights issues with bonus elements were obtained from the *Australian Financial Review, The Sydney Stock Exchange Gazette,* and *The Stock Exchange of Melbourne Official Record.* Rate-of-return data were obtained from the $N = 651$ version of the price-relative file compiled by Brown and described in Ball, Brown and Officer (1976a; reproduced as chapter 4 in this book—see especially note 9). This file consists of monthly rates of return (adjusted for changes in the basis of quotation) for industrial or commercial companies listed on the Melbourne or Perth stock exchanges, the constraint on the former generally being that their ordinary capital exceeded \$1 million in par value. The file extends over the period January 1958 to December 1970, and comprises data on 651 securities.

Capitalisation changes between 1960 and 1969 inclusive were studied, the latter date being chosen because we wanted to examine returns for a period of 12 months after the capitalisation changes, and 1970 was the last year for which price data were available.[9] Firms were required to be on the price file and to have sufficient price data to satisfy the needs of the risk estimation methods described below.

Estimation methods

Estimates of the monthly marketwide factors γ_{1t} and γ_{2t} were taken from Ball, Brown and Officer (1976a). The risk parameters β_{it}, $i = 1, \ldots, N$, were estimated by four methods.

First, they were estimated by Ordinary Least Squares over the whole period for which monthly returns were available for each share, with 50 monthly returns being the minimum accepted. Several studies on New York Stock Exchange data have suggested that a minimum of approximately 60 observations of monthly returns is required to obtain minimum-error estimates of relative risks[10]—the slopes of (2)—for the average share (i.e., not for selected groups which, for example, might experience greater stationarity in relative risk). Because the price-relative file limited the maximum number of observations to 155, and because not all firms had a full history of prices on the file, we reduced the cut-off to 50 monthly return observations. This method allowed samples of 155 bonus issues made by 114 firms, 81 splits by 80 firms and 193 rights issues by 132 firms.[11]

Second, a method of allowing for risk changes was examined. One limitation of the first approach is that it assumes relative risks are stationary over the entire period. If capitalisation changes are associated with risk changes, then the disturbances from equation (2), assuming constant regression slopes, will be confounded with market disequilibrium.[12] The possibility of risk changes seems more important for the rights sample, since rights involve investment by firms.

In the absence of hypotheses about changes in β_i's and since any systematic change for the sample as a whole could be expected to occur close to the share issue or split date, each security's price history was divided into two subperiods, each of at least 25 months, before and after the capitalisation change. Separate β's were then estimated before and after the change and were used in estimating the disturbances. This method resulted in a loss of observations, since securities which did not have price histories of 25 months before and 25 months after the capitalisation change were eliminated. The bonus, splits and rights samples were reduced in size to 100, 71 and 147 respectively.

Third, the slopes were estimated over the whole period for which monthly returns were available, subject to a minimum of 50 available observations, and if the t-statistic from comparing each β_i with the population mean of unity was less than 1.0, then that β_i was set equal to unity (an unbiased estimate in the absence of information); otherwise β_i was taken at its estimated value. This method produced a series of average residuals almost identical to that produced by the first method. Group sizes under method 3 were identical to those of method 1.

The fourth method was a combination of the second and third. Results from the second method indicated that the sample average relative risk, estimated over the period after the capitalisation change, was greater than that for the period before the event. But results from the third method indicated that it was not worthwhile discarding observations when the data criterion of the second method was not met. The fourth method, which produced all results reported below, therefore estimated separate β's before and after the capitalisation change, using a minimum of only 10 monthly observations for each period.[13] There were 150 bonus issues, 80 share splits and 193 rights issues which met the overall criteria.[14]

An additional problem is estimating the dispersion of the average residuals. The parametric t-statistic is inappropriate because it relies on the independently-and-identically-distributed assumption: it seems unlikely that the disturbances from equation (2) are identically distributed across time and across securities (Ball, Brown and Officer 1976a). We used the non-parametric Wilcoxon matched-pairs signed-ranks statistic, which does not rely on the assumption that returns are identically distributed.[15] For each share experiencing a capitalisation change (the "experimental" share), a control share was selected from the price-relative file. The control share was the one with the β nearest to that of the experimental share, but which did not itself experience a capitalisation change of any type in the 24-month period. Under the assumption that the capitalisation change was the only systematic difference between the groups of experimental and control shares, the difference between their average rates of return is an unbiased estimator of the effect of the capitalisation change.

Average rates of return were obtained for each experimental and control share over the period [−12; +12]. The statistic reported is the probability of observing the actual cumulative rate of return, under the null hypothesis of identical pairwise expected values of rates of return on experimental and control shares.

Share splits and the two factor model

A further experimental matter investigated was the possibility that one of the events under investigation, the announcement of a share split, was not independent of the market factors, γ_{1t} and γ_{2t}. If an event is not independent of (say) the market index, then part of the price response to the event is incorporated in the index itself, and the disturbance is not an unbiased estimator of the share price reaction to that event. The expected value of the post-announcement disturbance remains zero, given market efficiency, but the disturbance no longer captures the full price response. To evaluate market efficiency more fully, one would need to investigate the behaviour of the index itself.

A popular notion in the financial community just prior to Australia's conversion to decimal currency in February 1966 was that shares with a par value of one pound (converted to $2) should be split to either 2 shares of $1 or 4 shares of 50 cents, and in fact many Australian companies did so split their shares in or around February 1966.[16] Splits might not be independent of γ_1 and γ_2 if they tended to bunch in time and thus affect the index.

Share splits were analysed including and excluding firms which had effective split dates in the period 6 months before and after February 1966. Of the 23 splits in this period, 16 (about a fifth of the total number of share splits we studied) had split dates in February 1966. However, as their exclusion made "little" difference in the results, we report results when all splits were included.[17]

Summary of experimental design

The two-factor model separates securities' return variation into two components: marketwide factors which, given securities' relative risks, influence their returns; and disturbances, which incorporate all remaining variation. One interpretation is provided by the two-parameter model of equilibrium-expected returns, in which context the disturbance is an estimator for above- or below-equilibrium returns. An alternative interpretation is that the market portfolio is an experimental control, adjusted for market sensitivity, for the sample of securities with capitalisation changes. Whichever inter-pretation is chosen, an assumption underlying the experiment is that capitalisation changes were independent of the market factors.

Finally, we note that the results were insensitive to different methods of estimating relative risks, for the simple reason that the *ex post* risk premium for the period was not large (and that the sample apparently is relatively homogeneous).

Results

Bonus issues and valuation

The average and cumulative average residuals for the bonus issue sample are shown in columns (2) and (3) of table 23.1. The cumulative average residual for the period $[-12;0]$—i.e., the 13 months up to and including the month of the bonus announcement—was 20.2 per cent. Twelve of the thirteen monthly average residuals were positive. The Wilcoxon statistic assigned a probability of observing a CAR of this magnitude, under the null hypothesis that CAR is zero, of less than one in one thousand.[18] Although there could have been some anticipation of bonus issues or some "leakage" of the announcements, it is unlikely that either could account for average

Table 23.1   Bonus issues

(1) Month	(2) CAR	(3) AR
−12	0.013	0.013
−11	0.016	0.003
−10	0.013	−0.003
−9	0.014	0.001
−8	0.020	0.007
−7	0.044	0.024
−6	0.051	0.007
−5	0.062	0.011
−4	0.067	0.005
−3	0.074	0.007
−2	0.095	0.022
−1	0.114	0.018
0	0.202	0.088
1	0.215	0.014
2	0.204	−0.012
3	0.204	0.001
4	0.198	−0.007
5	0.190	−0.008
6	0.199	0.009
7	0.199	0.000
8	0.196	−0.003
9	0.197	0.000
10	0.201	0.005
11	0.208	0.007
12	0.204	−0.004

Sample size	150
Av. β_i before month 0	0.977
Av. β_i after month 0	1.082
Wilcoxon probability:	
(−12;0)	0.000
(+1;+12)	0.836
(β)	0.342

abnormal returns which were positive for 9 months prior to the announcement. A more likely explanation is that firms made bonus issues after favourable performance had become known to the share market, via such media as profit reports, dividend announcements, revaluations and general firm and industry news.[19]

The largest monthly average residual occurred in the announcement month, when almost half the yearly adjustment occurred.

We have hypothesised that abnormal returns accompanying announcements of bonus issues can be attributed to information effects rather than to bonus issues themselves. Fama et al. (1969) accepted changes in dividend payments as an experimental control for changes in future cash flows and hypothesised that abnormal returns accompanying share splits (they made no differentiation between bonus issues and share splits) is due to the market's anticipation of increases in future dividend payments. Brown, Finn and Hancock (1977) investigated firms making changes in dividend payments which were not accompanied by capitalisation changes, and found that positive dividend changes were accompanied by positive abnormal returns in the 12-month period up to their announcement. Thus, following Fama et al. (1969), we accept changes in dividend payments as a proxy for changes in future cash flows.

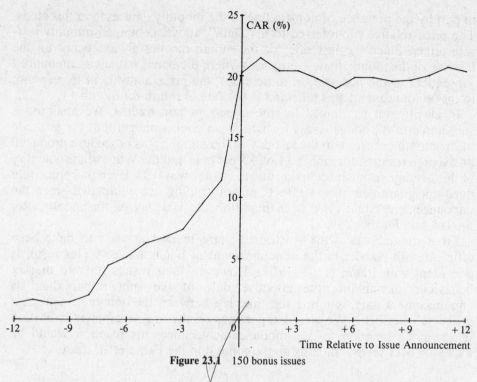

Figure 23.1   150 bonus issues

Dividends paid to shareholders in the 12 months subsequent to bonus issue announcements were compared with those paid in the previous 12 months. In 143 (92 per cent) of the 155 bonus issues initially selected, the total dollar amount paid on each "equivalent old share" after the announcement exceeded that paid before. The finding is inconsistent with the information-effect thesis; the pattern of average residuals in table 23.1 is consistent with this thesis as well.[20]

Firms frequently announced at the same time their intentions to increase total dividend payments and to make bonus issues.[21] In other cases, we infer from the 92 per cent relative frequency of dividend increases that the probability of a dividend increase, conditional on a bonus issue, was assessed in the market as being close to unity. Bonus issue announcements thus conveyed information to the market about changes in firms' future dividend payments, which in turn conveyed information about firms' future cash flows.[22]

Bonus issues and market efficiency

Table 23.1 shows the speed with which share prices change in response to information contained in bonus issue announcements, at least on a monthly basis. Subsequent to month 0, the average residuals in column (3) appear to have been randomly distributed around zero. The cumulative average residual changed by two tenths of 1 per cent over the year. Five of the twelve monthly average residuals were positive. The Wilcoxon probability of 0.836 for the period [+1;+12] suggests that any differences in returns between the bonus group and the control group were not systematic.

The positive average residual of 1.4 per cent in month +1 can be explained in part by the presence of non-trading in the monthly data used in this study. The price-relative file referred to in "Data", above, contained monthly last-sale prices. Since the last sale for the month did not always occur on the last day of the month, there were cases where the bonus issue was announced subsequent to the last sale. In these cases, the price adjustment in response to the announcement was reflected in the rate of return for month +1.

In an attempt to control for the effects of non-trading, we analysed a subsample of 83 bonus issues for which we could confirm that the last sale of the month occurred on the last day of the month. This procedure produced an average residual for month +1 of 0.5 per cent and the Wilcoxon probability of this average residual occurring due to chance was 0.34. Even this procedure does not guarantee all the effects of non-trading are eliminated since the announcement could have been made on the last day of the month after the last sale for that day.

From monthly data, the Australian share market appears to have been efficient with respect to the announcement of bonus issues.[23] This result is consistent with Fama et al. (1969). However, their results refer to market behaviour surrounding the effective date of the split rather than its announcement date, ignoring the time lag between the announcement of a split and its effect.[24] We would expect our results to give a better indication of the price reaction to the announcement, since this reaction would be averaged over several months up to month 0 in the Fama et al. study.

Rights issues and valuation

The average and cumulative average residuals for the sample of rights issues containing bonus elements are shown in table 23.2. Most of the conclusions drawn in the results for bonus issues apply here. Firms making rights issues with bonus elements experienced positive abnormal returns in the 12-month period up to the announcement month, the CAR at month 0 being 9.7 per cent. The largest average residual, 2.6 per cent, occurred in the announcement month. The Wilcoxon probability for period $[-12;0]$ indicated that the probability of this price behaviour occurring due to chance was close to zero. Each of the 13 months had a positive average residual.

Of the total of 193 rights issues, 177 or 92 per cent increased the effective dividend payment in the 12-month period following the announcement of the issue.[25] As was the case with the bonus issues, these results appear to be consistent with the information-effect hypothesis. In many cases dividend intentions were announced jointly with the rights issue,[26] and in cases where they were not announced jointly there was a high relative frequency of the dividend payment increasing subsequent to the rights announcement.

The differences in the magnitudes of the average price changes associated with the bonus and rights issues can be attributed to differences in the amount of information. If a dividend change conveys information about a firm's future cash flows, then the larger the dividend change, the greater is the expected change in share price. Brown, Finn and Hancock (1977) provide evidence in support of this proposition. In our study the mean ratios, of dividends

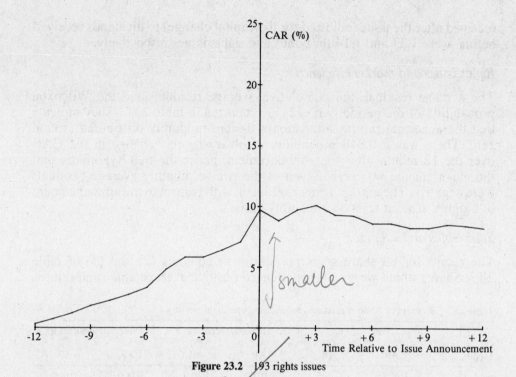

Figure 23.2   193 rights issues

Table 23.2   Rights issues

(1) Month	(2) CAR	(3) AR
−12	0.003	0.003
−11	0.007	0.004
−10	0.012	0.005
−9	0.018	0.006
−8	0.022	0.003
−7	0.027	0.006
−6	0.033	0.006
−5	0.048	0.015
−4	0.058	0.010
−3	0.058	0.000
−2	0.064	0.006
−1	0.071	0.006
0	0.097	0.026
1	0.088	−0.009
2	0.097	0.009
3	0.101	0.005
4	0.093	−0.008
5	0.092	−0.001
6	0.086	−0.007
7	0.086	0.001
8	0.082	−0.005
9	0.082	0.000
10	0.085	0.003
11	0.084	−0.001
12	0.082	−0.001

Sample size	193	Wilcoxon probability:	
Av. β_i before month 0	0.966	(−12;0)	0.000
Av. β_i after month 0	0.985	(+1;+12)	0.848
		(β)	0.741

received after the issue (adjusted for the capital change) to dividends received before, were 1.23 and 1.14 for bonus and rights issues respectively.

Rights issues and market efficiency

The average residual, the cumulative average residual, and the Wilcoxon probability for the period [+1;+12] are reported in table 23.2. They indicate that the abnormal returns after month 0 were randomly distributed around zero. There was a 0.848 probability of observing this change in the CAR over the 12-month after the announcement, under the null hypothesis that the mean change was zero. Seven of the twelve monthly average residuals were negative. The market appears efficient with respect to the announcement of a rights issue, at least on a monthly basis.

Share splits and valuation

The results for all share splits are shown in columns (2) and (3) of table 23.3. Shares which were split experienced positive average abnormal returns

Table 23.3   Share splits: Abnormal returns around announcement month

(1) Month	Total sample		Dividend increases		Dividend non-increases	
	(2) CAR	(3) AR	(4) CAR	(5) AR	(6) CAR	(7) AR
−12	0.005	0.005	0.010	0.010	0.000	0.000
−11	−0.005	−0.010	0.000	−0.010	−0.010	−0.011
−10	−0.002	0.003	0.001	0.001	−0.006	0.005
−9	0.008	0.011	0.014	0.013	0.002	0.008
−8	0.014	0.006	0.033	0.019	−0.007	−0.009
−7	0.020	0.006	0.048	0.015	−0.011	−0.004
−6	0.021	0.001	0.057	0.009	−0.018	−0.007
−5	0.019	−0.002	0.055	−0.001	−0.021	−0.003
−4	0.015	−0.004	0.054	−0.001	−0.028	−0.007
−3	0.028	0.013	0.073	0.019	−0.022	0.006
−2	0.033	0.005	0.079	0.007	−0.019	0.003
−1	0.049	0.016	0.107	0.027	−0.016	0.003
0	0.081	0.032	0.153	0.046	−0.001	0.015
1	0.086	0.005	0.163	0.010	−0.001	−0.001
2	0.080	−0.005	0.170	0.007	−0.021	−0.020
3	0.087	0.007	0.175	0.005	−0.012	0.009
4	0.083	−0.004	0.170	−0.005	−0.015	−0.003
5	0.082	−0.001	0.176	0.006	−0.024	−0.008
6	0.092	0.010	0.190	0.015	−0.018	0.006
7	0.090	−0.002	0.185	−0.006	−0.017	0.001
8	0.080	−0.010	0.185	−0.000	−0.038	−0.020
9	0.095	0.015	0.205	0.021	−0.029	0.008
10	0.100	0.005	0.209	0.004	−0.022	0.007
11	0.102	0.002	0.205	−0.004	−0.013	0.009
12	0.111	0.009	0.205	0.001	0.005	0.018
Sample size	80		42		38	
Av. β_i before month 0	0.873		0.871		0.875	
Av. β_i after month 0	1.036		1.027		1.047	
Wilcoxon probability:						
(−12;0)	0.011		0.009		0.712	
(+1;+12)	0.246		0.088		0.607	
(β)	0.341		0.099		0.486	

on or before the announcement, with the largest abnormal return occurring in the announcement month.

Columns (4) to (7) of table 23.3 show the market reaction to share splits followed by dividend increases and non-increases respectively. Share splits were followed by dividend increases in the subsequent 12 months in 42 cases (53 per cent) of the split sample. Of the firms in this category, approximately two-thirds made a bonus or rights issue in the 12 months period after the split announcement, and an effective dividend increase accompanied the later issue.[27]

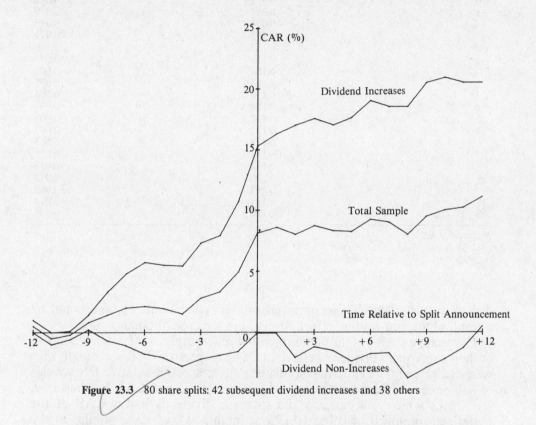

Figure 23.3 80 share splits: 42 subsequent dividend increases and 38 others

We suggest that the average residual of 3.2 per cent in the split announcement month was due to two complementary factors. First, although it was not mandatory in Australia for firms to announce intended dividend policy at the time of the split announcement, in some cases they were announced simultaneously.[28] Second, a bonus or rights issue was often announced at the time of the split announcement and, as stated earlier, it was the usual practice for firms to announce dividend intentions at that time.

To test the price behaviour around the dividend increase month, we redefined month 0 to be the month of the dividend increase. The average and cumulative average residuals around this redefined month 0 (see table 23.4) reveal that the average price change over the period up to the dividend increase month was positive and significant.[29] Although there was a positive average change after month 0, there is a 0.530 probability that a change of this order was

Table 23.4 Share splits with subsequent dividend increases: Abnormal returns around dividend increase month

(1) Month	(2) CAR	(3) AR
−12	0.027	0.027
−11	0.036	0.009
−10	0.042	0.006
−9	0.037	−0.005
−8	0.052	0.015
−7	0.054	0.002
−6	0.072	0.018
−5	0.081	0.010
−4	0.094	0.013
−3	0.115	0.021
−2	0.125	0.010
−1	0.159	0.033
0	0.168	0.009
1	0.193	0.025
2	0.198	0.005
3	0.194	−0.004
4	0.192	−0.002
5	0.182	−0.009
6	0.177	−0.005
7	0.189	0.011
8	0.174	−0.015
9	0.200	0.027
10	0.195	−0.005
11	0.181	−0.014
12	0.180	−0.001

Wilcoxon probability:

(−12;0)	0.000
(+1;+12)	0.530
(β)	0.378

due to chance. The change occurred primarily in month +1, and could be a result of the non-trading effect observed in the case of bonus issues.

The relative CAR's of the bonus issue and split samples were not independent of their subsequent dividend behaviours. The respective CAR's at month zero were 0.202 and 0.081, perhaps reflecting the respective relative frequencies of subsequent dividend increases, which were 0.92 and 0.53. Furthermore, split firms which subsequently did increase dividends had a CAR at the (redefined) month 0 of 0.168 (0.193 at month +1), which is similar to the figure for bonus issues. The evidence suggests a "cash flow explanation" of the magnitudes of the CAR's.

Finally, we note that, in the case of splits which did not subsequently increase dividends, the residuals wandered around zero in the pre- and post-split periods, which is consistent with a "cash flow explanation" and is inconsistent with splitting being valuable in its own right.

Share splits and market efficiency

The cumulative average residual in table 23.3 for all share splits shows a puzzling upward drift over the 12 following months. The estimated Wilcoxon probability that this was due to chance was only 0.246. However, the upward drift did not begin until approximately 6 months after the split announcement. In view of the market's efficient reaction to bonus and rights issues, it seems

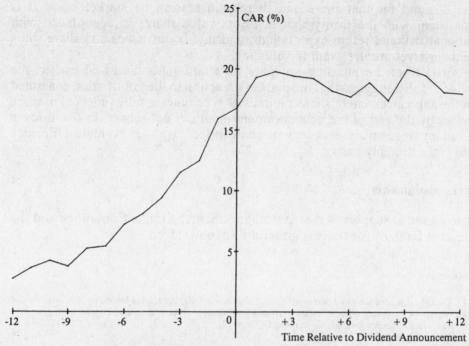

Figure 23.4   42 share splits with subsequent dividend increases

implausible that a reaction to share splits commenced 6 months after their announcements. This result is anomalous.

Summary and conclusions

This chapter reports abnormal returns on Australian share prices around the time of announcements of capitalisation changes through bonus and rights issues, and share splits. Following Fama, Fisher, Jensen and Roll, we argue that the observed abnormal returns were due to information concerning anticipated cash flows, and not to the increased number of shares which resulted from the capitalisation changes. Our experiment assumes that this information about anticipated cash flows was captured in subsequent changes in firms' dividend payments. The evidence from the experiment appears to be consistent with this information-effect hypothesis.

Share splits that were not accompanied by subsequent dividend increases provide further evidence on the information-effect hypothesis. The average residuals for this category were randomly distributed around zero both before and after the split announcements. This suggests the obvious conclusion that firms making share splits experienced no increases in value unless the splits were accompanied by subsequent increases in cash flow. Consequently, share splits by themselves appear to be of no value to investors, at least in the following 12-month period. At best, share splits appear to proxy for other factors.

This conclusion is contrary to the notion that the purpose of a split is to bring the price of a share into a "popular" trading range, thus increasing the demand for that share and thereby increasing its market price. It is consistent with the theory that investors value shares in accordance with rational risk and return expectations, and that bonus issues and share splits in themselves are irrelevant to valuation.

Apart from the puzzling anomaly for share splits discussed earlier, the evidence also suggests that the market's reaction to the information contained in the announcement of share capitalisation changes is fully reflected in share prices by the end of the announcement month, if not sooner. In the absence of more frequent observations of share prices, we can evaluate efficiency only on a monthly basis.

Ackowledgments

The financial support of the Australian Research Grants Committee and the Reserve Bank of Australia is gratefully acknowledged.

Notes

1. Asset revaluations are more common in Australia than in (say) the United States.
2. We ignore secondary considerations, such as administrative costs, and assume interest rates given.
3. *Australian Financial Review*, 6 September 1973, p. 19.
4. Ibid., 8 September 1972, p. 32.
5. See Murray (1970, p. 29).
6. For example, see Peterson (1971).
7. See Fama (1970a) for more detail. It is "efficient" in the sense that, conditional upon the supply of information, present share prices are minimum-variance. Market efficiency is thus a testable implication of the pure theory of exchange under uncertainty, with information assumed to be a public good once it is "announced".
8. This model is implied by multivariate normality; interpretation of its variables and constants is supplied by (1).
9. The Brown file has recently been expanded and updated to December 1973. It is to be further expanded to include all securities listed on Australian Associated Exchanges since January 1974.
10. See, for example, Gonedes (1973).
11. These are samples in the sense that we are sampling from processes over a limited time interval of ten years. We study the population of capitalisation changes, over the interval, which meet our data requirements.
12. For example, if β_i increased around the time of the capitalisation change, disturbances from equation (2) assuming a constant β_i for the whole period will be biased downwards before the event and upwards after the event. Ball (1972b) discusses this issue, but note that the extent of the bias normally is not important.
13. This does not imply that the risk shift occurred exactly at the time of the capitalisation change.
14. Using a maximum of 556 observations of weekly rates of return, Brown and Walter (1974) found that 35 of a random sample of 50 β's were significantly different from unity at the 10 per cent confidence limit, 29 at 5 per cent and 21 at 1 per cent. Our procedure resulted in 168 of the 300 subperiod β's for the bonus sample being set to unity, 202 of the 386 for the rights issue sample, and 103 of the 160 for the split sample.
15. The statistic is described in Siegel (1956). Note that the statistic does assume independence and hence, like the Student t, it tends to underestimate dispersion in this context.
16. "Investors Notebook", *Australian Financial Review*, 6 January 1966, p. 8.
17. For example, the CAR in month 0 increased from 0.081 to 0.093 when the 23 were excluded. Although 16 of the share splits occurred in February 1966, they were announced at various times between May 1965 and February 1966.
18. Note that the Wilcoxon statistic assumes independence and can be expected to underestimate dispersion in this context. The third Wilcoxon probability in table 23.1 tests the difference in the β's of the sample firms and their paired control firms. The probability of the differences in β's occurring by chance was 0.342, suggesting that the matching procedure was sufficiently accurate for the purposes of this study.
19. Brown, in chapter 18 of this book, has shown that firms which release "good" earnings reports experience positive abnormal returns in the 12-month period prior to the release of the report. Dividend

increases have similar and related effects, as shown in chapter 21 by Brown, Finn and Hancock. Sharpe and Walker (chapter 25) show similar and related results for asset revaluations, which tend to occur around the time of bonus issues.

20. Differences in the magnitudes of the price changes reported here and in the Brown, Finn and Hancock (1977) study can be attributed to differences in the magnitudes of the dividend changes.

21. Australian Associated Stock Exchanges, *Official List Requirements*, section 3.e(3), requires firms' dividend-per-share intentions to be announced jointly with announcements of new share issues. This section came into force on 1 September 1971 and so was not in force during the period studied here. However, it appears that, prior to September 1971, it was common practice to announce dividend intentions jointly with bonus issues, although the data sources indicate that this was not always the case.

22. The information-effect thesis could be tested further by analysing the average residuals separately for the dividend increase and non-increase categories. The results of this analysis are not reported here since the small size of the dividend non-increase category (12 observations) made it difficult to draw reliable conclusions. Notwithstanding the small size, the results were consistent with information-effect hypothesis, in that the average price change was uniformly negative for the 5 months following month 0 for the dividend non-increase category. (The share splits analysed below allow a better test of dividend increase and non-increase categories).

23. Evidence presented by Brown, Finn and Hancock (1977) on the adjustment of share prices to earnings and dividend announcements leads us to suspect that all the price adjustment to a bonus issue occurs within a day or so of the announcement.

24. Fama et al. (1969) hypothesised that this lag could be up to 5 months. They did analyse market behaviour around the announcement month for a random sample of 52 splits from their data, and found the behaviour of the residuals after the announcement date to be almost identical to that after the split date. This result is to be expected since the split month is the latest month in which the announcement could occur.

25. Dividends paid after a rights issue were adjusted for any bonus element in the issue. Thus dividends paid after the ex-rights date were adjusted by the factor $[1 + (\text{rights value}/\text{ex-rights price})]$.

26. The 1971 Australian Associated Stock Exchanges listing requirement discussed in note 21 above applies to rights issues as well as to bonus issues.

27. In some cases, this later issue was announced in the same month as the split.

28. The 1971 Australian Associated Stock Exchange listing requirement referred to in notes 21 and 26 does not apply to share splits.

29. Month 0 as redefined is the latest month in which a dividend increase is announced. Consequently, we expect to see smaller positive average residuals in several months up to and including month 0.

24 Audit qualifications and share prices: Further evidence

T.J. Shevlin and G.P. Whittred

Introduction

A number of recent studies have sought evidence on the information content of qualified audit reports through the behaviour of security prices around the time of release of audit qualifications. Firth (1978a) investigates United Kingdom qualifications, Ball, Walker and Whittred (1978) those in Australia and Chow and Rice (1978), Elliott (1982) and Dodd et al. (1983) have studied United States qualifications. With the exception of Firth (who studies both "not true and fair" and "subject to" qualifications), the principal concern of these researchers has been with "subject to" qualifications. Despite this homogeneity of interest, the question of whether or not "subject to" opinions *per se* convey information to the stock market remains unresolved. For example, Firth, Ball, Walker and Whittred, and Dodd et al. report little evidence of an adverse effect on share prices.[1] Chow and Rice argue that an adverse effect is observable for certain types of "subject to" qualifications (in particular those pertaining to "asset realisation"), and Elliott argues that if there is an impact it is small by comparison to that of the related uncertainty itself.

Of course there are numerous possible explanations for these differences. The studies were conducted in different countries with (possibly) differing institutional environments, they use data from different time periods, and although they all employ one variant or another of the standard "market model" methodology there are marked differences in the exact manner of its application and in the choice of related experimental controls. Indeed, Dodd et al. (1983) argue that it is in the latter dimension that most difficulties are likely to arise. These authors identify three critical aspects in the experimental design of such studies: (a) the identification of the public announcement date of the qualification, (b) the choice of controls for the market's expectations/prior disclosures and (c) concurrent disclosures. Their review of the existing United States studies points out deficiencies in one

Reprinted from the *Australian Journal of Management* 9, no. 1 (June 1984), 37–52, by permission of the authors and the publisher.

or more of these respects in each. However, their criticisms apply with equal force to both of the non-United States studies.

This chapter brings additional evidence to bear on the information content of audit qualifications by employing an experimental design which overcomes some of the limitations of these earlier studies. Our experimental design is similar (in principle) to that of Elliott (1982). Our results are generally consistent with those of Dodd et al. (1983).

Data

The sample of "subject to" qualifications employed in this study was selected from a data file constructed by Whittred, Walker and Birkett (1978).[2] Only the first in a sequence of identical qualifications was included. This procedure was adopted since repeated qualifications seemed likely to have lost their "surprise" element, and thus unlikely to have any major effect on price. Qualifications occurring on companies which went into receivership or liquidation at any time during the 14 years covered by the file, and qualifications occurring within 6 months of a takeover were also deleted. These procedures clearly discard potentially significant qualifications— particularly on companies entering financial distress. However, they were adopted because both Ball, Walker and Whittred (1979) and Birkett and Walker (1971) observe that the financial statements of many failed companies do not receive their first qualification until just prior to the announcement of failure, and we desired to minimise the effect of such potentially confounding events.[3]

To be eligible for inclusion companies must also have appeared on the "909" version of Brown's price relative file.[4] The final sample comprises some 106 qualifications on 99 companies.[5] Sample attributes are disclosed in table 24.1 and discussed below in the section "Information Variables and Portfolio Formation".

Table 24.1   Distribution of "subject to" audit qualifications by subject matter and year

Subject matter	1964–69	1970	1971	1972	1973	Total
Depreciation on buildings	—	1	1	30	18	50
Valuation of assets	2	—	3	2	3	10
Adequacy of provisions (assets overstated/ liabilities understated)	1	—	5	4	1	11
Miscellaneous	4	1	1	1	10	17
Multiple	3	1	2	4	8	18
Total	10	3	12	41	40	106

Experimental design

The principal feature of our experimental design is that it compares the "abnormal" or "excess" returns on a control portfolio of firms with those of portfolios of qualified companies. The power of these tests is critically dependent upon our ability to accurately identify the date of release (or announcement) of the qualifications and to control for the effects of contemporaneous events. In an Australian context, and in comparison with the United States, the latter represents more of a problem than the former. The manner in which we address these problems is discussed below.

Announcement dates and event periods

Let t_0 be the month in which the audit qualification first becomes public. Detailed search procedures lead us to believe that for every instance in the present study this was the annual report month (i.e., the date the annual report was received by the Sydney Stock Exchange). Detailed searches of both stock exchange files and Australia's leading financial daily (*Australian Financial Review*) for the 12 months preceding this date for each company revealed no references to impending qualification. Neither the preliminary profit reports or such other interim reports or company releases as existed[6] contained any references, direct or indirect (at least in our interpretation), to the possibility of qualification. Such references to qualifications as appeared in the financial press did so (usually) within a day or so of the stock exchange receipt date and appeared, in the majority of cases, to be "unremarkable".[7] These observations are consistent with those of the United States experience reported in Elliott (1982) and Dodd et al. (1983).

A 25-month test period centred on t_0 was adopted to investigate possible market reaction associated with this event. Within this total period several different time periods were studied (refer table 24.2).

Table 24.2 Test periods based on event time

Test Period	Month of Announcement				
	−12	−6	0	+6	+12
1.	|<---	---|---	---|---	---|---	--->|
2.	|<---	---|---	--->|		
3.			|<---	---|---	--->|

Test period 1 represents the entire test period which is then broken into two subperiods. The period (−12, 0) tests for any prior association between qualification and firm performance. A study of the price behaviour in the period (+1, +12) allows us to draw inferences regarding the efficiency of the stock market's response to this event and serves as a check on the appropriateness of a maintained hypothesis of the study (i.e., capital market efficiency). Since the "event periods" described above may actually average out any unique effects associated with the release of the qualifications in month zero, we also examine price responses in this month.

Concurrent events

To capture the marginal effect of audit qualifications it is necessary to control for the effect of any concurrent disclosures. The likelihood of such disclosures depends to a large degree on the length of the period chosen to measure abnormal returns. One way to solve this problem (as in Dodd et al. 1983) is to work with very short time periods—days for example. However, in the absence of a daily price relative file (and given the high costs of establishing one even for a study of this size) the only other feasible control strategy is to factor any contemporaneous event/signal directly in to the experiment.

We do not control, in the event-month tests that follow, for the information contained in the annual report that is released concurrently with the auditor's qualification. Rather we rely on the standard assumption that if there are any effects associated with the information contained therein they "average out".

However, it is necessary to control for the approximately contemporaneous (on a monthly basis) release of companies' preliminary profit reports. Whittred's (1980) study of the reporting behaviour of companies receiving "subject to" qualifications reveals that, on average, their preliminary profit reports are released some 12 weeks after the end of the financial year. Their annual accounts follow some 5 weeks later. These average results clearly allow the possibility that a company's preliminary profit report and its annual report reach the Sydney Stock Exchange in the same month. Of course, there could be as much as a 2-month (or more) difference between these events. Thus, while the audit qualification release month is definitely t_0, it is also true that the preliminary profit report could have been released any time between months -2 to 0 inclusive.[8] The manner in which we control for this possibility is discussed subsequently.

Information variables and portfolio formation

As discussed above, the experimental design compares the "abnormal" returns on a control portfolio with those of portfolios constructed on the basis of the realisations of selected information variables. Of interest here are the realisations of two information variables—annual earnings (strictly, the unexpected component of these earnings) and the audit qualification pertaining to those earnings.

Table 24.3 depicts the manner in which information or sample portfolios are formed. Sample firms were grouped initially into three portfolios, according

Table 24.3 Construction of sample portfolios

	Subject matter of qualification	Earnings variable	Portfolio number
	Depreciation	$(\tilde{E}_{it}^{+}$	1
		$(\tilde{E}_{it}^{-}$	2
Set of 106 Securities	Valuation	$(\tilde{E}_{it}^{+}$	3
		$(\tilde{E}_{it}^{-}$	4
	Other	$(\tilde{E}_{it}^{+}$	5
		$(\tilde{E}_{it}^{-}$	6

to whether they received "depreciation on buildings", "valuation" or "other" qualifications.[9] In November 1970 Institute Statement D5, "Depreciation, Depletion and Amortisation of Fixed Assets", required firms to calculate and report depreciation on buildings, contrary to common Australian practice. There were few qualifications for non-compliance with this requirement. However, following the release in May 1971 of Institute Statement K1, "Conformity with Institute Technical Statements", such qualifications became commonplace. Valuation qualifications include those qualifications identified as such in table 24.1, as well as the "adequacy of provisions" qualifications. The latter usually implied that either assets were overstated or liabilities were understated, and the former contained explicit statements that shares in or amounts due from other companies, stocks, debtors or land and buildings were overstated. The "other" category is comprised of approximately equal numbers of "multiple" and "miscellaneous" qualifications. The former category includes any company the accounts of which were qualified in more than one respect in a given year. Note that it is possible for either or both of "valuation" and "depreciation" qualifications to appear in this category— as in fact some did. Qualifications classified as miscellaneous related to a much wider variety of circumstances including those for accounting treatment (e.g., inadequate or incorrect charging of provisions and capitalisations), inadequate records, incorrect classifications, internal control weaknesses and so on.

A control portfolio comprising 50 companies was randomly selected, but so as to ensure these companies were (a) unqualified, (b) on the Brown price-relative file and (c) of the same time distribution as reported in table 24.1. Within each of the 4 portfolios (3 sample, 1 control) firms were subsequently grouped according to the sign of their unexpected earnings estimated in the manner described below.

Unexpected earnings variables

We are interested in controlling, not for income *per se*, but for the amount of new information conveyed to the market by the (approximately) contemporaneous income number. Following Ball and Brown (1968), this can be approximated by the difference between the actual change in EPS and the market's conditional expectation of this change. The procedure employed was to compare actual and predicted changes in EPS, the latter being estimated from a "naive" version of the following model:[10]

$$E(Y_{i,t}) = \hat{a}_{it} + \hat{\beta}_{it} Y_{m,t}$$

where:
- E = an expectation operator;
- $Y_{i,t}$ = net change in EPS for firm i in period t;
- $Y_{m,t}$ = the market index of changes in net earnings per share, the "non-diversifiable" or "economy-wide" component of firms' income;
- $\hat{a}, \hat{\beta}$ = OLS regression parameters, representing the average relationship of firm income to the market over time.

The market index of EPS changes was taken from Whittred (1978). Briefly, it is computed as the equally weighted average of changes in net EPS for

70 to 104 firms per year over the interval 1960–74, and is independent of the qualified companies studied here. Because of the lack of extended time series on individual firms' EPS, apart from those contained in the index above, we employ a "naive" version of this cross-sectional model in earnings i.e., we assume $\alpha = 0$, $\beta = 1$.

Given the existing evidence on the time series behaviour of accounting earnings,[11] unexpected earnings were also defined relative to expectations generated by martingale and submartingale models—the drift for the latter being estimated using up to 11 years of prior data.[12] Table 24.4 contains summary statistics for only the first procedure, since the conclusions reached here, and in subsequent sections, are the same for each model.[13]

Table 24.4 Summary statistics and significance tests for the homogeneity of unexpected earnings (cents per share)

	Portfolio							
	Control		Depreciation		Valuation		Other	
Statistic	E^+	E^-	E^+	E^-	E^+	E^-	E^+	E^-
Mean	3.86	−3.10	2.80	−4.42	4.91	−6.85	8.26	−5.52
Median	2.85	−2.10	1.57	−2.66	3.68	−4.41	2.30	−4.98
Standard deviation	3.91	4.71	3.27	5.53	4.44	7.96	10.81	5.44
N	27	23	22	28	7	14	10	25

E^+ : $F(3, 62) = 2.469$, probability $= 0.0702$
E^- : $F(3, 86) = 1.432$, probability $= 0.2392$

Although our porfolio groupings control for the sign of unexpected earnings (refer table 24.3), they do not control for the magnitude of same. Hence table 24.4 reports the results of a one-way analysis of variance over E^+ and E^- for the cross-sectional model. Although some variation in the mean unexpected earnings for each portfolio is apparent (in particular, "other E^+") the median values are much more stable and our test statistic reveals that we cannot strictly reject the null hypothesis of no difference in the magnitude of unexpected earnings at $\alpha = 0.05$.

The reported F statistic on E^+ is, however, sufficiently large to be a source of some concern. This result is due almost entirely to a very large unexpected earnings for one company in the "other E^+" portfolio (some 33.25 cps). To illustrate, if we were to exclude this company, the mean and standard deviation of unexpected earnings for this portfolio would drop to 5.49 and 6.68 respectively, resulting in an F statistic of 1.044 (probability 0.3797). Similarly, the use of a non-parametric analysis of variance reduces the effect of this outlier and reveals no significant difference at conventional levels.[14]

In summary, apart from the immediately preceding exception, it appears that our portfolios are relatively homogeneous with respect to both the sign and magnitude of unexpected earnings. Thus, without engaging in the prohibitive exercise of one-on-one matching, we appear to have achieved reasonable controls (at least at the portfolio level) on both these variables.[15]

Estimating abnormal returns

As indicated earlier, the ultimate variable of interest is the mean abnormal return for each portfolio over defined event periods. The abnormal return for each portfolio was computed as the arithmetic average of the component firms' abnormal returns estimated from the well-known market model. Estimation of individual companies' relative risk was conducted using the 60 monthly rates of return ending in the 13th month preceding the announcement of its qualification. Brown's arithmetic monthly return index was used as a proxy for the market. For the 19 securities with less than 24 monthly observations over this interval, β_i was set to unity (an unbiased estimate in the absence of other information). These 19 securities were distributed uniformly across portfolios.

Briefly, the randomly selected control portfolios E^+/E^- had betas of 1.0038/ 0.8948 respectively. The remaining E^+ portfolios, depreciation, valuation and other (1, 3 and 5 in table 24.3) had betas of 0.8554, 1.0640 and 1.1102. The betas of the corresponding E^- portfolios (2, 4 and 6 in table 24.3) were 1.0406, 1.1320 and 1.0747 respectively. These differences in portfolio risk do not, however, present any problems when it is realised that the variable of concern is the mean portfolio risk-adjusted return.

Testing the significance of event-period abnormal returns computed as described above presents something of a problem. Standard significance tests rely on the assumptions that these returns are independently and identically distributed, over time and across securities. It is unlikely that all of these conditions will be met. The manner in which we attempt to overcome these problems is described in the appendix. Following Gonedes (1975), we adopt a multivariate analogue to the standard Students' t-test. This procedure not only adjusts for cross-sectional dependence but also controls our type 1 error rate—a matter of some importance in the case of multiple comparisons.

Results

Table 24.5 provides T^2 results relevant to the realisation of the information variables for each of the defined test periods. These results are based on the portfolios resulting from the adoption of the naive cross-sectional model of unexpected earnings and after employing the standardisation procedures described in the appendix.[16] For the 24 months surrounding the release of an audit qualification (test period 1) the reported T^2 and associated F statistic indicate that we cannot reject the null hypothesis that there is, for all comparisons simultaneously, no difference between sample and control portfolios.

Before proceeding to a discussion of our remaining results a number of points about table 24.5 warrant comment. First, it is important to recall that the estimated mean differences are not excess returns in the usual sense of the word, but rather represent mean differences between standardised portfolio abnormal returns. As such they have no strict economic interpretation but do facilitate the significance tests reported here. Second, the estimated standard deviation for each portfolio varies across test periods depending on M, the number of standardised return vectors observed in each period.

Table 24.5 T^2 Results and summary statistics for differences $(\tilde{d})$ between monthly standardised abnormal returns on information and control portfolios

Portfolio	Estimated mean $\hat{u}\,(\tilde{d})$	Estimated standard deviation $\hat{\sigma}\,(\tilde{d})$	$t\,(\hat{u})$	$F(v_1, v_2)$	Normalised weights implied by T^2
		Test period 1 (−12, +12)			
1	0.0435	0.3486	0.6237	0.0513	−1.0782
2	0.0118	0.3342	0.1761	0.0041	−0.5765
3	0.0060	0.4524	0.0663	0.0006	0.0830
4	−0.0119	0.5337	−0.1118	0.0016	−0.3253
5	−0.0420	0.4193	−0.5008	0.0331	1.3243
6	−0.0576	0.3881	−0.7419	0.0726	1.5728

Value of $T^2 = 1.8746$, value of $F_{(6,\,19)}$ corresponding to $T^2 = 0.2473$

Portfolio	Estimated mean	Estimated standard deviation	$t\,(\hat{u})$	$F(v_1, v_2)$	Normalised weights
		Test period 2 (−12, 0)			
1	−0.0074	0.2528	−0.1058	0.0011	0.4220
2	0.0231	0.1612	0.5155	0.0258	0.1101
3	−0.0588	0.4323	−0.4904	0.0234	−0.0013
4	−0.1336	0.2659	−1.8114	0.3190	0.0012
5	−0.0359	0.4615	−0.2800	0.0076	0.0518
6	−0.1410	0.3003	−1.6925	0.2785	0.4161

Value of $T^2 = 39.5797$, value of $F_{(6,\,7)}$ corresponding to $T^2 = 3.8480$

Portfolio	Estimated mean	Estimated standard deviation	$t\,(\hat{u})$	$F(v_1, v_2)$	Normalised weights
		Test period 3 (+1, +12)			
1	0.0986	0.4347	0.7859	0.0561	1.6844
2	−0.0005	0.4636	−0.0000	0.0000	−0.9126
3	0.0762	0.4819	0.5474	0.0272	1.1647
4	0.1199	0.7126	0.5827	0.0309	0.4225
5	−0.0487	0.3886	−0.4338	0.0171	−1.9881
6	0.0328	0.4614	0.2464	0.0055	0.6291

Value of $T^2 = 1.9754$, value of $F_{(6,\,6)}$ corresponding to $T^2 = 0.1796$

Values of fractiles of the F distribution:

df	Fractiles		
	0.90	0.95	0.99
6,6	3.055	4.284	8.466
6,7	2.827	3.866	7.191
6,19	2.109	2.628	3.939

Third, while there is some variation across portfolios in the estimated standard deviations for any given test period, the T^2 procedure relies on the assumption of equal covariance structures and is relatively robust—given equal and "fairly large" sample sizes (Harris 1975, p. 85)—to violations of the homogeneity of covariance assumptions. Finally, the univariate t statistics are those resulting from the adoption of the alternative weight vectors discussed in the appendix. Note that related F's are adjusted for a different number of degrees of freedom (that is, this statistic is calculated assuming the comparisons/contrasts are post-hoc).

The results for test period 2 imply a difference between sample and control portfolios. For 5 of the 6 comparisons standardised returns on the sample portfolios are less than those for the control portfolio and the overall F is significant at very near the 95 per cent level. A portfolio-by-portfolio analysis reveals the most likely source of this inconsistency with the null to be portfolios

4 and 6. These portfolios have by far the largest t's and F's, though the latter do not approach conventional significance levels. At this stage, one's inferences depend on whether the t's or the F's are deemed the appropriate statistic on which to rely. Our interpretation rests on the t's since our experimental design was explicitly tailored to assess the effect of particular types of audit qualifications—i.e., the contrasts are not post-hoc. The results of our event-month tests are summarised in table 24.6. Recall that in these tests the preliminary profit reports may appear in any of the months $(-2,0)$ though (-1) would be the more usual.

Table 24.6 Standardised abnormal returns event months

| | | Month | |
Portfolio	-2	-1	0
1	0.1606	−0.0924	0.4825
	(0.5248)	(−0.3019)	(1.5768)
	(0.4607)	(−0.2650)	(1.3842)
2	−0.1926	0.1880	0.2196
	(−0.6930)	(0.6764)	(0.7901)
	(−0.5764)	(0.5626)	(0.6572)
3	−0.0908	−0.3504	0.7775
	(−0.2067)	(−0.7974)	(1.7694)
	(−0.2007)	(−0.7745)	(1.7185)
4	−0.2192	−0.1727	−0.3284
	(−0.7169)	(−0.5646)	(−1.0736)
	(−0.4108)	(−0.3236)	(−0.6153)
5	0.4478	−0.9836	−0.0142
	(0.8768)	(−1.9258)	(−0.0278)
	(1.0679)	(−2.3457)*	(−0.0338)
6	−0.3165	0.1582	−0.7056
	(−1.0675)	(0.5334)	(−2.3806)*
	(−0.8157)	(0.4076)	(−1.8192)

* Significant at $\alpha = 0.5$

Numbers in parentheses represent univariate t statistics calculated using estimates of standard deviation taken respectively from pre-event $(-42, -13)$ and event $(-12, +12)$ time. Generally speaking, and with the possible exception of the "other E^-" portfolio (6), the release of the audit qualification *per se* does not appear to have an impact on share price.

Summary and conclusions

Most existing studies into the stock market effects of an audit qualification suffer from an inability to identify precisely when the qualification was announced. Differences in institutional requirements and in the reporting behaviour of Australian companies provide an opportunity to investigate this issue without a major identification problem. However, this experimental advantage is at least partially offset by the necessity of working with monthly return data—which increases the problem of controlling for concurrent announcements, in particular the preliminary earnings announcement. We attempt to overcome this problem by factoring unexpected earnings directly into the experiment. Once again, data limitations force us to employ what might be regarded as relatively unsophisticated models of unexpected earnings. Yet the results are robust to at least three alternative expectations models (martingale, submartingale and "naive" cross-sectional).

The results support the following general conclusions. For the sample of companies studied here (recall repeated qualifications and those on companies in distress have been excluded) there is no substantive evidence that qualification affects equity prices (though our tests in this respect may not be very powerful). However, with the exception of relatively technical or non-compliance qualifications, there is evidence that firms experience negative abnormal returns prior to the release of the qualification—perhaps reflecting the uncertainties that ultimately resulted in the auditor's decision to qualify. The extent of this abnormal performance appears to vary depending on the type of qualification.

These results reinforce those of Dodd et al. (1983) which stand in contrast to most existing studies in this area. The conclusions, at least with respect to pre-announcement behaviour, are also consistent with those of Elliott (1982) whose experimental design is very similar to that adopted here.

Appendix: Significance tests

As observed in the section "Estimating Abnormal Returns", standard testing procedures rely on the assumptions that security returns are independently and identically distributed—both over time and across securities—and it is unlikely that all of these conditions will be met.

We attempt to overcome the identically distributed problem by standardising each security's abnormal returns by an estimate of that security's residual standard deviation taken over the interval $(-72, -13)$, which is the interval over which securities' relative risks were estimated. These standardised returns are then pooled cross-sectionally to form t statistics for each portfolio for each month relative to month zero.

However, this procedure does not control for any cross-sectional dependence which may exist in the portfolio abnormal returns—a possible problem because our sample (cf. control) securities are not selected randomly and tend to bunch in the later years under study. Fortunately, Hotelling's T^2 test permits multiple comparisons in the presence of cross-sectional dependence (Bolch and Huang 1974, p. 76). Unfortunately, this methodology does not handle the possible serial correlation induced in portfolio returns by working in event time, with the result that our estimates of variance/covariance may still be biased. Working in residuals should, however, reduce this problem.

Let $\hat{R}_{1t}$ and $\hat{R}_{2t}$ be 6 x 1 vectors of (standardised) abnormal returns from $t-1$ to t on the sample and control portfolios respectively. The null hypothesis is:

$$W^T[E(R_t) - E(R_{2t})] = 0 \qquad (1)$$

for all values of the 6 x 1 weight vector W. Hotelling's T^2, a multivariate analog to Students' t is calculated as:

$$T^2 = \max_W t^2(W) = M(\hat{\mu}_1 - \hat{\mu}_2)^T S^{-1}(\hat{\mu}_1 - \hat{\mu}_2) \qquad (2)$$

where:

$$t(W) = \frac{W^T (\hat{\mu}_1 - \hat{\mu}_2) \sqrt{M}}{\sqrt{W^T S W}}$$

μ_1 and μ_2 are the sample estimates of $E(\hat{R}_{1t})$ and $E(\hat{R}_{2t})$ respectively; S is the sample variance/covariance matrix of $R_{1t} - R_{2t}$; and M is the number of standardised return vectors in the sample.

Note that the use of S ensures that any cross-sectional dependence in the samples will be taken into account in the calculation of our test statistics. Note also that since the test examines simultaneously the equality of all components of the vector of standardised return differences to zero, the type I error rate is controlled. The T^2 thus computed is based on a weight vector which maximises the value of the squared t statistic. The weight vector implicit in the calculated statistic can be "normalised" so that its components sum to unity, thus representing valid portfolio proportions.[17]

A significant T^2 acts as a screening device to determine whether further analysis is warranted. We will also be interested in ascertaining which types of audit qualification are driving such a result. This can be achieved by specifying alternative values for the weight vector W^T in (2). For example, applying the weights $W_1^T = [1\ 0\ 0\ 0\ 0\ 0]$, $W_2^T = [0\ 1\ 0\ 0\ 0\ 0]$ and so on reduces Hotelling's T^2 to the familiar Students' t. Further, given the manner in which T^2 is calculated, the individual t's reported will be automatically adjusted for any lack of independence.

When the null is true, T^2 has the F distribution with degrees of freedom $M-N$ where N is the dimensionality of the mean difference vector. The value of F is calculated as

$$F_{N,M-N} = \frac{M-N}{N(M-1)} \tilde{T}^2 \tag{3}$$

Note that M, the number of standardised return vectors observed in each period, varies from 25 in test period 1 to only 12 in test period 3.

Of course, such procedures are inappropriate when the event period is a single month (in this case $M = 1$). In such comparisons we are forced to rely on univariate t statistics. Two such statistics were calculated—the first employing a standard error estimated over the 25 months of the entire test period $[-12, +12]$; the second estimated over the 30 months immediately preceding this period $[-42, -13]$.

Notes

1. Firth does, however, report a significant negative effect for "not true and fair" qualifications. Dodd et al. (1983) also report a negative share price revision for "disclaimers of opinion", though their sample is very small ($n = 5$).
2. The file contains all major qualifications occurring in the consolidated accounts of industrial and commercial companies which had their common stock listed on the Sydney Stock Exchange at any time between March 1961 and December 1974. In all, the file contains some 613 qualifications on 337 companies.
3. Statistics made available by Alan Craswell (University of Sydney) indicate that of the 35 listed companies that entered distress between 1950-79 only 12 were qualified—2 in the year of, 10 in the year preceding, the announcement of bankruptcy.

4. The file contains monthly rates of return on 909 listed industrial and commercial companies over the period January 1958 to December 1973.

5. Approximately 30 per cent of this sample overlaps with the sample used by Ball, Walker and Whittred and the majority of these qualifications relate to depreciation on buildings.

6. Over the period of this study financial reporting on anything other than a semi-annual basis was rare, and although half-yearly reports have been required by the stock exchanges since 1964 the extent of the required disclosures has been minimal and the degree of compliance highly variable.

7. Unremarkable in the sense that they seemed to generate little surprise or critical comment by the financial journalist reviewing the accounts.

8. In fact, the frequency distribution of preliminary profit reports in the present sample took the following form:

relative time	t_{-3}	t_{-2}	t_{-1}	t_0
% preliminary reports released	5	21	41	33

Thus a substantial number of preliminary profit reports (33 per cent) reached the stock exchange in the same month as the company's annual report containing the audit qualification.

9. This was the finest partitioning of the sample space that could be achieved without introducing significant problems regarding the homogeneity of cell variances (refer appendix).

10. Note that this model is consistent with the capital asset pricing model which is implicit in our subsequent use of market-model residuals as measures of "information content", i.e., we employ a "market model" in earnings that is a direct analogue of that in returns (Ball 1978c).

11. For Australian evidence, refer to Whittred (1978) and Finn and Whittred (1982, reproduced in this book as chapter 20). More generally refer to Foster (1978b, ch. 4).

12. The figure 11 was arbitrarily selected, but is based on Finn and Whittred's (1982) findings that (a) submartingale models incorporating drift factors estimated over a large number of prior years consistently outperform those estimated using fewer observations and that (b) it was not until $\delta > 6$ that the submartingale model started to significantly outperform the martingale model.

13. The estimates of median and mean unexpected earnings exhibited remarkable stability across each of the eight portfolios and three forecasting models employed. The major effect of the adoption of the cross-sectional model was a much more even distribution of companies in the E^+/E^- categories for both the control and depreciation portfolios.

14. The Kruskal–Wallis H statistics for E^+ and E^- comparisons were 4.46 and 7.08 respectively. The critical value for H with $\alpha = 0.05$ and 3 degrees of freedom is 7.82.

15. Following Beaver, Clarke and Wright (1979), Elliott (1982) achieves a one-on-one matching on forecasting errors scaled by the standard deviation of prior EPS changes. He also manages to match on the basis of a 4-digit SIC industry classification. Although the former procedure is desirable the preceding discussion highlights its impracticability in the present context. That essentially the same results obtain when we use both martingale and submartingale models is a source of some "comfort". There were no obvious industry effects in the present sample.

16. Our results were not affected by the standardisation procedure described in the appendix. Comparisons of non-standardised, or simple, abnormal return distributions, over the same event periods using Hotelling's T^2 procedures yielded the same conclusions. In these particular comparisons we also experimented with pre-event covariance (cf. event-period covariance) matrices as the S in equation (2), in the belief that these might represent more efficient estimates of the underlying covariance structure. The results were not sensitive to the choice of the period used to estimate S.

17. From Gonedes (1975, p. 226) the normalised weight vector can be derived from the fact that the normalised weights implicit in the observed T^2 value are proportional to $S^{-1}(\hat{\mu}_1 - \hat{\mu}_2)$. To calculate the normalised weights we divide the vector $Z = S^{-1}(\hat{\mu}_1 - \hat{\mu}_2)$ by a scalar which is the sum of the components of the vector Z (i.e., $\Sigma_j^n Z_i$).

25 Asset revaluations and stock market prices

I. G. Sharpe and R. G. Walker

Several recently reported studies have considered whether changes in accounting methods by firms whose securities are publicly traded have led to any discernible response in the form of shifts in share prices.[1] These studies have been framed in differing terms and have looked at share price movements under a variety of conditions. But a common finding has been that changes in accounting methods *per se* do not appear to have been associated with substantial changes in stock market prices. This paper presents some evidence of changes in accounting method which are associated with shifts in stock prices. It describes an examination of movements in share prices of a sample of relatively large Australian public companies which announced upward asset revaluations during the period 1960–70. This examination revealed that announcements of asset revaluations were associated with substantial upward movements in stock prices, and that these shifts in stock prices were generally sustained in the post-announcement months. Furthermore, the stock market appears to digest this new information quickly into stock prices as the adjustment was almost complete at the close of the announcement month. Additional analysis suggested that the observed movements in stock prices could not be attributed entirely to such additional information signals as earnings and dividend changes, nor were the results explained by induced changes in volatility which could conceivably result from the release of revaluation information. Given that the revaluations reflected changes in the worth of assets which had predominantly taken place but had not been recorded during prior accounting periods, the findings are consistent with claims that the failure of accounting to *systematically* provide contemporary information about the affairs of firms can deprive the stock market of useful information.

Asset revaluations

The upward revaluation of "fixed" assets is commonplace in Australia,[2]

Reprinted from *The Journal of Accounting Research* (Autumn 1975), 291–331, by permission of the authors and the publisher.

familiar in the United Kingdom,[3] but effectively banned in the United States.[4] Australian asset revaluations are carried out at the discretion of company managements. There are no explicit guidelines concerning the basis or comprehensiveness of these revaluations either in companies' legislation, stock exchange rules or pronouncements of professional bodies. [*Editor's note:* This was the situation at the time this article was written. Current accounting standards include AAS10 and ASRB1010.] Some revaluations are conservative. For example, managements may disclose that the new asset figures are still well below appraisal values or that they have reported properties at the level of out-of-date "valuations" prepared for the use of rating authorities. However, it appears that most revaluations bear some relationship to "current values" in the sense of current resale prices. Hence, the announcement of an upward revaluation typically recognises gains from holding assets that have previously been ignored in financial statements prepared in accord with "generally accepted accounting principles".

We know of no previous studies aimed at investigating the effect of asset revaluations on share prices. However, there is some related evidence available from an examination of Australian experience with takeover bids during 1960–70.[5] Frequently, takeover bids have been the occasion for directors of offeree firms to comment on the extent to which book values diverged from "current values". A comparison between the gross share price movements of a sample of firms which released "new information" in response to takeover bids and the shifts in the share prices of all offeree firms for which the movement in month-end prices before and after the bid could be obtained produced the following findings.[6]

Share price movement (pre/post bid)	Firms which released new information	All offerees
Decreases 1–80%	2	108
Increases 0–20%	7	241
21–40%	14	156
41–60%	6	77
61–80%	4	49
81% over	8	57
	41	688

The distribution of share price movements of the two groups differed significantly,[7] thereby suggesting that the release of contemporary information in these instances may have had some bearing on share price movements. But these announcements occurred in conjunction with takeover contests, so the subsequent price movements cannot be directly attributed to the release of "new information" about the net worth of the offeree firm. Moreover, since a proportion of these responses concerning the differences between book figures and current values were unquantified, it is impossible to assess the "significance" of the announcements in relation to prior accounting reports. Finally, these announcements were not always followed by a formal adjustment of a firm's accounting records for inclusion in subsequent financial statements.

In contrast to this study of takeover bids, the study reported below focuses on the effect of announcements of asset revaluations on share prices, especially in cases where these changes in accounting method could be interpreted as constituting significant revisions of prior accounting representations of the position and performance of firms.

The sample

A number of formal asset revaluations were selected from cases recorded on a file compiled by the Department of Accounting, University of Sydney, from a review of the Sydney Stock Exchange "Investment" and "Mining" Services. Asset revaluations were located from an examination of balance-sheet summaries together with a review of "capital changes". The latter source was used since asset revaluations followed by bonus issues which immediately "capitalised" revaluation reserves would not necessarily show up clearly in year-end balance sheets.

With the object of ensuring that any price movements which might be associated with the asset revaluations were not attributable to takeover contests, the sample period was limited to the 1960s, for which particulars of takeover activity were available. The sample was also limited to asset revaluatioins of some "size"—a $1 million "increase" was selected initially, but this was later lowered to $900,000 in order to increase the size of the sample. To further ensure that the changes in method constituted important changes in the manner in which a firm's affairs were depicted by accounting reports, the cases were also restricted to those in which the revaluations constituted an addition of at least 10 per cent to shareholders' funds (as indicated in the most recent balance sheet prior to the revaluation). Some additional limitations were imposed. Revaluations of holding companies' investments in subsidiary companies were excluded, on the ground that the prior presentation of consolidated statements would have provided some indication of the distortion previously embodied in cost-based valuations of these assets. Revaluations of marketable securities were also excluded on the ground that information about the market value of these assets would have been disclosed in notes to annual balance sheets in compliance with Australian disclosure laws.[8] Of the cases which fitted these prescriptions, several were found to have been made by firms whose stock exchange listing was limited to senior securities. These cases were rejected so that the sample would be composed entirely of announcements by firms whose common stock was publicly traded in Australia. Finally, the form of analysis adopted led to the exclusion of several cases in which multiple revaluations occurred within a period of three years perhaps producing a downward bias in the pre- and post-revaluation residuals. This left a sample of 34 asset revaluations by 32 listed companies. The dates on which these revaluations were announced were obtained from Sydney Stock Exchange files, and (in some instances) cross-checked against newspaper reports.

A comparison of the list of revaluations with the list of takeover bids[9] indicated that only one of the 34 revaluations occurred within three years of a takeover offer being directed at the revaluing firm. This case was that of APA Holdings Ltd, which revalued in October 1968, and in December 1968 was subject to a first-come-first-served bid for 10 per cent of its issued shares. This bid was unsuccessful and did not attract a counter offer. These circumstances did not suggest that the case should be excluded from the sample; subsequent examination of the data indicated that its retention had not noticeably influenced the results.

Examination of the revaluation announcements indicated that the majority related to properties and investments:

Assets revalued

"Land and buildings", "freehold property", "properties"	13
"Investments", "shares in associated companies"	8
"Plant and equipment"	3
Other descriptions (e.g. "fixed assets", "capital assets") or combinations of items (e.g., "freeholds and leaseholds", "properties and plant")	10
Total revaluations	34

In this respect it is important to note that, until recently, it was uncommon for Australian firms to provide for depreciation on buildings.[10] Hence, during the 1960s the upward revaluation of properties would not normally have led investors to expect that subsequent periods would face increased depreciation charges.

The basis of revaluation was not always indicated in unambiguous terms. The following is a selection of extracts from the revaluation announcements:

Directors [of G. E. Crane Holdings Ltd] reported that the fixed asset figures shown in the accounts increased during the year, due to additions and a revaluation of certain freeholds and plant. Two of the company's properties were revalued to agree in the company's books with the Valuer General's most recent assessment. In addition to this, some items of plant were raised to bring them closer to present-day values after depreciation.[11]

Just prior to the close of the financial year the Board [of Castlemaine Perkins Ltd] caused a valuation to be made by well-known valuers of certain of its properties and, guided by that valuation, revalued these properties in the Company's books . . .[12]

. . . the directors [of McPherson's Ltd] advise that acting on valuations received from the Company's Valuers they have revalued the Company's freehold properties.[13]

[Silverton Transport and General Industries Ltd] has revalued its terminals and Broken Hill Cockburn railway line from £290,239 to £1,781,744. The Assets are not necessarily expected to realise this enhanced figure.[14]

The analysis

Share price movements around the date of the revaluations were examined using what has come to be known as the "market model".[15] This method of analysis eliminates the effect of marketwide influences on individual stock prices. For each company in the sample, an equation of the form

$$R_{it} = \alpha_i + \beta_i R_{mt} + l_{it} \tag{1}$$

was estimated using the ordinary least-squares regression technique where
R_{it} = the monthly return for company i in month t calculated from end-of-month prices (obtained from the Sydney and Melbourne Stock

Exchange Gazettes) and including dividends. Appropriate adjustments
were made for stock splits, bonus issues, and "rights";

R_{mt} = the "market" rate of return (represented by the average monthly rate
of return on a portfolio consisting of some 500 Australian stocks traded
on the Melbourne Stock Exchange assuming dividends are reinvested
and adjustments made for capital changes);[16]

α_i = a constant, equal to a riskless rate of return;

l_{it} = a random error term for month t; and

β_i = a measure of volatility of the return on company i's shares relative
to the market return.

Approximately 60 monthly observations were used to estimate the parameters
α_i and β_i. These did not include 12 observations before and 12 observations
after the announcement month since it was assumed that responses to asset
revaluations would be reflected in share prices within this period. Inclusion
of these observations for the purpose of estimating the coefficients α_i and
β_i in equation (1) would have violated the ordinary least-squares assumption
that the expected value of the error term, l_{it}, is zero.

Table 25.1

Company	Revaluation date(s)		Dividends*	$\hat{\beta}$†		R^2
Elec. Equipment	Aug.	1969	D	0.086	(0.42)	0.014
Dunlop Rubber	Mar.	1963	I	1.138	(5.81)	0.382
G. E. Crane	Sept	1960	D	0.942	(3.15)	0.185
Concrete Industries	Apr.	1960	I	1.476	(4.18)	0.250
Castlemaine Perkins	Aug.	1960	I	0.891	(5.13)	0.414
Brickworks Ltd	Sept.	1961	S	0.645	(2.44)	0.120
BHP	Sept.	1960	S	0.685	(3.83)	0.224
Fairymead Sugar	Aug.	1960	I	0.808	(2.24)	0.111
Comeng	Nov.	1960	I	0..859	(2.81)	0.182
Broons	Apr.	1969	I	0.424	(1.54)	0.045
Adelaide Cement	Aug.	1961	S	0.650	(2.96)	0.124
	Jan.	1969	I			
Advertiser News	Oct.	1963	I	1.081	(3.41)	0.172
Aust. United Investments	July	1967	I	0.274	(1.19)	0.042
Bennett & Fisher	Feb.	1967	S	0.355	(2.09)	0.080
Wynyard Holdings	Aug.	1963	S	0.481	(1.20)	0.063
Trustees Executors	Aug.	1963	I	0.122	(0.94)	0.057
Howard Smith	Jan.	1960	I	0.731	(3.28)	0.197
Qld Cement & Lime	June	1967	I	0.452	(2.70)	0.130
Provincial Traders	May	1969	S	1.087	(4.95)	0.306
Perth Arcade	Sept.	1967	I	0.157	(1.07)	0.021
Myer	Oct.	1969	I	1.182	(6.24)	0.481
Mt Isa Mines	Apr.	1960	S	0.724	(3.31)	0.180
	July	1963	S			
McPhersons	May	1961	S	0.863	(5.75)	0.393
Silverton	Oct.	1964	S	0.798	(2.29)	0.117
Hardie Holdings	July	1960	I	0.499	(1.91)	0.071
John Martin	Oct.	1969	S	0.905	(3.18)	0.157
Industrial Engineering	Oct.	1967	D	0.287	(1.25)	0.045
Mauri Bros.	Oct.	1960	I	1.050	(4.44)	0.314
Malleys	Oct.	1964	I	0.278	(0.80)	0.017
Aust. Paper Manuf.	Jan.	1962	I	1.148	(7.05)	0.474
APA Holdings	Oct.	1968	D	0.574	(2.81)	0.222
North BHP	Jan.	1960	D	1.008	(2.68)	0.178

* I = Increase, S = Steady, D = Decrease.

† t statistic of β in parentheses.

Table 25.2

Month relative to announcement date	Average residuals (%)	Cumulative average residuals (%)
−12	1.47	1.47
−11	−0.62	0.85
−10	−0.74	0.11
−9	0.44	0.55
−8	0.66	1.21
−7	0.90	2.11
−6	3.56	5.67
−5	0.33	6.00
−4	0.76	6.76
−3	0.23	6.99
−2	0.90	7.89
−1	2.15	10.04
0	9.59	19.63
1	1.44	21.07
2	−1.57	19.50
3	1.64	21.14
4	−1.58	19.56
5	−2.24	17.32
6	−1.46	15.86
7	1.78	17.64
8	0.49	18.13
9	−0.57	17.56
10	−0.41	17.15
11	1.48	18.63
12	0.32	18.95

The revaluations announcement month was numbered month zero. Using the estimated values of α_i and β_i and known values of R_{mt}, predicted values of R_{it} for the excluded months ($t = -12$ to $+12$) were calculated. These predicted values were then subtracted from the actual monthly returns in those months producing residuals $\hat{l}_{it}$ for $t = -12$ to $+12$. These were then averaged across all the 34 revaluation cases to produce a series of average residuals:

$$\mu_t = \frac{1}{34} \sum_{i=1}^{34} \hat{l}_{it}$$

Findings

The results of the application of the "market model" are summarised in tables 25.1 and 25.2 and in figure 25.1. They indicate that an announcement of a revaluation of assets was accompanied, on average, by a cumulative average increase in return of about 18 per cent or 19 per cent above that expected from the general state of the stock market. Approximately half of this took place prior to the announcement date (the shift at month −6 can perhaps be attributed to the publication of the 6-month report). But there was an unmistakable jump in the average residual of the announcement month, and the cumulative average residuals (CAR) indicate that this response was sustained over the twelve post-announcement months.

Prima facie these results indicate that the release of information about upward revaluations (which usually implies that previous financial statements

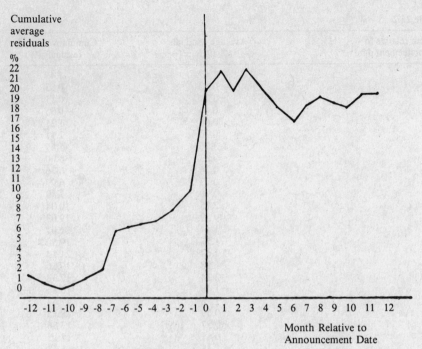

Figure 25.1   *Source:* Table 25.2

had "undervalued" assets) was both accompanied and preceded by a strong increase in the price of the company's shares. To the extent that the share price movements were attributable to the revaluations, then it may be argued that buyers and sellers in the stock market regard revaluation announcements as information of significance.

Earnings or dividends changes

It might be supposed that the results in table 25.2 could be attributable to factors other than asset revaluations. In particular, investors might have responded to announcements of reported earnings rather than to the disclosure of asset revaluations. Calculations were made of the rate of increase in earnings reported by the revaluing companies. Earnings for the accounting period ending closest to the announcement month were related to earnings reported in the preceding year, after due allowance for capital changes. These calculations revealed that the sample was comprised of companies with an average rate of increase in reported earnings in the revaluation year somewhat greater than the average for all companies in Australia.

The cases of revaluation announcements were divided into two groups, corresponding to the upper and lower halves of the distribution of the rates of changes in earnings. The mean rates of change in earnings for the two groups were 34 per cent and −2 per cent while the mean beta coefficients were 0.828 and 0.589 respectively. In contrast, the mean annual rate of growth of net profit for Australian companies in the fiscal years 1959–60 to 1969–70 was 7.7 per cent. Thus the two groups roughly corresponded to better-than-average (or market) and worse-than-average performers in terms of rates of growth of earnings of all companies. However, there was also a tendency for the returns of the companies in the better-than-average earnings group to be more volatile, relative to the market, than the poorer earnings performers.

The stock market's reaction to an earnings report will depend upon whether the reported earnings were "better" or "worse" than expected. If we postulate that the market expects a company's earnings to grow (decline) by the same percentage in the revaluation year as in the preceding year, then the lower half earnings sample consists of fourteen "worse"-than-expected earnings cases and three slightly "better"-than-expected earnings cases. On the other hand, the upper half earnings sample is composed of fourteen cases where earnings were "better" than expected and three cases where earnings were slightly "worse" than expected. Thus, in terms of the postulated definition of expected earnings, the 34 revaluations appear to be evenly distributed between "better"- and "worse"-than-expected earners. A significant positive residual in the revaluation announcement month for the lower half earnings sample would clearly be inconsistent with the anticipated negative residual due to the "worse"-than-expected earnings performance of this sample.

Average residuals were calculated for the two groups; the results are shown in table 25.3. These results must be evaluated cautiously because of the smallness of the samples. Asset revaluations accompanied by "high" (above average) increases in reported earnings were associated with a cumulative

Table 25.3

Month relative to announcement date	Lower half rates of change in earnings sample		Upper half rates of change in earnings sample	
	AR	CAR	AR	CAR
−12	1.67	1.67	1.27	1.27
−11	−0.73	0.94	−0.51	0.76
−10	0.81	1.75	−2.29	−1.53
−9	−0..68	1.07	1.56	0.03
−8	1.40	2.47	−0.08	−0.05
−7	0.00	2.47	1.80	1.75
−6	2.39	4.86	4.73	6.48
−5	−1.11	3.75	1.77	8.25
−4	0.58	4.33	0.94	9.19
−3	−1.29	3.04	1.75	10.94
−2	0.82	3.86	0.98	11.92
−1	−0.16	3.70	4.46	16.38
0	10.47	14.17	8.71	25.09
1	1.91	16.08	0.97	26.06
2	−1.15	14.93	−1.99	24.07
3	0.06	14.99	3.22	27.29
4	−1.81	13.18	−1.35	25.94
5	−2.43	10.75	−2.05	23.89
6	−3.84	6.91	0.92	24.81
7	2.32	9.23	1.24	26.05
8	−1.81	7.42	2.79	28.84
9	−3.32	4.10	2.18	31.02
10	0.05	4.15	−0.87	30.15
11	1.11	5.26	1.85	32.00
12	−0.68	4.58	1.32	33.32

average residual of approximately 30 per cent; approximately half of this adjustment took place prior to the announcement date. Asset revaluations accompanied by "low" (below average) increases in earnings also experienced substantial share price movements; the average residual in the announcement month for this group was 10.47 per cent, but the cumulative average residual drifted downwards in later months to around 5 per cent twelve months after the revaluation date. For both groups, 6-month interim reports may have influenced the pattern of the residual both before and after the revaluation date. While differences in earnings performance and/or average betas could explain the difference in the pattern of residuals between the upper and lower earnings groups, it seems unlikely that the positive average residual in the announcement month for the latter (worse-than-average performance) group was attributable to earnings performance.

Some of the asset revaluation announcements were accompanied by announcements of changes in dividend rates; in other cases reports of changes in dividend policies were announced around the time of the revaluation. These reports of dividend changes may have had some effect on share prices. Apart from the supposition that dividend changes *per se* affect share prices, it could also be argued that changes in dividend payouts could be interpreted as signals of forthcoming reports of improved earnings.

Table 25.1 refers to the relative level of dividend distributions subsequent to the revaluation announcements. The classification was generally based upon an examination of dividend payouts in the 12 months following the revaluation, after allowing for capital changes. In some cases a shift in dividend patterns just prior to the revaluation was the determining factor. In other cases, the issue of bonus shares with accompanying promises of overall rises in dividends was categorised as an "increase" even though the share did not rank for dividends for some time so that, strictly speaking, changes in distribution levels were not discernible within the 12 months following the revaluation. Using this basis of classification, there were 18 cases where the revaluations were associated with higher dividends, 11 cases of steady dividend payouts, and 5 declines.

A disaggregation of the residuals by dividend performance is shown in table 25.4. Again these results must be evaluated cautiously because of the smallness of the samples. Asset revaluations accompanied by increased dividends were associated with a CAR in excess of 25 per cent; about two-thirds of this adjustment took place prior to the announcement date. Revaluations in the "steady" and "decreasing dividend" classes were initially grouped because of the smallness of the sample. The CAR for this group was roughly 10 per cent, equivalent to the average residual in the announcement month. Finally, residuals were averaged for 10 cases in which revaluations were accompanied by "steady" dividends. (This sample excluded Wynyard Holdings, which at the time of revaluation had yet to pay a maiden dividend). The CAR after the revaluation amounted to between 25 per cent and 30 per cent; approximately half of this adjustment occurred before the revaluation date.

As noted above, the rate of increase of reported (operating) earnings of a substantial number of the revaluing companies was considerably less than the average for all companies in Australia during the period under review.

Table 25.4

Month relative to announcement date	Dividend increases (18 revals.)		Dividend steady or decrease (16 revals.)		Dividend steady (10 revals.)	
	AR	CAR	AR	CAR	AR	CAR
−12	1.986	1.986	0.885	0.885	2.82	2.82
−11	1.917	3.903	−3.468	−2.583	0.21	3.03
−10	−0.153	3.750	−1.412	−3.995	−2.61	0.42
−9	0.662	4.412	0.184	−3.811	−0.48	−0.06
−8	−0.576	3.836	2.059	−1.752	4.30	4.24
−7	1.626	5.462	0.091	−1.661	−0.99	3.25
−6	3.117	8.579	4.068	2.407	7.15	10.40
−5	1.978	10.557	−1.531	0.876	−1.15	9.25
−4	0.206	10.763	1.339	2.215	0.51	9.76
−3	−0.141	10.622	0.643	2.858	−0.01	9.75
−2	1.641	12.263	0.064	2.922	0.47	10.22
−1	3.050	15.313	1.143	4.065	1.93	12.15
0	8.437	23.750	10.893	14.958	9.39	21.54
1	−0.369	23.381	3.471	18.429	4.90	26.44
2	−1.402	21.979	−1.752	16.677	−0.58	25.86
3	3.823	25.802	−0.820	15.857	1.24	27.10
4	−0.973	24.829	−2.272	13.585	−1.43	25.67
5	−1.960	22.869	−2.561	11.024	0.93	26.60
6	−2.507	20.362	−0.286	10.738	2.90	29.50
7	1.901	22.263	1.650	12.388	4.08	33.58
8	1.905	24.168	−1.106	11.282	−0.28	33.30
9	2.060	26.228	−3.519	7.763	−4.14	29.16
10	0.107	26.335	−0.935	6.828	−0.34	28.82
11	−0.425	25.910	3.625	10.453	5.52	34.34
12	0.297	26.207	0.345	10.798	2.32	36.66

For example, the mean rate of increase of earnings for the companies included in the "lower half" sample of table 25.3 was −2 per cent compared with the mean annual rate of growth of net profit for all Australian companies between 1959-60 and 1969-70 of 7.7 per cent.[17] Moreover, it is evident from table 25.1 and note 16 that a majority of revaluations were undertaken when relatively high rates of increases in earnings were being reported. In an attempt to produce a sample of revaluations by firms whose earnings performance was more in line with that being recorded by other firms whose stocks were publicly traded, the data for the "lower half" earnings cases were combined with the data for the lowest 13 cases in the "upper half" of the distribution. The mean rate of increase of earnings of the companies in this sample of 30 revaluations in the announcement period was 10 per cent, roughly equivalent to the rate of change of earnings for the market as a whole in the corresponding years.[18] AR (average residuals) and CAR for this sample are shown in table 25.5. The average rate of increase of earnings of this group of 30 revaluation cases was very much influenced by a large decline in the earnings reported by Wynyard Holdings Ltd. Hence, another sample was devised consisting of all companies in the "lower half" of the distribution, except Wynyard Holdings Ltd, plus the lowest 7 cases in the "upper half" of the distribution. The 23 cases in this sample also reported increases in earnings averaging 10 per cent. Residuals for this sample are reported in table 25.5.[19]

The adjustments underlying tables 25.3, 25.4 and 25.5 are admittedly somewhat crude. Furthermore, there were several revaluations where the asset

Table 25.5

Month relative to announcement date	Sample of 30 cases (See text)		Sample of 23 cases (See text)	
	AR	CAR	AR	CAR
−12	1.52	1.52	2.12	2.12
−11	0.84	2.36	0.27	2.39
−10	−0.44	1.92	−0.06	2.33
−9	−0.33	1.59	−1.06	1.27
−8	1.08	2.67	1.60	2.87
−7	0.02	2.69	0.92	3.79
−6	3.70	6.39	2.72	6.51
−5	0.69	7.08	0.55	7.06
−4	0.37	7.45	−0.02	7.04
−3	−0.65	6.80	−0.24	6.80
−2	0.70	7.50	0.64	7.44
−1	2.40	9.90	2.02	9.46
0	9.15	19.05	8.98	18.44
1	1.72	20.77	1.70	20.14
2	−1.84	18.93	−0.71	19.43
3	2.04	20.97	2.44	21.87
4	−1.90	19.07	−2.41	19.46
5	−2.11	16.96	−2.25	17.21
6	−1.87	15.09	−1.76	15.45
7	2.05	17.14	1.33	16.78
8	−0.11	17.03	−0.73	16.05
9	−1.00	16.03	−0.59	15.46
10	−0.46	15.57	−2.01	13.45
11	1.74	17.31	3.09	16.54
12	−0.03	17.28	0.06	16.60

revaluation announcement month did not correspond with the earnings or dividend announcement month. If the stock market is efficient,[20] then, in these cases, an earnings or dividend effect would not be expected in the revaluation announcement month. Despite these obvious shortcomings of the analysis, it seems improbable that the upward movements in stock prices in the revaluation announcement month evident in the residuals of the subsamples (i) the "lower half" earnings companies where the average rate of growth of earnings was considerably less than for all companies in Australia (table 25.3), (ii) dividend steady or decline cases (table 25.4), and (iii) samples where the rate of growth of earnings was roughly equivalent to the market as a whole (table 25.5), were attributable to the release of earnings or dividend information. Thus the evidence is consistent with the related hypotheses that asset revaluation announcements influence share prices and that such announcements convey information which has not previously been incorporated into stock prices as a result of other information sources.

Limitations of "market model" analysis

It might be claimed that the above results arise from weaknesses in the "market model" or in its application,[21] and as such do not in fact reflect a sustained response to announcements of asset revaluations. Figure 25.2 shows the timing of the revaluations relative to market movements—depicted for this purpose by the Sydney Stock Exchange All Ordinaries Index. Sixteen

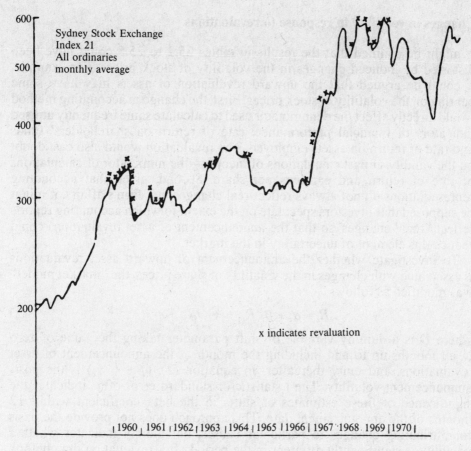

Sydney Stock Exchange
Index 21
All ordinaries
monthly average

x indicates revaluation

| 1960 | 1961 | 1962 | 1963 | 1964 | 1965 | 1966 | 1967 | 1968 | 1969 | 1970 |

Figure 25.2

of the 34 revaluations occurred around the market peaks of 1960 and 1969, while the remainder were fairly equally distributed over the intervening years. In view of this spread, and because relatively few firms make asset revaluations at any one time, it seems unlikely that objection could be made to the results on the grounds of either distortion of the market index of systematic "errors" in anticipation of the market index.

Another assumption implicit in the application of the market model is that the "riskless" rate of return [that is, α_i in equation (1)] remains constant over time. In order to minimise any bias in this respect, the observations used to estimate equation (1) were limited to a 5-year period, and whenever possible, centred on the revaluation date. In this latter respect, the primary exceptions were the regressions for the 1960 and 1969 revaluations which used post- and pre-revaluation data, respectively, because of data limitations.

Finally, as emphasised earlier, in the light of *a priori* beliefs about likely stock price adjustments in obtaining regression estimates of equation (1), 12 observations were excluded on either side of the announcement date. As Ball[22] has emphasised, the number of observations excluded can influence the general pattern of residuals. However, it appears extremely unlikely that this factor alone could account for the very large average residual in the announcement month which is so obvious in tables 25.2 to 25.5.

Changes in volatility in response to revaluations

It might be claimed that the results in tables 25.2 to 25.5 could have been distorted by induced changes in the volatility of stock prices. For example, it could be argued that the upward revaluation of assets may have some bearing on the volatility of stock prices. First, the change in accounting method would directly affect the denominator used to calculate some frequently utilised indicators of financial performance: rate of return on shareholders' funds and rate of return on assets employed. The revaluation would also cast doubt on the validity of past calculations of income—the numerator of calculations of rate of return and earnings per share. Second, given that accounting representations do not always reflect real changes in a firm's affairs, it might be supposed that investors speculate on the extent to which accounting reports reflect "real" changes, so that the announcement of asset revaluations could reduce this element of uncertainty in the market.

To investigate whether the announcement of upward asset revaluations is associated with changes in the volatility of share prices, the "market model" was modified as follows

$$R_i = \alpha_i + \beta_i^a R_m + \gamma_i D R_m + e_i \qquad (2)$$

where D is a dummy variable or shift parameter taking the value of zero in all months up to and including the month of the announcement of asset revaluations, and unity thereafter. In equation (2), $(\beta_i^a + \gamma_i)$ is the post-announcement volatility. The t statistic or standard error of γ_i indicates the significance of these estimates of shifts in the beta coefficient within 12 months of the announcement date. This approach does not provide the basis for attributing changes to particular causes, but merely indicates whether volatility is significantly different in the period after revaluation than before. Also, this procedure may only be used when the regression equation includes both prior- and post-announcement data to estimate α_i and β_i the sample used here was accordingly limited to 16 cases, and for the purpose of applying this test it was necessary to add up to 12 observations of monthly returns for some companies. The findings from the application of this technique are shown in tables 25.6 and 25.7.

Of the 16 $\hat{\gamma}_i$ coefficients in table 25.6, 7 are negative and 9 positive, suggesting that there was no systematic positive or negative change in volatility. On the other hand, 10 of the 16 coefficients indicates that the post-revaluation volatility was closer to unity than previously. However, only 3 of the $\hat{\gamma}_i$ coefficients were significantly different from zero at the 95 per cent confidence level, so that little confidence can be placed on these findings. Recalculation of the residuals for these 16 cases provides a check on whether the results in tables 25.2 to 25.5 were distorted by the changes in volatility that did take place for individual stocks. Table 25.7 sets out the cumulative average residuals for these 16 revaluations as initially calculated, and then as calculated allowing for volatility changes. It is evident that the adjustment for volatility changes has had very little effect on the pattern of cumulative average residuals. Consequently, it is extremely unlikely that our earlier results were biased in any way by instability in the volatility coefficient, β, over time.

Table 25.6*

Company	$\hat{\beta}_i^a$†	$\hat{\gamma}_i$†	R^2
Dunlop Rubber	1.595 (5.72)	−0.846 (2.23)	0.433
Brickworks Ltd	0.224 (0.63)	0.456 (1.08)	0.135
Advertiser News	1.299 (2.82)	−0.417 (0.65)	0.179
Australian United Investments	0.174 (0.43)	0.148 (0.30)	0.044
Bennett & Fisher	0.063 (0.18)	0.378 (0.93)	0.095
Wynyard Holdings	0.399 (0.44)	0.101 (0.10)	0.063
Trustees Executors	0.420 (2.30)	−0.562 (2.25)	0.136
Qld Cement & Lime	0.508 (1.65)	−0.079 (0.22)	0.131
Perth Arcade	0.006 (0.02)	0.236 (0.77)	0.032
McPhersons	0.837 (4.05)	−0.079 (0.31)	0.354
Silverton	0.991 (2.02)	−0.360 (0.56)	0.122
Hardie Holdings	0.560 (1.07)	0.024 (0.04)	0.097
Industrial Engineering	0.486 (1.27)	−0.310 (0.65)	0.052
Mauri Bros.	0.542 (1.43)	0.578 (1.33)	0.290
Malleys	0.129 (0.35)	0.752 (1.19)	0.055
Aust. Paper Manuf.	0.226 (1.31)	1.133 (4.84)	0.494

* Pre-announcement volatility = $\hat{\beta}_i^a$. Post-announcement volatility = ($\hat{\beta}_i^a + \hat{\gamma}_i$).
† t statistics in parentheses.

Table 25.7

Month relative to announcement date	Sample of 16 (see table 25.6)			
	Unadjusted for volatility change		Adjusted for volatility change	
	AR	CAR	AR	CAR
−12	3.95	3.95	4.15	4.15
−11	−0.08	3.87	−0.11	4.04
−10	−0.48	3.39	−0.75	3.29
−9	0.08	3.47	0.34	3.63
−8	1.11	4.58	1.30	4.93
−7	0.31	4.89	0.43	5.36
−6	3.44	8.33	3.41	8.77
−5	−0.44	7.89	−0.64	8.13
−4	0.16	8.05	0.04	8.17
−3	−0.43	7.62	−0.52	7.65
−2	1.58	9.20	1.44	9.09
−1	2.55	11.75	2.53	11.62
0	6.28	18.03	6.25	17.87
1	2.26	20.29	2.31	20.18
2	−1.77	18.52	−1.72	18.46
3	2.79	21.31	2.91	21.37
4	1.07	22.38	1.23	22.60
5	−1.11	21.27	−0.90	21.70
6	−2.08	19.19	−2.03	19.67
7	1.35	20.54	1.29	20.96
8	1.26	21.80	1.45	22.41
9	−1.42	20.38	−1.60	20.81
10	1.89	22.27	1.86	22.67
11	0.63	22.90	0.62	23.29
12	−0.20	22.70	−0.47	22.82

Conclusion

The findings of this study must be viewed cautiously in view of the small sample involved, the nature of the market model (which does not permit the identification of the factors causing the observed pattern of residuals), and the association of asset revaluations with above-average rates of increase in reported earnings. Bearing in mind these reservations, the principal findings are: (i) after adjusting for any possible changes in volatility and standardising somewhat crudely for earnings and dividend behaviour, the results are consistent with the hypothesis that the market regards an announcement of an asset revaluation as information of significance; (ii) the market appears to absorb the information content of asset revaluations quickly into security prices; and (iii) there is little evidence to support the view that the announcement of asset revaluations is associated with systematic changes in the volatility of a stock's return relative to the market.

Acknowledgments

This chapter was prepared with the assistance of Dorothy Simons and P. T. Triong, R. Ball and R. R. Officer of the University of Queensland.

Notes

1. See Ball (1972a); Archibald (1972); Baskin (1973); Kaplan and Roll (1972).
2. For some data on the incidence of revaluations in Australia 1950–70, see Chambers (1973, pp. 52–53).
3. The incidence of asset revaluations among UK listed companies "engaged primarily in manufacturing and distribution" is reported in Whittington (1971, pp. 59–63).
4. Evidently on an interpretation of S.E.C. Release No. 4 (1938) which states that financial statements would be presumed "misleading or inaccurate" if they had been prepared in accord with accounting methods which lacked "substantial authoritative support". See Benston (1973).
5. Walker (1973).
6. Ibid., p. 42.
7. That is, using the chi-square statistic at the 10 per cent significance level (after grouping scores for price increases of 41 per cent and above).
8. For example, NSW Companies Act, 1961, as amended, 9th Schedule.
9. See note 4.
10. The change was prompted by the release by the Institute of Chartered Accountants in Australia of a revised version of Statement on Accounting Practice D5 ("Depreciation, Depletion and Amortisation of Fixed Assets") in November 1970 and the subsequent release of Statement K1 ("Conformity with Institute Technical Statements") in May 1971 (revised February 1972).
11. Sydney Stock Exchange, Investment Service, File 640A.
12. Circular to shareholders, 30 August 1960.
13. Sydney Stock Exchange, Investment Service, File M71.
14. *Australian Financial Review*, 28 September 1964.
15. The test used by Fama, Fisher, Jensen and Roll (1969) to analyse price movements in connection with stock splits.
16. This series was published as an appendix to a paper presented by R. Ball at the Portfolio Management Seminar sponsored by Macquarie University and the NSW Branch of the Australian Society of Security Analysts, May 1973. The series was developed by P. Brown of the University of Western Australia.
17. The annual rates of growth of net profit were:

1969–70	10.1	1963–64	11.4
1968–69	10.4	1962–63	14.3
1967–68	8.8	1961–62	7.0
1966–67	10.9	1960–61	−13.6
1965–66	0.9	1959–60	13.9
1964–65	10.1		

Source: Reserve Bank of Australia, *Statistical Bulletin Company Supplement*. The main source of information for the supplement was the Investment Service of the Research and Statistical Bureau of the Sydney Stock Exchange. Other sources included accounts published by companies and returns lodged with registrars of companies. It covers accounts of non-finance public companies but excludes companies primarily engaged in mining or primary industry and companies operating mainly overseas.

18. Weights were applied to the rate of growth shown in note 17 in accordance with the number of revaluations in the respective periods.

19. In view of the fact that the average β of the revaluing companies listed in table 25.1 is 0.71, , somewhat less than the weighted market average of unity, it may be argued that a sample should have been selected with an average rate of increase of earnings less than the 10 per cent selected for table 25.5. Residuals were in fact calculated for several samples with average rates of growth in earnings varying between −2 per cent and 10 per cent. The CAR's for these samples were bounded on the low side by the CAR results of the "lower half" earnings sample shown in table 25.3 and on the high side by the CAR results of table 25.5.

20. That is, in the semi-strong sense as defined by Fama (1970a).

21. For a rigorous discussion of the limitations of the "market model" see Ball (1972b, pp. 343-53).

22. Ibid., p. 347.

26   Asset revaluations and stock prices: Alternative interpretations of a study by Sharpe and Walker

Philip Brown and Frank J. Finn

In 1975, Sharpe and Walker reported from a study of the behaviour of stock market prices around the time of 34 asset revaluation announcements[1] made by 32 Australian public companies. (This paper is reproduced in this book as chapter 25.) They found the announcements "were associated with substantial upwards movements in stock prices" (1975, p. 293), after abstracting from marketwide effects. Sharpe and Walker recognised the possibility that the stock price increases they observed might have been due to other events, such as earnings (p. 300) or dividend announcements (p. 303), or volatility changes (p. 308) which occurred at the time of the revaluation announcement. Nevertheless, they felt their results were "consistent with the related hypotheses that asset revaluation announcements influence stock prices and that such announcements convey information which has not previously been incorporated into stock prices as a result of other information sources" (p. 305).

This chapter explores further two alternative interpretations of their results.

Interpretation one. One interpretation is that announcements of changes in asset book values cause security analysts to change their assessments of the current values of these assets, and consequently to change the equilibrium prices of rights to participate in the cash flows which those assets generate—i.e., to change stock prices.

Interpretation two. An alternative interpretation is either that current values of assets are irrelevant (i.e., stock prices are independent of them), or that Sharpe and Walker's asset revaluation announcements were not newsworthy and that other contemporaneous and relevant events occurred.

As we noted above, Sharpe and Walker recognised the possibility of interpretation two, but preferred interpretation one as the explanar of their results. Interpretation two seems extreme, given the experimental controls they used. We argue, however, that it is not implausible.

The case for interpretation two

Few would argue that current values of assets are irrelevant, *ceteris paribus*, and we are not among them anyway. It is not obvious to us, however, that the asset revaluation announcements studied by Sharpe and Walker were newsworthy.

Sharpe and Walker note (1975, pp. 296–97) that the majority of the announcements they studied related to the revaluation of property or investments. Information concerning these assets is very often readily available to stock market agents at low marginal cost. A corporation's major holdings of property and investments frequently are common knowledge among security analysts. Indeed, information often can be obtained readily from public records. Again, Sharpe and Walker limited their study to revaluations of assets which, because of the relatively large dollar amounts involved,[2] would be likely to have come under the scrutiny of security analysts during their visitations, luncheons with executives and so forth. The likelihood that security analysts could have made unbiased assessments of the difference between book and current values would have been increased by the fact that many of the revalued assets had been held for some years.[3]

It is plausible, then, to conclude that security analysts had an incentive to predict current values, and that they could have done so in an unbiased way before the revaluation announcements were made. As plausible as this conclusion may be, it does mean that Sharpe and Walker's interpretation and conclusion contradict the Efficient Market Hypothesis—an hypothesis which has described well the behaviour of Australian stock prices (e.g., Ball, Brown and Finn 1977, and Hancock 1975)—unless other explanations for positive excess returns[4] can be found.

Earnings reports, dividend changes, and bonus issues

Earnings reports

In referring to earnings forecasts, Sharpe and Walker (1975, p. 302) postulated "that the market expects a company's earnings to grow (decline) by the same percentage in the revaluation year as in the preceding year", and argued that half the revaluations were associated with negative forecast errors and half with positive forecast errors. Average and cumulative average excess returns were then found to be large and positive for each earnings group.

A potential problem with the Sharpe and Walker classification is highlighted when we note that the mean estimated beta-coefficients of their upper and lower earnings groups were 0.829 and 0.529 respectively (1975, p. 301). If there is an association between beta-risk and its earnings analog, it is unlikely that the two groups were homogeneous with respect to earnings expectations.

Although Sharpe and Walker undertook a lengthy justification for their procedure, it does yield relatively inefficient predictions.[5] A more efficient forecasting assumption is that earnings this year will be unchanged.[6] The Sharpe and Walker sample included 29 cases where the accompanying earnings report was "favourable" (that is, earnings per share adjusted for capital changes increased).

Even if Sharpe and Walker did understate the proportion of "favourable" earnings reports, those reports, taken alone, are unlikely to explain more than perhaps a quarter of Sharpe and Walker's cumulative average excess return (compare table 18.3 in chapter 18).

Table 26.1   Summary of asset revaluations and related announcements

Company	Revaluation month[1] Sharpe & Walker	Revised	Bonus issue status[2]	Dividends[3]	Earnings[4]	Financial report[5]
1. Elec. Equipment	6908		S (1/2)	I	I (6906)	6908 (A)
2. Dunlop Rubber	6303		S (1/4)	I	I (6306)	6303 (I)
3. G. E. Crane	6009		N	D	I (6006)	6009 (A)
4. Concrete Industries	6004	6103	S (1/3)	I	I (6106)	6103 (I)
5. Castlemaine Perkins	6008		S (1/4)	I	I (6006)	6009 (A)
6. Brickworks Ltd	6109		X	I	I (6106)	6109 (A)
7. BHP	6009		S (1/2)	I	I (6005)	6008 (A)
8. Fairymead Sugar	6008	6005	S (1/1)	I	I (5912)	6005 (A)
9. Comeng	6011	6010	NL	D	I (6006)	6010 (A)
10. Broons	6904		S (1/4)	I	I (6906)	6902 (I)
11. Adelaide Cement	6108		S (1/1)	I	I (6105)	6107 (A)
12. Adelaide Cement	6901		S (1/4)	I	D (6905)	6901 (I)
13. Advertiser News	6310		S (1/1)	I	I (6312)	6402 (A)
14. Aust. United Investments	6707		S (1/2)	I	I (6706)	6707 (A)
15. Bennett & Fisher	6702		S (1/2)	S	I (6706)	6702 (I)
16. Wynyard Holdings	6308	6010	NA	NA	NA	NA
17. Trustees Executors	6308		X	I	I (6306)	6308 (A)
18. Howard Smith	6001		S (1/4)	I	I (5912)	6004 (A)
19. Qld Cement & Lime	6706		S (1/2)	I	D (6707)	6708 (A)
20. Provincial Traders	6905		C	I	I (6906)	6905 (I)
21. Perth Arcade	6709	6708	S (1/5)	I	I (6706)	6708 (A)
22. Myer	6910		X	S	I (6907)	6909 (A)
23. Mt Isa Mines	6004	5811	S (1/8)	D	D (5806)	5811 (A)
24. Mt Isa Mines	6307		S (3/2)	S	I (6306)	6309 (A)
25. McPhersons	6105		S (1/2)	I	D (6106)	6109 (A)
26. Silverton	6410	6409	N	S	I (6406)	6409 (A)
27. Hardie Holdings	6007		S (2/5)	I	I (6006)	6007 (A)
28. John Martin	6910		N	I	I (6907)	6909 (A)
29. Industrial Engineering	6710		S (1/4)	I	I (6706)	6708 (A)
30. Mauri Bros.	6010		S (1/4)	I	I (6006)	6009 (A)
31. Malleys	6410		X	S	I (6406)	6409 (A)
32. Aust. Paper Manuf.	6201	6112	S (1/4)	I	I (6206)	6201 (I)
33. APA Holdings	6810	6812	S (1/1)	I	I (6809)	6811 (A)
34. North Broken Hill	6001	5911	S (9/1)	S	I (5906)	5909 (A)

1. Month of revaluation announcement; revised when differs from SW (see note 9); 6908 is the 8th month of 1969, etc.

2. Bonus issue status:
   S = Simultaneous bonus issue announcement.
   N = No indication of bonus issue given.
   X = Announced that a bonus issue not intended.
   C = Announced "considering" a bonus issue: bonus issue was announced 6909.
   NL = Bonus issue not allowable under a trust deed.
   Figures in brackets are the terms of the bonus issue, e.g. (1/2) is a 1-for-2 bonus issue.

3. Dividends after the revaluation announcement month compared with dividends before, as described in the text.
   I = Increase; S = Steady; D = Decrease

4. Change in earnings per share for the fiscal year ending closest to the revised revaluation month. Month in brackets is the relevant balance date.
   I = Increase; D = Decrease

5. Announcement month for results of financial report released (to the stock exchanges) closest to the revised revaluation month. Brackets indicated annual (A) or half-yearly interim (I) report.

NA: Wynyard Holdings was a subsidiary company in 6010.

Dividend changes

Column 6 of table 26.1 classified all revaluations according to the status (increase/steady/decreasee) of the related dividend payout. Dividends per share (DPS) in the 12 months following the revaluation announcement month were compared with DPS, adjusted for capital changes, in the 12 months up to the announcement month. Our classification rule indicated 24 revaluations were accompanied by dividend increases, on 6 occasions dividends remained steady, and on 3 occasions they decreased.[7]

As with earnings reports, the proportion of dividend increases, taken alone, cannot explain more than a proportion of, perhaps at most half, Sharpe and Walker's cumulative average excess return (compare table 21.1 and figure 21.1 in chapter 21).

Bonus issues

Details of Sharpe and Walker's revaluation announcements and related bonus issue, earnings and dividend announcements, together with financial report dates, are summarised in table 26.1.[8]

In previous research (Ball, Brown and Finn 1977), we noted (but did not document) the fact that Australian corporations often announce bonus issues and asset revaluations simultaneously. The Sharpe and Walker selection is not atypical in this regard. Of 33 revaluation announcements, 24 were accompanied by a simultaneous bonus issue announcement, and on another occasion the firm announced that its board of directors was "to consider" a bonus issue (details of the issue came four months later).

As with stock splits in the United States (Fama et al. 1969), bonus issues in Australia have been shown to be associated with higher dividend payments and significant positive excess returns. Ball, Brown and Finn (1977), for example, found cumulative average excess returns of approximately 20 per cent over the 13 months up to the end of the bonus issue announcement month, and that almost half the 20 per cent occurred in the announcement month itself. *Ceteris paribus*, the incidence of bonus issues should have led Sharpe and Walker to observe some positive average excess returns in the period up to the revaluation announcement month. Sharpe and Walker report a 19.63 per cent cumulative average excess return over the 13 months up to the end of the asset revaluation announcement month, with 9.59 per cent occurring in the announcement month.

Unfortunately, we do not know if bonus issues can explain entirely Sharpe and Walker's excess returns. Apart from the difficulty of small sample inference, the answer partly depends on whether the association between excess returns and the announcement of a bonus issue is independent of the announcement of an asset revaluation as well.

Conclusion

How do we choose between interpretation one and interpretation two? In 30 out of 33 cases[9] studied by Sharpe and Walker, the corporation concerned either released an annual or interim report (containing earnings and dividend details) in the month of revaluation announcement, or announced a bonus issue in that month. In the remaining three cases, the annual report was released in the month immediately prior to the revaluation announcement. Of the 33 revaluations, 25 could be identified with bonus issues, 29 with increased earnings per share, and 24 with increased dividends per share.

Taken alone, bonus issues or dividend reports or profit reports might not explain fully Sharpe and Walker's results. But the fact of the matter is that they occurred jointly and within the time frame of reference of Sharpe and Walker's asset revaluation announcements. Thus, we suggest that interpretation two cannot be dismissed as a plausible explanation of their findings.

The question of whether asset revaluations *per se* affect stock prices cannot be answered until we understand better why asset revaluations occur and, in particular, how they are related to bonus issues, and dividend and earnings reports. In short, a sound theory, and better evidence, are needed to solve the puzzle posed by Sharpe and Walker.

Acknowledgments

This paper has benefited from the comments of Ray Ball and George Foster.

Notes

1. An asset revaluation occurs when an asset's book value is changed in the accounting records to reflect its "current value" (refer Sharpe and Walker 1975, p. 297).
2. Sharpe and Walker's (1975, p. 296) selection criteria required the revaluation to be at least $900,000 and to add 10 per cent to shareholders' funds.
3. For example, "During the year the Board obtained valuations of the Company's freehold premises in Melbourne and Sydney . . . to show the value of the assets concerned at more appropriate figures than those based on original cost some twenty-five years ago." (From the 1963 Annual Report of the Trustees Executors and Agency Co. Ltd, p. 11.)
4. Sharpe and Walker measured excess returns by cumulating the average residual from the "market model" (following Fama, Fisher, Jensen and Roll 1969).
5. Using Canadian data, Finn (1975) found that a zero growth forecast outperformed all other mechanical rules tested, including the rule used by Sharpe and Walker. Also Whittred (1978) found that changes in earnings per share for a sample of 104 Australian firms over the period 1960–74 were essentially independent.
6. We compared the "no change" forecasting model and Sharpe and Walker's model, using Whittred's (1978) data. In every year (1962 to 1969, the period common to Sharpe and Walker's and Whittred's data) the "no change" rule yielded a more accurate average forecast, the overall accuracy ratio being 5:3 (i.e., in 5 out of 8 occasions the "no change" rule was more accurate). On those occasions when the rules gave different results for the sign of the earnings forecast error, the accuracy ratio was 2:1 in favour of the "no change" forecast rule. Because the "no change" rule tends to overstate the proportion of "favourable" earnings reports, we also tested a second naive model, which was to predict that next year's earnings per share equals this year's plus the change since last year. The accuracy ratios in favour of the "no change" model were the same as above.
7. We tested the sensitivity of our dividend classifications by using three other rules: dividends in the 12 months beginning with the revaluation announcement month, to previous 12 months; and two half-yearly analogs to the annual dividend rules. The results were consistent with those reported here.
8. Some of our dates and figures differ from those in Sharpe and Walker's table 25.1 in chapter 25. Complete data are available on request.
9. We exclude Sharpe and Walker's revaluation 16, because the firm was an unlisted subsidiary at the time of revaluation.

27 Identifying some issues in current cost accounting

Ray Ball and Philip Brown

Postponement of current cost accounting (CCA) could be seen as evidence of a vacillating accounting profession. Alternatively, it could be evidence that the accounting profession must respond to the political and market pressures inherent in the nature of its policy choices and that it is the various political and market forces which are uncertain. A third explanation is that the practical issues in CCA implementation are greater than the profession believed. Whichever way it is viewed, the postponement does provide an opportunity to canvass the issues more widely, and to that extent it is to be welcomed.

We enter the debate, not because we support the introduction of CCA in the manner proposed by the Statement of Provisional Accounting Standards of October 1976, but because we believe that two allegedly major consequences of the introduction of CCA are relatively unimportant. In particular, we argue that the introduction of CCA will not significantly affect inflation, nor will it significantly affect the sharemarket averages.

There are several other significant issues, however, which do warrant careful debate. We discuss them in the context of the costs and benefits of introducing CCA, and the difficulties that policy makers face when assessing whether CCA's benefits are likely to exceed its costs.

CCA and inflation

There is a fear that the introduction of CCA will exacerbate inflation. A version of the argument runs as follows.

Businesses base their pricing decisions on buyer demand and product replacement cost, such that the higher the product replacement cost, the higher the price. If businesses do not know replacement costs, they base their pricing decisions on the available measure, namely historical costs (book values) of the products.

Reprinted from the *Australian Accountant* 47 (August 1977), 413–21, by permission of the authors and the publisher.

When CCA is introduced, many businesses will know for the first time the replacement costs of the products they sell. Since "inflation" implies costs on average are rising through time and since businesses typically hold stocks for some time before they are sold, products' replacement costs at the time of sale, on average, exceed their historical costs (book values). On the basis of their new knowledge—that product costs are higher—many businesses will raise their product prices, thus exacerbating inflation.

Key assumptions in this argument are that many businesses are unaware of replacement costs so that the introduction of CCA will bring a significant number of surprises, and that the net effect of those surprises will be biased in a particular way—namely, towards *increased* costs. But how many businesses do not already know, approximately, their product replacement costs? Do the guesses which are now being made tend to over- or under-estimate replacement costs?

If there is a widespread commercial incentive to provide internal information to managers on product replacement costs, is it not more reasonable to assume, as a working hypothesis, that replacement costs are already accessible by management, *whether or not they are supplied in a routine fashion by an accounting system?*

We argue, then, that even if there were an inflationary impact due to businesses becoming aware of the excess of replacement over historical cost, that impact would be felt long before the time of CCA's introduction. To argue otherwise is to argue that the average business is underestimating inflation. We submit that most businesses have a rough idea of replacement costs, even if those costs are not routinely reported in the accounts. Further, we would expect the "rough guesses" to be unbiased—to be overestimates about half the time and underestimates for the other half.[1]

Suppose the introduction of CCA is linked to its introduction for income tax purposes such that lower CCA profit figures are associated with reduced taxable incomes. Then one possible equilibrium solution is for lower rather than higher product prices, the crucial parameters being how, and to what extent, the government acts to maintain its total revenue.[2]

In arguing that CCA is inflationary, some seem to assume the implied target rate of return under CCA is much the same as under conventional (historical cost) reporting. It is unclear to us, however, that decision makers who use CCA's figures will choose to exclude from profit the holding gains on stock and equipment, as the profession's Provisional Standard proposes. Even if they do so choose, why should their target rates of return bear any close resemblance to their target rates under conventional reporting? It may well be the case, for example, that the current target rate of return under CCA is low or even negative for many firms, to be consistent with the rational depletion of capital stock in a situation of continuing excess of supply of investment assets.

In our opinion, there are good grounds for believing CCA's introduction will have little effect on inflation.

CCA and the share market

It is well known that the introduction of CCA will result in lower disclosed profits (and lower earnings per share) for most companies. But can the share market averages be expected to fall as a result? We believe the answer is, by and large, "No". Our reasoning is, once again, based on our belief that the market makers have made unbiased guesses about the effects of inflation, in this case on share values, and hence CCA cannot be *expected* to affect the share market averages in any particular direction. There seems as much reason to expect the market to overestimate the effect of inflation on profits as there is to expect it to underestimate the effect. Which way share prices will be affected by CCA reports seems an even-money bet.

In addition, we can't see much reason for the market's guess to be far wrong in either direction. It is not uninformed. Appreciation of CCA's effects on disclosed profits is widespread. Many accountants in commerce and industry (in share market terms "insiders") have looked closely at the question of how much difference CCA will make to the profits of companies with which they are associated closely. Inevitably, their conclusions will be reflected, if only indirectly, in the overall structure of share prices. The important point is that the share market is *presently* making guesses, however well informed they may be on an individual company basis, of the effect of inflation on the levels of company profits.

Numerous companies have disclosed CCA's effects on their profit figures including, for example, BP, CSR, Ford, Direct Acceptance, John Fairfax, Philips, and B. Seppelt & Sons (only some of these are listed on Australian stock exchanges).

Finally, security analysts and other share market "outsiders" have not ignored the situation. For example, J. M. Bowyer & Co. have published widely quoted estimates for "Australia's 50 largest companies by market capitalisation (excluding Woodside and Pancontinental)", which showed that reported profits would have averaged 37 per cent less if CCA had been adopted by each company for its financial year ending in 1976.

Thus, the share market is hardly ill-informed on the matter. The Bowyer estimates emphasise this point—they were derived from publicly available data and from estimates of asset purchase patterns and depreciation rates, without recourse to companies' internal records.

Belief in a general awareness of the average impact of CCA on corporate profits, coupled with the observation that market makers act quickly on useful information (and have an enviable tendency to ignore data that *ex ante* are useless), leads us to predict that the introduction of CCA will not affect the share market *averages* by any discernible amount, other things being equal. If CCA information is useful, some share prices will undoubtedly rise and others will fall, as the individual company profit results either exceed or fall short of the analysts' predictions. Thus, even if the share market finds CCA information to be useful in valuing individual shares, the share *averages* should not be affected significantly by CCA reports.

In an attempt to gain some limited appreciation of the effect of CCA profit reports on share prices, we computed the price movements which occurred when the Bowyer estimates were announced. Prices were observed two weeks before and two weeks after the day upon which the estimates were released. Appropriate allowance was made for dividends and other

Table 27.1   Share price reaction to J. M. Bowyer & Co. estimates of CCA pre-tax profits

	Bowyer Profit estimates		Share prices		Per cent changes	
	Historical ($m)	CCA ($m)	5/1/77 ($m)	2/2/77* ($m)	Profits (%)	Share prices (%)
CUB	27.4	20.8	1.70	1.65	−24.1	−2.9
Castlemaine	15.4	13.7	3.60	3.60	−11.0	0.0
Swan	12.1	10.7	1.28	1.31	−11.6	2.3
Tooth	18.6	16.0	1.61	1.58	−14.0	−1.9
Ansett	24.8	14.7	1.10	1.16	40.7	5.5
Brambles	16.8	13.2	1.40	1.50	−21.4	7.1
TNT	21.5	19.4	1.56	1.50	−9.8	−3.8
Coles	40.2	23.7	1.32	1.44	−41.0	9.1
Grace Bros.	14.7	8.3	1.70	1.80	−43.5	5.9
Myer	73.5	52.6	1.96	2.00	−28.4	2.0
Woolworths	30.9	12.9	1.20	1.24	−58.3	3.3
Ampol	15.6	5.8	0.66	0.68	−62.8	3.0
ACI	22.8	(1.3)	1.47	1.45	−105.7	−1.4
APM	24.8	6.8	1.24	1.32	−72.6	6.5
CIG	20.5	15.6	2.55	2.83	−23.9	11.0
Repco	26.1	13.4	1.30	1.35	−48.7	3.8
Boral	20.5	13.6	1.77	1.82	−33.7	2.8
Concrete Ind	14.5	10.8	1.28	1.36	−25.5	6.3
J. Hardie	25.1	20.6	5.30	5.40	−17.9	1.9
Pioneer Concrete	18.5	14.5	1.10	1.13	−21.6	2.7
AMATIL	24.8	(1.0)	1.56	1.50	−104.0	−3.8
P. Morris	43.6	32.3	8.30	8.20	−25.9	−1.2
Bougainville	78.0	73.2	1.25	1.29	−6.2	3.2
Comalco	28.9	12.7	2.25	2.50	−56.0	11.1
CRA	164.4	103.5	3.02	3.09	−36.9	2.3
EZ	12.0	1.3	2.85	2.85	−89.2	0.0
Hamersley	66.4	40.9	2.80	2.85	−38.4	1.8
MIM	44.7	19.4	2.42	2.55	−56.6	5.4
North BH	11.8	9.2	1.07	1.13	−22.0	5.6
Peko	9.6	1.2	4.30	4.40	−87.5	2.3
Thiess	15.0	8.8	2.10	2.00	−41.3	−4.8
Utah	240.9	231.5	4.80	4.68	−3.5	−2.5
WMC	20.5	5.9	1.60	1.48	−71.2	−7.5
ANZ	83.4	80.9	3.48	3.25	−3.0	−6.6
AGC	49.1	49.1	1.40	1.38	0.0	−1.4
Bank of NSW	109.0	106.1	5.08	4.80	−2.7	−5.5
CBA	35.5	34.6	2.52	2.50	−2.5	−0.8
CBC	23.6	22.7	1.88	1.58	−3.8	−16.0
IAC	7.1	6.9	0.75	0.68	−2.8	−9.3
National	74.5	73.4	2.65	2.50	−1.5	−5.7
BHP	284.6	129.3	7.60	7.40	−54.5	−2.6
Burns Philp	15.1	2.9	2.05	1.98	−80.8	−3.4
CSR	77.0	50.4	3.84	3.50	−34.5	−8.9
Dunlop	26.1	4.8	0.96	0.99	−81.6	3.1
Elder Smith	14.2	5.8	1.88	2.10	−59.2	11.7
Herald & W.T.	21.3	17.8	1.88	1.93	−16.4	2.7
Howard Smith	13.7	11.5	3.50	3.12	−16.1	−10.9
ICI	45.3	10.1	1.75	1.81	−77.7	3.4
Lend Lease	18.2	14.9	2.25	2.30	−18.1	2.2
Reckitt	16.7	13.0	3.00	3.32	−22.2	10.7
Average					−36.6	0.3

* Adjusted for dividends and rights (i.e., the only changes in the basis of share capitalisation).

changes in the basis of quotation for each share. Table 27.1 and figure 27.1 reveal what happened.

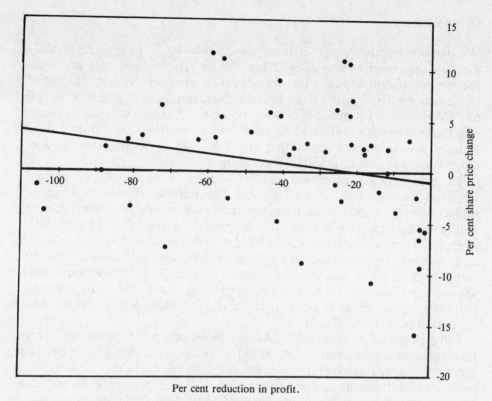

Figure 27.1   Relation between Bowyer CCA estimates and share prices

The general picture is that nothing happened. On average, prices rose moderately by about 1 per cent, compared with the average profit reduction under CCA of 37 per cent. The share market as a whole rose by about the same percentage (the Statex-Actuaries Accumulation Index rose by one twentieth of 1 per cent less than the average of the 50 Bowyer & Co. companies). Based upon the average price behaviour of the 50 shares, the share market does not seem to have been perturbed by the CCA estimates.

At the individual share level, there was, if anything, some tendency for price movements to be inversely related to the change in reported profit: the greater the reduction in profit from historical cost accounting to CCA, the better the average price performance.[3] This tendency is shown by the downward-sloping line on the graph, which is the best estimate of the relation which occurred between share prices and the CCA estimates. However, the tendency to move in the opposite direction (than that which most observers would expect) is slight. On average, a 10 per cent reduction in profit under CCA was associated with only a four-tenths of 1 per cent increase in share price. It would be close enough to say that *individual* share prices were unaffected by the Bowyer & Co. estimates.

There seems little evidence in these data to support the view that investors will be penalised in the share market if CCA is introduced. Either the Bowyer & Co. estimates are not perfect, or the share market disregards CCA figures, or the share market anticipates CCA figures with considerable accuracy, or (as seems likely) some combination of these effects occurred.

Other issues

We wonder whether some of the opposition to CCA can be explained by the fact that most of the alleged benefits of replacement cost accounting are already obtainable at a less formal level, whereas the costs of formally implementing CCA are yet to be met. Incidentally, the potential benefits of CCA include the promise of taxation relief, which some company executives might now consider is obtainable regardless of methods used in accounting to investors. As pointed out earlier, much depends upon the extent to which the government acts to maintain its revenue.

There is growing awareness of CCA's costs. Some costs are "internal", for example the costs of staff training, accounting system development, replacement price data acquisition, and increased auditor involvement; others will be imposed externally, such as the increased costs of policing by regulatory agencies. There are also costs associated with renegotiating agreements, such as borrowing contracts (e.g. adjustments to debenture trust deeds), executive compensation plans and other incentive schemes, and contractual profit-sharing arrangements such as partnership agreements. The costs are many, and they are not insignificant to users. The accounting policy makers would do well to study them closely.

Some potential benefits of CCA defy measurement. Suppose we accept, for argument's sake, that CCA would increase economic efficiency. How are we to satisfy ourselves that it is achieved? While there may be something to be said for the disclosure provisions of the CCA proposal, are the empirical research techniques sufficiently advanced to allow a follow-up study which can draw valid conclusions?

There is also the question of equity. The tax reform proposals, which bear some resemblance to the CCA proposal, reduce the general level of company tax. However, some companies (notably those with substantial investments in "monetary items" such as cash, accounts receivable, loans, and fixed-interest securities) will not experience noticeable tax reductions. This can be seen from the Bowyer & Co. estimates in table 27.1—the smallest reductions in profit under CCA are for the banks and finance companies. If the company tax rate is increased to maintain the government's revenue, then these companies will pay *more* tax under the tax reform proposals. Since CCA and the tax reform proposals are not divorced, banks and finance companies could be excused for believing that CCA is inequitable. Why should *their* profits appear to be higher?

Finally, there is the dubious relevance of replacement costs in an economy which is not replacing its capital. The conventional argument for replacement costs goes along the lines that non-replacement of capital is "bad" and that replacement-cost accounting is needed to alert managers and investors to this fact. This argument falls down if non-replacement of the capital stock is a rational occurrence.

If investors assess investments as now being riskier than when initially undertaken, as we believe they have in recent experience, then non-replacement of the capital stock is rational. We suggest this as an explanation of the current depression of investment activity. And if it is not worth replacing capital (i.e., if the total capital stock is to be run down), then on average the market worth of capital must be less than its replacement cost. In such times, how relevant is replacement cost information to investors?

Conclusion

The suggestions that CCA will reduce share prices and increase inflation seem wildly impractical. Managers, investors and other users of accounting reports are making implicit or explicit estimates of the effects of inflation, whatever they may be, at this very moment. It is feasible that those estimates are too high—that CCA income will be greater than currently expected; but it is also feasible that they are too low. Either way, we do not expect CCA's introduction will have much impact on either share prices or inflation.

The impact issues lie elsewhere. Perhaps the accounting profession has underestimated the direct and indirect costs of CCA. We believe that it has also overestimated the relevance of replacement costs in the present economic climate.

Notes

1. An alternative version of the argument is that business will act to restore their profit levels, however calculated, and that they will therefore raise product prices if CCA profits are reported. This version seems to assume that prices can be raised at will.
2. It could also be argued that the introduction of CCA might slightly reduce inflation through its effect on risk. If CCA provides information superior to that now available to investors and managers, then its introduction will eliminate some investor and management guesses—that is to say, it will reduce uncertainty. Now, ignoring for the moment the cost involved in CCA, a greater certainty consequent upon CCA's introduction, other things being equal, will lead risk-averse suppliers of capital to accept a *lower* expected return on investment, and this lower cost of capital will be passed on in the form of *reduced* product prices.
3. For the statistically minded, the Spearman rank-order correlation coefficient was -0.32, which (on the basis of a two-tailed t-test) is significant at the 0.05 level. We note that the t-statistic probably is overestimated, due to dependence among shares' rates of return. The product-moment coefficient was -0.21; and the r-square from the regression plotted on the graph was 4 per cent.

28 Takeovers: The Australian evidence

Peter Dodd and R. R. Officer

Introduction

Two fundamental questions arise in the context of takeovers: (1) What conditions give rise to takeovers? (2) Who benefits and/or who loses from takeovers?

The level of interest in takeovers depends on the level of takeover activity as the press, other financial commentators and politicians question the value of takeovers and seek answers to the questions posed above and related issues. In an earlier study (Dodd and Officer 1986) we have addressed many of these issues at an analytical level; in the current research we seek to resolve some of the empirical questions. This paper presents a preliminary summary of those empirical results. The complete report of the research appears in Bishop, Dodd and Officer (1987).

The pattern of takeover activity

It is frequently asserted that economic theory has an inadequate or no explanation for takeovers at an aggregate level. This is wrong as a generalisation, but a significant number of issues relating to takeovers are yet to be resolved. In theory, a merger of two enterprises (or a takeover) will occur when there exists some synergy between the enterprises, i.e. the value of the combination is greater than the value of the individual parts making up the takeover or merger. As a consequence we should be able to observe that the value of the ultimate enterprise is greater than the sum of the values of the enterprises going into the combination. We will be addressing this issue shortly. It still does not explain why there should be patterns or waves of takeover activity.

"Waves" of takeover activity have been noted for many years in the economics literature; moreover, these waves appear to transcend national

Reprinted from *Takeovers and Corporate Control*, proceedings of conferences on 9 June 1986 (Auckland) and 13 June 1986 (Sydney), Centre for Independent Studies, 1987, pp. 129–52, by permission of the authors and the publisher.

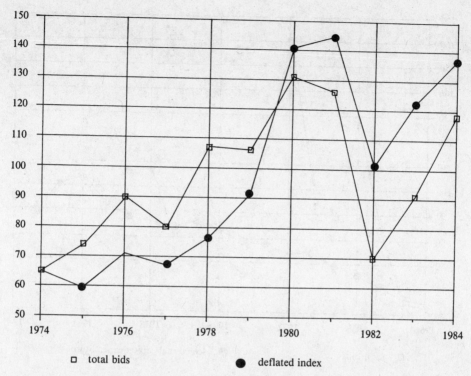

Figure 28.1   Total number of takeover bids and deflated Statex Actuaries Accumulation Index

boundaries. For example, the first episode of intense merger activity in the United States was observed early in the twentieth century, the second in the 1920s, another wave was noted in the late 1960s and more recently we have seen another wave of growth in takeovers in the 1980s. The latest wave appeared to start early in the 1980s, then slacken off slightly, but it has proceeded with renewed intensity in the mid-1980s. A similar pattern can be observed in Australia, although the analysis contained in the chapter commences only in 1972.

In theory, the motivation underlying a takeover is to increase company profitability, but this still does not explain why there should be cyclical movements in takeovers. Tobin (1969) advanced a theory that when the market value of a firm's assets is greater than the replacement cost of those assets, the firm will be induced to invest in more of those assets since the value of the new capital investment would exceed its replacement cost. Tobin's measure has become known as the q-ratio (q = market capitalisation of all the firm's assets/the replacement cost of those assets in the physical market). A related implication of Tobin's theory is that firms with q-values greater than the q-values of firms with similar assets would be inclined to take them over, i.e. $q^B > q^T$ where B is the bidding firm and T the target firm. No Australian evidence on q-values is available as yet, but in a recent United States study Hasbrouck (1985) reports that target companies are characterised by low q-values. This theory is consistent with synergy as the driving mechanism for takeovers, but it does not explain why these differential valuations should go in waves.

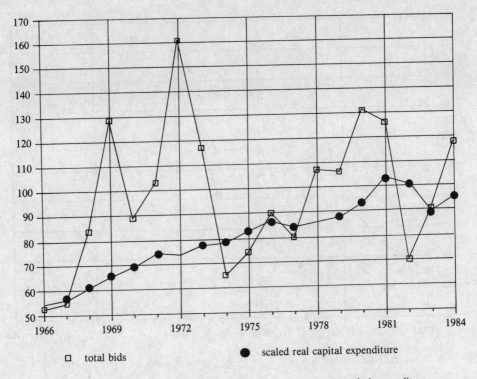

□ total bids   ● scaled real capital expenditure

Figure 28.2   Total number of takeover bids and scaled real gross capital expenditure

The relationship between the number of successful takeovers and the deflated Statex Actuaries Accumulation Index is depicted on figure 28.1 for the period 1974-84. Clearly, there is a close relationship between the buoyancy of the stock market and the number of successful takeovers; this evidence is also consistent with that found overseas and reported in Melicher, Ledolter and D'Antonio (1983).

A number of possible explanations can be given for the relationship between the state of the share market and the number of takeovers, but as yet we have not had time to explore them in sufficient detail to give a satisfactory conclusion. The explanation we prefer, on analytical grounds, is that periods of stock market boom are periods of optimism for investment, and firms can increase their investment by either internal or external (takeovers) means. This theory requires that the opportunities for synergy between two companies increase during periods of stock market buoyancy and decrease when the stock market falls. This is quite plausible in that the expanded demand for real goods in the economy that created the stock market boom also creates various economies of scale, which could lead to synergy between firms. Our theory would require investment decisions to be pro-cyclical, i.e., a positive correlation between the stock market index and internal and external investment decisions of firms (and also Tobin's q). Again, preliminary support for the theory is evident in figure 28.2, which graphs the relationship between successful takeovers and real capital expenditure.

Who benefits, who loses?

If one were to judge takeovers on the basis of the press comments surrounding them, particularly adverse comments, and the many calls for the regulation of takeovers, particularly the requirement for disclosure of financial and other information by bidding companies, one would be led to the conclusion that it is the target company's shareholders who are likely to lose as a result of a takeover. However, the evidence is overwhelmingly in the opposite direction: if there is one group who benefits from takeovers, it is the shareholders of target companies. To our knowledge there has not been a single study examining the effects of takeovers that has documented evidence that, as a generality, the shareholders of target companies do not benefit from takeovers. This includes studies from around the world, using a variety of experimental techniques to examine the effect of takeovers.

However, the evidence with respect to the wealth effects on the shareholders of bidding companies as a result of takeovers is not as clear. For example, Jensen and Ruback (1983), in a survey of the evidence from the United States, conclude that "the target company's shareholders benefit, and that bidding firm shareholders do not lose". One of the reasons for the apparent uncertainty with respect to the benefits that bidding company's shareholders receive is that bidding companies are usually much larger than target companies. This means that if the benefits of a takeover were to be shared equally between the bidding company's shareholders and the target company's shareholders, the target company's shareholders would receive a higher return on their investment in the company than the bidding company's shareholders. We would expect, under these circumstances, the greater dilution of the benefits to the shareholders of bidding companies to make it more difficult to detect benefit of the takeover to this group of shareholders.

In this study we will restrict our examination of the effects of takeovers to the shareholders of acquiring and target companies. Other groups that may be affected by takeovers, such as the consumers of the products of the companies involved in the takeover (who may be adversely affected by a reduction in competition), management, and employees, will not be examined, although we have explored the possible effects on such groups in another paper (Dodd and Officer 1986). However, we should note in passing that there is no consistent or unambiguous evidence suggesting that any of these groups are adversely affected by takeovers.

Measuring the effect of takeovers on shareholders

There are two basic ways in which the effect on shareholders of takeovers could be examined. One way is to examine the accounting records of companies before and after the takeover to see whether reported earnings, assets and other variables respond positively to the effect of the takeover. The other way is to examine the shareholders' dividends and capital gains that can be attributed to the takeover.

There are a number of severe problems in using accounting numbers to examine the effect of takeovers.

(a) The effect of a takeover may take some years to be fully reflected in accounting earnings, so that the accounting returns would need to be examined for an extended period after the takeover. Moreover, because the effect of a takeover is likely to be felt at different intervals of time after the takeover for different firms, any aggregation of the effects is likely to be diluted, making it more difficult to analyse.

(b) Accounting practices vary enormously between companies. Even companies in the same industry, operating under the same accounting standards, can adopt accounting methods that lead to significant differences in reported earnings. Aggregating the effect of a variety of accounting practices on companies under takeover will lead to ambiguity and possible bias.

(c) Any bias in reported accounting numbers, particularly earnings, is not necessarily self-correcting as is any bias in capital market rates of return. There is no obvious arbitrage strategy that can be adopted by shareholders and other investors if it is perceived that reported accounting earnings are consistently biased relative to "true" earnings. Shareholders cannot trade accounting numbers. Any bias that is detected would be immediately impounded or corrected in share market prices, so that although capital market rates of return are unbiased, accounting numbers could be significantly biased. This does not imply that accounting numbers are useless, or that they are not the main source of information for share market investors. It is the relative changes in a company's reported earnings that are important to investors when they assess whether a company's shares are over- or undervalued, not the absolute level of accounting income.

(d) Acquiring companies that pay a premium in a takeover relative to the target company's net tangible assets report that premium as "goodwill" in the asset account. Under existing accounting standards, such goodwill must be written off through the profit and loss account within 20 years. Moreover, the company will usually write up the value of other assets. The consequence is likely to be a reduction in the reported earnings of the company after the takeover. The ratio of accounting earnings divided by net tangible assets after a takeover is likely to be a biased measure of the "true" rate of return. In general, accounting figures are not satisfactory measures of rates of return.

The preferred method of measuring the effect of takeovers on shareholders is through capital market rates of return after adjusting for capital changes such as stock splits, bonus issues and rights issues, and adding back any cash distribution such as dividends to capital changes. This methodology is also not without its problems. Share prices reflect the expectations of future cash flows. Future benefits are capitalised into the current share price. This implies that current shareholders are able to obtain the benefit of capital appreciation in their shares. However, it is always possible that the expected benefits of a takeover will not be realised. In these circumstances the share price would overvalue the benefit of a takeover. The converse is also true: the benefit of a takeover may be underestimated in the share price. In short, we cannot be sure that the change in share price that capitalises the expectations of the effect of a takeover will accurately reflect the true effects of takeover on the fortunes of a company and its shareholders.

Nonetheless, although the share returns of a specific company undergoing a specific takeover may be wrong, we would not expect any consistent bias in returns across all companies. In other words, the share market prices and the capital market rates of return estimated from these will be unbiased estimates of the future benefits arising as a result of takeovers. Should any bias develop, then there is an opportunity for investors to capitalise on that bias by adopting profitable trading strategies. The effect of such trading strategies would eliminate the bias. Therefore, although it is possible to criticise the market's expectation of the effect of a takeover on the performance of a company in a specific instance, such criticism is not legitimate in aggregate or over extended periods of time. The statistical law of large numbers ensures that measurement errors that are independent and therefore not a result of any consistent bias will cancel each other out in an aggregate sample of firms involved in takeovers. The use of capital market rates to assess takeovers has none of the disadvantages that were listed above for accounting numbers.

A suitable control

In any scientific study it is necessary to establish a suitable control against which the symptoms or effects under study can be assessed. We are concerned with isolating the effect of a takeover on the performance of companies from all the other effects on company performance. One method of approaching this problem is to adopt a control firm so that every firm that has undergone a takeover, either as target or acquirer, would have assigned to it a similar firm that has not undergone a takeover.

The problem with this approach is finding a firm that is similar. The fact that one firm is involved in a takeover and the other is not is likely to indicate substantial prior differences between the firms apart from the mere fact of the takeover. For example, firms that have a cash surplus or borrowing potential but are limited in the amount of internal investment (e.g. plant expansion) that they can undertake are likely to expand their operations by external investments, i.e., takeovers. The converse is true for firms with internal growth potential. The two firms may be equally good investments, so that their returns may be identical. A comparison between the two firms would suggest that the takeover did not benefit the firm that grew by external investment; however, such an inference would be wrong because the firm that grew by takeover did not have the opportunity to grow by internal investment.

In general, we would not expect external investment, that is, investment by takeovers, to be a superior strategy to internal investment, that is, growth by investment in plant and equipment. It depends on the circumstances facing companies. If takeovers were a superior investment strategy, we would expect more and more companies to enter the takeover game until the rewards were diminished and the returns were consistent with alternative forms of investment. The converse is also true. Therefore, a matching-firm control is hazardous because of the difficulty in finding the correct matching firm, viz., the firm that could have and should have grown by takeover but did not, but was identical to the firm involved in the takeover in all other respects.

An alternative approach to the matching-firm control is to form separate portfolios of bidding firms and target firms, and then compare the performance of these portfolios with the portfolio that incorporates the market for all equities (shares). The notion behind this control is that all the other factors that affect share prices, such as the state of the economy, government policy, etc., will be captured in the market portfolio. Therefore, the only distinguishing feature between the market portfolio and the portfolio of acquiring or target companies will be takeover activity.

There are a number of useful alternative models that adopt the market portfolio as the basic control. These are variously known as the capital asset pricing model, the unconstrained market model, the constrained or zero-one market model, and various multifactor models that incorporate the market as the main factor. The models have various attributes and disadvantages. It would be digressive to discuss the advantages and disadvantages of each. It suffices to comment that we adopted the zero-one market model on the grounds of its simplicity. This makes the interpretation of the results more straightforward than if other, more sophisticated models had been used.

The unconstrained market model is described as:

$$r_{pt} = \alpha_p + \beta_p r_{mt} + u_{pt} \tag{1}$$

where

r_{pt} is the portfolio return over time period t;

α_p is a constant or intercept term;

β_p is a slope coefficient that measures the sensitivity of the portfolio return to the market return;

r_{mt} is the market return over time period t; and

u_{pt} is the portfolio's residual return, i.e., that part of its return that is unexplained by the market. By definition, the unconditional u_{pt} of all firms making up the market portfolio has an expected value of zero.

The zero-one market model constrains the intercept term to zero and assigns the value of 1 for the beta coefficient.

The effect of a takeover on the portfolio is measured by the residual or abnormal return u_{pt}, which represents the part of the return that is unexplained by the market. Since our portfolio differs from the market only in that it was involved in a takeover, u_{pt} represents the effect of the takeover on the portfolio's return. The u_{pt}'s are calculated over a period of time around the takeover to measure the cumulative abnormal return or the full effect of the takeover as it is capitalised into share price returns.

If all the information about a takeover were capitalised into the share price at one point in time for all firms, relative to the public announcement date of a takeover, then we would need to observe only one value for u_{pt}. However, the share market's expectations of the effect of the takeover are modified as news of the takeover becomes impounded into price around the period of the takeover. Because this information becomes impounded into share prices at different times for different firms, it is necessary to accumulate the abnormal return over the period during which news relating to takeovers is released. We will have more to say about this in our discussion of the results.

Data

The sample of takeovers covers the period from January 1972 to December 1985, and is derived originally from the Sydney Stock Exchange's publications *Current Offers* and *Takeover Offers*. The sample includes only offers for ordinary shares and excludes schemes of arrangement and other non-takeover transactions. The relevant details of the offers were collected from the files of the Sydney Stock Exchange, from the financial press, and from surveys of individual companies involved. These details include:
* the date of the initial public announcement of the offer;
* the price offered;
* the percentage of issued shares sought in the offer;
* the percentage of issued shares held by the bidder prior to the offer;
* the closing date of the offer; and
* the outcome of the offer in terms of the percentage of shares held after the close of the offer as well as the date at which that outcome was publicly available.

For some offers it was not possible to collect a complete set of data required from the above sources. Offers that fell into this category were used only when there was sufficient data available for a particular class of firm involved in a takeover.

The sample includes offers for target firms listed on the Sydney Stock Exchange as well as offers by bidders listed on the exchange for unlisted target firms. Therefore, some transactions are included where either the bidder or the target firm was not listed. To be included in the analysis, sample firms had to have available stock price data on the files of the Centre for Research and Finance at the Australian Graduate School of Management.

Each takeover offer was classified as to its outcome using the following rule: If the offer was not withdrawn and the bidder held over 50 per cent of the target company's issued shares after the bid (and did not hold over 50 per cent prior to the bid), the offer was defined as "successful". If the offer was not withdrawn and the bidder held less than 50 per cent after the offer, the offer was defined as "unsuccessful". We recognise that this definition is subject to misclassification, especially when a bidder is able

Table 28.1 Sample breakdown

Targets	Successful	506
	Unsuccessful	117
	Withdrawn	136
	Outcome unknown	214
	TOTAL	973
Bidders	Successful	419
	Unsuccessful	82
	Withdrawn	114
	Outcome unknown	139
	TOTAL	754

to achieve an effective operating control of the target with less than 50 per cent of the issued shares. However, for the purposes of the analysis it is impractical to inspect each transaction on a case by case basis.

The sample that met the above data requirements and is used in the analysis is shown in table 28.1.

The average relative market capitalisation (measured in $000) six months before the announcement of takeover is shown in table 28.2.

Table 28.2 Capitalisation of sample

	Mean	Median
Targets	28,359	5,291
Bidders	108,168	29,341
Target as a % of bidder	26.2	18

The difference in average capitalisations suggests that the bidding companies are of the order of four to five times larger than the target companies. Also, it is worth noting that the extreme differences between the mean and median reflect the very strong positive skewness in the distributions of the size of both the target and bidding companies.

Results

The results are shown first as graphs of cumulative abnormal returns (CAR's), i.e., cumulative abnormal residuals of the zero-one market model described as u_{pt} in equation (1) above. These graphs start accumulating the abnormal returns 36 months before the announcement of a takeover. The announcement month is shown as zero, so that three years before the takeover would be designated as -36 months; similarly $+4$ indicates four months after the announcement date.

The announcement date is when it is assumed that the takeover is announced publicly. In many cases the imminent announcement of a takeover is anticipated by the market so that the market tends to react before the formal announcement. Further, the probability that the takeover will be consummated is usually less than 1 at the announcement date. This means that it is not surprising to see the cumulative average residuals rise after the announcement date as the probability that the takeover will be consummated comes closer to certainty. Where the CAR's flatten out in the graph it is an indication that there is no longer a positive accumulation of abnormal returns; the abnormal returns are approaching zero, which is expected for the market as a whole. Note also that the graph is an average of the market reaction to takeovers. For individual takeovers the market reaction is not as smooth as is depicted in the graph. The graph does, however, depict the typical or average market reaction.

The results are also presented in tables describing in more detail the characteristics of the cumulative abnormal returns at particular times. In effect, these tables describe the distributional properties of the CAR's for the time interval indicated. Because of uncertainty about the properties of the distributions of these CAR's, the distributions are described by the mean, median, first quartile, third quartile, number of positive abnormal returns, and number of negative abnormal returns. Because of the problems associated with the distribution of abnormal returns we have not attempted to derive any form significance tests of the returns. We believe that the information provided allows the reader to clearly assess whether or not the takeover has benefited a particular shareholder group whose abnormal returns are described by the tables.

All bidding companies

Figure 28.3 shows the abnormal returns to all the bidding companies in the sample from three years before the formal announcement of the takeover offer to two years after the announcement. The graph shows that starting from three years before the takeover, the average abnormal returns for all the bidding companies accumulate to peak at approximately one month after the formal announcement. The CAR is about 25 per cent over the 38 months, i.e., 36 months before the takeover and approximately 2 months after the formal announcement. The graph indicates that approximately 2 months after the formal announcement there are no abnormal returns, on average, to the bidding companies.

Because it is unlikely that a takeover would be anticipated a full three years before its announcement, the almost monotonic increase in the CAR's over the three-year period suggests that bidding companies are typically companies who have been doing well. This, to some extent, confounds the actual effect of the takeover on a bidding company. However, as we might expect, once companies have made a bid and therefore have clearly identified themselves as being companies with abnormal returns, allowing the effect of the bid to be impounded into share prices (which we assume has occurred by two months after the announcement of the takeover), the companies no longer earn abnormal returns. If the abnormal returns were to continue after this date there would be a clear strategy open to investors to invest in companies that make bids for other companies to earn abnormal returns. The fact that the abnormal returns do not continue after the completion of the takeover offer indicates that such a strategy would not yield abnormal returns, and therefore the market can be judged as being efficient with respect to the information surrounding a takeover offer.

Table 28.3 describes the cumulative abnormal returns over specific time period for all bidding companies. The first column in the table records the cumulative abnormal return from three years before the announcement to one year before the announcement. This column indicates that on average bidding companies over this two-year period had cumulative abnormal returns of around 12 per cent. The bottom 25 per cent of the bidding companies had less than −15 per cent abnormal return, and the top 25 per cent had greater than 45 per cent abnormal return. Further, there were about 60 per cent more companies with positive CAR's over this period than with negative CAR's. Overall, it would be reasonable to conclude that from three years to one year before the announcement of a takeover, bidding firms experienced, on average, positive abnormal returns.

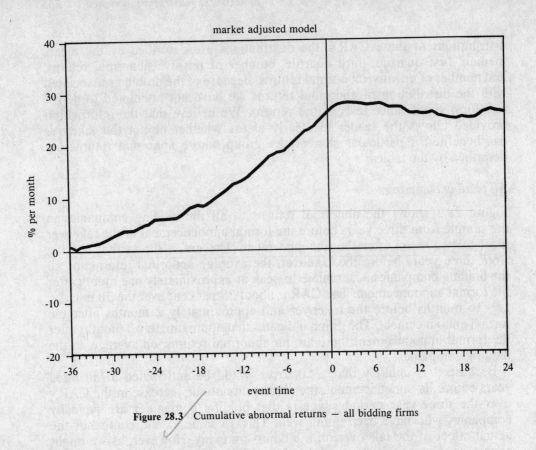

Figure 28.3 Cumulative abnormal returns — all bidding firms

Table 28.3 The returns to shareholders of all bidding firms (CAR's over specific time intervals)

	Period of the cumulative abnormal return relative to the takeover announcement month (month 0)			
	−36 to −11	−11 to 0	+1 to +2	−3 to +3
Mean	12.6	12.1	1.4	6.0
Median	12.4	10.8	0.7	5.2
25th percentile	−15.2	−7.9	−6.2	−10.0
75th percentile	45.9	33.1	8.7	21.5
No. +ive CAR's	468	468	397	465
No. −ive CAR's	295	295	353	315

A similar interpretation can be made for the second and third columns of table 28.3 where the CAR's are examined for the twelve months before the announcement up to and including the announcement month, and from the announcement month to two months after the announcement. The final column looks at the abnormal returns three months before the announcement month to three months after. This seven-month period probably captures most of the information surrounding a takeover that is relevant to a bidding company. The results indicate that, on average, bidding firms benefit from a takeover, although not all bidding firms experience positive abnormal returns over this period—40 per cent of the sample experienced negative abnormal returns.

Successful bidding companies

Figure 28.4 depicts the cumulative abnormal return behaviour of companies that successfully took over the target company. The sample is a subset of the previous all-bidding-company sample. The pattern of CAR's is very similar to the all-bidding sample and the same points made with respect to that sample are relevant.

Table 28.4 describes the CAR's over specific time intervals for successful bidding companies. The results are broadly similar to those for all bidding firms and the conclusions remain much the same: in general, successful bidding companies earn abnormal returns and these returns can be associated with the takeover.

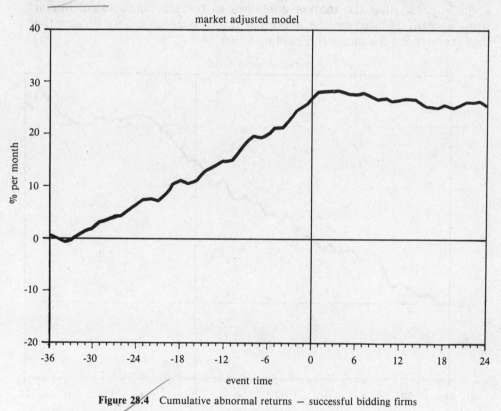

Figure 28.4 Cumulative abnormal returns — successful bidding firms

Table 28.4 The returns to shareholders of successful bidding firms (CAR's over specific time intervals)

	Period of the cumulative abnormal return relative to the takeover announcement month (month 0)			
	−36 to −11	−11 to 0	+1 to +2	−3 to +3
Mean	11.8	12.1	1.6	7.9
Median	9.9	10.5	1.3	7.5
25th percentile	−18.5	−7.9	−5.6	−8.4
75th percentile	45.2	32.4	7.7	22.6
No. +ive CAR's	208	238	202	236
No. −ive CAR's	154	132	161	133

Unsuccessful bidding companies

Unsuccessful bidding companies are companies that made a bid but were unable to acquire 50 per cent of the target company's issued shares. We could expect that a significant proportion of these companies would become locked into the target company's share register but without control. In such circumstances we would expect the market to review adversely the performance of these firms, which should result in abnormal losses and a consequential downturn in the CAR's.

Figure 28.5 depicts the CAR's of unsuccessful bidding companies. In contrast to the above expectations, the CAR's continue to increase after the announcement month for about six months and then appear to plateau. The graph suggests that the market continues to revalue unsuccessful bidding firms upwards. Moreover, the abnormal return is considerably greater than that experienced for successful bidding firms.

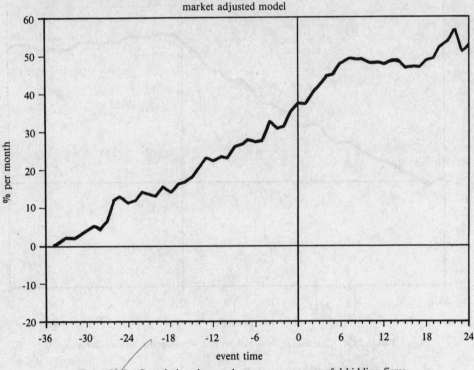

market adjusted model

Figure 28.5 Cumulative abnormal returns — unsuccessful bidding firms

Table 28.5 The returns to shareholders of unsuccessful bidding firms (CAR's over specific time intervals)

	Period of the cumulative abnormal return relative to the takeover announcement month (month 0)			
	−36 to −11	−11 to 0	+1 to +2	−3 to +3
Mean	21.8	14.8	2.5	10.0
Median	20.1	15.1	−0.7	6.5
25th percentile	−3.9	−4.4	−8.7	−4.5
75th percentile	52.9	30.2	13.1	23.0
No. +ive CAR's	64	59	37	58
No. −ive CAR's	25	30	44	30

One explanation of this apparently anomalous result is that the unsuccessful bidding firms are bought out of their holding at a higher price than their offer price; in effect, the firms represent successful "greenmailers". A number of companies like Industrial Equity Ltd have a successful history of making takeover offers and then being bought out of their holdings at a considerable profit. The persistent increasing post-offer abnormal returns in the graph are again due to the averaging effect across bidders, where abnormal returns from greenmail occur at different points in time relative to the initial takeover announcement.

Table 28.5 shows the CAR's for unsuccessful bidding companies over specific time intervals. It is clear from these results, particularly the first column, that unsuccessful bidding firms are firms that have significant positive abnormal returns well before the takeover offer. These positive returns could reflect the fact that many of these firms, and in fact bidders in general, make a succession of takeover offers, and that the market has capitalised the expectation that they will continue to make offers and be bought out at considerable profit to themselves. Also, it should be noted that the number of firms in this category (about 80) is much smaller than that in other categories. The table also indicates a significant increase in abnormal returns after the announcement date. These results are consistent with a proportion of these unsuccessful bidders being successful greenmailers.

Bidding companies that withdrew their bids

Figure 28.6 depicts a pattern of abnormal returns for companies that made a bid but then withdrew it. The results indicate that the abnormal returns

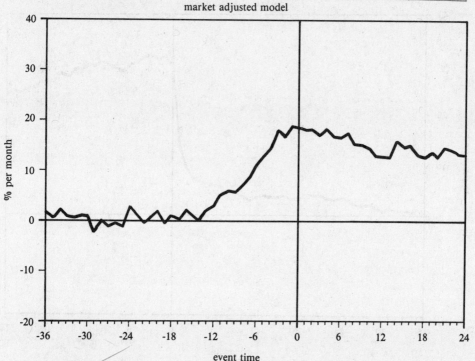

Figure 28.6　Cumulative abnormal returns — bidding firms that withdrew their bids

Table 28.6 The returns to shareholders of bidding firms that withdrew their bids (CAR's over specific time intervals)

	Period of the cumulative abnormal return relative to the takeover announcement month (month 0)			
	−36 to −11	−11 to 0	+1 to +2	−3 to +3
Mean	8.7	16.1	−1.5	1.8
Median	18.5	20.1	0.0	3.3
25th percentile	−10.4	−6.3	−9.8	−19.2
75th percentile	45.6	40.4	5.9	16.1
No. +ive CAR's	84	90	60	74
No. −ive CAR's	43	39	64	56

leading up to the offer are considerably lower than for other categories within the sample of bidding firms; moreover, abnormal returns begin to appear only a little over twelve months before the announcement of the offer. Further, there is some suggestion that the market revises its estimate of the value of such companies in that the CAR's tend to drop in the period after the offer.

The results in table 28.6 confirm the results depicted by figure 28.6.

All target companies

Figure 28.7 depicts the behaviour of CAR's for all target companies in the sample (approximately 980 companies). The results indicate that most of the large positive abnormal returns occur in the six-month period prior to

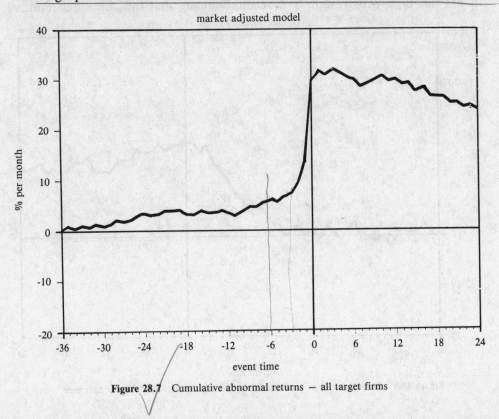

Figure 28.7 Cumulative abnormal returns — all target firms

Table 28.7 The returns to shareholders of all target firms (CAR's over specific time intervals)

	Period of the cumulative abnormal return relative to the takeover announcement month (month 0)			
	−36 to −11	−11 to −7	−6 to +1	−3 to +3
Mean	2.0	1.7	22.2	21.0
Median	3.9	0.1	20.8	16.7
25th percentile	−26.3	−12.4	0.9	0.3
75th percentile	33.5	13.5	43.2	39.6
No. +ive CAR's	436	388	626	638
No. −ive CAR's	384	382	207	207

the announcement of the offer. The abnormal returns show a premium of about 35 per cent, but there is some suggestion of a revised estimate after the announcement of the takeover in that the CAR's tend to fall. The reason for this will be explained when the behaviour of withdrawn bids is examined.

Table 28.7 confirms the general impressions derived from figure 28.7. Nearly all the abnormal returns to the portfolio of target companies is achieved over the seven-month period from three months before the target has received its offer to three months after. The results unambiguously indicate high returns to target company shareholders: on average the shareholders receive about 22 per cent positive abnormal return over this period.

Successful target companies

Successful target companies are those in which the offerer company gains a shareholding greater than 50 per cent during the offer. The pattern of

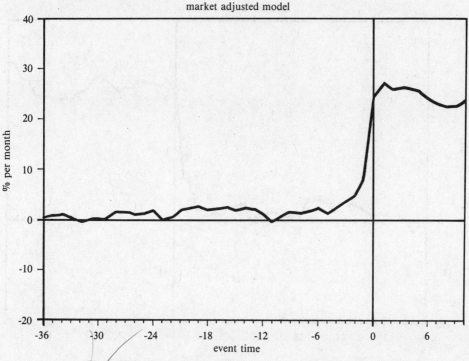

Figure 28.8 Cumulative abnormal returns − successful target firms

Table 28.8 The returns to shareholders of successful target firms (CAR's over specific time intervals)

	Period of the cumulative abnormal return relative to the takeover announcement month (month 0)			
	−36 to −11	−11 to −7	−6 to +1	−3 to +3
Mean	−0.4	0.4	21.9	20.1
Median	2.4	−0.3	21.3	16.5
25th percentile	−27.2	−12.7	2.2	0.5
75th percentile	32.4	12.2	43.1	39.3
No. +ive CAR's	240	216	362	360
No. −ive CAR's	220	221	108	113

the CAR's for successful target comanies (figure 28.8) broadly reflects the pattern of returns for the total sample of target companies as described in figure 28.7. Table 28.8 confirms the results: target companies that are subject to a successful bid for more than 50 per cent of their issued equity capital earn significant abnormal returns for their shareholders.

Unsuccessful target companies

Companies that were targeted for takeover but in which the bidding company obtained less than 50 per cent of the issued equity capital show abnormal returns not dissimilar to those of successful target companies. From figure 28.9 it appears that the target companies where the offerer was unsuccessful in gaining control do not suffer in terms of the valuation placed on them by the share market. Table 28.9 confirms these results.

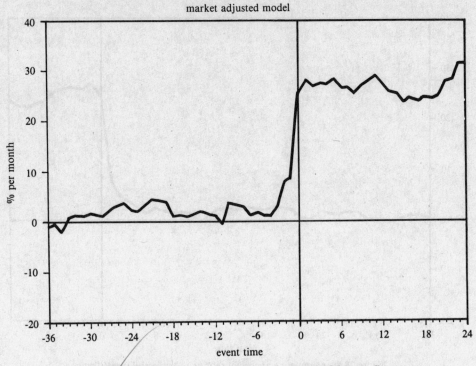

Figure 28.9 Cumulative abnormal returns − unsuccessful target firms

Table 28.9 The returns to shareholders of unsuccessful target fir...

	Period of the cumulative abnorma... to the takeover announcement month (...			
	−36 to −11	−11 to −7	−6 to +1	
Mean	−0.3	−0.1	22.6	
Median	0.4	0.8	19.4	17.7
25th percentile	−29.7	−15.9	−2.3	0.4
75th percentile	26.5	10.9	42.8	35.2
No. +ive CAR's	39	35	59	67
No. −ive CAR's	37	34	22	15

The evidence is that target companies subject to unsuccessful takeover offers do not suffer adverse market reaction relative to successful offers. This may suggest that the synergy between the target and the offer company is not the prime reason for the revaluation of the target company. A likely explanation is that the market expects these target companies to be subject to successful offers at a later date.

Withdrawn bids: Target companies

Figure 28.10 depicts the pattern of CAR's of target companies that had the bid for their shares withdrawn by the offerer companies. The graph indicates that this sample of companies was performing abnormally well before the offerer made the bid, or more accurately before the capital market

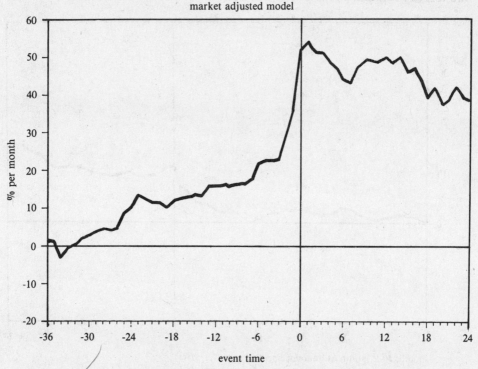

market adjusted model

Figure 28.10 Cumulative abnormal returns — target firms whose bid was withdrawn

...se bid was withdrawn (CAR's over specific

	Cumulative abnormal return relative ...ver announcement month (month 0)		
	−11 to −7	−6 to +1	−3 to +3
	1.2	30.5	23.3
	0.7	30.5	18.0
	−12.3	4.4	3.6
	13.0	50.4	44.0
	50	82	81
42	43	20	23

...m the offerer company. The results are confirmed by

...evidence of a downward revision in the market's value of such t... ...mpanies: CAR's decline slightly in the months following a withdraw. .id. The decline is not significant but it does suggest some downward revision in the market's value of the company, possibly reflecting a change in the expectation that such companies are going to be subject to another bid.

Conclusion

The overriding conclusion of this study is that takeovers, on average, are value-creating investments. The results show that shareholders of bidding and target companies earn positive abnormal returns at the time of a takeover.

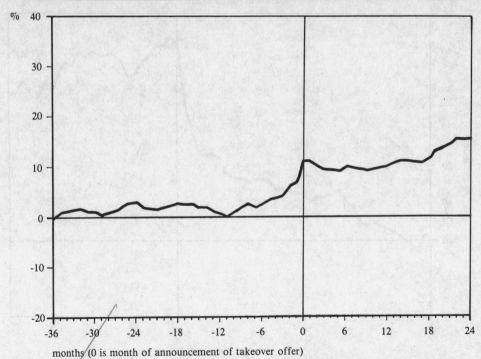

Figure 28.11 Cumulative abnormal returns — value-weighted portfolio of all sample firms engaged in takeover activity

Perhaps the most succinct representation o̶f̶ ̶
figure 28.11. As noted earlier, bidding firms on a̶
than targets. To account for this size discrepancy and ̶
results are not overstated by that discrepancy, the abnormal ̶
bidders and all targets are weighted by their relative market capit̶a̶
and then aggregated. This result is presented in figure 28.11. In effect t̶h̶
is the performance of a value-weighted portfolio of all sample firms engaged
in takeover activity. Such a portfolio earns large positive abnormal returns
from takeover offers and this result is evidence of the benefits accruing to
shareholders from takeover effects.

The evidence on takeovers in Australia is clear: as the economic theory
presented in Dodd and Officer (1986) predicts, takeovers are value-creating
investments. On the basis of this evidence, regulatory proposals to restrict
takeovers must be severely questioned. Such proposals cannot be sensibly
premised on arguments that takeovers waste resources. Indeed, inhibiting
takeovers is tantamount to restricting transactions that increase the economy's
wealth.

block transactions on share
stralian evidence

Frank J. Finn

The Sydney Stock Exchange (SSE) offers an unusual opportunity to study the effects of large transactions on share prices. First, the SSE is "small" and "thin" by world standards, so we are able to analyse a sample of block trades ranging in size from 1 to 60 days' normal trading volume. Both the average size of these blocks and the dispersion in their size are relatively large, so the various hypotheses can be put to a good test. Second, the trading mechanism on the SSE allows us to eliminate any price effects due to brokers providing liquidity services. According to Kraus and Stoll (1972, pp. 570–71), liquidity effects could be difficult to distinguish from the effects of size per se. We are able to avoid liquidity effects because the SSE is an auction market, not a dealer market, and has no designated specialists in trading particular stocks, so there is no formal mechanism whereby brokers provide liquidity services. In addition, the Exchange's reporting requirements allow us to identify and eliminate from our sample all trades in which a broker "acted as a principal" (i.e., traded on own account), so for this sample of block trades there is no informal mechanism whereby brokers are providing liquidity services: all of the trades are conducted between non-broker investors. The SSE thus allows an unusually clean test of the effect of quantity on price — that is, of the "perfect substitution" and the "price pressure" hypotheses.

The research design is an adaptation of Scholes (1972) and Kraus and Stoll (1972). We encounter, and suggest solutions to, several research design problems that hitherto have not been raised in this context. They include the apparent log-normality of block size variables, which appears to cause severe misspecification in Kraus/Stoll regressions of returns on block size.

The first section of this chapter develops the effect of block transactions on share prices under the competing hypotheses. The second section describes the institutional setting for block trading on the SSE, and the third describes the data. The fourth section discusses several research design problems and the design used in this study. Results and conclusions are contained in the final two sections.

Reprinted from the *Journal of Banking and Finance*, by permission of the authors and the publishers.

Large transactions and share prices: hypotheses

Four hypotheses concerning the effect of large transactions on share prices emerge from the work of Kraus and Stoll (1972) and Scholes (1972). This section describes those hypotheses, with a view to establishing differential predictions that can be used to empirically discriminate among them.

The "competitive market" or "substitution" hypothesis

This hypothesis states that, in equilibrium, all securities are priced as perfect substitutes for one other. Hence, "large" orders to buy or sell a particular share have infinitesimally small effects on its price, other things remaining equal, since these individually "large" orders create only infinitesimally small changes in the supply or demand for securities in aggregate. All market participants thus are price-takers, at least in regard to the size of their trades per se. The assumption that securities are priced to be perfect substitutes underlies most models of equilibrium security pricing, including the Present Value and Capital Asset Pricing models, so the "substitution" hypothesis occupies a central position in the literature.

The "segmented market" or "price pressure" hypothesis

This hypothesis states that securities are not perfect substitutes and implies that the size of a trade per se is an important determinant of price. In a seller-initiated transaction, the seller of a "large" block (large relative to "normal" volume offered for sale) faces a downward-sloping excess demand curve, whereas the buyer of a "large" block, in a buyer-initiated transaction, faces an upward sloping excess supply curve. Hence, attempts to sell "large" blocks tend to decrease price *temporarily*, and attempts to buy "large" blocks tend to increase price *temporarily*, other things remaining equal. Prices revert to prior levels once "normal" market volume is restored, because "normal" patterns of supply and demand are restored after the block has been cleared. The initial effect on price is a function of block size, and so the post-block reversal therefore also is a function of block size.[1]

The "short-run liquidity costs" hypothesis

Under this hypothesis, there exist liquidity or immediacy costs of trading a block, even if willing buyers or sellers exist, owing to costs of finding the willing parties. Liquidity services can be provided by specialists who hold inventories of stock, out of which they trade with buyers or sellers who otherwise cannot immediately locate matching sellers or buyers, respectively. "Dealer" markets, such as the New York Stock Exchange, have formal mechanisms for providing liquidity services through specialist brokers. Kraus and Stoll (1972, pp. 570–71) argue that brokers incur the costs of holding inventories to provide clients with liquidity and therefore earn compensation in the form of trading with the public at "a price away from the equilibrium price". This is particularly relevant to block trades: investors seeking to buy or sell a larger quantity of stock are less likely to find matching traders immediately. If block trades involve brokers providing liquidity, then this argument implies that the block price is lower than surrounding prices for a seller-initiated block and higher for a buyer-initiated block, other things remaining equal. The argument also implies that price reverts to equilibrium after the transaction has occurred, the price change reflecting the broker's compensation. This hypothesis thus implies price reversals around the block trade and the "liquidity cost" hypothesis might appear indistinguishable from the "price pressure" hypothesis.

We are not concerned with the "liquidity cost" hypothesis in this study for several reasons. First, the argument appears to overlook the equilibrium reward for holding inventory. The equilibrium expected return on a security appears to precisely cover the broker's opportunity cost of holding stock in inventory, ignoring bookkeeping costs (which should be a trivial percentage of a block transaction), so we are not convinced that brokers need to trade at off-equilibrium prices. The immediate pre-block price therefore includes the equilibrium reward to the specialist for holding inventory up to the time that price is observed, so there seems to be no reason to expect inventory holding costs to influence the difference between the immediate pre-block price and the block price (or any subsequent price change, for that matter). In addition to inventory holding costs, the broker also incurs costs of locating buyers and sellers, but these are covered by the normal brokerage commission. We therefore see no non-trivial reason for liquidity services to cause trades at non-equilibrium prices. Second, we will be studying the effect of block trades on rates of return (and therefore on percentage price changes) and there is no reason to expect the *percentage* cost of liquidity services to increase with the amount of stock provided. The percentage might even decrease, however trivially, due to fixed costs in bookkeeping. Third, for reasons outlined in the section on institutional setting, we are confident that our sample does not contain trades where brokers have provided liquidity services. For these reasons, we ignore liquidity effects and focus on the "price pressure" and "substitution" hypotheses.

Information effects

Scholes (1972) observes that the effect of size per se on price could be confounded by the effect of information implied by the decision to trade. Seller-initiated trades could occur around the time of "bad news" reaching the market, and buyer-initiated blocks could be associated with "good news". The block transaction itself might be the medium supplying the information to the market, in which case we would expect to see prices revised precisely at the time of block transactions. Alternatively, other information media could trigger price revisions at around the same time. Further, the more extreme the news, the larger the block is likely to be.[2] Thus, a price effect related to block size could be consistent with information effects, the price pressure hypothesis, or both. Consequently, our research design attempts to discriminate between information and selling pressure effects.

Prior evidence

Scholes (1972) studies a sample of registered and unregistered secondary distributions (block trades). Unregistered distributions are publicly announced on the day of the trade, whereas registered distributions are required to be registered with the Securities and Exchange Commission twenty days prior to the trade. His results are consistent with information being released to the market via the block trade.

Scholes finds a negative average price change at the time of large secondary distributions, which he attributes to information effects related to the identity of the seller of the block. He finds no post-block price reversals, nor any relation between price change and block size, and interprets these results as supporting the substitution hypothesis. For the registered distributions separately, he finds negative price changes prior to the actual distribution and no subsequent price reversals, which he also attributes to information effects.

Kraus and Stoll's (1972) results tend to support a less than perfectly elastic excess demand curve for "seller-initiated" block trades. They find it difficult to determine whether this is due to price pressure or liquidity cost effects, but they lean toward the latter. Note, however, that our evidence from SSE data suggests that their conclusions are based upon a misspecified relation between block size and stock returns.

Mikkelson and Partch (1985) examine price changes around the earliest announcement dates of secondary distributions. They find a negative price change at the announcement date and weak evidence of a negative relation between price change and the size of the block. They offer two interpretations as being consistent with their results: (1) block size is a proxy for unfavourable information; and (2) the demand for a firm's shares is less than perfectly elastic.

It is worth nothing that we are dealing with trades in the secondary market only. In relation to primary or new issues of stock as studied by Hess and Frost (1982) and Asquith and Mullins (1986), the price pressure hypothesis might imply a relatively permanent effect on price owing to the permanent increase in supply. In contrast, a block trade in the secondary market implies only a temporary shift in supply or demand; shifts in supply or demand are removed as soon as the market is cleared, that is, as soon as the transaction is executed. Note also that secondary market supply and demand can only be defined meaningfully in terms of volume *per period*. Thus, the block trades in our sample are selected because they are large relative to normal trading volume: the median proportion of shares outstanding is only two-tenths of one percent of the number of shares outstanding, but the median is eleven days' normal trading volume (see table 29.1). While a primary distribution alters a stock variable (the number of shares outstanding), a trade in the secondary market can alter only a flow variable (the rate of excess demand per unit of time — that is, volume of trading over a discrete period such as one day). This distinction forms the basis of the prediction, in the following subsection, that under the price pressure hypothesis there is only a temporary shift in price.

Discriminating among hypotheses

To discriminate among competing hypotheses we identify the actual block prices and then focus on *post*-block rates of return to investigate whether any price reversals occur.

The first requirement is to control for information effects. Without information effects, the substitution hypothesis predicts that a block sale has no first-order effect on price, whereas the price pressure hypothesis predicts an initial price effect followed by a reversal. In the presence of information effects, however, the distinction is not so clear-cut, but a differential prediction can be obtained by focussing on post-block price behavior. The substitution hypothesis predicts a negative (positive) price effect at the block trade for a seller-(buyer-) initiated block, followed by no price reversal. The price pressure hypothesis predicts an initial price effect in the same direction, followed by reversals when volume reverts to "normal". In addition, the size of any price reversal is a function of the block size, since any initial price-pressure effect is size-related. The distinguishing prediction therefore is in relation to post-block price *reversals*, and whether any reversal is a function of the size of the block.

Institutional setting

Trading on the Sydney Stock Exchange

Under SSE rules, large orders need not be filled on the trading floor. Until 7 March 1976, by-law 54A of the SSE required a broker to offer stock on the trading floor unless the market value of the order was $100,000 or more, in which case the shares could be crossed by the broker off-market as a "special" transaction. Alternatively, the shares could still be traded on the floor as an "ordinary" transaction. As from 8 March 1976, the rule was amended to provide a minimum consideration for off-market crossings of $250,000 and at the date of writing the minimum consideration was $500,000. Buyers and sellers do not save commissions in a "special" sale; each pays a commission to the broker handling the transaction.[3] The rules for reporting "ordinary" and "special" transactions to the exchange are discussed in the next subsection.

The SSE operates an auction market for securities. An intending buyer or seller places an order with a broker who satisfies the order by auction on the trading floor of the exchange. The buyer and seller each pay their respective broker an agency commission. In contrast to the New York Stock Exchange (NYSE), there are no dealer or specialist members of the SSE, although brokers can fulfil a dealer's function by trading on their own account as principals. When brokers trade as principals they must declare so to the exchange.

We confine ourselves to a test of the substitution and price pressure hypotheses by excluding all block trades where brokers acted as principals.[4] It would have been difficult to determine whether brokers trading on their own account were acting as market makers, similar to specialist NYSE dealers, or whether they were simply investing. For example, we cannot determine whether they retained beneficial ownership of the traded shares. To control for cases where the transaction price might reflect any liquidity costs of a broker, we therefore excluded all cases where brokers traded on their own account.

Thus, for all trades in our sample, brokers acted as agents for the buying and selling parties, each party paid a brokerage commission, and there was no inventory held by any broker. In no case was a dealer or specialist interposed between the buying and selling parties. All block trades occurred in an auction market.[5]

Block trades and data errors

The research design, described below, involves testing for post-block price reversals and this is sensitive to some types of data errors. It is well known that data errors in a random price series induce negative first-order serial correlation in the observed return series.[6] Consider the effect of errors in recording either the correct block price (our day 0 price) or the correct chronological date of the block trade. Each of these errors introduces misclassification when trades are classified on the basis of the sign of the price change from the pre-block to the block price, as required by the Kraus and Stoll research design (described in the section below on identification of "buying pressure" and "selling pressure"). Even in a random series, observed price change from the pre-block to the block price on average will appear to be reversed at the post-block price. Errors in recording block trades thus generate price reversals that appear consistent with price pressure effects. Note, however, that recording errors are unlikely to be related to the size of the block.

"Special" transactions (described above in the section on trading on the Sydney Stock Exchange) are crossed off-market by the broker and present considerable data error problems, because SSE regulations do not require a special transaction to be reported as occurring on its actual date. The regulations allow a special transaction to be reported up to 10 days after the transaction occurred.[7] The effect is to induce errors of opposite sign in measuring price changes at day 0 (the day of the block trade) and the following day.[8] Therefore, we exclude specials from the sample and concentrate on blocks traded on the floor of the exchange as ordinary transactions. Ordinary transactions are recorded immediately after they occur on the floor of the exchange and are publicly disclosed in the record of the day's trading.[9]

Data

Details are obtained from the transactions records of the SSE of all block transactions during the period 1 July 1974 to 30 June 1977, excluding all cases where brokers traded on their own account as principals and all off-market special transactions. We define a block transaction as a minimum of 10,000 shares with a minimum value of $100,000 (all amounts are in Australian dollars).[10] This results in 176 block transactions in 93 companies. Of these, 70 blocks are specials, leaving us with 106 blocks traded on the floor of the exchange as ordinary transactions. This is the population of such transactions on the SSE for the 3-year sample period.

Three measures of the size of a block are collected:
1. dollar value of amount of block, expressed in Australian dollars;
2. proportion of the firm's outstanding shares traded in the block; and
3. number of shares traded in the block, scaled by the average daily volume

of sales for that issue during the 25-day period from day -32 through day -8, where day 0 is defined as the day of the block transaction. (We interpret this variable as the size of the block relative to normal trading volume in that stock over a 25-day period prior to the block transaction.)

The price pressure hypothesis is vague in specifying an explicit size variable, reference usually being made to "large" blocks relative to "normal" demand or supply. We suspect that variable 3 above is closest to the spirit of the hypothesis. Nevertheless, we investigate the three size specifications to allow any size effects to reveal themselves.

Details of the size distributions for our sample are shown in table 29.1. The minimum size is $100,850, the maximum is $850,000 and the mean and median sizes are $156,653 and $140,400 respectively. By way of comparison, the SSE (1977) reports the mean dollar value of all transactions in 1975, 1976 and 1977 as being $1,122, $1,229 and $1,258. The blocks range from approximately 1 to 60 days normal trading volume for these firms, where normal volume is measured over days -32 through -8 relative to the block transaction, and the mean and median blocks are 14.7 and 10.99 days normal volume, respectively. Both the average and the *range* of the block sizes thus are large, relative to normal supply or demand, which should allow any differential effects of size on price to be observed.

Table 29.1   Distribution of block size variables

Decile	Dollar value	Proportion of firm	Number of days' normal volume
.1	108,470	0.00037	3.08
.2	113,970	0.00087	5.09
.3	122,460	0.00128	7.22
.4	134,400	0.00167	9.35
.5	140,400	0.00200	10.99
.6	155,850	0.00276	14.10
.7	166,400	0.00345	18.76
.8	180,000	0.00465	21.92
.9	200,000	0.00756	28.27
Mean	156,653	0.00350	14.70
Minimum	100,850	0.00011	0.94
Maximum	850,000	0.02076	60.60

Daily returns are calculated for the period extending from the close of trading 33 trading days prior to the block sale to the close of trading 32 days after: 65 rates of return in all, 32 before and after "day 0", the recorded day of the block. The returns are adjusted for dividends, splits, etc., and "days" are defined as trading days during which trades actually occurred (i.e., days with zero turnover were ignored).[11] All rates of return are continuously compounded. The day 0 price is defined as the actual block price. Thus the return for "day 0" denotes the rate of return from the closing price on the trading day prior to the block trade through to the block price, and the return for "day 1" denotes the rate of return from the block price through to the closing price on the trading day after the block trade.

The market index used is the Statex-Actuaries Accumulation Index, an equally weighted index of the highest market capitalisation and highest turnover shares on the SSE, which is adjusted for dividends and splits, and is the only available index of daily rates of return in Australia over our sample period.[12]

Research Design

We control for exogenous marekt-wide price changes around the dates of the block transactions, using the market model. Market model residuals (and prediction errors), cumulated over pre- or post-block trade periods, then are regressed cross-sectionally on various measures of the size of the block. In this regard, we adopt similar techniques to Kraus and Stoll (1972) and Scholes (1972), with the refinements discussed below.

Identification of block price

In their within-day-0 analysis, Kraus and Stoll use the actual block price and investigate price changes immediately before and after the block trade. They find significant reversals for "minus tick" blocks and conclude that their results supported the liquidity cost hypothesis. In their cross-sectional regressions investigating the effect of block size on price, both Scholes and Kraus and Stoll use, as the dependent variable, the price change from the opening price to the closing price over the day of the block trade.[13] This procedure has inherent limitations because it does not involve identifying the actual block price and thus cannot directly observe the effect of size on price. We use the actual block price in all tests; we run separate cross-sectional regressions using price changes up to the actual block price and price changes subsequent to the actual block price, rather than a single regression using the price change over a single period which straddles the block.

The distinction between pre- and post-block price change is important in testing for any price pressure effects. If a price change and a subsequent reversal occur within the day, the rate of return over the entire day, using opening and closing prices for that day, will not detect the price pressure effects. Also, if the block trade occurs at a price different from the opening price for the day, a non-zero price change over the full day could be due to either a partial reversal or no reversal after the trade. Since the price change from open to close on the day of the block trade includes any information effect, which could be associated with block size, a positive relation between size and the absolute price change over the full day is consistent with the substitution hypothesis, together with information effects, as well as with the price pressure hypothesis. In addition, a single regression using price change over the day of the block trade would not detect price pressure effects if reversals occurred over a period longer than a single day.[14]

Because the time frame for any reversal is undefined by the price pressure hypothesis, we run separate cross-sectional regressions using, as dependent variables, pre- and post-block price changes over periods ranging from one to five trading days. That is, we run separate cross-sectional regressions using block size as the independent variable and dependent variables defined as price changes over the periods: [day -1: block price] and [block price: day + 1]; [day -2: block price] and [block price: + 2]; through to [day -5: block price] and [block price: day + 5].

Identification of "buying pressure" and "selling pressure"

Empirical estimation of price–volume relations typically encounters an identification problem, arising from the joint presence of supply and demand effects. Research in the securities markets is unlikely to be immune to this problem. Kraus and Stoll classify block transactions as buyer- or seller-initiated, based on whether they traded on "plus ticks" or "minus ticks" (that is, whether the block prices respectively exceed or are exceeded by the last traded price before the block transaction). The assumption is that "plus tick" block trades result from shifts in the demand for securities per unit of time and that "minus tick" block trades result from equivalent shifts in supply. However, for plus ticks the supply schedule, if one does exist for individual securities, might not be held constant as is assumed: there could have been shifts in both supply and demand. Similarly, the demand schedule that the price pressure hypothesis assumes to exist for individual securities need not be constant when a minus tick is recorded. Consequently, there is a loss in power/efficiency in relation to the price pressure hypothesis: the researcher observes only the joint and offsetting effects of supply and demand variation.

This problem is inherent in the Kraus/Stoll research design and possibly also in that of Scholes. We attempt to reduce the problem by defining plus ticks and minus ticks in terms of the sign of the market model residual: positive and negative respectively. This procedure has two advantages. First, eliminating the market factor reduces the amount of exogenous variance in the variable used to identify the direction of movement, which is justifiable because (by definition) price pressure effects are security-specific. There is a trade-off, however, because securities' relative risks are measured with error. Second, this procedure allows us to include the 45 per cent of all cases in which the block was traded at exactly the prior day's closing prices.[15]

We report a specification check on the above classification procedure by examining unadjusted returns, for transactions that are classified as plus or minus ticks based on the actual block price compared to the closing price of the prior day. We thus investigate whether any post-block reversals in market model residuals also exist in unadjusted returns. In addition, we examine the volatility of stock returns before and after the block trades, as a check on the estimation of the post-block regressions.

Distribution of size variables

The size distribution of many economic variables conforms closely to the log-normal or Gibrat distribution.[16] We investigate three measures of block size and find that each is better described as Gibrat than as Gaussian. Furthermore, we observe that cross-sectional regressions of securities' abnormal returns on block sizes are poorly specified and that log transformations of the size variables produce well-behaved regressions.[17] The results are described below.

Results

Are there post-block reversals on average?

Market-model regressions are run for individual securities over the modified daily return period [-32 days: to +32 days] relative to the day of the block sale, excluding days (-7: +7).[18] The estimated regression parameters are used to generate conditional expectations over the interval [-7: +7], producing prediction errors for that interval also. These are averaged across securities, producing a time series of average residuals and prediction errors in event time. We use the term "abnormal return" (denoted as AR) to encompass both residuals and prediction errors. Cumulated abnormal returns (denoted as CARs) are reported in table 29.2 for the plus and minus tick categories, as defined in the section on identification of "buying pressure" and "selling pressure". Cross-sectional t statistics for the daily average residuals (ARs) also are reported in table 29.2.[19] Note that the sum of the average residuals (as distinct from the prediction errors over the interval [-7: +7]) is zero by construction, so that the individual-day results over [-32:-8] and [+8: +32] can give only a picture of the time series of residuals for the average block-trade security. However, the prediction errors over [-7: +7] should provide unbiased estimates of the relation between block trades and excess returns on a daily basis.

Table 29.2 Cumulative average residuals and daily *t* statistics*

	Plus ticks ($N = 55$)		Minus ticks ($N = 51$)	
Day	CAR	t for AR for day shown	CAR	t for AR for day shown
−30	−0.00255	−0.943	0.00159	1.296
−25	−0.00745	1.215	−0.00024	−0.927
−20	−0.00872	2.323	−0.00337	−1.231
−15	−0.01017	−0.918	0.00512	0.685
−10	0.00344	2.086	0.00875	−0.755
−5	0.00691	0.068	0.01613	−0.101
−4	0.00784	0.343	0.01591	−0.099
−3	0.00970	0.451	0.02007	1.668
−2	0.01775	2.332	0.01808	−0.976
−1	0.02117	1.242	0.01803	−0.023
0	0.03737	8.643	0.00192	−8.844
1	0.03727	−0.032	0.00102	−0.372
2	0.03552	−0.455	0.00062	−0.166
3	0.03361	−0.801	0.00103	0.166
4	0.03267	−0.292	−0.00322	−1.387
5	0.03507	0.690	0.00036	1.430
10	0.02819	−0.867	−0.00048	−0.054
15	0.03633	−0.181	−0.00382	−1.175
20	0.03862	−0.443	−0.00594	0.793
25	0.04541	0.932	−0.01442	0.021
30	0.04310	0.353	−0.01632	0.704

* CAR = Cumulative average market model residual
  AR = Average market model residual

For plus tick blocks, the AR on day 0 is 1.6 per cent (it is positive by construction), while for day +1 it is virtually zero, indicating no within-day reversal (recall that we have denominated day 0 as the block trade and day 1 as the closing price on the day after the trade). At days 0 and +1, the cross-sectional t statistics are 8.64 (again, positive by construction) and -0.03 respectively. Over longer periods, there is no evidence of systematic reversal. For example, the CAR at day +5 is 3.5 per cent compared with 3.7 per cent at day 0 (i.e., at the block trade). The minus tick category shows a similar picture. The AR for day 0 is large (-1.6 per cent with a t statistic of -8.84, both negative by construction) and for day +1 it is a negligible -0.009 per cent. There is thus no evidence of systematic reversal, on average, for either plus or minus ticks during the immediate period after the block trade. These results are consistent with the competitive market or substitution hypothesis, together with block transactions being associated with price changes due to release of information: good news in the case of buyer-initiated blocks and bad news for seller-initiated blocks. The results are inconsistent with the price pressure hypothesis.

As a specification check, table 29.3 reports cumulative average unadjusted returns (denoted as CAURs) for plus and minus ticks, classified on the basis of the actual block price compared with the closing price of the prior day. These data do not use the market model in any way; and the 49 cases in which the block price equals the previous day's closing price cannot be used.

Table 29.3 Cumulative average unadjusted returns and daily *t* statistics*

	Plus ticks (N = 27)		Minus ticks (N = 30)	
Day	CAUR	t for AUR for day shown	CAUR	t for AUR for day shown
−30	−0.00260	−2.266	0.00084	0.866
−25	−0.00038	1.013	0.00788	−0.793
−20	−0.00071	2.763	0.00227	−1.661
−15	−0.00620	−1.813	0.00212	−0.587
−10	0.01360	2.375	−0.01031	−1.476
−5	0.03765	1.375	−0.00151	−0.001
−4	0.04159	0.696	−0.00825	−1.730
−3	0.04211	0.074	−0.00822	0.013
−2	0.04856	1.163	−0.01005	−0.744
−1	0.05372	1.145	−0.01404	−0.927
0	0.08377	11.719	−0.03831	−10.974
1	0.08100	−0.364	−0.03986	−0.504
2	0.08555	0.858	−0.03721	0.824
3	0.08244	−0.694	−0.03626	0.277
4	0.07820	−0.849	−0.03765	−0.334
5	0.07796	−0.045	−0.03243	1.571
10	0.07567	0.532	−0.03510	−0.812
15	0.08629	3.324	−0.04509	−0.339
20	0.09302	−0.781	−0.04291	0.995
25	0.09616	0.520	−0.05119	1.095
30	0.09784	−0.655	−0.05967	1.118

* CAUR = Cumulative average unadjusted return
  AUR = Average unadjusted return

Table 29.4 Standard deviations of mean daily returns

	Pre-block (including day 0)	Pre-block (excluding day 0)	Post-block	F^* ($\hat{\sigma}^2$ pre/$\hat{\sigma}^2$ post)
1. Mean daily unadjusted returns	0.00299	0.00304	0.00194	2.375
2. Mean daily residual returns	0.00270	0.00274	0.00206	1.718

* Degrees of freedom (32, 31). The $\hat{\sigma}^2$ pre is for the pre-block period including day 0.

The results are not qualitatively different from those in table 29.2, where the plus and minus ticks are classified on the basis of market model residuals. There is no systematic reversal for either plus or minus ticks in the 30-day post-block trading period.

It might be argued that our finding of no reversals after block trades could be due to increased volatility of returns following block trades. Standard deviations of pre- and post-block returns therefore are reported in table 29.4. Row 1 shows the standard deviations of the mean daily unadjusted returns in the pre- and post-block periods for the total sample, and Row 2 shows the standard deviations of the mean daily residual returns for the same periods. If anything, there is a decrease in volatility of mean daily returns following the block trade. The F statistic for a two-tailed test of no difference in variances is significant at the 2 per cent level for Row 1 and is not significant at the 10 per cent level for Row 2. Thus, the variance of mean daily returns does not appear to increase after the block trades.[20]

These specification checks suggest some confidence in the method of classifying block trades by the sign of the market model residual, and in the finding of no average reversals following block trades. We use the residual-based classification of plus and minus ticks in the further tests below.

Distribution of size variables

We argue in the previous section on distribution of size variables that block size variables are likely to conform to the log normal distribution. Normal probability plots of the three size variables reveal that the three size variables are highly skewed. We report the plots for block size measured relative to normal trading volume. Figure 29.1 displays the normal probability plot for this variable, which is right-skewed. Figure 29.2 shows that, after log transformation, this block size variable closely approximates normality, indicating that it conforms to the Gibrat law. Similar results are obtained for the other block sales variables. Block size measured as percentage of the firm traded also closely conforms to the lognormal distribution. However, the distribution of the dollar value of the block remains skewed after log transformation.

Are there post-block reversals as a function of size?

To test if the observed residual return is a function of the size of the block

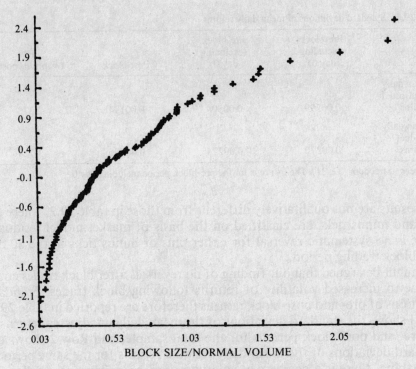

Figure 29.1 Normal probability plot of block size/normal volume

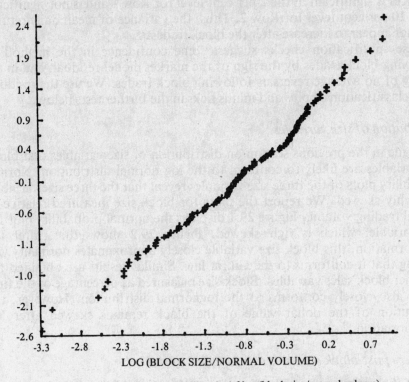

Figure 29.2 Normal probability plot of log (block size/normal volume)

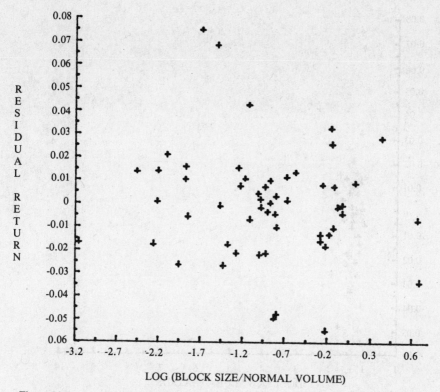

Figure 29.3 Post-block residual return and log of block size relative to normal volume (plus ticks)

transaction, we run a series of cross-sectional regressions of residual return over different time periods (as described in the section on the various block size variables). Following the above section on distribution of size variables, we are concerned with the specification of regressions using untransformed block size variables, in this study and in prior studies of the effect of block transactions on price.

Plots of residual returns against the log transformed and untransformed size variables show that the best specified regressions are for the log of block size relative to normal volume and the log of proportion of the firm. The plot for the log of block size relative to normal trading volume is shown in figure 29.3. The plots for the other size variables exhibit varying degrees of heteroscedasticity, as indicated by Bartlett's test of the homogeneity of the disturbance term, and the regressions tend to be dominated by small numbers of outliers. The regressions using the untransformed dollar value of block, shown in figure 29.4, are especially poorly specified. This is the variable used by Kraus and Stoll (1972). Similar specification problems could exist in their regressions if lognormality applies universally to block size distributions, as we suspect it does.[21]

In the results below we report only the regressions using the two well-behaved size variables, that is, the log transformations of both block size relative to normal trading volume and percentage of the firm traded. For the sake of brevity, we confine reported results to residual returns measured over 5 days and 1 day before and 5 days and 1 day after the block trade. Results of

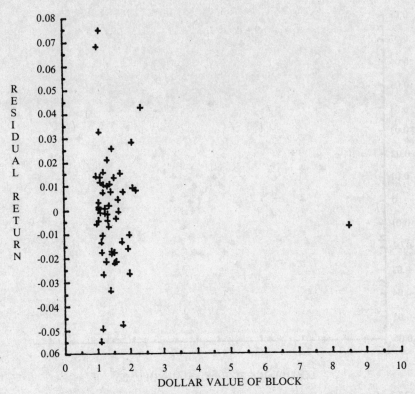

Figure 29.4   Post-block residual return and dollar value of block (plus ticks)

the regressions for the periods up to the block trade are given in table 29.5. Note that in panels B and C the mean dependent variable (residual return) by construction is negative for minus ticks and positive for plus ticks for the period [day -1: block price], and that the panel A means are not independent of this effect.

We argue in the first section that a positive relation between block size and price change *up to* the block trade is consistent with information effects, the price pressure hypothesis, or both. If the *post-block* price effects are inconsistent with the price pressure hypothesis, then we can conclude that any pre-block relation between price change and block size is best explained by information effects. Panel A of table 29.5 therefore reports statistics from regressions of residual returns over the period [day -5: block price] on the log of block size relative to normal volume. There is little association between the residual return over the 5-day period up to the block trade and the size of the block. The adjusted coefficients of determination (RSQs) are close to zero and, as can be seen by comparing the intercept terms with the mean dependent variables, the intercepts capture most of the mean residual returns.

Although the signs of the slope coefficients are consistent with information and/or price pressure effects, being negative for minus ticks and positive for plus ticks, the accompanying t statistics are not significant at conventional significance levels. In addition, the coefficients are very small. Since the slope coefficients are implied price elasticities, the largest estimate (for plus ticks) implies a price elasticity of only 0.0125.[22]

Table 29.5   Cross-sectional regressions of residual return up to the block trade on block size

Panel A: Residual return over [day −5: block price]
Independent variable = log of block size relative to normal volume

	N	α	$t(\alpha)$	β	$t(\beta)$	Adj. RSQ	ρ_1	Bartlett's statistic	Mean independ. variable	Mean residual return
Minus ticks	51	−0.0187	−3.156	−0.0058	−1.151	0.006	0.072	1.498	−0.7737	−0.0142
Plus ticks	55	0.0420	3.068	0.0125	1.128	0.005	−0.034	11.254	−0.9232	0.0305

Panel B: Residual return over [day −1: block price]
Independent variable = log of block size relative to normal volume

	N	α	$t(\alpha)$	β	$t(\beta)$	Adj. RSQ	ρ_1	Bartlett's statistic	Mean independ. variable	Mean residual return
Minus ticks	51	−0.0134	−5.583	0.0034	1.674	0.035	−0.058	1.759	−0.7737	−0.0161
Plus ticks	55	0.0184	6.426	0.0023	1.007	0.000	−0.084	0.027	−0.9232	0.0162

Panel C: Residual return over [day −1: block price]
Independent variable = log of proportion of firm

	N	α	$t(\alpha)$	β	$t(\beta)$	Adj. RSQ	ρ_1	Bartlett's statistic	Mean independ. variable	Mean residual return
Minus ticks	51	−0.0086	−0.741	0.0013	0.662	0.000	0.106	0.089	−6.045	−0.0161
Plus ticks	55	0.0380	3.926	0.0034	2.294	0.073	−0.012	3.578	−6.365	0.0162

Key: α = intercept coefficient; $t(\alpha)$ = t statistic for α; β = slope coefficient; $t(\beta)$ = t statistic for β; Adj. RSQ = adjusted coefficient of determination; ρ_1 = first-order autocorrelation coefficient; Bartlett's statistic = F statistic for Bartlett's test.

In panels B and C, the dependent variable is residual return for the period [day -1: block price], and the independent variable is log of block size relative to normal volume in panel B and log of proportion of firm in panel C. Again, the RSQs are close to zero and the regression slopes are very low. For the plus ticks in panel C, the t statistic for the slope is as large as 2.29, and the RSQ is 0.073, but even in this case the price elasticity of demand implied by the slope is only 0.0034. In sum, block size appears to have little effect on residual return up to the time of the block transaction. We do not detect any significant information and/or price pressure effects.

Results for the post-block regressions are in table 29.6. We argue in the first section that this provides the most discriminating test between the hypotheses. In panel A, the mean residual returns over the 5-day period following the block trade are very small and the signs are inconsistent with reversals. The mean residual returns are negative for both minus and plus ticks, -0.16 per cent and -0.23 per cent respectively. The regressions for both the minus and plus ticks show no size-related effects. The 1-day results are in panels B and C. Again, the mean residual returns indicate no reversals. The RSQs essentially are zero and the regression slopes are insignificant, except perhaps for the minus ticks in panel B with an RSQ of 0.05 and a t statistic of 1.9. But even here the price elasticity implied in the slope of 0.0052 is such that a block equal to 25 days' normal trading volume has a price effect of only 0.5 per cent.

Table 29.6   Cross-sectional regressions of residual return after the block trade on block size

Panel A: Residual return over [Block price: day +5]
   Independent variable = log of block size relative to normal value

	N	α	$t(\alpha)$	β	$t(\beta)$	Adj. RSQ	ρ_1	Bartlett's statistic	Mean independ. variable	Mean residual return
Minus ticks	51	0.0044	0.579	0.0076	1.191	0.008	0.065	2.911	−0.7737	−0.0016
Plus ticks	55	−0.0050	−0.426	−0.0029	−0.306	0.000	0.026	0.049	−0.9232	−0.0023

Panel B: Residual return over [Block price: day +1]
   Independent variable = log of block size relative to normal value

	N	α	$t(\alpha)$	β	$t(\beta)$	Adj. RSQ	ρ_1	Bartlett's statistic	Mean independ. variable	Mean residual return
Minus ticks	51	0.0031	0.976	0.0052	1.907	0.050	−0.049	0.175	−0.7737	−0.0009
Plus ticks	55	−0.0037	−0.765	−0.0039	−0.994	0.000	0.175	0.681	−0.9232	−0.0001

Panel C: Residual return over [Block price: day +1]
   Independent variable = log of proportion of firm

	N	α	$t(\alpha)$	β	$t(\beta)$	Adj. RSQ	ρ_1	Bartlett's statistic	Mean independ. variable	Mean residual return
Minus ticks	51	0.0114	0.747	0.0020	0.816	0.000	0.042	0.154	−6.045	−0.0009
Plus ticks	55	−0.0006	−0.037	−0.0001	−0.032	0.000	−0.140	4.945	−6.365	−0.0001

Key: α = intercept coefficient; $t(\alpha)$ = t statistic for α; β = slope coefficient; $t(\beta)$ = t statistic for β; Adj. RSQ = adjusted coefficient of determination; ρ_1 = first-order autocorrelation coefficient; Bartlett's statistic = F statistic for Bartlett's test.

The post-block results thus indicate no reversals on average and no relation between residual returns and block size, over either 1-day or 5-day post-block periods. The evidence is inconsistent with price pressure effects. The sample of large block transactions behaves like a random sample of transactions, as is implied by the competitive market hypothesis, despite their relatively large average size and their substantial variation in size. Because the price pressure hypothesis does not specify the time period within which any price reversals might occur, we have run cross-sectional tests over post-block intervals ranging from 1 to 5 days and have found no price pressure effect over any interval.

Conclusions

Several research design problems arise in attempting to assess the effect of large transactions on security prices. Those problems can be surmounted with one possible exception, which is the difficulty of completely avoiding the confusion of supply and demand effects: the classical identification problem. Following Kraus and Stoll (1972), we adopt the procedure of assuming that plus and minus tick block transactions are buyer-initiated and seller-initiated respectively. While we differ from Kraus and Stoll in defining plus and minus tick blocks in terms of market model residuals, we replicate their definition as a specification check.

A robust and testable implication of the price pressure hypothesis is that post-block price reversals are related to block size and that, after controlling for information effects, the post-block cross-sectional regressions provide unbiased estimates of price elasticity. The evidence from large block transactions on the Sydney Stock Exchange suggests low price elasticity for individual securities. No reversals are found after the block trades, nor is there any reliable evidence of a relation between returns and block size, as would be implied by the price pressure hypothesis. For a sample of transactions that ranges from 1 to 60 days normal trading volume, the absence of apparent effects of block transactions on price is marked. In the Sydney equity market, an auction market which is small and thin by some standards, relatively large blocks do not themselves appear to affect prices. Large blocks either have no direct price effect, or they are broken up into blocks of the relatively large size observed in our sample in order to escape price effects, with the costs of doing so not affecting prices.

Acknowledgments

This paper has benefited from the comments of Michael Barclay, Robert Holthausen, Alan Kraus, Richard Leftwich, Merton Miller and a referee. We also wish to acknowledge the collaboration of Philip Brown and Neil Gould. Financial support was provided by the Managerial Economics Research Center at the University of Rochester and the John M. Olin Foundation.

Notes

1. See also Scholes (1972, p. 191) in referring to secondary distributions, or seller-initiated trades: "The price pressure hypothesis implies that the larger the secondary distribution, the greater the necessary inducement. We can then test to see if the abnormal return subsequent to the distribution is also a function of the size of the sale."
2. This statement implies some untested beliefs concerning the process of information supply. Certainly we expect the size–news relationship to be non-negative.
3. Throughout the sample period, the sum of brokerage commission and transaction tax (called "stamp duty") was approximately 1.6 per cent, 1.2 per cent and 1.1 per cent to each side of the trade (buyer and seller) for transactions of $100,000, $200,000 and $300,000.
4. Kraus and Stoll (1972, pp. 573–74) argue that the liquidity cost effect arises through the dealer or market maker acting on his own account, and that the effect is likely to be less for a buyer-initiated trade than for a seller-initiated trade, because market makers rarely go short to facilitate the former. In the case of the latter, the reversal is said to occur through a sequence of trades first at the dealer's bid price and then at the dealer's ask price.
5. This does not preclude a non-broker from providing a liquidity service. In particular, institutional investors hold inventories of stock and could provide liquidity if it were possible to do so. Because our data exclude brokers trading as principals, we have at best only a "weak" test of the liquidity cost hypothesis. Nevertheless, we argue below that block trades on the SSE have little or no effect on share prices, apart from possible informational effects.
6. For example, see Officer (1975).
7. See, for example, rule 6.17, paragraph (5), *Memorandum and Articles of Association, By-Laws and Regulations,* Sydney Stock Exchange (Aguust 1977), which allows reporting of "special" transactions up to 10 days after the actual transaction.
8. Testing of the specials, using the same procedures as those described in subsequent sections for the ordinaries, showed that they exhibited immediate and virtually complete reversals, and that the magnitude of the reversals was not related to block size during either 1-day or 5-day post-block periods. We interpret these as error-induced reversals.
9. The daily trading record shows the price of each transaction for each stock. Cumulative records are posted at the exchange several times during each trading day and the record for the day's trading is reported in the morning press on the next day.

10. As discussed previously, the rules of the SSE up to 7 March 1976 defined "large" transactions as those involving $100,000 or more.

11. When this trading-day definition resulted in a period of multiple calendar days, the same calendar period was used for the market index in the market-model regressions reported later.

12. Because continuous observations of the index are not available, the independent variable is the index return over the entire trading day. Possible nonsynchronous trading in our day 0 block return and the day 0 index return has the potential to cause spurious reversals in the day 0 and day +1 residuals. Thus our procedure could be biased *against* the substitution hypothesis. However, as shown later, we find no evidence of reversals in either plus or minus tick blocks over post-block periods of one to five days.

13. Although Scholes does not explicitly state that he uses the closing price at the end of the day in which the block was traded, the notation used (especially p. 195, fn. 27) suggests this is the case. If he did use the actual block price, we are not told whether the regression uses price changes before or after the block trade. Kraus and Stoll (1972, pp. 578–82) make it clear that they did not use the actual block price. Mikkelson and Partch (1985) used the price change over the 2-day announcement period as their dependent variable.

14. The question arises as to the interpretation of our results if price reversals occurred over intervals of less than one day, as suggested by the evidence of Dann, Mayers and Raab (1977). Under these circumstances, the *dependent* variable in our cross-sectional regressions, the market-model residual return over the interval from the block trade to the close of trading on day +1, will measure the true effect of the block trade with additional noise. The variance of the additional measurement error will be the security return variance over the interval from the (unknown) time of the price reversal to the end of day +1. Because this error affects the dependent variable only, its effect is to reduce the RSQ. However, the regressions still produce unbiased estimates of the slope coefficients. Our conclusions rely upon the slope, so they are unaffected by this potential lack of specification in the price pressure hypothesis.

15. Kraus and Stoll (1972, p. 573) omitted zero tick blocks because they could result from the mechanics of clearing the specialist's book before executing the block trade, and this could occur for either seller- or buyer-initiated blocks. Note again that the SSE operates an auction system of trading, and there are no specialists or specialists' books. Each order is filled by auction.

16. The Gibrat law has been shown to describe accurately size distributions of, among other things, farm sizes, firm sizes and plant sizes. See Dixon and Sonka (1979) and Clarke (1979).

17. We suspect that the Gibrat law applies universally to block size distributions. There is noticeable skewness in the untransformed NYSE numbers reported in Kraus and Stoll (1972, table 1) for their sample. Consequently, the cross-sectional regression results of Kraus and Stoll (1972, p. 582), which use the arithmetic dollar values of blocks as the independent variable and which suggest price pressure for minus-tick blocks, could be unreliable, as they prove to be for our SSE data.

18. These days were excluded for the usual reason: if there are price effects of a block trade, the disturbance term will have a non-zero expected value and high variance at day 0 and possibly for several days around day 0. Since there is no daily price file available in Australia we confined our data collection to 65 daily returns.

19. By construction, the daily average residual for day 0 only is positive (negative) for plus (minus) ticks. The significance levels implied by the t statistics in table 29.2 should not be taken literally, because of possible violations of the i.i.d. assumptions in the cross-sectional residuals. Since the residuals represent drawings from different populations they are unlikely to be identically distributed. Also, residuals for securities with block sales in the same calendar period may be cross-sectionally correlated. However, Brown and Warner (1980) found that the cross-sectional t-tests performed well relative to more sophisticated tests, and that any differences between the empirical distribution of the test statistics and the t distribution were generally not large.

20. An alternative measure of volatility is the mean daily standard deviation of returns for all stocks in the sample. This measure was 0.0246 pre-block and 0.0252 post-block. The t statistic for difference in means was 0.046.

21. Kraus and Stoll (1972, p. 582) ran cross-sectional regressions using the arithmetic dollar value as the independent variable and the rate of return over the full day of the block trade as the dependent variable. They interpreted their results as supporting either the price pressure hypothesis or the liquidity cost hypothesis, especially for minus-tick blocks which showed a negative relationship between block size and the rate of return. Leaving aside the question of the appropriate distribution of the size variable, it was argued in the section "Identification of Block Price" that such a result, using price change over the full day of the block trade, could be consistent with the substitution hypothesis together with information effects. Scholes (1972) used log of dollar value and log of percentage of firm as the independent variable and rate of return over the full day of the block trade as the dependent variable. He found virtually no relationship between size and rate of return.

22. The table also shows the first-order autocorrelation coefficient, ρ_1, and Bartlett's statistic. Since the regressions are run on ranked estimates of block size, autocorrelation of the residuals indicates non-linearity. The values of ρ_1 indicate that autocorrelation is not a serious problem. The Barlett's statistic is the F statistic for Bartlett's test of the homogeneity of the variance of the disturbance term. The high F statistic for the plus ticks in panel A indicates heteroscedasticity.

PART 6

Evaluation of investment strategies

30 The investment performance of unit trusts and mutual funds in Australia for the period 1969 to 1978

G. N. Robson

Introduction

The aim of this research is to examine the investment performance of a sample of Australian unit trusts and mutual funds. The sample is larger and the period longer than previous research. The function of unit trusts and mutual funds (hereafer called funds) is to act as financial intermediaries. They re-package the collective capital of a large number of relatively small investors into mainly non-speculative and long-term investments. Over the past fifty years the funds' structure and portfolio composition have changed substantially. They now offer the investor a broad range of investment objectives and financial assets as well as allowing the fund manager the flexibility to adapt to changing market conditions.[1]

This chapter is organised as follows: first, it provides a brief review of the empirical evidence and the hypotheses to be tested; then it describes the data and collection procedures, discusses the measurement of investment performance and the results of the empirical tests, examines the financial characteristics of the funds and their risk and return, and finally provides a summary of the results.

Review of the empirical evidence and hypotheses

In table 30.1, five main conclusions from the empirical research on professionally managed funds are summarised. Column 1 lists the conclusions; the other columns reference the authors of research from the United States, United Kingdom and Australia respectively. The main conclusions have been that funds exhibit neither superior performance nor consistent performance; and that fund betas tend to be stationary, related to investment objective and less than 1. Funds also appear to be less than perfectly diversified.

Reprinted from *Accounting and Finance* 26, no. 2 (November 1986), 55–79, by permission of the author and the publisher.

Table 30.1   Five conclusions from the empirical research on funds in three countries

Conclusion	USA Research	UK Research	Australian Research
1. Funds on average earn a return commensurate with their risk.	Sharpe (1966) Jensen (1968, 1969) Friend, Blume and Crockett (1974) McDonald (1974) Joy and Porter (1974) Kim (1978) Mains (1977)	Ward and Saunders (1976) Firth (1978) Guy (1978)	Robson (1974) Leslie (1976) Praetz (1976c) Bird, Chin and McCrae (1983)
2. Funds do not exhibit runs on superior performance	Jensen (1969) Carlson (1970) Friend, Blume and Crockett (1970) Voorheis (1976)	Guy (1978) Firth (1978) Moles and Taylor (1977)* Gurney (1976)*	As above
3. The investment objective of a fund is significantly related to risk	Jensen (1969) Friend, Blume and Crockett (1970) McDonald (1974)	Ward and Saunders (1976) Moles and Taylor (1977)** Firth (1978)	Robson (1974)
4. The systematic risk levels (beta), on average, are less than one	All of the above	All of the above	Robson (1974) Leslie (1976) Praetz (1976c)
5. Fund betas are approximately stationary over time	Jensen (1969) Mains (1977)†	Ward and Saunders (1976) Moles and Taylor (1977) Firth (1978)‡	No research

*   Moles & Taylor and Gurney report some consistency
** Moles & Taylor found no relationship
†   Mains re-examined 70 of Jensen's 115 funds using monthly and not yearly data. He argues that the funds' betas were not stationary.
‡   The U.K. evidence is mixed but betas appear to be more stationary in the late 1970s.

Using previous empirical research as a guide, the following are the hypotheses to be tested:
1. The investment performance of the sample of funds was superior to a buy-the-market-and-hold strategy.
2. The funds exhibited consistent superior investment performance from one period to the next period or periods.
3. The systematic risk estimates of the funds were stationary over the 10-year period.
4. The stated investment objectives of the funds were significantly related to their systematic risk and total variability.
5. There was a significant relationship between fund risk and investment performance.

Data

Sample of funds

The sample consists of the majority of unit trusts and mutual funds in Australia which were continuously in existence for at least 5 years during the 10-

year period 1 January 1969 to 31 December 1978. There were three reasons for accepting only those funds with a minimum of 5 years' data. First, as discussed below, the lack of a suitable index for the entire 10-year period necessitated dividing the study into two equal subperiods of 1969 to 1973 and 1974 to 1978. Second, a 5-year period using monthly returns should provide unbiased estimates of the systematic risk (beta) and performance measures of the funds.[2] Third, a 5-year period should provide a sufficient period over which to evaluate investment performance of funds.

For each period the sample consists of the 4-weekly returns on the portfolios of those funds for which the repurchase price was available in the *Australian Financial Review*. Dividend distribution details of the various financial characteristics and investment objectives for each fund were obtained through personal interview and questionnaire. The response rate was excellent with no fund refusing to cooperate.

There is a small survivorship bias in the sample in that two funds were excluded from the study because they were put into liquidation during June–July 1971.[3] The final sample consists of 67 unit trusts and 9 mutual funds. Of this sample 9 unit trusts which have income as their investment objective were excluded from the analysis because almost all of their portfolio comprised fixed interest securities, cash and cash on deposit at call. Hence they could not be compared with a benchmark portfolio consisting of equity securities. In the first 5-year period there were 54 funds (49 unit trusts and 5 mutual funds) and in the second 5-year period 51 funds (42 unit trusts and 9 mutual funds). In existence over the entire 10-year period were 38 funds (33 unit trusts and 5 mutual funds).

The final sample, while not random, included the majority of unit trusts and mutual funds in existence over the period 1969 to 1978 for which at least 5 years data were available.[4]

Benchmark portfolios

The selection of a market proxy for this study over the period 1969 to 1978 proved difficult for two reasons. First, unlike the United States and the United Kingdom, there was no publicly available market index which included dividend distributions over the entire 10-year period. Only since March 1972 has the Statex-Actuaries Accumulation Index been published. As the name implies dividends are included in the calculation of the index. The second problem was that unit trust and mutual fund prices are published only once a week on each Monday. The prices calculated are based on the last sale price of the securities in the fund's portfolio on the Friday preceding the Monday publication. Thus, when calculating the returns for the market index the observation date for the market index must coincide with the observation date for the funds. This effectively precluded any index calculated on a monthly basis where the observation date was the last trading day of the month. Therefore, indexes used in other Australian studies, such as Ball, Brown and Officer (1976a), could not be used or meaningfully converted to a 4-weekly basis.

Consequently, this study was divided into two subperiods. In the first 5-year period of 1969 to 1973 an index which consisted of a random selection of 50 actively traded industrial shares listed on the Melbourne Stock Exchange was used. This index was developed by Terry Walter of the University of New South Wales and is reported in Brown and Walter (1974).

The index includes dividends, adjustments for bonus and rights issues, etc., and, based on weekly closing prices, the weekly rates of return were converted to a continuously compounded rate of return. The 4-weekly return for the Walter Index is the sum of the individual 4 weeks continuously compounded rate of return.

For the second 5-year period, 1974–78, the Statex-Actuaries Accumulation Index was used. The index is an equally weighted index comprising the 50 companies with the highest median monthly turnover (Australia wide) of its ordinary shares in the preceding year with all dividends accumulated. The 4-weekly returns on the Statex Index were calculated by taking the level of the index over the period and dividing by the level of the index at the beginning of the period, and then converted to a continuously compounded rate of return.

The third index used is an equally weighted index comprising all the funds in the sample (excluding income trusts). This is simply the average continuously compounded rate of return of all the funds in existence in any 4-week period. This index overcomes the problem of a portion of funds which have invested in fixed interest securities, where the two benchmark portfolios described above are based only on equity securities. The "Fund Index" represents an industry average against which a fund's performance and consistency can be evaluated. The number of funds in the index varied as funds entered the sample or terminated during the 10-year period. In fact, the number of funds in the sample ranged from a minimum of 51 at the end of 1978 to a maximum of 67 in the middle of the period. This Fund Index was used over the entire 10-year period as well as the two 5-year periods.

This Fund Index represents a portfolio that is a reflection of the average of investors' expectations or "consensus expectations" (Rosenberg 1981). Rosenberg argues that this type of index is a good surrogate for the market portfolio return. The index is a desirable benchmark because it represents a conspicuous investment alternative. The index is a "consensus portfolio" which reflects a passive portfolio strategy.

The Fund Index was deliberately constructed not to completely overlap each sample. The aim was to compare a sample of the funds with an industry index which was larger than the sample and representative of the industry. Thus the average return of each sample will not necessarily equal the return of the index over each period. Also the number of funds classified as superior or inferior to the index will not necessarily be equal.

One further index was used for testing the stationarity of systematic risk (beta) of each fund. This was the Melbourne All Ordinaries Index which was used as a market proxy for the entire 10-year period. Although the Melbourne All Ordinaries Index is just a share price index it is used to provide tentative evidence on the relative stationarity of beta from one 5-year period to the next.

Risk-free estimates

Ideally the rate of return should be a market-determined rate. However, because of the relative thinness of the market in government debt securities,

the annual yield to maturity on consecutive "New Issues" dates from Reserve Bank Bulletins was used. In all, four risk-free estimates were used. These were:
1. 13-week Treasury notes,
2. 26-week Treasury notes,
3. 2-year government bonds, and
4. 10-year government bonds.

The annual yields were converted to continuously compounded rates of return and the 4-weekly continuously compounded return calculated by dividing by 13. See appendix 1 for more precise definitions of the variables.

Measurement of investment performance

Rate-of-return approach

The simplest method to measure the investment performance of a managed portfolio is to use rate of return as the sole yardstick. Performance is then evaluated based on a comparison between the rate of return of a portfolio and the return of an index.

This approach implicitly assumes the relative riskiness of the index and portfolios are not significantly different. However, this is rarely the case. The evaluation should incorporate both return and risk.[5]

Risk and return approaches

Four main approaches which incorporate both risk and return have been used. These are:
1. The weighted index benchmark portfolio approach first used in the Wharton School *Study of Mutual Funds* (1962) and subsequently by Friend and Vickers (1965) and Kim (1976, 1978).
2. The risk-class benchmark portfolio approach adopted by Friend, Blume and Crockett (1970).
3. A stochastic dominance methodology discussed and developed by Porter (1973), and Joy and Porter (1974).
4. The risk-adjusted performance measures approach developed and used by Sharpe (1966), Treynor (1965) and Jensen (1968, 1969).

Each approach has advantages and disadvantages. Officer (1980) and Robson (1981) provide a detailed discussion of the practical and theoretical issues of each approach. The first three approaches were not used in this study because of data limitations, cost and unsuitability. The three risk-adjusted performance measures of Sharpe, Treynor and Jensen were used.

The three measures were closely related and provide very similar rankings of performance. In Robson (1981) all Spearman rank order correlations between the three measures (and rate of return) were significant at the 0.001 level. Only the Jensen measure and rates of return will be reported in this paper. The Jensen measure provides an estimate of a fund's abnormal return. A positive Jensen measure suggests superior performance to that which would have been expected for the level of systematic risk.

It is not intended to enter the theoretical debate of Roll (1977, 1978, 1979) and Mayers and Rice (1979) about the usefulness of the above measures which rely on the market model and the capital asset pricing model framework. Provided the indexes selected are broadly based and representative of an investor's portfolio choice, the performance measures will serve as useful tools to evaluate portfolio performance.

Also, Peterson and Rice (1980) demonstrate that using four different indexes made little difference to the rankings of mutual fund performance. They used a sample of fifteen mutual funds, the Sharpe and Treynor performance measures, two 5-year periods and both equally and value-weighted indexes. They showed that despite theoretical shortcomings of portfolio evaluation measures that use market indexes, the measures still have practical application. However, they do add that the measures should be used with caution and awareness of the potential ambiguity. The Fund Index (or consensus portfolio) should also yield useful performance measures.

Investment performance risk and return

In this section the empirical results for the two 5-year subperiods and entire 10-year period will be presented and discussed. Because of the similarity in the results between the four estimates of the risk-free rate of return, only the results using the 13-week Treasury notes will be presented.[6]

Investment performance

Tables 30.2, 30.3 and 30.4 present the summary statistics for the funds for the periods 1969–78, 1969–73 and 1974–78 respectively. The funds were classified into one of five investment objectives.[7]
1. Growth: Funds specifically investing in equity shares for capital appreciation.
2. Growth–income: Funds investing mainly for capital appreciation but with investments also yielding dividend or interest income.
3. Income–growth: Funds investing mainly for dividend or interest income but with some capital appreciation.
4. Balanced: Funds seeking approximately equal proportions of dividend and interest income and capital appreciation.
5. Income: Funds specifically investing in income producing investments, such as fixed interest securities, with little or no investment in equity shares.

10-year period 1969–78. From table 30.2 the overall average annual return of those funds in existence over the 10-year period was less than the index comprised of their peers. Further, the risk-free asset outperformed both the index and the average return of the funds. Only the income–growth and balanced funds outperformed the index and the risk-free asset. Only 14 of the 38 funds outperformed the index.

First 5-year period 1969–73. Table 30.3 reveals that compared with the Fund Index (hereafter called FUNDEX), 24 of the 54 funds outperformed FUNDEX. Compared with the Walter Index (hereafter called WALDEX), only 11 of the 54 outperformed the index. The income–growth funds and growth funds performed best and worst respectively.[8] The average return of the funds was greater than FUNDEX but less than both the risk-free asset and WALDEX.

Second 5-year period 1974–78. Table 30.4 shows that the average return of the funds was less than FUNDEX and Statex-Actuaries Accumulation Index (hereafter called STATDEX) but greater than the risk-free asset. Again

Table 30.2 Summary statistics for the 10-year period 1969–78*

Objectives of funds	Number of funds in group	Average** return (per cent)	Average Jensen measure	Average† beta	Average‡ R^2
Growth	9	3.71	−2.41	1.32	0.77
		(3.24)	(3.21)	(0.22)	(0.14)
Growth–income	15	5.30	−0.88	1.01	0.75
		(1.35)	(1.31)	(0.30)	(0.24)
Income–growth	7	8.54	2.33	0.83	0.50
		(2.65)	(2.62)	(0.34)	(0.24)
Balanced	7	7.02	0.76	0.59	0.54
		(1.93)	(1.89)	(0.26)	(0.19)
Overall	38	5.83	−0.35	0.97	0.67
		(2.75)	(2.71)	(0.37)	(0.24)
FUNDEX		6.18	0	1.00	—
		(3.61)			
Number > FUNDEX		14	14	20	—
Number < FUNDEX		24	24	18	—
Risk-free asset		6.37	—	—	—

* The figures in parenthesis are the standard deviations of the estimates for each group.
** Arithmetic average annual continuously compounded rate of return over the period.
† Systematic risk using FUNDEX as the market index.
‡ Percentage of variation in fund returns explained by FUNDEX returns.

Table 30.3 Summary Statistics for the 5-year period 1969–1973

Objective of funds	Number of funds	Average return (per cent)	R_m = FUNDEX**			R_m = WALDEX†		
			Jensen measure	Beta	R^2	Jensen measure	Beta	R^2
Growth	10	−1.62	−2.58	1.28	0.76	−7.37	0.95	0.63
		(6.66)	(6.01)	(0.25)	(0.12)	(6.67)	(0.15)	(0.14)
Growth–income	24	0.81	−0.79	1.07	0.81	−4.82	0.82	0.71
		(1.59)	(1.33)	(0.21)	(0.17)	(1.68)	(0.17)	(0.15)
Income–growth	7	7.25	4.92	0.83	0.45	1.79	0.63	0.39
		(3.96)	(3.41)	(0.42)	(0.28)	(4.12)	(0.29)	(0.23)
Balanced	13	4.78	1.90	0.66	0.57	−0.58	0.52	0.52
		(2.81)	(2.55)	(0.24)	(0.23)	(2.88)	(0.18)	(0.20)
Overall	54	2.15	0.27	0.98	0.70	−3.44	0.75	0.61
		(4.56)	(3.91)	(0.33)	(0.23)	(4.71)	(0.24)	(0.20)
FUNDEX		1.82	0	1.00				
Number > FUNDEX		27	24	30				
Number < FUNDEX		27	30	24				
WALDEX		5.79				0	1.00	
Number > WALDEX		11				11	8	
Number < WALDEX		43				43	46	
Risk-free asset		4.88						

* The figures in parenthesis are the standard deviations of the estimates.
** The statistics in these three columns estimated using FUNDEX as the market index.
† The statistics in these three columns estimated using WALDEX as the market index.

the funds failed to outperform either index on each of the performance measures used. Only 18 of the 51 funds outperformed FUNDEX, whereas 23 outperformed STATDEX. On average the balanced funds performed the best. However, there was no significant difference between the means of each measure of each objective group.

Table 30.4 Summary statistics for the 5-year period 1974–1978*

Objective of funds	Number of funds	Average return (per cent)	R_m = FUNDEX**			R_m = STATDEX†		
			Jensen measure	Beta	R^2	Jensen measure	Beta	R^2
Growth	21	9.75	−1.55	1.28	0.75	−0.52	0.77	0.68
		(3.38)	(3.53)	(0.20)	(0.16)	(3.47)	(0.13)	(0.18)
Growth-income	15	9.76	−0.77	1.00	0.74	0.01	0.60	0.69
		(1.13)	(1.76)	(0.34)	(0.28)	(1.52)	(0.20)	(0.25)
Income-growth	8	10.26	0.14	0.85	0.53	0.88	0.49	0.45
		(1.99)	(2.30)	(0.30)	(0.23)	(2.20)	(0.19)	(0.23)
Balanced	7	9.45	0.09	0.56	0.53	0.57	0.32	0.44
		(3.50)	(3.95)	(0.25)	(0.17)	(3.78)	(0.14)	(0.17)
Overall	51	9.79	−0.83	1.03	0.68	0.01	0.61	0.61
		(2.65)	(2.99)	(0.36)	(0.23)	(2.85)	(0.22)	(0.23)
FUNDEX		10.54	0	1.00				
Number > FUNDEX		17	18	30				
Number < FUNDEX		34	33	21				
STATDEX		11.01				0	1.00	
Number > STATDEX		12				23	1	
Number < STATDEX		39				28	50	
Risk-free asset		7.85						

* The figures in parenthesis are the standard deviations of the estimates.
** The statistics in these three columns estimated using FUNDEX as the market index.
† The statistics in these three columns estimated using STATDEX as the market index.

Two other points to note from tables 30.3 and 30.4 are the average systematic risk and R^2 estimates. The average beta using WALDEX and STATDEX is less than 1. The average beta using FUNDEX must necessarily be approximately equal to 1 with about half above and below 1. The R^2 estimate provides an indication of fund diversification. For both WALDEX and STATDEX estimates the R^2 values indicate that only 61 per cent of next month's return of the averge fund was attributable to the market factor. The average R^2 of 61 per cent is consistent with McDonald (1974) who reported a similar average R^2 with monthly data.

In this section the results of testing the first hypothesis were presented. Using four measures of investment performance the hypothesis was rejected. The funds did not outperform either a benchmark portfolio of their industry (as would be expected) or a market portfolio of equity securities. At best the funds were neutral performers depending upon the time period and the benchmark portfolio used. Income-growth funds appeared to consistently outperform the other groups and benchmarks. Growth funds appeared to do worst.

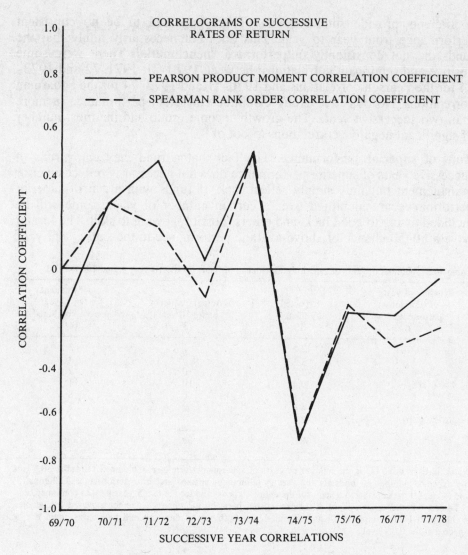

Figure 30.1 Correlograms of successive rates of return

Consistency of fund performance

There remains the possibility that a few funds may consistently outperform the market owing to superior performance. That is, a fund with superior management should exhibit runs of successive years of superior performance.

Consistency from year to year. To test for consistency in fund performance from year to year, the Spearman Rank Order and Pearson Product Moment Correlation Coefficients of successive rates of return from 1969 to 1978 were calculated. Rates of return were used because the evidence mentioned earlier revealed that all four performance measures were highly correlated. Rates of return also have fewer possible estimation errors.

Figure 30.1 plots correlograms over the 10-year period. The sample size for each correlation ranged from 38 to 64 funds. The two correlation coefficients provide similar results. <u>There appeared to be no consistent performance from year to year.</u> This does not necessarily imply that the funds did not consistently outperform a "benchmark". There were some positive and significant correlations[9] between 1970–71, 1971–72 and 1973–74 for the Pearson correlations and 1970–71 and 1973–74 for the Spearman correlations. No objective group exhibited consistent performance in more than two successive years. The growth–income group had the most number of significant negative correlations (5 out of 9).

Runs of superior performance. The fact that a fund may enjoy runs of successive years of superior performance does not necessarily reflect superior management but may simply reflect luck. If funds with a run of superior performance are identified over a certain number of years, some will be included owing to good luck, and others (possibly) owing to skill. The former have a 50–50 chance of above-average performance in the subsequent year;

Table 30.5   Number of years of superior performance of funds for the 10-year period 1969–1978

Number of years of superior performance (1)	Expected frequency (2)	Actual frequency entire 10 years (3)	Actual frequency for two 5-year periods combined (4)
0–2	2.1	1	2
3	4.4	6	4
4	7.8	10	9
5	9.4	10	11
6	7.8	6	8
7	4.4	2	1
8–10	2.1	3	3
	38.0	38	38

Notes: In each table (1) is the number of years of superior performance. Column (2) in table 30.5 lists the expected number of funds for the various number of years of superior performance. Columns (3) and (4) report the actual frequencies for the entire 10 years and for the two 5-year periods combined.

To test whether a significant difference existed between the *observed* and the *expected* frequencies, a chi-squared one-sample test was performed. For both sets of data the null hypothesis could not be rejected at the 0.05 level.

Table 30.6   Number of years of superior performance of funds for the 5-year period 1969–1973

Number of years of superior performance (1)	Expected frequency (2)	Actual frequency	
		R_m = FUNDEX (3)	R_m = WALDEX (4)
0	1.7	0	6
1	8.4	4	18
2	16.9	20	21
3	16.9	21	4
4	8.4	8	4
5	1.7	1	1
	54.0	54	54

Notes: In table 30.6 columns (3) and (4) report the actual frequencies using FUNDEX and WALDEX respectively. The results for FUNDEX revealed no significant difference between expected and observed. But for WALDEX the actual distribution was significantly worse than expected. (The null hypothesis would have been rejected at the 0.001 level.)

the latter a better than 50–50 chance. This will be evidenced in the subsequent year with a disproportionately large number of the funds in such a group achieving superior performance.

The measure of superior performance used for this analysis was the Jensen measure. The first procedure was to observe the number of funds with superior performance each year. If it is assumed that there is an equal chance of a fund having a Jensen measure less than or greater than zero (the null hypothesis), then the probability of the number of years of superior performance can be assessed. Notice that, initially, it is not the runs of success but the number of successes that is being evaluated. The results for the 10-year period are set out in table 30.5 and for the two 5-year periods in tables 30.6 and 30.7 respectively.

Table 30.7 Number of years of superior performance of funds for the 5-year period 1974–1978

Number of years of superior performance (1)	Expected frequency (2)	Actual frequency	
		R_m = FUNDEX (3)	R_m = STATDEX (4)
0	1.6	2	1
1	8.0	6	4
2	15.9	25	20
3	15.9	12	19
4	8.0	6	6
5	1.6	0	1
	51.0	51	51

Notes: For the second 5-year period the chi-squared test revealed no significant difference between the frequencies for both benchmark portfolios. However, for FUNDEX, there were more funds than expected with zero years of superior performance; the majority had only 2 out of 5 years superior performance. The funds perform better for the STATDEX comparison with a greater than expected number of funds with 2 and 3 years superior performance.

The above results and discussion simply analysed the number of years of superior performance. The next part will examine whether funds exhibited any greater than or less than consecutive years of superior performance than expected, assuming a 50–50 chance of being superior. Over the 10-year period there were 380 Jensen Measures calculated (10 for each of the 38 funds). Of these, 184 (48.42 per cent) were positive and 196 were negative. The binomial test was performed to determine whether the observed distribution of positive and negative Jensen measures was significantly different from that expected. That is, the null hypothesis was that the probability of a positive or negative Jensen measure is equal to 0.5. Using a two-tailed test, the null hypothesis could not be rejected at the 0.05 level of significance. Over the entire 10-year period there was no evidence of inferior or superior investment performance.

Table 30.8 reports the record of the funds' consistency over the 10-year period 1969–78. The record provides no support for the hypothesis that a significant number of funds consistently outperformed the benchmark portfolio with equal risk. Only one fund (No. 30: Scottie Balanced Fund) performed consistently with eight successive superior performances from 1971 to 1978. The binomial test was performed on the first four categories in table 30.8

(the remaining categories having too few observations). The only significant result was for funds with one year of superior performance followed by another. That is, the 39.13 per cent of instances was significantly worse than expected. Alternatively, consistency could be examined by observing the performance of funds which were successful in any one year through subsequent years. Table 30.9 records the results of this analysis. Apart from the Scottie Balanced Fund no fund had a run of superior performance of more than 4 years. Only in the period 1976 to 1978 did the funds exhibit some consistency. The results confirm that funds on average did not exhibit any consistent superior performance in this period.

Table 30.8   Runs of consecutive superior performance for funds over the 10-year period 1969–1978

Number of years of superior performance (Y)	Number of instances (N)	Number of instances with superior performance subsequent year (NS)	Percent of instances (NS/N)
1	184	72	39.13*
2	72	29	40.28
3	29	12	41.38
4	12	4	33.33
5	4	3	75.00
6	3	2	66.67
7	2	1	50.00
8	1	0	0
9	0	0	0

* Significant at the 0.05 level using a two-tailed binomial test.

One further test for consistency of investment performance was used. It is based on the runs test concept. However, the one-sample runs test described in Siegel (1956) and the runs tests used by Fama (1965) were not applicable to the data, since the data are not continuous with too few observations for each fund. The methodology used is described fully in Robson (1981). It is based on observing the number of changes of positive and negative Jensen measures for each year over each period.[10] The chi-squared one-sample test and the Kolmogorov–Smirnov one-sample test were used to test for a difference between the observed distribution and expected distribution of changes.[11] One problem in using these tests is that the assumption that each observation (fund) was independent may be violated. This was due to the fact that some of the funds had the same management company which could be making the investment decisions for the funds in the group.

Table 30.10 shows the distribution of the number of changes in Jensen measures for the 38 funds for the 10-year period 1969–78. The null hypothesis that the sample has been drawn from the specified theoretical distribution was rejected for both tests. This implies the assumed theoretical distribution is mis-specified. That is, there was not an equal probability of a fund having a positive or negative Jensen statistic each year.

However, from table 30.10 it is noticeable that the funds tended to exhibit a great number of changes in the 6 to 9 categories and less in the 0 to 5 categories. If the funds did exhibit consistent yearly investment performance,

Table 30.9 Consistency of superior performance of funds for subperiods over the 10-year period 1969–1978

Base year	No. of funds with superior performance ($J_{it} > 0$) in base year (N_B)	Per cent ($N_B/38$)	No. of funds with two consecutive $J_{it} > 0$ (N_2)	Per cent (N_2/N_B)	No. of funds with three consecutive $J_{it} > 0$ (N_3)	Per cent (N_3/N_2)	No. of funds with four consecutive $J_{it} > 0$ (N_4)	Per cent (N_4/N_3)	No. of funds with five consecutive $J_{it} > 0$ (N_5)	Per cent (N_5/N_4)
1969	16	42.1%	4	25.0%	3	75.0%	3	100.0%	0	0
1970	14	36.8	9	64.3	6	66.7	1	16.7	0	0
1971	28	73.7†	16	57.1	5	31.3	1	20.0	1	100.0*
1972	19	50.0	5	26.3	1	20.0	1	100.0	1	100.0
1973	21	55.3	9	42.9	2	22.2	1	50.0	1	100.0
1974	11	28.9†	2	18.2	1	50.0	1	100.0	1	100.0
1975	18	47.4	8	44.4	4	50.0	4	100.0		
1976	19	50.0	7	36.6	7	100.0				
1977	21	55.3	10	47.6						
1978	17	44.7								
	184									

* Fund 30 (Scottie Balanced Fund) had eight consecutive $J_{it} > 0$ from 1971–78 which are not shown after the fifth consecutive superior performance.

† Significant at the 0.05 level using a two-tailed binomial test.

then there should have been a larger number of cases with 0 to 3 changes. However, this was not the case. In fact, the funds tended to have more changes than expected.

Table 30.10   Distribution of changes in fund Jensen statistic for the 10-year period 1969–1978

Number of changes	Observed frequency (O_i)	Binomial probability $(n = 9 \, p = 0.5)$	Expected frequency (E_i)	Theoretical cumulative distribution $F_0(X)$	Observed cumulative distribution $S_{38}(X)$	$\|F_0(X){-}S_{38}(X)\|$
0	0	0.0020	0.0760	0.0020	0.0000	0.0028
1	1	0.0176	0.6688	0.0196	0.0263	0.0067
2	2	0.0703	2.6714	0.0899	0.0789	0.0110
3	2	0.1641	6.2358	0.2540	0.1316	0.1224
4	9	0.2461	9.3518	0.5000	0.3684	0.1316
5	5	0.2461	9.3518	0.7461	0.5000	0.2461
6	15	0.1641	6.2358	0.9102	0.8947	0.0155
7	3	0.0703	2.6714	0.9805	0.9737	0.0068
8	1	0.0176	0.6688	0.9981	1.0000	0.0019
9	0	0.0020	0.0760	1.0000	1.0000	0.0000
	38	1.0002	38.0076			

The results for the first 5-year period, 1969–73, reveal that the funds' performance was strikingly inconsistent. Only one fund (No. 28, 3rd Federal Flexible Trust) has a positive Jensen measure for all the 5 years irrespective of the index used.

The second 5-year period 1974–78 saw the funds' consistency improve, especially after 1975. One fund (No. 30, Scottie Balanced Fund) had 5 years of superior performance. From 1975 four of the funds had 4 consecutive years of superior performance.

In summary, the evidence in this section suggests that the majority of funds did not exhibit any investment performance consistency from year to year. There was no correlation between the funds' rates of return from year to year or years. Nor did a significant number of funds consistently outperform a passive benchmark portfolio with equivalent risk.

Stationarity of systematic risk estimates

An important consideration when using performance measures which incorporate systematic risk, beta, is its stationarity over time. If beta is relatively stationary then conditional expectations of future returns on portfolios and individual securities can be made. The level of systematic risk will have varying effects on the Jensen and Treynor measures for different estimates of the risk-free asset returns.[12] Moreover, for any given rate of return an underestimated level of systematic risk will result in an overestimation of the Jensen.

Leaving aside the issue of the number of observations needed (daily, weekly, monthly, etc.) and over what period (yearly, 5-yearly, etc.) the question in this section is whether the estimates of beta for the funds were relatively stable over the 10-year period. To test for stationarity of the beta estimates in different periods, regressions and correlations between betas of other periods were performed. The analysis was necessarily restricted to the 38 funds which were in existence over the entire 10-year period. Further, because only FUNDEX spans the entire 10-year period, the Melbourne All Ordinaries Index was also used to estimate fund betas to test for stationarity of beta. The Melbourne All Ordinaries Index (hereafter called MELDEX) is simply a price index and does not include dividend distributions. As such MELDEX will underestimate the returns on a market index. It was felt necessary to include betas estimated using a market index to provide tentative evidence of whether fund betas exhibited stationarity over time (rather than rely solely on FUNDEX which comprised the funds themselves).

The results of all correlations[13] between the betas of different periods and different indexes were all significant at the 0.001 level. That is, the systematic risk characteristics of the funds were relatively stationary over time. This stationarity of fund betas is encouraging for investors because it means they can be reasonably sure of the risk attitude of the fund management. It also implies that risk-adjusted performance measures which use beta in the estimation of the performance statistic may be less liable to estimation errors.

The relationship between the standard deviations of the rates of return of funds in different periods was also examined. Similar to the results for the betas, the standard deviation of returns of the funds appeared not to change significantly over time.

Risk and investment objectives

In the United States a fund's investment objective can be taken from the Wiesenberger classification scheme. However, in Australia, no classification scheme exists. Another difficulty is that the names of the funds often do not provide any guide to the funds' specific investment objective. To overcome this difficulty each fund in the sample was specifically asked to state which of five investment objective categories the management thought was most appropriate. The five objectives were: (1) growth, (2) growth–income, (3) income–growth, (4) balanced, and (5) income. Because income funds were excluded from the study, only the first four are included in this section. However, initial estimates of income fund betas were found to be the lowest of the five.

Tables 30.2, 30.3 and 30.4 show the relationship between objectives and risk of the funds. The relationship between investment objective and systematic risk (beta) was consistent with expectations. That is, funds with an "aggressive" objective such as "growth" exhibited relatively higher systematic risk than those with a more conservative risk profile such as "balanced", irrespective of which index was used to estimate beta. However, there was a substantial overlap in betas between objective groups.

This was especially the case for the growth–income and income–growth groups. In all periods a t test for differences between means of the betas of each of the groups revealed that they were not significantly different at 0.05 level of significance. For the 10-year period and first 5-year period there also appeared to be no significant difference in the means of the income–growth and balanced groups.

The relationship between objectives and total variability was not as clearly defined as with systematic risk. Again there appeared to be little difference between the growth–income and income–growth groups. There also appeared to be substantial overlap in the standard deviation of returns between the groups. Despite this imprecision, if an investor was able to ascertain the investment objective of the funds, there appeared to be substantial information content in estimating future systematic risk and total variability, as the relative risk for each group tended to increase with successively more "aggressive" investment objectives.

Risk and investment performance

This section will examine the relationship between fund investment performance and risk. The expectation is that fund performance should be an increasing function of both systematic risk and total variability.

Summary statistics on the performance of the funds by objective groups are shown in tables 30.2, 30.3 and 30.4 for the periods 1969–78, 1969–73 and 1974–78 respectively.

As noted in the section on investment performance there appeared to be a negative relationship between risk and return as well as with the risk-adjusted performance measures over the 10-year period and the first 5-year period, although the relationship was not perfect. For example, the income–growth group which had the third lowest average systematic risk and second highest average total variability, outperformed all other objective groups no matter which performance measure was used. In the second 5-year period there appeared to be a consistent negative relationship between risk (both systematic risk and total variability) and the Jensen measure, whereas there appeared to be no discernible relationship between risk and rate of return.

The results of this and the previous section suggest that whereas the beta for each investment objective group increased with successively more aggressive objectives (to a lesser degree for total variability), the funds with a relatively higher risk level did not exhibit higher returns than those funds with a lower risk level. This was particularly noticeable in the second 5-year period where the market returns were greater than the returns on all the risk-free asset estimates. Given R_m was greater than R_f there should be a positive relationship between risk and return. As further evidence on these findings, the funds were grouped by beta quartile rather than by investment objective group (between which there is considerable overlap in the risk estimates). The summary statistics, for each of the three periods, are shown in table 30.11).

Over the 10-year period which included periods when the equity market was declining and rising, table 30.11(a) reveals that there was an inverse relationship between risk and return and the Jensen measure. For the entire 10-year period the mean return of FUNDEX (6.18 per cent) was slightly less than the mean return of the risk-free asset (6.37 per cent). Thus a negative relationship between risk and return would be expected, but not as pronounced as in table 30.11(a).

The first 5-year period relationship between risk and return and the Jensen measure in table 30.11(b) reveals an inverse relationship. Over this period FUNDEX return was 1.82 per cent and the risk-free asset return was 4.88 per cent. An inverse relationship was therefore expected for risk and return.

Table 30.11 Risk and performance measures

Risk quartile	Mean beta*	Total variability	Mean yearly return	Jensen measure†
(a) 10-year period 1969–1978				
4	1.40	5.48	3.41	−2.70
3	1.14	4.66	5.29	−0.89
2	0.83	4.33	7.31	1.10
1	0.46	2.76	7.67	1.39
Overall means	0.97	4.35	5.83	−0.35
(b) 5-year period 1969–1973				
4	1.37	4.81	−2.05	−2.74
3	1.12	4.00	0.94	−0.51
2	0.88	3.76	4.60	2.41
1	0.53	2.45	5.23	1.97
Overall means	0.98	3.77	2.15	0.27
(c) 5-year period 1974–1978				
4	1.42	6.35	9.06	−2.61
3	1.22	5.46	9.89	−1.25
2	0.95	4.83	9.72	−0.67
1	0.50	3.13	10.56	1.37
Overall means	1.03	4.98	9.79	−0.83

* Systematic risk using FUNDEX as the market index.
† Jensen measure estimated using FUNDEX as the market index.

However, there was not a perfect inverse relationship between risk and the Jensen measure.

Over the second 5-year period the equity market was increasing with the return on FUNDEX (10.54 per cent) greater than the return on the risk-free asset (7.85 per cent). A positive relationship between risk and return was therefore expected. However, there was a slight, but not perfect, inverse relationship. Also there was an inverse relationship between risk and the Jensen measure.

The regrouping of funds into beta risk revealed that the lowest risk quartile group, on average, outperformed all other quartile groups. In some instances the superiority was quite marked. Funds with relatively high risk levels did not extract higher returns (and risk-adjusted returns) than funds with relatively low risk levels. Two possible reasons may be that: (1) the return on the market portfolio was less than the return on the risk-free asset. However, this does not explain the results in the 1974–78 period; and (2) the fact that there was no significant difference in risk levels and therefore returns of the classes. Alternatively, it may be that the high risk funds generate too many transactions costs trying to outguess the size of the fund, its age or other financial characteristics that influence a fund's risk and return.[15]

Financial characteristics, performance and risk

The aim of this section is firstly to describe some relationships between the funds' financial characteristics and secondly to examine the relationship between fund performance and risk and their financial characteristics. The financial characteristics were obtained from each fund's 6-monthly distribution report. These were: (1) size, (2) number of investors, (3) number of investments, (4) age, (5) initial service fee, and (6) percentage of equity shares, fixed interest securities and cash in the fund's portfolio.

The analysis is described fully in Robson (1981). The main conclusions were as follows:
1. The larger the size of the fund the greater the number of investors and number of securities in the portfolio.
2. Older funds were *not* larger than younger funds.
3. There was no relationship between size, initial service fee and percentage of funds invested in equity shares, fixed interest securities and cash.
4. There was no relationship between size and the risk-adjusted performance of a fund.
5. Funds with higher initial service fees performed better than those which charged lower initial fees.
6. The best predictor of a fund's beta was the percentage of funds invested in equity shares (positively) and the percentage invested in fixed interest securities (negatively). This was expected, but none of the other characteristics were useful in predicting risk.

Conclusion

This study examined the investment performance of unit trusts and mutual funds in Australia over the 10-year period 1969–78. The major findings of the study were:
1. The overall investment performance of the funds in each of the periods was inferior to both market indexes and an industry average as calculated here. "Income–growth" funds consistently outperformed the other funds.
2. The funds did not exhibit any consistency in their relative investment performance from one period to the next period or periods. Nor did the funds exhibit any runs of superior investment performance over and above that expected, assuming an equal probability of being superior or inferior. However, a few funds exhibited a number of years of consecutive superior performance. Given a sample of the size in this study one would expect by pure chance that some funds would show a consecutive number of years of superior performance. Nonetheless, it cannot be ruled out with any certainty that such funds' results were due to superior skill rather than luck.
3. The evidence, while not conclusive, did reveal that the systematic risk values of the funds were relatively stationary over time. Similarly, the standard deviations of the returns of the funds did not appear to change significantly over time.
4. The relationship between investment objective and systematic risk values was consistent with expectations. The group of funds with the most aggressive investment objective exhibited the highest average beta value and funds with the most conservative investment objective exhibited the lowest average beta value. However, there was a degree of overlap between

the objective groupings. The relationship between investment objective and total variability was less clearly defined.

5. There appeared to be a negative relationship between fund risk levels (beta or total variability) and fund investment performance. Low risk funds appeared to outperform the high risk funds in each of the three time periods. In the second 5-year period, 1974–78, there was no significant relationship between risk and rate of return. However, this could be a function of the market indexes used and more particularly the time period of the research.

6. Overall financial characteristics of the funds such as size, age, etc., would not be useful for an investor in predicting future investment performance of the funds.

Appendix 1: Definition of variables

The following are the definitions of the variables used in the estimation procedures:

W_{tj} = Weekly continuously compounded rate of return of the Walter Index during the jth week of the tth 4-weekly period for the subperiod January 1969 to December 1973; $t = 1, \ldots, 65$.

S_t = Level of the Statex-Actuaries Accumulation Index at the end of the tth 4-weekly period for the subperiod January 1974 to December 1978; $t = 1, \ldots, 65$.

F_t = Level of the Fund Index at the end of the tth 4-weekly period for the period January 1969 to December 1978; $t = 1, \ldots, 130$.

R_{mt} = $(lnw_1 + lnw_2 + lnw_3 + lnw_4)_t$ Jan 69–Dec 73
$$t = 1, \ldots, 65$$

$\quad ln(S_t) - ln(S_{t-1})$ Jan 74–Dec 78
$$t = 1, \ldots, 65$$

$\quad ln(F_t) - ln(F_{t-1})$ Jan 69–Dec 78
$$t = 1, \ldots, 130.$$

Continuously compounded rate of return on the benchmark portfolio M during the tth 4-weekly period for each of the periods.

r_{yt} = Annual yield to maturity on a government security between consecutive "New Issue" dates, $t = 1, \ldots, 10$ years.

R_{ft} = $ln(r_{yt}) / 13, t = 1, \ldots, 130$.
Continuously compounded rate of return on the risk-free asset f during the tth 4-weekly period over the 10-year period January 1969 to December 1978.

P_{it} = Repurchase price per unit/share of the ith fund at the end of the tth 4-weekly period over which the fund was in existence.

D_{it} = Dividend per unit share paid by the ith fund during the tth 4-weekly period. That is, the period in which the unit/share went "ex-dividend".

R_{it} = $ln(P_{it} - P_{i,t-1} + D_{it}) - ln(P_{i,t-1})$
Continuously compounded rate of return on the ith fund during the tth 4-weekly period for the period over which the fund was in existence. (Adjusted for unit/share splits where appropriate.)
Systematic risk was estimated through the "market model" using

ordinary least-squares regression of a fund's rate of return (R_i) on the market rate of return (R_m) over time (t).

Acknowledgments

I am indebted to Professor R. R. Officer and two anonymous referees for comments on earlier drafts. I am also indebted to Terry Shevlin for his computer programming assistance. I also thank the managements of those Unit Trusts and Mutual Funds who so willingly provided information relevant to the study.

Notes

1. See Robson (1981) for a more detailed analysis of the role, growth and structure of the funds.
2. Alexander and Chervany (1980) report that an optimal estimation interval was generally four to six years.
3. Although the loss of two funds represents less than 3 per cent of the final sample, the two funds were relatively small compared with the other funds.
4. A number of funds were excluded from the sample because they were either property trusts or fully invested in another trust within the same management group.
5. See Officer (1980) for a discussion of why returns should be adjusted for risk differences when evaluating portfolio performance.
6. In general, the results were worse for the longer-term risk-free estimates. That is, because the longer-term risk-free rates of return were higher the funds' excess returns were lower (or more negative). However, the overall rankings between the performance measure did not change significantly.
7. The funds were asked to specify which objective best described each fund's investment policy.
8. Statistical tests to determine if the means of each performance measure were significantly different between objective groups were performed. Students t-test for difference between means (one-tailed test) and a one-way analysis of variance between groups were used. There were significant differences but the results are not reported here.
9. Two-tailed test at the 0.05 level.
10. For example, if a fund over the period 1969–73 had the Jensen measures of $+ - + - +$ this would count as four changes.
11. The Kolmogorov–Smirnov test avoids the problem of small expected frequencies in some categories.
12. Similarly, the standard deviation of the rate of return will have an impact on the Sharpe measure.
13. Spearman Rank Order and Pearson Product correlations were used.
14. In the interest of brevity, only the results using FUNDEX as the market index are shown. The relationships are the same for WALDEX and STATDEX.
15. Another reason may be that the risk-adjusted performance measures may be biased. See Friend and Blume (1970).

31 Superannuation fund managers —how do they rate?

R. Bird, H. Chin and M. McCrae

Praetz in a previous issue of this journal reported on the performance of Australian mutual funds and unit trusts.[1] He concluded that the performance of these institutions was poorer than expected, which is a similar conclusion to other studies evaluating the same institutions.[2] In this study we evaluate the performance of another group of investment managers—those who manage superannuation funds.

The data on quarterly returns earned by superannuation funds from January 1973 to June 1981 was supplied by Campbell and Cook.[3] By June 1981, 380 individual funds under the control of 27 management organisations (hereafter called managers) were included in the Campbell and Cook survey. We aggregated the individual funds under the control of each manager in order to obtain a measure of the quarterly returns of the portfolio under the control of each manager. In this study we report on the performance of 15 managers for whom there was data for a reasonably sized portfolio over the entire data period.

We used the two performance evaluation techniques—the Sharpe and Treynor techniques—used by Praetz and also a third technique developed by Jensen. It proved that the performance measures for each manager, and their rankings, were very highly correlated under all three techniques so the findings reported in this paper are restricted to those obtained when using the Jensen measure.

The Jensen measure is a derivative of the risk premium form of the capital asset pricing model (CAPM). According to the CAPM, the expected excess return on any asset (portfolio) is represented by the following equation.

$$E(R_i) - R_f = \beta_i \left[E(R_m) - R_f \right] \tag{1}$$

where
$$E(R_i) = \text{the expected return on portfolio } i$$
$$R_f = \text{the return on the risk-free asset}$$
$$E(R_m) = \text{the expected return on the market portfolio}$$
$$\beta_i = \text{portfolio } i\text{'s (relative) systematic risk.}$$

Reprinted from *JASSA* 4 (December 1982), 9–11, by permission of the authors and the publisher.

If investors' expectations are realised on the average, then equation (1) can be approximated by the following equation:

$$\bar{R}_{it} - R_{ft} = \beta_i [\bar{R}_{mt} - R_{ft}] + \bar{e}_{it} \tag{2}$$

where all the variables are measured *ex post* for each period, t, and the expected value of the error term, e_{it}, is zero.

Jensen's performance measure is derived from the following time series regression:

$$R_{it} - R_{ft} = \alpha_i + \beta_i [R_{mt} - R_{ft}] + e_{it} \tag{3}$$

Since the CAPM asserts that the intercept term in equation (3) should be zero, this intercept term (α_i) is the Jensen performance measure. A statistically significant positive (negative) intercept term can be interpreted as evidence of superior (inferior) performance.

In order to estimate equation (3) we had to obtain measures of the quarterly returns on the risk-free asset and the market portfolio. As an estimate of the return on the risk-free asset we used the yield on 13 week Treasury notes. In order to be in strict accordance with the CAPM, the return on the market portfolio is the return on a market value weighted portfolio of all assets. As such a measure is unobtainable we used the following proxy:

$$R_{mt} = 0.1\, X_{1t} + 0.1 X_{2t} + 0.1 X_{3t} + 0.7\, X_{4t} \tag{4}$$

where
X_{1t} = the yield on 13-week Treasury notes in period t
X_{2t} = the yield on government bonds, with 5 years to maturity, in period t
X_{3t} = the yield on semi-government securities, with 5 years to maturity, in period t
X_{4t} = the rate of return on the Statex-Actuaries Accumulation Index, in period t.

This proxy was chosen as it is consistent with restrictions on the investment alternatives available to the managers since all funds in our sample were subject to 30/20 requirements. The resulting Jensen measure for each manager measures his performance relative to a policy of investing 10 per cent of available funds in each of short-term government securities, medium-term government securities and medium-term semi-government securities and the remaining 70 per cent in an index fund based on the Statex-Actuaries Accumulation Index.

The results are reported in table 31.1. We found that only 1 of the 15 managers had a positive Jensen measure. Applying a 90 per cent confidence interval, the Jensen measure for this manager was significant but only one manager had a significant negative Jensen measure. Based on this evidence, it would be difficult to accept the hypothesis that the overall performance of managers was superior to that which would have been achieved if they had invested their funds in the proxy market portfolio. In fact, we found this to be true when we calculated the Jensen measure for a composite of the portfolios under the control of each manager.[4]

Our finding that superannuation fund managers were unable to outperform the simple strategy of effectively investing in an index fund after satisfying

Table 31.1 The managers' Jensen performance measures

Manager	Jensen measure	β value	R^2
1	−0.427	0.760	0.899
2	−0.895*	0.698	0.943
3	−0.196	0.716	0.930
4	−0.429	0.652	0.936
5	−0.179	0.677	0.898
6	−0.031	0.500	0.640
7	−0.502	0.654	0.800
8	0.927*	0.624	0.773
10	−0.165	0.568	0.888
13	−0.165	0.429	0.774
14	−0.452	0.486	0.839
15	−0.021	0.319	0.785
16	−0.550	0.510	0.804
17	−0.154	0.463	0.863
19	−0.029	0.555	0.823

* Significant using a 90 per cent confidence interval.
Note: The beta values in all cases were significantly different from both zero and 1.

the 30/20 requirements is somewhat damning.[5] However, it must be recognised that there are two countervailing biases inherent in our analysis. Our analysis is biased against the managers as the returns on our proxy market portfolios are gross of all charges whereas our returns for the managers are net of transactions costs incurred with respect to the investment of new funds. On the other hand it is also biased in their favour as the simple strategy inherent in the index would involve lower management costs (and supposedly fees) and transaction costs to those currently incurred.

The question posed in the title of this chapter was how do superannuation fund managers rate? On the basis of our evidence, the answer is not very well. However, this answer may be unreasonably damning of the managers as we found that their poor performance was confined to the early years covered in our study. The Jensen measure for the composite portfolio of all managers was −2.025 per cent per quarter (and significant) over the first nine quarters (i.e., January 1973 to March 1975) but +0.406 per cent per quarter (but not significant) over the remaining 25 quarters (i.e., April 1975 to June 1981). Maybe the answer should be, not so good but getting better.

Notes

1. P. Praetz, "The Measurement of Mutual Fund Performance in Australia", *JASSA*, September 1976, 8–10.
2. See M. Leslie, "The Performance of Equity-Based Unit Trusts and Mutual Funds in the period 1968–1975", unpublished MBA thesis, University of Queensland, 1976; and G. Robson, "The Investment Performance of Unit Trusts and Mutual Funds in Australia in the Period 1969 to 1978", unpublished M.Ec. thesis, Monash University, 1981.
3. The data were supplied by Campbell and Cook (Consulting Actuaries) on the basis that the names of individual funds and managers would not be disclosed.
4. The Jensen measure for the composite portfolio was −0.38 per cent but it was not statistically significant using a 90 per cent confidence interval.
5. One scenario which suggests the managers would not be expected to earn abnormal returns (i.e., have significant positive Jensen measures) is that the capital market is strong form efficient. A second scenario is that the capital market is only semi-strong form efficient but the managers arrive at their investment decisions on the basis of publicly available information. Assuming the second to be correct, it may suggest the managers devote too many resources to analysing publicly available information.

32 Internal performance evaluation and institutional security analysts

Frank J. Finn

Introduction and overview

Over the past two decades or so, numerous studies have investigated the performance of the share portfolios of actively managed investment funds. These studies have generally concluded that actively managed portfolios have not outperformed the market index on a risk-adjusted basis. Very few studies, however, have investigated the performance of actively managed funds at internal levels.

This chapter describes an evaluation of the internal research performed by security analysts employed in a major Australian institutional investor. The analysts' research was prepared exclusively for use within the institution and was at no time made public. The institution, referred to as Institution X, is an Australian life insurance office and pension fund manager and is one of the largest 10 life offices in Australia. The method followed here is one approach by which a managed fund can evaluate its research and other internal fund management procedures.

The analysts' earnings forecasts taken as a whole were similar to those of other market participants and could not be used to identify potentially profitable investment opportunities after the forecast period. However, when classified according to logical steps in the research procedure followed within Institution X, certain categories of the analysts' forecasts and recommendations were potentially profitable. These results point to a productive role played by the analysts in that they exhibited substantive predictive skills in certain instances. The results also were responsible for some changes in the research procedures with Institution X.

Analysts' research procedure

Each analyst was charged with preparing two reports per year on each of a limited number of assigned companies.[1] The reports contained a point estimate of annual earnings per share and a recommendation in one of the categories of buy, hold/buy, hold, hold/sell, sell. The first report for the year (called first-half forecast) was made some time after receipt of the company's annual report for the preceding year and prior to receipt of the interim report for the current year.[2] After receipt of the interim report, the procedure called for the analyst to visit the company, interview company executives, and then prepare his second report (called second-half forecast). However, because of the sheer volume of work involved, preparation of two reports and a visit for every company was regarded as exceptional, and no analyst completed 100 per cent of reports and visits in any year of the 5-year period studied.

The portfolio manager of Institution X measured accuracy of earnings forecasts as a quantitative evaluation of the analysts' research. However, since only second-half forecasts were assessed for accuracy, the system created an incentive for analysts running short of time to complete second-half forecasts at the expense of first-half forecasts.[3] More is said about this later.

Details were obtained of all research reports prepared by the analysts of Institution X over the 5-year period 1974–78. These comprised 834 reports prepared for 144 companies listed on the Australian Associated Stock Exchanges. To allow comparisons with earnings forecasts of other professional analysts, all stockbrokers' forecasts of earnings per share kept in the company files of Institution X were also obtained. This resulted in 2,070 forecasts by 50 brokerage firms on the same companies.

Forecast consensus and accuracy

A brief profile of the consensus and accuracy of the two groups of analysts' forecasts is given below. Comparisons are shown of forecasts made by the two groups before and those made after the announcement of the interim profit figure, and also those made for the same company in the same month.

Table 32.1 shows the correlation between forecasts of the two groups of analysts for the forecast variable defined as forecast percentage change in EPS.[4] Table 32.2 compares the accuracy of the two groups for forecasts on the same firm in the same month, using mean absolute and mean square error metrics for forecast percentage change in EPS.

Table 32.1 Correlation of forecasts of Institution X and brokers (forecast percentage change in EPS)

	1st half	2nd half
Forecasts in same half of year	0.71 (558)	0.92 (803)
Forecasts in same month	0.87 (83)	0.96 (78)

Note: Product moment correlation coefficient. Number of observations in parentheses.

Table 32.2 Accuracy of forecasts on same firms in same month (forecast percentage change in EPS)

	1st half			2nd half		
	Inst. X	Brokers	Z stat	Inst. X	Brokers	Z stat
Mean absolute error	0.47	0.41	0.74	0.09	0.10	0.44
Mean square error	2.63	2.02	0.68	0.02	0.02	0.38

Note: Z stat = Z statistic from the Wilcoxon matched-pairs signed-ranks test.

The forecasts of the two groups were very highly correlated. Forecasts made after the interim profit announcement were more highly correlated across analysts than those made prior to the interim announcement. Table 32.2 shows that there was no significant difference in forecast accuracy when the internal analysts' forecasts were compared with those made by the brokers in the same month.[5] In summary, the earnings forecasts of Institution X's analysts were very similar to those of other market participants, as represented by brokers' forecasts.

In considering forecasting accuracy, the relevant issue is not how accurate the forecasts turn out to be, but how accurate they were when made relative to the forecasts incorporated in market price at that time. The high degree of consensus in the forecasts of the analysts and brokers and the lack of any superior forecasting accuracy when the analysts were compared with the brokers suggest that the analysts' forecasts may be no more accurate than forecasts incorporated in market prices at the time the analysts made their forecasts. The issue of relative accuracy, or information content, is considered in more detail below.

Information content and methodology

The standard approach for investigating the effects of information contained in, say, a forecast variable is to examine share price adjustments of firms subject to the forecast around the forecast time. According to the capital asset pricing model of Sharpe and Lintner there is a positive linear relationship between a security's expected return and its systematic risk in the market. We can use this model to investigate information effects via securities' abnormal returns, or residuals, after controlling for systematic risk and for market factors.

Monthly closing prices were used throughout and the reference month, month 0, is the month in which a forecast or recommendation was made for a particular security. Abnormal returns were estimated for each security subject to a forecast or recommendation for each month in the period $[-12:+12]$, that is, 12 months before to 12 months after month 0. The average abnormal return, $AR[m]$, was computed in the usual way by averaging all residuals for each month m relative to month 0, and the cumulative average residual $CAR[p:q]$, cumulates the AR's from month p to month q.[6]

When a set of positive and negative forecasts or recommendations were evaluated, the signs of the residuals for the negative forecasts or recommendations were reversed in computing the AR's, CAR and test statistics. In this way a set of positive and negative forecasts or recommendations are represented by a single series of AR's and a single CAR rather than by one CAR for positive forecasts and another for negative forecasts. Any forecasting ability will be reflected as positive abnormal returns subsequent to the prediction date. The statistical significance of the results was estimated using t-$AR[m]$, the t statistic corresponding to $AR[m]$, and t-$CAR[p:q]$, the cumulative t statistic corresponding to $CAR[p:q]$.[7]

Earnings forecasts

To give an indication of Institution X's investment performance, month 0 was first redefined as the month of purchase. The CAR for the total purchases made during the evaluation period is shown in figure 32.1 and summarised below. The numbers in parentheses are the cumulative t statistics corresponding to the CAR's.

% CAR[−12:0]	% CAR[+1:+12]	N
8.29	−1.68	318
(3.80)	(−0.93)	

The shares purchased showed strong price increases in the months up to the purchase month. The post month 0 performance is consistent with the findings of the many studies of managed fund performance in that the stocks purchased showed average, or even slightly below average, performance subsequent to purchase. Based on this, the performance of Institution X appears to be typical of that of the managed funds investigated in the earlier studies.

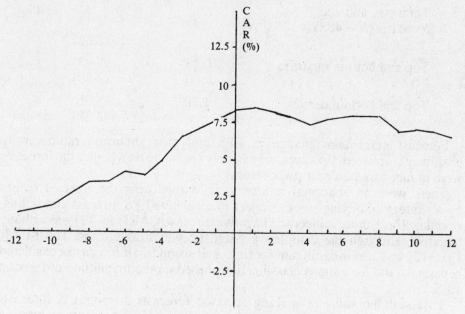

Month Relative to Month 0 (Month of Purchase)

Figure 32.1   Total purchases

Classification of analysts' forecasts into forecasts of "good" or "bad" EPS performance implies a measure of expected earnings against which predicted earnings are compared. Initially, a no-change expectation was assumed, and forecasts were classed as "good" earnings forecasts if forecast EPS was above actual EPS of the previous year, and vice versa for "bad" earnings forecasts.

Results for the complete group comprising all positive and negative EPS forecasts, with month 0 defined as the forecast month, are summarised below. Recall that the signs of the residuals for the negative forecasts have been reversed and added with the residuals for the positive forecasts.

% CAR[−12:0]	% CAR[+1:+12]	N
2.82	−2.55	718
(2.37)	(−1.41)	

The CAR and t statistic for the period [−12:0] indicate that the analysts discriminated between firms which had done well in the past and those which had performed poorly in the past in making their positive and negative EPS forecasts. Firms which were forecast to have earnings increases were firms which had shown positive abnormal returns over the months up to the forecast month, and vice versa for forecast EPS decreases. This also applied to the magnitude of forecast EPS. Firms which were forecast to have larger percentage changes in EPS were those which experienced larger abnormal returns in the past. For example, some results for the second-half forecasts are below:

	Mean absolute forecast % change in EPS	% CAR[−12:0]
Total pos. and neg. forecasts ($N = 405$)	0.48	4.32 (2.84)
Top and bottom quartiles	0.83	7.93 (2.80)
Top and bottom deciles	1.70	15.96 (4.30)

Forecast percentage change in EPS and past abnormal returns were positively correlated. However, we can only speculate on whether the forecasts were in fact based on past stock returns.[8]

There were no abnormal returns to be earned *after* the forecast month by a strategy of buying stocks subject to a positive EPS forecast and selling, or selling short, those subject to a negative forecast. CAR[+1:+12] was actually negative, although the cumulative t statistic was insignificant. The t-CAR [+1:+12] was also insignificant for first- and second-half forecasts considered separately and for various classifications based on the magnitude of forecast EPS.[9]

To assess the value of making accurate forecasts at month 0, forecasts were classified according to the subsequently realised percentage forecast error, defined as:

(Forecast EPS − Actual EPS) / Actual EPS.

Month 0 was still defined as the month of an analyst's forecast, whereas the actual error became known some time subsequent to month 0, when actual EPS was announced.

Consider the case where the forecast error as defined above was negative, which means that at month 0 the analyst underpredicted the subsequently announced EPS. If the analyst and the market were predicting the same EPS at month 0, we would expect positive abnormal returns to occur subsequent to month 0, as market participants became aware of the underprediction and market prices were revised accordingly. The CAR subsequent to month 0 shows the abnormal return which potentially could have been earned if the analysts were able to make accurate forecasts of the current year's EPS at month 0.[10] The post-month 0 results are summarised below:

	Mean absolute forecast error	% CAR[+1:+12]
Total pos. and neg. errors	0.226	6.23 (3.86)
Top and bottom quartiles	0.398	11.12 (5.40)
Top and bottom deciles	0.717	13.79 (4.00)

The potential abnormal return from perfect forecasting ability at month 0, averaged over all forecasts during the evaluation period, was 6.23 per cent, and the cumulative t statistic indicates that this return was statistically significant. Also, as is to be expected, the size of the CAR subsequent to month 0 was positively related to the magnitude of the forecast error. The obvious implication is that any ability of the analysts to improve on the consensus forecasts of the market at the time of making their forecasts would result in potentially large returns.

In evaluating the forecast error categories, any divergence in the AR's, in the direction of a negative AR for positive forecast errors and a positive AR for negative errors, prior to month 0, indicates that the analyst was "behind" the market in making his forecasts. Prices had adjusted prior to month 0 to any over- or underprediction in the analyst's EPS forecast. Any such divergence would be shown as a positive AR prior to month 0 for the combined group of positive and negative forecast errors.[11]

When first- and second-half forecast errors were considered separately, there was some suggestion that the analysts "missed" some information known to the market and already reflected in prices when making their first-half forecasts. Relevant AR's and t-AR's for month [−1] are:

	First-half forecasts % AR [−1]	Second-half forecasts % AR [−1]
Total pos. and neg. forecast errors	0.87 (2.21)	0.36 (0.84)
Top and bottom quartiles	2.66 (3.41)	0.35 (0.39)
Top and bottom deciles	3.40 (2.70)	0.42 (0.36)

The AR's for month [−1] were significant for the first-half forecast errors, suggesting that market prices had made some prior adjustment to the over or underprediction in the analysts' forecasts in month 0. The AR's for month [−1] for the second-half forecasts were small and insignificant. The sizes of the AR's for the different magnitudes of the first-half forecast errors suggests that more information known to the market at month [−1] was missed by the analysts for the larger errors.

It is worth noting again that during the whole period covered by this study, only the second-half forecasts were assessed for accuracy in evaluating the analysts' research. The procedure within Institution X has since been changed so that both first- and second-half forecasts are given equal weight in the evaluation system.

Forecast revisions and company visits

The reporting procedure within Institution X allowed the use of first-half forecasts of annual EPS as an alternative benchmark of expected earnings to that of the previous year's EPS. Thus second-half forecasts were classified as positive or negative revisions of first-half forecast EPS, when both forecasts were made for a company in the one year. Since approximately 37 per cent of all second-half forecasts in the evaluation period were preceded by a company visit, the second-half revisions were further classified according to whether or not they were prepared after a company visit. Comparisons of these categories over the period after month 0, the forecast month, should indicate the value of the company visit to the analysts in preparing their forecasts.

The results are summarised as:

	% CAR [−12:0]	% CAR [+1:+12]
Total pos. and neg. revisions *with* prior company visit (N = 103)	6.39 (1.75)	6.54 (1.99)
Total pos. and neg. revisions *without* prior company visit (N = 166)	8.19 (2.78)	−0.08 (−0.39)

The difference in the CAR's subsequent to the forecast month is striking. The abnormal return over the period [+1:+12] for the visit category is quite large, 6.54 per cent, compared with virtually zero for the no-visit category. The monthly AR's suggest that a large proportion of the price adjustment to information contained in the forecast revisions after a visit occurred in the first two months after the forecast month. CAR [+1:+2] was 3.78 per cent, with t-CAR [+1:+2] of 2.37.

The CAR's for positive and negative revisions in the visit category are shown separately in figure 32.2. The CAR's for the period [+1:+12] were of the correct sign for information content and of a similar order of magnitude, being 6.76 per cent and −6.50 per cent for the positive and negative revisions respectively.

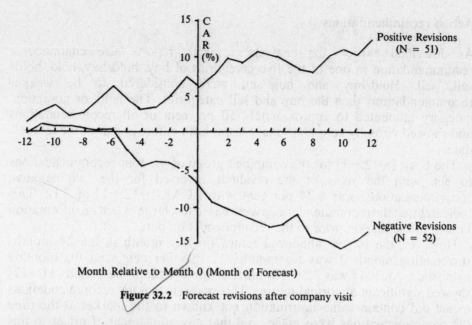

Figure 32.2 Forecast revisions after company visit

These results imply that the company visit did make a difference to the analysts' forecast revisions. An alternative explanation may be that the analysts possessed some advance specialised knowledge about which firms to visit, rather than the visit itself causing the positive CAR [+1:+12]. In either case, the visit was associated with subsequent large abnormal returns, and thus becomes a valuable tool for Institution X and its analysts in forming their forecasts. Averaged across all forecast revisions in the visit category, abnormal returns of approximately 6.5 per cent could have been earned by acting on the buy and sell signals implicit in the revisions.[12]

Forecasts in this category numbered 14.4 per cent of total earnings forecasts produced by the analysts during the period studied. Questioning within Institution X indicated at least two reasons for not visiting a company prior to the second-half forecast: (a) some firms would not agree to a visit and others discouraged the analyst by creating blocks such as the repeated unavailability of staff at mutually convenient times; (b) sheer volume of work made it almost impossible for an analyst to visit each assigned company each year, and a view expressed by analysts was that if in-house opinion was in line with brokers' opinions a visit could be a waste of time since it would be covering "information already known".

One obvious area of future investigation within Institution X's research procedure is to follow up and evaluate the reasons for visiting or not visiting a company. An *a priori* hypothesis is that a firm doing poorly is more reluctant to grant a visit than a firm doing well. Since the reasons for not conducting a visit had not been recorded in the analysts' reports, this was not investigated further. However, reasons for visiting or not visiting a company are now formally included in the analysts' research reports in the procedure currently being followed within Institution X.

Action recommendations

As described earlier, the analysts' research reports also contained a recommendation in one of the five categories of buy, hold/buy, hold, hold/sell, sell. Hold/buy and hold/sell were considered to be weaker recommendations then the buy and sell categories. The hold, or no-action, category amounted to approximately 50 per cent of all recommendations and showed virtually zero abnormal returns both before and after the forecast date.

The CAR [−12:−1] for the combined group of the four recommendations to act, with the signs of the residuals reversed for the two negative recommendations, was 6.24 per cent with t-CAR [−12:−1] of 3.12. This indicates that the recommendations were based to a large extent on information known to the market prior to the recommendation date.

However, the largest abnormal return for any month in the 24 months surrounding month 0 was for month +1, 1.98 per cent, and the monthly t statistic t-AR [+1] was 3.56. No other single month in the period [+1:+12] showed significant abnormal returns. This suggests that the recommendations to act did contain some information not known to the market at the time the recommendations were made, and that any adjustment of prices to this information occurred in the month after the recommendation month.

This is reinforced by AR [+1] for each of the four recommendation categories considered separately. The numbers in parentheses are for t-AR [+1].

	% AR [+1]	% of total recommendations
Buy	1.11 (1.83)	21
Hold/buy	1.36 (1.70)	12
Hold/sell	−3.49 (−1.96)	6
Sell	−3.56 (−2.47)	11

The negative recommendations, hold/sell and sell, appeared to contain more information than the positive recommendations, in the sense that the abnormal return in the month following the negative recommendations was almost three times that for the positive recommendations. The negative recommendations also comprised a smaller proportion of the total recommendations. The AR [+1] was 1.20 per cent averaged over the positive categories accounting for 33 per cent of all recommendations made during the period studied, whereas AR [+1] was −3.53 per cent averaged over the negative categories accounting for 17 per cent of all recommendations.[13]

It is interesting to consider possible reasons the analysts' negative recommendations might contain more information. Casual evidence suggests that stockbrokers in Australia have been reluctant in the past to issue sell recommendations.[14] However, the brokers' buy recommendations are widely circulated among clients and institutions. Therefore, it appears that there is more scope for the internal analysts to dig out negative information not incorporated in share prices than is the case for positive information.

Further analysis combining the recommendation categories, or revisions of recommendations, with forecast revisions after a company visit was not done because there was only a very small number of observations in any combined category.[15]

Conclusions

This study has attempted to evaluate the research function of a major Australian institutional investor by looking for efficiencies and inefficiencies in the research procedures followed within the organisation. The analysts' research reports were not made publicly available at any time, but were prepared for the exclusive use of the fund employing the analysts.

The method used involved identifying the analysts' activities which make up the research function, and also identifying the times at which forecasts were made. The activities making up the research function were then evaluated by analysing share price movements of the relevant companies over periods surrounding the forecast dates. This method is also appropriate for evaluating other internal management processes which make up a fund's total investment performance, such as the fund's purchasing or selling functions.[16]

An interesting conclusion from the forecast error analysis is that the analysts' forecasts were more up to date for second-half forecasts than for first-half forecasts. This was attributed to the internal evaluation procedure within Institution X during the study period, whereby second-half forecasts were formally assessed for accuracy but first-half forecasts were not. For first-half forecasts, there was evidence of less than complete extraction of information from market prices in that the forecast errors included information reflected in prior months' prices.

The results indicate a productive role for certain categories of the analysts' research. Potential abnormal returns were associated with revisions of forecast EPS following a company visit and with the analysts' action recommendations, especially the negative or sell categories.

As shown earlier, the total purchases of Institution X during the period of the study showed average, or even slightly below average, returns subsequent to purchase. The term "potential" abnormal return has been used throughout for the company visit and recommendation categories. The value of forecasts containing information may have been lost at subsequent stages of the fund management procedures, that is, at stages between the research and purchasing functions. Alternatively, the fact that an informed investor, the institution, wishes to buy at a "good" price could cause sellers to raise the price to the point at which the stock is not a "good" buy, in which case the fund did not actually have the opportunity to claim the potential abnormal return. If this was the case, the role of the analysts' research may be one of advising management which stocks *not* to buy, via the negative revisions and recommendations, so that a normal return could be earned on those actually bought.

Although the results point to substantive predictive skills of the analysts in certain instances, we should be cautious in generalising from these results. No attempt was made to analyse whether the number of analysts employed within the institution was appropriate given the opportunity of potential abnormal returns, and also, the analysis was conducted within one institution. However, there was no obvious reason Institution X or the analysts in Institution X were atypical of the organisations and individuals undertaking active investment management.

Acknowledgments

The comments of R. Ball, P. Brown, R. Dukes, L. Lookabill, R. Officer, W. Sharpe and G. Waymire on earlier versions of this paper are gratefully acknowledged.

Notes

1. The number of companies assigned to each analyst was between 40 and 45 during the period of this study.
2. Listing requirements of the Australian Associated Stock Exchanges require companies to issue two earnings reports per year. The interim report covers the first six months' results, and the annual report covers results for the full year.
3. This was possible since many companies have different balance dates during the year.
4. The variable used was $(\hat{E}_{it}/E_{i,t-1})$, where $\hat{E}_{it}$ is forecast EPS for firm i for year t, and $E_{i,t-1}$ is actual EPS for year $t-1$. The variable is unity plus the forecast percentage change in EPS. The distribution of this variable was truncated by omitting (a) observations where $E_{i,t-1}$ was zero or negative, and (b) the top 1 per cent of observations. Two additional variables were also tested, with virtually the same results: $\log (\hat{E}_{it}/E_{i,t-1})$ and forecast change in EPS scaled by the standard deviation of past EPS changes.
5. The lack of any significant differences is seen from the low z statistics from the Wilcoxon matched-pairs signed-ranks test.
6. Abnormal returns were estimated by using a portfolio-matching technique. Each sample security which experienced a forecast was matched with a portfolio of securities which did not experience forecasts and which were weighted to produce the same systematic risk as the sample security. The average difference between the returns of the sample securities and the relevant control portfolios was used as an estimate of the average abnormal return for that period. Details are contained in F. J. Finn, *Evaluation of the Internal Processes of Managed Investment Funds*, Greenwich, Connecticut: JAI Press Inc., 1984.
7. These t statistics were estimated by forming portfolios across time, in a manner similar to that first used by J. F. Jaffe, "Special Information and Insider Trading", *Journal of Business*, 1974, pp. 410–28; and G. Mandelker, "Risk and Return: The Case of Merging Firms", *Journal of Financial Economics*, 1974, pp. 303–35. This approach attempts to control for any cross-sectional dependence in securities subject to a forecast in the same month. The portfolio residuals were standardised by the portfolio standard deviation, and the average standardised abnormal return becomes the estimate of t-AR $[m]$. The t-CAR $[p{:}q]$ was obtained by cumulating the monthly t statistics and dividing by $\sqrt{n}$, where n is the number of months in the cumulating period.
8. Brown, Foster and Noreen present similar evidence for analysts' earnings forecast revisions in the United States. Upward forecast revisions were preceded by positive security returns, and vice versa. See P. Brown, G. Foster and E. Noreen, *Security Analyst Multi-Year Earnings Forecasts and the Capital Market*, Sarasota, Fla.:American Accounting Association, 1985.
9. Similar conclusions applied to the brokers' EPS forecasts:

% CAR [−12:0]	% CAR [+1:+12]	N
4.48	−0.39	2070
(2.66)	(−0.88)	

10. For a group of positive and negative forecast errors, the signs of the residuals were reversed for the positive forecast errors. Thus the CAR for the complete group is expected to be positive subsequent to month 0, and shows the average abnormal return which potentially could have been earned from the complete group of forecasts.

11. Note that this test is biased downwards as a measure of the extent to which the analyst was behind the market, since month 0 includes a period prior to the actual forecast date.

12. It should be noted that these results were for virtually the population of cases during the evaluation period in which an analyst made a first-half forecast and then conducted a company visit prior to his second-half forecast. Only four cases of zero revisions following a visit were excluded.

13. The four recommendation-to-act categories totalled 351 recommendations, accounting for approximately 50 per cent of total recommendations.

14. For example, the senior research partner of a large Melbourne broker has said: "You are a little limited on a sell recommendation because if you say a stock is overpriced, you can only talk to people who are the main shareholders in that stock. There is no point in talking to people who don't hold the stock." Another possible reason for reluctance was connections, such as underwriting, brokers and the companies may have had. These and other possible reasons are discussed in *Business Review Weekly*, Nov. 19–25, 1983, pp. 40–45.

15. Recommendations were combined with positive and negative earnings forecasts relative to last year's actual EPS. When the directions of the earnings forecast and the recommendation conflicted, the results pointed to information content in the recommendation, in terms of a significant AR[+1], rather than in the direction of the EPS forecast. This is consistent with the earlier conclusion that there was little information content in the earnings forecasts classified as positive or negative relative to last year's EPS.

16. See Finn (note 6) for an evaluation of these functions within Institution X.

33 Published investment recommendations and share prices: Are there free lunches in security analysis?

Ray Ball, Philip Brown and Frank J. Finn

We have all received "free" investment advice. Much of it is only "approximately" free, coming at the price of (say) a newspaper, a magazine or a call to a stockbroker. The question immediately arises: do we get something for nothing? Are there any free lunches in security analysis?

In this chapter, we investigate what happens to share prices before, at, and after 1,059 recommendations to buy or sell specific shares listed on the Melbourne Stock Exchange. Our aim is to determine whether recommended shares outperform the market as a whole, and whether the advice is timely or late. We chose recommendations which were published in two sources because we were unable to locate a continuous and unbiased sample of recommendations from other sources. Strictly speaking, the results which we report below apply only to the 1,059 recommendations investigated—we leave it to readers to decide whether to generalise these results to other sources (e.g., stockbrokers' recommendations, and reports from security analysts to investment managers) or to other recommendations from the same sources (e.g., more recent recommendations).

We begin by discussing the recommendations that we investigated and the source of the share price data used. Then we discuss the method of investigating whether or not the recommendations increase one's return on investment. The method seems simple and valid to us, and has been used many times over in Australian, American and other studies of the share market, but we explain it nevertheless so that readers can accept or reject our results if they accept or reject the method. Finally, we discuss the results and the conclusions that might be drawn from them.

Data

We analysed buy and sell recommendations published in two sources by four different tipsters. We have disguised the identities by calling them Source

Reprinted from *JASSA* 2 (June 1978), 5-10, by permission of the authors and the publisher.

A and Source B. For reasons that will become apparent, we collected recommendations made during the period 1959 through 1969. Share rate-of-return data (including dividends plus price changes) were obtained from the "$N = 651$ version" of the computer file compiled by Philip Brown.

Share price data

The "$N = 651$ version" of Philip Brown's price file contained monthly rates of return (adjusted for changes in the basis of quotation) for 651 industrial and commercial companies listed on the Melbourne Stock Exchange, and with ordinary capital exceeding \$1 million in par value. The file extended over the period January 1958 to December 1970.[1]

Because we wanted to investigate share price behaviour before and after (as well as at the time of) the recommendations, the availability of share price data over 1958–70 restricted us to recommendations over the smaller period 1959–69. In addition, we obviously restricted the analysis to recommendations concerning the 651 Melbourne-listed shares. This restriction does not seem onerous, since the 651 companies on the file are the largest of the Melbourne industrial and commercial issues.

Source A recommendations

Analysts making investment recommendations can be divided somewhat loosely into two groups: (1) fundamentalists, who study information such as profit reports, dividend announcements, industry reviews, etc., in attempting to gain insights into a firm's future earnings potential; and (2) chartists or technicians, who believe security prices move according to certain patterns and thus study past prices and/or trading volumes.

During the period 1959–69, Source A published two separate types of investment recommendations. The first was associated with a general section on investments, and typically contained reviews of selected companies' activities, earnings, etc. It made recommendations based largely upon fundamental factors. We classified recommendations from this source as being of a "fundamentalist" type.

We investigated only those cases which could reasonably be taken as either buy or sell recommendations. We ignored cases in which the recommendation was not unequivocal. For example, the following were classified as buy recommendations.

> The 50 cent shares reached a peak of \$1.88 in 1964, but by late '65 was as low as 80 cents. The current \$1.21 for a 5.1 per cent yield represents a strong recovery; if Waltons continues on its upwards earnings trend, which seems likely, prices could rise appreciably higher yet.

> Further price growth [for G. J. Coles and Co. Ltd] from the present \$1.34 (yield: not too low at 4.3 per cent) can be expected. In the longer term, the formidable chain of variety stores and supermarkets is a remarkable asset that seems to ensure success.

We identified 366 buy recommendations from this "fundamentalist" source for which we had share price data. No clear sell recommendations were found.

Examples of cases rejected as not being clear recommendations were:

> It now remains to be seen if [David Jones Ltd] can shake off whatever problems it has

and return to something like the buoyancy of earlier years. If an appreciable rise in earning rate is achieved this current year, the scrip could be worth buying for price recovery prospects. The interim report should be carefully studied by prospective investors.

Though, based on earnings growth in recent years, the $1 scrip [of ICIANZ Ltd] is far-over-priced at $2.02 for a 3.7 per cent yield, it seems possible that asset expansion could shortly begin to pay off. The better rise in profit last year suggests that this process might have already begun.

The second type of recommendation in Source A was made by the "trader", and was offered as advice for chart followers and market technicians. Recommendations by the "trader" began in September 1964, and were clearly based on technical factors, with comments such as "strict adherence to trend is essential" and "if the chartist sticks to price trends, he cannot go far wrong" appearing frequently in the discussions. Buy recommendations were typically cases where the stock was in a "well-defined uptrend" or "the uptrend is intact", and vice versa for sell recommendations. We identified 173 buy and 85 sell recommendations made by the "trader" and for which we had share price data.

Source B recommendations

Several types of recommendations were published in Source B from time to time. Analyses in two different sections were based on fundamental factors such as earnings and dividends. We identified 269 buy recommendations for which we had share price data, and included them under the heading "analyst". Again, analyses which could not reasonably be taken as recommendations for action were ignored. No clear sell recommendations were found.

We also selected another regular feature, which we called the "speculator". This section maintained a portfolio of shares and periodically purchased new shares and sold shares purchased some time previously. Purchases and sales were based on many factors, both fundamental and technical, rumours, and even intuition or whim. We excluded all cases where a stock was bought and sold in the same month. We studied 166 cases where a stock purchased in a particular month was not sold until at least the following month and for which we had share price data. The average holding period for the stocks included was between 2 and 3 months, although some stocks were held for considerably longer periods, up to 10 months in three cases.

Data summary

The 1,059 recommendations were from the only continuous and unbiased sample of recommendations available to us. The recommendations need not be typical of recommendations in general, nor even of earlier or later recommendations from the same sources. We are therefore restricted in generalising from the results. The requirement that the recommended shares be represented on Philip Brown's data file imposed another restriction. Consequently, we offer the results from this limited study as being of interest in their own right and leave inferences concerning their generality to the reader.

Method of analysis

Our aim is to determine whether or not recommended shares outperform the market as a whole. In addition, we would like to see how timely the recommendations are. The obvious difficulty arises as a result of differences among shares in risk. This implies that the market performance as a whole might not be a valid standard to compare the recommended shares against: the recommended shares might be riskier or less risky than the market. Futhermore, different analysts might tend to recommend shares of different risks, and their results might not be comparable.

There would be no problem if there were no relationship between risk and a share's performance. But there are good reasons to expect that higher-risk shares are *expected* (not guaranteed, of course, or there would be no risk!) to outperform the market as a whole. Furthermore, for the Melbourne shares on Philip Brown's file over the period we are studying (1958–70), there was in fact a significant relationship between average returns and risks.[2]

This problem is not a new one. The method that we used to get around it is not new either: it has been used in studies of share market performance since the mid-1960s. It simply consists of comparing the rate of return earned on the share with the risk-adjusted return on the index. The method of adjusting for the effect of risk differences upon rates of return is the "market model" first used by Fama et al. (1969) in their study of stock splits. More specific details are provided in our study of bonus issues and splits (see chapter 23).

The results were summarised in terms of a "cumulated average abnormal return", which was calculated as follows:

1. All rates of return, both for individual shares and for the index, were calculated as dividends and capital gains/losses, expressed as a percentage of opening price, with complete adjustments made for bonus issues, splits, bonus elements of rights issues, etc.
2. The index used was a simple average of the rates of return on all of the shares on Philip Brown's file.
3. The abnormal return for a particular share in a particular month was calculated as the difference between the rate of return on the share in that month and the risk-adjusted rate of return on the index in that month.
4. For each of the 1,059 recommendations we investigated, "month 0" was defined to be the month in which the recommendation was made. Because the recommendations occurred over an 11-year period, "month 0" was a different *calendar* month for different recommendations. But since we wanted to see what happened in the market place *around the time of the recommendations*, we calculated the average abnormal return at month 0 by averaging the abnormal returns in the different calendar months at which the different recommendations were made.
5. The process was repeated for "month +1", which was defined to be the month after the recommendations (different *calendar* months for different shares), for "month +2" (two months after), etc. This gave us a series of average abnormal returns, beginning twelve months before the recommendations and ending at various intervals after them. This series was designed to uncover the abnormal price movements of the average

recommended security, and to identify the months (relative to the recommendations) when the price movements occurred.
6. To gain some appreciation of the total price movement over time, we cumulated them (i.e., we added them together over time). The resulting "cumulative average abnormal returns" are plotted in figures 33.1 and 33.2.

This method of calculating and plotting cumulative average abnormal returns has been in use since the mid 1960s and has proven to be a sensitive device for uncovering share price movements due to dividend announcements, earnings announcements, bonus issues and other share market events.

As we shall now see, it also uncovered some abnormal price behaviour for shares that were the subject of the 1,059 recommendations.

Results

Figure 33.1 plots the cumulative average abnormal returns for both sources of recommendations from Source A. The period reported is 25 months: the month of the recommendation (month 0) and the 12 months on either side. Figure 33.2 reports similar statistics for the recommendations in Source B, over various time periods which we explain below.

The "fundamentalist"

Two features of the "fundamentalist's" recommendations stand out. First, he recommended the purchase of shares which had on average experienced positive abnormal returns. Over the 13 months up to the end of the month of the recommendations, the cumulative average abnormal return was +3.6 per cent. Thus, we can conclude that the "fundamentalist" and the share market were backing the same shares.

Second, the recommendations appear to have been too late to have earned investors abnormal returns. Of the +3.6 per cent cumulative abnormal return up to the end of month 0, only +0.6 per cent occured in month 0, compared with +2.7 per cent occurring in the prior 3 months and +0.3 per cent in the 9 months before that. These results suggest that the "fundamentalist's" recommendations were based on factors previously made public, such as profit or dividend announcements. If the "fundamentalist's" recommendations did contain any new information not previously made public, share prices adjusted rapidly to that information. No opportunities for profit remained for investors acting after the month of the recommendation.

The "trader"

As discussed previously, the "trader's" recommendations were based largely on established "trends" in prices. Judging from the abnormal returns plotted in figure 33.1, this is exactly what happened, but the "trends" did not continue as hoped.

First, it is clear from the plots that the "trader's" recommendations were shares which had experienced substantial price movements over the previous 12 months. As in the case of the "fundamentalist", there was little abnormal behaviour in the month of the recommendations: a slight average increase

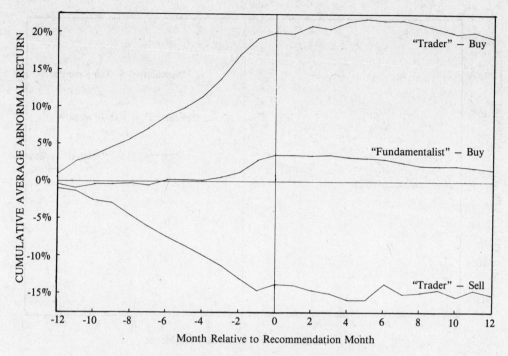

Figure 33.1   Recommendations from source A

for *both* the "buy" and "sell" recommendations. Most of the 15–20 per cent average abnormal return occurred in the 12 months prior to the recommendation month.

Second, over the 12 months following the recommendations, there was little average abnormal behaviour for either category—the graphs in figure 33.1 are quite "flat" in the post-recommendation period. The "trends" upon which the recommendations were based did not persist beyond the month of their publication.

The "analyst"

Results shown in figure 33.2 for the "analyst" were similar to those for the "fundamentalist". First, most of the average abnormal return occurred in the 12 months prior to the recommendation month: the average in month 0 was +0.9 per cent, compared with +3.3 per cent during the previous 3 months and +1.9 per cent in the 9 months prior to that.

Second, there was a tendency for the recommended shares to earn negative abnormal returns (i.e., below-average, risk-adjusted returns) in the 12 months following the month of recommendation.

The "speculator"

Two plots are shown in figure 33.2 for the "speculator". The first, labelled "1 to 10 months", is for the total 166 recommendations studied. The graph does not extend beyond 10 months, since this was the longest any share was held before resale. The 166 cases were held for varying periods from

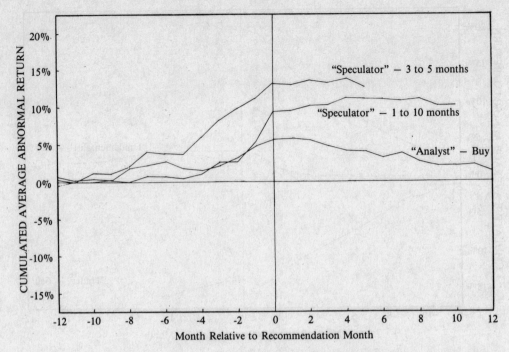

Figure 33.2   Recommendations from source B

1 to 10 months before resale. One limitation of the analysis is that we excluded all cases where a share was bought and sold in the same month. Thus the graph excludes any potential profit from these cases. The second plot for the "speculator" is for the 50 (of the 166) cases bought in month 0 and sold in months 3, 4 or 5. Those shares therefore were held for a minimum of 2 clear months after purchase. The two conclusions are by now familiar.

First, the "speculator" appears to have recommended the purchase of shares which have experienced average abnormal returns in the order of 10–15 per cent. Second, there is little evidence of abnormal returns beyond the month of the recommendation.

Conclusions

Surprisingly little is known about the profitability of published investment recommendations. We have studied recommendations from several published sources, and have found the results to consistently support the following conclusions.

The first and most obvious conclusion is that there are gains that can possibly be made from security analysis. In terms of the graphs we report, an earlier and more accurate source of information will allow the investor to experience some of the average abnormal returns prior to our "month 0".

The second conclusion is that most or all of the potential gains could not have been captured by waiting for the public announcement of the recommendations that we studied. For this sample at least, the recommended shares did not outperform the market (risk-adjusted).

These conclusions, strictly speaking, apply only to the 1,059 recommendations we studied. They might not apply to recommendations from other sources, or to other recommendations from the same source. We leave the reader to decide whether to extrapolate them to other samples, other time periods, other methods of "picking the winners", and other methods of deciding whether or not they are winners.

We finish by stating how these results fit into the much-maligned "efficient markets" viewpoint. This hypothesis suggests the following: (1) in a well-functioning, competitive marketplace, returns should be consistent with efforts (there should be no free lunches); (2) the effort involved in using publicly available information is "small" (an example would be last year's profit figure); and (3) thus, if the share market works well, the the returns from using publicly available information should be "small".

Numerous studies have supported this viewpoint. The present study adds one more piece of evidence: there were no free lunches from the sources we investigated.

Notes

1. The file has since been expanded to include 909 companies and has been updated to December 1973. The newer version was not available when we conducted this study.
2. A summary of the evidence is contained in: Ball, Brown and Officer (1976b and 1976c).

PART 7
Contingent claim pricing

34 Modelling option prices in Australia using the Black–Scholes model

R. L. Brown and T. J. Shevlin

Introduction

A substantial volume of research in the United States, Australia and elsewhere has made use of the Black–Scholes (1973b) option pricing model. For example, in the United States the efficiency of stock option markets has been investigated by Black and Scholes (1972), Galai (1977) and others. In Australia, efficiency has been investigated by Castagna and Matolcsy (1980). Similarly, the use of the Black–Scholes model to generate implied standard deviations (ISD's) has been studied by Latane and Rendelman (1976) and by Schmalensee and Trippi (1978) in the United States and subsequently by Brown (1978) in Australia. However, there has not yet been published in Australia any paper which has attempted to answer directly the deceptively simple but important question of how well the Black–Scholes model fits the actual pricing behaviour of the Australian options market. The most that has appeared is some indirect evidence in Brown (1978) and in Chiarella and Hughes (1978). In the United States, the question has been tackled by MacBeth and Merville (1979) using data for six underlying stocks in 1976. Accordingly, our aim in this chapter is to document the ability of the Black–Scholes model to track option prices determined in the Australian options market. The time period studied is from February 1976 to December 1980.

The remainder of the paper is constructed as follows. The Black–Scholes model is briefly presented below, and then the problem of estimating the standard deviation rate is considered. Data sources and collection methods are outlined and the major empirical findings are presented. Finally, the last section summarises our findings and conclusions.

The model

The Black–Scholes equation is: $w^* = S\,N(d_1) - Ce^{-rT}N(d_2)$ \hfill (1)

Reprinted from *Australian Journal of Management* 8, no. 1 (June 1983), 1–20, by permission of the authors and the publisher.

where:
$$d_1 = [ln(S/C) + (r + \frac{1}{2}\sigma^2)T]/\sigma\sqrt{T}$$
$$d_2 = d_1 - \sigma\sqrt{T}$$
w^* = model option price
s = stock price
C = exercise price
r = interest rate
σ = standard deviation of rate of return on the stock
T = option term to maturity
$N(\,.\,)$ indicates cumulative standard normal distribution function.

The model assumes that the option is of the European type (that is, the option may not be exercised prior to the maturity date) and that the stock does not pay dividends during the life of the option. Where dividends are not payable, Merton (1973c) has shown that the American/European distinction is irrelevant. However, where a dividend is payable during the option's life and where options are in fact of the American type (as in the Australian options market), some adjustment to the model is desirable. The procedure adopted here follows the suggestion of Black (1975). In this procedure, there are initially two model values calculated for each option. The first assumes that the option is exercised prematurely at the ex-dividend date. Accordingly, this model value is based on current stock price and an option term equal to the term from the date of valuation to the ex-dividend date. The second model value assumes that the option is held through the ex-dividend date to maturity[1] and therefore the stock price variable is measured by the observed (current) stock price less the present value of the forthcoming dividend.[2] The appropriate model price is then the larger of these two alternative model prices. The appropriate measure of the "term" is the value of T associated with the larger option price.

Estimation of the standard deviation rate

In option valuation, the estimation of the standard deviation rate (σ) is often of critical importance to the researcher. It is the only variable in the Black–Scholes model which is likely to be subject to significant measurement error; indeed, stock volatility is described by Black (1975, p. 36) as the "big unknown" in the option valuation formula. Because of its importance we have investigated a number of alternatives. Methods to estimate standard deviation rate fall into two broad groups. The first group uses some set(s) of historical stock prices and the second uses the model itself to generate so-called implied standard deviations (ISD's).[3]

There are a large number of variations available to the researcher within the general framework of historically based estimates. In contrast to the model-based estimates, the historically based estimates have the feature of being completely independent (in both time and construction) of the model itself. This seems desirable from a methodological viewpoint but, as shown below, will not of course necessarily produce the best fit between model prices and actual prices. In the "classical" version, the historical estimate ($\hat{\sigma}_{jt}$) is given by:

$$\hat{\sigma}_{jt} = [\frac{1}{\tau-1} \sum_{t=-\tau}^{-1} (R_{jt} - \bar{R}_j)^2]^{0.5}$$

where R_{jt} is the return on stock j at time t and the estimation period consists of τ time periods prior to the valuation date. There is, of course, an almost unlimited choice as to prior time period over which estimation could be performed. If the standard deviation rate is constant (as the model assumes) then there is reason to hope that the estimates should not prove too sensitive to choice of time period. A choice must also be made as to whether returns should be measured in their continuous or arithmetic form. Given the continuous-time framework in which the model is usually presented, we have concentrated on the continuous return definition. Other choices also face the researcher. Boyle and Ananthanarayan (1977) suggest that in a Bayesian framework the estimate could be adjusted as follows:

$$\hat{\sigma}_{jt}^{**} = \hat{\sigma}_{jt} [(\tau-1) / (\tau-3)]^{0.5}$$

Finally, Black (1975, p. 40) suggests that in reaching an estimate of standard deviation, more weight might be given to more recent return observations. An infinite variety of such weighting patterns exists. One of the simplest and most obvious is a linear weighting scheme in which the most recent return is given a weight of N, the next most recent a weight of $(N - 1)$, and so on, back to a weight of 1 for a return observed N periods ago, and a zero weight thereafter.[4]

Within the historically based group, but outside the "classifical" method, there are more complex estimators which make use not only of closing stock prices but also of data on such factors as high, low and opening prices. Garman and Klass (1980) present a number of these estimators but they suggest that, although these estimators are in principle more efficient than the classifical estimator, they are also rather more sensitive to the number of transactions between observations. We have not pursued this line of estimation because of data deficiencies (including lack of data on the number of transactions between observations).

We report below the results of a number of tests which make use of a standard deviation rate estimated in the "classical" fashion from past returns. In most of these tests we have used a rate referred to as HISTSD1, which is based on the following choices: the estimation period consists of 60 monthly adjusted returns ending the month prior to the option valuation date; the return definition adopted is the continuous (logarithmic) return; no Bayesian adjustment is used; and no differential weighting scheme (equivalently, equal weights) is applied to the past return series. However, we also present in table 34.2 evidence on the sensitivity of our results to the method used to estimate the standard deviation rate from past returns.

The second group of estimation procedures relies on using observed option prices to solve the model to obtain "implied standard deviations" (ISD's). These individual ISD's are then usually weighted and averaged to form a weighted implied standard deviation (WISD$_{jt}$) for stock j at time t. If WISD$_{jt}$ is then used to price options—as in, for example, Latane and Rendleman (1976), Chiras and Manaster (1978), MacBeth and Merville (1979) and Castagna and Matolcsy (1980)—then there is an obvious element of circularity involved in the procedure. For example, $WISD_{jt}$ will pick up not only errors in volatility measurement but also the influence of any relevant variable(s) omitted from the model. The problem is somewhat reduced if WISD is calculated at a point in time prior to the calculation of the option prices. In the tests reported below we use $WISD_{j, t-1}$ to value options traded at time t. However, even with this improvement we regard the procedure with suspicion and find it unsatisfying from a methodological viewpoint. There are, nevertheless, two reasons for investigating it empirically. First, for some purposes, it may be desirable to maximise model accuracy almost without regard to the method of estimation. For example, one may wish to value an option at a point in time when the option was not actually traded in the market. Second, a number of papers have used the approach without in every case documenting its ability to price options accurately. To use an Australian example, Castagna and Matolcsy (1980) were mainly interested in market efficiency and their analysis "*assumes* that all investors price options with the Black and Scholes model" (p. 2, emphasis added).

In this chapter we investigate only one method for calculating ISD's but we do document results for a number of different weighting schemes (including as a special case the use of equal weights). Evidence on using ISD's was first published by Latane and Rendleman (1976) and the procedure for their calculation is now well understood. Accordingly, we do not discuss this in any detail. In line with Black's approximation method, alternative ISD's are calculated, one with respect to each ex-dividend date and one with respect to maturity. It is, however, very unlikely that any ex-dividend date except the last is likely to be important. As shown by MacBeth and Merville (1979, pp. 1179-80) the appropriate ISD is the smallest one produced.

Various weighting schemes have been suggested to calculate the WISD of stock j at time t, including the following:

$$WISD1 = \frac{\sum\limits_{k=1}^{K} (ISD_k\, q_k)}{\sum\limits_{k=1}^{K} q_k} \qquad\qquad (2)$$

Brown (1978)

$$WISD2 = \left[\frac{\sum\limits_{k=1}^{K} (ISD_k\, q_k)^2}{\sum\limits_{k=1}^{K} (q_k^2)}\right]^{0.5} \qquad (3)$$

Latane and Rendleman
(1976, 1979)

$$WISD3 = \frac{\sum\limits_{k=1}^{K} ISD_k\, n_k}{\sum\limits_{k=1}^{K} n_k} \qquad\qquad (4)$$

Chiras and Manaster (1978)

where

$$q_k = \frac{\partial w_k}{\partial v_k}\Big|_{v_k = \text{ISD}_k}$$

$$n_k = \frac{\partial w_k}{\partial v_k} \cdot \frac{\text{ISD}_k}{w_k} \text{ is an elasticity measure}$$

$k = 1, \ldots, K$ is the number of options traded on stock j at time t.

w_k = the market price of option k.

In addition, there is also the equally weighted average,

$$\text{WISD4} = \frac{1}{K} \sum_{k=1}^{K} \text{ISD}_k \tag{5}$$

Schmalensee and
Trippi (1978); and
Patell and Wolfson (1979)

As mentioned above, to avoid some of the problems of circularity we estimate standard deviation rate by

$$\hat{\sigma}_{j,t} = \text{WISD}_{j,t-1}$$

In most of the tests which make use of the WISD concept we employ the weighting scheme defined by WISD1 above. However, we also present in table 34.6 evidence on the sensitivity of our results to the weighting scheme employed.

Data

Option prices in the Australian options market were collected from all trades occurring on the final trading day of each month over the period February 1976 to December 1980 (inclusive). The earlier date is the first month in which the Australian options market was open for trading and the later date was imposed by the time of data collection. This information was collected from the daily quote sheets of the Sydney Stock Exchange. An option price was recorded in the sample if, and only if, both of the following conditions were fulfilled:

(a) an option trade actually occurred (as evidenced by non-zero entries in the "volume traded" column and in the daily high/low columns); and

(b) the "last sale" option price was within the closing bid/ask spread for that option.

The intention of these rules for data selection is to minimise the problem of non-synchronous observations between option prices and the price of the underlying stock.

The underlying stocks chosen were the four which were listed in the Australian options market for the whole of the sample period. These were: Broken Hill Proprietary (BHP), CSR Ltd, Western Mining Corporation (WMC) and Woodside Petroleum Ltd (WPL). The sample consisted of over 1,500 option prices. Closing stock prices were also collected from the quote sheets, and information on dividends and capitalisation changes was collected from various stock exchange records. The Options Clearing House provided information on option maturity dates. Interest rates used were the prime rates published by the Australian Merchant Bankers Association.

Empirical findings

Prices using historical standard deviation estimates

Model option prices (w^*) were calculated using Black's adjustment to the Black–Scholes model and using HISTSD1 to estimate the standard deviation rate. We then calculate for each option the pricing difference, Δ, defined as model price less market price. That is, $\Delta = w^* - w$. The expected value of Δ is zero. The null hypothesis $H_0: \bar{\Delta} = 0$ is tested using a t statistic calculated for dependent (or matched) samples.[5] In addition, we calculate P, which is the percentage of the pricing differences which are positive. The expected value of $\bar{P}$ is 50 per cent. The null hypothesis $H_0.\bar{P} = 50$ per cent is tested using a simple binomial test (as approximated by the normal when $N_p \geqslant 5$ and $N(1 - p) \geqslant 5$ where N is sample size and p is sample proportion).[6] We also calculate the percentage pricing difference (D) is defined as

$$D = 100 \; \Delta \, / \, w = 100(w^* - w) \, / \, w$$

The three measures Δ, P and D are used extensively in the discussion of our results and in the supporting tables.

To summarise the overall "fit" of the model to the market, we present in table 34.1 information on mean prices, mean and standard deviation of pricing differences (Δ) and median[7] percentage pricing differences (D). Comparing the mean market price with mean model price shows that the model tends to underprice options by, "on average", a few cents (the lowest is about 3.5 cents for WPL and the highest about 7 cents for BHP). Although this may not appear a very great difference it is, nevertheless, a clear tendency towards underpricing. The associated t statistics indicate that there is virtually a zero probability that the "true" mean pricing difference could be zero. More formally, the null hypothesis of $\bar{\Delta} = 0$ can be rejected at a significance level of α at most of 0.0005. Median percentage differences range from about -3 per cent to -13 per cent and confirm this conclusion. The second-last column of the table reports results found for variable P. A P-value greater (less) than 50 per cent suggests that the model is tending to overprice (underprice) options relative to the market. These percentages range from 26 per cent (WMC) to 42 per cent (BHP). The final column reports the

Table 34.1 Pricing ability using historical estimates of standard deviation rate (HISTSD1), all options

Stock	Mean market price ($\bar{w}$) ($)	Mean model price ($\bar{w}^*$) ($)	Mean pricing difference ($\bar{\Delta}$) ($)	Standard deviation of Δ ($)	$t(\Delta)$	Prob [$\bar{\Delta}=0$] (%)	Median percentage pricing difference (D)	$P =$ percentage of $\Delta > 0$ (%)	Prob [$P=50$]
BHP	1.263	1.194	−0.069	0.199	−7.64	0.000	−2.81	41.9	0.000
CSR	0.633	0.585	−0.048	0.090	−7.86	0.000	−6.92	32.1	0.000
WMC	0.463	0.417	−0.046	0.068	−12.97	0.000	−12.73	26.0	0.000
WPL	0.359	0.324	−0.035	0.067	−11.07	0.000	−8.25	32.8	0.000

probability that the true percentage is 50 per cent using a simple binomial test. These results also indicate a significant tendency towards model underpricing. Equivalently, this underpricing is consistent with the argument that the estimates of standard deviation rate may be inaccurate; in particular, these estimates may be too low.

Table 34.2 provides evidence on the sensitivity of this finding to the method used to estimate the standard deviation rate from historical data. We investigate four possibilities (in addition to HISTSD1 used above) and in general find that there is little difference. Method 2 retains all the choices made in the calculation of HISTSD1 except that it uses a 30-month (instead of 60-month) estimation period. Similarly, Method 3 is equivalent to Method 1 except that arithmetic returns are used; Method 4 uses the adjustment suggested by Boyle and Ananthanarayan (1977) and Method 5 uses a linear weighting scheme to give greater weight to more recent observations. For space reasons we do not present full counterparts to table 34.1 and instead report mean Δ and variable P (the percentage of positive Δ's). There is a strong consistency between methods. All mean pricing differences are negative and in no case is there any chance (to three decimal places) that the true mean difference is zero. Although we do not perform any significance tests for differences *between* methods, it is apparent that the choice of method (insofar as we have tested the alternative) is not crucial.

This evidence may be compared with the little available from previously published Australian studies. Brown (1978) suggested that the model showed a strong tendency to underprice CSR, WMC and WPL options (BHP options were not included in that study). It was also suggested that with the possible exception of CSR, this tendency persisted in less extreme form into the first half of 1977, at which point the sample terminated. Chiarella and Hughes (1978) were not primarily concerned with a comparison of Black–Scholes prices with market prices. However, a limited comparison can be made by

Table 34.2 Comparison of pricing ability using different historical estimates of standard deviation rate

Stock	Measure	Estimation method number				
		1	2	3	4	5
BHP	$\bar{\Delta}(\$)$	−0.0694	−0.0958	−0.0596	−0.0618	−0.0939
	$P(\%)$	41.9	32.7	44.0	43.1	34.8
CSR	$\bar{\Delta}(\$)$	−0.0484	−0.0348	−0.0464	−0.0445	−0.0392
	$P(\%)$	32.1	32.1	34.0	34.0	29.7
WMC	$\bar{\Delta}(\$)$	−0.0464	−0.0416	−0.0389	−0.0435	−0.0448
	$P(\%)$	26.0	21.6	27.4	26.5	23.5
WPL	$\bar{\Delta}(\$)$	−0.0348	−0.0448	−0.0262	−0.0325	−0.0419
	$P(\%)$	32.8	19.1	36.9	34.1	23.3

Notes:

$\bar{\Delta}$ is mean pricing difference.

P is percentage of Δ's which are positive.

Method 1(i.e., HISTSD1) is described in detail in the section "Estimation of the Standard Deviation Rate" of the text. Methods 2 to 5 are identical with Method 1 except in each case, in one (different) respect. The differences are given in the section "Prices Using Historical Standard Deviation Estimates" of the text.

For all methods and stocks the value of Prob[$\bar{\Delta}$=0] was zero to three decimal places.

referring to their table 2 (p. 47), in which all 20 reported BHP option prices and 19 of the 20 WMC option prices were *overpriced* by the model. These prices relate entirely to trading in the second half of 1977. A year-by-year summary of our results is presented in table 34.3. Our results are essentially consistent with both of the previous studies referred to above. Model underpricing of CSR, WMC and WPL in 1976 is again evident.[8] By 1977 this tendency has been reversed and overpricing is evident, especially in the case of BHP. In the last three years (1978–80) the tendency was again towards underpricing by the model although not to the same extent as in 1976. Overall, therefore the tendency is towards underpricing except in 1977. Possible reasons for the anomalous overpricing are examined below.

Table 34.3 Pricing ability using historical estimates of standard deviation rate: (HISTSD1) by calendar year

Stock		$\bar{\Delta}(\$)$	Prob[$\bar{\Delta}$=0]	Median D(%)	P(%)	Prob[P=50]
BHP	1976	−0.005	0.731	1.13	54.41	0.467
	1977	0.083	0.000	23.21	85.48	0.000
	1978	0.004	0.806	1.20	52.38	0.626
	1979	−0.104	0.000	−6.62	31.85	0.000
	1980	−0.223	0.000	−11.66	11.82	0.000
CSR	1976	−0.091	0.000	−19.61	10.42	0.000
	1977	0.032	0.033	9.63	76.92	0.092
	1978	−0.014	0.161	−3.26	38.09	0.275
	1979	−0.015	0.065	−2.46	43.48	0.378
	1980	−0.063	0.000	−6.94	29.76	0.000
WMC	1976	−0.046	0.000	−22.90	10.00	0.000
	1977	0.017	0.003	15.03	74.36	0.002
	1978	−0.027	0.000	−17.63	26.32	0.004
	1979	−0.057	0.000	−12.13	22.32	0.000
	1980	−0.066	0.000	−11.74	22.33	0.000
WPL	1976	−0.031	0.000	−13.22	16.88	0.000
	1977	0.008	0.000	7.09	65.22	0.012
	1978	−0.006	0.154	−9.06	41.51	0.218
	1979	−0.025	0.000	−5.17	40.98	0.047
	1980	−0.080	0.000	−17.29	14.18	0.000

MacBeth and Merville (1979) found consistent relationships between, on the one hand, the size and direction of the pricing difference and, on the other hand, the type of option being valued. For example, they found that the model tended to underprice (overprice) options which were in (out) of the money.[9] They also found that pricing errors were smaller for short-term options and the error increased as the term to maturity increased. Panel A of table 34.4 disaggregates our results according to whether the option being valued is in-the-money or out-of-the-money. Panel B disaggregates the results according to whether the effective term of the option is "short" (less than or equal to three months) or "long" (greater than three months).[10] The model underprices significantly both in-the-money and out-of-the-money options but only in the case of BHP options is it possible to distinguish statistically[11] between the average performance of the model in pricing these two option types. Note that although in dollar terms there is little difference in pricing performance, the model records much larger percentage pricing

Table 34.4 Pricing ability using historical estimates of standard deviation rate: (HISTSD1) by option type

Panel A: "In-the-money" versus "out-of-the-money"

Stock	Type	$\bar{\Delta}(\$)$	Prob[$\bar{\Delta}=0$]	Prob [$\bar{\Delta}$IN=$\bar{\Delta}$OUT]	Median $D(\%)$	$P(\%)$	Prob[P=50]
BHP	In	−0.084	0.000		−2.76	39.75	0.000
	Out	−0.042	0.002	0.024	−5.84	46.20	0.340
CSR	In	−0.042	0.000		−4.15	36.36	0.001
	Out	−0.061	0.000	0.151	−23.87	23.14	0.000
WMC	In	−0.044	0.000		−4.84	30.05	0.000
	Out	−0.050	0.000	0.372	−30.73	20.13	0.000
WPL	In	−0.034	0.000		−5.00	36.69	0.000
	Out	−0.036	0.000	0.711	−19.09	26.55	0.000

Panel B: Short (⩽ 3 months) versus long (> 3 months)

Stock	Type	$\bar{\Delta}(\$)$	Prob[$\bar{\Delta}=0$]	Prob [$\bar{\Delta}$SH=$\bar{\Delta}$LO]	Median $D(\%)$	$P(\%)$	Prob[P=50]
BHP	Short	−0.047	0.000		−1.35	44.64	0.109
	Long	−0.089	0.000	0.022	−4.81	39.45	0.001
CSR	Short	−0.026	0.001		−5.51	39.39	0.035
	Long	−0.068	0.000	0.001	−8.44	25.66	0.000
WMC	Short	−0.030	0.000		−8.41	27.66	0.000
	Long	−0.057	0.000	0.000	−15.15	24.89	0.000
WPL	Short	−0.013	0.005		−3.06	41.28	0.022
	Long	−0.048	0.000	0.000	−11.20	27.56	0.000

errors for out-of-the-money options. This result is not surprising and reflects the fact that market prices of out-of-the-money options are much lower than in-the-money options.

On a short versus long basis (Panel B) there is again underpricing of both option types, but there is statistically significant tendency for the model to be even less successful (in dollar terms) in valuing long options rather than short options. This result is to be expected given that both Black–Scholes model prices and market prices converge to the minimum of zero or S–C as term to maturity approaches zero.[12]

These results raise the possibility that the anomalous overpricing in 1977 as reported in table 34.3 can be explained by, say, an unusually large proportion of 1977 trades being in an option type which the model tends to overprice regardless of year of trade. To check this possibility we analysed the 1977 trades but did not observe such a domination by any single option type. In addition, all four option types were overpriced by the model in 1977. The explanation of the 1977 results must therefore lie elsewhere.

In principle, it is possible to explain differences between model values and actual values by invoking measurement error in the variables and/or omitted variables. Researchers into option pricing have usually regarded the standard deviation rate as the variable most likely to be measured with error. Thus our results suggest that the Black–Scholes model may be misspecified. The number of variables which might have been improperly omitted is indefinitely large but might include, for example, taxation variables. As noted previously in this chapter, the concept of an implied standard deviation has, in one form or another, commonly been employed as a supposed means of correcting for these problems. In the next section, we examine the extent to which such procedures improve the empirical fit of the model.

Prices using "implied" standard deviations

The overall picture presented by the results reported in the previous section is one of model underpricing. In this section we present our findings on the ability of the model to price options when volatility is measured by the lagged value of WISD. Tables 34.5 and 34.8 are counterparts[13] to tables 34.1 and 34.4.

Tables 34.5 uses lagged WISD1 (the simple weighted average ISD) to estimate standard deviation rate and is constructed so as to permit direct comparison with table 34.1 (which used historical estimates of standard deviation rate). Mean pricing differences are now positive for all four stocks and much lower in absolute value (less than half of 1 cent for BHP, WMC and WPL and 1.2 cents for CSR). Median percentage pricing differences are around 1 per cent or less. The t statistics are much lower, and, using the conventional standards of significance tests, none is significant at $\alpha = 0.05$. The same is true of the proportion of errors which are positive. In summary, the overall picture now is one of much greater accuracy than was found using the historical estimates of standard deviation rate. However, the tendency has switched from underpricing to a slight, but not statistically significant, tendency to overprice options by the model, relative to the market.

Table 34.5 Pricing ability using lagged values of WISD1 to estimate standard deviation rate: all options

Stock	Mean market price ($\bar{w}$) ($)	Mean model price ($\bar{w}*$) ($)	Mean pricing difference ($\bar{\Delta}$) ($)	Standard deviation of Δ ($)	$t(\bar{\Delta})$	Prob [$\Delta=0$]	Median percentage pricing difference (D) (%)	$P =$ percentage of $\Delta > 0$ (%)	Prob [$P=50$]
BHP	1.272	1.273	0.001	0.185	0.09	0.931	0.42	51.0	0.679
CSR	0.691	0.703	0.012	0.095	1.73	0.085	0.81	54.2	0.262
WMC	0.477	0.482	0.004	0.069	1.12	0.263	0.39	51.2	0.666
WPL	0.370	0.373	0.003	0.052	1.47	0.143	1.10	53.8	0.114

To test the sensitivity of our results to the particular definition of WISD employed we re-ran the analysis using the other three definitions of WISD given in equations (3) to (5) inclusive. Summary statistics obtained are given in table 34.6. In general, the findings are not particularly sensitive to the definition employed. If, instead of using WISD1, we had used either of the other two "unequal weighting" formulae (WISD2 or WISD3), our inferences would be unaltered. As would be expected, the performance of WISD4 (the equally weighted definition) is noticeably different, but even so, the inference of overpricing is unchanged and the performance using WISD4 is still better than that achieved using the particular historical estimates tested.

In table 34.7 we present results by year. Recall that under HISTSD1 options were underpriced in all years 1976–80, except 1977 in which they were

Table 34.6　Comparison of pricing ability using different definitions of WISD

Stock	Measure	WISD definition			
		WISD1	WISD2	WISD3	WISD4
BHP	$\bar{\Delta}(\$)$	0.0007	−0.0034	−0.0014	0.0284
	Prob[$\bar{\Delta}$=0]	0.931	0.676	0.873	0.009
	P(%)	51.0	50.0	49.5	54.5
CSR	$\bar{\Delta}(\$)$	0.0123	0.0123	0.0091	0.0211
	Prob[$\bar{\Delta}$=0]	0.085	0.089	0.212	0.006
	P(%)	54.2	54.2	55.3	59.2
WMC	$\bar{\Delta}(\$)$	0.0041	0.0034	0.0061	0.0091
	Prob[$\bar{\Delta}$=0]	0.263	0.350	0.093	0.017
	P(%)	51.2	51.2	53.2	54.3
WPL	$\bar{\Delta}(\$)$	0.0036	0.0030	0.0045	0.0066
	Prob[$\bar{\Delta}$=0]	0.143	0.210	0.062	0.019
	P(%)	53.8	54.5	55.6	55.6

Notes:

$\bar{\Delta}$ is mean pricing difference.
P is percentage of Δ's which are positive.
For WISD definitions see equations (2) to (5) in the text.

significantly overpriced. The first point to note from table 34.7 is that there is no consistent significant under- or overpricing in any year. In 1977 all of the mean pricing errors are positive although only WPL is significantly different from zero (at $\alpha = 0.05$).[14] The only other statistically significant mean pricing errors are recorded in 1978 by both BHP and WPL suggesting a tendency for the model to underprice.

Table 34.7　Pricing ability using lagged values of WISD1 to estimate standard deviation rate: by calendar year

Stock		$\bar{\Delta}(\$)$	Prob[$\bar{\Delta}$=0]	Median D(%)	P(%)	Prob[P=50]
BHP	1976	−0.013	0.566	3.04	50.82	0.898
	1977	0.009	0.379	−3.39	48.39	0.800
	1978	−0.026	0.026	−2.81	43.81	0.205
	1979	0.008	0.658	1.69	58.52	0.048
	1980	0.021	0.387	−0.19	50.00	1.000
CSR	1976	0.006	0.768	1.25	51.35	0.870
	1977	0.044	0.280	22.06	75.00	0.318
	1978	−0.014	0.253	−4.91	33.33	0.197
	1979	0.017	0.232	0.81	56.41	0.424
	1980	0.016	0.098	1.80	59.14	0.191
WMC	1976	0.004	0.497	−2.15	47.62	0.706
	1977	0.008	0.142	4.04	64.71	0.087
	1978	−0.006	0.188	−8.50	47.06	0.732
	1979	−0.005	0.345	−0.66	46.43	0.450
	1980	0.016	0.125	0.74	55.34	0.279
WPL	1976	0.001	0.793	2.77	54.67	0.419
	1977	0.006	0.031	2.80	58.73	0.166
	1978	−0.012	0.004	−7.89	37.21	0.094
	1979	0.002	0.354	1.42	59.02	0.047
	1980	0.011	0.154	0.13	51.49	0.730

The results suggest that the observed anomalous model overpricing in 1977 was in part due to an incorrect estimate of the standard deviation rate. The Black–Scholes model is an increasing function of volatility and if the model price exceeds the market price this suggests that the market is using a lower estimate of volatility than that used in the model. As outlined previously the market's estimate of volatility is the "big unknown". A comparison of HISTSD1 with WISD1 (where we are interpreting WISD1 as our "best" estimate of volatility)[15] for the year 1977 indicates that HISTSD1 is greater than WISD1 in 78 per cent of the cases. Using a simple binomial test the probability that the true percentage is 50 per cent is zero.

Finally, in table 34.8 we present results for options classified by type of option (that is, whether in or out of the money and whether short or long). The inferences to be drawn from this table are rather different from those drawn from its historically based counterpart (table 34.4). Naturally, given the results presented in table 34.5, the overall tendency in table 34.8 must be towards overpricing but, unlike table 34.4, the overall tendency is not necessarily true of each subcategory. There are some negative mean errors and some percentage *P*-values less than 50.

Table 34.8 Pricing ability using lagged values of WISD1 to estimate standard deviation rate: by option type

Panel A: "In-the-money" versus "out-of-the-money"

Stock	Type	$\bar{\Delta}(\$)$	Prob$[\bar{\Delta}=0]$	Prob $[\bar{\Delta}\text{IN}=\bar{\Delta}\text{OUT}]$	Median $D(\%)$	$P(\%)$	Prob$[P=50]$
BHP	In	−0.012	0.295		0.05	50.00	1.000
	Out	0.026	0.020	0.034	0.77	52.87	0.472
CSR	In	0.013	0.143		0.48	54.10	0.365
	Out	0.011	0.372	0.892	2.40	54.39	0.508
WMC	In	0.006	0.247		0.60	53.17	0.364
	Out	0.002	0.756	0.581	−2.15	48.23	0.674
WPL	In	0.004	0.232		1.14	55.72	0.060
	Out	0.003	0.390	0.805	0.27	50.60	0.877

Panel B: Short ($\leqslant$ 3 months) versus long ($>$ 3 months)

Stock	Type	$\bar{\Delta}(\$)$	Prob$[\bar{\Delta}=0]$	Prob $[\bar{\Delta}\text{SH}=\bar{\Delta}\text{LO}]$	Median $D(\%)$	$P(\%)$	Prob$[P=50]$
BHP	Short	0.003	0.737		1.01	52.70	0.421
	Long	−0.002	0.900	0.764	0.37	49.40	0.849
CSR	Short	0.015	0.089		0.69	55.17	0.335
	Long	0.010	0.369	0.763	1.29	53.26	0.532
WMC	Short	−0.000	0.964		0.30	51.85	0.667
	Long	0.007	0.186	0.346	1.14	50.71	0.837
WPL	Short	0.008	0.060		2.52	61.68	0.003
	Long	0.001	0.772	0.155	−0.41	48.89	0.715

In table 34.4 the mean "in-the-money" pricing difference was closer to zero than the mean "out-of-the-money" pricing difference for CSR, WMC and WPL whereas the reverse was true for BHP. In table 34.8 the exact opposite is found. "Out" options are, on average, more accurately priced than "in" options for CSR, WMC and WPL and the reverse is true of BHP options. However, except for BHP, these differences are not statistically significant. Again, in table 34.4 the average pricing difference for long options exceeded that on short options, to a degree which is statistically significant. The finding in table 34.8 is that all mean errors are in absolute terms "small" (less than 1.5 cents) and in three cases out of four, the mean error for the long options is slightly smaller than the mean error for the short options (although not significantly smaller).[16]

Summary and conclusion

Although both the Black–Scholes option pricing model (as adjusted by Black to incorporate dividend effects) and the Australian options market have been in existence for some years there are now published results on how well the model can explain (or "fit") prices in the Australian market. We have investigated this question using approximately 1,500 option prices from the period February 1976 to December 1980. Using an historical estimate of standard deviation rate we find that the model tends to underprice options significantly, relative to the market. This result was robust to several alternative procedures for estimating standard deviation rate and on average applied to options regardless of whether in-the-money or out-of-the-money and whether short or long. In terms of mean pricing difference, long options seemed to be particularly troublesome for the model. One interpretation is that in determining option prices the market in Australia may use more information than is contained in historical estimates of standard deviation rate. It also suggests that care should be exercised in research which relies on model prices (based on historical standard deviation rates) as a control mechanism, since it may be that the control itself is biased).

As would be expected, model accuracy is greatly improved when lagged WISD values are used to estimate standard deviation rate. Very few mean pricing differences remained statistically significantly different from zero and were in absolute terms quite "small" (often less than 1 cent). The overall tendency was slightly towards model overpricing but this was not true of all option types. The model's previous difficulty in pricing long options virtually disappeared using WISD's. Where the need is for an accurate pricing formula (without regard for methodological virtue) the use of lagged WISD values can be recommended insofar as our results are representative of the Australian experience. Overall, however, the main implication of our findings is that the version of the Black–Scholes model investigated in this paper is misspecified and that the omitted variables (whose effects are taken up by the WISD) are relevant to option pricing in Australia.

Acknowledgments

For helpful comments on an earlier draft, the authors are grateful to Michael Brennan, Bob Officer, Graham Peirson, Norm Sinclair and an anonymous referee. All remaining errors are the authors'.

Notes

1. For ease of exposition, the explanation in the text assumes there is only one ex-dividend date during the life of the option. In fact there may be two such dates. A different option value is then calculated with respect to each ex-dividend date and with respect to the maturity date. It is, however, exceedingly unlikely that the option value with respect to the earliest ex-dividend date would be the greatest of the three.
2. The present value is calculated at the riskless rate over the time period from date of trade (observation) to dividend payment date, which typically falls several weeks after the ex-dividend date.
3. For examples of the former, see Black and Scholes (1972) or Galai (1977). On the latter see Latane and Rendleman (1976), Chiras and Manaster (1978), Schmalensee and Trippi (1978) and MacBeth and Merville (1979). A third group might also be distinguished. The standard deviation rate can be estimated using those prices at which the stock actually traded during life of the option. We have not used this method, partly because it uses a significant amount of information not available to the market at the time of trade and, more pragmatically, partly because of the greater volume of data required.
4. This is a common time-weighting scheme. For example, a similar system is used to weight bond coupon payments in the Macaulay definition of bond duration. See, for example, Van Horne (1978, pp. 118–20).
5. See Chou (1969, pp. 391–93). The standard error $S_{\bar\Delta}$ is estimated as $S_{\bar\Delta}^- / (N - 1)^{0.5}$ where $S_{\bar\Delta}^-$ is the standard deviation estimated as $\Delta[\Sigma(\Delta - \Delta) / (N - 1)]^{0.5}$ and N the number of pricing differences. The ratio of $\bar\Delta$ to its standard error is distributed as the Student's distribution with $N = 1$ degrees of freedom. The test is two-tailed as $H_1 . \bar\Delta \neq 0$.
6. See Chou (1969, p. 317). The test is again two-tailed as $H_1 : P \neq 50\%$.
7. Because option prices can be very low in absolute terms, the percentage pricing differences contain some outliers. We therefore use median to indicate central tendency. The mean percentage pricing differences for each company were BHP 4.04 per cent, CSR −11.75 per cent, WMC −14.12 per cent, and WPL −9.23 per cent. Non-parametric probabilities for the median $D = 0$ per cent were not estimated as the parametric significance tests on $\bar\Delta$ and P are more powerful and in any event provide consistent results here.
8. Note that data for each of the studies were collected independently.
9. We follow the suggestion of Merton (1973c, p. 145) and define an "in-the-money" option as one for which the current stock price exceeds the present value of the exercise price. In this calculation, present value is measured at the riskless rate over the effective term to maturity.
10. We define "three months" to be one-quarter of a 365-day year: i.e., 91.25 days.
11. To test the difference in pricing errors between short and long options (and between in and out) two-tailed probabilities were estimated using a t statistic with a pooled standard error estimate. See Chou (1969, pp. 389–91).
12. Given the significant difference in pricing errors for the short/long classification, a four-way classification of option type was examined so as to control for this difference. The results are not reported here, as they are consistent with the results of the two-way classification in table 34.4. For each company, except BHP, the smallest pricing error both in dollar and percentage terms is recorded for the in/short classification which is consistent with our expectations. After controlling for term to maturity, there were still no significant differences (at $\alpha = 0.05$) in the pricing of in- and out-of-the-money, long-term options were still more significantly underpriced than short-term options.
13. However, the samples differ slightly owing to the use of lagged values. For example, no lagged value is available for the first trading month.
14. The reader needs to exercise caution in interpreting the results for 1977, 1978 for CSR, because of very small sample sizes. In all other years $N \geqslant 34$.
15. Given WISD1 is implied from the model, any measurement error in the other input variables will be taken up in the WISD's. Therefore, although the model's pricing performance improved using WISD, this does not mean the other variables are free of measurement error, nor does it remove the possibility of omitted variables from the Black–Scholes model.
16. A four-way classification of option type was also examined. The results are not reported here, as the four-way classification gives results which are consistent with those of the two-way classification reported in table 34.8.

References

Abdel-Khalik, A. R., and Thompson, R. B. 1978. Research on Earnings Forecasts: The state of the art. *Accounting Journal*, Winter: 180–209.

Agmon, T. 1972. The relations among equity markets: A study of share price co-movements in the United States, United Kingdom, Germany and Japan. *Journal of Finance* 27: 839–55.

Agmon, T. 1978. The country risk: The significance of the country factor for share-price movements in the United Kingdom, Germany and Japan. *Journal of Business* 46: 24–32.

Albrecht, W. S., Lookabill, L. L., and McKeown, J. C. 1977. The time-series properties of annual earnings. *Journal of Accounting Research*, Autumn: 226–44.

Alexander, G. J. and Chervany, N. L. 1980. On the estimation and stability of beta. *Journal of Financial and Quantitative Analysis* 15: 123–37.

Alexander, S. S. 1961. Price movements in speculative markets: Trends or random walks. *Industrial Management Review* 2: 7–26.

Alexander, S. S. 1964. Price movements in speculative markets: Trends or random walks, No. 2. *Industrial Management Review* 5: 25–46.

Altman, E. I. 1968. Financial ratios, discriminant analysis and the prediction of corporate bankruptcy. *Journal of Finance* 23: 589–609.

Archibald, T. R. 1972. Stock market reaction to the depreciation switchback. *Accounting Review*, January: 22–30.

Ariel, R. A. 1983. A monthly effect in stock returns. Unpublished manuscript, University of Chicago, Graduate School of Business.

Ariel, R. A. 1984. A monthly effect in stock returns. Working paper, Massachusetts Institute of Technology.

Asquith, P., and Mullins, D. W. 1986. Equity issues and offering dilution. *Journal of Financial Economics* 15: 61–89.

Ball, R. 1972a. Changes in accounting techniques and stock prices. *Empiricial Research in Accounting: Selected Studies.* Supplement to *Journal of Accounting Research* 10: 1–38.

Ball, R., 1972b. Risk, return and disequilibrium: An application to changes in accounting techniques. *Journal of Finance*, May: 343–53.

Ball, R. J. 1974. Filter rules: Experimental problems and Australian evidence. Unpublished manuscript, University of Queensland.

Ball, R. 1976. Anomalies in relationships between securities' yields and yield-surrogates. Unpublished paper, University of New South Wales.

Ball, R. 1977. A note on errors in variables and estimates of systematic risk. *Australian Journal of Management* 2: 79–84.

Ball, R. 1978a. Anomalies in relationships between securities' yields and yield-surrogates. *Journal of Financial Economics* 6: 103–26.

Ball, R. 1978b. Filter rules: Interpretation of market efficiency, experimental problems and Australian evidence. *Accounting Education* 18(2): 1–17. [CHAPTER 16]

Ball, R. 1978c. Market model studies: Justification, interpretation and experimental problems. Unpublished manuscript, Australian Graduate School of Management.

Ball, R. 1979. When are capital gains/losses taxed? Unpublished manuscript, Australian Graduate School of Management.

Ball, R., and Bowers, J. 1986a. A corrected Statex–Actuaries Daily Accumulation Index. Manuscript, Australian Graduate School of Management.

Ball, R., and Bowers, J. 1986b. Daily seasonals in equity and fixed-interest returns: Australian evidence and tests of plausible hypotheses. Unpublished manuscript, Australian Graduate School of Management.

Ball, R., and Brown, P. 1968. An empirical evaluation of accounting income numbers. *Journal of Accounting Research* 6: 159–78.

Ball, R., and Brown, P. 1977. Identifying some issues in CCA. *Australian Accountant* 47: 413–21. [CHAPTER 27]

Ball, R., and Brown, P. 1978. Market efficiency, random walks and seasonals in Australian equity prices. *Accounting Education* 18: 1–17.

Ball, R., and Brown, P. 1980. Risk and return from investments in the Australian mining industry: January 1958–February 1979. *Australian Journal of Management* 5: 45–66. [CHAPTER 5]

Ball, R., Brown, P., and Finn, F. J. 1977. Share capitalisation changes, information and the Australian equity market. *Australian Journal of Management* 2: 105–25. [CHAPTER 23]

Ball, R., Brown, P., and Finn, F. J. 1978. Published investment recommendations and share prices: Are there free lunches in security analysis? *JASSA* 2: 5–10. [CHAPTER 33]

Ball, R., Brown, P., Finn, F. J., and Officer, R. R. 1979. Dividends and the value of the firm: Evidence from the Australian equity market. *Australian Journal of Management* 4: 13–26.

Ball, R., Brown, P., and Officer, R. R. 1976a. Asset pricing in the Australian industrial equity market. *Australian Journal of Management* 1: 1–32. [CHAPTER 4]

Ball, R., Brown, P., and Officer, R. R. 1976b. Risk and return in the share market—part 1: Theory and evidence. *Australian Accountant* 46: 68–75.

Ball, R., Brown, P., and Officer, R. R. 1976c. Risk and return in the share market—part 2: Some implications. *Australian Accountant* 46: 138–42.

Ball, R., Lev, B., and Watts, R. 1976. Income variation and balance sheet compositions. *Journal of Accounting Research*, Spring: 1–9.

Ball, R., and Officer, R. R. 1978. Try this on your chartist. *Superfunds*, June. [CHAPTER 17]

Ball, R., Walker, R. G. and Whittred, G. P. 1979. Audit qualifications and share prices. *Abacus* 15: 23–34.

Ball, R., and Watts, R. 1968. The behaviour of earnings through time. Unpublished paper presented to the Workshop in Accounting Research, University of Chicago, 23 April.

Ball, R., and Watts, R. 1972. Some time series properties of accounting income. *Journal of Finance* 27: 663–82.

Ball, R. and Watts, R. 1979. Some additional evidence on survival biases. *Journal of Finance* 34: 197–205.

Bank Administrative Institute 1968. *Measuring the investment performance of pension funds.* Park Ride, Illinois: B.A.I.

Banz, R. W. 1981. The relationship between return and market value of common stocks. *Journal of Financial Economics* 9: 3–18.

Baskin, E. F. 1973. The communicative effectiveness of consistency exceptions. *Accounting Review*, January: 38–51.

Basu, S. 1977. Investment performance of common stocks in relation to their price-earnings ratios: A test of the efficient markets hypothesis. *Journal of Finance* 32: 663–82.

Basu, S. 1983. The relationship between earnings' yield, market value and return for NYSE common stocks. *Journal of Financial Economics* 12: 129–56.

Beaver, W. 1968. Alternative accounting measures as predictors of failure. *Accounting Review*, January: 113–22.

Beaver, W. H., Clarke, R., and Wright, W. F. 1979. The association between unsystematic security returns and the magnitude of earnings forecast errors. *Journal of Accounting Research*, Autumn: 316–40.

Beaver, W., Kettler, R., and Scholes, M. 1970. The association between market-determined and accounting-determined risk measures. *Accounting Review* 45: 654–82.

Beaver, W., Lambert, R., and Morse, D. 1980. The information content of security prices. *Journal of Accounting and economics*, March: 3–28.

Beaver, W., and Manegold, J. 1975. The association between market-determined and accounting-determined measures of systematic risk: some further evidence. *Journal of Financial and Quantitative Analysis* 10: 231–83.

Beedles, W. L. 1979. On the asymmetry of market returns. *Journal of Financial and Quantitative Analysis* 14: 653–60.

Beedles, W. L. 1984. Asymmetry in Australian equity returns. Unpublished manuscript, Monash University.

Beedles, W. L. 1986. Asymmetry in Australian equity returns. *Australian Journal of Management* 11(1): 1–12. [CHAPTER 3]

Beedles, W. L., and Simkowitz, M. A. 1980. Morphology of asset asymmetry. *Journal of Business Research* 8: 457–68.

Benston, G. J. 1973. Required disclosure and the stock market; An evaluation of the Securities Exchange Act of 1934. *American Economic Review*, March: 133.

Bildersee, J. W. 1975. The association between a market-determined measure of risk and alternative measures of risk. *Accounting Review* 50: 81–98.

Bird, R., Chin, H., and McCrae, M. 1982. Superannuation fund managers—how do they rate? *JASSA* 4: 9–11. [CHAPTER 31]

Bird, R., Chin, H., and McCrae, M. 1983. The performance of Australian superannuation funds. *Australian Journal of Management* 8: 49–69.

Birkett, W. P., and Walker, R. G. 1971. Response of the Australian accounting profession to company failures in the 1960s. *Abacus* 7: 97–136.

Bishop, S., Dodd, P., and Officer, R. R. 1987. *Takeovers: The Australian evidence 1972–1985.* Sydney: Centre for Independent Studies.

Black, F. 1972. Capital market equilibrium with restricted borrowing. *Journal of Business* 45: 444–55.

Black, F. 1975. Fact and fantasy in the use of options. *Financial Analysts Journal* 31: 36–41 and 61–72.

Black, F., Jensen, M. C., and Scholes, M. 1972. The capital asset pricing model: Some empirical results. In *Studies in the theory of capital markets*, edited by M. C. Jensen, pp. 79–121. New York: Praeger Publishers.

Black, F., and Scholes, M. 1972. The valuation of option contracts and a test of market efficiency. *Journal of Finance* 27: 399–418.

Black, F., and Scholes, M. 1973a. The behaviour of security returns around ex-dividend days. Unpublished manuscript, University of Chicago and M.I.T.

Black, F., and Scholes, M. 1973b. The pricing of options and corporate liabilities. *Journal of Political Economy* 81: 637–54.

Blume, M. E. 1970. Portfolio theory: A step toward its practical application. *Journal of Business* 43: 152–73.

Blume, M. E. 1971. On the assessment of risk. *Journal of Finance* 26: 1–10.

Blume, M. E. 1975. Betas and their regression tendencies. *Journal of Finance* 30: 785–95.

Blume, M. E. 1980. Stock returns and dividend yields: Some more evidence. *Review of Economics and Statistics* 52: 567–77.

Blume, M. E., and Friend, I. 1973. A new look at the capital asset pricing model. *Journal of Finance* 28: 19–33.

Bolch, B. W., and Huang, C. J. 1974. *Multivariate statistical methods for business and economics.* Englewood Cliffs: Prentice Hall.

Booth, L. D., and Johnson, D. J. 1984. The ex-dividend day behaviour of Canadian stock prices: Tax changes and clientele effects. *Journal of Finance* 39: 457–76.

Box, G. E. P., and Jenkins, G. M. 1970. *Time series analysis forecasting and control.* San Francisco: Holden–Day.

Box, G. E. P., and Pierce, D. A. 1970. Distribution of residual autocorrelation in autoregressive integrated moving average time series models. *Journal of the American Statistical Association* 65: 1509–25.

Boyle, P. P., and Ananthanarayan, A. 1977. The impact of variance estimation in option valuation models. *Journal of Financial Economics* 5: 375–87.

Branch, B. 1977. A tax loss trading rule. *Journal of Business* 50: 198–207.

Brealey, R., and Myers, S. 1984. *Principles of corporate finance.* 2nd ed. New York: McGraw-Hill.

Breeden, D. T. 1979. An intertemporal asset pricing model with stochastic consumption and investment opportunities. *Journal of Financial Economics* 7: 265–96.

Brennan, M. 1970. Investor taxes, market valuation and corporate financial policy. *National Tax Journal*: 417–27.

Brenner, M. 1979. The sensitivity of the efficient market hypothesis to alternative specifications of the market model. *Journal of Finance* 34.

Brown, P. 1969. The stockmarket in retrospect. *Economic Activity* 12: 7.

Brown, P. 1970. The impact of the annual net profit report on the stock market. *Australian Accountant* 60: 277–83. [CHAPTER 18].

Brown, P. 1972. Those half-yearly reports. *Australian Society of Accountants* Society Bulletin no. 13.

Brown, P. 1974. Unpublished, untitled manuscript, University of Western Australia.

Brown, P., Finn, F. J. and Hancock, P. 1977. Dividend changes, earnings reports, and share prices: Some Australian findings. *Australian Journal of Management* 2: 127–47. [CHAPTER 21]

Brown, P., Foster, G., and Noreen, E. 1985. *Security analyst multi-year earnings forecasts and the capital market.* Sarasota: American Accounting Association.

Brown, P., and Hancock, P. 1977. Profit reports and the sharemarket. In *Capital income and decision making: Introductory readings in accounting,* edited by I. Tilley and P. Jubb. Sydney: Rinehart and Winston. [CHAPTER 19].

Brown, P., Keim, D. B., Kleidon, A. W., and Marsh, T. A. 1983. Stock return seasonalities and the tax-loss selling hypothesis. *Journal of Financial Economics* 12: 105–27. [CHAPTER 7].

Brown, P., and Kennelly, J. W. The information content of quarterly earnings: A clarification and an extension. Available from the authors.

Brown, P., and Kennelly, J. W. 1972. The information content of quarterly earnings: An extension and some further evidence. *Journal of Business* 45: 403–15.

Brown, P., Kleidon, A. W., and Marsh, T. A. 1982. Size related anomalies in asset returns: Australian evidence. Unpublished manuscript.

Brown, P., Kleidon, A. W., and Marsh, T. A. 1983. New evidence on the nature of size-related anomalies in stock prices. *Journal of Financial Economics* 12.

Brown, P., and Walter, T. 1974. Fifty betas. *JASSA*, October, 1–7.

Brown, P., and Walter, T. S. 1986. Ex-dividend day behaviour of Australian share prices. *Australian Journal of Management* 11: 139–52. [CHAPTER 22]

Brown, R. L. 1978. A test of the Black and Scholes model of option evaluation in the Australian options market. *Australian Journal of Management* 3: 17–35.

Brown, R. L., and Shevlin, T. J. 1983. Modelling option prices in Australia using the Black–Scholes model. *Australian Journal of Management* 8(1): 1–20. [CHAPTER 34]

Brown, S. J., and Warner, J. B. 1980. Measuring security price performance. *Journal of Financial Economics* 8: 205–58.

Brown, S. J. and Weinstein, M. I. 1983. A new approach to testing asset pricing models: The bilinear paradigm. *Journal of Finance* 38: 711–44.

Bruce, R., McKern, B., and Pollard, I. (eds). 1983. *Handbook of Australian corporate finance.* Sydney: Butterworths.

Butlin, S. 1962. *Australian domestic product, investment and foreign borrowings 1861–1938/9.* London: Cambridge University Press.

Campbell, J. A., and Beranek, W. 1955. Stock price behaviour on ex-dividend dates. *Journal of Finance* 10: 425–29.

Carlson, R. S. 1970. Aggregate performance of mutual funds 1948–1967. *Journal of Financial and Quantitative Anaylsis* 5: 12.

Cass, D., and Stiglitz, J. E. 1970. The structure of investor preferences and asset returns, and separability in portfolio allocation: A contribution to the pure theory of mutual funds. *Journal of Economic Theory* 81: 122–60.

Castagna, A. D. 1976. An outline of the method adopted to establish a computerized data bank of Australian companies. *Accounting Education* 16: 1–7.

Castagna, A. D., and Matolcsy, Z. P. 1976. Financial ratios as predictors of company acquisitions. *JASSA*, 6–10.

Castagna, A. D., and Matolcsy, Z. P. 1977. An empirical analysis of Australian corporate failures. Seminar paper presented to the Department of Accounting and Public Finance, Australian National University, Canberra.

Castagna, A. D., and Matolcsy, Z. P. 1978a. The relationship between accounting variables and systematic risk and the prediction of systematic risk. *Australian Journal of Management* 3(2): 113–26. [CHAPTER 11]

Castagna, A. D., and Matolcsy, Z. P. 1978b. Source and prediction of systematic risk. Paper presented at the AAANZ conference, University of Otago, Dunedin, New Zealand.

Castagna, A. D., and Matolcsy, Z. P. 1980. The efficiency of the Australian traded stock options market: Some preliminary results. Paper presented at AAANZ conference, Townsville.

analysis on large asset markets. *Econometrica* 51: 1281–304.

Chambers, R. J. 1973. *Securities and obscurities.* Melbourne: Gower Press.

Chen, N. 1983. Some empirical tests of the theory of arbitrage pricing. *Journal of Finance* 38: 1393–414.

Chen, N., and Ingersoll, J. E., Jr. 1983. Exact pricing in linear factor models with finitely many assets: A note. *Journal of Finance*: 985–88.

Chen, N., Roll, R., and Ross, S. 1984. Economic forces and the stock market. University of Chicago working paper.

Chiang, A. C. 1967. *Fundamental methods of mathematical economics.* New York: McGraw-Hill.

Chiarella, C., and Hughes, W. R. 1978. Option valuation: Some empirical results. *Australian Journal of Management* 3: 37–48.

Chiras, D. P., and Manaster, S. 1978. The information content of option prices and a test of market efficiency. *Journal of Financial Economics* 6: 213–34.

Cho, D. C., Elton, E. J., and Gruber, M. J. 1984. On the robustness of the Roll and Ross arbitrage pricing theory. *Journal of Financial and Quantitative Analysis* 19: 1–10.

Chou, Ya-lun. 1969. *Statistical analysis with business and economic applications.* New York: Holt, Rinehart and Winston.

Chow, C. W., and Rice, S. J. 1982. Qualified audit opinions and share prices—an investigation. *Auditing: A Journal of Practice and Theory*, Winter: 35–51.

Clark, R. 1979. On the lognormality of firm and plant size distributions: Some U.K. evidence. *Applied Economics* 11: 415–33.

Cohn, R. A., and Pringle, J. J. 1973. Imperfections in international financial markets: Implications for risk premia and the cost of capital to firms. *Journal of Finance* 28: 59–66.

Collins, D. J., and McKeown, J. C. 1979. The market model: Potential for error. Faculty working papers, University of Illinois at Urbana-Champaign.

Collins, D. W., Kothari, S. P., and Rayburn, J. D. 1987. Firm size and information content of prices with respect to earnings. *Journal of Accounting and Economics* 9: 111–38.

Connor, G. 1985. Arbitrage pricing theory: The way forward. *Australian Journal of Management* 10: 109–30.

Constantinides, G. M. 1979. Capital market equilibrium with personal taxes. *Econometrica* (forthcoming).

Constantinides, G. M. 1980. Admissible uncertainty in the intertemporal asset pricing model. *Journal of Financial Economics* 8: 71–86.

Constantinides, G. M. 1982. Optimal stock trading with personal taxes: Implications for prices and the abnormal January returns. Unpublished manuscript, University of Chicago.

Cornell, B. 1981. The consumption based asset pricing model—a note on potential tests and applications. *Journal of Financial Economics* 9: 103–8.

Cross, F. 1973. The behavior of stock prices on Fridays and Mondays. *Financial Analysts Journal* 29: 67–69.

D'Agostino, R., and Pearson, E. S. 1973. Tests for departure from normality. *Biometrika* 60: 613–22.

Dann, L. Y., Mayers, D., and Raab, R. J. 1977. Trading rules, large blocks and the speed of price adjustment. *Journal of Financial Economics* 4: 3–22.

Dhrymes, P. J., Friend, I., and Gultekin, N. B. 1984. A critical reexamination of the empirical evidence on the arbitrage pricing theory. *Journal of Finance* 34: 323–46.

Dimson, E. 1979. Risk measurement when shares are subject to infrequent trading. *Journal of Financial Economics* 7: 197–226.

Dixon, B. L., and Sonka, S. T. 1979. A note on the use of exponential functions for estimating farm size distributions. *American Journal of Agricultural Economics* 61: 554–57.

Dodd, P. 1976. Company takeovers and the Australian equity market. *Australian Journal of Management* 2: 15–36.

Dodd, P., and Officer, R.R. 1987. Takeovers: The Australian Evidence. In *Takeovers and corporate control*, conference proceedings, pp. 129–52. Sydney: Centre for Independent Studies. [CHAPTER 28]

Dodd, P., Dopuch, N., Holthausen, R., and Leftwich, R. 1983. Qualified audit opinions and stock prices: Information content, announcement dates, and concurrent disclosures. *Journal of Accounting and Economics*, April: 3–38.

Dodd, P., and Officer, R. R. 1986. *Corporate control, economic efficiency and shareholder justice*. Sydney: Centre for Independent Studies.

Douglas, G. W. 1969. Risk in the equity markets: An empirical appraisal of market efficiency. *Yale Economic Essays* 9: 3–45.

Dryden, M. M. 1969. A source of bias in filter tests of share prices. *Journal of Business* 42: 321–25.

Dryden, M. M. 1970. Filter tests of U.K. share prices. *Applied Economics* 1: 261–75.

Dunsdon, W. K. 1973. Australian government bonds and their relationship with the capital asset pricing model. Unpublished MBA thesis, University of Queensland.

Durand, D., and May, A. M. 1960. The ex-dividend behaviour of American Telephone and Telegraph stock. *Journal of Finance* 15: 19–31.

Dyer, J. C. 1975. A descriptive analysis of the distribution of returns from Australia (ordinary) shares. *Accounting Education* 15: 7–26.

Dyl, E. A. 1977. Capital gains taxation and year-end stock market behavior. *Journal of Finance* 32: 165–75.

Eades, K. M., Hess, J., and Han Kim, E. 1984. On interpreting security returns during the ex-dividend period. *Journal of Financial Economics* 13: 3–34.

Elliott, J. 1982. 'Subject to' audit opinions and abnormal security returns: Outcomes and ambiguities. *Journal of Accounting Research*, Autumn (Part 2): 617–38.

Elton, E. J., and Gruber, M. J. 1970. Marginal stockholder tax rates and the clientele effect. *Review of Economics and Statistics* 52: 68–74.

Elton, E. J., and Gruber, M. J. 1972. Earnings estimates and the accuracy of expectational data. *Management Science*, April: B409–23.

Elton, E. J., and Gruber, M. J. 1984. Non-standard CAPM's and the market portfolio. *Journal of Finance, Papers and Proceedings* 39(3): 911–24.

Elton, E. J., Gruber, J., and Rentzler, J. 1984. The ex-dividend day behaviour of stock prices: a re-examination of the clientele effect: Comment. *Journal of Finance* 39: 551–56.

Epps, T. W., and Epps, M. L. 1976. The stochastic dependence of security price changes and transaction volumes: Implications for the mixture-of-distributions hypothesis. *Econometrica* 44: 305–21.

Evans, J. L. and Archer, S. H. 1968. Diversification and the reduction of dispersion: An empirical analysis. *Journal of Finance* 23: 761–67.

Faff, R. 1986. An empirical examination of the arbitrage pricing theory in the Australian equity market. Discussion paper 9, Monash University.

Fama, E. F. 1965. The behaviour of stock market prices. *Journal of Business* 38: 34–105.

Fama, E. F. 1968. Risk, return and equilibrium: Some clarifying comments. *Journal of Finance* 23: 29–41.

Fama, E. F. 1970a. Efficient capital markets: A review of theory and empirical work. *Journal of Finance* 25: 383–417.

Fama, E. F. 1970b. Multiperiod consumpion–investment decisions. *American Economic Review* 60: 163–74.

Fama, E. F. 1976. *Foundations of Finance*. New York: Basic Books.

Fama, E. F., and Babiak, H. 1968. Dividend policy: An empirical analysis. *Journal of the American Statistical Association* 63: 1132–61.

Fama, E. F., and Blume, M. 1966. Filter rules and stock market trading profits. *Journal of Business (Special Supplement)* 39: 226–41.

Fama, E. F., Fisher, L., Jensen, M. C., and Roll, R. 1969. The adjustment of stock prices to new information. *International Economic Review* 10: 1–21.

Fama, E. F., and MacBeth, J. D. 1973. Risk, return and equilibrium: Empirical tests. *Journal of Political Economy* 81: 607–36.

Fama, E. F., and MacBeth, J. D. 1974. Tests of the multiperiod two-parameter model. *Journal of Financial Economics* 1: 43–66.

Fama, E. F., and Miller, M. H. 1972. *The theory of finance.* New York: Holt, Rinehart and Winston.

Finn, F. J. 1975. Mechanical models and earnings per share forecasts. Unpublished paper, University of Queensland.

Finn, F. J. 1984. *Evaluation of the internal processes of managed investment funds.* Greenwich: JAI Press.

Finn, F. J., and Whittred, G. P. 1982. On the use of naive expectations of earnings per share as experimental benchmarks. *Economic Record*, June: 169–73. [CHAPTER 20]

Firth, M. 1978a. Qualified audit reports: Their impact on investment decisions. *Accounting Review*, July: 642–50.

Firth, M. 1978b. Unit trusts: Performance and prospects. *Management Decision* 16: 94–176.

Fisher, I. 1930. *The theory of interest.* New York: MacMillan. Reprinted by Augustus M. Kelley, New York, 1970.

Fisher, L., and Lorie, J. H. 1968. Rates of return on investments in common stock: The year-by-year record, 1926–1965. *Journal of Business* 41: 291–316.

Foster, G. 1978a. Asset pricing models: Further tests. *Journal of Financial and Quantitative Analysis* 39–53.

Foster, G. 1978b. *Financial statement analysis.* Englewood Cliffs: Prentice Hall.

Francis, J. C., and Archer, S. H. 1971. *Portfolio analysis.* New Jersey: Prentice Hall.

Freeman, R. 1987. The association between accounting earnings and security returns for large and small firms. *Journal of Accounting and Economics* 9: 195–228.

French, K. R. 1980. Stock returns and the weekend effect. *Journal of Financial Economics* 8: 55–69.

Friedman, M., and Savage, L. J. 1948. The utility analysis of choices involving risk. *Journal of Political Economy* 61: 279–304.

Friend, I., and Blume, M. 1970. Measurement of portfolio performance under uncertainty. *American Economc Record* 60: 561–75.

Friend, I., Blume, M., and Crockett J. 1970. *Mutual fund and other institutional investors: A new perspective.* New York: McGraw-Hill.

Friend, I., and Westerfield, R. 1980. Co-skewness and asset prices: A new approach. *Journal of Finance* 36: 897–914.

Friend, I., and Vickers, D. 1965. Portfolio selection and investment performance. *Journal of Financial Economics* 20: 391–415.

Galai, D. 1977. Tests of market efficiency of the Chicago Board Options Exchange. *Journal of Business* 50: 167–99.

Garman, M. B., and Klass, M. J. 1980. On the estimation of security price volatilities from historical data. *Journal of Business* 53: 67–78.

Gibbons, M. R. 1982a. Multivariate tests of financial models: A new approach. *Journal of Financial Economics* 10: 3–27.

Gibbons, M. R. 1982b. Discussion. *Journal of Finance* 37: 474–76.

Gibbons, M. R., and Hess, P. J. 1979. An investigation into day effects in assets returns— a progress report. Unpublished manuscript, University of Chicago.

Gibbons, M. R., and Hess, P. 1981. Day of the week effects and asset returns. *Journal of Business* 54: 579–96.

Gonedes, N. J. 1973. Evidence on the information content of accounting numbers: Accounting-based and market-based estimates of systematic risk. *Journal of Financial and Quantitative Analysis* 8: 407–43.

Gonedes, N. J. 1974. Risk, information and the effects of special accounting items on capital market equilibrium. Unpublished manuscript, University of Chicago.

Gonedes, N. J. 1975. Risk, information and the effects of special accounting items on capital market equilibrium. *Journal of Accounting Research*, Autumn: 220–56.

Gonedes, N. J., Dopuch, N., and Penman, S. H. 1976. Disclosure rules, information-production, and capital market equilibrium. The case of forecast disclosure rules. *Journal of Accounting Research* 14.

Greenwood, R. 1983. Brokers try the harder sell, buy and hold. *Business Review Weekly*, 19–25 November: 40–45.

Griffin, P. A. 1976. Competitive information in the stock market: An empirical study of earnings, dividends and analysts' forecasts. *Journal of Finance* 31: 631–50.

Grossman, S. J., and Stightz, J. E. 1976. Information and competitive price system. *American Economic Review*: 246–53.

Grubel, H. C. 1968. Internationally diversified portfolios: Welfare gains and capital flows. *American Economic Review* 58: 1299–314.

Gultekin, M. N., and Gultekin, N. B. 1982. Stock market seasonality and end of the tax year effect. Unpublished manuscript, University of Pennsylvania.

Gurney, J. P. 1976. Rank correlation of unit trust performance 1971–1975. *Investment Analyst*, December: 28–30.

Guy, J. R. F. 1978. The performance of the British investment trust industry. *Journal of Finance* 33: 443–55.

Hall, A. R. 1963. *The London capital market and Australia 1870–1914*. Canberra: ANU Press.

Hamada, R. S. 1969. Portfolio analysis, market equilibrium and corporation finance. *Journal of Finance* 24: 13–31.

Hamada, R. S. 1972. The effect of the firm's capital structure on the systematic risk of common stocks. *Journal of Finance* 27: 435–52.

Hancock, P. 1975. Dividend policy changes, profit reports, and share prices: Some Australian findings. Unpublished M.Com. thesis, University of Western Australian.

Harris, R. J. 1975. *A primer of multivariate statistics*. New York: Academic Press.

Hasbrouck, J. 1985. The characteristics of takeover targets. *Journal of Banking and Finance* 9.

Hess, A. C., and Frost, P. A. 1982. Tests for price effects of new issues of seasoned securities. *Journal of Finance* 36: 11–25.

Hess, P. J. 1982. The ex-dividend day behaviour of stock returns: Further evidence on tax effects. *Journal of Finance* 37: 445–56.

Hirshleifer, J. 1970. *Investment, interest, and capital*. Englewood Cliffs: Prentice Hall.

Holthausen, R. W. 1976. Further test of the association between market determined and accounting determined risk measures. Unpublished manuscript, Graduate School of Management, University of Rochester.

Huber, P. J. 1964. Robust estimation of a location parameter. *Annals of Mathematical Statistics* 34: 73–101.

Huberman, G. 1982. A simple approach to arbitrage pricing theory. *Journal of Economic Theory* October: 183–91.

Ingersoll, J. E., Jr. 1984. Some results in the theory of arbitrage pricing. *Journal of Finance* 39: 1021–39.

Institute of Chartered Accountants' Statement of Accounting Practice D5. 1970. *Depreciation, Depletion and Amortization of Fixed Assets*. November.

Institute of Chartered Accountants' Statement of Accounting Practice K1. 1971. *Conformity with Institute Technical Statements*. May. Revised February 1972.

Jaffe, J. F. 1974. Special information and insider trading. *Journal of Business* 47: 410–28.

Jaffe, J. F., and Westerfield, R. 1985. The week-end effect in common stock returns: The international evidence. *Journal of Finance* 40: 433–54.

Jensen, M. C. 1968. The performance of mutual funds in the period 1945–1964. *Journal of Finance* 23: 389–416.

Jensen, M. C. 1969. Risk, the pricing of capital assets and the evaluation of investment portfolios. *Journal of Business* 42: 167–247.

Jensen, M. C. 1972. The foundations and current state of capital market theory. *Bell Journal of Economics and Management Science* 3: 357–98.

Jensen, M. C., and Benington, G. A. 1970. Random walks and technical theories: Some additional evidence. *Journal of Finance* 25: 469–82.

Jensen, M. C., and Ruback, R. 1983. The market for corporate control. *Journal of Financial Economics* 11.

Johnston, J. 1972. *Econometric methods*. 2nd ed. New York: McGraw-Hill.

Joy, O. M., and Porter, R. B. 1974. Stochastic dominance and mutual fund performance. *Journal of Financial and Quantitative Analysis* 9: 25–31.

Kalay, A. 1982. The ex-dividend day behaviour of stock prices: A re-examination of the clientele effect. *Journal of Finance* 37: 1059–70.

Kalay, A. 1984. The ex-dividend day behaviour of stock prices: A re-examination of the clientele effect: A reply. *Journal of Finance* 39: 557–61.

Kaplan, R. S., and Roll, R. 1972. Investor evaluation of accounting information: Some empirical evidence. *Journal of Business*, April: 225–57.

Karmel, P. H., and Polasek, M. 1970. *Applied statistics for economists*. 3rd ed. Melbourne: Pitman.

Keim, D. B. 1982. Further evidence on size effects and yield effects: The implications of stock return seasonality. Unpublished manuscript, University of Chicago.

Keim, D. B. 1983. Size-related anomalies and stock market seasonality: Further empirical evidence. *Journal of Financial Economics* 12.

Keim, D. B., and Stambaugh, R. F. 1984. A further investigation of the weekend effect in stock returns. *Journal of Finance* 39: 819–40.

Kendall, M. G. 1953. The analysis of economic time series—part I: Prices. *Journal of Royal Statistical Society* 96: 11–25.

Kendall, M. G., and Stuart, A. 1968. *The advanced theory of statistics*. Vol. 3. Los Angeles: Griffen.

Kim, T. 1976. Investment performance of college endowment funds. *Quarterly Review of Economics and Business* 16: 73–83.

Kim, T. 1978. An assessment of the performance of mutual fund management: 1969–1975. *Journal of Financial and Quantitative Analysis* 13: 385–406.

King, B. F. 1966. Market and industry factors in stock price behaviour. *Journal of Business* 39: 139–90. Special supplement.

Korajczyk, R. 1982. Stock market seasonality: Some international evidence. Unpublished manuscript, University of Chicago.

Krasker, W. S., and Welsch, R. E. 1979. Efficient bounded-influence regression estimation using alternative definitions of sensitivity. *Journal of the American Statistical Association* (forthcoming).

Kraus, A., and Litzenberger, R. H. 1972. Skewness, preference and the valuation of risk assets. Unpublished manuscript, Stanford University.

Kraus, A., and Litzenberger, R. 1976. Skewness preference and the valuation of risk assets. *Journal of Finance* 31: 1085–1100.

Kraus, A., and Litzenberger, R. 1983. On the distributional conditions for a consumption-oriented three-moment CAPM. *Journal of Finance* 38: 1381–91.

Kraus, A., and Stoll, H. R. 1972. Price impacts of block trading on the New York Stock Exchange. *Journal of Finance* 27: 269–88.

Kuhn, T. S. 1969. *The structure of scientific revolutions*. Chicago: University of Chicago Press.

Kwon, Y. K. 1985. Derivation of the capital asset pricing model without normality or quadratic preference: A note. *Journal of Finance* 40: 1505–9.

Lakonishok, J., and Levi, M. 1982. Weekend effects on stock returns—a note. *Journal of Finance* 37: 883–89.

Lakonishok, J., and Vermaelen, T. 1983. Tax reform and ex-dividend day behaviour. *Journal of Finance* 38: 1157–79.

Lamberton, D. 1958. *Share price indices in Australia*. Sydney: Law Book Company.

Latane, H. A., and Rendlemen, R. J. 1976. Standard deviations of stock price ratios implied in option prices. *Journal of Finance* 31: 369–81.

Latane, H. A., and Rendlemen, R. J. 1979. Corrections to 'Standard deviations of stock price ratios implied in option prices'. *Journal of Finance* 34: 1083.

Leroy, S. F. 1982. Expectations models of asset prices: A survey of theory. *Journal of Finance* 37: 185–217.

Leslie, M. K. 1976. The performance of equity based unit trusts and mutual funds in the period 1968–1975. Unpublished M.B.A. thesis, University of Queensland.

Lessard, D. R. 1973. International portfolio diversification: A multivariate analysis for a group of Latin American countries. *Journal of Finance* 28: 619–33.

Lev, B. 1974. On the association between operating leverage and risk. *Journal of Financial and Quantitative Analysis* 9: 627–64.

Levy, H., and Sarnat, M. 1970. International diversification of investment portfolios. *American Economic Review* 60: 668–75.

Lintner, J. 1956. Distribution of incomes of corporations among dividends, retained earnings and taxes. *American Economic Review* 46: 97–113.

Lintner, J. 1965a. The valuation of risk assets and the selection of risky investments in stock portfolios and capital budgets. *Review of Economics and Statistics* 47: 13–37.

Lintner, J. 1965b. Security prices, risk and the maximal gains from diversification. *Journal of Finance* 20: 585–615.

Litzenberger, R. H., and Ramaswamy, K. 1979. The effects of personal taxes and dividends on capital asset prices: Theory and empirical evidence. *Journal of Financial Economics* 7: 163–95.

Litzenberger, R. H., and Ramaswamy, K. 1980. Dividends, short selling restrictions, tax-induced investor clienteles and market equilibrium. *Journal of Finance* 35: 469–82.

Long, J. B., Jr. 1974. Stock prices, inflation and the term structure of interest rates. *Journal of Financial Economics* 1: 131–70.

Lorie, J. H., and Neiderhoffer, V. 1968. Predictive and statistical properties of insider trading. *Journal of Law and Economics* 11: 35–51.

Luedecke, B. P. 1984. An empirical investigation into arbitrage and approximate *K*-factor structure on large asset markets. Unpublished manuscript, AGSM, University of New South Wales.

MacBeth, J. D., and Merville, L. J. 1979. An empirical examination of the Black–Scholes call option pricing model. *Journal of Finance* 34: 1173–86.

Mains, N. E. 1977. Risk, the pricing of capital assets, and the evaluation of investment portfolios: Comment. *Journal of Business* 50: 371–84.

Makridakis, S. G., and Wheelwright, S. C. 1974. An analysis of the interrelationships among the major world stock exchanges. *Journal of Business Finance and Accounting* 1: 195–215.

Mandelbrot, B. 1966. Forecasts of future prices, unbiased markets and martingale models. *Journal of Business* 39: 242–55.

Mandelker, G. 1974. Risk and return: The case of merging firms. *Journal of Financial Economics* 303–35.

Markowitz, H. M. 1952. Portfolio selection. *Journal of Finance* 7: 77–91.

Markowitz, H. M. 1959. *Portfolio selection.* New York: John Wiley and Sons.

Marsh, T. 1977. Insider trading: Issues and analysis. Unpublished manuscript, University of Chicago.

Marsh, T. 1980. Intertemporal capital asset pricing and the term structure of interest rates. Unpublished manuscript, Massachusetts Institute of Technology.

Masulis, R. W. 1980. The effects of capital structure change on security prices: A study of exchange offers. *Journal of Financial Economics* 8: 139–77.

Mayers, D. 1972. Nonmarketable assets and capital market equilibrium under uncertainty. In *Studies in the theory of capital markets*, edited by M. C. Jensen, pp. 79–121. New York: Praeger Publications.

Mayers, D., and Rice, E. M. 1979. Measuring portfolio performance and the empirical content of asset pricing models. *Journal of Financial Economics* 7: 3–28.

McDonald, J. G. 1974. Objectives and performance of mutual funds 1960–1969. *Journal of Financial and Quantitative Analysis* 9: 311–33.

McInish, T. H., and Puglisi, D. J. 1980. The ex-dividend behaviour of preferred stocks. *Review of Business and Economic Research*: 81–90.

Melicher, R., Ledolter, J., and D'Antonio, L. 1983. A time series analysis of aggregate merger activity. *Review of Economics and Statistics.*

Merton, R. 1971. Optimum consumption and investment rules in a continuous time model. *Journal of Economic Theory*: 373–413.

Merton, R. C. 1973a. An intertemporal capital asset pricing model. *Econometrica* 41: 867–87.

Merton, R. C. 1973b. A re-examination of the capital asset pricing model. In *Risk and return in finance*, edited by I. Friend and J. D. Bicksler, pp. 141–59. Massachusetts: Ballinger.

Merton, R. C. 1973c. Theory of rational option pricing. *Bell Journal of Economics and Management Science* 4: 141–83.

Mikkelson, W. H., and Partch, M. M. 1985. Stock price effects and costs of secondary distributions. *Journal of Financial Economics* 14: 165–94.

Miller, M. H., and Modigliani, F. 1961. Dividend policy, growth and the valuation of shares. *Journal of Business* 34: 411–33.

Miller, M. H., and Modigliani, F. 1966. Some estimates of the cost of capital to the electric utility industry, 1954–1957. *American Economic Review* 56: 333–91.

Miller, M. H., and Scholes, M. 1972. Rates of return in relation to risk: A re-examination of some recent findings. *Studies in the theory of capital markets*, edited by M. C. Jensen, pp. 47–78. New York: Praeger Publications.

Miller, M. H., and Scholes, M. 1978. Dividends and taxes. *Journal of Financial Economics* 6: 333–64.

Moles, P., and Taylor, B. 1977. Unit trust-return performance. *Investment Analyst*: 34–41.

Moore, A. B. 1962. Some characteristics of change in common stock prices. In *The Random Character of Stock Market Prices*, edited by P. Cootner. Cambridge: M.I.T. Press.

Morgenstern, O. 1963. *On the accuracy of economic observations*. Princeton University Press.

Morris, B. E. 1980. *The Commonwealth Bank Bond Indices*.

Mossin, J. 1966. Equilibrium in a capital asset market. *Econometrica* 34: 768–83.

Murray, I. 1970. Where companies go wrong in financial management. *Rydges* 43(6): 21–24.

Neiderhoffer, V. 1965. Clustering of stock prices. *Operations Research* 13: 258–65.

Neiderhoffer, V. 1966. A new look at clustering of stock prices. *Journal of Business* 39: 309–13.

Neiderhoffer, V., and Osborne, M. 1966. Market making and reversal on the stock exchange. *Journal of the American Statistical Association* 61: 897–916.

Nelson, C. R. 1973. *Applied time series analysis*. San Francisco: Holden-Day.

Noti, G. 1977. Share price behaviour on ex-dividend dates. *Securities Institute Journal*: 11–15.

O'Brien, J. R., and Young, I. C. 1985. Rates of return on rights and shares. Unpublished manuscript, Macquarie University.

Officer, R. R. 1972. The distribution of stock returns. *Journal of the American Statistical Association* 67: 807–12.

Officer, R. R. 1975. Seasonality in Australian capital markets: Market efficiency and empirical issues. *Journal of Financial Economics* 2: 29–51. [CHAPTER 15]

Officer, R. R. 1979. The stock market: An introduction to market concepts and Australian evidence. In *Share markets and portfolio theory* (1st ed.), edited by R. Ball, P. Brown, F. J. Finn and R. R. Officer. St Lucia: University of Queensland Press.

Officer, R. R. 1980. Performance measurement. In *Share markets and portfolio theory* (1st ed.), edited by R. Ball, P. Brown, F. J. Finn and R. R. Officer. St Lucia: University of Queensland Press.

Officer, R. R. 1985. Inflation, rates of return to equities, yields on select securities and their interrelationships. Unpublished manuscript. Monash University.

Osborne, M. F. M. 1962. Periodic structure in the Brownian motion of stock prices. *Operations Research* 10: 345–79.

Patell, J. M., and Wolfson, M. A. 1979. Anticipated information releases reflected in call option prices. *Journal of Accounting and Economics* 1: 117–40.

Pearson, E. S., and Hartley, H. O. (eds). 1966. *Biometrica tables for statisticians*. 3rd ed. Vol. 1. Cambridge: Cambridge University Press.

Peirson, C. G., and Bird, R. G. 1976. *Business finance*. New York: McGraw-Hill.

Peters, S. C., Samdrov, A. M., and Welsch, R. E. 1982. Computational procedures for bounded-influence and robust regression (TROLL: BIF and BIFMOD). Technical report no. 30. Cambridge: M.I.T. Center for Computational Research in Economics and Management Science.

Peterson, D., and Rice, M. L. 1980. A note on ambiguity in portfolio performance measures. *Journal of Finance* 35: 1251–65.

Peterson, R. 1971. Bonus issues, share splits and rights issues. *Chartered Secretary* 23: 198–207.

Pettit, R. R. 1972. Dividend announcements, security performance and capital market efficiency. *Journal of Finance*, December: 993–1007.

Pettit, R. R. 1976. The impact of dividend and earnings announcements: A reconciliation. *Journal of Business* 49: 86–96.

Porter, R. B. 1973. An empirical comparison of stochastic dominance and the mean-variance portfolio choice criteria. *Journal of Financial and Quantitative Analysis* 8: 587–608.

Poterba, J. M., and Summers, L. H. 1984. New evidence that taxes affect the valuation of dividends. *Journal of Finance* 39: 1397–415.

Praetz, P. D. 1969. Australian share prices and the random walk hypothesis. *Australian Journal of Statistics* 11: 123–39.

Praetz, P. D. 1973a. Growth rate estimators for economic time series. *Australian Journal of Statistics* 15: 118–27.

Praetz, P. D. 1973b. Analysis of Australian share prices. *Australian Economic Papers* 20: 70–78.

Praetz, P. D. 1976a. Some effects of errors on the independence and distribution of stock price returns. *Australian Journal of Management* 1: 79–83.

Praetz, P. D. 1976b. Rates of return on filter tests. *Journal of Finance* 31: 71–75.

Praetz, P. D. 1976c. The measurement of mutual fund performance in Australia. *JASSA* 3: 10–16.

Praetz, P. D., and Wilson, E. J. G. 1978. The distribution of stock market returns: 1958–1973. *Australian Journal of Management* 3: 79–90.

Pratt, J. W. 1964. Risk aversion in the small and in the large. *Econometrica* 32: 122–36.

Reinganum, M. R. 1981a. Misspecification of capital asset pricing: empirical anomalies based on earnings' yields and market values. *Journal of Financial Economics* 9: 19–46.

Reinganum, M. 1981b. The arbitrage pricing theory: Some empirical results. *Journal of Finance* 36: 313–21.

Reinganum, M. R. 1983. The anomalous stock market behaviour of small firms in January: Empirical tests for tax-loss selling effects. *Journal of Financial Economics* 12.

Reserve Bank. 1982. *Australian economic statistics.* Occasional paper no. 8A.

Robson, G. N. 1981. The investment performance of unit trusts and mutual funds in Australia for the period 1969 to 1978. Unpublished Masters thesis, Monash University.

Robson, G. N. 1986. The investment performance of unit trusts and mutual funds in Australia for the period 1969 to 1978. *Accounting and Finance* 26(2): 55–79. [CHAPTER 30]

Rogalski, R. 1984. New findings regarding day of the week returns over trading and non-trading periods. Manuscript, Dartmouth College.

Roll, R. 1973. Assets, money and commodity price inflation under uncertainty. *Journal of Money, Credit and Banking*, November: 903–23.

Roll, R. 1977. A critique of the asset pricing theory's tests, part 1: On past and potential testability of the theory. *Journal of Financial Economics* 4: 129–76.

Roll, R. 1978. Ambiguity when performance is measured by the securities market line. *Journal of Finance* 33: 1051–69.

Roll, R. 1979. Testing a portfolio for ex ante mean/variance efficiency. In *Studies in the management sciences*, edited by E. Elton and M. Gruber. Amsterdam: North Holland.

Roll, R. 1983. Vas is das? The turn-of-the-year effect and the return premia of small firms. *Journal of Portfolio Management*, Winter: 18–28.

Roll, R., and Ross, S. A. 1980. An empirical investigation of the arbitrage pricing theory. *Journal of Finance* 35: 1073–102.

Rosenberg, B. 1981. The capital asset pricing model and the market model. *Journal of Portfolio Management*, Winter: 5–16.

Ross, S. A. 1976. The arbitrage theory of capital asset pricing. *Journal of Economic Theory* 13: 341–60.

Ross, S. A. 1977. Return, risk and arbitrage. In *Risk and return in finance*, edited by I. Friend and J. I. Bicksler, pp. 189–218. Massachusetts: Ballinger.

Ross, S. A. 1978a. Mutual fund separation in financial theory—the separating distributions. *Journal of Economic Theory* 17: 254–86.

Ross, S. A. 1978b. The current status of the capital asset pricing model (CAPM). *Journal of Finance* 33: 885–901.

Rozeff, M. S., and Kinney, W. R., Jr. 1976. Capital market seasonality: The case of stock returns. *Journal of Financial Economics* 3: 379–402.

Rubinstein, M. E. 1973. A mean-variance synthesis of corporate financial theory. *Journal of Finance* 28: 167–81.

Samuelson, P. A. 1965. Proof that properly anticipated prices fluctuate randomly. *Industrial Management Review* 6: 41–49.

Samuelson, P. A. 1973. Proof that properly discounted values of assets vibrate randomly. *Bell Journal of Economics and Management Science* 4: 369–74.

Schmalensee, R., and Trippi, R. R. 1978. Common stock volatility expectations implied by option premia. *Journal of Finance* 33: 129–47.

Scholes, M. J. 1969. The effect of secondary distributions on price. Unpublished Ph.D. dissertation, University of Chicago.

Scholes, M. J. 1972. The market for securities: Substitution versus price pressure and the effects of information on share prices. *Journal of Business* 45: 179–211.

Scholes, M. J. and Williams, J. 1977. Estimating betas from nonsynchronous data. *Journal of Financial Economics* 5: 309–27.

Shanken, J. 1982. The arbitrage pricing theory: Is it testable? *Journal of Finance* 37: 1129–40.

Sharpe, I. G., and Walker, R. G. 1975. Asset revaluations and stock market prices. *Journal of Accounting Research* 13: 293–310. [CHAPTER 25]

Sharpe, W. F. 1963. A simplified model of portfolio analysis. *Management Science* 9: 277–93.

Sharpe, W. F. 1964. Capital asset prices: A theory of market equilibrium under conditions of risk. *Journal of Finance* 19: 425–42.

Sharpe, W. F. 1966. Mutual fund performance. *Journal of Business* 39: 119–38.

Sharpe, W. F. 1981. *Investment.* 2nd ed. Englewood Cliffs: Prentice Hall.

Shevlin, T. J. 1981. Measuring abnormal performance on the Australian securities market. *Australian Journal of Management* 6(1): 67–107. [CHAPTER 12]

Shevlin, T., and Whittred, G. 1984. Audit qualifications and share prices: further evidence. *Australian Journal of Management* 9(1): 37–52. [CHAPTER 24]

Shultz, P. 1983. Transaction costs and the small firm effect: A comment. *Journal of Financial Economics* 12: 81–88.

Siegel, S. 1956. *Non-parametric statistics for the behavioural sciences.* New York: McGraw-Hill.

Simkowitz, M. A., and Beedles, W. L. 1978. Diversification in a three moment world. *Journal of Financial and Quantitative Analysis* 13: 927–41.

Simkowitz, M. A., and Beedles, W. L. 1980. Asymmetric stable distributed security returns. *Journal of the American Statistical Association* 80: 306–12.

Sinclair, N. A. 1981. An empirical examination of the required number of leading and lagged variables for ACM beta estimation. *Australian Journal of Management* 6(2): 119–26. [CHAPTER 13]

Sinclair, N. A. 1982. An empirical test of the arbitrage pricing theory. Unpublished Ph.D. dissertation, Australian Graduate School of Management, University of New South Wales.

Sinclair, N. A. 1987. Multifactor asset pricing models. *Accounting and Finance* 27(1): 17–36. [CHAPTER 9]

Smirlock, M., and Starks, L. 1983. Day of the week effects in stock returns: Some intraday evidence. Manuscript, University of Pennsylvania and Washington University.

Solnik, B. H. 1973. *European capital markets: Towards a general theory of international investment.* London: Lexington Books.

Solnik, B. H. 1974. Why not diversify internationally rather than domestically? *Financial Analysts Journal* 30: 48–54.

Stambaugh, R. F. 1982. On the exclusion of assets from tests of the two-parameter model. *Journal of Financial Economics* 10: 237–68.

Stapleton, R. C., and Subrahmanyam, M. 1978. A multiperiod equilibrium asset pricing model. *Econometrica* 46: 1077–96.

Stigler, G. J. 1966. *The theory of price.* 2nd ed. London: Macmillan.

Stokie, M. D. 1982a. The distribution of stock market returns: Tests of normality. *Australian Journal of Management* 7: 159–78. [CHAPTER 2]

Stokie, M. 1982b. The testing of Australian stock market indices for mean-variance efficiency. *Accounting and Finance* 22: 1–18.

Stokie, M. D. 1983. Parameter stationarity in the distribution of stock market returns. *Australian Journal of Management* 8: 83–90.

Stoll, H. R., and Whaley, R. E. 1983. Transactions costs and the small firm effect. *Journal of Financial Economics* 12: 57–79.

Sunder, S. 1976. Discussion of Griffin (op. cit.). *Journal of Finance* 31: 680–84.

Sydney Stock Exchange Limited. 1977; 1978. *Annual Report.* Sydney: S.S.E.

Thompson, D. J. 1976. Sources of systematic risk in common stock. *Journal of Business* 49: 173-88.

Tobin, J. 1958. Liquidity preference as behaviour towards risk. *Review of Economic Studies* 25: 65-86.

Tobin, J. 1969. A general equilibrium approach to monetary theory. *Journal of Money, Credit and Banking* 1.

Treynor, J. L. 1965. How to rate management of investment performance. *Harvard Business Review*, Jan.-Feb.: 63-75.

Treynor, J. L., and Mazuy, K. K. 1966. Can mutual funds outguess the market? *Harvard Business Review* 44: 131-36.

Tsiang, S. C. 1972. The rationale of the mean-standard deviation analysis, skewness preference and the demand for money. *American Economic Review* 62: 354-71.

Van Horne, J. C. 1978. *Financial market rates and flows.* Englewood Cliffs. Prentice Hall.

Vasicek, O. A. 1973. A note on using cross-sectional information in Bayesian estimation of security betas. *Journal of Finance* 28: 1233-39.

Voorheis, F. L. 1976. How well do banks manage pooled pension portfolios? *Financial Analysts Journal*: 35-40.

Wachtel, S. B. 1942. Certain observations on seasonal movement in stock prices. *Journal of Business* 15: 184-93.

Walker, R. G., and Hartman, R. J. 1973. *Takeover bids and financial disclosure.* Melbourne: Accountancy Research Foundation.

Ward, C. W. R., and Saunders, A. 1976. U.K. unit trust performance 1964-1975. *Journal of Business Finance and Accounting* 3/4: 83-99.

Watson, J., and Dickinson, J. P. 1981. International diversification: An *ex post* and *ex ante* analysis of possible benefits. *Australian Journal of Management* 6(1): 125-34 [CHAPTER 6]

Watts, R. 1973. The information content of dividends. *Journal of Business* 46: 191-211.

Watts, R. 1976. Comments on the impact of dividend and earnings announcements: A reconciliation. *Journal of Business* 49: 97-106.

Watts, R. L., and Leftwich, R. W. 1977. The time series of annual accounting earnings. *Journal of Accounting Research*, Autumn: 253-71.

Wharton School of Finance and Commerce, University of Pennsylvania. 1962. *Study of mutual funds.* Washington D. C.: U.S. Government Printing Office.

Whittington, G. 1971. *The prediction of profitability and other studies of business behaviour.* Cambridge: Cambridge University Press.

Whittred, G. P. 1978. The time series behaviour of corporate earnings—some Australian evidence. *Australian Journal of Management*, October: 195-202.

Whittred, G. P. 1980. Audit qualification and the timeliness of corporate annual reports. *Accounting Review*, October: 563-77.

Whittred, G. P., Walker, R. G., and Birkett, W. P. 1978. Audit qualifications in Australia, 1961-1974. Unpublished manuscript, University of New South Wales.

Winkler, R. L., and Hays, W. L. 1975. *Statistics, probability, inference and decision.* New York: Holt, Rinehart and Winston.

Working, H. 1960. Note of the correlation of first differences of averages in a random chain. *Econometrica* 4: 916-18.